Economic Policy and Microeconomic Performance
in Inter-War Europe
The Case of Austria, 1918–1938

Beiträge zur Unternehmensgeschichte

Herausgegeben
von Hans Pohl
und Günther Schulz

Band 25

Jens-Wilhelm Wessels

Economic Policy and Microeconomic Performance in Inter-War Europe

The Case of Austria, 1918–1938

Franz Steiner Verlag Stuttgart 2007

Gedruckt mit Unterstützung des Bundesministeriums für Bildung, Wissenschaft und Kultur in Wien, der Wirtschaftskammer Österreich, der Industriellenvereinigung Tirol sowie der Firmen Böhler-Uddeholm AG, Mondi Business Paper Holding, Siemens AG Österreich und Voestalpine AG

Bibliografische Information der Deutschen Nationalbibliothek
Die Deutsche Nationalbibliothek verzeichnet diese Publikation in der Deutschen Nationalbibliografie; detaillierte bibliografische Daten sind im Internet über <http://dnb.d-nb.de> abrufbar.

ISBN 978-3-515-08476-5

ISO 9706

Gedruckt auf säurefreiem, alterungsbeständigem Papier. Druck: Printservice Decker & Bokor, München
Printed in Germany

CONTENTS

Part III

LIST OF FIGURES

LIST OF TABLES

VORWORT

Das Verhältnis zwischen Wirtschaft und Politik zählt zu den interessantesten, wenn auch endgültig kaum zu beantwortenden Fragen der Wirtschaftsgeschichte. Dank der Omnipräsenz der Politik in den modernen Medien ebenso wie in der traditionellen Geschichtsschreibung kann leicht der Eindruck entstehen, dass sie auch das wirtschaftliche Geschehen in hohem Maße mit bestimmt und mit bestimmte. Umgekehrt tendieren auf Karl Marx zurückgehende Vorstellungen, wonach nicht das Bewusstsein das Sein, sondern das Sein das Bewusstsein bestimme, dazu, die Politik letztlich als von der Wirtschaft abhängig zu betrachten. Was im einen wie im anderen Fall zu wenig bedacht wird, ist die Tatsache, dass sich die wirtschaftliche Entwicklung eines Landes aus der Summe millionenfacher Einzelentscheidungen zusammensetzt, die zumindest in einem marktwirtschaftlichen Umfeld von einer Vielzahl von Faktoren bedingt sind und ausgelöst werden. Unter ihnen stellen die politischen Rahmenbedingungen nur einen von vielen derartigen Faktoren dar.

Dennoch kann ihr Einfluss bald stärker, bald schwächer ausfallen. Es war daher ein Hauptziel der nachstehenden Analyse zu untersuchen, wie sehr die tatsächliche Entwicklung ausgewählter österreichischer Großunternehmen zwischen den beiden Weltkriegen von der Wirtschaftspolitik der damaligen Regierungen beeinflusst wurde oder vielleicht eher anderen, sich je nach Konjunkturlage verändernden, insbesondere marktwirtschaftlichen „Gesetzen“ folgte. Jens-Wilhelm Wessels legte die Arbeit im Mai 2001 am Institut für Geschichte der Universität Innsbruck als Dissertation vor. Er wählte mit Absicht die englische Sprache, um seine Untersuchung als eine in ihrer Aussagekraft über Österreich hinausreichende Fallstudie einem breiten, auch nicht-deutschsprachigen Publikum leichter zugänglich zu machen. Herr Wessels hatte selbst die Absicht, die Arbeit für die Drucklegung noch einmal zu überarbeiten, was durch seinen tragischen und viel zu frühen Unfalltod am 29. März 2005 verhindert wurde.

Dank großzügiger Unterstützung durch das Bundesministerium für Bildung, Wissenschaft und Kultur in Wien, die Wirtschaftskammer Österreich, die Industriellenvereinigung Tirol sowie einige Nachfolgeunternehmen der in der Arbeit behandelten Firmen (Böhler-Uddeholm AG, Mondi Business Paper Holding, Siemens AG Österreich, Voestalpine AG) war es möglich, dem Wunsch des Autors und seiner Eltern nachzukommen und die Arbeit beim ebenfalls überaus kooperativen Franz Steiner Verlag zu veröffentlichen. Ihnen allen sei ebenso von Herzen gedankt wie Herrn Prof. Dr. Hans Pohl, der sich schon zuvor spontan bereit erklärt hatte, den Band in die von ihm und Herrn Prof. Dr. Günther Schulz herausgegebene Reihe „Beiträge zur Unternehmensgeschichte“ aufzunehmen.

Innsbruck, im Frühjahr 2007 Franz Mathis

1. INTRODUCTION

The main aim of this study is to discern the relationship and interconnection between economic policy and macroeconomic as well as microeconomic development and growth in Europe during the inter-war period, i.e. the relation between economic policy and performance. It is attempted to ascertain the impact of economic policies on long-term economic development in various European countries and in Austria specifically. For the inter-war period, this means to analyse the effects of monetary and orthodox policies on real economic development. In addition, this paper seeks to detect the main determinants of economic growth and development at that time. This means that theories which include classical monetary, Keynesian and structural approaches have to be discussed and considered. Essentially, this study finds a structural approach to analyse, interpret and explain policy-making and macroeconomic and micro-economic development as most useful in understanding the enormous economic changes of the time. The impact of monetary and intentional political factors will be relativised. The aim is a reinterpretation of economic development and policy by utilising structural theories and microeconomic data.

The principal motivation comes from the challenge to attempt to write the economic history of such an interesting and stratified time as the inter-war period by analysing and employing microeconomic empirical data of Austria and comparing these with macroeconomic information and economic policy of various European countries. This was especially interesting as this method has not been used very much in historical research of the economic history of the interwar period.[1] By and large, to understand and interpret this period, macroeconomic data (such as data on national income, interest and investment rates, employment or international trade flows) in combination with an examination of economic policy measures and political events have been employed.[2] This method has been near at hand as such data as well as policies can be more easily registered and analysed.

The great disadvantage of such an approach is the tendency to overestimate the impact of intentional political and monetary factors on national economic performance. Political events, measures of economic policy and monetary mechanisms have often been considered as some of the primary causes of economic stagnation and crisis.[3] Primarily, researchers have looked at the higher political decision making

1 Most historical studies of business history almost exclusively focus on microeconomic development or on an aspect of it. See for example Alois Mosser's detailed analysis *Die Industrieaktiengesellschaften in Österreich 1880–1913. Versuch einer historischen Bilanz- und Betriebsanalyse*, Vienna 1980. See also: Helmut Wiesbauer, *Die österreichischen Aktiengesellschaften 1918–1938, unter Berücksichtigung betriebswirtschaftlicher und rechtlicher Aspekte*, dissertation, Linz 1977.

2 See bibliographical references in various chapters.

3 See for exampleWolfram Fischer, *Weltwirtschaftliche Rahmenbedingungen für die ökonomische und politische Entwicklung Europas 1919–1939*, Wiesbaden 1980.

bodies of governments, national banks and international organisations, as vital factors influencing not only policy, but also economic performance and development. For the inter-war period, deflationary policies, restrictive currency policies, distortions of the international capital market and faulty monetary systems, such as the inter-war gold standard, are usually considered as some of the main determinants of performance.

Not only the writing about European and American inter-war economic history, but also the research of economic history of inter-war Austria overemphasised the importance of intentional political factors and macroeconomic data, which often tend to provide a rough and blurred picture of economic development. As most historians have noted the extreme foreign control of the League of Nations and its principle powers on Austrian policy-making and the seemingly extreme orthodox and deflationary economic policy of Austria, most writers have attributed a disproportionally great significance to the effects of policy-making and monetary mechanisms on stagnant Austrian economic growth and development.

In contrast, this work attempts to write a structural economic history. This is done by employing Schumpeter's business cycle theory and by attempting to describe his concept of the permanent "process of creative destruction" as it unfolded in various European countries. The analysis and interpretation of Austrian microeconomic data in the framework of the European economy forms an essential component of describing the "second industrial revolution" in Europe that led to the emergence of the consumer oriented, advanced classical 20th century economy. The distortion of this process during the inter-war period is regarded as the primary cause for economic stagnation in Europe. However, the strength of statement of this approach and this work clearly has its limitations. Similar to many historical studies that try to explain and understand large scale and long-term developments, essentially the process of attempting to provide a structural explanation is determined and constrained by theoretical preconceptions. Fundamentally, this study and all other attempts of an explanation and theoretical approaches do not just explain, but primarily describe the same complex process in different ways.[4]

The structure, method and the application of sources of this paper are adapted to the structural approach. Therefore, economic policies are discussed and alternative structural interpretations of economic history of different European countries are presented with the help of macroeconomic data as well as that of secondary literature which has applied a similar approach. On the other hand, a reinterpretation of the economic history of inter-war Austria is sought, also with the help of secondary literature and macroeconomic data, but primarily with the analysis and discussion of extensive microeconomic data of 24 Austrian industrial joint-stock companies. These are divided into traditional, stagnant and modern, expanding industrial sectors. The development and performance of these Austrian enterprises are incorporated into the framework of the general equivalent development and growth of industrial sectors in the economies of other European and peripheral countries.

For the discussion of comparative European economic policy and performance (which includes such intricate and heterogeneous topics as disintegration, inflati-

4 See also ibid, 31.

on, the gold standard, deflationary policies, the Great Depression and rearmament policies of authoritarian states), extensive secondary literature and contemporary statistics have been used. Some statistical data have been taken from historical statistics. Yet, the publications of the contemporary Austrian and German institutes of economic research (Österreichisches Institut für Konjunkturforschung and the German Institut für Konjunkturforschung) and the official Austrian and German statistical offices (Österreichisches Statistische Zentralamt and the German Statistisches Reichsamt) provided the most important statistical material. The most significant Austrian publications are the official statistical handbook (*Statistisches Handbuch für die Republik Österreich*), the report on Austrian inter-war foreign trade published after the Second World War (*Der Aussenhandel Österreichs in der Zeit zwischen den beiden Weltkriegen. Beiträge zur Österreichischen Statistik*) and the special issue of 1965 of the monthly reports of the Austrian institute for economic research, *Österreichs Volkseinkommen von 1913 bis 1963*.

Even better material could be extracted from the contemporary publications of the German Institut für Konjunkturforschung and the Statistisches Reichsamt. They not only provided valuable statistical material, but also reliable reports and analysis on contemporary economic issues. The most important sources are the German statistical yearbooks of 1924–1938 (*Statistisches Jahrbuch für das Deutsche Reich*), the German quarterly journal of business cycle research (*Vierteljahreshefte zur Konjunkturforschung*), the special issues of statistics (*Einzelschriften zur Statistik des Deutschen Reiches*), the economic journal of the statistical office (*Wirtschaft und Statistik*), and finally, the weekly reports of the German institute of economic research (*Wochenbericht des Instituts für Konjunkturforschung*). Furthermore, various contemporary and post-World War Two doctoral dissertations which covered various economic issues of the inter-war period have been used as well.

As the method of the utilisation of secondary literature and macroeconomic data is clear, only the procedure of the analysis and application of microeconomic data has to be elucidated. The main source of information on microeconomic development of Austrian industrial joint-stock companies is the contemporary Austrian version of the economist *Der Österreichische Volkswirt* and its supplement *Die Bilanzen* (the balance sheets). The weekly published supplement discussed the latest annual business reports, balance sheets and profit and loss accounts of the most important Austrian joint-stock companies. Fortunately, this periodical was published between 1918 and 1938 and remained nearly untouched by state censorship in the 1930s. For all bibliographical references that relate to these periodicals, I retained the German method of dating.

To analyse economic development of joint-stock companies, the financial data from *Die Bilanzen* was used to create time series diagrams of balance sheets and profit and loss accounts for those companies whose data were available for most of the period. The diagrams are alphabetically listed in the appendix. Thus, when discussing the financial standing and general development of Austrian companies, it is advisable to consult the time series diagrams in the appendix. For some companies, production data diagrams are also included. The financial time series diagrams vary slightly, but nearly all balance sheet diagrams include at least balance sheet value, accounts receivable (debtors) and liabilities (creditors). In some cases the data for capital stock and reserve, losses and bonded debts are included. All profit and loss account diagrams include data of gross profit, net profit, and total expenses. Some of the profit and loss account diagrams also include data for investment, depreciation and costs for servicing interest payments.

Combined with annual business reports, the financial time series diagrams allow an indirect analysis of the actual development of business activities. The balance sheets largely give rough clues about the changing volume of business, as well as the general financial standing. Most important determinants are the relation of liabilities to debtors and the change of balance sheet value. Besides the business reports, the profit and loss accounts have the greatest value for interpretation and demonstration of the development of any company. In most cases their financial standing directly reflected the real economic development. These time series diagrams of profit and loss accounts partially reveal investment behaviour as well as earning power. The rough development of earning power, i.e. profitableness, is discerned by calculating the relation of net profit to gross profit. In some cases this does not really work, as the nature of production and sales of some companies allowed for a more favourable relation of gross to net profits. It is essential to notice that the time series diagrams have their greatest advantage in revealing long-term developments. Therefore, in most cases, contemporary falsifications of annual financial data can be easily recognised. Yet, the primary source of information remained the annual business reports.

The basic organisation of this study consists of an alternation between discussions of economic theory, policy and macroeconomic development on the one hand, and discussions of Austrian microeconomic development embedded into general industrial European development on the other. The paper is divided into three parts, each incorporating a period of time with a distinctive type of economic development and growth. These specific periods and topics are disintegration, inflation and stabilisation until 1925; moderate prosperity and restrictive policies until 1930; and the years of the Great Depression until 1938. Apart from the first, part two and three include two chapters. One of these respective chapters discusses comparative macroeconomic development and policy. The second chapter in each part examines microeconomic development and includes a conclusion. Due to the difficult nature of the main topic and unreliable statistics, the first part only includes one chapter.

PART I

2. ECONOMIC POLICY AND DEVELOPMENT IN THE IMMEDIATE POST-WAR PERIOD, 1918–1924: DISINTEGRATION, INFLATION AND STABILISATION.

To begin the story of economic policy, performance and microeconomic development with a period which included the end of World War One, the disintegration of three empires, excessive inflation, sudden monetary stabilisation and the enormous social and economic turmoil that went along with these processes, is extremely difficult. First of all, these topics are far too complex and diffused to fit into the framework of this study. Secondly, as economic growth and development was highly influenced by inflation, available statistics, business reports, balance sheets and profit and loss accounts are unusually unreliable and difficult to scrutinise.

With these methodological difficulties in mind, this chapter will only attempt to answer very broad and general questions about the impact of three vital processes of this period on microeconomic development. Therefore, this first part just consists of one chapter (unlike parts II and III), which only incorporates a general and introductory discussion of comparative economic policy and Austrian microeconomic development. These processes are the disintegration of a traditional economic area, inflation and hyperinflation, and economic stabilisation.

2.1. DISINTEGRATION

After the war, the situation of the new Austrian Republic was exceptionally unique and problematical. It was the only advanced industrialised country involved in the war that not only experienced political and social turmoil, but also hyperinflation, the initial disintegration of old economic ties, the initial loss of traditional markets as well as of material resource bases. Its future economic and political prospects seemed meagre. Therefore, the issue of the Austrian development after 1918 has been the subject of heated debate, and the belief in economic nonviability ("Lebensunfähigkeit") remained vital not only for most contemporaries,[1] but also for many

1 Even well-informed contemporaries did not believe in the economic viablility of the Austrian Republic. Gustav Stolper, for example, the most important proponent of economic journalism, considered either a union with Germany or a Federation of the Danubian states (Donauföderation) as a solution. "Die einzelnen Erkenntnisse, zu denen sie [die Darstellung] gelangte, fügte sich zu dem lückenlosen Schluß von der Lebensunfähigkeit eines deutschösterreichischen Staates – dies nicht als wehleidige Protestphrase, sondern als objektiv begründete und begrifflich eindeutig umschriebene Tatsache gemeint." Gustav Stolper, *Deutschösterreich als Sozial- und Wirtschaftsproblem*, Vienna 1921, preface, XI. See also: Gustav Stolper, "Der Friedensvertrag von St. Germain in seinen wirtschaftlichen Wirkungen," in: *Schriften des Vereins für Sozialpolitik*, vol. 162, Gustav Stolper (ed.), *Deutsch-Österreich. Neue Beiträge über seine wirtschaftlichen Verhältnisse*, Munich and Leipzig 1921, 1–12. Friedrich Hertz was one of the few contemporary

modern historians and politicians.[2] Considering the short-term implications of the war after 1918, the calling into question of economic viability and the overestimation of war effects on Austrian economic development in the inter-war period is hardly surprising.

2.1.1. The Short-term Effects of the War

The short-term effects of the war were seemingly far more profound in Austria than in most other successor states.[3] Czechoslovakia, which inherited a greater share of the developed industrial areas, appeared to have had a much more balanced economy than Austria, and more easily faced the economic problems of the inter-war period.[4] This was partially due to its stronger nationalist movement and confidence, whereas in Austria there was a strong initial pessimism after the war and public opinion favouring a union with Germany.

Indeed extreme economic nationalism, in combination with massive war-time devastation and shortages, resulted in immediate and short-term economic problems. One of these included an acute fuel shortage and a lack of natural resources and raw materials,[5] which had to be expensively imported after 1918, especially as the inflation grew more fierce. During the times of the monarchy, coal was delivered from the mines in Silesia and Bohemia, territories which belonged to Poland and

scholars that had an affirmative opinion about Austria's economic viability. See his writings: *Ist Österreich lebensfähig?*, Vienna 1921; and "Zahlungsbilanz und Lebensfähigkeit Österreichs", in: *Schriften des Vereins für Sozialpolitik*, vol. 167, M.J. Bonn (ed.), *Probleme der deutschen Zahlungsbilanz*, Munich and Leipzig 1925, 3–62.

2 Hans Seidel, Secretary of State of the Austrian Ministry of Finance, wrote in 1981: "The Republic of Austria, which was founded after the breakdown of the Austro-Hungarian monarchy in 1918, was not considered economically viable and in fact was not viable. In the 1920s the economy could only be kept running with the aid of foreign loans." See Seidel's article: "The Austrian Economy: An Overview," in: Sven Ardt (ed.), *The Political Economy of Austria*, Washington, D.C., 1982, 7.

3 The literature on the collapse of the Austro-Hungarian Empire and the effects on Austria and the successor states is very extensive. For example: Jonathan Bloomfield, "Surviving in a Harsh World:Trade and Inflation in the Czecheslovak and Austrian Republics 1918–1926," in: Gerald D. Feldman, Carl-Ludwig Holtfrerich, Gerhard A. Ritter and Peter-ChristianWitt (eds.), *The Experience of Inflation. International and Comparative Studies*, New York 1984.

4 Of the Austrian part of the Habsburg Monarchy, the territory of the Austrian Republic had an average share of the national income of 4466 million crowns of a total income of 15,024.6 million crowns between 1911 and 1913. The Czech share was 6710.3 million, the Polish share 2267.7, the Yugoslavian 536.8 and the Romanian 236.1 million crowns. Norbert Schausberger, *Der Griff nach Österreich*, Vienna 1978, 82. Very detailed data about Austrian and Czecheslovak economic conditions after the war provide Karl Bachinger and Vlastislav Lacina, "Wirtschaftliche Ausgangsbedingungen", in: Alice Teichova and Herbert Matis (eds.), *Österreich und die Tschechoslovakei 1918–1938. Die wirtschaftliche Neuordnung in Zentraleuropa in der Zwischenkriegszeit*, Vienna 1996, 51 ff.

5 More about this: Peter-Robert Berger, *Der Donauraum im wirtschaftlichen Umbruch nach dem Ersten Weltkrieg. Währung und Finanzen in den Nachfolgestaaten Österreich, Ungarn und Tschechoslovakei 1918–1929*, dissertation, Vienna 1982, 183 ff.

Czechoslovakia after 1918. Now, coal and other raw material had to be imported from Czechoslovakia under high costs, until the immediate and harsh trade restrictions were lowered in the early 20s. For example, domestic production could only deliver 13% of railway requirements, one of the largest consumers of coal.[6] Not only did the railway system suffer from extreme lack of coal, but also the whole Austrian economy, especially in 1919,[7] as minimum annual supplies could not be met. Since the export oriented finishing industry constituted a large portion of the total industrial sector, Austria particularly suffered from a high dependence on raw material and semi-finished products imports.[8] Traditional conditions of industrial division of labour and trade were also torn apart. An example, often employed by historians, is the case of the textile industry.[9] The spinning and finishing processes, which had been located in Austria, were suddenly cut off from the weaving process, which was situated in Czechoslovak territory after 1918.

Another allegedly large problem arising out of the seemingly arbitrarily erected borders was the intersection of traffic lines and the loss of part of infrastructure. This was more severe for the Czechoslovak Republic than for Austria, because most railway lines concentrated on Vienna. Yet, both states lost their easy connection to the ports of Trieste and Rjeke, now located in Italy and in the newly established Yugoslavia.[10] Another harsh immediate problem for Austria was a serious shortage of foodstuffs in the years 1919 and 1920. Only insufficient relief credits, especially from Great Britain, France and Italy,[11] were provided.

However, the Austrian economic position should not have been regarded as negatively as contemporaries believed it to be. After all, with its new borders, Austria possessed about one eighth of the total territory and population and one third of the industry of the former monarchy. Therefore, it was the best developed country of the successor states, besides the Czechoslovak Republic, which incorporated about one fifth of the territory, one fourth of the population and far more than half of the industry of the monarchy.[12] The other, underdeveloped successor states, faced even

6 On the situation of the Austrian railway see: Hans Freihsl, *Bahn ohne Hoffnung. Die österreichischen Eisenbahnen von 1918 bis 1938. Versuch einer historischen Analyse*, Vienna 1971.

7 For example, Austrian coal production was 155,437 tons in December 1918, while the overall requirement was 12.5 million tons. Karl Bachinger and Herbert Matis, "Strukturwandel und Entwicklungstendenzen der Montanwirtschaft 1918–1938," in: Michael Mitterauer (ed.), *Österreichisches Montanwesen. Produktion, Verteilung, Sozialreformen (Sozial und Wirtschaftshistorische Studien)*, Vienna 1974.

8 Fritz Weber, "I. 2. Die wirtschaftliche Entwicklung," in: Emmerich Tálos, Herbert Dachs, Ernst Hanisch and Anton Staudinger (eds.), *Handbuch des politischen Systems Österreichs. Erste Republik 1918–1933*, Vienna 1995, 29.

9 Bloomfield, 234.

10 Ibid.

11 These countries borrowed 19 million US dollars from the US Treasury. This was spent on Austrian food relief. Austria, as a former central powers nation, was not entitled to help from the American Relief Administration which supported Eastern and Central European countries. Bloomfield, 239.

12 Dieter Stiefel, *Konjunkturelle Entwicklung und struktureller Wandel der österreichischen Wirtschaft in der Zwischenkriegszeit. Forschungsbericht Nr. 135*, Vienna 1978; and Alice Teichova, "A Comparative View of the Inflation of the 1920s in Austria and Czechoslovakia," in: Nathan

harsher problems, as their predominantly obsolete agricultural economies were no longer part of a protected, nearly self-sufficient large economic unit. For the first time, they were forced to integrate into a highly competitive world economic system.

2.1.2. Trade Policy and Disintegration

The greatest long-term change for Austria and the other successor states was the transformation from the large and tariff protected economic unit of the Austro-Hungarian Empire, incorporating over 50 million inhabitants, to a small export oriented and dependent economy. The impact of this major shift has long been a subject of contemporary and historical debate. As this change entailed harsh, immediate economic nationalism of the mostly underdeveloped successor states and an Austrian economy with an unprotected domestic market that was surrounded by trade barriers, contemporaries in Austria often attributed the economic misery of their country to disintegration and its consequences.[13]

After the war until 1925, Austria pursued a very liberal trade policy.[14] Even the first post-war tariffs that were introduced in 1925–27 were mild compared to the import duties in the neighbouring countries. One reason for this was the strong dependence of the economy on imports of fuel, raw materials and foodstuffs, especially after the war. Another reason was the stipulations of the peace treaty, which discarded the idea of the most-favoured nation principle and enforced unilateral and discriminative trade relations on the former Central Powers countries for the first five years after 1919. Yet, one of the main factors for liberal Austrian trade policy was the high dependence of the economy on foreign sales to be able to use the industrial capacity sufficiently. During the time of inflation the old, quite low customs tariffs of 1906 could be maintained, because the extreme currency depreciation made higher protection of the domestic market unnecessary.[15]

At the same time, the successor states' trade policies pursued the exact opposite principles. As structural shifts in the world economy tended to force these states to advance domestic industrialisation after the war, they turned to economic nationalism of which protective trade policies were an essential component.[16] These states either attempted to protect an underdeveloped industry and market, or trade policies were designed to assist the execution of a deflationary currency policy, as in the case

Schmukler and Edward Marcus (eds.), *Inflation through the Ages: Economic, Social, Psychological and Historical Aspects*, New York 1983.

13 For example: Gustav Stolper, *Deutschösterreich*.

14 Hermann Gross, "Mitteleuropäische Handelspolitik 1890–1938 und der Donauraum," in: *Der Donauraum. Zeitschrift des Forschungsinstitutes für den Donauraum*, vol. 7, 1962, 100–114.

15 Österreichisches Statistisches Zentralamt *Der Aussenhandel Österreichs in der Zeit zwischen den beiden Weltkriegen*, no. 1, Vienna 1946, 14.

16 Alice Teichova,"Die Wirtschaftspolitik der kleinen Nationen in Mittel- und Osteuropa. Sachzwänge und Handlungsspielräume in der Zwischenkriegszeit," in: Wolfram Fischer (ed.), *Sachzwänge und Handlungsspielräume in der Wirtschafts- und Sozialpolitik der Zwischenkriegszeit*, St. Katharinen 1985, 116 ff.

of Czechoslovakia. These policies included all sorts of import bans and restrictions, as well as nostrification, i.e. the nationalisation of Austrian foreign assets in the former belligerent countries and the successor states. Right after the war, the allies attempted to maintain a small amount of economic cohesion in the area, by forcing Hungary and the Czechoslovak Republic to continue their exports of coal and foodstuffs to Austria. This was stipulated in the peace treaties.[17] It was also conceded to the core successor states, Austria, Hungary and the Czechoslovak Republic, to conclude agreements on preferential customs tariffs outside of the multilateral most-favoured nation clauses. Yet, immediately after the conclusion of the peace treaties, the successor states kept up their protectionist policies, enhanced by the artificial and short-term market autarky caused by the war.

Many historians have been inclined to overestimate the effects of this political disintegration on economic development and trade. Disintegration and nationalisation have been predominantly considered as harmful to the economies of the area in the long run. The new borders in Central and Eastern Europe (determined by the Treaty of St. Germain), which had little relation to economic cohesion and traditional trade patterns, have been regarded as the most important reason for Austria's seemingly great economic disadvantage and non-viability after the war. It is maintained that this exogenous shock on economic structures had greater negative economic repercussions for Austria than in other states. It is said to have caused exceptionally severe structural economic distortions, resulting in unusually pronounced economic stagnation. The successor states' new extreme political and economic nationalism is said to have intensified these problems, as it limited export trade of the Austrian industry.[18]

However, in more recent literature a more differentiated view has been supported, which underlines the structural continuity of trade patterns and economic interdependencies in Central and South-Eastern Europe before and after the First World War. These authors have been stressing that this area remained one of the most closely interwoven economic units in the world, despite political forces that pressed economic disintegration forward.[19] Jürgen Nautz, in his monograph on

17 Gertrude Enderle-Burcel and Eduard Kubu, "Die österreichisch-tschechoslowakischen Handelsbeziehungen in der unmittelbaren Nachkriegszeit," in: Alice Teichova and Herbert Matis (eds.), *Österreich und die Tschechoslowakei 1918–1938*, 113–130.

18 Fritz Weber, "Die wirtschaftliche Entwicklung," 29–32.

19 "Die politische Entwicklung des Donauraumes nach 1918 ließ – wie bereits gezeigt worden war – keine wirtschaftliche Integration mehr erwarten: Neugegründete, autonome Staaten mit ungeheurer politischer Zentrifugalkraft, entgegengesetzte Bündissysteme, kriegerische Auseinandersetzungen um Grenzziehungen, Verschiedenartigkeit der neu enstandenen politischen Systeme (von der Räterepublik bis zum Königreich) usw. ließen eine ähnliche Desintegration auch in den witschaftlichen Beziehunngen erwarten. Die vorliegende Untersuchung liefert dazu allerdings gegenteilige Ergebnisse. [...] Wie in der Untersuchung für das Hochkonjunkturjahr 1928 gezeigt werden konnte, bildeten die Nachfolgestaaten der ehemaligen Habsburgermonarchie einen Handels-Integrationsraum ersten Ranges, stärker als er etwa zwischen den nordischen Staaten (ohne politische Hemmnisse) vorlag." Stefan Karner, Ingris Kubin and Micheal Steiner, "Wie real war 'Mitteleuropa?' Zur wirtschaftlichen Verflochtenheit des Donauraumes nach dem Ersten Weltkrieg," in: *Vierteljahrschrift für Sozial- und Wirtschaftsgeschichte*, vol. 74, no. 2, 1987, 153 ff.

Austrian trade policy, also supports this view. He believes that the consequences of economic disintegration have been overestimated.[20] Another author notes that none of the new national states could afford to pursue a policy of complete autarky over a longer period of time. It is asserted that open trade intercourse re-established itself after a few post-war years of initial isolation.[21]

This study attempts to support this view with its empirical data on company histories. Even though the Austrian economy underwent these drastic changes and suffered from discriminating policies of its neighbouring countries, the negative results were soon overcome or circumvented. In most cases, nostrification was ineffective and import tariffs had limited results, either because of Austrian inflationary competitive advantage or because of their ineffectiveness against advanced products. Old trade links with Eastern and South Central Europe were usually re-established, at least by the mid 20s. In addition, after the immediate war-time shortages had been met in the area, trade and trade policy tended to nearly return to normalcy.

Several factors limited the effectiveness of protectionist trade policies. As we shall see below, tariffs generally only tended to be high for products of the traditional industries, whereas the successor states' dependence on modern industrial finished goods was high. These must have enjoyed lower tariffs even in the immediate post-war years, as can be seen indirectly through company exports and sales development. Thus, as many Austrian companies exported advanced finished products, they were hardly affected by trade limitations. In addition, the rapidly depreciating crown parity rendered an easy circumvention of import barriers for most industrial sectors possible.

As companies' histories prove below, there were also many ways of circumventing nationalisation of foreign Austrian assets. One way, for instance, was to establish or buy subsidiary companies with sales organisations and production plants in the respective countries. These were often owned by nationals only pro forma. Another way was to create holding companies based in neutral or Entente countries. One example of such an Austrian-owned holding company was the Färbereien und

20 Jürgen Nautz, *Die österreichische Handelspolitik der Nachkriegszeit 1918–1923. Die Handelsvertragsbeziehungen zu den Nachfolgestaaten*, Wien 1994, 22; and in his article he also states that until recently the economic effects of economic disintegration had been overestimated and that economic unity continued in the face of political fragmentation, "Between Political Disintegration and Economic Reintegration. Austrian Trade relations with the successor states after World War I," in: David F. Good (ed.), *Economic Transformations in East and Central Europe. Legacies from the Past and Policies for the Future*, New York 1994, 261 ff.

21 Herbert Matis, "Disintegration and multi-national enterprises in Central Europe during the post-War Years (1918–23)," in: Alice Teichova and P.L. Cottrell, *International Business and Central Europe 1918–1939*, New York 1983, 75. Strong persistence of trade flows after World War One and close relations especially between the triangle Austria-Hungary and Austria-CSR is also emphasised by Jan Stankovsky, "Foreign trade in Austria and East-Central Europe. Retrospective and perspective," in: Teichova, *International Business*, 281 ff. Felix Butschek also does not regard the creation of tariff walls and other trade restrictions as effective as has been presumed. These measures "did not much change the direction of foreign trade because the trade relations among the successor states remained very close." Butschek, "External Shocks and Long-Term Patterns of economic growth in Central and Eastern Europe," in: Good, *Economic Transformations*, 31.

Druckereien Trust AG, established in Switzerland (Chur) in 1921. It controlled all branches of the former Vereinigte Fäbereien AG from Vienna in the new states.[22]

Moreover, harsh trade policies were not as harmful, because the first two or three years after the war, strong trade interconnections were not necessary anyway. Due to the war, domestic demand for all kinds of products was extremely high in all of these economies, which resulted in full capacity employment of these nations.[23] Shortages of raw materials were great. Therefore, domestic demand for finished products was high, so that it was easy to maintain high trade barriers. Nevertheless, as the more recent literature emphasised, this initial isolationism was not maintained for long, and as soon as immediate post-war domestic demand fell and urgent shortages were overcome, trade, division of labour and production, and exchange of goods and raw materials returned. Certainly, it returned on a more limited basis, and on a very selective basis with differentiated customs tariffs.

Thus, already after 1920 and 1921, interest for more liberal trade arrangements grew, especially in Austria and Czechoslovakia, which attempted to direct its trade more to Western Europe. These years introduced a return to normalcy in trade relations. The conference of Portorose established the will of the successor states to improve trade conditions. Austria and the CSR concluded the first trade and transport agreements, and in 1920, Austria signed trade treaties with Yugoslavia, Romania and Germany.[24] On May 4, 1921, another trade agreement was signed between Austria and the Czechoslovak Republic, including bilateral most-favoured nation treatment. The treaty was not immediately ratified because Czechoslovakia would have suffered a serious trade disadvantage due to price distortions from the Austrian inflation. However, after hyperinflation was terminated and once the League reconstruction of October 1922 began, the trade treaty was ratified in November and came into effect in the beginning of 1923. In December 1922, as an attempt to stimulate exports, the Austrian government invited Italy, the Czechoslovak Republic, Yugoslavia, Romania and Poland and all other nations which had had treaties with Austria before the war, to a trade conference.[25]

Following that, various customs tariffs with Italy, France, and Belgium were agreed upon. New tariffs with France lowered duties on certain Austrian imports in March 1923; in June, a new trade agreement included most-favoured nation treatment, and France and Austria granted each other minimal tariffs for various products. Most other trade agreements included most-favoured nation treatment. In 1923 and 1924, further treaties were signed with Denmark, Iceland, Japan, the Netherlands, Portugal, Russia, Sweden, Norway, Latvia, Romania and Turkey.[26] Customs tariffs were revised with Czechoslovakia in November 1924, and came into effect at the beginning of 1925. This considerably lowered customs tariffs barriers with one of

22 Matis, "Disintegration and multi-national Enterprises," 79 ff.

23 Andreas Resch and Zdenek Sládek, "Integrations- und Desintegrationstendenzen. Die Handelsbeziehungen 1921–1937," in: Teichova and Matis, *Österreich und die Tschechoslowakei*, 256 and 257.

24 Resch and Sládek, 262/263.

25 Nautz, *Handelspolitik*, 533 ff. Resch and Sládek, 266.

26 Nautz, *Handelspolitik,* 536.

Austria's most important trade partners.[27] This was certainly also part of a general European trend, after the Franco-German confrontation of 1923, of introducing the return to economic normalcy and the end of reconstruction.

2.2. INFLATION

After the First World War, inflations of various degrees occurred in many areas of Europe. Generally, there were three groups of countries with distinct courses of currency development. Only among the countries of the first group no inflations occurred at all. These are the countries that tried to maintain or return to the pre-war gold parities of their currency. These were the United States, Great Britain, Switzerland, the Netherlands, Spain, and the Scandinavian countries. The second group consisted of those nations that experienced only moderate inflations and which stabilised their currencies at a lower gold parity than before the war. These countries were France, Belgium, Italy and Czechoslovakia. The third group were the countries which not only underwent inflations, but suffered from hyperinflations. They allowed the total depreciation of their currencies and required currency reforms. These were Germany, Austria, Hungary, Poland and Russia.[28]

2.2.1. Theories of the Causes of Inflation

Besides the Great Depression of the 1930s, the post-war inflations in Germany, Russia and Central Europe probably constituted the most horrifying economic experiences of the inter-war period. The essential mechanisms that caused these inflationary processes seemed to have been very similar in these countries, even though their political circumstances were very different. Specifically, the causes of the German and Austrian inflations are comparable, as both countries were highly advanced and encountered similar political and economic conditions.

In Austria, contemporary discussion about the causes of inflation generally evolved around two contrary approaches. The supporters of the money quantity theory believed that running budget deficits and the massive expansion of the national money stock entailed currency depreciation and inflation. The second group of contemporary theoreticians regarded the chronically passive national balance of payments situation that resulted from the structural difficulties of a small state as the primary cause of inflation. Orthodox and liberal economists and politicians, such as Alexander Spitzmüller[29] and Viktor Kienböck,[30] tended to adhere to the former

27 Resch and Sládek, 268.

28 Gerald D. Feldman, Carl-Ludwig Holtfrerich, Gerhard A. Ritter, Peter-Christian Witt, "Einführung. Inflation und Wiederaufbau in Deutschland und Europa 1914 bis 1924. Ein Forschungsprojekt," in: Gerald D. Feldman, Carl-Ludwig Holtfrerich, Gerhard A. Ritter, Peter-Christian Witt (eds.), *The German Inflation Reconsidered. A Preliminary Balance*, New York 1982, 4.

29 President of the Austro-Hungarian Bank. See: Alexander Spitzmüller, ... *und hat auch Ursach es zu lieben*, Vienna 1955.

theory and believed in a policy of currency reform that could end the inflationary process. The latter theory was usually supported by those who considered the viability of the new Austrian state as unrealistic.[31]

Modern theories of the causes of inflation either emphasise the cost-push factor (for example the rise of prices for wages and raw materials) or the demand pull factors (demand enormously exceeds supply).[32] In their attempt to explain the inflations of the early 20s, historians have tried to utilise current theories and emphasised the intricate and stratified causes of currency devaluation at different stages of the inflationary processes. In the case of the German and Austrian inflations, remarkable similarities of their courses have been ascertained. This is also the case when one compares the more moderate French inflation until 1926.

Bachinger and Matis regarded the result of the appalling disproportion of the massive increase of the money supply and the continuous lack of goods as the cause for inflation.[33]

Most historians have seen the inflationary finance of war costs after 1914 as the initial cause of inflation. Governments financed their expenses and deficits with domestic public loans and state money creation through the national banks that had suspended their bank rates. The consequence was an enormous expansion of the money supply during the war. This occurred in all belligerent countries. Only in Britain a large proportion of the war costs were financed with taxes.

The enormous acceleration of inflations, especially in Germany and Austria, is often considered as caused by domestic political constrains after 1919. In both countries, massive social uprisings occurred at the end of 1918. Therefore, economic policy of the new governments was constrained by the efforts to maintain social peace and initiate resumption of economic growth at all costs. That entailed the introduction and maintenance of expensive programmes of social relief, such as high unemployment support, work creation programmes, labour support for the enforcement of wage increases and other types of social support. Furthermore, the repatriation of armies and large raw material and foodstuffs imports were also financed by massive government spending. This expenditure could only be maintained by sustaining the war-time inflationary financing of state deficits.

Thereafter, inflations seemed to become increasingly controlled by the changing political situation. As the harsh clauses of the peace treaties became public, the value of the Austrian crown and the German mark tended to decline. In early 1920, currency depreciation slowed down as the political situation seemed to calm down. In Austria, for instance, the rumours of the possibility of large scale Allied relief credits resulted in capital repatriation and currency stabilisation. As soon as it became clear that there was no foreign help and as the German reparation sum was determined, inflation intensified again. In Austria, it turned to hyperinflation after

30 He became president of the Austrian central bank in the 30s. See: Viktor Kienböck, *Das österreichische Sanierungswerk*, Vienna 1925.

31 Karl Bachinger and Herbert Matis, "Die österreichische Nachkriegsinflation 1918–1922," in: *Beiträge zur Historischen Sozialkunde*, No. 3, 1986, 88–89.

32 Ibid., 89.

33 Ibid., 83.

May 1922, once a government crisis lowered the probability of foreign relief credits. In Germany, hyperinflation became extreme, because passive resistance against the French occupation of the Rhineland was supported by extreme intentional currency depreciation. Until November 1923, the German currency had depreciated to four billion marks to one dollar. By the end of 1922, 14.4 thousand Austrian paper crowns were worth one pre-war gold crown.[34]

Roughly, most of these inflation theories tend to attribute the causes and severity of inflations in the early 1920s to political factors that pushed economic policy-making to pursue inflationary monetary policies which entailed negative economic consequences.

Among all of these factors, a post-World War Two study of the League of Nations has considered the expenses of post-war reconstruction requirements and the inability to finance these by restricted consumption and increased taxation as one of the most vital elements that supported inflation. Railway, military and social expenses rose tremendously, whereas the "country's productive resources [were] close to being fully employed"[35] for unrestrained domestic private consumption. Instead of concentrating the countries' economic efforts on reconstruction alone, so it was argued, the populations of many states indulged in private consumption and dissaving. Therefore, public reconstruction expenses which were not backed-up by sufficient taxation and saving could only be financed with increasing inflation. This was a more structural approach to explain the roots of rapid inflation.

Another structural historical hypothesis of inflation causes, in close relation to previous analyses, can be discerned. Indirectly, it reveals the insignificance of economic policy, as it was constrained and controlled by secular, long-term structural socio-economic shifts that were intensified by the war. It also shows that the same large scale socio-economic processes not only constrained and dominated economic policy-making, but were also the main determinants of inflations in several European countries at this time. Essentially, extreme inflation was not only a political phenomenon, but an expression of, and a reaction to, extreme socio-economic shocks of the economy.

In this view, the existence of a socio-economic inflation-consensus ("Inflationskonsens")[36] within a country's population is considered a pre-condition for rapid currency depreciation. Especially, Schuker employed this approach in explaining the

34 Far more detailed accounts of the inflationary processes in Germany and Austria are given by Bachinger and Matis, "Nachkriegsinflation", 84-86, and Gerald D. Feldman, "Der Historiker und die deutsche Inflation," in: *Beiträge zur Historischen Sozialkunde*, no. 3, 1986, 69–70. See also W.F. Hallgarten and Joachim Radkau, *Die Deutsche Industrie und Politik von Bismark bis in die Gegenwart*, Frankfurt a.M., 1974, 171 ff, and Walré de Bordes, *The Austrian Crown. Its Depreciation and Stabilisation*, London 1924.

35 League of Nations, Economic, Financial and Transit Department (ed.), *The Course and Control of Inflation. A Review of Monetary Experience in Europe after World War I*, reprinted edition (original publication: 1946), New York 1978, 5. See also chapter 1: Financing Post-War Reconstruction.

36 Feldman, "Der Historiker," 70.

run-on French inflation until 1926.[37] In this view, the population of a country with inflationary war finance was essentially unwilling to carry the financial burden of the war after the end of hostilities. As inflation could only be stopped by reducing or ending the expansion of the national debt, subsequent public expenditure either had to be extremely restricted or taxation had to be increased in order to finance social and reconstruction spending. In those countries where the social and economic disruptions of the war had been extremely harsh (Germany, Austria, Central and Eastern European countries and Russia), the unwillingness of the population to tolerate increasing taxation and/or falling expenditure was especially pronounced. Therefore, governments' economic policies in these countries were extremely constrained by inflation-consensus of the population. Governments had no choice but to resort to continuous war-time financing and massive spending.

Inflations worsened as the system of credibility and cooperation between fiscal policy and the most influential socio-economic interest groups declined. As compelled inflationary government currency policy continued, the trust of the population in its national currency deteriorated. As long as important socio-economic interest groups kept benefiting from the advantages of inflationary finance, currency depreciation was protracted. The process continued to a point where the disadvantages of inflation predominated and the currency could not be used as a means of payment.[38] Until then, inflation had worked as an undifferentiated, unavoidable and arbitrary method of indirect taxation of weak governments on those sections of society that based their wealth primarily on capital.[39] Great internal public debts, based on war bonds, were cancelled. Then, a complete currency stabilisation became the most expedient policy, supported by stabilisation consensus ("Stabilisierungskonsens") of the greater part of the population.[40]

In countries with mild but prolonged inflation, very similar processes took place. However, in these cases, inflations never became extreme as it was possible at an early point in time to find a political, social and economic consensus for stabilisation. In France, run-on inflation until the mid 20s was also caused by the reluctance of the population to accept the financial burden of the war. Yet, with increasing political and economic stability after 1925, cooperation and credibility was restored. Unlike Austria, in Czechoslovakia, the currency reform of April 1919 and political independence established credibility and cooperation of the population in public fiscal

37 Stephen A. Schuker, *The End of French Predominance in Europe. The Financial Crisis of 1924 and the Adoption of the Dawes Plan*, North Carolina 1976.

38 Charles P. Kindleberger provides a good discussion of structural and monetary inflation theories. Kindleberger, "A Structural View of the German Inflation," in: Feldman, Holtfrerich, Ritter, Witt, *Experience of Inflation*.

39 John Maynard Keynes in 1924: "Eine Regierung kann durch dieses Mittel [public money creation] leben, wenn sie durch kein anderes mehr leben kann. Es ist diejenige Form der Besteuerung, der das Publikum am schwersten auszuweichen vermag, und die selbst die schwächste Regierung durchsetzen kann, auch wenn sie sonst nichts mehr durchsetzen kann." Cited in: Carl-Ludwig Holtfrerich, "Die deutsche Inflation 1914–1923 und ihre Verteilungswirkungen," in: *Beiträge zur Historischen Sozialkunde*, no. 3, 1986, 75.

40 Feldman, "Der Historiker," 71.

policy right after the war and considerably mitigated the inflation.[41] Banknotes were stamped to 1% of their nominal value, and 50% of privately held banknotes and of banks and savings accounts were converted into a 1% compulsory public loan. It is assumed that due to the monetary reform, about one quarter of money circulation was taken out of the economy.[42] As the state was able to float large domestic loans (for example the national liberation loan), increased taxes and was not responsible for war debts, it was partially possible to cover the national debt[43] and to limit consumption, expenditure and inflation successfully.[44]

2.2.2. Implications of Inflation

Inflations had long-term effects on economic policy-making. They caused an inflation phobia in the inter-war period, which uncompromisingly forced economic policy after the mid 20s into a static, neoliberal deflationary policy, even in the face of severe economic depression in the early 30s. Most countries that underwent mild or rapid inflation adhered to orthodox policies during the depression.

At first glance, inflation in Austria and Germany seemed to have had positive implications on macroeconomic levels. While there was a short, but violent worldwide economic recession in 1920/21, especially harmful to the British and American economies, Germany and Austria experienced rapid economic growth and full employment.[45] Meanwhile, between 1920 and 1924, Austrian GNP was growing 7.5% annually. Industrial production expanded at rates around 10% or more. In comparison, in the period of relative prosperity, between 1924 and 1929, national income was only growing 3.5% annually.[46] A very similar development took place in Germany, when an inflationary boom of iron and steel production, ship-building, rebuilding of railways and an increase of consumption supported rapid economic growth after 1920.

In addition, rapid inflation resulted in a competitive export advantage. As the Austrian crown and the mark depreciated, their relative national price levels dropped in comparison to world market prices. Inflation caused low prices for Austrian

41 Josef Faltus and Alice Teichova, "Die Nachkriegsinflation. Ein Vergleich," in: Teichova and Matis, *Österreich und die Tschechoslovakei*. On monetary policy of the successor states see also: Friedrich Steiner, "Erster Teil. Notenbankpolitik und staatliche Anleihepolitik in den österreichisch-ungarischen Nachfolgestaaten," in: *Schriften des Vereins für Sozialpolitik*, vol. 166, Franz Eulenburg (ed.), *Deutsche Zahlungsbilanz und Stabilisierungsfrage*, Munich and Leipzig 1924, 3–80.

42 Teichova, "Inflation in Austria and Czechoslovakia," in: Schmukler, Nathan and Edward Marcus (eds.), *Inflation through the Ages*, New York 1983, 538.

43 Alice Teichova, "Die Inflation der 1920er Jahre in Mitteleuropa im Vergleich," in: *Beiträge zur Historischen Sozialkunde*, no. 3, 1986, 68.

44 League of Nations, *The Course and Control of Inflation*, 65.

45 Holtfrerich, "Die deutsche Inflation," 78. Feldman, "Der Historiker," 69.

46 Österreichisches Institut für Wirtschaftsforschung, *Monatsberichte des Österreichischen Instituts für Wirtschaftsforschung, special issue 14, Österreichs Volkseinkommen 1913 bis 1963*, Vienna 1965, 5.

and German goods, and export industries began to thrive temporarily. France and Great Britain suffered from the German exchange dumping export.[47] In Austria, this competitive export advantage was only effective after mid 1920, after most short-term effects of the war were overcome and when the world economy experienced a slump.[48] The more contemporaries became aware of these advantages for economic growth, the more the social inflation consensus was strengthened. Not only industrialists, but primarily the lower income groups benefited from a favourable redistribution of income.[49]

However, these inflationary booms only brought superficial economic benefits. Even though inflations helped to initiate economic growth after the war and rendered possible full employment, German national income of 1923 was only 72% and Austrian only 79% of 1913 levels.[50] At the same time the advanced countries reached or surpassed pre-war growth levels. Moreover, economic growth rates in countries with extreme inflations were primarily so rapid because they started from very low post-war growth levels. Inflations tended to support the growth process, but were not the primary cause for recovery. The competitive export advantage only lasted for short periods of time, and the volume of export trade during the inflation was still far lower than during the stabilisation process between 1923 and 1925. Before that, between 1920 and 1922, the annual average value of Austrian exports was 1412.6 million schillings (981 million gold crowns).[51] In 1925, when the economy was still suffering from stabilisation crisis, the export value amounted to 2167 million schillings.[52]

Thus, inflations seemed to have had ambivalent implications. On the one hand, they offered great short-term advantages, such as the export advantage, low labour costs, easily attainable (but often diluted) capital, cheap investments and quick returns. On the other hand, as stabilisation proved, there were many long-term disadvantages, such as massive misinvestment, low and insufficient investment, and therefore, in the long-term, low productivity and competitiveness. To what degree these symptoms of inflations affected economic subjects is difficult to judge.

Very little historical research has been conducted in the field of company history and inflations of the early 20s.[53] The results of studies of inflation effects on real economic development have been equivocal. Many economists have asserted that inflation intensified structural distortions. Yet, a study on German heavy industry concluded that the history of the iron and steel industry during the inflation was a story of success. Companies rebuilt their plants and expanded their production capacity.[54] Other studies have shown that, compared to the pre-war era, investments were

47 Hallgarten and Radkau, *Deutsche Industrie und Politik*, 159

48 Bachinger and Matis, "Nachkriegsinflation," 86.

49 Ibid., 87–88. See also Holtfrerich, "Die deutsche Inflation."

50 Holtfrerich, "Die deutsche Inflation," 78. Österreichisches Institut für Wirtschaftsforschung, *Monatsberichte 14*, 43.

51 Bachinger and Matis, "Nachkriegsinflation," 86.

52 *Volkseinkommen*, 42.

53 Gerald D. Feldman and Heidrun Homburg, *Industrie und Inflation*, Hamburg 1977.

54 Gerald D. Feldman, *Iron and Steel in the German Inflation 1916–1923*, New Jersey 1977, 12.

far lower during the inflation in Germany.[55] The stronger inflation became, the more companies' domestic bank deposits declined. Investment rates dropped. In Germany, this was especially the case after the summer of 1922, when hyperinflation set in. Firms only held domestic bank credit and deposits abroad.

Microeconomy analysis of Austria shows that a few large companies were able to benefit from the positive symptoms of inflation. This depended on numerous factors, such as the type of company, its business and trade policy, the time of capital accumulation and allocation for investment. Most companies, however, could not take advantage from inflation as it made a proper readjustment of economic structures to a new post-war world market very difficult or nearly impossible. This depended on the type of company. As this paper attempts to divide the industrial sector into the modern 20th century industrial branches and traditional pre-war sectors, a trend of performance during the inflation becomes apparent.

Usually, companies of the modern sectors of the economy tended to perform better than traditional firms. Unlike their German counterparts,[56] the Austrian traditional heavy industry, for example, did not seem to do very well. It also seemed that larger companies benefited more from the financial advantages than smaller firms.[57] The inflation seemed to intensify the process of stagnation for traditional industries and expansion for modern sectors. Thus, the notion that industrial structural distortions from the war were intensified during the inflation cannot be fully supported.

2.3. STABILISATION

Stabilisation will only be briefly addressed here, as its repercussions on policy and performance will be discussed in chapter two and three. For microeconomic analysis in chapter one, only the short-term effects of stabilisation crisis will be discussed.

2.3.1. The Mechanism of Stabilisation

In all countries with inflation, the end of rapid currency depreciation and the introduction of stabilisation meant an extreme policy regime shift.[58] The key to currency stabilisation of all of these countries was a shift in policy so that credibility and cooperation between fiscal policy-making and the population was restored. Basically, the stability of currencies depended on "trust and faith" of the population in the state to secure its debts. Policy makers in the government ministries and central banks had to ensure that the national debt was covered by the ability and obligation of

55 Dieter Lindenlaub, "Maschinenbauunternehmen in der Inflation 1919 bis 1923. Unternehmenshistorische Überlegungen zu einigen Inflationstheorien," in: Feldman, Holtfrerich, Ritter and Witt, *German Inflation*, 49 ff.

56 Feldman, "Der Historiker." See also: Feldman, *Iron and Steel.*

57 Bachinger and Matis, "Nachkriegsinflation," 86.

58 Thomas J. Sargent, "Die Beendigung vier großer Inflationen," in: Feldman, Holtfrerich, Ritter and Witt, *Experience of Inflation*, 39 ff.

the state to maintain taxation on an appropriate level. This ensured coverage of the future national debt. An important element of this policy regime shift and return of credibility was the re-establishment of the pre-war gold standard. After the inflation ended, policy makers in France, Germany, Austria and Central Europe adopted a harsh deflationary monetary policy in order to once again peg their currencies to a gold parity. The pegging to gold only meant that governments accepted the obligation to fulfil their future debts. This way, they automatically limited and constrained their future financial, currency and economic policy, especially during times of stagnant economic growth. This will be the topic of chapter two.

In order to facilitate the change of policy, some countries, such as Austria, received reconstruction loans from the League of Nations.[59] Thus, as Austria was a country where this regime shift was enforced most pronounced after 1923 as a model for stabilisation,[60] its economic policy can be clearly divided into two periods of extremes: The time of inflationary policy from the war until the end of 1922 and the time of restrictive and very deflationary policy thereafter until 1938.[61]

2.3.2. Implications of Stabilisation

The vital fact for microeconomic analysis of this chapter is that the sudden shift from extreme inflation to sudden currency stability resulted in a severe shock on the national economies of Austria, Germany and many Eastern European countries. Stabilisation was part of the general inflation phenomenon. With its extremity, it led to an inevitable crisis. All nations experiencing strong inflation, also had to undergo a painful period of short, but abrupt stagnation due to extreme deflation. The stronger inflation had been, the more painful the stabilisation process and crisis. This was not so much the case in France, where inflation had been comparatively mild. Generally, this sudden extreme shift of economic policy had strong effects on economic performance.

The great export advantage due to the extremely depreciating currency, which had helped to overcome protective trade barriers, was suddenly lost. This was a shock to the export oriented economy of Austria. Another problem was the necessary extreme shift of national monetary policy. It entailed periods of eminently restrictive credit availability. The overall result of stabilisation was that countries with extreme inflation suffered from erratic short-term economic slumps in the mid 20s. Germany

59 Countries that received loans were: Austria (1923), Belgium (1926), Bulgaria (1928), Danzig (1925), Estonia (1927), Germany (1924), Greece (1928), Hungary (1924), Poland (1927), Romania (1929), Yugoslavia (1931). League of Nations, *The Course and Control of Inflations*, 98.

60 League of Nations stabilisation schemes were modelled to the Austrian reconstruction process. For example, Hungarian stabilisation in 1924 was very similar. Berger, *Der Donauraum*, 496 ff.

61 Karl Bachinger, "Teil II: Österreich 1918–1945. 4. Der Staat und dieWirtschaft," in: Karl Bachinger, Hildegard Hemetsberger-Koller and Herbert Matis (eds.), *Grundriss der österreichischen Sozial- und Wirtschaftsgeschichte von 1848 bis zur Gegenwart*, Vienna 1987, 77 ff.

had several stabilisation crises in late 1923, as well as in several months in 1924, 1925 and 1926. Hungary suffered from a stabilisation crisis in the same years, Poland much later in 1926/27, and Austria in 1923 and 1924.

2.4. MICROECONOMIC DEVELOPMENT DURING DISINTEGRATION, INFLATION AND STABILISATION

2.4.1. Traditional and Modern Industries

Now, we will turn to a discussion of company histories until 1924/25. In order to detect patterns of economic development and growth of the 21 companies that have been analysed here, they are divided into traditional industries of the 19th century, and modern industrial branches that saw their large scale application in the 20th century. In turn, traditional and modern industries are divided into industrial sectors. The same method has been used in chapters 3 and 5. This method is utilised in order to support a theory of endogenous economic growth, based on long-term and large scale transformations of industrial structures. These transformations are determined by the different rate of the constant application of new innovations and technology among industrial sectors and the change of consumption patterns. This approach will be further elaborated in chapters 2 and 4. For understanding microeconomic development during disintegration, inflation and stabilisation, it is important to note that growth rates of modern sectors tended to exceed those of the traditional industries, as a result of the permanent transformation of the consumption and production processes and patterns in advanced industrialised capitalist countries. Moreover, modern sectors tended to deal with exogenous shocks, such as inflation, much better than traditional industries. They suffered more from international structural changes and disproportions after the war.[62]

2.4.2. Traditional Industries

2.4.2.1. Iron and Steel Producing and Processing Industry

a. Alpine The first industrial sector to be discussed is the iron and steel industry, mainly represented by the largest Austrian company, the Österreichisch-Alpine Montangesellschaft. The other two are Gebrüder Böhler and Schoeller-Bleckmann. Before the war, the Alpine Montan had concentrated its production on raw materials (coal and iron ore) and semi-finished products (steel, rolled steel), and possessed

62 Theoretically, this approach is based on Joseph A. Schumpeter's business cycles theory. See section 4.3. Literature that employed a similar approach and on which this work builds on is listed in footnotes of 2.1.2 and 4.3. A similar structural approach has been employed by Ingvar Svennilson, *Stagnation and Growth in the European Economy*, United Nations, Economic Commission for Europe, Geneva 1954.

coal mines in Fohnsdorf, Köflach, Seegraben and in Orlau (Silesia), ore mines in Eisenerz and Hüttenberg, iron ore mines in Hieflau and Vordernberg, steel works in Donawitz and Neuberg and refineries in Donawitz, Kindberg, Neuberg and Zeltweg. Alpine had about 17,000 workers and employees before the war.[63] However, due to the post-war disturbances production and employment fell rapidly, from a workforce of 19,000 during the war to 12,500.[64]

Not only was employment uncertain, but also ownership conditions. After the state sold 50 thousand shares to the notorious speculator Camilio Castiglioni in 1919, and after 200 thousand shares had been in the hands of the Italian car manufacturer Fiat, the Italian banks Credito Italiana and the Banka commerciale Italiana,[65] the German steel combine of Hugo Stinnes controlled the majority of Alpine shares after 1921.[66] After the Stinnes combine collapsed, the majority of shares remained in the hands of the largest European steel trust, the German Vereinigte Stahlwerke.

The Alpine was one of the firms which experienced the negative effects of war, immediate post-war shortages, inflation and sudden stabilisation most severely. Suddenly, after it already had experienced distortion from the war economy, it had to rely on massive fuel and raw material imports. Alpine suffered from coal shortages, exhaustion of plant, declining production and low productivity. Production of metallurgical engineering declined the most and was only one fifth of peace time production in 1920. Although coal demand was high, its production was 20% below the pre-war level.[67] After disintegration, Alpine iron and steel production had to face international market forces, while the firm suffered from the harsh, immediate effects of the war. For example, the connection between Styrian iron ore and the Bohemian coal mines had been interrupted,[68] causing severe coal shortages in 1919 and 1920, and continued to disturb production until the spring of 1921. It was attempted to compensate the sudden import dependence by establishing affiliated companies in the successor states. In 1923, the Alpine created the Ferro AG in Budapest and the Montansyndikat in Zagreb as footholds in Eastern Europe. Management also bought shares of the Silesian-Polish Bismarckhütte and the Kattowitzer Bergbau und Eisenhüttenbetrieb to secure coke supplies.[69] However, most of the coke requirements came from the German Stinnes steel combine after April 1921, which finally allowed for higher raw iron production.

The development of the Alpine was a classical example of the problems that the European iron and steel industry, as a traditional sector, suffered from during the inter-war period.[70] Actual demand for iron and steel and its products did not decline

63 Franz Mathis, *Big Business in Österreich. Österreichische Großunternehmen in Kurzdarstellungen*, Vienna 1987, 25.

64 Helmut Fiereder, "Die Österreichisch-Alpine Montangesellschaft (OeMAG) von 1881 bis 1938. Technologie, Konzernierung und besitzrechtliche Verhältnisse im alpenländischen Hüttenwesen", in: *Scripta Mercuaturae*, vol. 15, no. 1, 1981, 68 ff.

65 Bachinger and Matis, "Montanwirtschaft," 110.

66 Mathis, 25 and 26. Fiereder, 68.

67 Ibid, 109.

68 Matis, "Disintegration and multi-national enterprises, 79.

69 Matis, "Disintegration and multi-national enterprises, 80.

70 Svennislon, 119 ff.

after the war, but the expansion of demand was on a much lower level that before 1914. During the war, European production capacity had been increased. Yet, after the end of hostilities, capacity was expanded even more. For example, French plants were built up during the war in areas outside of North Eastern France, where those plants had been either in occupied or combat areas. After the war, these factories were quickly rebuilt and France left the war with much higher production capacity than before. In Germany, production capacity increased during the war and thereafter, because the plants in Alsace-Lorraine, the Saar and Upper Silesia were lost to France. British production capacity was also considerably expanded. In addition, the much more modern factories that had been built, were much larger and productive, due to technical reasons. Furthermore, national expansion of plant capacity was supported by governments, as iron and steel production was considered vital for military demands and national defence. Capacity increases were also enhanced by high expectations of entrepreneurs, who hoped for the same expansion of demand that had existed before the war. Thus, by the mid 20s, capacity of steel production on the European continent was probably 50% higher than before the war,[71] whereas demand had not risen commensurately.

The consequence of this development was fierce competition on the European and world iron and steel markets. International prices tended to fall permanently, and often precipitously, while national prices were maintained at high levels, to the detriment of national processing industries and consumers. This extremely competitive environment was especially harmful to a capital intensive industry that suffered from low price elasticity. Finally, this process led to cartelisation, the emergence of ever larger industrial combines and extreme national protectionism. Alpine Montan suffered from these major structural problems in particular, because it had not been exposed to the world market before the war, and because it was situated in a small export dependent country. Moreover, its productivity was lower than that of other European national producers. Especially, productivity of ore production in Styria was low.[72]

The sudden forceful shift from a large and protected domestic market to open fierce and world-wide competition, in combination with the structural problems of the European iron and steel industries, made the Alpine particularly vulnerable to economic policy, policy changes and economic crises not only during the time directly following 1918, but also in the long-term. Its overall development was determined by the crisis that iron, steel and coal production was undergoing during the inter-war period. Therefore, the subsequent description is a mirror image of these structural faults.

As the main firm of the older industries that suffered from structural deficiencies, it was also one of the main companies that put the greatest pressure on the enforcement of a policy of protectionism in Austria. Thus, structural shifts that pressured large sectors of national producers, moved politics to protective trade and currency policy on the national level, to attempt to alleviate the consequences of the war for

71 Ibid, 124.

72 Bachinger and Herbert, "Montanwirtschaft," 118.

their domestic industries. The development of the Alpine shows how little these political measures were functional and helpful. Internationally, policy measures, especially of protectionism and competitive currency depreciation, were harmful for all and enhanced stagnation and crises. Alpine is a perfect example of this development, since it suffered extremely from the protectionist policies of its neighbour countries, from its weak position after the war and its greater export dependence. Other national iron and steel industries, in Germany, Great Britain, and France, did not suffer from the structural faults and policy measures as much, because these national industries could rely on a fairly large domestic market ensuring at least moderately sufficient demand.

Business Activity

Unlike many other companies, the Alpine[73] could not take advantage from the depreciation of the crown at all. Business activity was already very low in 1921. Export sales were stagnating and almost impossible in the successor states, because of high customs tariffs and administrative obstacles. Export prices were also far too low for the firm's production costs, and it became necessary to sell under prime cost price, while much cheaper Czechoslovak iron was imported. Capital availability was a serious problem. In the following year, two capital increases of more than 100 million crowns were carried through to finance running costs and investment. Yet, as capital was quickly diluted and profits were low, the financial situation continued to be precarious. The following capital increases also proved to be insufficient for capital intensive investments and debt coverage. Rate of issues were too low and rapid inflation quickly depreciated balance sheet value. In 1922, business improved slightly, but debts were increasing, because the imported Czechoslovak coke had not been paid. The management was urgently looking for foreign credit.

With more extreme inflation, sales development exactly followed along the lines of the falling crown in 1922, and as soon as stabilisation materialised in the autumn of that year, the already low export volume declined rapidly. Once the crown was stabilised, the Austrian market was flooded with cheap imported iron from Czechoslovakia and Hungary. Thus, dismissal of 3000 workers, the shut-down of two plants and short working became necessary. In 1922, management complained about the much too high tariff walls of the successor states, while foreign competition was allegedly easily able to infiltrate the Austrian market. The leadership demanded multilateral most-favoured nation trade terms. Yet, once this was finally established in 1925, the Alpine export conditions still had not improved.

The Ruhr crisis in Germany and the dramatic decline of German iron, coal and steel production resulted in a brief and moderate boom. Already by January, when the Belgian and French troops began the occupation of the West German industrial area, Alpine production began to thrive again. Especially raw ore, and to lesser degree, iron ore production increased. Belgian and German competition on the Austrian market came to an end and exports increased. Production capacity was utilised to almost 100% and the workforce was larger than in the last pre-war year. Most exports went to Germany, while the old sales areas of Italy, Switzerland and the Balkans

73 *Bilanzen*, 28.10.1922, 2.12.1922, 9.12.1922, 16.12.1922, 27.1.1923, 24.2.1923, 9.6.1923, 7.6.1924, 11.10.1924, 1.11.1924, 18.7.1925, 19.6.1926, 3.7.1926. See also A.2 and A.3.

became almost insignificant, either because of high tariffs, because of small demand, or because of competition, especially from Belgian firms. These were able to export more cheaply to the Balkan area by sea, than Alpine, which was directly positioned in the neighbouring country. Clearly, this shows the dramatic loss of productivity and competitiveness of the Alpine Montangesellschaft. With the end of the Ruhr crisis, Alpine business activity also declined. It only proved to be a brief, specious boom.

1924 was a serious crisis year as its earning power fell precipitously. The currency stabilisation crisis, which lowered domestic demand, coincided with the end of the artificial demand from Germany, after the Ruhr crisis terminated. Once again, short working had to be introduced and blast furnaces were shut down in a plant for iron ore and in a plant for steel production in Donawitz. Furthermore, one plate rolling mill and one steel plant had to be closed. In late 1924, the downswing continued. Apart from the coal mines, almost all plants had to be shut down in October, and only by November did business activity resume growth at low levels. Slowly, orders for railtracks and railway carriage springs were placed by the Austrian federal railways. Yet, exports remained low in spite of efforts to sustain low market prices. Tariffs in Germany and the successor states were too high and prices were too low. In 1922 and 1923, only 60% of pre-war production was maintained. It dropped to 40% in 1924. In 1925, Alpine sales rose slightly, but only two out of five blast furnaces and 10 out of 17 open hearth furnaces were employed. Only less than 50% of production was exported.

Finally, under competitive pressure and under the impression of the continuing currency depreciations of France and Belgium, the first international iron and steel cartel agreements were concluded in 1924 and 1925. The Czechoslovak iron and steel firms concluded an export agreement with the Alpine, which partitioned export markets of the areas of Hungary, Yugoslavia, Italy, Albania, Greece, Bulgaria, Romania, Poland and the European parts of Turkey. The ratio of the total market share was 4 to 6 in favour of the Czechoslovak firms. Negotiations for an international iron and railtrack cartel among Germany, France, Belgium and Luxembourg were progressing, with the aim to end beggar-thy-neighbour exports of countries with depreciating currencies. Especially exports from Belgian and French plants had been able to take advantage of their moderate domestic inflations. However, by the mid 1920s, they showed willingness to adjust their prices to gold parity. Yet, none of these agreements resulted in an improvement of Alpine business, as its position as a national producer on international markets was too small.

As it reflected the massive structural problems of the Alpine, its financial standing developed alarmingly. Due to inflation and high expenses, profitableness, i.e. the net profit percentage share of total income, fluctuated extremely. In 1913, 52.8% of gross profits remained net profits; in 1918, this dropped to 19.5%. In 1919, earning power was back to 28.4% and dropped again slightly in 1920. Finally, in 1921, when inflation seemingly offered no more advantages and trade barriers constituted a serious problem, profitability fell quickly to 11.2%. In 1922, the year with hyperinflation, almost no profit was made. The profitability rate fell to 1.3%. Thus, in this case inflation did not enhance profits at all and could not stop the decline of investments.

To compensate for falling profits, several capital increases were executed, more bank loans were raised and money was saved by not reimbursing Czechoslovak coke deliveries during the inflation years, while the Czechoslovak crown only depreciated slightly. In 1923, profitability recovered to 26.4%, because of the artificial boom generated by the German demand during the Ruhr crisis. In the crisis year 1924, the ratio dropped to 1.85%. In 1925, almost no profit was made (0.8%). Eventually, earning power did not recover until 1928. Surprisingly, finances improved slightly in 1923, after an older credit was reimbursed and the Alpine received a 500 thousand pound sterling loan. Yet, bank debts were still almost as high as the British loan. In the same year, Czechoslovak coke debts increased again, because the Austrian crown increasingly depreciated against the Czechoslovak crown.

Only by 1923 was the company able to commence post-war investment for modernisation. Management purchased and installed an electrical lift for one of the mines, a gas power plant, and a transmission line from Eisenerz to Donawitz. Moreover, thermodynamics installations were improved and Alpine began to build its own electricity power plants. Nevertheless, much more investment was necessary to increase productivity. Finally, in 1925, Alpine was able to acquire another foreign loan, which made it a little more independent of expensive domestic bank capital. The Alpine received a five million US dollar credit to pay off old bank debts. Still, expensive bank loans amounted to more than half of total capital.

To sum up, it can be maintained that Austria's largest company had turned into a financially highly unstable and highly unprofitable firm with obsolete plant equipment and low productivity. While, for example, the sales value of 1923 was almost as high as 1913, even though production was between 20 and 30% lower (which meant increased prices), gross profit of the same year only amounted to 26% and net profits only 13% of 1913 levels. Whereas net profits were above the value of expenses in 1913, the situation had reversed right after the war. It was barely possible to keep expenses below gross profits level during the inflation, and only in 1923, under special conditions, was it possible to reach an acceptable rate of profitability. During the inflation, investment and depreciation were far too low. Depreciation on plant completely stagnated during inflation and did not follow income development.

b. Böhler Unlike Alpine, Gebrüder Böhler & Co AG Wien[74] and Schoeller-Bleckmann Stahlwerke AG had already been much more export oriented before the war and were able to maintain, or to recover, their foreign sales and production subsidiary firms afterwards. Due to their wide production range, these firms were not only iron and steel producers, but also processors. They produced high grade steel, tool steel, specialised steel of various sorts, dynamite, tungsten and tungsten steel, chromium, non-corroding, heat and acid resistant steel, magnet steel, drilling steel, ball bearing steel, springs, steel sheet, steel tools and pneumatic tools of all kinds.

Böhler, with up to 5000 employees before the war, was larger than Schoeller-Bleckmann.[75] Information on Böhler business activity for the period right after the war and during inflation times is quite scarce, but the development of its foreign

74 *Bilanzen*, 1.3.1924, 15.12.1928.
75 Mathis, *Big Business*, 57–60.

holdings and the effects of nostrification can be shown. Apart from its plants in Austria, it had subsidiary sales companies in Berlin, Frankfurt, Leipzig, Düsseldorf, Stuttgart, Milan, Prague, Budapest, Brussels, Paris, Sheffield, Moscow, St. Petersburg, Jekaterinburg, Shanghai, Tokyo, Osaka, Sidney, Melbourne and Buenos Aires. Furthermore, Böhler had shares in Bohemian coal mines, owned complete steel plants in Sheffield, Düsseldorf and Ratibor (Upper Silesia), a file factory in Remscheid (Germany), and an armament factory in Brescia (Italy).

During the war, Böhler lost all of its possessions in England, France, Belgium and Russia.[76] In order to avoid further consequences of nostrification, the firm completely reorganised itself in 1923. New, separate corporations were established in each country where assets had been held. The new corporations were subordinated to a Swiss holding company, called Vereinigte Böhlerstahlwerke AG in Zurich. Although separate companies existed in Germany, Hungary, Yugoslavia, Romania, Czechoslovakia, Switzerland, Japan, China and Argentina, they were still under the central leadership of Böhler AG in Vienna. Among the foreign firms, only two had productive capacity (in Ratibor and in Düsseldorf). The rest were sales corporations. In 1923, the Austrian workforce amounted to 3000 and the German to 800.

In all, disintegration only slightly harmed Böhler, since only one production plant in England and some foreign sales corporations were lost. Politics could be fairly easily circumvented by founding a holding corporation in a neutral country. Böhler seemed to have gone through inflation quite well. Its advantage was its strong export orientation, that had existed already before the war, with a large foreign export organisation, and its wide range of very specialised products. Because of the high development and technological content of Böhler steel products, the firm could not necessarily be counted as part of the older industries.

c. Schoeller-Bleckmann Schoeller-Bleckmann Stahlwerke AG[77] was similar to Böhler, only smaller and not quite as successful. Before the war, these were two separate companies, both with foreign sales subsidiary firms that were still maintained after disintegration by transforming them into seemingly independent limited corporations. Their firms were in Switzerland, Holland, Belgium, Sweden, Norway, Germany, Russia, Romania, Italy, Shanghai, Rio de Janeiro and in the United States. Thus, before the onset of the war, Schoeller and Bleckman had already established themselves as highly export oriented companies. Production included quality and specialised steel of all kinds, such as construction steel, steel sheet, sheet iron, sheet for transformers and generators, pieces for machinery up to 70 tons of weight, steel for railway material, files, anvils, and tools. This firm could also be counted as part of the iron and steel processing industry. The formal merger was carried through only by 1924, because of delayed ratification of a new merger bill in parliament. Yet, in actuality, the merging process was already begun in 1922.

In the same year, the strong currency fluctuation of the crown, the German mark and the appreciation of the Czechoslovak crown caused problems for exports. Inflation also considerably augmented freight and raw material costs. During the Ruhr

76 The factory in Italy had been sold before the war, ibid, 59. Mathis, *Big Business*, 159.

77 *Bilanzen*, 2.6.1923, 7.7.1923, 14.11.1925, 7.8.1926. See also A.19.

crisis, between February and May 1923, Schoeller-Bleckmann briefly benefited from an improvement of sales in Germany. Then, the negative effects of the interruption of German production was noticed, initiating a crisis. Business activity only recovered slowly, and only by the end of 1924 did employment begin to increase again. Only 60% of capacity was utilised, and prices were low. 65% of production was exported.

Yet, despite these difficulties, the financial standing of Schoeller-Bleckmann remained fairly stable. Inflation distorted earning power, which was very high until 1925, the year when the reconstruction balance was introduced. In 1922, 72.5% of gross profits remained net profits. In 1923, due to the crisis in Germany, only 53%. In 1924, it was still 66.4 %. Yet, in 1925, the company had a small net loss of 25 thousand schillings. This suggests that profitability had actually suffered during inflation, that depreciation levels had been too low, and that accounting had been unsound during the inflation. The first larger investments were carried through only by 1925.

Overall, both, Schoeller-Bleckmann and Böhler, were affected by stabilisation, but only mildly compared to Alpine. Moreover, both remained internationally competitive after inflation, unlike Alpine. Thanks to strong export orientation and highly developed products both firms remained economically viable, and were much less affected by disintegration, inflation and stabilisation.

2.4.2.2. Iron and Steel Processing Industry

a. Hutter & Schrantz Following the analysis of the iron and steel producing and processing industry, the traditional iron and steel processing industry and its performance and development during inflation will be dealt with. This sector is represented by four firms: Enzesfelder Metallwerke, Brevillier-Urban, Ditmar-Brünner and Hutter & Schrantz. The latter, as one of the oldest firms in Austria,[78] was not only the most successful firm within this industrial sector, but one of the most successful companies in Austria. Hutter & Schrantz AG Siebwaren und Filztuchfabriken[79] was hardly affected by disintegration, inflation and stabilisation. Part of its secret was its high long-term export orientation, making this enterprise much less dependent on the weak domestic market. Another credit point was its wide range of production, including different types of felt, metal cloths, wire grating and screen filters and sieves. Many of these simple products were used in paper mills and made the firm slightly dependent on the paper industries' business cycles.

In 1913, Hutter & Schrantz possessed five factories. Three located in Austria, one on the territory of the future Czechoslovak Republic and one in Hungary. None of these were lost after war and disintegration. The firm was even able to enlarge its manufacturing capacity by purchasing one more factory in Czechoslovakia, setting

78 Mathis, *Big Business*, 159.

79 *Bilanzen*, 5.5.1923, 10.5.1924, 1.8.1925, 10.7.1926. See also A.15 and A.14.

80 Mathis, *Big Business*, 160.

up a new plant in the Burgenland area and investing in modern plant equipment. The former plant was for the supply of metal cloth to the Czechoslovak market.[80] In all, Hutter & Schrantz possessed four factories in Austria, two in the Czechoslovak Republic and one in Hungary after the war. Compared to the pre-war years, production and production capacity were much greater.

Business activity experienced a long-lasting upswing after the first post-war years. Whereas plant capacity was fully employed, considerable investment could be sustained. By 1922, all plant equipment had undergone technical reconstruction, and modernisation was completed. Moreover, Hutter & Schrantz was able to maintain its former export markets. Trade connections were kept with all European states, Russia, and with neighbouring and overseas countries. Employment was allocated to its foreign companies according to economic conditions of markets. When plants in Czechoslovakia suffered from industrial stagnation due to deflation, the Austrian parent firm passed on export orders to its Czechoslovak subsidiary firms. In 1923, more sales markets abroad were opened up; in East India, Brazil and North America. Trade connections to Russia and the Eastern European countries were intensified. 1924 was also a good year. In spite of its high export rate, the trade barriers of the successor states seemed to have had no results on sales figures and turnover. The same can be said about the policy regime shift and the stabilisation period, which did not harm business activity at all. In 1925, turnover increased 10% and production was twice as high as annual pre-war production.

The financial standing of Hutter & Schrantz[81] was also remarkably stable and successful, despite difficult general economic conditions. Soon after the inflationary drop, the pre-war balance sheet value was recovered, and by 1925, it was 62% above pre-war value and consisted of 59% capital and reserves. Despite large investments, debts were low, which suggests that investment capital must have come from profits during inflation. Profits and loss accounts also revealed the enormous inflation figures, depreciated to thousand schillings. In 1922, gross profits increased 18 times, taxes 27 times, and total expenses 13 times. Yet, investments seemed to have been fairly high. In 1922, earning power rose quickly, when expenses only came to 60% of gross profits. Already in 1923, pre-war net profit value was surpassed, while gross profits were not even half of their 1913 value. This shows an amazing increase of profitability after stabilisation had set in. Thereafter, earning power only fell slightly and never decreased below pre-war levels. Financially, 1923 remained the best year. Debts were lower than before the war and only one-quarter consisted of bank credits.

Hutter & Schrantz is an amazing example of how economic policies, even the drastic war time changes, with disintegration, inflation and stabilisation, did not necessarily have to affect microeconomic development negatively. Only the Hungarian subsidiary firm had problems acquiring foreign exchange for the purchase of material. Success of Hutter & Schrantz lay in its strong export orientation, and furthermore, in the wide distribution of export sales. Unlike many subsequent enterprises, it was not limited to the markets of the successor states, as exports were sent

81 See appendix.

almost all over the world. When demand in one market dropped, sales in another could be increased or new markets were opened up. In addition, the war with the consequent increase in capacity of world paper industry lifted demand for Hutter & Schrantz products. This would explain the opening up of new overseas markets. Production capacity expansion was also possible as investment benefited from inflation. Expansion was financed with credits at an early stage of the inflation, when capital was not yet diluted. After the investments had been carried through, paper crown credits had depreciated to only a fraction of their original value.

b. Enzesfelder Contrary to the previously reviewed firm, Enzesfelder Metallwerke AG[82] was strongly influenced by the war, disintegration and inflation. As it was one of the main munitions factories of the Empire, it had enormously expanded during the war. After 1918, it faced massive problems. Production capacity was oversized and soon obsolete, whereas the transformation from war to peace time production was problematical.

After disintegration, the firm began to sell parts of its large mechanical equipment to industries in Poland and Yugoslavia. Still, complete capacity utilisation was not possible throughout the inter-war period, even though the manufacturing and repair of railway rolling stock was introduced with modern plant equipment in 1922. Moreover, clients in the successor states paid reluctantly for export orders. With its new production branch, Enzesfelder became highly dependent upon orders from the federal railway, which gave away its limited orders to Grazer Waggonbau and to the Simmeringer, the other two railway carriage producers in Austria.

Other smaller production branches were the manufactures of a rolling and a tube rolling mill and of a department for metal wares.[83] These had sufficient export orders in 1922, also from Czechoslovakia. In 1923, business appeared to be going quite well and export orders were coming in, but again clients paid reluctantly and slowly, causing interest costs to rise. The very moderate upswing and the late investment for the carriage department in the inflation turned out to be a failure. In 1924, the stabilisation crisis showed its full impact on Enzesfelder and revealed the low apparent book profits that were made during the specious prosperity of the inflation years. Exports to the successor states dropped, and the number of employees sunk from 1300 in 1923 to 900.

The profit and loss accounts showed the inflationary development of income. While gross profits and expenses rose steadily, net profits stagnated and depreciation on plant equipment remained insufficient.

c. Brevillier Like its name suggests, the company Schrauben- und Schmiedewarenfabriks AG Brevillier & Co. und A. Urban und Söhne[84] fabricated hardware and screws. Before the First World War, it had become one of the largest firms in the Austro-Hungarian Empire, with a workforce between 3000 and 4000 employees and

82 *Bilanzen*, 22.9.1923, 20.9.1924.

83 Mathis, *Big Business*, 95.

84 *Bilanzen*, 16.6.1923, 20.9.1924, 26.9.1925, 10.7.1926. See also A.6.

workers.[85] During the war, the workforce increased to 5000, when production was adjusted to the war economy. Before the war, Brevillier owned a Hungarian screw manufacturing plant. In 1922, it acquired a second factory in Budapest. In the Polish towns Sporysz and Ustron, Brevillier also possessed two hardware manufacturing plants.

Disintegration and nationalisation did not cause the loss of any foreign assets. Yet, eventually the management of five plants in three countries increased operating costs. Though, the greatest problem was the change from a large protected market to sudden export dependence, because its productivity was below international standards and markets suffered from overcapacities. After the war, up to 75% of sales were exported.

The firm also did not benefit very much from inflation, as business activity was smaller in 1922 than before the war. From the beginning of 1922, full capacity utilisation was not possible any longer and sales stagnated during the summer. Export sales were retarded by the fall of the German mark and by German export exchange dumping. In the following year, sales still stagnated. Exports did not improve; in France and Belgium the currency depreciation seemed to offset the low value of the crown. In 1924, the situation was not much better. By then, the workforce had fallen to 1800. Up to 80% of production was exported, but prices were low because of competition from Belgian and German firms. Customs trade barriers also resulted in profits decline. Furthermore, sales in Poland and Hungary were very moderate, because of the monetary crises in these countries. Although new currencies had been introduced in 1920, inflation continued, which turned into hyperinflation by 1924 in both countries.[86]

Only by 1925 did business activity rise again as a response to the general improvement of currency and trade conditions in Europe. Yet, generally, Brevillier continued to suffer from overcapacities. Therefore, competition was fierce, prices were low and just a fairly small part of plant was fully employed.

Only because financial policy remained cautious during inflation and thereafter did its financial standing not turn into disaster. Any capital diluting was prevented. Similar to many other firms, depreciation on plant was kept on low levels during the inflation, but gross profits and expenses rose, which still allowed for a moderate increase of net profits. However, once stabilisation manifested itself, foreign competition became more fierce and it was more difficult to keep up with low international price levels. While gross profits and expenses increased, net profits stagnated well into the 20s. Balance sheet value declined because of inflation and was recovered with the reconstruction balance of 1925. Still, the debts situation worsened. Before the war, liabilities had not even been one tenth of gross profits. After stabilisation in 1924, creditors almost reached gross profits value. The balance of 1925 changed this disproportion.

85 Mathis, *Big Business*, 69.

86 Alice Teichova, *Kleinstaaten im Spannungsfeld der Großmächte. Wirtschaft und Politik in Mittel- und Südosteuropa in der Zwischenkriegszeit*, Vienna 1988, chapter 8: Kapitalbildung und Auslandsanleihen, 115.

Thus, the foreign holdings of Brevillier were not affected by disintegration. The financial development clearly showed its lack of productivity and competitiveness right after the end of the inflationary export advantage. As it was not export oriented before the war, Brevillier had great difficulties to face the challenges of a small economy dependent upon foreign trade.

d. Ditmar-Brünner Lampen- und Metallwarenfabriken R. Ditmar, Gebr. Brünner AG[87] produced petroleum lamps, fittings and various sorts of hardware, and was very export oriented already before the First World War. Sales outlets were in Vienna, Graz, Lemberg, Trieste, Budapest, Berlin, Munich, Milan, Rome, Paris, Lyon, Warsaw, Moscow and Bombay.[88] This company is a good example of how management, sales organisation and production were adjusted successfully to the changing economic conditions and policy shifts of post-war Europe. Since only simple products were sold before, production was quickly adjusted to the new market situation. Before the war, luxury items were fabricated and sold. After the early 20s, these were only produced on order, and manufacturing turned to cheap mass-produced articles. For example, so-called "storm lamps" for two schillings a piece became quite important for overseas export sales.

After the war, the majority of sales continued to be exported. Yet, war and disintegration resulted in the loss of all sales outlets outside of the former territories of the monarchy, apart from the one in Italy. This caused a financial loss of five million gold crowns, which were fully written off already during the war. By 1924, only one agency in Prague remained. However, the re-establishment of new agencies abroad was not considered to be expedient, as it was possible to use foreign commercial establishments, traders and its own sales representatives to maintain exports.

Already by 1921, its foreign business activity throve again, especially in East India. Of course, for 1921 the results of the profit and loss accounts are difficult to measure. Profits increased 9 times, whereas expenses grew 20 times and amounted to 75% of income. Before the war, expenses never came to more than one third of total income. Thus, inflation retarded earning power. The business year 1923/24 was also satisfactory and demand rose in the second half of 1923. In 1924, the export rate came to 75%, whilst domestic demand was stagnant. However, turnover was much higher than during the last pre-war year. Finances developed satisfactorily, the former export markets were regained and new foreign markets, never before contacted, were opened up. In 1925, around 60% was exported.

Even though turnover was higher than before the war, balance sheet value did not even reach pre-war figures. Yet, financial standing was good, as liabilities remained below debtors' value. Management conducted a cautious business policy. As foreign sales flourished, financial standing was stable, despite lower post-war profitability, due to inflation. Fortunately, most of the pre-war debt claims were compensated in the form of Austrian pound sterling obligations, giving the company significant reserves, which helped to finance rationalisation and to re-establish foreign trade connections. This supported the transformation of the production process that en-

87 *Bilanzen*, 28.10.1922, 3.1.1925, 8.8.1925, 14.8.1926. See also A.9.

88 Mathis, *Big Business*, 84.

abled the company to produce cheap mass products and to fight competition from the United States and Germany.

Hence, within the iron and steel producing industry, the firms which had been quite export oriented already before the war, like Hutter & Schrantz and Ditmar-Brünner, were able to encounter long and short-term post-war problems most easily. Even though Ditmar-Brünner had lost its pre-war export organisation, it was able to resume world-wide exports through different means. Companies that had focused more on the market of the former Empire, faced serious problems of overcapacities and protectionism. They suffered from structural problems of the old European industries, as well as from the new frontiers. Furthermore, the new international competition was much more fierce for these firms as their productivity was much lower. This was partially the consequence of having relied on the large protected market of the monarchy.

2.4.2.3. Traditional Machine Building Industry

a. Hofherr-Schrantz and Land Reforms in Eastern Europe Hofherr-Schrantz-Clayton-Shuttleworth, landwirtschaftliche Maschinenfabrik AG in Vienna,[89] and its Hungarian counterpart, the Hofherr-Schrantz-Clayton-Shuttleworth, Ungarische Maschinenfabrikswerke AG, were joint stock companies that chiefly produced agricultural machinery. The Austrian Hofherr had two departments, one for agricultural machinery and one for tobacco machinery. The former was much larger. Before the war, when it was still one company, it sold about half of its products within the Austro-Hungarian Empire. Exports primarily went to the agricultural states of Eastern and South-Eastern Europe: Romania, Bulgaria, the territories of Poland in the hands of Germany and to Czarist Russia. After the war and inflation, the larger Austrian branch sold only about one-third of its production on the domestic market, which developed fairly steadily. Hence, also Hofherr turned into a heavily export oriented company. Due to its sales structure and its high dependence on the purchasing power of the agricultural population of Eastern Europe, Hofherr-Schrantz was to a maximum extent affected by the disintegration of the Empire, the erection of trade barriers by the successor states, the Russian Revolution, the revolutions in Eastern Europe, land reforms in all of these countries, and by the inflation and deflation crises of Eastern Europe.

Unlike most of the companies of the iron and steel industry, Hofherr lost the majority of shares of its foreign assets; in this case, its possessions in Hungary. The pre-war sales and production agreements were terminated, and the Hungarian firm became virtually independent with the majority of its shares in Hungarian hands. However, both continued to share their export organisation in Eastern Europe, which was still owned by the Austrian firm. Sales agencies were in Prague, Sofia, Cracow, and Lemberg. In March 1925, the agency in Romania (Lemberg) had to be handed over according to assessed value, asserted in front of the Allied reparations commis-

89 *Bilanzen*, 8.9.1923, 23.8.1924, 5.9.1925, 18.9.1926. See also A.13.

sion, to a native financial group. Technical experience, patents and development of new machinery was still in the hands of the Viennese firm.

Before the war, business volume was greater. The company shrunk according to its business decline, from 2000 employees and workers in 1913 to between 1200 to 1400 in the 20s. In 1922, sales were still satisfactory, but after the end of autumn a decline set in, obviously due to currency stability. In this year, Hofherr was extremely reliant on exports, as domestic sales only amounted to about 15% of total sales.

Yet, exports were not flourishing, since one of the largest former markets, Russia, had completely retrenched. In addition, sales in Romania and Poland were much lower than before and remained depressed throughout the inter-war period. The decline of these markets can be largely attributed to political and economic turmoil in those areas. Furthermore, these countries' purchasing power was undermined as they also underwent inflation at this time, while the Austrian crown appreciated, especially after 1923. Thus, Hofherr could not take much advantage of the depreciating crown in 1922. Protective measures of the successor states also showed their effects.

In the next year, business did not improve very much, even though Eastern European harvests were much better. According to estimates, sales only amounted to half of pre-war value of about 14 million gold crowns. In 1923, three countries that constituted important markets experienced dramatic economic and political changes that affected Hofherr sales negatively. In Germany and Poland, massive currency depreciation resulted in a complete halting of sales to those areas. In Bulgaria, a revolution broke out before the beginning of the harvest, the prime season for sales.[90] Also Russia and Romania, formerly the most important sales areas, had little demand, and Hungary completely shut off its market for imports of agricultural machinery, as it protected its own industry. Exchange control, customs tariffs increases and other protective measures further retarded exports in 1923.

In 1924, business prospects remained piteous, as the results of the land reforms, especially in Russia, Romania, and to a lesser degree, in Poland and in the Czechoslovak Republic, were added to the implications of political turmoil and inflations in Eastern Europe. The repercussions of the land reforms were really noticed after the end of Austrian stabilisation. The decline in sales of all Eastern European countries probably had its main cause in the agricultural land reforms,[91] enforced right after the end of the war and in the early 20s under immense social pressure, fear of revolution and peasant revolts. The first reforms commenced in December 1918 in Yugoslavia and Romania. Since the main motivation was socio-political pressure from peasants, almost all of these reforms caused a decline in agricultural production, reintroduction of older and more primitive methods of cultivation, and basically, a return to small peasant holdings. This entailed stagnation of growth, development and

90 In June 1923, the Bulgarian Prime Minister and leader of the revolutionary peasant party, A. Stambolijski, was overthrown by army officers and killed soon after. The new government under A. Zankow ruled until 1926. In September 1923, a communist uprising, led by W. Kolarow and G. Dimitrov, was suppressed. Thereafter, the revolutionary peasant and communist parties were surppressed. See: L.A.D. Dellin, *Bulgaria*, New York 1957.

91 Teichova, *Kleinstaaten*, chapter: Bodenreformen und landwirtschaftliche Entwicklung, 39 ff.

capital accumulation in these countries. With very little capital and little government support these small peasant holdings soon went into debt, nearly turned to subsistence farming, and many did not participate in the market economy at all. This was most expressed in Yugoslavia and Romania, formerly two very important markets of Hofherr, whose sales before the war must have heavily relied on the financially stable large landowners that were integrated into the market economy.

In Poland, agricultural purchasing power for machinery was also damaged by reforms, although these were often executed sluggishly and moderately. Therefore, many old landowners remained. Reforms in Hungary were more harmful to production, but also here mostly the former owners remained, employing one of the proportionally largest agricultural workforces of Europe.[92] In Bulgaria, reform was begun in 1921 and was forcefully advanced by the radical peasant leader Alexander Stambolijski. It was extremely harmful to growth of agricultural production. In the long run, agricultural production was harmed by land reforms and agriculture failed to be a source for capital accumulation for industry in most Eastern European countries.[93] Therefore, as purchasing power was low, demand for machinery declined. This resulted in stagnant business of the Austrian and Hungarian Hofherr for the rest of the inter-war period. Both firms had to rely on the remaining demand of the landowners that had not been expropriated, and on state orders from Soviet Russia which reached significant sales in the late 20s.

In the Czechoslovak Republic, initially land reforms also had socio-political motives, but were enforced under more economic specifications. Organisation was much better, and agricultural capital formation did not suffer as heavily. Thus, agricultural purchasing power for machinery and other products from industry was maintained in the long run. Yet, Hofherr did not benefit as much from this, as the Czechoslovak Republic closed off its market much more and supported the domestic machinery industry.

In 1924, Eastern European harvests were not as successful as the previous year. Hofherr hoped for an improvement of the trade situation after the revision of import tariffs, as part of the new trade agreements with the successor states. At the same time, management also demanded higher protection of its domestic market. Finally, in 1925, the situation improved and business activity increased, even though capacity was still only utilised up to 65%. Export to Russia and to the Eastern European countries rose, because of better harvest and a more settled political and economic situation in the area, despite continuing land reforms. Hungarian and Austrian Hofherr exported goods to Russia worth 250 thousand US dollars. To lower the dependence on Eastern European countries' demand, new export outlets were opened up in the markets of Greece, Spain and South Africa. In 1924, 60% of sales were exported and pre-war value of turnover was almost reached again. Yet, prices were low, and costs for raw materials were much higher than in 1913. This clearly explains the development of profit and loss accounts. While turnover was fairly high, profits never reached pre-war value again and stagnated. This suggests that profitableness and competitiveness had declined.

92 Ibid, 48.
93 Ibid, 53.

Balance sheets and profit and loss accounts revealed the enormous contraction of business activity after the war and inflation and its only slow and limited recovery until 1925, when stagnation followed until the depression. The diagrams also show the inflationary monetary depreciation and the drop of earning power. Gross and net profit value of 1913 was not even nearly reached again during the inter-war period, even though turnover was almost as high as before the war. The same can be said for balance sheets, debtors and creditors. The balance sheets suggest an apparently financially consolidated firm during the inflation. But its capital was highly diluted by several increases. Indeed, gross profits rose until 1925 and net profits until 1923, but interests payment almost doubled, taxation payments quadrupled in 1923 and debt became disproportionally high. Three quarters of liabilities consisted of bank credit and rose faster than debtors.

Financial standing did not improve until the collapse during the depression. In this case, inflation was certainly harmful to the company, but the main problem was the decline of the main sales areas and the availability or non-availability of credit for the firm. Prices were low and payment conditions of Hofherr clients were very difficult, due to the results of land reforms. Before the war, when credit availability and credit conditions for Austrian companies were much more favourable, terms of payment had even been up to three and a half years. After 1918, terms of payments often incorporated a deadline of two years, while the company had to live on very expensive bank credits to finance production and development. Thus, in the 20s, expenses included a large chunk of interest payments. It is difficult to judge if it would not have been better for Hofherr to find other sources of capital, to avoid dependence on bank credit. Perhaps it would also have been advisable to even cut down business activity.

Below, it will be shown that electrical engineering companies received credit under more favourable conditions from other sources of finance. This was possible because their earning power was much higher, so that a large portion of their sales returns were utilised for investment. Their financial position was also better because a large section of their customers (public and semi-public institutions) paid immediately and reliably. These firms had a fairly stable source of income, rendering possible far easier domestic and foreign credit availability, especially after 1925. For Hofherr, the situation was just contrary, as customers paid reluctantly and income was uncertain. As its markets were disturbed by political and social turmoil and future business expectations were poor, the willingness to grant credit was weak.

The Hungarian Hofherr,[94] with 1800 employees, was slightly bigger than its Austrian counterpart. Initially, it seemed to suffer much more from disintegration and protectionism of its neighbour countries. The agrarian reforms in Hungary also decreased demand. Comments in the business reports reveal the dissatisfaction with the reforms, as the firm suffered from the fall of investment of peasants and landowners.[95] Yet, this company did better than the Austrian Hofherr, because it was less

94 *Bilanzen*, 8.9.1923, 18.9.1926.

95 The report for 1922 states that it was shown in Hungary as well as in Poland, "daß nicht nur der kolonisierte Zwergbauer weniger investiert als der Großgrundbesitzer, sondern auch daß

dependent on export sales, since the Hungarian domestic market was bigger than the Austrian. As still 80% of the population still lived on farming, and the Hungarian protectionist trade barriers also helped to close off the domestic market from foreign competition, the Hungarian Hofherr could soon rely on its home market. By the mid 20s, it was also able to augment its exports, which were directed to Yugoslavia, Romania (these markets were shared with the Austrian Hofherr) and Turkey.

b. Engine Factories The engine factories suffered very badly from the structural changes of the post-war European economy and from inflation and stabilisation crisis. Production capacity within the Austro-Hungarian Empire and in all of Europe had been very high already before the war. After disintegration, the Austrian engine companies lost their large protected domestic market and were forced to face fierce international trade. Meanwhile, the successor states began to build up their own locomotive industries, imported cheaper engines from other countries, and their demand declined. As business reports show, as long as inflation offered fairly low prices compared to products from other countries, the successor states and other Eastern European countries continued to purchase from Austrian firms, to restock their rolling railway material cheaply after the war. Yet, as soon as stabilisation materialised, Austrian exports of engines fell quickly. In addition, compared to other European national producers, the productivity of Austrian engine companies was low. In the long run, though, the main problem constituted the obsolete 19th century technology that was employed. Increasingly, steam engine locomotives were replaced by electric engines. The attempts to compensate this shift by diversifying production to other applications of steam power were unsuccessful. In all, demand fell while capacity was very high, and all companies remained permanently underemployed.

Of the six firms that primarily concentrated on engine production for the market of the Austro-Hungarian Empire, with an annual output of approximately 600 steam locomotives before the war, only four survived the collapse in 1918. Among them were the three largest producers, the Lokomotivfabrik der Staatseisenbahngesellschaft (Steg), the Wiener Lokomotivfabriks AG, and the AG der Lokomotivfabrik, vormals S. Sigl, Wiener Neustadt.[96] The latter was the smallest and merged with the Wiener in 1930.

At first, it seemed that inflation compensated for losses of Neustädter[97] during the war, when the re-equipping of rolling stock had been neglected. During the inflation, the profit and loss accounts showed a steady rise of gross and net profits until the business year 1922/1923. Only once during inflation time, the year 1921/1922, did the value of expenses surpass net profit. Despite the beginning of deflation at the end of 1922, employment for orders from foreign markets still maintained satisfactory business activity. The crisis came in 1923/1924, when inflationary profits finally terminated and employment shrunk. Gross profit dropped 6%, expenses increased one and half times and net profits fell 25%. Attempts were made to extend the pro-

dieser in der Ungewißheit über sein künftiges Schicksal Investitionen auf das unumgänglich Notwendige beschränkt."

96 *Bilanzen*, 30.10.1926.

97 *Bilanzen*, 6.1.1923, 5.1.1924, 28.2.1925. See also time series diagrams of balance sheet and profit and loss accounts in appendix.

duction range, by manufacturing industrial boilers and machinery. In 1924/1925, the figures of the loss and profit account declined considerably, revealing the contraction of business activity. Thereafter, expenses remained above the value of net profits. Hence, the inflation had artificially increased exports and had concealed low earning power, from which this firm had to suffer until the merger.

The Wiener Lokomotivfabriks AG,[98] as the largest locomotive engine producing company in continental Europe, underwent similar development. During the inflation, business volume was much lower than before the war. Business activity was erratic and comparably high compared to the post-stabilisation era. Profits rose fast and collapsed at the end of the inflation. The short export upswing was a fictitious boom that lasted until 1923. Meanwhile, depreciation on plant and investment had been neglected.

In 1921, sales were comparably high for inter-war standards. 104 engines and 113 tenders were sold on foreign markets. Exports were high and resulted in short-term financial successes, until foreign orders and sales dropped suddenly and short time work became necessary in the last months of 1922. Investment, financed with profits and capital increases, for plant enlargement had been high during inflation, which increased capacity even more. This revealed that the management was blinded by the specious export boom of this time. In 1923, demand continued to drop, as the stabilised crown offered no more low-priced material for the importing countries. Suddenly, international competition for export orders became fierce for the Wiener, as the inflationary advantage was gone and its productivity had been neglected and distorted during the inflation. After 1923, only small orders for repairs and the fabrication of frames for electric locomotives offered employment. In 1924, business was at a minimum, because the company could not accept international orders since prices were below production costs. Also, in this case, attempts were made to increase the range of production, as the firm began to start investments for the manufacturing of high-pressure steam boilers for factories and power plants.

c. Simmeringer The next firm that was part of the Austrian machine building industry was the Maschinen- und Waggonbaufabrik AG in Simmering, vorm. H.D. Schmid.[99] This company owned factories in Vienna and the Brünn-Königsfelder Maschinenfabrik in the Czechoslovak Republic, whose majority of shares was owned by the Simmeringer. The Brünn-Königsfelder was almost half of the size of its Austrian counterpart, but expanded considerably in the late 20s. Both primarily fabricated railway carriages, and also various types of machinery as subsidiary branches of production. For the Brünn-Königsfelder, the department of machinery production was larger than railway carriage output. It was also more export oriented than its parent company in Vienna.

The attempt of nostrification of Czechoslovak assets of this firm was a good example of how the consequences of disintegration on ownership and control were circumvented and could not be enforced by policy. The Czechoslovak government wanted the production plants on its territory to be separated from the Austrian lea-

98 *Bilanzen*, 7.4.1923, 30.8.1924, 15.8.1925, and Notizen 28.2.1925. See also A.26.

99 *Bilanzen*, 18.8.1923, 20.9.1924, 8.8.1925, 29.10.1927, 21.7.1928. See also A.22.

dership in Vienna, which still kept the majority of shares. Until 1925, no agreement was reached between the Czechoslovak authorities and the Austrian management. Despite the possibility of separation, the management still wanted to maintain a unified control and leadership of the business of both companies, allegedly to share the costs for the sales and purchasing departments and to achieve a better utilisation of capacity of both plants. Orders were accepted jointly, and depending on capacity utilisation, were passed either to the Czechoslovak branch or to the Austrian plant.

Negotiations continued until December 15, 1926, when a conclusion was finally reached, according to which the Brünn-Königsfelder was turned into an independent joint stock company. Of its total stock of 75 thousand shares, the Simmeringer was only allowed to hold 15 thousand. The rest had to be offered on the Czechoslovak capital market to potential private share holders. For the business year of 1926, the profits of the Czechoslovak plant were still included in the profit and loss account of Simmeringer. Nevertheless, eventually, despite the effort of Czechoslovak authorities, only 22 thousand shares of the Brünn-Königsfelder had been sold on the market by 1927, so that the Viennese management still held 53 thousand shares of the total stock of 75 thousand. Thus, it successfully kept the controlling interest of the Czechoslovak company for the rest of the inter-war period. This was a perfect example of how political forces could not enforce their own policies against economic structures and financial conditions. In this case, the majority of shares could not be bought by domestic financial groups, either due to lack of interest or lack of capital.

During the war, production capacity was expanded in both countries. Thereafter, both firms heavily relied on public orders for rolling stock. Because of the inflation, the Viennese plants received plenty of orders until late 1922 and had good sales until early 1923. Compared to the last pre-war year, turnover was much higher. Brünn-Königsfelder had more problems, because domestic orders were low and exports were problematical as a result of deflationary Czechoslovak currency policy. When a deflationary policy was pursued while the neighbouring countries underwent inflation, policy regime was obviously noticed on the microeconomic level.

For the Simmeringer, the decline of incoming orders continued in the business year 1923/24, since demand from the federal railways stagnated. Repairs and orders from the Viennese tram service did not suffice to compensate for the loss of railway carriage demand. Yet, by mid 1924, business activity throve again, because of orders that resulted from the electrification of the Viennese municipal railway. In addition, the machine building department received orders from the wood processing industry.

In 1924/25, business really began to improve, when Simmeringer received an order from the federal railways for the delivery of 500 passenger carriages and orders from the Viennese tram services. These clients paid great advances and financial standing improved. The departments of crane production and machinery worked for orders from foreign customers. The business of Brünn-Königsfelder improved as well, since the Czechoslovak state railways ordered carriages.

The collapse of the Empire, inflation and deflation did not seem to have resulted in a serious deterioration of its financial standing. The inflationary period of the profit and loss accounts indicated a moderate rise of profits, while net profits barely remained above expenses. As this was reversed in 1924/1925, profitability seemed to drop with the end of inflation. However, as for most other companies, inflation profits were only fictitious and stabilisation revealed the realistic earning power. Overall, by the mid 20s, the financial standing of Simmeringer was stable and in a better position than before the war. Profitability had also not declined, as in 1923/1924 net profit value was above the 1913 level. After the war, expenses were lower than in 1913.

The development of Simmeringer proves uncharacteristic, because apart from its obvious dependence on public and municipal orders, it seemed to have been unaffected by war consequences. As mentioned, the Czechoslovak government had been unable to enforce nationalisation, and the Viennese firm kept its foreign possessions. In the second half of the 20s, the Simmeringer could not successfully decrease its reliance on orders of the railways and was severely hit by the depression.

2.4.2.4. Mining Industry

a. Veitscher A very typical example of the change and decline of the position of the European industry in the world after the war, is the Veitscher Magnesitwerke AG.[100] It was also a typical example of how little companies and whole branches of industry, in this case the magnesite industry, were influenced by politics and economic policy. It is apparent how little disintegration, inflation, deflation, and economic and currency policy regime shifts had to do with the development of Veitscher. For the management, the loss of formerly very important markets, the creation of world-wide overcapacities, cartel agreements and the international business cycles of the various national iron and steel industries were of major concern, as these factors essentially determined performance. Trade barriers did become an important issue, but they were only a symptom of structural deficiencies.

Unlike many other firms of the mining industry, in fact unlike any other branch of industry or company in Austria, the development of the Austrian magnesite industry was quite unique. It was the only industrial sector that held a special position of strength within the world industry, as it possessed a key role in the supply of a vital material for the world-wide iron and steel industry. Magnesite, in its various forms, was a very important material for the production of iron and steel, because it formed the basis of the heat resistant material for blast furnaces. As this material had to be permanently renewed with continuing iron and steel production, constant demand was ensured. Therefore, magnesite production completely dependend on the business cycle development of the international iron and steel industry.

Before the war, this raw material was processed in large and high quality amounts almost exclusively in Austria. Before the war, the Austrian magnesite industry was the oldest and largest of its kind[101] and held world monopoly status. The

100 *Bilanzen*, 21.10.1922, 25.11.1922, 20.1.1923, 29.12.1923, 17.1.1925. See also A.24.

101 Walter Hermann, *Der Magnesit in der Weltwirtschaft unter besonderer Berücksichtigung Österreichs. Eine wirtschaftsgeographische Untersuchung*, Vienna 1937, 67.

boom of this industry culminated in the year 1913. Major customers were the United States and the West European iron and steel industries. Of course, the First World War temporarily overthrew this market system, as the Austrian monopolist was suddenly cut off from world trade, and as iron and steel industries abroad began to explore and exploit other sources of magnesite supply. Before the end of the war, the American iron and steel industry had started to haul magnesite of lower quality from Washington state.[102] The Western European countries also had built up their own magnesite mining industries. However, these were inefficient and the mines were of low quality, so that they could only exist because of the conditions of war economies. Moreover, mines in the US and in Western Europe were not able to satisfy market demands. Therefore, these markets were partially recovered by Austrian firms.

However, overall, the Austrian magnesite mining industry had lost large shares of the world market, as capacities had not only been developed in the US and Europe, but also in Asia. Russia, for example, had the largest magnesite deposits in the world and became the largest producer in the 1930s. Also in Manchuria, large deposits were found and exploited. The result were overcapacities in world-wide magnesite production in the inter-war period. Asian markets, especially the important Japanese market, were lost for the Austrians and the vital markets of the United States and Western Europe had to be shared with other domestic producers. However, since Veitscher was the largest magnesite producing company within the Austrian magnesite industry, it continued to be one of the largest suppliers of magnesite in the world. Thus, it was in a fairly safe position, even though it could not regain its pre-war market position and production volume. Essentially, the company was financially prosperous, while its real economic development stagnated. Production was modernised and rationalised, but it was far lower than pre-war output. Capacity could never be fully employed.

As a whole, the central European magnesite mining companies faced a similar situation as the European iron and steel industry after the war. In addition to the structural problems, Veitscher suffered from the immediate short-term results of the war, such as lack of coal and infrastructure. This seriously impeded production until 1921. Between 1919 until early 1921, compensation trade agreements, which basically meant barter trade, was the only way for Veitscher to attain coal from abroad.[103]

Moreover, after the war, part of the former Austro-Hungarian magnesite industry turned into Italian and Slovenian companies, that tried to close off their markets. Yet, their attempts of exclusively supplying their domestic markets were of little success as their magnesite prices were considerably higher. The new foreign firms in this area were much smaller, had much less developed plant equipment, and therefore, much lower productivity. After all, price relations and productivity were more important than nationalistic concerns. With the help of very low prices, supported by inflation, the Austrian companies, among them of course Veitscher, were able to circumvent the high trade barriers of the successor states and Italy. Eventually, the companies

102 Hermann, 71 ff.

103 Friedrich Walter, *Veitscher Magnesitwerke Actien-Gesellschaft 1881–1951*, without data on location and year, chapter: "Die Zeit zwischen den Weltkriegen 1919–1938," 200 ff.

in the Central European countries succumbed to market pressure and later became part of the Central European magnesite cartel, under strong Austrian influence. The Veitscher and the other Austrian firms, such as the Österreichisch-Amerikanische Magnesitgesellschaft in Radenthein, as the largest national producers in Europe, clearly dominated this cartel. Moreover, the company in Radenthein furnished very close financial ties to the American magnesite industries, which tried to enhance its influence on Austrian production, as it was unable to satisfy US demand on its own.[104] Thus, the Radentheiner was very well equipped with American capital, was able to invest in modern plant equipment, and became the only serious competitor of the Veitscher within Austria.

By autumn 1921, the immediate problems of the war were overcome by Veitscher, and "normal" business could be resumed. Because of its strong export orientation, Veitscher was much less dependent on the condition of the Austrian economy. When it underwent an inflationary boom in 1920/21, Veitscher suffered from the business cycle downturn in the United States and Western Europe, which also affected iron and steel production. Yet, 1921/1922 was a good business year, with production reaching 67% of the pre-war volume.[105] Of total production, 37.5% was delivered to the United States, almost 11% sold in Austria and 47.9% was exported to the rest of Europe. In the same year, Veitscher founded the Eglinton Magnesite Brick Co. Ltd in Glasgow, with stock capital of 50 thousand pounds. The purpose of this formation was the circumvention of the British magnesite syndicate. With this new company, Veitscher indirectly became part of the British sales cartel and was able to sell its products in Britain through Eglinton.

However, the upswing of sales, from 3500 tons to 30,000 tons in 1921/1922,[106] did not have an enduring nature. The extremely high sales to the United States, in the summer of 1922, were largely due to collective preventive sales as a reaction to the pending raises of American customs tariffs on imported magnesite of 11.5 US dollars per short ton (907 kilograms).[107] The magnesite import tariff was increased on September 21, 1922, probably as a reaction to pressure from national American magnesite producers. As the American market was vital, Veitscher management feared an enormous fall of turnover in the next year. At the same time, inflation and the sudden policy regime shift to deflation was a minor issue for Veitscher sales.

Right after the coming into force of the new American tariff, exports to the United States stopped altogether. Yet, the Austrian management was not inclined to react to higher tariffs by lowering its prices and hoped American customers would accept cost increases. The main reason for this static pricing policy was a substantial Austrian export duty ("Exportabgabe") of seven gold crowns (about 11 schillings) per ton of magnesite. This did not allow for price reduction without seriously harming profitability. Thus, negotiations with US importers began, to find a way to circumvent high tariffs or to conclude a compromise with American producers.

104 Hermann, 70.
105 120,000 tons in 1913, and 80,000 tons in 1921/1922.
106 Walter, 213.
107 Walter, 202.
108 Prices were lowered and the market was divided. Ibid, 155.

The Harbison Walker Refractories Co. was the American importer and intermediate trader for imported European magnesite to the American customers, the iron and steel firms. After the implementation of the tariff, Harbison feared competition from domestic producers and suppliers of magnesite and considered its market position to be endangered. Thus, a counter strategy was developed. To have a chance to regain the US market, all major European magnesite producers were incorporated into what would later become the Central European magnesite cartel. It was able to offer lowered prices,[108] while the American intermediate trader was able to reorganise the US market.[109] This prevented the exclusion of the European producers from the very important American market.

The new cartel included, as mentioned, all major European producers with their subordinated plants: Veitscher Magnesit AG, Steirische Magnesit AG (Austrian), Österreichisch-Amerikanische Magnesit Gesellschaft (Austro-American), Societa Lavelli Pisa (Italian), Stella Werke AG Breslau (German), WB Caolin & Schamotte Fabrik Prag (Czechoslovak), Magnesit AG Bratislava (Czechoslovak) and N.W. Magnesit Co Chewellah (American).[110] It had a common sales company in Basel (Switzerland) that divided demand among its members. Since the Austrian branches dominated the cartel as the largest national producers in Europe, it can be concluded that the cartel was basically under Austrian leadership. Another clue to that assumption provides the fact that the cartel concluded delivery agreements with such major German iron and steel corporations as the Vereingte Stahlwerke, Krupp in Essen and the Klöckner combine, giving the Austrian firms the exclusive delivery right and guaranteeing demand from the largest European national producer, the German iron and steel industry.[111]

Therefore, despite a sudden fall of American sales due to a policy measure, the business year 1922/1923 turned out to be satisfactory. Total sales were even higher than the previous business year, with nearly 39,000 tons exported to the US.[112] On the Western European market, sales were also successful despite the opening of the Ruhr crisis. Symptoms of which were already noticed by falling German demand. In 1923, inflation directly supported business. Veitscher covered its production costs in depreciating Austrian crowns, but income came mostly from exports returns in the form of stable foreign exchange. This helped to maintain a good financial standing and to place new investments.

The following business year 1923/24 was a time of a short, but intense crisis that had numerous origins. The stabilisation crisis in Austria was probably only to a minute degree the cause for the poor business activity, since most sales were outbound. In 1924, total sales declined 31%. The main reason for this downswing must be sought in a recession of the iron and steel industry. Generally, employment in the world iron and steel industry was lower in 1924. This was especially the case in Germany, the economy of which underwent a stabilisation crisis. The Veitscher

109 Ibid, 202.
110 Hermann, 75.
111 Ibid, 74.
112 Walter, 213.

balance sheet[113] revealed the brief crisis; total balance sheet value and debtors dropped, while liabilities almost remained the same. Gross profit also stagnated, whereas net profits declined 21%. Moreover, the firm had to pay high profit and income tax at an early moment in 1924, after months of futile negotiations with the Austrian ministry of finance. This was one of the very few moments when the firm actually needed bank credit.[114] Under the impression of the crisis, production costs were lowered considerably. Because of the enlarged production capacity caused by the war, the magnesite industry especially suffered from overcapacities when sales were low. Veitscher production capacity was actually between 150,000 and 160,000 tons of magnesite annually. In 1913, output had amounted to 120,000 tons. The firm had not enlarged its plants, but modernisation and rationalisation had improved capacity. Now, in the crisis year of 1923/1924, only 65,000 tons were produced, which was about 41% of its potential. In the next year, the magnesite industry recovered slightly, and Veitscher reached the production figures of 1922/1923.

In all, this firm had an extraordinarily stable financial standing, even during the hard times of disintegration, inflation and stabilisation. Investment was maintained during inflation, but capital increases had never been necessary. Profits had been used for investment, which enabled the firm to be one of the most modern magnesite producers in the world. Thus, productivity was also sustained notwithstanding inflation. Earning power fluctuated annually, depending on the change of expenses. Right after the war, 21% of gross profits remained net profits, the following year 44%, and even during the crisis year it was still 27%.

2.4.3. Modern Industries

2.4.3.1. Rubber Industry

a. Semperit Many firms of the former Austro-Hungarian Empire turned into multinationals. By far the largest, purely Austrian multinational enterprise was the Semperit, Österreichisch-Amerikanische Gummiwerke AG.[115] It was the largest company of the Austrian and Central and Eastern European rubber industry, with one of the most extensive industrial combines distributed all over the area of the successor states. Its business was quite successful during the war and the post-war period, despite the dramatic political and economic changes. In the years before 1923, its business was going through a general upswing. It was one of the most profitable and most consolidated firms in Austria, which had been able to apply large war-time profits for useful investment in order to modernise and expand production facilities massively.

Progressively, Semperit was in the position to specialise its production process and to acquire more domestic, as well as foreign manufacturing plants of other

113 See appendix.

114 Ibid, 203.

115 *Bilanzen*, 26.5.1923, 8.12.1923, 12.7.1924, 12.9.1925, 17.7.1926. See also A.20.

rubber producers. These were either shut down, or incorporated into its production process. In 1922, all stocks of the Vereinigte Gummiwarenfabriken Harburg-Vienna were acquired. In the following year, the Fama Gummiwerke AG was purchased. Semperit also had a large share of the Hungarian rubber works. In the early 20s, the Cordial Kautschuk- und Balata-Werke AG in Preßburg (Czechoslovakia) were bought up. Thus, even before the end of stabilisation, Semperit controlled almost the whole rubber industry of Austria, Czechoslovakia and Hungary. Compared to the pre-war years, the actual gold value of its assets had even increased.

Semperit was also able to re-establish its old foreign connections. The annual reports up to 1924 also show that inflation enabled this firm to overcome import bans and protective tariffs of the successor states. Yet, once the Austrian crown stabilised, in August and September of 1922, it became increasingly difficult to circumvent the trade barriers. As a whole, though, it was able to remain fairly competitive on the world market and was able to export not only to the neighbouring states, but also to markets abroad, for example, to the US and Great Britain.

Profit and loss accounts showed a decline of gross profits from 6.65 million in 1913 to 4.43 million schillings in 1923. The decrease of net profits was much smaller, from 1.2 million in 1913 to about 1 million schillings in 1923. The only minute decline of debtors and creditors, between 1913 and 1923, suggest that an actual reduction of turnover did not occur. It seems that production expanded while prices had dropped. Already in 1924, Semperit enjoyed a remarkable recovery of income, as gross profit was 60% and net profits 87% higher than in 1923. Expenses only increased 40%. The upward trend continued until the first half of 1925. Thereafter, a sudden reduction of plant activity became necessary, as the consequences of the stabilisation crisis affected the rubber company. The management blamed the economic crisis, the unstable currency situation and the customs increase in the marketing area.

In the case of Semperit, the disruption of trade patterns were hardly a problem. Inflation tended to support exports and helped to overcome the trade barriers of the successor states. Also nationalisation was not an issue for this firm, as it was able to enlarge its foreign holdings considerably. This also represented the trend of the modern rubber industry toward more concentration.

2.4.3.2. Electrical Engineering Industry

a. Felten & Guilleaume The first electrical engineering firm to be discussed, Felten und Guilleaume, Fabrik elektrischer Kabel, Stahl- und Kupferwerke AG,[116] was a German company, as the majority of its stocks were in the hands of the German mother company with the same name in Cologne-Mühlheim. It was much more severely hit by the implications of the war economy and inflation than all other electrical engineering companies.

116 *Bilanzen*, 31.3.1923, 3.5.1924, 1.5.1926. See also A.12.

Its financial development reflected the deterioration of its business. Gross profit of 1922 was not even one quarter of its 1913 level. It took the company until 1929 to surpass its pre-war gross profit level. Throughout the inter-war period, net profit figures remained below pre-war value. Before the war, net profit was higher than expenses. Yet, after 1922, this relation was completely reversed and net profits remained below expenses for the rest of the inter-war period. Dividend payments were also far below pre-war figures. In 1913, they amounted to 60 or 70 gold crowns, whereas they only came to about two gold crowns in 1923. Thus, earning power had suffered very much from war, inflation and stabilisation. Depreciation on plant was also far lower than in 1913. Between 1922 until 1924, it was near zero and increased only slowly after 1925. It can be assumed that depreciation was also near zero during the inflation period.

According to the report for 1922, business activity followed exactly along the lines of monetary depreciation. During inflation and hyperinflation sales and activity were rising until August and September of that year. Thereafter, sales of consumer goods declined rapidly. Sales suffered severely after the summer of 1922, due to the inability to compete against imported foreign products and on foreign markets. Investment was begun in this year, but seemed to be belated. In the inflationary period, the investment rate was very low and insufficient. Since the company suffered from foreign competition, its business report for 1922 blamed tariff barriers, import bans, and exchange control of the neighbouring countries for its poor performance.

In the spring of 1923, the occupation of the Ruhr showed its results in the loss of German competition. Slowly, the volume of incoming orders increased and business was satisfactory. Yet, in all, sales remained just as poor as the time following currency stabilisation. Only one Styrian plant was still able to take advantage from the political turmoil and economic disruption in Western Germany. After May 1923, the main plant in Vienna could partially use its capacity for orders for cables. Due to the weak domestic demand, it was necessary to sell on foreign markets for low prices.

Eventually, inflation caused financial losses, very low depreciation and investments, which entailed a decline of productivity and competitiveness after stabilisation. Net profits must have shrunk enormously during hyperinflation. Felten & Guilleaume came out of the inflation with a competitive disadvantage on foreign markets, and only troubles in Germany helped to overcome sales stagnation. Business activity and turnover must have remained fairly stagnant in 1922 and 1923.

b. AEG The following two companies to be discussed also had German parent companies: AEG and Siemens-Schuckert. After the war and the disintegration of the monarchy, the renewal of the business agreement between AEG Union Elektrizitäts-Gesellschaft in Austria[117] and its German parent company in Berlin became imperative. The former territories of the Monarchy continued to be the only primary sales area of the Austrian AEG. It could also continue to utilise all technical experience, patents, and construction types of AEG Germany and the affiliated General

117 *Bilanzen*, 14.7.1923, 19.7.1924, 10.10.25. See also A.1.

Electric Corporation. It also maintained its trading posts and workshops throughout Eastern Europe after the war, with trading joint stock companies in Zagreb, Belgrade, Bucharest, Athens, Sofia, Celje, Cracow, Warsaw and Budapest. Workshops were located in the Czechoslovak Republic and in Hungary.

AEG moderately expanded its production capacity during this time, suggesting low but constant investment. Expansion was in the field of the department of thermodynamics technology, as AEG was the only company with the license to built "Ruthspeicher"[118] in the successor states, apart from the industry in Czechoslovak Republic. Despite stabilisation crisis and complaints of many industrial sectors about capital scarcity, AEG invested heavily for expansion and development of transformer technology, creation of Geax (a factory for insulation material), and the enlargement of testing and switchboard systems. Compared to pre-war times, AEG had greatly expanded the quality and size of its plants and production capacity.

Between 1922 and 1924/25, the business activity of AEG and Siemens revealed the differential structure of import tariffs of the successor states. Whereas tariffs were high for most imports, the electrical engineering firms seemed to have little trouble in surpassing them. The underdeveloped economies of the successor states were dependent on imports of finished goods with high technological content. One exception was the CSR, which had its own, still young, but developed electrical engineering industry that needed to be protected from foreign competition. Thus, Czechoslovakia also implemented high tariffs on imports for the products of AEG, Siemens, and the other Austrian electrical engineering companies.

At first glance, comparing the balance sheet of AEG and Siemens, the former survived war, inflation and stabilisation much better than Siemens. Between 1913 and 1922, its gross profits dropped immensely by 90%. In 1923, income only recovered to 24% of pre-war value. AEG on the other hand, fared much better, as its gross profits only dropped 47% until 1923. In 1922, the year of hyperinflation, AEG business activity was high, due to orders for the electrification of parts of the railroads in the Alps and due to expanding sales in consumer goods. The sales of consumer goods was strongly affected by the policy regime shift and currency stabilisation. In November 1922, high demand declined rapidly. This decline was enhanced by inflationary distortion. As the flight to commodity values reached excessive proportions during rapid currency depreciation, dealers and shopkeepers fanatically bought and stored electrical consumer goods for value preservation. However, after the crown ended its fall, the market was flooded with cheap electrical durable consumer goods, and prices continued to fall. Hence, AEG had to terminate the barely introduced mass production of electrical consumption goods.

Unlike consumer sales, the production of large products for the big projects, such as hydroelectric power plants and railroad electrification, remained high and hardly affected by stabilisation crisis. This would more or less be the case for all electrical engineering companies in Austria. Orders regularly came from domestic power plant projects of the large electricity supply companies, railroad electrification of the federal railroad and the Vienna city railroad, and from the federal postal services for the instalment of transmission lines. The advantage of public and semi-public em-

118 This system improved steam accumulation for boiler plants.

ployment were continuously incoming orders, despite general economic disruptions caused by the shift from inflation to stabilisation. These orders often demanded the production and delivery of large, often custom-made, highly developed pieces of machinery, which development and fabrication required high-end technology and high capital intensity. This was financed by anticipatory credit and other forms of pre-financing. AEG enjoyed a high business activity for such large pieces. The great disadvantage of this type of employment was the virtual impossibility of even and constant utilisation of all departments of any firm. Many times, one department was overemployed while other capacity of other departments lay idle. In other cases, the delivery deadline demanded overtime, while the company was underemployed months later. This caused higher production costs and very difficult financing, especially when orders did not come in frequently.

As private industrial investment remained low, AEG continued to rely heavily on orders from the public and semi-public institutions and corporations, the railways and electricity supply companies. During the first year of stabilisation, 1923, orders for machinery, transformers, switchgear systems for power plants and electrification of railroad remained satisfactory. Soon, stock capital increases became necessary to finance further investment for production expansion. Export business to its old markets were expanded. Only the Czechoslovak Republic caused great obstacles for exports with its high import tariffs. Yet, products were successfully sold to former Serbia, Bulgaria, Romania, Greece and Poland. For the German parent company, orders were accepted for exports to Luxembourg, Denmark and also to Japan, India, South America and Egypt. Orders from private industrial investment were also slowly coming in. For example, electrical lifting gear, electrical transport systems, metallurgical ovens and electrical heating systems for industrial plants were delivered and installed. The department of thermodynamics technology received orders from steam power plants.

In 1924, the effects of stabilisation were still not showing results, even though only 50% of plant capacity was utilised and factories were shut down for eight weeks because of two strikes. The extent of plant expansion, compared to the last pre-war year, was obvious, because turnover was as high as in 1913, even though only 50% of plant capacity was employed. Again large pieces for hydroelectric power plants were delivered, and engines and electric locomotives were built for the federal and Vienna city railways. Employment was uneven. The department for steam turbines was primarily employed for outbound trade. Even though some orders came in from the domestic industries, such as the Alpine Montangesellschaft and the textile, oil and metal industries, these orders still did not suffice to render possible constant employment of all departments or for full utilisation of capacity.

Generally, AEG maintained a very high investment rate during inflation, and the firm was not disturbed by policy regime change in 1923. Investments were financed by exhausting a large portion of its capital reserve and increasing share capital. This type of financing was apparent in the sharp loss of balance sheet value and capital reserve and stock between 1913 and 1923. As the financial basis shrunk, the overall financial standing improved slightly. After the inflation, debtors' value was higher than liabilities.

c. Siemens Information about this firm until stabilisation is scarce. Foreign trade of the Österreichische Siemens-Schuckert Werke[119] was also constrained by its German parent firm which held the majority of shares. The agreement with the German Siemens-Schuckert included export rights to the successor states. A subsidiary company was located in Preßburg, Czechoslovakia, and Siemens also had shares of the German Siemens foundations in Yugoslavia, Romania, Bulgaria, and Hungary. No foreign assets were lost in the war. Nevertheless, its export business was limited, and it suffered from foreign competition.

As mentioned before, Siemens-Schuckert fared much worse than AEG. It was much more influenced by currency depreciation and stabilisation. By 1922, a sales crisis occurred that was intensified in 1923 by the fall of the German mark, which encouraged stronger German competition. As it was much more difficult to deal with international competition than for many other electrical engineering companies, Siemens experienced a greater fall of investment and productivity during war and inflation. Profit and loss accounts revealed a dramatic fall of gross profits and expenses, and only a slight fall of net profits, which nearly went into deficit. This suggests defective balance sheet policy, which employed capital reserves to cover losses. In reality, net profits were far lower than reported. Moreover, share capital was extremely diluted as it was increased several times. Its overall financial standing was more difficult than AEG finances, because liabilities remained higher than debtors after 1923.

In 1923, Siemens experienced a crisis. In April and May, only 30% of workers were employed, and the 48 hour week was only resumed by November. To have any employment at all, any kind of order had to be accepted. Only after a great number of orders for large projects came in, from power plants and the federal railroad, business slowly began to recover in 1924. However, utilisation of the different departments was uneven. Constant orders from industry for mass-produced electrical engines and machinery did not materialise. Still, compared to 1923, turnover rose 60% in 1924.

d. Elin In the inter-war period, one of the most successful companies of Austria was the Elin Aktiengesellschaft für elektrische Industrie.[120] Compared to other enterprises, its performance was truly remarkable, as it proved to possess the ability of ingenuity, flexibility and a strong drive to explore export sales outlets, to overcome and survive successfully the most severe economic conditions.

Elin was much smaller than Siemens and about the size of AEG Austria. During the inflation years and thereafter, especially in 1922 and 1923, it enormously expanded and diversified its range and volume of production, and export markets. By 1922, capital was increased to establish new production departments. For example, the building of electrical railway engines and the construction of large pieces of machinery, such as turbines and transformers, were introduced. At the same time, while the nostrification polices of the successor states started to take effect, the export

119 *Bilanzen*, 14.7.1923, 20.12.1924, 5.12.1925. See also A.21.

120 *Bilanzen*, 13.10.1923, 20.10.1923, 9.8.1924, 3.10.1925. See also A.10.

organisation expanded rapidly. Subsidiary sales companies were located in all of the successor states, especially in Yugoslavia (Zagreb, Marburg and Belgrade) and the Czechoslovak Republic (Brüx). Other sales companies were in Amsterdam, Milan, Bucharest, and also in South American countries. In addition, Elin also possessed power plants in Austria, Poland, Yugoslavia and Romania. The Romanian was located in Ragusa and was the only one under sequestration until July 1924.

To advance sales to Soviet Russia, Elin founded, in combination with other large Austrian companies, the Austro-Russian Industrial and Trade Company (the so-called "Russawstorg"),[121] which was transformed into the Austro-Russian Industry Ltd in July 1923.[122] The Elin was the leader of this syndicate, which included Brevillier, Böhler, the steelworks Schmidt & Co. and other machine building companies. This Austrian association of firms had concluded a sales license contract with the Soviet government, stipulating that Russia held a 25% share of the total capital stock of 100 thousand schillings.

Thus, by 1924 the industrial combine of Elin included the following shares of sales and industrial subsidiary companies: Austro-Russische Industrie AG (8,3% share), "Elin" Nederlandsche Mij in Amsterdam (100%), "Fulgur" in Zagreb (100%), "Elin" Yugoslavia (100%), "Elin" Gesellschaft für elektrische Industrie GmbH Maribor (100%), Österreichische Telephon-Automaten-Gesellschaft (100%), Bechmann GesmbH (100%), Möllersdorfer Eisengießerei GesmbH (100%), "Kontakt" AG (majority of shares), "Meteor" Glühlampenfabrik (majority), Grazer Tramway Gesellschaft (majority),Wiener Lokalbahnen (30%), and finally the Steirische Wasserkraft- & Elektrizitäts AG (Steweag, 6%). The latter was an electricity supply company. Elin was also the leader of Belgian, Dutch, Austrian, and Greek financial groups and had influence on the Compagnie Hellénique d'Electricité in Athens.

Altogether, Elin was hardly affected by nationalisation and disintegration, as it was possible to expand foreign holdings and to enlarge the volume of export business activities. Only the Czechoslovak Republic seemed to cause major problems to export business. However, the business report of 1924 proved that sales to Czechoslovakia improved with the resumption of normal trade relations in the early 20s, after coming into force of new trade agreements. Several trade agreements came into effect after 1922, mainly to re-establish old trade links, to overcome the initial post-war isolationism of the successor states and to terminate the one-sided unfavourable trade relations determined by St. Germain. These agreements with the successor states included the unilateral most favoured-nation clause. Therefore, by 1924, equal preference treatment was established with the Czechoslovak Republic, which seemingly directly affected Elin exports to that country positively.[123] And after the removal of differential customs in Spain, exports also to this area expanded.

In 1922, business activity was better than in the previous year, even though Austrian industrial growth had been higher in 1921. Similar to AEG and Siemens, also Elin accepted large orders from the railway and power plant projects. For example,

121 The so-called "Russisch-Österreichische Industrie- und Handels-Gesellschaft." *Bilanzen*, 10.2.1923 and 21.7.1923.

122 Austro-Russische Industrie AG.

123 Berger, *Der Donauraum*, 199 ff.

it built the power lines for rail-tracks on the Arlberg, for the tracks Zirl-Landeck in Tyrol and finished several projects for power plants. In the next year, further orders came from various electricity supply companies. For Maconi Wireless Telegraph Co Ltd, the complete heavy current engineering for high frequency transformers for the first wireless telegraphy station in Austria was finished. In 1924, orders also came from the city power plants and railways of Vienna. Future domestic employment prospects were seen positively, since all of the power plant projects and railway electrification programmes were far from completion. Positive future expectations were also raised by the fact that the majority of Austrian industrial plant had not yet been electrified. It was believed that these investments would be placed as soon as an economic upswing would start. As we shall see, this hope was to be fulfilled only to a limited extent.

Unlike the two German firms, its engagement in large scale electrification projects on foreign markets, mostly financed by foreign public and semi-public institutions, was far greater. In 1922, products were exported to, and construction projects were begun in, the Balkans, Poland, Hungary, Italy, Belgium, Spain, Portugal and South America. In the following year, sales were also directed to Palestine. Elin foreign trade and business expanded even more in the later 20s.

Its financial standing was remarkably stable and seemed to have improved during war and inflation. Between 1913 and 1923, balance sheet value declined. However, whereas debtors remained stagnant, liabilities declined, which suggests that the level of business activity was maintained and that financial standing improved. Apparently, its earning power was lower than profitableness of AEG. Yet, the low net profit figures throughout the 20s suggest a much more honest accountancy method and a much higher investment rate. Expansion of the early 20s and the pre-financing of large pieces of machinery for power plant projects, especially in the successor states, made high reinvestments of large portions of gross profits necessary. The moderate decline of gross profits and the simultaneous increase of net profits were remarkable. Management also sustained appropriate depreciation on plant during the inflation.

Contrary to Lindenlaub's theory, investments and expansion were quite high in the case of Elin. Capital increases were not just employed for increased production costs, but for higher investments. The price of this high investment and expansion was lower profitability.

e. Brown-Boveri The last electrical engineering firm under review, for the period 1913–1923, is the Österreichische Brown-Boveri Werke AG.[124] It was the smallest of the Austrian electrical engineering companies and was partially a foreign owned company. The Swiss Brown-Boveri was its parent company, but only held 15% of shares. After the war, both firms established several Brown-Boveri branches in all of the successor states, in the form of national joint stock companies, of which the shares in Hungary and in the Czechoslovak Republic were completely in the hands of the Austrian Brown-Boveri. The branch in Brünn included a production plant for the Czechoslovak market. This was a method to circumvent high Czechoslovak

124 *Bilanzen*, 9.8.1924, 29.8.1925. See also A.7.

import tariffs. After production was moved to that country, it was lawfully nationalised, but the majority of shares remained in Austrian hands and profits continued to be on the Austrian Brown-Boveri account. The Austrian firm also had a 30% share of the Polish and 50% of the Yugoslavian branches. In all, the cooperation with the Swiss Brown-Boveri was advantageous, as the Swiss firm attracted plenty of orders for large projects, which employment was redistributed. Moreover, running costs were lowered by sharing the development and testing departments for electrical engineering.

Information about Brown-Boveri during the inflation years is scarce. In the last peace time year, business was not going well, and losses of 762 thousand schillings were made. Unlike Siemens, AEG and Elin, there was no expansion of the production plant during war and inflation. Despite currency stabilisation, business activity remained steady, once again because of semipublic and public orders from the railroads and power plants. Brown-Boveri specialised in the installation of heavy electrical engineering equipment for the power plant projects and also delivered rail-track equipment, rectifier plants, train engines and other equipment, while business in transformers and smaller engines was increasingly taken over by smaller firms.

In 1924, "normal business", as the production and sale of ordinary commercial products was called, almost came to a standstill. Just as for the other firms, domestic consumer and industrial demand for electrification equipment was low. Brown-Boveri exclusively relied on a few large orders from domestic railway and power plant projects and on large orders from the successor states. While 70% of products were delivered to the area of the Czechoslovak Republic in 1913, the export rate was only 50% in 1923 and 1924. Some turbo aggregates were directed to Czechoslovak industrial companies.

As for other companies, the balance sheet value of Brown-Boveri declined. Debtors only declined moderately and remained above the number of liabilities. Therefore, financial standing continued to recover from the losses of 1913. Comparing profit and loss accounts of 1913 with 1922/23, a sharp increase in gross and net profits is evident.

Overall, Brown Boveri came out of war and inflation in good standing, due to large public orders and continuos demand from the successor states. The same can be said for the whole Austrian electrical engineering industry. Domestic demand for consumer and small and medium pieces of electric equipment for industry remained low. Thus, all four concentrated on supplying the large public construction projects in Austria and in the successor states. This explains the overall good financial position, as orders came from the government funded federal railways, the municipal railway and trams, and from power plant projects. All these clients paid well and on time, despite inflation, stabilisation and deflation.

Performance of the electrical engineering companies was quite different. As most of them focused on their stagnant home market, their development was mediocre. Only Elin was able to expand, while Siemens was underemployed. This was possible because Elin not only extended its employment in Austria, but was heavily engaged in business throughout the successor states and the rest of Eastern Europe. As a purely Austrian firm, without constraints from any parent company, Elin was able to choose export markets freely in Eastern and South Eastern Europe, despite protectionism and capital scarcity in these countries.[125]

An advantage for this branch of industry was the high technological content of its finished products, which could not be produced in the successor states (apart from the CSR) and in the other Eastern European countries. This type of production demanded development, testing and experience and not only capital investment, neither of which were available in these countries. Therefore, the dependence of these areas of post-war Poland, Hungary, Bulgaria, Romania, Yugoslavia and Greece on these imports could not be removed with disintegration, nationalisation or protective trade policies, as the necessary complex economic structures for the manufacturing of high-end technology, which had been developed in the industrialised countries before the war, were non existent. As soon as the initial post-war policies were removed, these states turned to a very selective protective economic policy. This became even more obvious after 1925. Their dependence on these imports entailed a reduction of import tariffs for products of high technology. Thus, the Austrian firms of the electrical engineering industry were only mildly affected by disintegration and the shift to protectionism.

2.4.3.3. Motor Industry

For the third modern industry, the automobile and utility vehicle industry, the changes and economic consequences of the war had a greater impact. Disintegration was not a main problem for most firms, but inflation and stabilisation were not as easily dealt with as the rubber or the electrical engineering industry faced these obstacles to economic growth. The main reasons for its vulnerability were the long-term structural changes within, and of the position of, the developed European industry,[126] from which the Austrian motor industry particularly suffered. Until 1913, Europe was the world's leading manufacturer of industrial goods.[127] After the war, this changed as the United States had become the leading industrialised nation in the world. Its industries constituted strong competition for many European industries. This was especially the case for the superior and highly productive American motor industry. The Americans had adopted much sooner much more modern, cheaper and efficient production processes and could export to Europe effectively, despite protective customs barriers.

As the European automobile industry faced serious American competition, national producers enforced strong protectionism to shut off, and retrench to, each other's markets. The Austrian motor industry, as a producer in a small country dependent on foreign trade, was one of the weakest links in this system. It was not only pressured by US competition, but also by the greater market power of other European, especially German, producers in large countries. Austrian vehicles suffered from protectionism and low competitiveness. These structural problems, apparent

125 Teichova, *Kleinstaaten*.
126 Svennilson, 18 ff.
127 Svennilson, 17.

in increasing protectionism and retrenchment, intensified in the later 20s and after the depression.

a. Daimler In the inflation years, the Österreichische Daimler Motoren AG[128] precisely reflected this general economic malaise of post-war Europe. As all assets and plants were within the territory of the Austrian Republic, disintegration and nationalisation did not affect Daimler.

Yet, stabilisation had greater repercussions as its sales declined quickly once the crown stopped its devaluation. It took until the summer of 1923 for demand to recover. Moreover, the war had caused large short-term overcapacities, and world-wide competition was fierce. Prices were depressed. In addition, raw materials had to be imported expensively while the company suffered from capital scarcity. During the inflation, several capital stock increases did not overcome the lack and dependence on bank credit, while investment remained low. Due to the reliance on the credit of four banks, payment for interests were excessively high, using up to 60% of gross profit.

In 1922, the export situation was satisfactory, but finances represented the extreme distortion of capital development. Superficially, high profits were made; however these were really just apparent book profits. Gross profit increased more than 20 times, taxes 6.5 times, social security expenses 40 times, general expenses 16 times and net profit 45 times. There was a heavy disproportion of capital stock and debts. For the period between 1913 and 1922, the balance sheet shows a fall of balance sheet value and an almost unchanged value of liabilities. The financial position was alarming.

To stay competitive and to render possible an improvement of its financial standing in the long run, major reforms of production were undertaken in 1923. All workers were dismissed for several weeks, production was rationalised and various production processes were adjusted. Then, re-commencement of production was prolonged due to the Ruhr crisis, as raw materials from Germany were not available. However, gross and net profits increased after all. Sales in Germany, Western Europe, Scandinavia, overseas and Poland were satisfactory, whereas they stagnated in the successor states. Prices were depressed because of American competition.

In the following year, the stabilisation crisis really began to take effect, as the backlog of productivity and competitiveness that had mounted during the inflation became apparent. As the debt burden was already high, the extraordinary rise of interests rate was especially harmful. Since business activity declined right after fairly high, but necessary investments, expenses surpassed gross profit by nearly 100 thousand schillings in 1924.

In this year, foreign trade to Germany declined, corresponding to the German deflation crisis and consequent fall of demand. Demand on the Austrian market dropped simultaneously. Daimler management saw the crisis of the Austrian stock exchange market and the newly introduced automobile tax as the main reasons. The

128 *Bilanzen*, 28.7.1923, 19.7.1924. See also A.8.

peak of the Austrian stock exchange boom was around the turn of 1923/1924.[129] A large part of the capital for speculation came from repatriated Austrian capital and from foreign speculators that wanted to make quick profits. At the beginning of 1924, the French franc became an object of speculation because of its perpetual depreciation. Exchange and produce deals against the franc were concluded on a massive scale, with the hope that it would continue to depreciate. Along with the speculative stock exchange boom, a fairly large section of the Viennese population prospered overnight, stimulating demand for luxury goods and expensive cars. Firms such as Daimler and Gräf & Stift, which usually produced utility vehicles, returned to their pre-war production of luxury cars under the impression of the stock market boom, supporting their mediocre sales of 1923 and 1924.

This high, but brief demand suddenly ended when the Viennese stock exchange market crashed in March 1924, after the bank syndicate of J.P. Morgan lent 100 million US dollars to the French government to stop the fall of the franc. This led to the stock market crash and sudden disenchantment of business circles in Austria. Apart from the loss of demand for Daimler, Gräf & Stift and other mostly Viennese firms, the greater problem was the loss of capital to the Austrian economy. The boom was also one of the reasons for the extremely high interest rates that were offered to Austrian enterprises, especially during the inflation years until the mid 20s.

Daimler management placed great hopes in the new Austrian customs tariffs, to protect its domestic market from foreign competition.[130] This kind of calculation was typical of all firms with problems of productivity and competitiveness. The new tariff was passed by parliament on September 5, 1924, and came to force on January 1, 1925. It introduced Austria's slow movement towards moderate protectionism.[131] Yet, for Daimler the slow and moderate change of Austrian trade policy offered no improvement of sales, as cheap foreign automobile imports did not decline. The new policy did not keep the firm from facing superior foreign competition in the 20s.

b. Steyr The Steyr Werke, as the largest car manufacturing firm (its name was still Österreichische Waffenfabriks-Gesellschaft Steyr),[132] had the highest export rate among companies of this industrial sector, usually far above 50% of turnover value. Before the war, Steyr was one of the best consolidated weapons and vehicle producers in Austria and enjoyed a boom during the war. High war profits were employed to expand the plants for automobile production. Steyr was insofar in a better position

129 Hans Kernbauer, *Währungspolitik in der Zwischenkriegszeit. Geschichte der Oesterreichischen Nationalbank von 1923–1938*, Vienna 1991, 97/98.

130 "Wenn der Absatz nicht zurückgeht und wenn sich die Hoffnung erfüllt, daß nach Inkrafttreten der neuen Zollsätze die ausländische Konkurrenz, die heute den österreichischen Markt etwa zur Hälfte versorgen soll, von ihm mehr zurückgedrängt wird, so darf man heuer hoffen, daß auch bei rigorosen Rückstellungen bereits ein kleiner Überschuß verbleibt." *Bilanzen*, 19.7.1924.

131 Ernst Haas, *Die Außenhandelspolitik der ehemaligen Republik Österreich während der Weltwirtschaftskrise bis zum Anschluß unter besonderer Berücksichtigung der Handelsvertragspolitik*, dissertation, Hochschule für Wirtschafts- und Sozialwissenschaften, Nürnberg ,Würzburg, 1939, 30.

132 *Bilanzen*, 3.11.1923, 28.6.1924, 30.5.1925. See also time series diagrams of balance sheet and profit and loss accounts in appendix.

than Daimler, as it produced its own semi-finished products, whereas Daimler was dependent on expensive imports. Production remained steady in the years of inflation, with approximately between 2500 to 3000 vehicles produced annually. Yet, plant was hardly improved or expanded. In compliance with Lindenlaub's theory of low investment during inflation times, capital scarcity forced a limited expansion of Steyr's production capacity.

In 1922, its lower productivity was still covered by the low crown parity. Before the production process became more concentrated, Steyr seemed to be much more competitive than Daimler. Despite disintegration and high tariffs, it exported to its traditional markets in the area of the successor states, as well as to Germany, Sweden, Switzerland, Spain, Bulgaria, the Balkans, and very little to Great Britain and France. Furthermore, exports also went to Soviet Russia and its neighbouring countries. Domestic sales also increased, due to the inflationary boom, and amounted to about 30% of total sales.

As trade between Austria and the Czechoslovak Republic fell under the most favoured-nation clause, trade agreements between states that were not immediately connected to Austrian exports could improve Steyr's foreign trade position. In the framework of the Czechoslovak westward trade orientation, this country concluded a customs tariffs agreement with allied France in August 1923, after the first preliminary trade agreement had been signed in 1920.[133] After its conclusion, Steyr exports to the CSR also improved, since the agreement lowered tariffs on all Czechoslovak car imports.

In the first stabilisation year, 1923, deficiencies of productivity that had been covered by inflation exports became obvious. Now the competition of foreign automobile firms was increasingly noticed also on the domestic market. As a reaction, Steyr management complained about insufficient protection from prohibitive tariffs. Austrian tariffs on imported cars were only 10 to 12% of value, while some foreign tariffs were up to between 45 and 85% of value. In 1923, attempts were made to increase competitiveness, and further concentration of production, rationalisation and investment in plant were advanced with the help of capital increases. Volume of production was sustained, and two thirds of sales were exported. To overcome trade barriers, products were often sold at cost-price.

Steyr was finally hit by the stabilisation crisis in 1924. Sales declined by a few hundred units, while domestic demand declined. Exports also slowed down even though trade connections were improved in 1923 and 1924. Yet, Steyr continued to pursue an aggressive business policy. In the face of the sales crisis, management even raised dividend payments to prove its competitiveness and to raise faith of its stockholders. The hope for higher sales in the following years was fulfilled.

The development of its financial standing revealed its unusual course of business. The balance sheet development after 1921 is quite unlike those of any other firm that has been reviewed so far. For 1921, the deflated crown figures, depreciated to thousand Austrian schillings, seemed really small and revealed the sudden upward spiral of inflation. All figures doubled, tripled or increased 10 times or more. Expenses rose as quickly as gross profits. For example, in 1922 gross profit increased

133 Resch and Sládek, 263.

25 times, while social expenses increased 175 fold. For management it was possible to cover financial weaknesses and to distort the balance sheets and profit and loss accounts. Expenses were reported far lower than their actual value, while in actuality the firm was living on its financial substance.

Between 1921 to 1922, the sudden increase of liabilities is obvious. Another increase followed after 1923, which continued until 1928. This suggests that Steyr followed a risky business policy, expanding with the help of credit and capital increases and hoping for higher returns and good sales. This policy proved to be fatal when the depression began. Whether this was a deliberate policy, or whether conditions compelled management to finance massive expansion on credit is difficult to judge. Forceful foreign competition and the pressure for investment and expansion to compete with the world-wide market, must certainly have played a great role in the fairly risky car industry business of the 20s, which suffered from international overcapacities, constant rationalisation and falling prices.

The Steyr profit and loss account is also exceptional. Gross profits and expenses increased enormously at the same rates between 1921 and 1928, whereas net profits only rose slightly. This means a quickly and steady increasing business activity and turnover since inflation times, without an interruption by stabilisation. Activity and profits were virtually unaffected by currency stability and the major change of currency policy regime. This is truly remarkable, and can only be explained by the high export content of sales, which must have been steady despite the negative business account of 1924.

c. Gräf & Stift The companies of the motor industry that produced utility vehicles were less exposed to international market pressure and focused more on the domestic market. Therefore, disintegration and inflation were less harmful. Truck and bus production was not as risky as automobile production, but it was also less profitable. This was also the case for the Wiener Automobilfabrik AG vorm. Gräf & Stift.[134] It could easily continue to sell its main war product on the market, the five ton workshop truck. During inflation and high stock exchange profits, the firm briefly returned to its former peace-time production of luxury cars. After the end of inflation and once American car imports pressured the Austrian market, Gräf & Stift easily turned back to utility vehicle production. Very little was exported, as the firm nearly exclusively relied on its home market. A lot of specialised trucks were purchased by the public, the postal services, the army, the federal railway and by the municipal fire departments. Financial standing was fairly safe, since the balance sheet value declined only slightly, liabilities fell and debtors increased between 1913 and 1925. Earning power seemed to be somewhat higher before the war, despite an increase of gross profits by 30% between 1913 and 1924.

d. Austro-Fiat After the end of the war, the Österreichische Automobil-Fabriks-AG, vorm. Austro-Fiat,[135] also returned to utility vehicle production. Its production

134 *Bilanzen*, 19.9.1928. See also A.11.

135 *Bilanzen*, 2.10.1926, 14.5.1927. See also time series diagrams of balance sheet and profit and loss accounts in appendix.

range included normal, fire, army and ambulance trucks and other special utility vehicles as well as buses. Austro-Fiat also built its own gears and tools. Bank credit seemed to have been very small or was very quickly repaid. The expansion of plant was moderate and it disposed of its possessions in Hungary. Also this firm almost exclusively supplied the domestic market. Capital stock reserve was 50% higher in 1925 than before the war. During war and inflation, gross profits declined more dramatically than net profits until 1922. In 1923, finances improved until the crisis of 1924 caused a fall of demand and a sharp fall of gross profits.

Both, Gräf & Stift and Austro-Fiat, were only moderately affected by war and inflation, especially compared to Austro Daimler and Steyr. Both pursued a safe and conservative business policy of retrenchment. As they relied on the home market, protectionism and disintegration were of little influence on them. For the utility vehicles producing firms, the domestic market was vital, and therefore, the fluctuating growth and stabilisation crises of the Austrian economy had the greatest implications on these companies. These occurred sharply, but briefly in 1923 and 1924. After stabilisation crises, moderate domestic demand began to thrive again. These were also the only firms of the new modern industries that were not export oriented at all.

The modern automobile industry can be divided into the less risky, but less profitable, domestic market reliant utility vehicles producing firms, and the risky and export depending car industry. Naturally, it was affected by the fall in domestic demand in 1924 to a lesser degree, but had to face fierce international competition, overcapacity and protective trade barriers. These barriers must have been of more significance in the developed nations with higher purchasing power for such durable goods, than in the successor states. In fact, as will be shown, their tariffs were moderate compared to the ones of the industrialised nations. The low purchasing power of the markets of the successor states was a greater problem than protective trade. Therefore, policy was less significant than were structural economic circumstances.

2.5. CONCLUSION

By and large, disintegration and nationalisation had minor implications on most companies. Of the 21 companies analysed here, only four lost their foreign assets. These where Hofherr-Schrantz, Ditmar-Brünner, Alpine and Böhler. The last company only lost a small portion of its foreign holdings and was able to keep the majority by founding a foreign holding company under its leadership. Among the companies of the modern sectors, no foreign holdings were lost. Nine companies did not lose any subsidiary sales or production branches abroad. Among these, Semperit and Elin, belonging to the modern industries, even successfully expanded their foreign holdings. Simmeringer kept the majority of its foreign holding, despite Czechoslovak efforts of nostrification. Eight enterprises did not have any foreign assets before the war.[136]

136 Mathis also emphasised continuity despite political changes. In his study, he comes to the conclusion that companies which kept, expanded or newly acquired foreign assests in the successor states were more numerous than firms that lost foreign holdings. Franz Mathis, "Das Jahr 1918

As will be seen in subsequent chapters, modern industries tended to perform and weather crisis situations better than traditional industries. Clearly, the financial situation reflects this trend. Even though the financial standing of all industrial sectors deteriorated between 1913 and 1925, chiefly the enterprises belonging to the traditional sectors tended to endure the poorest financial conditions. Among ten companies with poor or, at utmost, satisfactory financial standing, only four were part of the modern sectors: Steyr, Austro-Daimler, Felten & Guilleaume and Siemens. Among nine companies with good or stable financial standing only three belonged to the traditional sector: Hutter & Schrantz, Ditmar-Brünner and Veitscher.

The long-term structural transformation of the European economy mainly determined economic performance. This process was apparent in increasing production capacities abroad and in a shift to modern modes of production. The severity and nature of the impact of these changes on industrial sectors determined economic performance of individual companies. As the traditional sectors tended to be affected negatively by these processes, almost only companies from the traditional sectors suffered from structural long-term changes, intensified by war and inflation. The enterprises where this process was most conspicuous were Alpine, Veitscher, the engine factories, Simmeringer, Hofherr-Schrantz, Enzesfelder and Brevillier. As all of them suffered from fierce foreign competition and overcapacities after inflation granted no more competitive export advantage, the symptoms of structural change for traditional sectors were low earning power, productivity and competitiveness. Not only were most of the firms unable to regain competitive productivity and earning power, but they also permanently suffered from protectionism as their domestic and international market position was often weak.

In contrast, companies that had been highly export oriented before the war endured disintegration, inflation and stabilisation most successfully. These were Ditmar-Brünner and Hutter & Schrantz. The two firms that had been export oriented *and* belonged to the modern sectors, Semperit and Elin, not only enjoyed favourable performance, but also underwent massive expansion. These four companies were the only firms that were able to improve their sales conditions until 1925. For nearly all other enterprises, inflation only resulted in a minor upswing of sales. Thereafter, traditional as well as many modern companies faced much harsher market conditions than before the war and were hit by stabilisation at different points in time. Only Veitscher, Hutter & Schrantz and Ditmar-Brünner were not at all affected by stabilisation crisis as their performance depended on foreign markets. Most electrical engineering firms were only minutely hit by stabilisation crises.

To make any assertions about the change of the productive sector is more difficult. By and large all industrial sectors suffered from initial overcapacities and did not expand their plant until after the mid 20s. However, evidence suggests that modern sectors had a greater inclination to modernisation, rationalisation and expansion than traditional industries. Most changes of the productive sector were made after the end of the inflation. Only very few were able to make profitable and effective

und die österreichischen Großunternehmen. Neubeginn oder Kontinuität?", in: Othmar Pickl and R. Metlar (eds.), *Zerfall und Integration*, Vienna 1995.

investments during the inflation. Some changed to the manufacture of slightly different products, some modernised and rationalised, and only very few companies enlarged their productive capacities.

Only Ditmar-Brünner successfully changed its production to simple mass consumption goods. For Enzesfelder, the shift to railway carriage production turned out to be a failure. For the engine factories to continue to rely on railway orders was a mistake. Due to continuous and unrelenting international market pressure after stabilisation, Steyr, Daimler, AEG, Böhler, Schoeller-Bleckmann and Veitscher partially or completely modernised and rationalised their production processes. Only three companies, two of them modern enterprises, not only modernised, but also enlarged their production capacities. These were Hutter & Schrantz, Semperit and Elin. In some cases, these firms must have invested heavily before the onset of the extreme inflationary process. Thereafter, their investments were completed while their debts, still raised in paper crowns, were nearly cancelled when depreciated to schillings. This development was especially pronounced for the semi-public electricity supply companies that carried out hydro-electric power plant construction.[137] As they suffered most extremely from structural shifts of the European industry, exclusively traditional companies experienced massive misinvestment, constant overcapacities and in some cases contraction of their productive sector. The most prominent among them were Alpine, the engine factories, Enzesfelder, Hofherr-Schrantz and Brevillier.

137 See chapter 3, subheading 3.3.1. b).

PART II

3. THE YEARS OF MODERATE PROSPERITY, 1925–1930. NEO-LIBERAL CURRENCY AND BUDGET POLICIES, THE GOLD STANDARD, AND ECONOMIC PERFORMANCE IN EUROPE

3.1. GENERAL ECONOMIC DEVELOPMENT, THEORY AND POLICY

The theme of this section is concerned with the main two spheres that dominated economic development of companies: economic theory and economic policies applied, and the changing structure of the international economy and the national economies of Europe. Subjects of analysis are the Austrian companies. For comparison, the policy and performance of France and Belgium, Great Britain, Germany and policy and microeconomic performance of Austria will be interwoven into the discussion of company histories. Compared to the first chapter, this chapter will address the more subtle influences of policy on economic performance as there were no such extreme policy regime shifts from highly inflationary policies to stabilisation.

This section addresses a part of the inter-war economic history that represented the most prosperous and calm years of the period overall and of the 1920s. In spite of this, the inter-war period was a time when European industrial output per capita rose only 1% annually, and overall performance was poor.[1] Before and after the two World Wars, European economic growth was much higher. When viewing overall performance covering the period of 1913 until 1938/39, it is obvious that economic growth was very uneven and low in Europe compared to the pre-war and post-World-War Two periods.[2] This development manifested itself most clearly in countries with weak performance. At first glance, one of the main reasons for poor performance seemed to have been the effects of the war. The First World War lasted until 1918, but its immediate consequences on the world economy lasted until the mid 20s for many countries. Only by this time, most European countries recovered their pre-war level of production or barely surpassed it. The end of this era (1929/30) was also the peak of national income for most countries, and most would barely be able to recover or surpass the 1929/30 level in the 1930s. Specifically the losing states of World War One fared the worst in this process. For those nations that had undergone severe inflation, only the post-stabilisation era rendered possible proper reintegration and partial recovery. Therefore, it took until the mid 20s for Austria and Germany to be once again fully reintegrated into the world economy, and it took until the late part of the decade for them to reach pre-war GNP levels.

1 Angus Maddison, "Economic Policy and Performance in Europe 1913–1970," in: Carlo M. Cipolla (ed.), *The Fontana Economic History of Europe, Volume 5, The Twentieth Century*, Sussex 1977, 442 ff.

2 Paul Bairoch, "Europe's Gross National Product: 1800–1975," in: *The Journal of European Economic History*, 2, Vol. 5, 1976, 273–340.

In the inter-war period, a clear difference of economic performance existed between the countries that had experienced extreme inflations and those that belonged to the Entente or had been neutral. The course of performance and growth in Germany and Austria, the most important countries of the first group, was nearly synchronised. Total German and Austrian performance was poor, and only during the time of the boom of the late 20s was their development within the average European growth curve. Figures 3.1 and 3.2 reveal the high rates of growth of these countries, but their low levels of growth compared to 1913 levels.

In addition, although annual macroeconomic data suggest a fairly smooth development of the German economy in the late 20s, in reality the economic development distinguished itself by an unusual succession of hectic upswings and downswings between inflation, stabilisation and the beginning of the Great Depression. The years 1923/24 marked a downswing due to stabilisation, then followed a brief upswing until mid 1925, then a short recession followed until the spring of 1926. After that, a moderate boom occurred, which reached its peak at the end of 1927. The first signs of the depression were already noticed by the summer of 1929.[3]

Austrian fluctuating growth nearly exactly followed the business cycle pattern of Germany; the only difference was that inflation ended and stabilisation began a year sooner. In 1923, some of its industrial sectors benefited from the near collapse of the German economy. Compared to growth patterns in other industrialised countries, Austrian growth, during the inter-war period, was extreme. Between 1913 and 1929, the annual growth rate was only 0.3%, but was among the highest in Europe between 1920–1929, when the years of war are excluded. In fact, the Austrian annual average compound growth rate between 1920–1929 was quite high with 5.2%, only surpassed by Finland (5.3%), Czechoslovakia (6%) and the average Eastern European level (6.3%).[4] Yet, in 1925, Austrian growth began from a fairly moderate level and did not surpass its 1913 per capita income level.[5] Nevertheless, other advanced countries did not perform much better, as can also be said for such major economic powers as Germany, the United Kingdom and the USSR.[6] In the 30s, however, the Austrian rate of growth was among the lowest in Europe, falling again dramatically to 0.5% between 1929–1938.[7]

This fluctuating annual average growth reveals the difficulty the Austrian and German economies were undergoing in facing structural shifts in a hostile environment. Growth rates of all other Western European countries were much more even, but lower and more moderate. At the same time growth levels tended to be higher. To conclude, it can be maintained that German and Austrian economic performances were among the poorest in Europe overall, and that growth levels were low, but that rates were above average in the late 20s. However, growth and development of

3 Rainer Meister, *Die große Depression. Zwangslagen und Handlungsspielräume der Wirschafts- und Finanzpolitik in Deutschland 1929–1932*, Stuttgart 1991, 91–99.

4 Maddison, "Policy and Performance," 451.

5 Only by 1950 was the 1913 per capita income level surpassed. Ibid, 449.

6 Bairoch, "Europe's Gross National Product," chart: B2 Volume of total and per capita GNP by individual countries: 1913–1950.

7 Maddison, "Policy and Performance," 451.

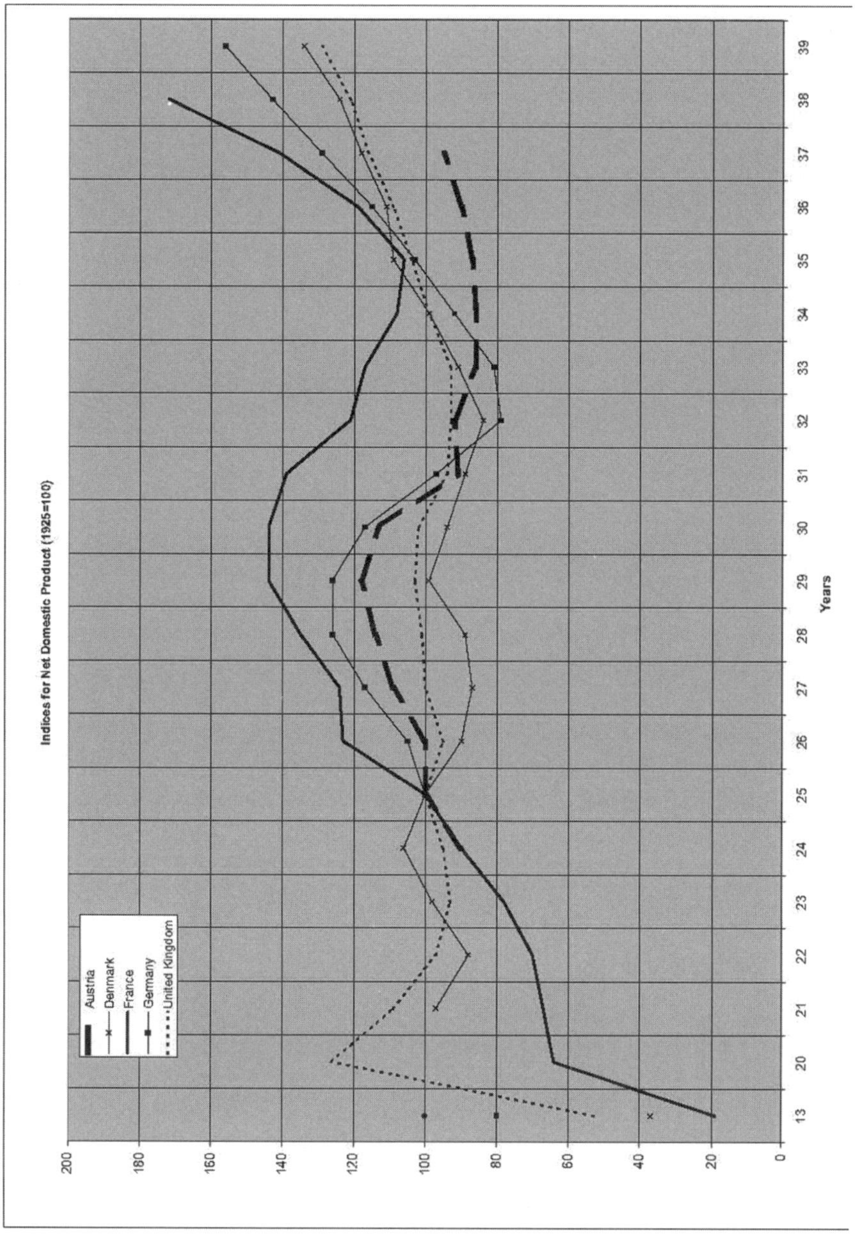

Figure 3.1.: Indices for Net Domestic Product (1925=100). Source: Indices calculated from Peter Flora, Franz Kraus and Winfried Pfenning, *State, Economy, and Society in Western Europe 1815–1975. A Data Handbook in two Volumes. Volume 2. The Growth of Industrial Societies and Capitalist Economies*, Frankfurt 1987, chapter: Growth of National Product, 337 ff.

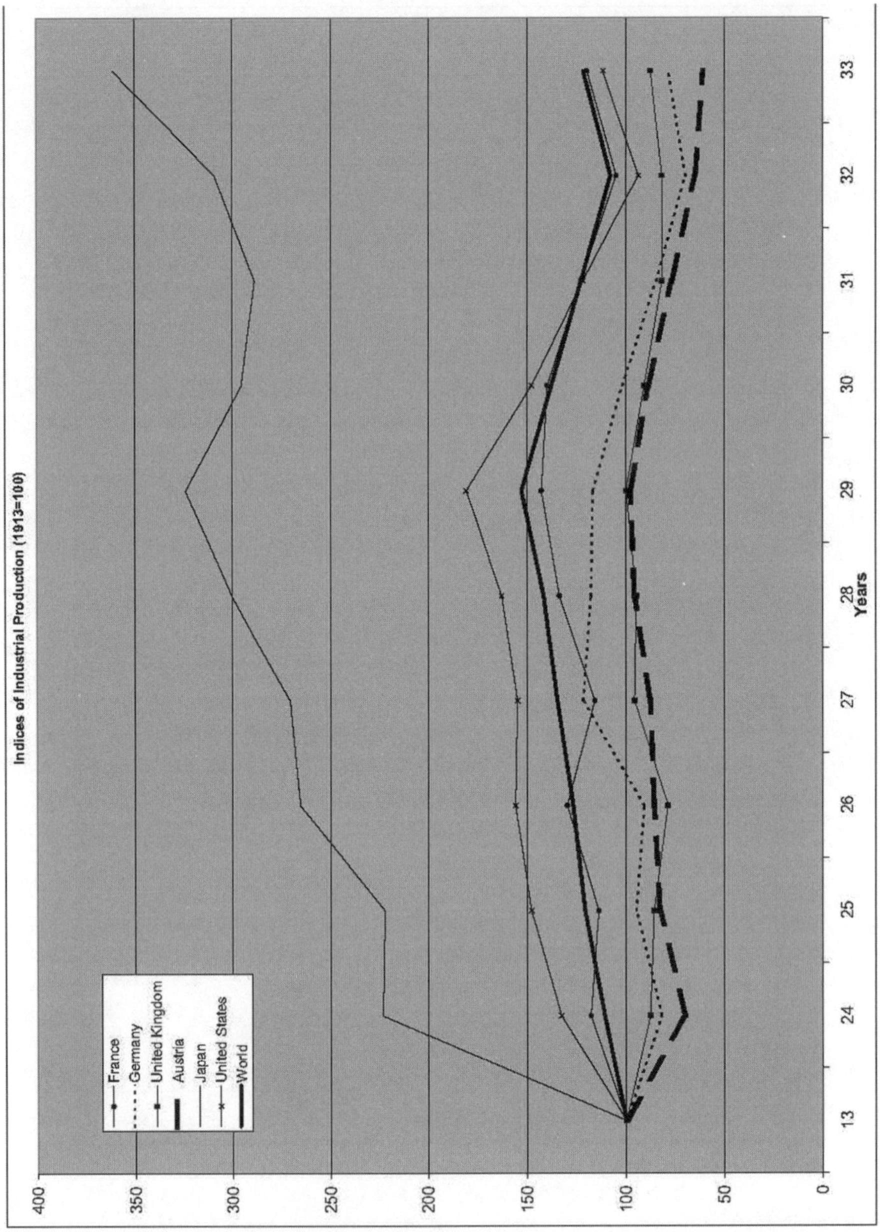

Figure 3.2.: Indices of Industrial Production (1913=100). Sources: League of Nations (ed.), *Industrialization and Foreign Trade*, Geneva 1945. W. Abelshauser and D. Petzina, „Krise und Rekonstruktion," in: W.H. Schröder and R. Spree (ed.), *Historische Konjunkturforschung*, Stuttgart 1981, 75–114. Meister, *Die große Depression*, 94. Österreichisches Institut für Wirtschaftsforschung, *Monatsberichte 14*, 40.

other industrialised countries was not remarkably better, but reached a higher level than in Germany and Austria. How can these below average performances of these two countries be explained? National economic policy, international protectionism and the inability to overcome the results of the First World War have often been blamed.

Among the major Entente countries, the remarkably good performance of France and Belgium in surpassing pre-war production was outstanding. In contrast, British performance was poor in the 20s, as it only slightly overcame 1913 production. When viewing the development of net product at current prices, the differences in British and French development are obvious. While the French economy was growing rapidly until 1929, British development stagnated. The situation was almost reversed in the 1930s, when France only started to recover by 1935.

When regarding economic policy of the 1920s, it is hard to see how political and monetary factors influenced this overall poor performance. The time after 1924/25 revealed the attempt of the leading economic powers to re-establish pre-war conditions, as economic theory of policy-making in nearly all countries was dominated by neo-classical, liberal economic theory, which formed the essential theoretical basis of this effort. Until the late 20s, it was still considered realistic to return to pre-war economic and monetary conditions in the framework of the classical gold standard. The goal was to return to a system of fixed exchange rates, to support international division of labour, trade and economic growth, as existed before 1914. In 1925, with economic stabilisation and more political stability, as a result of the Dawes settlement in 1924, the outlook of contemporaries regarding production, trade and financial stability, was positive.[8] Leading the attempt to establish pre-war conditions were, of course, the representatives of American and Western European financial interests, the central banks, such as the American Federal Reserve, the Bank of England or the Bank of France, and first and foremost, the Financial Committee of the League of Nations as a representative of Entente economic interests. These institutions had the strongest financial and political economic leverage and attempted to guide the other European governments of the advanced industrialised countries toward the restoration of the traditional economic and financial systems with the help of orthodox policy. Their political and economic pressures and goals, moreover, were warmly received by the mostly bourgeois and rightist post-1924 governments and central banks of the other highly developed nations in Europe.

Generally, government economic policy tried to follow the theoretical concepts of classical economics and laissez-faire. Nevertheless, theory could only be applied to a very limited extent. Eventually, most governments essentially practised a policy that was a compromise[9] between the attempt to re-establish the conditions before

8 Joseph S. Davis, "Economic and Financial Progress in Europe, 1924–25," in: *The Review of Economic Statistics and Supplements*, Vol. 7, Cambridge, Massachusetts 1925, conclusion 85. The League of Nations experts that evaluated Austrian economic condition in 1925 also regarded future economic development for Austria as positive. See: W.T. Layton and Charles Rist, *Die Wirtschaftslage Österreichs*, Vienna 1925.

9 "The interwar years were transition years between the belief in the viability of a self regulating market system and the recognition that a substantial, deliberate policy of economic control was

the First World War and the mostly half-hearted and mediocre efforts to alleviate the economic and social problems from which their countries suffered. These emanated from the structural changes that the European economy was undergoing, while the state's share of national income rose in most countries, indicating that the public sector became increasingly involved and responsible for economic growth and social security.

Although the states' share of GNP remained relatively small and policy tended to be orthodox and passive, historiography has primarily made national and international neo-liberal economic policy responsible for poor economic growth of this period, by way of restricting credit expansion and generating insufficient demand via state investment. The general move of most countries' trade policy toward protectionism in the 20s, and even more so in the 1930s, has also been regarded as a major factor contributing to stagnant international trade, low investment rates, and therefore, to low economic growth. In view of this interpretation, the essential question remains the actual impact of the political and monetary sector as a major tool of policy on the real economic development and to what degree changes in economic structures dominated development and performance. This is an attempt to explore this question for European, and specifically Austrian, policy and economic development.

However, economic performance and its influencing factors prove extremely difficult to judge as general development had to face numerous problems, apart from shifts in structure. Such problems included the destruction of the international monetary system and the failure to find a substitute, a fundamental payments disequilibrium of many countries, lack of international co-operation, protectionism, and worst of all, the pursuit of traditional pre-war policy objectives which had little relation to the economic realities of the 20s.[10]

3.1.1. Theories of Economic Development in Germany and Austria

For this low and unusual development in Germany and Austria in the 1920s and the dramatic fall and severity of the depression in these countries, generally two explanations have been offered. The first is based upon classical economic theory and the second is more under the influence of a Keynesian paradigm.[11] The former hypothesis, mostly supported by Knut Borchardt,[12] attempted to elucidate the policy options available to the Brüning administration in a position of constraint in early

essential to stability." Benjamin Ward, "National Economic Planning and Policies in Twentieth Century Europe 1920–1970," in: Cipolla, *The Fontana Economic History of Europe 5*, 701.

10 Maddison, "Policy and Performance," 453.

11 In Meister, *Depression*, Borchardt's thesis is briefly explained, 88–99. The Keynesian explanation is presented 98–102.

12 Knut Borchardt, "Zwangslagen und Handlungsspielräume in der großen Weltwirtschaftskrise der frühen dreißiger Jahre. Zur Revision des überlieferten Geschichtsbildes," and "Wirtschaftliche Ursachen des Scheiterns derWeimarer Republik," in: Knut Borchardt (ed.), *Wachstum, Krisen und Handlungsspielräume der Wirtschaftspolitik. Studien zur Wirtschaftsgeschichte des 19. und 20. Jahrhunderts*, Göttingen 1982.

1930. Despite clear signs of an economic slump, the German government turned to measures which, from the viewpoint of modern economic policy, supported recession tendencies. The same policy was followed in Austria with similar vigour, in both cases essentially supporting the downswing that led to the intensification of socio-economic conflicts and the dissolution of parliament. Spending was cut, taxes raised and a restrictive deflationary currency policy was pursued in the face of a severe depression. The aim was to lower the costs of production and to raise prices. In contrast to many modern economists, Borchardt suggests that this policy option was the right choice, and that a solution of the economic problems was not possible within the framework of the classical capitalist system. Policy was in a position of constraint ("Zwangslage") marked by contracting world trade, a default currency system, reparations, war debts and the repercussions of inflation.

The core of his thesis asserts that the struggle for the distribution of the slowly growing national income ("Einkommensverteilungskonflikt") caused the economic mechanism, which from a neo-liberal point of view always had the tendency to turn back to full employment equilibrium, to be disturbed by non-system conform behaviour. Simply outlined, the struggle of distribution was fought out on two levels: Between employees/workers and entrepreneurs/capitalists as well as between the private and public sectors of the economy over the amount of duties, taxes and their redistribution over transfer payments. Regarded in retrospect, the state, forced to intervene actively into the distribution process, tended to favour employees and workers in its decisions. At the same time, taxes were continuously raised. In the late 20s, the essential result was that wages tended to rise faster than aggregate productivity of the economy. In the long run, this caused company income and net profits to decline. This, according to Borchardt, was the main cause for low investment rate, which is regarded as the main motor for economic growth.[13] In addition, the development of declining international market prices, the system of fixed exchange rates and high national discount rates made it more problematical for companies to clear themselves of the increasing wage and tax expenses by augmenting the prices of their products. The situation was quite unfavourable for private enterprises as the consequence of the distribution conflict resulted in proportionally low investment, which, in turn, was considered the main cause of low economic growth in the 1920s. The outcome was a grotesque boom with high public and private consumption, low profits and investments, falling prices, high unemployment, relatively low export volume and low economic growth. This, on the other hand, only intensified the distribution conflict, causing further disturbance of the economic system.

13 Theodor Balderston agrees that wages grew faster than productivity, but states, in constrast to Borchardt, that productivity improvement in Germany was quite favourable compared to foreign and especially American productivity performance. He concluded that "Even although the wage rises outstripped productivity gains, so that unit costs and export prices rose, (...) there is no evidence of deterioration in German competetivity, even in 1930." He also claims that "the ratio of productivity improving to purely capacity extending investment" was unusually high in the late 20s. But he sees the causes of the economic crisis in Germany partially in investment. Theodor Balderston, *The Origins and Course of the German Economic Crisis. November 1923 to May 1932*, Berlin 1993, 80 and 400 ff.

The second thesis[14] places emphasis on the level of aggregate international and domestic economic demand as the major factor determining employment. This is a Keynesian approach. According to this theory, the disproportion between supply and demand was not caused by a low investment rate, but resulted mainly from low foreign demand, great income losses of the middle class due to inflation and a low domestic consumption level between 1927–29. Other factors were low utilisation of capacity, the defaults of the international currency system and increasing cartelisation. However, the uneven distribution of national income, lower income among the masses, which resulted in a lower consumption rate, cannot necessarily be regarded as the main problem that caused poor performance. In Germany during the second half of the 20s, real consumption was 6% higher than before the war. Public consumption was more than 3% higher than in 1913.[15] In Austria, private consumption increased 17.4% between 1913 and 1929. In the same time span, public consumption rose 12.8%.[16] In contrast, the overall net investment rate was much lower in both countries in the late 20s.

The representatives of the Keynesian approach would then place emphasis on the lack of foreign demand, on the relative decline and contraction of international trade and on demand during the inter-war period. The core of the argument is low international demand, which is said to have been caused by increasing protectionist policies.[17] The misfunctioning of the international gold standard, which resulted in deflationary policies in most countries and easily disseminated economic recession tendencies from country to country, has been considered closely interconnected with the spread of low international market demand. Moreover, the system lacked credibility and co-operation in trade and currency policy[18] and a counter-cyclical interventionist state policy to counteract low demand.

3.1.2. Theoretical Concepts applied: National and International Structural Transformations

This paper attempts to suggest that neither disproportionally increasing wages and taxes (which seemed to have caused a relative decline in productivity) nor protectionist policies, nor the misfunctioning of the gold standard (lowering international demand) were the main causes for poor growth, development and performance in

14 Meister, *Depression*, 98 states Petzina, Abelshauser, Krohn, Holtferich, Maier and Plumpe among others as the main representatives of this approach. See also Werner Abelshauser and Dietmar Petzina, "Zum Problem der relativen Stagnation der deutschen Wirtschaft in den zwanziger Jahren," in: Hans Mommsen, Dietmar Petzina and Bernd Weisbrod (eds.), *Industrielles System und politische Entwicklung in der Weimarer Republik*, vol. 1, Düsseldorf 1974.

15 Meister, *Depression*, 100.

16 Österreichisches Institut für Wirtschaftsforschung, *Monatsberichte 14*, 43.

17 See for example: Abelshauser and Petzina, "Krise und Rekonstruktion", 95.

18 See Barry Eichengreen, *Golden Fetters. The Gold Standard and the Great Depression, 1919–1939*, Oxford 1995, Introduction.

Austria and other countries. Insufficient international demand was, in fact, the main problem, but it was not induced by a default currency system and economic policy, i.e. protectionist trade policy, but instead, by real economic factors.

The cause for declining trade and low international demand lay in structural disproportions of the world economy and of the modern national economies in Europe and the US. It is suggested that the most dominating factors of economic development and performance were two endogenous structural transformations taking place, one on an international level and one taking place on a national level in the older industrialised countries in Europe and the United States. It is also suggested that protectionist trade policies, limiting the exchange of goods, were a result, a political reaction of a general structural change of the world economy, partially ignited and speeded up by war and inflation. This change in structure, manifesting itself in falling international demand and higher competition, was the main cause of poor European, and in particular, Austrian economic performance.

To understand these structural shifts, it is necessary to look at trade and industrialisation before and after the war. Before the First World War, the world economic trade system was still dominated by the three main industrialised countries of Europe: Germany, Britain and France. Trade of finished products was dominated by these three European countries, and most of world trade occurred among these three industrial nations and the United States.[19] Trade between industrialised countries and the economic periphery of the world mainly consisted of trade of finished products from Europe to the rest of the world and of primary products, or at utmost, of basic semi-finished products to Europe or the United States.

After the war, these traditional trade patterns shifted. The decline of Europe's economic strength was a result of the stagnation and partial contraction of its traditional industries, such as textiles, paper, shipbuilding, iron and steel, and traditional machine building industries. This stagnation, in turn, was a consequence of structural shifts within the economies of the advanced countries, visible in increasing pressure and competition from intensifying industrialisation and the building-up of production capacities in the periphery countries of the world industry, especially in Eastern Europe, India, China, Japan, the British colonies, South American countries and also the United States and Canada. These new production capacities of the old and more simple industries, which had been applied in Europe on a massive scale in the 19th century (such as textiles, paper, shipbuilding, traditional machine building based on steam power and iron and steel) had developed during or after the war in the periphery under more favourable conditions. The new producers had been cut off from European competition and dependence, while the old industrialised countries invested their whole economic effort into the battlefields of World War One. After the war, the traditional industries in Europe were pressured by enlarged and partially superior production capacities abroad, but also by increased plant facilities within the old industrialised countries in Europe created during the war.

19 See Svennilson, 16–18.

The total result of this development were serious overcapacities[20] in the world among most older and traditional industries of the late 19th century, which were based on iron and steam technology. This caused a tendency of overproduction, declining prices, and falling demand in the 1920s, after the immediate high post-war demand had been met. Protectionist trade policies only enhanced these developments and were only a political reaction of governments to pressure from national producers of the various declining industries. Countries that had undergone inflation, endured high indebtedness and were not export oriented before the war, especially suffered from this. The overall consequence of this long-term development, accelerated by the war, was very moderate growth of trade[21], slower than growth of world production. The decline of trade was the strongest among semi-finished and finished products of textiles, paper, iron and steel. Other older primary products industries, such as mining, declined in many countries, not only because of overcapacities, but also because new sources of energy were available, such as oil and electricity. Some traditional industries also declined because artificial substitutes, developed by the chemical industries, replaced their products.

Whereas the new industrialising countries in the periphery contributed to overproduction, higher competition and falling prices, the permanent "industrial revolution" of the old industrialised countries that was generated by the development and application of new technologies and sources of energy, underwent serious distortions. The usual process, a perpetual economic revolution[22] taking place within the most advanced national economies of Europe and the US, was at a vital junction in the inter-war period that caused a structural long-term imbalance. The modern industries in the industrialised countries led this revolution away from the 19th century economy, which was supported by coal, iron, steel and textiles, toward the introduction of the highly developed, classical 20th century economy dominated by automobiles, electrical engineering, flexible energy availability, chemicals and durable mass consumer goods industries. Therefore, one author claims, "it was mainly

20 In a similar fashion this has already been suggested by studies of the League of Nations. "While this surplus capacity is being built up, the older industrial states are not able to adapt their own economic structure and their exports of manufactured goods to a shift in foreign demand as they can in normal times because the disturbances which have given rise to the surplus simultaneously curtail all international demand. In consequence the surplus caused by industrial expansion in certain areas proves detrimental to older industrial countries." League of Nations, *Industrialization and Foreign Trade*, 81.

21 This is also briefly mentioned in Meister, *Depression*, 111. "Das geringe Wachstum des Welthandels wird unter anderem auf die durch den Ersten Weltkrieg bewirkte Störung der internationalen Arbeitsteilung zwischen den industrialisierten Staaten West- und Mitteleuropas und der übrigen Welt zurückgeführt." This was also recognised by contemporaries; see section on development of world textile industry 3.2.1.; and Rolf Wagenführ, "Die Industriewirtschaft. Entwicklungstendenzen der deutschen und internationalen Industrieproduktion 1860 bis 1932," in: Deutsches Institut für Konjunkturforschung (ed.), *Vierteljahreshefte zur Konkjunkturforschung*, special issue 31, Berlin 1933.

22 Joseph A. Schumpeter, *Konjunkturzyklen. Eine theoretische, historische und statistische Analyse des kapitalistischen Prozesses*, 2nd volume, Göttingen 1961, chapter 14: Die „Industrielle Revolution" der zwanziger Jahre, 806 ff.

technological progress which changed the structure of many existing industries and created others by introducing new products and services, materials or processes"[23] in the 20s. The modern industries, such as car manufacturing, electricity and chemicals, had proportionally much higher growth rates than all other industrial sectors. While the old industries enjoyed high growth rates in the periphery countries, they declined or stagnated in Europe; whereas, in the meantime, the new industries in this area and in the United States expanded quickly.

However, this change in industrial structures suffered from structural distortions. Countries in which the economy only partially experienced this transformation of increasing application of new technologies and services suffered more from stagnation of their older industrial sectors. Furthermore, by the nature of their technologies, investment of new industries tended to be more rationalising than expansive, making a compensation of the stagnation of the older industries even more difficult. Naturally, old industrialised countries that went through this process of shifting economic structures profoundly and quickly, underwent the most well-balanced economic development. The best example of this case was the United States' development until the depression. It had the best of both changes. This does not mean that overall growth had to be higher than in other countries. Growth rates, as defined by the increase of national product, tended to be higher in the periphery, where more primitive industries were being developed and where growth levels had been low before. Growth rates were either much lower or stagnating in Europe, since the shift to new industries was slower and growth levels had previously been high. Furthermore, growth in Europe was also slower, because the shift to modern and complex industries was capital and technology intensive and more inward oriented, directed to technological development of domestic economies and increasing dependence on domestic consumer purchasing power. On a large and profound scale, this process required big, advanced national markets and a favourable distribution of wealth. This is especially obvious in the case of the large modern European economies of France, Britain and Germany.[24] Growth and development shifted more toward internal development of the various national economies, while trade stagnated or grew only moderately. For example, the car industries were almost exclusively inward oriented. Sales were only on the domestic market, and only the automobile manufacturers in small countries, such as in Austria, had to export a substantial portion of their production. In all of Europe, these changes meant a decline in the position of international trade for the national economies.

This theory, which bases economic growth on industrial change and innovation, has its roots in Schumpeter's theory of long-term business cycles, as the expression of long-term secular industrial transition, as the main force advancing economic growth and development in a capitalist economic system. It basically describes economic changes by employing a concept of endogenous growth theory, on which

23 Sidney Pollard, *The Development of the British Economy, 1914–1980*, 3rd edition London 1962, 57.

24 Svennilson, chapter: Transformation and Growth of Early Industrialised Countries, 44 ff.

a massive amount of literature is based today.[25] This structural theory of economic growth has also been applied to explain economic stagnation. Therefore, it is possible to base stagnation hypotheses, in turn, on the idea of an insufficient structural shift within the industrialised economies, from traditional to modern industries, resting on new technologies. This concept is closely interconnected with a phase of industrial revolution that has been called "Stalemate in Technology" and is also based on Schumpeter's evolutionary business cycle growth theory as a "Process of Creative Destruction"[26]:

> "It begins when many lines of business based on mature technologies turn stagnant, capital withdraws from it but cannot (temporarily) find profitable reinvestment opportunities in new types of technology, and while stagflation indicates structural readiness for radical innovations, these don't emerge instantly, don't come in the right time and place, and don't 'fall from the sky' in the most convenient quantity and quality. Eventually, the mounting need for innovation produces a swell of basic innovations, and that highlights the recovery and puts an end to the stalemated situation."[27]

The empirical data presented here in the form of company histories partially support the "Imbalanced-Technical-Change-Hypothesis (ITCH)" of Mensch and Schnopp[28], *suggesting an interconnection between economic stagnation and innovation and assuming that the 1920s crisis, at least in modern industrialised countries, was to large degree the result of a temporary maturation of technology, and an imbalance between expansive and rationalising innovations. However, the main problem was not a lack of basic innovations in the inter-war period, but rather their slow large scale application and the rationalising tendencies of new industries unable to compensate for losses of growth among the traditional industries. A slowing down of the application of new technologies resulted in distortions of industrial structures.*

Another probable factor, which cannot be analysed here, was the fragility of large scale mass consumer markets, on which new industries increasingly relied. The combined effect of these shifts in advanced countries, together with economic disadvantages of small advanced countries with small markets and minor national producers and of the international structural change, can be regarded as the major factors contributing to economic stagnation in Austria and other European countries in the inter-war period. The development and business activity of Austrian companies clearly reflected the results of these two structural revolutions.

25 One of the latest works, based on Schumpeter: Philippe Aghion and Peter Howitt, *Endogenous Growth Theory*, Cambridge, Massachusetts 1998.

26 Joseph A. Schumpeter, *Kapitalismus, Sozialismus und Demokratie*, 4th edition, Munich 1950, chapter 7: "Der Prozeß der schöpferischen Zerstörung", 134–142.

27 Gerhard Mensch and Reinhard Schnopp, "Stalemate in Technology, 1925–1935: The Interplay of Stagnation and Innovation," in: Schröder and Spree, *Historische Konjunkturforschung*, 61.

28 Ibid, 64 ff.

In front of this background of structural transformations, the role of state interference was slowly modifying in an economy that was dramatically changing and transforming toward the typical modern 20th century economy. Due to these shifts and the changing relationship between state and economy, the booming years of 1925 until 1929 were a period of very unusual economic growth, as some historians and economists have noted.[29] Typical characteristics of this upswing were strong rationalisation movements in the new industries, cartelisation (especially among the older industrial sectors), an increase of industrial production, a fall in prices more dramatic for primary goods than for semi-finished and finished products, but not a full utilisation of industrial capacity. In many ways, this boom was unlike any other before, because whereas production rose, prices for goods fell, large overcapacities still existed, large resources were not employed and high unemployment remained in most countries. Thus, the symptoms of this boom did not fit into the theoretical framework of classical economic theory and could, therefore, not be dealt with by classical policy. Moreover, in some countries the boom was partially artificially induced by external finances and caused serious balance of payments problems. In the long run, it led to an unstable international economic system, partially accelerating the downfall in 1929/30.

Generally, policy did not play such a major role in generating the poor economic performance in Austria, as has been often suggested,[30] because economic structural problems were out of the reach of national economic policy. Moreover, it will be shown below that Austrian economic policy, at least in the 20s, was quite similar to that of other European states. Still, other nations with similar policy regimes performed slightly better. Austrian economic policy was in no way any more restrictive than in other countries. Therefore, policy was not the major problem and should be regarded in the international contemporary framework. The major reason for the Austrian and European demise was the change of the economic structures of industrialised Europe and the consequential intensifying competition of the periphery. It will be shown that this transition was much more difficult to face for smaller countries than for industrialised nations with large domestic markets that were able to maintain a financial market to support technological development and to generate enough consumer purchasing power to have at least sufficient demand for the new, large industrial combines. Thus, smaller nations had to be much more export oriented, but in the face of growing trade barriers and declining world trade, this was difficult to maintain. Furthermore, Austria was in a particularly difficult position as its exports were still partially oriented toward the underdeveloped markets of the

29 For example Derek H. Aldcroft, *Die zwanziger Jahre. Von Versailles zur Wall Street, 1919–1929*, Munich 1978, chapter 8: Die Hochkonjunktur der späten zwanziger Jahre, 216 ff.

30 In literature policy is often criticised, but not put into contemporary international perspective. Instead interwar policy is often compared with post-World War Two policy and then harshly judged. "Aber das Schicksal der Zweiten Republik [...] zeigt mit einer exemplarischen Deutlichkeit, daß Fatalismus, fälschlich als Liberalismus ausgegeben, keine für die Wirtschaftspolitik akzeptable geistige Grundhaltung darstellt." Eduard März and Maria Szecsi, "Stagnation und Expansion. Eine vergleichende Analyse der wirtschaftlichen Entwicklung in der Ersten und Zweiten Republik," in: *Wirtschaft und Gesellschaft*, 2, 1982, 330 and 331.

Eastern and South-Eastern European states, whose economic position was weak and purchasing power low.

Even though fairly similar economic policies were chosen in all of Europe, as we will see below, performance was quite different. How can this be explained, other than with the fact that different economic structures and conditions existed among these nations, some more able to deal with the transitions taking place in the 20s than others that were stagnating? Britain suffered in the 20s not only because of its absolute strict adherence to the gold standard and the resulting deflationary policy,[31] but because the shift to the new industrial revolution was most difficult for this country. At first glance, in France and Belgium, this painful change seemed to have been postponed by the government financed reconstruction boom and by mild inflation until the late 20s. The German and Austrian economies only reintegrated into the world economy and trade after the end of inflation. Only after the stabilisation crisis in Austria (1924) and in Germany (1926), did the structures of these economies begin to adjust. Both slowly overcame the inflationary distortions, and their economies participated in the growth and moderate boom of the late 20s, marking the final shift toward modern industries and consumption. For Germany, this was much more the case than for Austria. Whereas in Germany, the boom was much more obvious with gross domestic product rising 25.6% between 1925 and 1929[32] , in Austria, growth was much more moderate with 17.4%.[33] This certainly also had to do with the difficulty in transformation for small countries that were heavily export oriented.

3.1.3. Contemporary Economic Theory

Before discussing economic policies and performances, the dominant contemporary economic theory and its impact on policy-making should be briefly deliberated. Contemporary theoreticians in Austria, like Joseph A. Schumpeter, Ludwig von Mises, Friedrich von Hayek, Fritz Machlup or Oskar Morgenstern, were, certainly, strongly influenced by 19th century Austrian Economics,[34] just as the schools of economics in other states to a greater or lesser degree. To measure the influence of contemporary theory on policy-making of the inter-war period is impossible, but its dominant role is obvious. Directly, economists rarely influenced policy-making, and it was only by the late 20s when institutes for economic research were founded, which had the objective to quantify and describe business cycles with the help of useful statistics. In Austria, the institute for business cycle research[35] was founded in 1927. Its Ger-

31 The Sterling exchange rate has been regarded as too high, thus lowering the expansion of exports. Carlo Zacchia, "International Trade and Capital Movements 1920–1970," in: Cipolla, *The Fontana Economic History of Europe 5*, 516.

32 See Flora, Kraus and Pfenning, *State, Economy, and Society 2*, 350.

33 Flora, Kraus and Pfenning, *State, Economy, and Society 2*, 340.

34 Austrian economics was dominated by the thought of Carl Menger, Friedrich vonWieser and Eugen von Böhm- Bawerk. See for example: Robert B. Ekel und and Robert F. Hébert, *A History of Economic Theory and Method*, 2nd edition, New York 1975, 276 ff.

35 Österreichisches Institut für Konjunkturforschung.

man equivalent had been established two years before in Berlin.[36] In the US, the Harvard business cycle barometer was developed, which was published monthly in the "Review of Economic Statistics." These institutions regarded themselves, at most, as advisory organisations, which only observed the economic process without explaining it,[37] not to speak of interfering in policy-making. Business journals published part of their publications and were read by entrepreneurs and national banks for possible business expectations and predictions.

Economists themselves saw their field as a pure science[38] which observed the economic process and attempted to support and modify the classical laws that had been layed down in the 19th century. Once theories were established, they were then superimposed on the current conditions. This is exactly what happened when the Great Depression set in. This science was meant to be free of value and judgement, and believed in formalism, functionalism, market laws and price mechanisms. In the changing social and economic circumstances of the 20s and 30s, neo-classical economic liberalism was an anachronism. The complex socio-economic process was framed into a mechanistic and classical scientific world-view, and the economic laws that had been discovered seemed to many as impeccable as the laws of physics.

Therefore, state intervention, for the first time on a massive scale during the First World War, was regarded as a cardinal fault. Economists believed that intervention distorted the natural mechanistic process, and that any further subsequent state interference on the social and economic sphere was the primary cause for the problems that occurred in the 20s and 30s. It was presumed that as long as the price, wage and interest mechanisms were flexible, the real economic world would always swing back to the full employment equilibrium. At the core of this thinking seemingly existed the notion that the monetary sphere would control real economic development and business cycles.

An integral part of the classical business cycle theory was a view of an economic system, controlled by endogenous forces, that would automatically swing back to an equilibrium of full employment after a recession. It was believed that only exogenous factors, such as a major war or non-system conform economic policy, would disturb this balance. Thus, for the analysis of recession origins the concept of disproportionality, either due to overproduction or overinvestment, was central to understanding and interpretation. Strangely enough, the concepts of underconsumption and lack of investment were hardly considered. Ususally, when crisis symptoms set in, theoreticians considered production to be too high for demand.

36 The Deutsche Institut für Konjunkturforschung was founded in 1925 under the chairmanship of Ernst Wagemann and was closely connected with the Statistische Reichsamt, the statistical office of the German government. The first publication of the Konjunkturforschungsinstitut came out in January 1926. See: Rolf Krengel, *Das Deutsche Institut für Wirtschaftsforschung (Institut für Konjunkturforschung) 1925–1979*, Berlin 1986, 8 ff and 12.

37 Especially the publication of the early years until the depression were only descriptive. Ibid, 13

38 The following is based on Gerhard Kroll, *Von der Weltwirtschaftskrise zur Staatskonjunktur*, Berlin 1958, 135 ff.

The course of business cycles was roughly interpreted as follows: Low interest rate and low labour costs would induce investment after a recession, production would increase, pressing forward a boom period with rising interest rates,[39] and perhaps, increasing stock market speculation. Soon, at the end of the upswing, credit would become short, and interest rates, as well as production costs, would rise. At some point, overcapacity would cause overproduction, then prices would fall and production would decline, introducing a recession again. The crisis would cleanse the economic distortions of the productive sectors that had grown under booming and mildly inflationary conditions. Prices, wages and interest rates would fall again, allowing for increasing investment and introducing the next upswing. A dramatic decline of sales, due to a fall in demand during a depression, was not seen as cause for a downturn, but only as a crisis symptom. This was, primitively explained, the classical business cycle theory. It was almost regarded as a clockwork, a mechanistic and self-regulating process; therefore, even monetary government interference was considered as a distorting element for the mechanism of prices, wages and interests, not allowing for the evolution of ideal conditions for entrepreneurs to introduce another upswing.

This directly relates to Borchardt's idea of non-system conform behaviour, which depressed investment rates inWeimar Germany. This creed in the self-regulating mechanism, disturbed by government interference, occasioned Ludwig Mises to demand the end of unemployment relief in 1931 at the beginning of the peak of the depression.[40] He was convinced that state intervention had caused high labour and production costs and thought that inflationary policy had prolonged the cleansing crisis, which would distort the system and preclude the usual recession and upswing. The new interventionism, even though very moderate by today's standards, was regarded as inflationary, making credit too easily available. Thus, overproduction and "unhealthy" enterprises (companies that were created under boom conditions and regarded as inefficient) would remain that would usually have been eliminated in the recessionary process.

Theories postulated that governments would have to balance their budgets, just like private enterprises, and that authorities, especially the central banks, should do anything to avoid inflationary monetary expansion by keeping credit tight. A stable currency with stable exchange rates, exactly as during the period of the pre-war gold standard, was seen as an essential part of this mechanism. This led to, what many economists today consider, a policy that enhanced recession tendencies. For instance, when downswings set in 1921 and 1929 in the United Kingdom and the US, or in 1923/24 in Germany and Austria, authorities tended to restrict the money supply even more. Contemporary theory did not regard the damaging effects of monetary policy on the real economic world when credit was restricted while stagnating tendencies were obvious. Credit was restricted, because any other policy move was believed to be inflationary. Today, after Keynes, the view is that credit expansion

39 The economist Gustav Cassel gave the interest and leading discount rate a central role in the development of the business cycles.

40 Ludwig Mises, *Die Ursachen der Wirtschaftskrise*, Vienna 1931.

during recession periods, entailing underutilisation of capacity and unemployment, has no inflationary effects, but instead, helps to overcome the depression.

Economic journalism in Germany and Austria was also largely adherent to classical economics and believed in the self-regulating powers of the economic process.[41] Only with mounting problems in the 20s and the onset of the depression, did they slowly realise that this mechanism no longer functioned, partially because of inflationary distortions. Gradually, it became clear that more state interventionism was inevitable. Still, the public research institutes strictly believed in neo-liberal economics. Statistics of all kinds were used to show the apparent repetative wave movement of short-term business cycles.[42] During the time of the Great Depression, when economic advice and possible business forecasts were especially needed, only descriptions of the economic malaise were presented. Among the main five sectors dealing with economics (economic practice, economic journalism, university economics, and the bureaucracy of the ministries of economics) this was an integral part of published business cycle research.[43] Most of these only had an influence on changing opinion and expectations of the economic subjects. In reality, only the government ministries, besides the national bank, had an actual impact on policy-making.

By and large, restrictive policies were followed, but were also compromised by necessary moderate state investment and social expenditure. In spite of this, these deflationary measures must have at least retarded growth and certainly did support a downswing, but were not the primary cause for stagnation in the inter-war period. These theoretical principles were the guide to economic policy, not only in Austria, but in all nations and must be understood in the framework of the political and economic circumstances, after some countries had undergone extreme inflationary experiences. Of course, the utilisation of the League of Nations' loans and the

41 Gustav Stolper, one of the main editors of *Der Österreichische Volkswirt* besides the chief editor Walter Federn, left Austria to found the German equivalent of this journal, *Der Deutsche Volkswirt*, on June 16, 1926. These journals were probably among the most influential publications of economic journalism in Germany and Austria. Stolper was considered an expert among journalists on German and Austrian economic development in these years. Even though he considered state investment as positive, he still trusted in the self-regulating mechanism of economics and in the theories of disproportionality at the height of the depression in Germany. In September 1932, he wrote: "Jede Krise ensteht durch eine Störung des Gleichgewichts der wirtschaftlichen Kräfte, jeder Aufschwung setzt die Wiederherstellung dieses Gleichgewichtes voraus. Es ist das Wunder der kapitalistischen Gesellschaft, daß sie, wenn man sie walten läßt, von sich aus dieses Gleichgewicht wieder herstellt und noch die schwerste Krise zum Motor des wirtschaftlichen Fortschritts werden läßt." Cited in: Barbara Sattler, *„Der Deutsche Volkswirt" 1926–1933*, dissertation, Kiel 1982, 198.

42 Österreichisches Institut für Konjunkturforschung, *Monatsberichte des Österreichischen Institutes für Konjunkturforschung*, 1st volume, Vienna 1927, 5.

43 Kroll, 131 ff. See also Andreas Korsch, "Der Stand der beschäftigungspolitischen Diskussion zur Zeit der Weltwirtschaftskrise in Deutschland. II. Die Auseinandersetzung mit der zeitgenössischen Wirtschaftslehre," in: G. Bombach, H.J. Ramser, M. Timmermann and W. Wittmann (eds.), *Der Keynesianismus I. Theorie und Praxis keynesianischer Wirtschaftspolitik. Entwicklung und Stand der Diskussion*, New York 1976, 37 ff.

poor attempt at reintroducing the pre-war gold standard were also guided by these principles.

Small wonder that theory did not provide active economic advice for policy-making and that the eventual measures taken turned out to be half-hearted. All economic policies (apart from rearmament and war economies), including the New Deal, were essentially a compromise between an attempt to implement these theoretical principles and the attempt to face the social and economic problems of the inter-war period actively. In the end, no clear policy line was pursued. Interestingly enough, this mediocre policy was carried out by right or bourgeois governments in all European states, after the left socialist movements had retrenched.[44] In Austria, the great coalition between Christian democrats and social democrats disintegrated in 1922, and a year later, the drastic policy regime shift of deflationary stabilisation set in. In Germany, the social democrats lost power in 1920, and after the Ruhr struggle over reparations ended, the government and specifically, the Reichsbank pursued a restrictive credit policy. Similar development occurred in Britain, where labour was replaced by the conservatives in 1924. Of course, the regime shift in this case was not as extreme as in Germany or Austria. There was no inflation, and everything was done to return to pre-war pound gold parity. In France, the mild inflation was terminated after the "cartel de gauches" lost power, and the bourgeois politician, Poincaré, took over. Essentially, Keynesian or pre-Keynesian economics was not introduced until the late 30s, and then, was only very moderately applied. These kinds of models and ideas to overcome the problems arose by the late 20s, but were usually heavily criticised by contemporaries. In 1932, the Austrians, Otto Deutsch and Alexander Vértes, published a paper on state intervention suggesting large public works programmes that would generate a multiplication effect in the economy and would overcome massive unemployment.[45] Yet, this suggestion was either not well received or ignored. Also Keynes' "Treatise on Money" was heavily criticised by Austrian economists and journalists.[46]

3.1.4. Economic Policy, the Gold Standard and International Lending

In order to grasp the origins of the motives of economic policy-making, it is not only necessary to look at contemporary theory, but also to understand the re-emergence and eventual collapse of the inter-war gold standard system. As already mentioned, the re-establishment of a system of fixed exchanged rates, the classical gold standard, was a central aspect of the attempt to return to the economic conditions of the late 19th century. That meant, on a national level, to re-adjust domestic currencies to their pre-war conditions. In the 20s, this attempt was at the core of economic policy, which was largely a currency policy. After the war, a myth concerning the pre-war gold

44 See: Charles S. Maier, *Recasting Bourgeois Europe. Stabilisation in France, Germany, and Italy in the Decade after World War I*, New Jersey 1975.

45 Otto Deutsch and Alexander Vértes, *Aufbau nicht Abbau*, Vienna 1932.

46 Felix Butschek, "Präkeynesianismus in Österreich," in: *Wirtschaft und Gesellschaft*, 19, 1993, 176 ff.

standard and prosperity had emerged, idealising the pre-war international monetary system. The main problem with this was that the causes and effects of the system were confounded. It was not clear that the existence of the gold standard had only been possible because of stable real economic conditions before 1914, and not vice versa. Extremely portrayed, it was believed that with the re-establishment of a currency system fixed to gold, economic growth and prosperity would return and that structures would adjust automatically.

The theory of the system implied that gold coins would be used in domestic economies, while other money was easily convertible into gold at any time. The national bank would hold a certain amount of gold reserves that could be converted under demand. The idea was that a balance of payments equilibrium would be maintained among all countries by altering the amount of available gold in various countries accordingly.[47] The amount of the national gold reserves would determine the money supply in any one country. The money supply would, in turn, be determined by demand, which was conditioned by national income, prices and interest rates, set by the world market. It was believed that the money supply, thus, the supply of gold, would define price levels in a national economy. Hence, would a balance of payments disequilibrium occur in any country, the theory expressed that it was expedient to deflate the economy, meaning the national bank would have to raise its interest rate to restrict credit in order to attract the inflow of gold and credit from abroad until the national price level would be lowered to the international level. This deflationary monetary policy could work as a break on the economy, but tended to bring national balance of payments back into equilibrium.

The myth that dominated post-war policy-making48 was the belief that the rules of the gold standard were pursued consciously before the war, by the various national banks, especially by the Bank of England. In fact, this was not the case, just as the actual influence of the Bank of England was much smaller than had been previously thought.[49] Furthermore, the system did not work as smoothly as believed. Its functioning, to a large degree, was due to extremely favourable circumstances, when the world economy and trade were expanding rapidly, and when the centre of this system, the industrialised European countries, still dominated the world economy and trade. Therefore, exchange rates had been stable before 1914. The system never had to face severe stresses or crises and could rely on credibility and co-operation

47 In 1918, the report of the British Cunliffe Committee strongly advocated the reintroduction of the gold standard and explained the mechanism of the system with the goal to maintain the balance of payments equilibrium. See: "Cunliffe Committee on Currency and Foreign Exchanges after the War," in: Barry Eichengreen (ed.), *The Gold Standard in Theory and History*, New York 1985, 169 ff.

48 On the myth of the gold standard and its influence on policy-making in the inter-war period see: Gerald D. Feldman, "Politik, Banken und der Goldstandard in der Zwischenkriegszeit," in: Manfred Pohl (ed.), *Vom Goldstandard zum Multireservewährungsstandard. Neuntes Nationales Symposium zur Bankengeschichte am 18.10.1985, im Hause der Deutschen Bank A.G.*, Frankfurt am Main 1987, 11–20.

49 Donald N. McClokey and J. Richard Zecher, "How the gold standard worked, 1880–1913," in: Eichengreen, *The Gold Standard*, 64 and 65.

among the core countries of this system: Great Britain, Germany and France.[50] In addition, the theory oversimplified the international process of prices, wages, income and interest rates changes.[51] Another fault was the overestimation of the role and the influence of interest rates on price levels and wages. Instead of lowering the price level, higher interest rates and credit restrictions could help to slow down economic expansion. Regarding economic policy in the 20s and 30s, many authors argue that manipulating interest rates, to deflate the economy with the goal to adjust price levels, to a high degree retarded growth. It is important to note that the idea of the strong influence of interest rates was very important in forming policy in most countries in the inter-war period.

The essential objective of policy efforts in the 20s was the restoration of a system of fixed exchange rates to minimise the risk of exchange fluctuations for international economic undertakings, the movement of capital and goods. Very similar motives lay behind the implementation of the Bretton Woods system afterWorld War Two.[52] Yet, the greatest disadvantages of implementing such a system were the consequences of the necessity of central banks to intervene actively and on a massive scale on capital markets. This was particularly the case when economic growth was low and when economies had undergone severe inflations. Moreover, an even greater disadvantage resulted from the consequences for national policy to maintain the same currency parity for long periods. This effort made restrictive fiscal policies absolutely necessary, as they had a strong impact on the state of national currencies. The result were national economic and social policies strongly compromised and constrained by policy efforts to maintain stable currencies and balanced budgets. These policy goals were especially difficult to attain under conditions of weak economic growth, particularly during the inter-war period. When growth was weak or stagnating, it was harder to compromise national social and economic policy with currency policy. National economic and social interests came into serious conflict with the effort to sustain a stable international currency system. Before the war, these problems never arose, but this is exactly what happened after 1925, leading to the collapse of the gold standard system in the early 30s.[53]

Unfortunately, there were two factors, one intentional and one functional, that had dramatically changed since 1913 and made the implementation of the pre-war system unrealistic. These changes were not triggered, but instead were accelerated by the war. The first factor was the breakdown of the pre-war currency system and the loss of European financial strength during the war. The second, more important, factor was the drastic change in the position of the European economy in the world

50 Eichengreen, *Golden Fetters*, 30.

51 Aldcroft, *Die zwanziger Jahre*, chapter: Der Goldstandard der Nachkriegszeit, 185, 186.

52 The gold standard not only led to the adoption of the gold exchange standard in 1922, but also to the Bretton Woods international monetary system in an attempt to turn back to long lasting currency stability and economic growth. See Gerd Hardach and Sandra Hartig, "Der Goldstandard als Argument in der internationalen Währungsdiskussion," in: *Jahrbuch für Wirtschaftsgeschichte. Währungs- und Finanzgeschichte*, 1, 1998, 125–141.

53 Barry Eichengreen, *Vom Goldstandard zum Euro. Die Geschichte des internationalen Währungssystems*, Berlin 1997, 130.

and the structural shifts of the advanced economies after the war. In fact, it could be argued that the former was a consequence of the latter.

After the war, stabilisation basically lasted until the end of the 20s.[54] In most countries, the new gold standard was a gold exchange standard, which meant that central banks could hold reserves in foreign exchange, mostly US dollars or pound sterling, as well as in gold. Stabilisation was uncoordinated and carried out by various means, in some cases lasting almost a decade with parities of all kinds of ratios. The way the currency system was re-established, and the parities of the national currencies were set, is of some importance to economic development, so it has been largely argued by many authors. It is also claimed that the parity of a national currency determined, to a large degree, the competitiveness of a national economy. When regarding microeconomic activity, this is true only to a limited degree. Only when currency parity was really inflationary did it seem to have results on economic activity. The effects of the shift of economic structures had a much greater impact on economic performance than parity ratios or, for that matter, interest rates, as we will see below.

Only a few countries regained their pre-war parities, among them were Britain, and the neutrals: Switzerland, the Netherlands, Denmark, Sweden and Norway. Their currencies are said to have been overvalued, causing a disadvantage in international competition and possibly resulting in stagnating economies. All countries that experienced severe inflation, the ones discussed in the first chapter, had to introduce completely new currencies. These countries were Germany, Austria, Hungary, Poland and Russia. After their inflationary experience, both Austria and Germany tried their utmost to maintain a strong currency with a restrictive, conservative monetary policy. France, Belgium, Italy, Romania, Bulgaria, Yugoslavia, Czechoslovakia and Finland set their parities to only a fraction of their pre-war parities, often reluctantly after years of domestic political and economic struggle in the attempt to regain the old parity. The old pre-war gold parity was seen as a matter of national reputation and pride. The countries of the last group are often said to have had an undervalued currency, which supposetly offered these economies an inflationary competitive advantage, and, in the case of France and Belgium, a major contribution to growth.

Another important factor influencing currency stabilisation and the restoration of an international currency system was the structure and size of international lending in the 20s.[55] The war had caused huge international debts between the European Allies, especially France and Great Britain and the United States. These were war debts. The larger problem was the German reparations problem and the German debt situation after the stabilisation of 1924. It is not necessary to discuss the whole aspect of war debts and reparations in the small framework of this paper, but the debts problem[56] and financial deficiencies in the late 20s of Germany, Austria and Eastern Europe are of relevance in understanding the effects of policy and performance in

54 Derek H. Aldcroft, *The European Economy 1914–1990*, 3rd edition, London 1995, chapter: Inflation and Currency Stabilisation, 49 ff.

55 Ibid, 57 ff.

56 Aldcroft, *Die zwanziger Jahre*, chapter 10: Schuldnernationen und internationale Anleihen, 274 ff.

these countries. This aspect of the financial situation in Europe is also important since most Austrian companies found their export sales markets in these areas. Specifically for Austria and Eastern Europe, it is claimed that deliberate credit restrictions, by the central banks in order to attract foreign credit, caused insufficient and too expensive credit availability, leading to the faults in these economies by way of restricting investments. Another fault of Austrian and German capital markets is said to be the size and structure of international lending to these countries. This will be discussed under subheading 2.4. In the United Kingdom, France and Belgium, and in most of the neutral countries, credit restrictions were not as severe and are not said to have disturbed growth and development.

That the re-establishment of the pre-war system of fixed exchange rates became unrealistic was only realised during the Great Depression. To most governments and decision makers it became clear that economic structures had changed, but instead of turning to a more fruitful international co-operation, policy in the 30s moved toward more protectionism and intensifying nationalism. Instead of finding an alternative to the gold standard system, nations changed to policies of besieged economies. Interventionist policies were only very moderately introduced, but these were often half-hearted and ineffective. The only really effective interventionist policy during the 30s was government financed rearmament and the beginnings of war economy. These policy changes will be the topic of the last two chapters, as will be shown that these policy shifts and the more hostile international economic environment was very harmful to a small nation like Austria, a nation without the capacities to generate large economic programmes for a raise in demand.

3.2. POLICY AND DEVELOPMENT IN FRANCE

Let us now move to economic policy and performance in some European countries during the 20s to suggest some alternative explanation for growth and development and to have an international background for company history. French and Belgian economic growth was very similar in the inter-war period.[57] Among the industrialised countries, both had relatively high growth levels in the 1920s, the development of both countries was above pre-war levels, and both were not as severely hit by the depression as most other countries. France and Belgium also had similar performance in the 30s, when both suffered from very low growth rates and only very moderate recovery. French economic structure was unlike that of the other highly industrialised countries, because, on the one hand, very modern large industries were developing in the 20s while large, older industries still existed. Yet, on the other hand, the agricultural sector still made up a far higher proportion of national product than in comparable, advanced Western economies. Furthermore, also dissimilar to other

57 André Armengaud, Sidney Pollard and Guido L. de Brabanter, "Die Wirtschaft: Großbritannien, Irland, Frankreich, Belgien, die Niederlande, Luxemburg, 1914–1980/83," in: Wolfram Fischer (ed.), *Handbuch der Europäischen Wirtschafts- und Sozialgeschichte. Band 6. Europäische Wirtschafts- und Sozialgeschichte vom Ersten Weltkrieg bis zur Gegenwart*, Stuttgart 1987, 344 ff.

modern economies, many industries, especially textiles, still consisted of a great number of small factories and workshops, as family firms. Many of these small masters and artisans still produced under obsolete conditions. Production methods were often backward and productivity was low.[58]

In spite of this, the economy was buoyant in the first post-war decade. This has basically been attributed to two factors as essential components of economic policy: Post-war inflationary government finance of a large reconstruction scheme for the devastated areas of North Eastern France, and the run on, compared to Germany or Austria, very mild depreciation of the French and Belgian franc that was initiated by war finance and lasted until late 1926. It is said to have improved the competitive position of these economies.

As in other countries with inflation, inflationary development in France depended, to a very high extent, on the trust of the population in the government to repay its war debts. About 20% of war time government expenditure had been financed by taxes, the rest was deficit financed[59] by selling war bonds to the French population. This method of financing the war was similar to the beginning of the inflationary processes in Germany and Austria. Only in Britain was a much greater proportion of the war financed with taxes. After it had already lost a substantial part of its value during the war, the franc remained stable immediately after the war and until April 1922.[60] It was supported by Allied, especially American, credit, only until 1919, when these were withdrawn. After the war, the government could only finance running expenditure by renewing state bonds.[61] Yet, the ability of the government to sell or renew bonds depended once again upon the likelihood of public debt repayment.

The war reparations issue was closely connected to France's financial problems. Initially, French politicians and the population expected the reconstruction of the areas devastated by warfare to be financed by German reparation payments. In view of this expectation, the French government pre-financed a large reconstruction scheme with an enormous floating public debt, mainly in the form of short-term obligations. After it definitely became clear, at the end of the Ruhr crisis in 1923, that German payment would not materialise on the expected scale, French government expenditure increasingly relied on the renewal of the floating public debt.[62] The ever-increasing scale of the floating debt, connected with the erosion of public finance, the decreasing expectancy of the population in the restoration of the pre-war parity of the French franc, slowly eroded the trust in governmental finance, and

58 Tom Kemp, *The French Economy 1913–1939. The history of a decline*, London 1972, 68.

59 Barry Eichengreen, "The Bank of France and the Sterilisation of Gold, 1926–1932," in: Francois Crouzet (ed.), *The Economic Development of France since 1870*, Volume 1, Aldershot 1993, 471.

60 Barry Eichengreen, "Did Speculation Destabilize the French Franc in the 1920's?" In: Crouzet, *Economic Development* 1, 442.

61 A very good description and explanation of the inflationary French finances and the socio-political background is given by Stephen A. Schuker, *The End of French Predominance. The Financial Crisis of 1924 and the Adoption of the Dawes Plan*, North Carolina 1976.

62 Schuker, 13 ff.

therefore, decreased its value. This manifested itself in capital flight and speculation against the franc. Thus, the realisation that the burden of war and reconstruction finance would have to be carried by the French population along with the inability to establish a sufficient level of taxation caused mistrust in public finance and the fall of the franc.

Eventually, the government increasingly had to rely on advances from the Bank of France to finance mounting deficits. This led to a rise in note circulation and increased depreciation.[63] Several speculative offensives of capital markets against the franc, especially in early 1924, resulted in further devaluation. After Poincaré was back in government in that year, the government managed to obtain a foreign loan from influential American financial circles, which helped to stabilise the franc in March and April. The following year, further devaluation set in, partially due to a scandal between the new, left Herriot government and the Bank of France in combination with a general crisis of confidence. In the summer of 1926, the most drastic speculative attack and depreciation took place, which was ended when the new conservative government under Poincaré returned to power with a reputation of fiscal conservatism. A fiscal and monetary reform was concluded, limiting the issue of new notes and de-facto stabilisation materialised in December.[64]

Even though full pre-war parity was the goal of the initial plan, the dramatic devaluation resulted in the restoration of the franc with only one-fifth of its old pre-war gold value. Nevertheless, this inflationary development was very mild compared to the experiences of Germany and Austria. In spite of this, mild inflation combined with government financed reconstruction of the North Eastern areas are said to have made a major contribution to the rapid economic growth that took place in France.[65] The low and depreciating parity of the franc is said to have increased international competitiveness of French export trade. Contemporary decision makers also seemed to have believed this, since E. Moreau (governor of the Bank of France) and Charles Rist (a renowned French economist) advised Poincaré in 1926 to refrain from restoring pre-war parity, hoping that this might maintain an international advantage in production and trade. In actuality, the restoration of the old parity had been totally unrealistic anyway in the face of the changes caused by the war. The new parity only meant a slight undervaluation of the real value of the franc, which represented the decreased economic strength of the country. In fact, there seems to be some truth in the fact that the large scale destruction of industrial equipment which had opened up great possibilities for new profitable investment, had increased growth and investment at least until the pre-war level of production was reached once again in 1923 and 1924.

However, currency devaluation and initial reconstruction finance cannot be the full explanation for rapid French growth throughout the decade, lasting almost until

63 Eichengreen, "Did Specualtion Destabilize the French Franc in the 1920's?‘

64 Kemp, 80.

65 Claude Fohlen, "Die Entwicklung Frankreichs," in: Carlo M. Cipolla, *Europäische Wirtschaftsgeschichte. The Fontana Economic History of Europe in 5 Bänden, Deutsche Ausgabe herausgegeben von Knut Borchardt, Die europäischen Volkswirtschaften im zwanzigsten Jahrhundert*, Stuttgart 1980, 107 and 108.

1931. Two factors run contrary to this. First of all, the advantages due to the depreciation of the French franc were partially offset by the depreciation of other European currencies, and secondly, the French economy was still much less integrated into the world economy than other Western European nations, making exports less vital for growth. Some proof remains in the still great protectionist tendencies, expressed in high tariff rates. Even though it was becoming more integrated into the world economy than before the war, it was less export oriented than Germany, Britain, Austria and Belgium. Therefore, the boom was probably much less export oriented as well. The expansion of the 20s was due mostly to internal growth, which revealed the structural shift that most industrialised nations went through at this time.

After scrutinising the exchange rates in the 20s, it is obvious that only the franc parity of the dollar and the pound decreased dramatically until 1926, offering a possible export advantage until that time. In 1919, the dollar/franc parity was 1:7.26, and in 1921, 1:13.49. In fact, in 1922, the franc actually appreciated again to 1:12.33, but fell once more in 1926 to 1:31.44.[66] The following year, it appreciated again. Compared to pound sterling, the development was similar. Yet, compared to German marks, there was no advantage from devaluation until 1925, and thereafter, it was only slight. The same can be said for Swiss francs and Czech crowns. In comparison to Belgian francs, there was no advantage whatsoever. Compared to Austrian crowns and schillings, the franc only depreciated once in 1923 and 1924, when the crown stabilised. Hence, the export advantage for French companies with Austria only existed between these years and 1926, when the schilling actually depreciated against the franc.[67] When the German mark was falling between 1919–1922, the Ruhr industry could exert pressure on the export markets of the French and Belgian iron and steel industries, and protectionist tendencies increased in both countries in 1921, revealing that the franc did not seem to render possible a competitive advantage against German export industries. In 1924, the situation reversed with German regime shift, but again this advantage could have lasted only until the end of 1926.[68] That would have been only two years of serious currency advantage against the major competitor in iron and steel.

Therefore, growth could only have been induced by inflationary exports to a minor degree. Furthermore, despite ostensible export advantage of the depreciating currency, French customs tariffs were quite high in the 20s, between 21 and 30% of value of imports. This also suggests that there was no competitive advantage. Among the western European nations these were the highest tariffs.[69] In addition, growth

66 Alfred Sauvy, *Histoire Économique da la France entre les deux guerres. De l'armistice a la dévaluation da la Livre (1918–1931)*, Fayard 1963, 444.

67 Jürgen Schneider, Oskar Schwarzer and Markus A. Denzel (eds.), *Währungen der Welt II. Europäische und nordamerikanische Devisenkurse (1914–1951)*, Stuttgart 1997, 284.

68 Eric Bussière, "The Evolution of Structures in the Iron and Steel Industry in France, Belgium, and Luxemburg: National and International Aspects, 1900–1939," in: Crouzet, *Economic Development* 2, 166.

69 See: The Austrian National Committee of the International Chamber of Commerce (Österreichisches Nationalkomitee der Internationalen Handelskammer) (ed.), *Zollhöhe und Warenwerte. Eine vergleichende Studie über die Höhe der Zollbelastung für 402 Waren in 14 europäischen Staaten,* Vienna 1927, Introduction XV.

also seemed to have been much less inflation induced, because domestic inflation did not bring a massive increase in profits nor in investment finance and structure. Usually inflationary growth brought a massive increase in investment, financed through external sources. However, just as before the war, still 65% of investment finance was carried by gross earnings of companies.[70] Only growth in the early 20s could be explained by reconstruction supported by government finance, and by the initial high demand for manufactures, existing throughout Europe after the war.

The main factor advancing economic expansion was the long-term secular industrial transformation described above, i.e. the dramatic change and growth of the new modern industries and the partial shift of traditional industries to modern modes of production. Industrial investment and growth was mainly due to large technical changes of the new industries, reorganisation of production, the emergence of a mass consumer market and large scale investment in new equipment.[71] The French economy became much more diversified than before, and just as in Austria, Germany, and Britain, the older industries stagnated and the modern sectors became the main factor for economic growth and development. Unlike the British economic structure, growth and development of the new industries was not retarded by the dominance of old and long established industries. Among the three largest industrialised countries in Europe, France was the least developed. Thus, changing to new structures and surmounting obstacles and hesitations was easier.

The wood, fabric processing, and building industries stagnated. Textiles, leather, food, coal, glass, gas and iron and steel industries grew moderately. The industrial index for the iron industry, for example, declined from 100 in 1913 to 54 in 1921, and surpassed its pre-war level moderately in 1930, to 147. All of the branches of the textiles industries were below their pre-war production level in 1930.

Fortunately, the market of the French economy was large enough to maintain rapid internal growth, based on new and modern industries. The new and modern sectors of the economy, like metal processing, electricity, chemicals, petroleum and fuels, rubber, car manufacture and most consumer durable industries, were booming,[72] mainly supporting the rapid growth of the 20s. First and foremost among those were the electrical industries, that carried most of the new innovations with a new form of energy flexibility and were one of the main stimulants of the capital market. Another major supporter of growth was the automobile industry, the largest in Europe at this time. In the 20s, the "Big Three", Renault, Peugeot and Citröen, emerged as highly integrated firms that introduced American assembly line production methods. For the first time, they produced cheaply manufactured small cars, taking advantage of a large consumer market.[73] The automobile industry underwent rapid growth. The index level of 100 in 1913 increased to 238 in 1921 and was at

70 Francois Caron (Translated from the French by Barbara Bray), *An Economic History of Modern France*, London 1979, 256 ff.

71 This view is strongly emphasised by Francois Caron.

72 Ibid, 254.

73 Patrick Fridenson, "French Automobile Marketing 1890–1979," in: Crouzet, *Economic Development* 2, 233 ff.

637 in 1930.[74] Probably the government financed reconstruction helped to initiate the process until 1923/24,[75] but the main drive came from the new forms of industries themselves.

3.3. POLICY AND DEVELOPMENT IN GREAT BRITAIN

Economic performance of the United Kingdom was in sharp contrast to the French. While France was experiencing a moderate boom in the 20s, the British economy seemed to be stagnating. While the French economy was stagnating in the 30s, Britain's was expanding. When examining indices for net domestic product for the years 1925–1930, British growth performance was worse than Austrian and far worse than German or French. Only Denmark was not only stagnating, but declining. The highest rate of growth occured during the brief post-war boom of 1920. After that, the British economy hardly seemed to be able to recover from the international recession of 1921/22. It took until the end of the Great Depression (1932/33) for the economy to grow more rapidly. Growth during the inter-war period was very erratic and uneven; yet, certainly not as much as in Germany and Austria. In most years, it was stagnant. Though, in some years comparatively high and sharp drops of growth occurred in 1921 and 1931.[76] Annual growth of gross national product was only moderate, 1.9% between 1920 and 1929. At the same time, manufacturing expanded only 2.8%.[77] Furthermore, unemployment was high throughout the 1920s, higher than ever before.

At first glimpse, the primarily conservative economic policy of the 1920s seemed to have been responsible for this malaise. Right after the war, policy decision makers proclaimed their intention to set the pound sterling back to pre-war parity, which was $ 4.86 to the pound. This meant that the economy needed to be deflated from $ 3.40 in 1920 to the former parity.[78] The Cunliffe Committee (arranged by the Ministry of Reconstruction and the Treasury) came to this decision with the intention to restore a functioning international currency system, the pre-war gold standard, to counteract any further inflationary government finance that had been incited by the war, and to return to a balanced budget. Eventually, it took until 1925 to restore the pre-war parity, and therefore, to return to the gold standard. Until then, highly restrictive policy, complying with old classical theories, prevailed. To attempt to restrict credit, to attract gold and to lower the prices and wages to American levels, interest rates were maintained comparatively high.

74 See chart: Indices de la production des sous-groupes industriels, in: Sauvy, 466.

75 Kemp, 68.

76 For a general and introductory view on the growth and general development of the British economy during this time see Derek H. Aldcroft, *The British Economy between the Wars*, Oxford 1983.

77 Pollard, *The Development of the British Economy*, 51 ff. Also: K. S. Lomax, "Growth and Productivity in the United Kingdom," in: D. H. Aldcroft and Peter Fearon (eds.), *Economic Growth in Twentieth-Century Britain*, Suffolk 1969 (first published in 1964).

78 G. C. Peden, *British Economic and Social Policy. Lloyd George to Margaret Thatcher*, Oxford 1985, chapter 4: The Return to the Gold Standard, 60.

Most historians and economists[79] have considered this policy move as a major mistake, contributing a large degree to the stagnation. Already in 1925, none less than John Maynard Keynes claimed that the exchange rate was at least 10% too high, leading to uncompetetively high export prices and a forced irresponsible reduction of wages and prices. An export disadvantage would harm export oriented industries, unemployment would rise while imports would be encouraged.[80] Others have calculated the overvaluation to as much as 25 or 30% .[81] Some have also regarded the policy to return to gold as instigated and supported by the interest of the City financiers, in order to maintain their influence on foreign investments and to restore their pre-war role in world finances.[82] In this view, the interests of industry were sacrificed for those of influential financial circles. Whatever the reason, the interest of Treasury officials and of the Bank of England were in line with this deflationary policy. Both had lost power during the war.

Nevertheless, it is still problematical to claim that this policy was the main cause for stagnation and high unemployment.[83] The fact that the bank rate was at 6%, the government cut expenditure and ran surpluses, and that money supply was falling 1921 and 1922, does not mean that these factors caused the recession and unemployment throughout the 20s. In 1920, Britain and the US experienced a short post-war boom, mostly supported by high demand of manufactures after war time shortages. In this time, British unemployment was low (3.9%). The international recession of 1921 and 1922, which only did not affect the countries with enormous inflation, and the shift from war to peace economy were the primary reasons for high British unemployment these years (16.9% in 1921 and 14.3% in 1922). The short, but brief post-war boom of 1920/21 was incited by piled-up high consumer demand after war time restrictions. Once this demand was satisfied, recession tendencies set in. Furthermore, compared to international standards, interests rates in Britain were not very high. Already by 1922, the bank rate was back to 3.69% and only rose to around 5% or less after 1925.[84] In Germany and Austria, bank rates were up to 10 or 12% after inflation; yet their growth rates were still higher than in Britain. It is questionable if this economic policy harmed credit availability and investment. The argument of overvaluation, damaging British export industries and the economy, has also been very attractive, because the recession in these industries and the return to gold coincided. The reasons against the traditional view are similar to the argument

79 Ibid.

80 John Maynard Keynes, "Essays in Persuasion, 1931. The Economic Consequences of Mr. Churchill, (written ritgh after the return to gold in 1925)," in: Sidney Pollard (ed.), *The Gold Standard and Employment Policies between the wars*, London 1970, 27 ff. D. E. Moggridge has also critised the policy of classical economics and the overvaluation of the pound. *British Monetary Policy, 1924–1931: The Norman Conquest of $ 4.86*, Cambridge 1972.

81 J. Redmond, "The sterling overvaluation in 1925: a mulitlateral approach," in: *Economic History Review*, 2nd series, volume 37, 1984, 520–532.

82 Peden, 61, mentioned for this view Pollard, *The Gold Standard.*

83 Peden, 64.

84 See chart: Money and interest rates 1920–38, J. F. Wright, "Britain's Inter-War Experience," in: W.A. Eltis and P. J. N. Sinclair (eds.), *The Money Supply and the Exchange Rate*, Oxford 1981, 284.

against French policy effects. On the one hand, the exchange rate differences were too minute[85] to have had substantial long-term effects on exports, and on the other, the British economy was stagnating chiefly due to real economic factors. Exchange differences had much less effect on growth, because the importance of exports for expansion was declining, especially during the recovery of the 30s. Since the role of exports was declining and growth primarily came from domestic expansion, restrictive economic policy, which caused relatively high currency value with the return to gold, had little influence on total performance. Most inter-war growth can be contributed to internal economic growth, in particular the increase of the consumer market, and therefore, to the rise of demand for the production of modern industries. While exports accounted for 19.1% of the increase of GNP between 1932 and 1937, 46.7% accounted for the increase in consumer demand.[86]

A major obstacle to growth was the great preponderance of the British economy to declining old industrial sectors, which had been largely export oriented before the war. The problematical and slow change of industrial transformation was revealed in an obsolete economic structure that made the shift to an effective expansion of modern industries, which could pull overall growth to higher levels, very difficult. The downfall of traditional sectors was a result of the change in the world economy, part of which was the contraction of world-wide trade and the overcapacities created during the war outside of Europe. Britain had great difficulty coping with these changes. Part of the reason for this was the slow shift of economic structures from one system of production to a new system, with new technology, innovation, and with new market and demand structures. Compared to other large advanced nations, this transformation in Britain occured quite late and painfully slowly.

One reason for this process was that this country, as one of the oldest industrialised nations, had already employed a disproportionally large amount of economic resources in the old staple industries before the war,[87] which represented the contracting industrial sectors in the 20s and 30s. The change in world demand and the new peripheral overcapacities explain the stagnation of the old, staple export industries in the inter-war period. This process, in combination with the slow and late shift to new industrial production, explains the overall poor performance during the 20s. Wright has estimated the actual increase of growth to as much as 20% in the 20s, if the old industries were excluded from GDP calculation.[88]

It can be delicate to divide the economy between old, stagnating and new, modern and expanding industries, as Pollard has noticed.[89] Not all old industrial sectors

85 Only the Fench franc was drastically depreciating to the pound sterling. After 1924, the pound exchange rate was quite stable compared to the most important currencies. See: Schneider, Schwarzer and Denzel, 29 ff.

86 Pollard, *Development*, 56.

87 Aldcroft, *The British Economy between the Wars*, 2.

88 J.F. Wright, "Britain's Inter-War Experience," 291.

89 Pollard, *Development*, 54. He lists the literature on the discussion about old and new industries in inter-war Britain. Contemporaries also recognised the different development of industrial branches and also distinguished between contracting and expanding industries. See for example: *The Economist*, article: "Contracting and Expanding Industries," January 12, 1935, 60. Cotton, shipbuilding, coal mining, public works contracting, chemicals, boots and shoes, general

were stagnating, such as building in the early 30s.[90] Iron and steel processing also included very modern sectors, as was also the case for Austria with Gebrüder Böhler or Schoeller-Bleckmann. However, in all, this approach is reasonable, as long as one regards all of those sectors of the economy as modern that related directly and indirectly with the three main innovations that stimulated expansion: the internal combustion engine, electricity and the application of chemicals. In general, an industrial sector belonging to the modern industries, did not necessarily enjoy rapid growth, but its tendency to experience growth and rapid expansion was greater than that of traditional sectors.

This is not to say that the adherence to classical restrictive policy and the return to gold did not contribute at all to stagnation. Yet, the importance of monetary policy has been overemphasised[91] in the view of the transformations of real economic structures. Not only did the great disparity between the growth rates of modern and new sectors of the economy result in moderate growth in Britain, but also the slow application of new technology in the traditional sectors contributed to a moderate rise of GDP, of only 12.2% between 1924 and 1929 (industrial production grew 15.6%).[92] Especially older staple industries, such as shipbuilding, textiles and coal mining, depressed the overall growth rate and caused high unemployment. While these sectors declined and had to discharge workers, the modern industries, with much greater productivity, mechanisation and capital intensity, could not absorb the increasing workforce.

The old sectors of industry were declining. Home demand for the coal industry stagnated during the entire inter-war period. Due especially to the fact that its structure was still based on too many and too small collieries, its productivity was far below that of its foreign competitors, particularly compared to its American and German counterparts. Without much long-term success, cartels, formed by the government, attempted to raise prices and concentrate production. The British iron and steel industry was suffering from the same problems as the Alpine Montangesellschaft. High overcapacity after the war, unemployment (around 20%), low productivity and competitiveness, obsolete production methods, and too many and too small furnaces presented huge obstacles to recovery.[93] Shipping probably suffered most of all from the overcapacities of production. In the late 20s, production was just about three-quarters of its pre-war level. The depression depressed this sector to 7% of pre-war production!

engineering, woollen textiles were regarded as contracting industries with declining employment. Constructional engineering, electric wiring, silk manufacture and artificial silk weaving, brickmaking, commerce and finance, building, motor vehicles, hotels, pig iron and steel melting, road transport or electrical engineering, were considered as expanding industries with increasing employment in 1935. Statistics of the ministry of labour showed that many workers who had left coal mining went into the expanding building industry in the 30s. Still, not enough workers could be absorbed by the expanding industries.

90 Ibid.

91 J. F. Wright supports this view. He also regards the structural problems of the 20s as an important factor to stagnation. "Britain's Inter-War Experience," 282–305.

92 Ibid, 291.

93 Pollard, *Development,* chapter: The Old and Declining Industries, 66 ff.

Contrary to contraction and stagnation of traditional sectors, the new industries, apart from the aircraft industry, experienced much higher rates of growth and investment. While the contribution to the value in total net output increased for new industries, the older industries had a declining, but still very large share of total net output.[94] The structural problem of the 20s is also apparent in these numbers. In 1924, the share of the value of total net output was 14.1% for the modern industries and still 37% for the old industries. This shifted only slowly and very late. In 1935, the share was 21% for the new and 27.8% for the old industries.[95] In a way, this slow and late shift was the price paid in order to be the first industrialised nation. Pollard claims that a great part of the reason for the poor performance and high unemployment lay in the fact that "the new industries were unable to capture the export markets lost by the old staples."[96] In addition, the transformation was quite late compared to other industrialised countries and the conditions to regain large sectors of the world market were unfavourable, because of increasing protectionism.

Nevertheless, growth in the modern sectors of the economy was impressive. As in Austria, Germany and France, the production process in Britain was based around electricity, the internal combustion engine and chemicals; innovations of the late 19th century which were applied on a large scale for the first time in the 20s and 30s. In this time, these innovations were begun to be used in every day life and showed great capacity for internal growth. Electrical engineering and the supply of electricity offered a completely new and flexible form of energy, which in turn, initiated increasing application of electrical consumer goods, such as fans, toasters, refrigerators, or washing machines. The number of households with availability of electricity increased enormously, and many new firms evolved that were able to dominate large sections of the domestic market besides the increasing imports of German and American electrical goods.[97] The car industries proved to have just as much potential for growth. The number of firms declined, but large car manufacturing companies evolved[98] with more effective production methods using assembly lines and other methods of mass production. This new industry, in turn, made the rise of many other new industries possible and advanced the development of some older sectors, such as rubber, oil, glass, mechanical engineering, and metal processing. The chemical industry was also among the growing sectors of the economy, producing fibres, artificial clothes, or paint. Exactly as in Germany, it was soon dominated by very few large companies that expanded quickly; the Imperial Chemical Industries Ltd, being the largest among them, evolving from a merger in 1926.[99]

In conclusion, it can be maintained that the return to gold and restrictive economic policy in the 20s was much less influential on economic performance than often stated, as real economic factors, i.e. the distorted and imbalanced process of structural industrial change, were the main determinants for growth and develop-

94 Ibid.
95 Ibid, 54.
96 Ibid, 55.
97 Ibid, 59, 60.
98 The largest among them were Morris and Austin.
99 Ibid, 62.

ment. Moreover, it should be noted that policy was not as restrictive as has been claimed and was in general agreement with contemporary public, political opinions and expectations. The decisions that led to the return to gold and to pursue the necessary policies were made in order to revive the declining British export position. The Cunliffe Committee believed that deteriorated British trade was a direct result of the general stagnation of world trade. In turn, the financial dislocation and the disorganisation of currencies and exchange rate systems after the war were held responsible for stagnant international trade. Policy makers believed they could alleviate the unemployment problem by reviving exports for Britain and the world. This was only considered possible when world-wide currency stability was removed by a system of fixed exchange rates. Thus, as the British return to gold basically meant the restoration of the international gold standard, a return of the pound to pre-war gold parity was seen as essential to this revival.[100] The attempts of the Bank of England and the strong British influence on the Financial Committee of the League of Nations to advance the financial restoration and stabilisation of Central and Eastern European countries, must be seen in this framework. Furthermore, some economist and historians have claimed that a lower gold parity of the pound, for example $ 4.40, would not have made much of a difference to British economic problems in the 20s, because the economy was only slowly adjusting to post-war changes. Only a drastic, extremely inflationary, devaluation might have been able to bring an advantage in competitiveness, at least temporarily.[101]

3.4. ECONOMIC POLICY IN GERMANY AND AUSTRIA

France and Great Britain differed in economic policy. In Britain, the more tax-based finance of war expenditure made an early containment of the national debt and of inflationary tendencies possible much sooner than in France. In France, the mild and fairly long-lasting inflation was a result of unresolved government debts, due to war finances based on floating public loans and the unwillingness of the population to bear the costs for war and reconstruction by higher post-war taxes, supported by the early expectation that German reparations would cover the costs. Yet, there is no doubt that both nations attempted the re-establishment of the pre-war economic system, and that both were the most influential financial forces in Europe, besides the United States, to support this policy: Britain much earlier with the return to gold and France at least since 1928 with de-jure stabilisation. Therefore, both nations also supported the attempts of other European countries to enforce an economic policy along neo-classical, liberal and orthodox lines.

With the attempt to return to pre-war financial and economic systems, both also did their utmost to increase their financial and economic influence in such debt and inflation oppressed countries as Germany, Austria and the countries in Eastern

100 R. S. Sayers, "The Return to Gold 1925," in: Pollard, *The Gold Standard*, 89–91.

101 N. H. Dimsdale, "British Monetary Policy and the Exchange Rate 1920–1938," in: W. A. Eltis and P. J. N. Sinclair (eds.), *The Money Supply and the Exchange Rate*, Oxford 1981, 343.

Europe. These were the powers with the least financial and political economic leverage, that were practically financially dependent on capital imports from the West, especially from Great Britain and the United States. The economic policy of Germany, Austria and Eastern Europe, therefore, was, to a great extent, influenced, and in some cases dominated, by the financial interest of the Western powers. This manifested itself in Germany much less than in Austria and some Eastern European countries. This credit dependence from theWestern financial powers, as well as the pursuit of conservative economic policies supported by Britain and France with the assistance of the League of Nations' financial committee, was certainly not helpful to development and performance in these areas. It is also essential for understanding policy and performance in Austria and Germany. However, it is debatable if these policies and credit dependence were the main factors that limited economic growth and development in these areas. Was there always a causal connection between credit restriction, high discount rates (monetary policy) and economic downswings or upswings, as many historians and economists have suggested?

In the case of Germany, macroeconomic data do not suggest any disadvantages before 1929. Austrian performance was very moderate compared to other industrialised nations, but more plausible alternative explanations for economic stagnation can be offered. Despite difficult credit availability and capital imports, German growth performance in the 20s was better than in Britain. In fact, during the boom years 1925–1929, both German and Austrian growth rates were higher, which suggests that policy was much less influential than believed. Marcoeconomic data suggest that German, as well as Austrian, fiscal policies and economic development were similar to those of the Western economies, in spite of problems of their financial markets. Comparing the German structure of production of agriculture, raw materials, semifinished and finished products, as well as trade flow and terms of trade with structures of production and trade in France and Great Britain, Wolfram Fischer has come to the conclusion that, in fact, Germany had some substantial structural advantages, even though it had suffered inflation, stabilisation and problematic economic policies in the late 20s.[102]

The development of the terms of trade, for example, was quite similar in Europe. As all of Europe, all three nations, Germany, France and Britain, experienced a decline of their participation in world trade. Apart from France, the balance of trade was passive for all countries throughout the 20s. Between 1925 and 1929, German imports were 13.8% higher than exports. In Britain, imports were even 48.6% higher.[103] During times of recessions, German balance of payments improved, as was the case in 1926 and during the depression. The exact same occurred in Austria in 1925, the year of stabilisation, and in 1930, the first depression year. During the relative upswing, the terms of trade was extremely passive. Value of imports was

102 Wolfram Fischer, "Die Weimarer Republik unter den weltwirtschaftlichen Bedingungen der Zwischenkriegszeit," in: Hans Mommsen, Dietmar Petzina and Bernd Weisbrod (eds.), *Industrielles System und politische Entwicklung in der Weimarer Republik*, vol. 1, Düsseldorf 1974, 26 ff.

103 Ibid, 41.

around 50% above exports.[104] While Fischer regards the structure of production and terms of trade as similar, many saw the monetary sector and the international capital movements as disadvantageous for Germany. The same has been said for the Austrian monetary situation.

Regarding these circumstances of international influence and credit problems, German and Austrian economic policies were similar. Both experienced a dramatic policy regime shift from inflation to stabilisation, both turned to restrictive policies after stabilisation, which were in both cases supported by the influence of France and Britain. Both suffered from inflationary distortion of their economic structures, both had a cyclical pattern of performance during inflation that was different from the international business cycle,[105] and in both countries very large capital imports occurred during the second half of the 20s, while credit policy of the national banks was very restrictive after stabilisation. Even though policies tended to be conservative, maintaining stable currencies, the gold standard system and balanced budgets, both countries' economic policies were compromised by social concessions given in the revolutionary situation of the immediate post-war years and turned to very moderate state intervention in the economy. Despite great similarities of policies, German performance was considerably better between 1925 and 1929 than Austrian. In annual manufacturing production, though, performance was quite similar between 1913 and 1929.[106] Despite weak capital markets with massive indebtedness, high capital imports and constrained policies, German and Austrian growth performance was better than in Britain, a country without such economic and financial problems.

3.4.1. Foreign Influence, Capital Inflow and Restrictive Currency Policy in Germany

To understand foreign influence on economic policy-making in Germany as one basis for restrictive policy, it is necessary to look at the motives and forces behind German currency stabilisation after the end of passive resistance in late 1923 and the regime shift in 1924. Highly complex and stratified, these had political, and primarily, economic roots originating from domestic, as well as international forces. The main domestic political factor was the endangered political unity of Germany, threatened by the breakdown of the economy in 1923 and the complete collapse of the mark. This was interwoven with active and open French support of the separatists movements in the Rhineland area and toleration of the breakdown of the German economy, while it was forcefully attempted to enforce reparation payments. As a reaction, German politicians initiated diplomatic offensives to counter French

104 Own calculation, Österreichisches Statistisches Zentralamt, *Der Aussenhandel Österreichs*, 12.

105 For Germany, this is claimed until stabilisation. The same can be said for all countries undergoing hyperinflation. Dietmar Petzina and Werner Abelshauser, "Zum Problem der relativen Stagnation der deutschen Wirtschaft in den zwanziger Jahren," Mommsen, Petzina and Weisbrod, *Industrielles System*, 75.

106 See chart: Annual Manufacturing Production, 1913 to 1950, in: Svennilson, 304 and 305.

schemes in the Rhineland. Britain disapproved of French policy toward Germany, and leading German policy makers, such as Wilhelm Marx, Gustav Stresemann and Hjalmar Schacht as the most prominent, could count on British, and to a lesser extent, on American help to find a workable, realistic solution for the reparations problem, based on realistically assessed economic conditions.[107]

To discern the difference of French and British policy and the conditions that allowed for the enforcement of the Dawes plan and eventual German stabilisation, the very complex matter of the reparations issue has to be taken into consideration. Briefly explained, the astronomical reparation sums and annual payments demanded soon after the war could only be serviced by Germany when the Western industrialised nations, the most important importers of German manufactures before the war, did not restrict German exports to their domestic markets during the years of German inflation. Only under these conditions could France and Britain expect Germany to generate the balance of payments surpluses necessary for reparation payments. This ran contrary to the interest of most French and British industrial sectors, which had to cope with increasing German competition on their markets, because of lowered production and labour costs, which were the result of rampant German inflation. At the same time, British and French industries suffered from lower demand of the German market.[108] The German industry partially benefitted indirectly from high reparation demands, while it could take advantage of high domestic inflation. Realising this, the industrial interests groups in France and Britain put pressure on their governments, especially on the Poincaré government, to change their policy stance toward Germany and the reparations issue.

Thus, eventually, international economic conditions pressured politics to change policy, leading to German currency stabilisation. There was not only a German national, but also an international political and economic stabilisation consensus in 1923. Finally, a more moderate and realistic reparations policy was pursued leading to the agreements laid down in the Dawes plan of 1924, which stipulated that the annual amount of German payments had to depend on economic performance and the stability of the German mark. Only as long as the stability of the German currency was not endangered, the Allied reparation agent allowed the transfer of reparation payments.[109] German domestic economic factors for stabilisation consisted of the same forces as in all other countries in which inflations had ended. Already by the end of 1922, debtors, the government and industry could not take any more economic advantages from the depreciating currency. After the Ruhr crisis, the German economy and its various socio-economic interest groups were more than ready for currency stabilisation. The same can be said about French, British and other European industries. The support for the termination of the German inflation was in their best interest.

107 The literature on this topic is massive. For example: Harold James, "Die Währungsstabilisierung 1923/24 in internationaler Perspektive," in: Werner Abelshauser (ed.), *Die Weimarer Republik als Wohlfahrtsstaat. Zum Verhältnis von Wirtschafts- und Sozialpolitik in der Industriegesellschaft*, Stuttgart 1987, 63 ff.

108 Dietmar Petzina, *Die deutsche Wirtschaft in der Zwischenkriegszeit*, Wiesbaden 1977, 78.

109 Ibid, 79.

As in Austria, the primary force behind stabilisation in Germany was the unwillingness of the most influential socio-economic interest groups to continue to support the inflationary process, as it offered no more advantages, since the currency could not function any longer as an instrument of credit. Unlike Austria though, the eventually painful and destructive process continued in Germany until the second half of 1923, because of external political factors. It was finally terminated after the political battle between France and Germany ended and the German economy had come near to a total breakdown, pushing the Weimar Republic close to political disintegration. *Essential for our analysis is the fact that the compelled search of, and final settlement for, a reasonable agreement of the reparations issue was pre-determined by structural processes and laid the foundations for a sharp regime shift, currency stabilisation and subsequent restrictive policy in Germany, which was heavily supported by France and Great Britain.*

After the restoration of the German currency, in the form of the Rentenmark, the Reichsbank and the central government operated within the small framework of restrictive monetary policy.[110] The money supply was restricted, taxes raised considerably, and the public revenue system was centralised. It was attempted to lower government expenditure, credit was made expensive and the authorities prepared the currency for the return to gold. Turnover and income tax were raised, and the general tax burden increased from 9% in 1913 to 17% in 1925. The Reichsbank had already been made independent of government finance with the law of autonomy of 1922. The bank carried out a complete and radical shift away from inflationary policy after November 1923, with the introduction of the strictly limited issue of the Rentenmark.[111]

Subsequent Reichsbank policy, now independent from the central government, was dominated by Hjalmar Schacht, the president of the bank, whose conservative policy was strongly supported by Montagu Norman, the head of the Bank of England and by Benjamin Strong, the president of the American Federal Reserve.[112] Thereafter, the money supply was limited, and prices and the exchange rate were kept stable. The dollar parity of the new currency was vigorously defended between November 1923 and October 1924, resulting in extreme deflationary pressure on the German economy, which expressed itself in harsh credit shortage for industry, declining investment, falling prices and dropping production.[113] In Germany, economic fluctuation was extreme between 1922 and 1924. It was the answer of a disrupted national economy to extreme policy shifts, from excessive inflation to extreme deflation. In early 1924, a short economic upswing occurred until April 1924. From April until August, the Reichsbank turned once again to harsh credit restriction, in order to counter balance payments deficits, to defend the mark exchange rate and to avoid any inflationary tendencies.

110 Ibid, 84.

111 The following partially based on Gerd Hardach, *Weltmarktorientierung und relative Stagnation. Währungspolitik in Deutschland 1924–1931*, Berlin 1976, 21 ff.

112 Hallgarten and Radkau, 181.

113 Hardach, *Weltmarktorientierung*, 29 ff.

No more credit expansion took place, its volume was frozen by the central bank and indirect credit control was executed. The greatest part of central bank credit volume was given to the big private banks, that chiefly gave credit to large industrial enterprises. Schacht believed that too much credit expansion would induce speculation and inflation. Credit was only given away for productive endeavours. In reality, though, this could not be controlled at all. The overall result of this policy was only successful from the viewpoint of traditional monetary theory. The recession, as part of the stabilisation crisis, was tolerated and intensified, but the economic subjects were forced to liquidate their foreign exchange holdings accumulated as part of the capital flight during the inflation and turned them into central bank notes. Reichsbank policy seemed to be able to push balance of payments into an active account, at least for a short period of time. The amount of foreign exchange that the bank was holding increased considerably, improving the mark's exchange rate. From autumn of 1924, the economy recovered from stabilisation crisis.

The next goal was the return to gold parity, which was seen as a return to an international currency system and the final and proper reintegration of the German economy into world trade. This was regarded as a pre-condition to attract foreign capital to an economy suffering from credit shortage and as the basis for the resumption of economic growth. The intentions were similar to the goals of the Cunliffe Committee, with the policy to make a return to the old prewar gold parity possible. The previously practised harsh credit policy helped, since the dollar parity of the mark was artificially kept high. Already in March 1924, Schacht had prepared the return to gold by founding the "Golddiskontbank," with the help of dollar and pound loans. The new currency was pegged to the dollar, which had been on gold since the war, and the legal gold cover was 40% of the money in circulation.[114]

This process, in combination with the foundation of the new section of the Reichsbank and its harsh monetary policy, was closely interconnected with the Dawes reparations plan. International control systems were integrated into the Reichsbank to ensure restrictive policy in order to maintain the stability of the mark. Half of the members of the executive board were foreigners. Yet, the Reichsbank itself was still privately owned by 19,000 stock holders, mostly Germans.[115] The system of foreign control was not forcefully implemented, as most policy makers in the central bank, and to a lesser degree, in the government were already in accordance with this policy. This harsh policy was in full alignment with the interests of the French, British and American industry, because German competition would be limited by a stronger currency. This policy was also in full alignment with the interest of their financial circles, the private and central banks, because a strong German currency could only be maintained with relatively high interest rates. This, in turn, offered good capital investment opportunities. In addition, a proper payment of at least part of the reparation bill could still be expected.

114 Ibid, 51.
115 Ibid, 48.

3.4.2. Foreign Control and Currency Policy in Austria

The conservative policy of the German Reichsbank highly restricted economic policy and led to a conflict with economic policy requirements of the central government. Not only was even mildly inflationary finance impossible, but the ability of the central government to secure loans from the central bank was limited to such a degree that it was itself forced to practise harsh fiscal policies. This development had great similarities to the situation in Austria. Exactly as German stabilisation and subsequent tight and restrictive credit policy, Austrian stabilisation and economic policy during the 20s was to an even greater extent influenced and controlled by foreign powers.

In Austria, currency stabilisation and the subsequent restrictive policy also had an international aspect, but had little to do with reparations. The motives of Entente influence were mainly economic and financial control over Central and Eastern Europe and the political and economic containment of Germany in this area. Austrian political independence was a key to this influence. Stabilisation, with League support for Austria, was enforced to realise the Allies', especially British, dreams of re-establishing the international pre-war currency and economic system. Austria was considered a model case of compelled and guided conservative restoration of old economic systems by the League of Nations. Stabilisation and the return to conservative fiscal policies in Germany and Austria, therefore, were in direct alignment with British, French and American financial and economic interest. Stabilisation and international influence on Austria and Germany, after the end of their inflations, resulted in similar restrictive economic policies in both cases, with great problems on domestic financial markets.

In spite of all its disadvantages, foreign capital inflow and influence was desired by policy makers in Germany and Austria. The pursuit of neo-liberal policies in these countries after 1923/24 was seen as a necessary pre-requisite for capital imports from the West, believed to be essential for economic revival. This control went along the lines of the policy objectives of the new conservative Austrian government that was in power after 1922. Therefore, foreign control and domestic political forces, that pressed forward the implimentation of conservative economic policy, complemented each other. Compared to German policy, in Austria, economic policy was even harsher and credit restrictions were even greater. Yet, public expenditure was not lower. In addition, it will be shown in microeconomic analysis, that the effects of restrictive monetary policy were minute in the late 20s, because the main stimulant for economic revival could not come from a change in policy, such as credit expansion or investment increase, but from outside demand to stimulate exports. A direct causal connection between restrictive policy and poor performance is questionable.

Austrian economic policy of the First Republic has not only been heavily criticised by contemporary journalists,[116] the social democrat opposition, but also by many historians.[117] Austria has been attributed a particularly unusually restrictive

116 See numerous statements of *Der Österreichischer Volkswirt*.

117 For example Peter Berger has called it an irresponsible deflationist policy, "The Austrian Econo-

economic policy, which has been regarded as a major factor contributing to the dissatisfying performance.[118] In the light of policy pursued in other countries, though, and regarding microeconomic activity, the accusations seem unjust. Furthermore, any other economic policy was not possible, because of enormous economic and political constraints, such as international political and economic pressure and influence, domestic pressure after the inflation shock, limited financial means and no economic theory supporting any expansive new policy.[119]

Conservative currency policy was ensured in Germany by the central bank, which was buttressed by foreign influence as well as by domestic policy-makers. This, in turn, ensured not only a stable currency, but also a conservative fiscal policy with a balanced budget. In Austria, the situation was similar, only that foreign influence was not legitimised by the obligation to pay reparations. Legitimisation of influence and the harsh policy regime shift were provided by an international loan secured by the League of Nations.[120] As a return for financial help, the Geneva Protocols supplied the legal stipulations for extensive foreign control not only over the recently founded national bank, but also over parts of the financial ministry of the Austrian government. After it was clear in October 1922 that international financial help would be granted to Austria and the crown had stabilised in November, the new Austrian National Bank was founded in January 1923,[121] from the remnants of the

my, 1918–1938," in: John Komlos (ed.), *Economic Development in the Habsburg Monarchy and in the Successor States* (*East European Monographs*, No. 280), chapter 17, New York 1990, and also in: Herbert Matis (ed.), *The Economic Development of Austria since 1870*, Aldershot 1994, 273 and 274. Some of the harshest criticism against Austrian inter-war economic policy came from Alois Brusatti, *Österreichische Wirtschaftspolitik vom Josephinismus zum Ständestaat*, chapter: Wirtschaftspolitische Leitlinien der Ersten Republik, Vienna 1965.

118 "Den wirtschaftspolitischen Maßnahmen der Bundesregierung und der Oesterreichischen Nationalbank, die freilich sehr stark von ausländischen Einflüssen seiten des Finanzkomitées des Völkerbundes und der Bank von England abhängig waren, ist eine große Verantwortung für die unbefriedigende Wirtschaftsentwicklung zuzuschreiben." Hans Kernbauer, "Zur österreichischen Wirtschaftspolitik in der Ersten Republik: Ein Überblick," in: Alice Teichova (ed.), *Banken, Währungen und Politik in Mitteleuropa zwischen den Weltkriegen*, Vienna 1997, 45. Stiefel has a similar view: "Eine der Ursachen dieser zögernden wirtschaftlichen Erholung (between 1925 and 1929) war die in Österreich betriebene Wirtschaftspolitik, die mehr als in anderen Ländern am Wechselkurs orientiert war und auch nach Aufhebung der Völkerbundkontrolle den 'Blick auf die Finanzprobleme und auf die internationale Kreditfähigkeit Österreichs' konzentrierte." Dieter Stiefel, *Konjunkturelle Entwicklung und struktureller Wandel der österreichischen Wirtschaft in der Zwischenkriegszeit*, Vienna 1978, 38.

119 Gerald Schöpfer, "Möglichkeiten einer aktiven Konjunkturpolitik im Österreich der zwanziger Jahre," in: *Geschichte und Gegenwart*, 2, 1983, 24–46.

120 On details about the diplomacy between Austria and the Entente that led to the conclusion of the Geneva Protocols see: Klemens von Klemperer, *Ignaz Seipel. Christian Statesman in a Time of Crisis*, Princeton 1972; Gottlieb Ladner, *Seipel als Überwinder der Staatskrise vom Sommer 1922. Zur Geschichte der Entstehung der Genfer Protokolle vom 4. Oktober 1922*, Vienna 1964; Friedrich Renndorfer, *Ignaz Seipel. Mensch und Staatsmann. Eine biographische Dokumentation*, Vienna 1978. See also Lajos Kerekes, *Von St. Germain bis Genf. Österreich und seine Nachbarn 1918–1922*, Budapest 1979, 362 ff.

121 The following detailed information from Kernbauer, *Währungspolitik*, 99 ff.

old Austrian-Hungarian National Bank. It terminated its support of budget deficits on November 18, 1923. Its first goal was to keep the crown exchange rate stable, and to support a quick floatation of the international loan. Meanwhile, the budget was financed by government floated loans and short-term foreign loans from the Bank of England. The Austrian trust in foreign, especially British, support, also as a means to execute stabilisation policy against domestic parliamentary opposition and public opinion,[122] resulted in an exaggerated foreign control mechanism over the new bank and the government.

Since London had granted short-term loans in late 1922, the Bank of England demanded a supplement to the statute of the Austrian national bank, including a clause that would grant a special foreign committee influence over the executive of the new bank. Eventually, a foreign advisor was appointed that observed the actions of the bank and kept close contact with the Financial Committee of the League of Nations and the Bank of England. In fact, the Financial Committee basically represented the interest of the Bank of England, led by Norman. Besides dominating British influence, French, Dutch, Belgian and Scandinavian financial interests were represented in this committee.

The loan was finally successfully floated in June 1923, with net proceeds of 631 million gold crowns. The budget deficits for 1923 and 1924, that the loan was supposed to cover, were deliberately estimated far too high, with 520 million gold crowns. It is not clear if the estimates were set too high by the Austrians or by the League of Nations' Financial Committee during the Geneva Conference in 1922. Possibly by the latter, to make sure that financial help could support a certain degree of control. The actual deficits for these years were only 40% of the estimated amount, and only worth one third of the amount of the loan. Only 212.3 million crowns of the proceeds were used for the Austrian budget deficits of 1923 and 1924, and for the repayment of the short-term loans received after November 1922. A further 34.7 million were utilised for a partial repayment from the government for the loans from the central bank in 1922. The majority of the international loan, 351.3 million, was used by the government for state investment between 1923 and 1928.[123] The size and the unfavourable conditions of the loan, which made those public investments that were financed by the loan far more expensive, were heavily criticised. Public investment itself was seen by many as positive, but an investment loan of similar magnitude could have been obtained by the government under more favourable and cheaper market conditions.

The Geneva Protocols not only stipulated the statutes of the bank, but also determined tight control of government finances. After the conservative government managed the ratification of the protocols in parliament, following fierce discussions with the opposition, parliament basically gave up its right to control future fiscal policy. A large section of government finances and expenditure was under the control of the

122 "Die Regierung berief sich auf Zwänge von außen, um Akkzeptanz politischer Entscheidungen zu erlangen." Roman Sandgruber, *Ökonomie und Politik. Österreichische Wirtschaftsgeschichte vom Mittelalter bis zur Gegenwart*, Vienna 1995, 343.

123 Kernbauer, *Währungspolitik*, 111.

League of Nations commissioner, the Dutchman and former mayor of Rotterdam, Alfred Zimmermann, who sent frequent reports on the state of Austrian government finances and currency stability to the League of Nations' officials.[124] Only he could release part of the remnants of the League loan, still the majority of the proceeds, for state investments. During the second half of the 20s, Austrian government officials had to ask for releases of capital from the loan to finance the very moderate state investment schemes. Meanwhile, the majority of the capital was forced to lay idle in foreign banks with a lower interest rate (6 or 7%)[125] than the interest rate the state had to pay for its maintenance. The result of this rather ridiculous arrangement was a slow and moderate release of loan proceeds, giving the Austrian government only limited capital for investment, while still ensuring a balanced budget. Surprisingly, this expensive loan did not result in higher state debt service than in other countries, as we shall see below.

The overall effects for economic policy were the same as in Germany: the national bank statutes pressured the bank to maintain a stable currency and to limit the capabilities of the government in order to get loans for state expenditure. The secondary effect was that the state either roughly maintained a balanced budget or only ran minor deficits. The fact that the Austrian government formally lost control over economic policy-making is actually irrelevant and was only a political issue. It is doubtful if policy would have been different if League control had not existed. Since the League of Nations' and British and French policy goals were stable currencies and balanced budgets, the overall policy was, from the viewpoint of neo-liberal theory, extremely successful. After the successful introduction of policy regime shift in Germany in 1924 and in Austria in 1923, the outcome were very similar economic policies in both countries, until the take-over of the National Socialists in Germany in January 1933 and the dissolution of parliament in Austria during March of the same year. In Austria, state investment was slightly lower, and the bank rate was a little higher throughout the 20s than in Germany.

Before going further into an analysis of the effects of these policies in Austria on microeconomic development, policy measures in Germany and in Austria following the reconstruction until the depression must be discussed. They were the outcome of a struggle over the rate of credit availability between the German central government and its national bank, and between foreign financial institutions and the Austrian national bank and government in the second half of the 20s. The situation was particularly grim after March of 1924, when the Viennese stock market crashed after an extensive speculation with the French franc.[126] Increasingly, foreign capital outflow took place and the central bank had to support the crown exchange rate by raising the discount rate. At the beginning of June, it was raised from 9 to 12% and up to 15%

124 On the stabilisation process, League of Nations control and its limiting effects, see also: Hans Kernbauer and Fritz Weber, "Von der Inflation zur Depression. Österreichs Wirtschaft 1918–1934", in: Emmerich Tálos und W. Neugebauer (eds.), *"Austrofaschismus." Beiträge über Politik, Ökonomie und Kultur 1934–1938*, Vienna 1984, 11–16.

125 Kernbauer, *Währungspolitik*, 113.

126 Information on Austrian currency policy from Kernbauer, *Währungspolitik*, 131 ff.

until August. Part of the motive was also to attract foreign capital and to reduce the ever existing suspicion of the Financial Committee and the Bank of England.[127] The high central bank discount rate has been considered one major factor contributing to the only very moderate Austrian participation in the boom of the late 20s.

Austrian currency policy was closely observed byWestern financial institutions, since financial experts in the world regarded reconstruction in Austria as a model case of stabilisation. After 1924 until the depression, a constant struggle took place between the Austrian national bank and the Bank of England, and also between the Austrian central government and the League of Nations commissioner, Zimmermann. The national bank wanted to loosen strict credit conditions, while Norman regarded currency policy in Austria as not restrictive enough. The authorities of the central government required more capital from the remnants of the international loan for state investment, while the League control was limiting the state's possibility for investment. By mid 1924, Norman saw the implementation of further credit restrictions of the Austrian central bank, under the leadership of its president Richard Reisch, as much too late to counter the effects of the stock market boom and crash of that year. The British bank authorities demanded a much more restrictive policy and believed that the Austrian authorities' policies were too inflationary, particularly since the central bank was acting as a lender of last resort for the many banks in crisis, especially after the speculative boom and the collapse of the Depositenbank.[128] While Austrian industrial interest demanded a decrease in the discount rate to induce investments and growth, the conference of the League of Nations, in September 1924, demanded strict deflationary measures from the government. Norman was against any further reduction of the interest rate. Yet, since bank deposits were increasing and the exchange cover of the currency had improved, the discount rate was decreased to 13% in late 1924. When Reisch met Norman in London, he had to defend himself against accusations. Norman wanted a restriction of the money supply in order to lower the price level. He also wanted more restrictions on credit availability. Obviously, the Austrian central bank policy under Reisch was not as compliant as Schacht's, and the attempt of the Bank of England to co-ordinate and to adapt the central banks' policies of Austria and Germany is apparent. Essentially, Reisch had to give in,[129] and in spite of the recessionary symptoms in 1924, the central bank policy in Austria remained extremely restrictive.

On the basis of the stabilised paper crown, the schilling was introduced as the new currency on March 1, 1925. 14.4 thousand paper crowns amounted to one gold crown. 1.44 schillings equalled one gold crown. Between this date and July 1, 1926, all economic subjects had to adjust their accountancy systems to the new currency, which meant that the balance sheets of 1925 and 1926 of all banks and joint-stock companies had to be reconstructed on the basis of the new schilling gold parity.

127 The bank's report put it very nicely. It regarded the "Wiedergewinnung des Vertrauens der maßgebenden Kreise des Auslandes" as vital. Kernbauer, *Währungspolitik*, 134.

128 Ibid, 141.

129 "Wir werden uns nach Möglichkeit den Wünschen der Herren in England anzupassen versuchen müssen [...]." Ibid. 157.

These were the so called "Goldbilanzen" (gold balance sheets or reconstructed balances). Finally, the inflationary distortion of accounting was over, and the actual capital basis had to be revealed, or was at least partially revealed. Almost all balance sheets showed a massive loss of capital compared to their pre-war values. Especially, the capital basis of the large Viennese banks had decreased dramatically.

In spite of urgent and apparent need of capital for industry and the domestic capital market after stabilisation and currency reform, the central bank adhered to its high discount rate in 1925, of 13 and 15%. This, it hoped, would attract sufficient foreign capital. A further meeting of Reisch with the decision makers of the Bank of England, showed the same results as before. The request for help in the form of foreign loans was declined. By late 1925, the bank rate was still at 11%. In 1926, the situation slightly improved when the Financial Committee of the League of Nations terminated control of government finances June 7, 1926. After Zimmermann's powers were restricted, a new advisor for the central bank, Robert Charles Kay from the Bank of England, was supposed to improve relations. However, this was not the case. Norman disapproved of the discount rate reduction to 7.5% in March 1926, and to 7% in August. In February 1927, it was down to 6%, a rate comparable to the ones in the Western industrialised countries.[130]

The whole conflict between London and the Austrian central bank over percentage points of discount rate changes had little results, neither on the capital market, nor on microeconomic activity, as we will see. Between November 1924 and the beginning of 1927, the bank rate was lowered from 15% to 6%, but the inflow of short-term foreign capital was not limited, nor did investment increase significantly.[131] Already by March 1927, Austrian short-term foreign debt amounted to 1050 million schillings. 700 million were received by the very large banks, such as the Bodencreditanstalt and the Creditanstalt, 150 million went to the small banks, and 200 million were channeled directly to industrial enterprises and trade companies.[132] For the rest of the year and throughout 1928, the discount rate remained around 6 or 7%. As European capital markets became more restricted until 1929, due to the speculative stock market boom in the US, the Austrian discount rate only increased slightly to 7% and later, to 7.5% in 1929. In late 1929, it increased by one more percentage point, to 8.5%. It fluctuated constantly according to the international capital market situation. The fluidity of the international capital market improved considerably after the crash in October in New York, and by September of 1930, the Austrian discount rate was at its lowest point in the inter-war period with only 5%. The president of the central bank stood for an interest rate as low as possible to help industry. With this policy, he was in opposition to the large Viennese banks, which never went below 6%. Yet, as will be shown, discount rate percentage points were not the significant factor in changing industrial investment behaviour significantly. The main stimulant was demand on domestic, and first and foremost, on international

130 Ibid, 197 ff.

131 Gross investment remained fairly low, between 6% of national income in 1924, 8.7% in 1926 and 9.9% in 1929. In 1913, it had been 12.9%. Österreichisches Institut für Wirtschaftsforschung, *Monatsberichte* 14, 41.

132 Kernbauer, *Währungspolitik*, 196–199.

markets. Furthermore, domestic discount rates did not matter so much, because many investments were financed by foreign capital. Reisch himself was aware of this.[133]

3.4.3. Policy in Germany after 1924

In Germany, a similar course of policy took place. After the return of the mark to the classical gold standard in 1924, the main objective of the Reichsbank was to defend the German financial position in the international currency system. This was done with the help of credit restrictions after April 1924. In 1925, Reichsbank policy remained restrictive, even though it was clear that the economy still suffered from the stabilisation crisis and that companies tended to have very limited financial means.[134] A conflict developed between the central government, which demanded credit expansion, and the central bank that wanted to defend the parity of the mark. The central government and chancellor Luther were in favour of credit expansion, especially since the domestic price level was sinking. He believed that the high discount rate, set by the central bank, would only improve the bank's position, but that credit expansion would loosen the pressure on industry. In fact, the monetary situation had been in a great position, with a note cover of 82% in October and 116% in December of 1924.

Finally, by February 1925, the central bank was willing to lower its discount rate, but only by one percent from 10 to 9%. Only by mid 1926, the bank seriously began to relax its policy, answering to a recession that was at its lowest point in April. The discount rate was lowered to 8%, by January 1926. In July, credit was expanded from 1.6 billion to 1.7 billion marks, and after October, capital inflow from abroad expanded increasingly. By January 1927, while the economy picked up again, the discount rate was even down to 5%. During the recession of early 1926, the monetary situation had improved considerably. The balance of payments situation recovered and gold coverage of the currency increased. The opposite occurred as soon as another upswing set in late 1926.

Therefore, after very restrictive monetary policies between stabilisation in 1924 until mid 1926, credit policy had become more relaxed until 1929, expressing itself in a lower discount rate. While the Reichsbank could maintain the value of the mark on international markets and rendered possible acceptable credit conditions, it was unable to control the massive inflow of foreign credit and inconsiderate German lending. After 1923 and increasingly after 1925, capital inflow to Germany rose enormously, especially from the US. Between 1923 and 1929, 21 billion dollars flowed into the German economy. Approximately 4 billion dollars went to the state

133 Reisch claimed that "für die Nationalbank das Entscheidene immer die Erwägung bleibe 'ob nicht der Wirtschaft durch eine Ermäßigung der Bankrate eine Erleichterung gebracht werden könne. Wenn auch die Herabsetzung der Bankrate um einen halben Prozent keinen entscheidenen Einfluß auf die Lage der Industrie ausüben könne, zumal ein Großteil der in Anspruch genommenen Kredite in ausländischer Währung direkt hereingenommen werde, so bedeute sie doch eine Entlastung für alle Schillingschuldner der Banken [...].'" Ibid, 211.

134 The following information for Germany from Hardach, *Weltmarktorientierung*, 52 ff.

and municipal governments, 7 billion to large banks, and 10 billion was utilised by industrial firms directly.[135] A large part of this was comprised of short-term loans, used for long-term investment. Since often times incoming loans were utilised by state or municipal governments, the Reichsbank attempted to control the inflow and to direct the incoming capital to productive ventures of industry. Eventually, its control mechanisms were ineffective and the central bank turned to credit restrictions. This only induced more foreign capital inflow, and discriminated against small companies. These were often not able to receive large loans from abroad.[136]

However, capital inflow was not primarily used for productive investment, but either to finance the balance of payment deficit or to pay part of the reparations burden. In the same time span (1923–1929), roughly 21 billion dollars flowed out of Germany for these purposes, the largest sum for the balance of payments deficit (9.4 billion) and for investment abroad (7.7 billion). In spite of this, industry still invested 33 billion marks, with funds from various sources.[137] The overall outcome was that the German economy suffered from heavy foreign indebtedness, resulting in expensive credit availability. Germany depended on capital inflow in the second part of the 20s, and its restrictive policy was a pre-requisite for this.[138] On the other hand, the heavy inflow also rendered possible a compromised orthodox policy that included rising state investment. While imported money helped to pay reparations and balance of payment deficits, the government could employ a larger portion of its collected revenue for active intervention. That these policies and deformed capital flows contributed to the severity of the depression is without doubt, but performance in the late 20s was not harmed, nor was the late boom primarily a result of capital inflow.

3.4.4. Capital Inflow to Austria and the Viennese Banks

Again, in Austria the situation was very similar. While domestic financial institutions only slowly turned to more moderate discount rates after 1927, with rates between the very high ones in Eastern Europe and the rates offered in France, Britain or the US, heavy capital inflow took place in Austria itself. Capital inflow had a different structure than in Germany, but similar results. While in Germany a major portion went to industrial firms directly, and only a minor part was for foreign investments, in Austria, most of the capital directly went to the main Viennese banks[139] that had already established their position as the main providers of credit before the First World War for industry in the area of the successor states and the rest of Eastern

135 Friedrich-Wilhelm Henning, *Das industrialisierte Deutschland 1914–1992, 8. Auflage*, Munich 1993, 86

136 Hardach, *Weltmarktorientierung*, 57 ff.

137 Henning, 86 and 87.

138 Hardach, *Weltmarktorientierung*, 56.

139 Such as the Bodencreditanstalt, the Creditanstalt für Handel und Gewerbe, the Niederösterreichische Escomptegesellschaft and the Wiener Bankverein.

Europe. They had financed long-term investment and the floatation of new shares[140] of the rapidly rising numbers of joint-stock companies in the last two decades before 1914.[141]

During and after the war, the financial substance of the banks had decreased dramatically, and they faced only two options: Either they chose austrification of their banking policy (i.e. the reduction of banking business to the domestic economy) or they opted for the maintenance of business connections in the area of the former Empire, even though a strong effort of nostrification was taking place in the successor states. Yet, while most branches of the Viennese banks were taken over by national capital groups in the successor states, and whereas some big companies in the successor states searched for different sources of finance,[142] the most influential Austrian universal banks were able to keep a large portion of their financial influence, especially in those areas where local banking was not as developed.[143] This was partially possible because of their old connections and experience in business in this area. These large and still influential banks had maintained their strong influence on financing domestic, as well as industrial ventures in Eastern Europe and were used by Western investors as a means to distribute their investment funds in this area.

This structure of capital flow resulted from a marriage of convenience. While the Austrian banks needed foreign capital funds to maintain their policy and influence, Western foreign investors wanted lucrative investment opportunities, especially where discount rates were high. The banks were also a tool for the effort of Western financial circles, the central banks and governments of Britain and France, to establish and maintain their economic influence in this area. The financial ties between the large Viennese banks and Western capital groups were improved especially after war and during inflation. The share of capital of the banks belonging to foreigners had increased considerably until the end of the inflation.[144] The mid-sized Anglobank and the Länderbank, for instance, were fully in the hands of French and British capital.[145] After the end of inflation, almost half of the Bodencreditanstalt was in foreign

140 Two thirds of the share capital issued by new joint-stock companies between 1907 and 1913 were bought by the large Viennese banks. Hans Kernbauer and Fritz Weber, "Multinational banking in the Danube basin: the business strategy of the Viennese banks after the collapse of the Habsburg monarchy," in: Alice Teichova and Helga Nussbaum (eds.), *Multinational enterprise in historical perpective*, Cambridge 1986, 186.

141 Ibid, 185 ff.

142 For example, the Skoda works and the mining and metallurgic company of the Czecheslovak government found a new source of capital from the French Schneider Le Creuzot group. As we shall see later, this capital group also gained considerable influence over other industrial ventures in Eastern Europe, as well as in Austria. Ibid, 187.

143 Most clients were lost in Upper Italy and in the Czechoslovak Republic. In Yugoslavia and Poland, the banks' influence remained strong. Ibid, 187 and 188.

144 Alice Teichova, "Rivals and Partners: reflections on banking and industry in Europe, 1880–1938," in: *European Industry and Banking Between the Wars. A Review of Bank-Industry Relations*, Leicester 1992, 24.

145 This is supported by an extensive literature on the matter. For example Charlotte Natmeßig, *Britische Finanzinteressen in Österreich: Die Anglo-Österreichische Bank*, Vienna 1998; and Alice Teichova, "Versailles and the Expansion of the Bank of England into Central Europe," in: Norbert Horn und Jürgen Kocka (eds.), *Recht und Entwicklung der Großunternehmen im 19. und*

hands, one fifth of the Creditanstalt and over one third of the Niederösterreichische Escomptegesellschaft.[146]

The banks borrowed heavily in the West and pumped this foreign capital into industrial ventures mainly in Eastern Europe. A large portion of the capital inflow to Austria was redirected out of the domestic economy. Thus, while capital inflow took place, it was utilised for foreign investment, making credit relatively more expensive in Austria than in France, Britain or the US. Capital inflow, which largely came from theWest, mostly consisted of short-term credit, while the industrial clients of the banks needed funds for long-term investments.[147] Often, these funds were granted, and by the late 20s, the large Viennese banks were pursuing a dangerous policy,[148] which meant borrowing on a short-term basis from the West, but lending on a long-term basis to Eastern Europe and to the domestic capital market. This dramatically enhanced the faults of an Austrian financial system in which the banks' assets already increasingly consisted of falling industrial stocks, whereas their deposits, their capital bases, were insufficient.

While the banks accepted an ever-increasing share of the newly issued industrial stocks from companies, hoping for a future economic revival and an upswing on the stock exchange market, they also increased their direct influence on company management. Banks sometimes had accounting control, insight in financial documentation, chairmanship or strong representation in the board of directors.[149] By the late 1920s, the situation culminated in serious liquidity problems of the main Austrian banks, which tried to postpone or avoid their final breakdown by concentration and bank mergers, which expressed itself in bank crashes after 1924 and in the collapse of the Creditanstalt in May 1931. These pressures also explain their unwillingness to lower the bank rate below 6% and their eagerness to attract capital from Entente countries.[150]

frühen 20. Jahrhundert, Göttingen 1979. Robert Hoffman, "Die wirtschaftlichen Grundlagen der britischen Österreichpolitik 1919," in: *Mitteilungen des Österreichischen Staatsarchivs*, 30, 1977, 284 ff.

146 Kernbauer and Weber, "Multinational banking," chart on page 189. Extensively on Western penetration of the banking system and on banking policy after disintegration see: Eduard März, *Österreichische Bankpolitik in der Zeit der großen Wende 1913–1923. Am Beispiel der Creditanstalt für Handel und Gewerbe*, Vienna 1981. See also: Karl Ausch, *Als die Banken fielen. Zur Soziologie der politischen Korruption*, Wien 1968; and Hans Kernbauer and Fritz Weber, "Die Wiener Großbanken in der Zeit der Kriegs- und Nachkriegsinflation (1914–1922)," in: Gerald D. Feldman, Carl-Ludwig Holtfrerich, Gerhard A. Ritter and Peter-Christian Witt (eds.), *Die Erfahrungen der Inflation im Internationalen Zusammenhang und Vergleich*, Berlin 1984.

147 Fritz Weber, "Die österreichische Bankenkrise und ihre Auswirkungen auf die niederösterreichische Industrie," in: Andreas Kusternig (ed.), *Beiträge über die Krise der Industrie Niederösterreichs zwischen den beiden Weltkriegen (Studien und Forschungen aus dem Niederösterreichischen Institut für Landeskunde*, vol. 7), Vienna 1985, 126.

148 Fritz Weber, "Universal banking in interwar Central Europe," in: Harold James (ed.), *The role of banks in the inter-war economy*, Cambridge 1991, 23 ff.

149 Rudolf Nötel, "Money, Banking and Industry in Interwar Austria and Hungary," in: *Banks and Industry in the Interwar Period. The Journal of European Economic History*, vol. 13, number 2, special issue, Fall 1984, 140.

150 Between 1924 and 1930 the indebtness of Viennese banks to Western Europe and the U.S. had increased threefold. Teichova, "Rivals and Partners."

The situation seems to have been similar to that of German capital inflow after the Dawes plan. There as well, mostly short-term funds came in that were used for long-term investment. Also, in this case, this mechanism is said to have caused an economic revival of the late 20s, mainly induced by foreign capital and to have caused the severe economic downswing after 1929.[151] In the case of Austria, the boom is often considered to have been induced by similar causes. Between 1925 and 1928, the condition of easily available foreign funds, together with deflationary government policies, low domestic demand and a bad export market are considered as having caused a powerful, but unstable investment boom.[152]

Was the upswing in Germany and in Austria between stabilisation and depression nothing but an artificially induced boom with heavy monetary injection? The main supposition is that the influence of the so-called universal banks of Vienna and Germany, and the pressure of deflationary and protectionist monetary and trade policies of the central banks and the central government were extreme on the domestic economy and that industrial investment and growth depended primarily on the availability of finance.[153] Hence, the structural weaknesses of the credit system, expressed in high dependence on capital imports and growing indebtedness of the large banks is said to have had major implications on growth and performance of the Austrian economy, because industry allegedly seemed to have lost most of its "auto-financing potential."[154] It is maintained that especially after the stock market crash in 1924, larger industrial investments could only be carried through with the help of bank credit.[155]

This point of view will be relativized by two factors. On the one hand, the influence of banking on industry in Austria was much less extensive than has been assumed, and on the other, many companies were able to avoid dependence on bank credit. Quite contrary to the view that large investment of industry could only be carried out by bank credit,[156] firms either searched for new credit sources abroad, to induce lucrative investment, or profits proceeds were sufficient for new investment.[157] Demand conditions and long-term structural transformations seemed to

151 Theodor Balderston, "The Origins of Economic Instability in Germany 1924–1930. Market Forces Versus Economic Policy," in: *Vierteljahrschrift für Sozial- und Wirtschaftsgeschichte*, Volume 69, 1982, 512. C.T. Schmidt, *German Business Cycles, 1924–1933*, New York 1934. D.S. Landes, *The Unbound Prometheus*, Cambridge 1969, 370–372.

152 Nötel, "Money, Banking and Industry," 158.

153 This is emphasised by Alois Mosser and Alice Teichova, "Investment behaviour of industrial joint stock companies and industrial shareholding by the Österreichische Credit-Anstalt: inducement or obstacle to renewal and change in industry in inter-war Austria," in: Harold James (ed.), *The role of banks in the inter-war economy*, Cambridge 1991, 123 ff.

154 Nötel, "Money, Banking and Industry," 144 ff.

155 Fritz Weber, "Die österreichische Bankenkrise," 126.

156 Peter Eigner, "Die Verflechtung zwischen denWiener Großbanken und der Industrie 1855 bis 1938," in: Herbert Matis (ed.), *Historische Betriebsanalyse und Unternehmen. Festschrift für Alois Mosser*, Vienna 1997, 193.

157 Alois Mosser shows in his short study that most investments were self-financed by profit proceeds or were externally financed via the issue of new shares. Outside capital in the form of credit was rarely utilised. He also states that investment was quite low in the inter-war period

have been the major stimulants of investment and growth and not credit conditions and monetary policies.

In fact, the banks did increase their share of capital stock of Austrian joint-stock companies mostly before the end of the inflation, but only in the minority of the cases was the majority of shares of a firm in the hands of the banks. Of all the joint-stock companies statistically registered in Austria before the depression (roughly between 500 and 700),[158] the Creditanstalt had shares of 193 companies, mostly within the machine building, metal processing, textile, sugar, brewery and foodstuffs industries. The Bodencreditanstalt had shares of 166 firms, such as the Veitscher Magnesitwerke, Österreichische Brau AG, Schoeller-Bleckmann steel works, Maschinenfabrik Simmering and Neusiedler paper works. The Niederösterreichische Escomptegesellschaft had shares of 114 companies, mostly within the electrical engineering industries.[159]

These numbers, though, do not say very much about the banks' influence on these firms. As many authors who supported the view of a strong influence of banks state themselves, the banks' control over the utilisation of the credit they had given was highly limited. Moreover, some of the shares, such as the Veitscher shares, were quite lucrative and resulted in respectable income from high dividend proceeds. In addition, companies were aware of the high credit cost of bank capital. As we shall see below, firms with high competitiveness, productivity and sufficient demand were able to avoid any dependence on bank money by attracting favourable foreign loans, often had substantial bank deposits and could finance investments from profit proceeds. The firms, mostly part of the older declining industries, suffering heavily from the structural malaise of the European economy, were the ones that did not have any other option but to depend on bank credit.

and only the upswing in the late 20s led to moderate expansionary investment behaviour in the few years 1924/25 until 1927. See: "Wachtumsstrategie oder Krisenmanagement? Vom Investitionsverhalten der österreichischen Industrie in der Ersten Republik," in: Kusternig, *Beiträge*, 113/114.

158 The number of statistically registered joint-stock companies in Austria naturally varied. In 1926, there were 515; in 1927, 522; in 1928, 540 joint-stock companies. The low point came after the end of the depression with slightly over 400 in 1933, according to the Statistisches Reichsamt (ed.), *Statistisches Jahrbuch für das Deutsche Reich*, vol. 56, 1937, page 259 (international survey). The total number of joint-stock companies was 752 in 1926, 705 in 1927, 667 in 1928 and only 489 in 1934, according to Alois Mosser, "Wachstumsstrategie oder Krisenmanagement?' 109. Austrian statistics provide an even higher figure of industrial joint-stock companies for 1928 with 707. See: Bundesamt für Statistik, *Statistisches Handbuch für die Republik Österreich*, vol. 10, Vienna 1929, 86.

159 Numbers from Eigner, 195.

3.5. INTERNATIONAL TAX BURDEN, BUDGET POLICIES AND STATE INVESTMENT

3.5.1. International Comparison

Government fiscal policy has to be briefly reviewed, before turning to microeconomic analysis. Most macroeconomic signs, even during the time of a relative upswing between 1925 and 1929, showed a grim picture in Austria. Unemployment never went below the 10% mark, terms of trade were always in a substantial deficit and the rate of investment was far below pre-war figures.[160] Many authors have seen the causes of the stagnating economic development in Austria in the low private and public investment rate, the high discount rate and low exports, as a result of protectionst trade policies. This argumentation also attributes the poor performance to the restrictive national economic policy.[161]

Yet, seen in international perspective, it is obvious that Austrian development was part of an international European trend.[162] Similar macroeconomic signs were apparent in Germany and Britain, and much more so in Eastern Europe. In these countries, trade deficits were substantial and unemployment was hardly below 10%, while similar tax, budget and investment policies were pursued by most other nations. When discussing microeconomic development and performance, the reasons for the stagnating growth in inter-war Austria during this time become obvious. For companies, bank rates, trade tariff rates, public investment and budget policies were only relevant to a minor degree for everyday economic life. Primarily international market demand, competitiveness and productivity were the main determinants of microeconomic performance. Domestic market demand for large companies in a small advanced country was of secondary importance. International and domestic demand could definitely not be incited by a modification of national economic policy, which would have changed the discount rate or increased public expenditure. Neither would it have been possible for the government of a small country to raise sufficient revenue, nor to run a massive deficit spending policy in the face of coercive international neo-liberal policy.

A small, export dependent country as Austria needed an increase in European trade, therefore an increase of demand via exports. In an international environment in which world trade was declining, in which an ever increasing share of economic growth was oriented toward inward oriented growth and development in large countries with big markets as in Germany, Britain, France or the US, and in which Europe's economic position deteriorated, the Austrian economy had a small chance of growing just as rapidly as other industrialised nations. These are reasons to regard

160 See chart: Verwendung des verfügbaren Güter- und Leistungsvolumens, Österreichisches Institut für Wirtschaftsforschung, *Monatsberichte* 14, 41.

161 Kernbauer and Weber, "Von der Inflation zur Depression", 14.

162 Jürgen Nautz is one of the few authors that agrees on this point. He regards the Austrian economy as having developed along the lines of the world economy and believes that any other economic policy was not possible under these historical circumstances. See: *Handelspolitik*, 561.

economic policy and performance in Austria in a different light. Throughout the 20s, conditions that would have enabled policy makers to adjust structures, to lower unemployment, or to increase the investment and capital market deficiencies, as some authors believe,[163] did not exist. Economic policy that pursued the stability of the currency and a balanced budget was not the cause for unemployment. The causes lay in low competitiveness on the international market and in great difficulty of the Austrian economy to change its emphasis from older to more modern industries,[164] in order to adjust to the two structural changes.

In spite of this, strict Austrian budget policy and limited state investment has been assigned a major role in contributing to moderate performance.[165] In order to question the viability of this thesis, it will be attempted to compare European tax, budget and investment policies. Generally, to estimate the effects of budget policies, public tax burden and investment rate on the economy is very difficult, and to compare budget, taxes and investment of Austria with that of other nations also provides some serious methodological problems. Statistics are confusing, the organisation and structure of tax systems and budgets were different among countries and changed several times during the inter-war period. Moreover, the bases of various national statistical assessment methods of taxes and budget items were different, just as economic structures differed from country to country. For example, some government bureaucracies considered investment as a separate section of the budget and others did not specifically mention investment expenditure at all. A comparison of the level of tax burden on the economy, and on companies, among several countries also constitutes methodological problems, because the share of taxes and duties or charges (Gebühren) of state income varied from country to country. Moreover, in some countries, social security was financed by taxes and in others, by subscription. Therefore, the following comparisons and calculations have to be viewed with caution.

163 Kernbauer and Weber speak of a "Moment der Zwangsläufigkeit" within the Austrian economic development in the inter-war period, "in dem Sinn, daß die versäumten Möglichkeiten der frühen zwanziger Jahre den Handlungsspielraum in der Weltwirtschaftskrise so stark einengten, daß eine Krisenlösungspolitik nur mehr als Fortsetzung und Verlängerung des immer schon angestrebten Sozialabbaus ins faschistische hinein denkbar schien: Durch Lohnsenkung und die Beseitigung der sozialen Errungenschaften der österreichischen Revolution sollte die Konkurrenzfähigkeit der Industrie wiederhergestellt werden." In: "Von der Inflation zur Depression," 24.

164 Kernbauer suggests an indirect connection between restrictive policy and unemployment and the independence of the Austrian state in the 1930s. "Die Wirtschaftspolitik, die der Erhaltung des Geldwertes Priorität einräumte, hatte somit ihr Ziel erreicht, allerdings auf Kosten einer hohen Arbeitslosigkeit, die mit zu den Ursachen zählte, die den Glauben an den österreichischen Staat unterminierten." Kernbauer, "Zur österreichischen Wirtschaftspolitik in der Ersten Republik," 60.

165 Many authors have supported this view. "Eine wesentliche Ursache dieser wirtschaftlichen, gesellschaftlichen und politischen Misere war sicher nicht zuletzt eine falsche Wirtschafts- und damit auch Budgetpolitik." Alexander Fibich, *Die Entwicklung der österreichischen Bundesausgaben in der Ersten Republik (1918–1938)*, dissertation, Vienna 1977, 19. See also Fritz Weber, "Staatliche Wirtschaftspolitik in der Zwischenkriegszeit. Zum Investitionsverhalten der öffentlichen Hand 1918–1938," in: Emmerich Talos (ed.), *Handbuch des politischen Systems Österreichs. Erste Republik 1918–1933*, Vienna 1995.

Generally, statistics provide the picture that the Austrian level of state income, expenditure and investment effort was within the average trend of European industrialised countries. In some respects, the budget and fiscal development in relation to economic growth seemed to have been even better and much less deflationary in Austria and in Germany than in France, Belgium or Britain. Figures 3.3 – 3.8, which provide a rough comparative impression of the structure of public expenditure in several European countries, verifiy this view.

The level of debt service and state expenditure for defence, which can be considered as unproductive and deflationary, was much lower in Austria than in these countries. Britain, for example, utilised 45% of overall expenditure for debt service in 1927/28, 35.9% in 1932/33 (after the devaluation of the pound) and between 20 and 30% during the rest of the 30s. Most of these debts must have been internal debts on state bonds and war debts to the United States. In France and Belgium, debt service burden was also very high, because of war debts to the US and large public floating government loans. In Belgium, debt service share of overall expenditure was 48.6% in 1926, 23.3% in 1931 and 37.17% in 1935. In France, it amounted to 42.8% in 1926, and was at its peak in 1929 with 51.04%. In spite of reparations payments in the late 20s, German war debts only made up 11.6% of expenditure in 1927/28, and 14.8% in 1928/29. Even when the domestic central government debt of national floating bonds and central bank credit service is added to this, the ratio was only 16.8% and 19.8% respectively.[166] This had largely to do with the extinction of public debt during the inflation. Surprisingly, the Austrian debt service share of government expenditure was the lowest, even though the harsh payments conditions stipulated in the Geneva Protocols of 1922 for the League of Nations loan of 1923, which comprised the majority of government debt, had to be fulfilled. Its share of overall central government expenditure was at its highest in the 20s in 1928, with 10.5%, and declined to 4.3% in 1930. Even after another international loan was floated in 1932, the debt share was only 9.4%. Regarding these ratios, the spending policy in Austria was the least restrictive.

At first sight, when comparing tax income with national income, it seemed that the Austrian tax burden on the economy was within the lower European average at the time. Between 1924 and 1937, the percentage of central government tax of GDP varied between 10.3% and 14.9%. In France, the taxation level was higher, between 15.4% in 1924 and 20.5% in 1929, which was a year with high GDP level. In Germany, it varied between 9.8% in 1926 and 17.6% in 1937. In Belgium, the percentage of central government tax of GDP was similar to that in Austria, with 10.8% in 1924 and 14.9% in 1936.[167] These are only very rough estimates, though. A comparative analysis of company tax burden in different countries could reveal the impact of policy on performance.

166 See Statistisches Reichsamt (ed.), *Statistisches Jahrbuch für das Deutsche Reich*, 1927–1929.

167 Peter Flora, Jens Alber, Richard Eichenberg, Jürgen Kohl, Franz Kraus, Winfried Pfenning and Kurt Seebohm, *State, Economy and Society in Western Europe 1815–1975. A Data Handbook in two Volumes. Volume 1. The Growth of Mass Democracies and Welfare States*, Frankfurt 1983, 266.

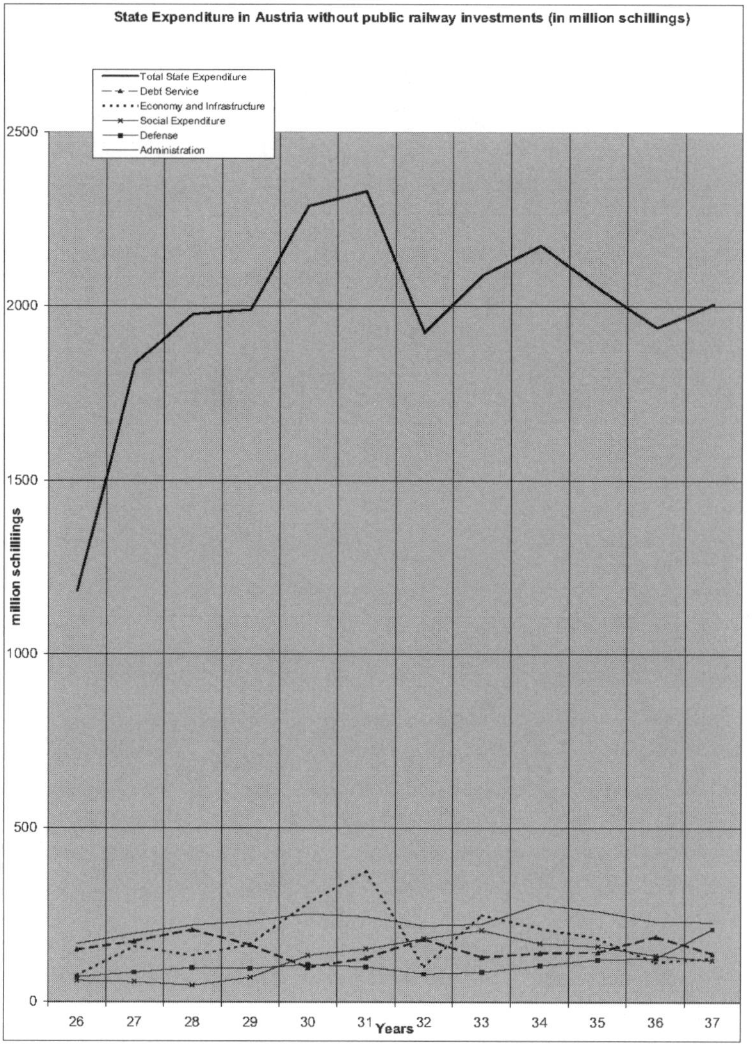

Figure 3.3.: State Expenditure in Austria without Public Railway Investments (in million schillings). Source: Statistisches Reichsamt (ed.), *Statistisches Jahrbuch für das Deutsche Reich*, vol. 56, Berlin 1937, 263.

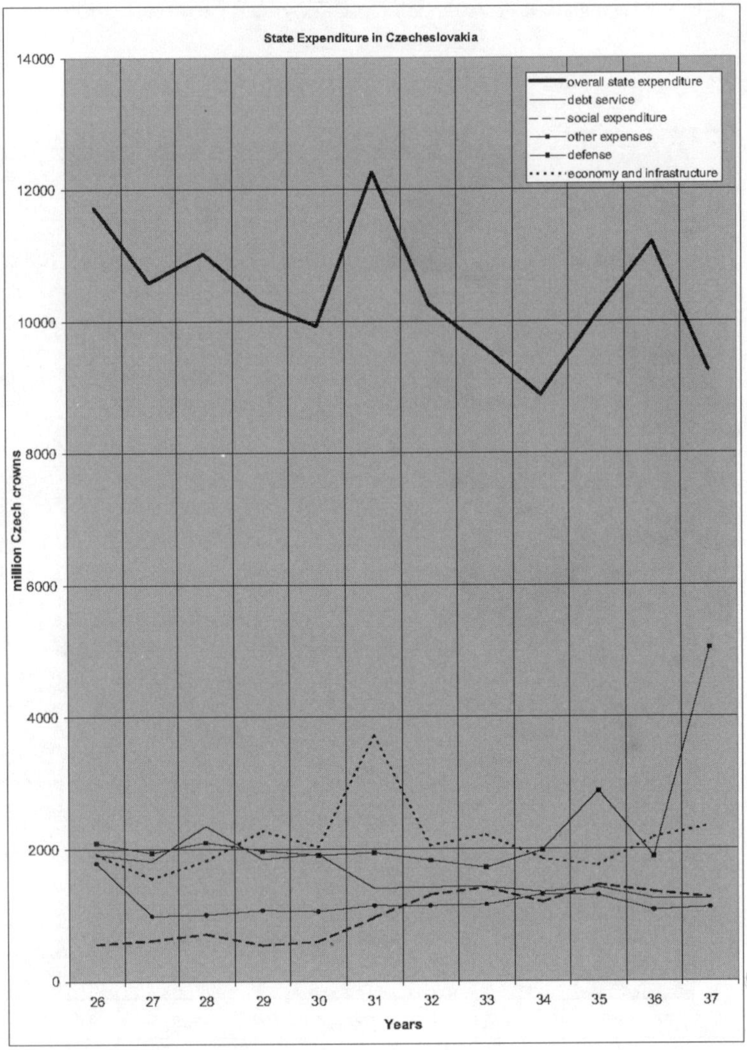

Figure 3.4.: State Expenditure in Czechoslovakia (in million Czech crowns). Source: Statistisches Reichsamt (ed.), *Statistisches Jahrbuch für das Deutsche Reich*, volume 56, Berlin 1937, 264.

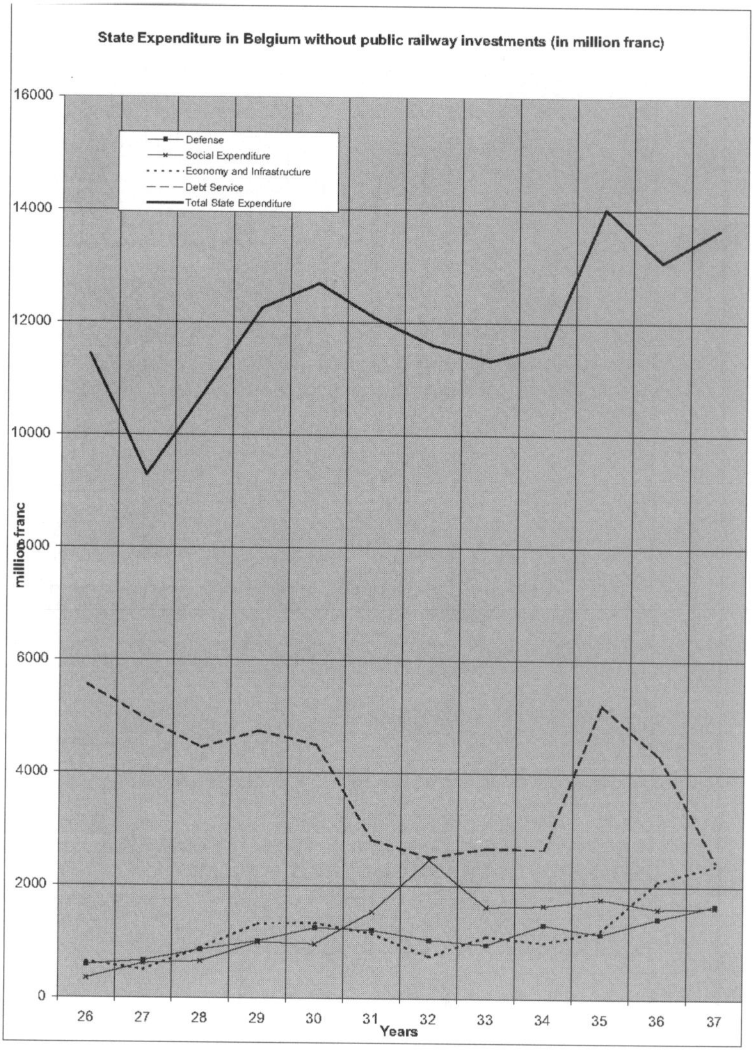

Figure 3.5.: State Expenditure in Belgium without Public Railway Investments (in million franc). Source: Statistisches Reichsamt (ed.), *Statistisches Jahrbuch für das Deutsche Reich*, volume 56, Berlin 1937, 260.

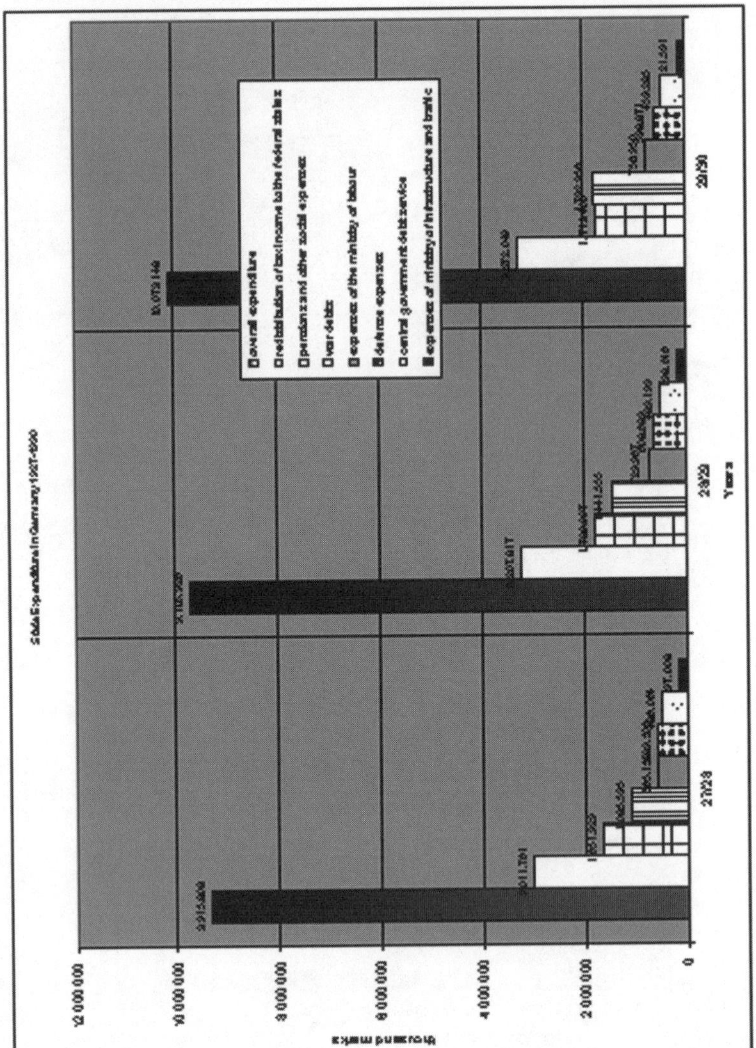

Figure 3.6.: State Expenditure in Germany, 1927–1930 (in thousand marks). Source: Statistisches Reichsamt (ed.), Statistisches Jahrbuch für das Deutsche Reich, volume 48, Berlin 1929, 415 ff.

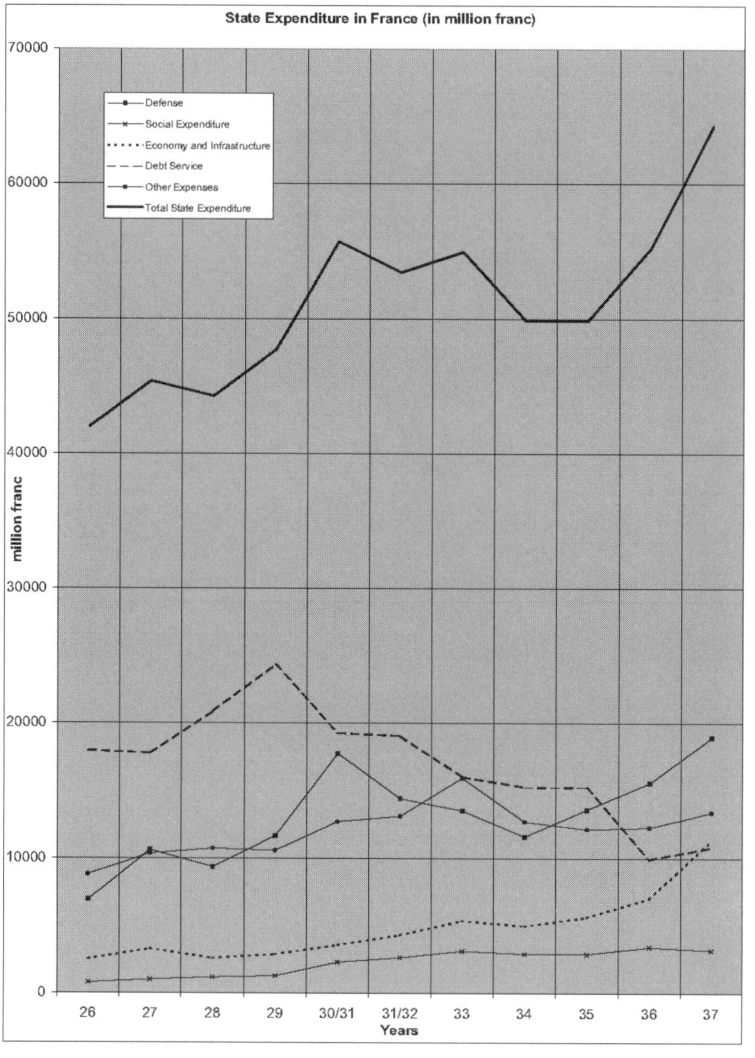

Figure 3.7.: State Expenditure in France (in million franc). Source: Statistisches Reichsamt (ed.), *Statistisches Jahrbuch für das Deutsche Reich*, volume 56, Berlin 1937, 261.

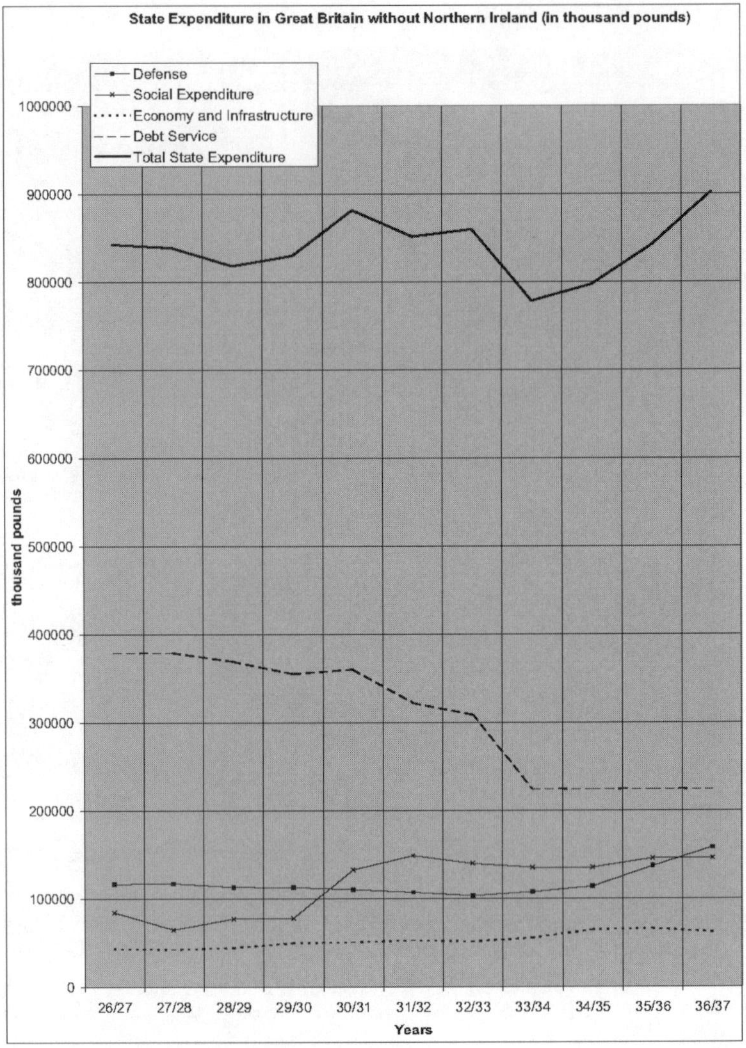

Figure 3.8.: State Expenditure in Great Britain without Northern Irland (in thousand pounds). Source: Statistisches Reichsamt (ed.), *Statistisches Jahrbuch für das Deutsche Reich*, volume 56, Berlin 1937, 261.

A study on Austrian joint-stock companies concluded that taxation of companies must have been extremely high and a burden to economic growth, as tax laws were traditionally anti-entrepreneurial.[168] Generally, the Austrian level of tax burden on business and industrial companies was comparable to that of Germany. Both countries had a tax burden level for enterprises quite above the European average. Thanks to a detailed study on comparative tax burden in several countries for the 1920s, conducted by contemporary German economists and based on extensive statistical material, we have detailed and reliable estimates.[169] The study concluded that overall tax levy for all forms of companies, including joint-stock companies, was highest in Germany.[170] Austrian taxation was nearly as high as German tax burden. In Austria, capital intensive enterprises, usually industrial companies, reached 80% of German taxation level. Labour intensive, i.e. firms within the services sector, and turnover intensive enterprises, i.e. firms mostly within the trading sector, reached between 90 and 97%. Generally, French taxation was between 47 and 33% below German levels. British, American and the majority of Italian taxation levels were 50% or more below German levels. To sum up, it is clear that German and Austrian tax burden on companies, including or excluding social security charges, was roughly twice as high as in France, Britain, Italy and the US.[171]

In contrast, general tax burden on wages and salaries was highest in Italy, Germany, France and Britain. Apart from the United States, taxation level on workers' and employees' income was lowest in Austria. This ranking shifts for higher income groups. In this case, German taxation level was the highest. Austrian tax burden was still the lowest.[172] On the one hand, Austrian taxation levels for enterprises were well above the European average, and on the other, the tax burden on employees and workers was the lowest. It seems that the productive sector was highly taxed, whereas private demand enjoyed an only mild tax load. However, it would be presumptuous to attempt to measure the effect of this on macroeconomic performance, but it is interesting to note that companies did not mention taxation levels as disproportionally burdensome.

Another vital aspect of state policy is public expenditure. A good contemporary source comparing state income and expenditure among the different sectors of several countries is the statistical yearbook published by the Statistisches Reichsamt. Its statistics allow an interesting comparative interpretation of the relation between fiscal policies and economic performance in Europe. At first glance, it is obvious how the relation between state income and state expenditure was similar in Austria, Great Britain, Belgium and France. This similarity is due to the effort in all these

168 Helmut Wiesbauer, *Die österreichischen Aktiengesellschaften 1918–1938, unter Berücksichtigung betriebswirtschaftlicher und rechtlicher Aspekte*, dissertation, Linz 1977, 90–119.

169 Statistisches Reichsamt (ed.), *Internationaler Steuerbelastungsvergleich. Die Steuer- und Soziallasten der gewerblichen und kaufmännischen Betriebe in Deutschland, Frankreich, Großbritannien, Italien, Österreich und den Vereinigten Staaten von Amerika. Einzelschriften zur Statistik des Deutschen Reichs*, Berlin 1933.

170 See: Die Hauptergebnisse der vorliegenden Untersuchung, ibid, 10.

171 Also see tables and comments in: Vierter Teil. Die Ergebnisse des rechtlichen und zahlenmäßigen internationalen Steuerbelastungsvergleichs, ibid, 593

172 See: Die Besteuerung der Löhne und Gehälter der Arbeitnehmer, ibid, 335 ff, 344 – 346.

countries to maintain a balanced budget and a stable currency, as a central part of the attempt to establish the pre-war gold standard.

According to the numbers of the Statistisches Reichsamt and of Fibich,[173] Austria seemed to have as much of an inclination for a small, but persistent government deficit than the other countries. The government intervention, due to the Creditanstalt crisis in 1931, is also very obvious. Spending policy was not much different. Britain was, in fact, very restrictive in the 30s, a time when its economy was booming. At the same time, French and Belgian expenditure was much higher than income in the 30s, when their economies were actually stagnating. Austrian spending policy was somewhat more moderate, but not as restrictive than British. The share of central government expenditure of national product was also very similar. In Austria, it was 16% of GNP in 1926 (or 12% of NDP), only slightly increased until the depression, and was 21.7% in 1936 (22.68% of NDP), but only because national product was much lower in the 30s.[174] In Germany, the share of central state expenditure of net domestic product in 1927/28 was around 11.8%,[175] but must have been considerably higher when expenditure of the federal state and the municipalities is included. In Britain, the share of NDP was much higher in 1928/29, with 18.8%, and remained on this level in the 30s.[176] In Belgium, where state expenditure policy was very similar to that of France,[177] the state expenditure's share of NDP was the highest, with 19.2% in 1927, 19.1% in 1930, and almost 21% in 1937.[178] Thus, Austrian spending and budget policy seemed to have been within the upper European level.

These numbers only provide a rough picture of the total central governments' involvement in the national economies of Europe and show that the restrictive currency and economic policies described above were compromised by increased public expenditure. In order to have a detailed look at economic policies, budget, expenditure and investment policies have to be regarded more closely. High state investment in infrastructure and in support for industry and export would reveal a more expansive, active and counter-cyclical policy. Such policies, though, did not exist in inter-war Europe. Not only in Austria, but in all states were budget policies restrictive, deflationary and pro-cyclical. There might have existed an interventionist under-current in the state administration,[179] but it never predominated policy-mak-

173 See figures 3.3 – 3.8 The figures for state expenditure of Austria from the Statistisches Reichsamt and from Fibich only vary slightly. Fibich has higher numbers for the years 1926, 1936 and 1937.

174 Own calculation with figures from Österreichisches Institut für Wirtschaftsforschung, *Monatsberichte* 14, Fibich and Reichsamt.

175 Own calculation with numbers from Reichsamt, 1929 and Flora, Kraus and Pfenning, *State, Economy, and Society* 2. The NDP level of 1927 and 1928 is taken from the average of the two years.

176 Own calculation with numbers from Reichsamt, 1929, and Peter Flora, ibid. NDP level of 1928/29 is taken from the average of the two years.

177 Reliable figures for France are not available to make a useful estimate of the ratio between expenditure and national product.

178 Calculated from Flora, Kraus and Pfenning, *State, Economy, and Society* 2. and Statistisches Reichsamt, 1937.

179 Fritz Weber suggests "die Existenz einer interventionistischen Unterströmung im Staatsapparat." Weber, "Staatliche Wirtschaftspolitik", 534.

ing. For example, the Geneva Protocols have been regarded as extremely restrictive for future policy-making in Austria, because financial funds for state investment were difficult to obtain.[180] Yet, observing state expenditure policy in other countries where no such restrictions existed, this claim seems to be overstated.

In Austria, where investment rates should have been very low, the share of state expenditure for economy and infrastructure of overall expenditure was 8.66% in 1927,[181] 6.7% in 1928, 16.3% in 1931 (due to the Creditanstalt crisis), and 8.9% in 1935. However, in Britain, the ratio was even lower, with 5.14% in 1926/27, 5.7% during the crisis in 1931 and was at its "peak" in 1936/37, with 6.8%. State expenditure for economy and infrastructure was somewhat higher in France, but not much, with a share of 7.17% in 1927, and 6.3% in 1930/31. It slowly increased during the stagnation in the 30s, to 11.2% in 1935 and 17.6% in 1937. As expected, the numbers were very similar in Belgium. The Czechoslovak Republic had, among the countries analysed, the highest share of investment in the economy and infrastructure of overall expenditure, with 14.68% in 1927, 30% in 1931, and 19% in 1936.[182] Generally, state investment behaviour in Austria was within the average European trend. At first sight, the inclination of the central German government for investment in infrastructure and economy seems to have been the lowest, with 1.47% of expenditure in 1928/29.[183]

Of course, all of these numbers have to viewed with caution, and a comparison such as this is very difficult. For Germany, for example, this is particularly the case since central government income from taxes was redistributed to the federal states, which in turn, must have spent a large portion of this sum in investments for various purposes. The redistributed sum for the states amounted to 32.3% of overall central government expenditure in the year 1927/28. How much of this went to productive investment is difficult to measure. It must be assumed that a very large portion went into road building, railway investment and municipal and other public construction. Therefore, the low rate of 1.47% is only correct for central government expenditure, but not for total public expenditure.

180 "Der Spielraum der staatlichen Wirtschaftspolitik war in den Jahren 1923 bis 1926 äußerst gering. Aus Furcht vor Konflikten mit dem Völkerbundkommissär wurden die Investitionsausgaben des Bundes von vornerein niedrig angestetzt und eine Reihe von Projekten überhaupt nicht in Angriff genommen [...]."Ibid, 538.

181 According to Fibich's numbers, the ratio would even be 10.68% in 1927, 10.77% in 1928. For 1931, Fibich excluded the costs for the Creditanstalt reconstruction, so that the share of investment of overall expenditure was only 4.2%. For 1935, only 5%.

182 For all these numbers see diagrammes expenditure in Britain, Austria, France, and Belgium. Figures for Czechoslovakia in Statistisches Reichsamt, *Jahrbuch* 1937, 264 (international survey).

183 Own calculation from figures in Statitisches Reichsamt (ed.), *Jahrbuch* 1929, vol. 48, 415 ff.

3.5.2. Public Investment in Austria and Germany

For Austria, though, detailed information on government investment is available.[184] Public investment behaviour can be clearly divided into two periods: The time after inflation and before 1931, and the time after the depression until 1937.[185] In the 20s, investment level was with around 9% of total budget expenditure much higher than in the 30s, with only around 3.2%.[186] Following the year 1923 until the depression, a large portion of investment costs went into investments for railway infrastructure. This amounted to 80% of all state investments in 1923, about 56% in 1926, 41% in 1928 and 61.3% in 1930. Between 1923 and 1930, 625.5 million schillings[187] were invested for railroad infrastructure; altogether that was not even 6% of the GNP of 1927. Most of these funds were used for two electrification programmes, that were backed up by the government decision of March 1920 to provide state financial support.[188] These programmes included the electrification of railway lines mostly in the Western part of the country,[189] the purchase of electrical engines and the construction of railway owned hydroelectrical power plants, such as those in Mallnitz, Stubachtal or Spulersee.[190]

Investment funds were very difficult to obtain, since the League of Nations commissioner was reluctant to give away capital for investment. In 1927, electrification programmes were almost terminated altogether, due to various interests. On the one hand, coal became cheaper as the successor states were interested in regaining the Austrian railway as one of their main customers after inflation, and on the other, funds from the League loan had been fairly expensive and were running-out by the end of that year.[191] The railroad electrification was indeed a major provider of demand for the four large Austrian electrical engineering companies in the 20s, and the threatened stop or reduction of electrification could have lowered business activity considerably. Therefore, at the beginning of 1928, these firms offered a plan to finance future electrification east of Salzburg. They offered a price of 150 million schillings and wanted to raise the capital for this themselves, as anticipatory credit to be repaid by the railroad. Eventually, the railroad management did not go along with this scheme and nothing came of it.

In spite of its significance for demand, railroad electrification remained fairly limited in Austria and not even 17% of tracks had been modernised by 1940.[192] Meanwhile, the electrical engineering industry found other sources of demand in

184 Thanks to Fibich's work *Die Entwicklung der österreichischen Bundesausgaben.*

185 Fibich, 149 and Weber, "Staatliche Wirtschaftspolitik," 531 ff.

186 Weber, ibid, 536.

187 Fibich, 143.

188 The "electrification law" was ratified July 23, 1920. Hans Freihsl, *Bahn ohne Hoffnung. Die österreichischen Eisenbahnen von 1918 bis 1938*, Vienna 1971, 73 ff.

189 The following tracks were electrified by 1930: Salzburg-Innsbruck-Arlberg-Bregenz, Wörgl-Kufstein, Innsbruck-Brenner, Feldkirch-Buchs, Attnang/Puchheim-Steinach/Irding. Fibich, 139.

190 Weber, "Staatliche Wirtschaftspolitik," 540 ff.

191 Freihsl, 79.

192 Fibich, 141.

the late 20s.[193] Not only this branch of industry benefited, but also rare orders for carriages provided large scale, but short-term, employment to such firms as Simmeringer and the Alpine. Only in 1924, when 1000 carriages were ordered, and in 1927/28, when 6700 carriages were ordered,[194] was domestic demand and business activity high enough for some of the companies of the machine building industry.

The government planned larger investments after the rest of the League loan was used up, and approval for a new loan was requested by the Austrian government from the financial control committee of the League. Investments on the scale of 722 million schillings were planned between 1927 and 1932, but not much came of it. At first, the approval for the loan came only by 1930, and secondly, the CA crisis and increasing depression the next year made further international floatation impossible. In 1930, the first slice of the international federal loan ("Internationale Bundesanleihe") released proceeds of 294.6 million schillings, the majority of which (248.4 million) went into investments for the railroad and the postal system.[195] Thus, 1930 was the year with the highest Austrian state investment in the inter-war period. The second slice could not be floated, because of the Creditanstalt crisis. The investments of 1928 and 1929 had to be financed by the running state budget. Thus, in 1930 once more heavy investment took place for electrification of the railroad and postal system with the help of this so-called investment loan. After this year though, central government investment became insignificant.

Usually, the rest of total state investment funds were utilised for the federal enterprises,[196] and almost all of these funds went to the federal postal system, the most significant of them. The others were insignificant and hardly worth their names. Between 1923 and 1930, 376.5 million schillings[197] were invested for the construction of long distance cables and the extension of the telephone system. Some of the funds came from remnants of the League loan, but the majority was provided by the running state budget. Some electrical engineering companies benefited from these investments. Yet, the sum invested was hardly 3.4% of the 1927 GNP.

Another form of investment was state and municipal support for housing construction, mainly in Vienna. This certainly helped many construction companies in the vicinity of the city. The central government only provided minimum funds for this, whereas the municipality of the city of Vienna invested higher sums for housing than the total value of state investment between 1924 and 1927.[198] Between 30 and 40% of the Vienna city expenditure was invested for housing construction only.[199] This was not an unusual situation in Europe and did not mark out the Austrian government as especially restrictive in this field. For example, the German central government invested only 5.79 million marks for housing in 1928/29, a minute fraction

193 Freihsl, 80.

194 Weber, "Staatliche Wirtschaftspolitik,"543.

195 Ibid, 544 and 545.

196 These were the postal system, federal forest districts, the federal coal iron and steel industries with only 350 employees, federal printing press, theatres among others. Fibich, 133.

197 Ibid, 143.

198 See figures from Weber, "Staatliche Wirtschaftspolitik," and Fibich..

199 Weber, ibid., 539.

of expenditure (not even one percent). Here, just as in Austria, most of housing was financed by the local municipalities. In the fiscal year 1927/28, 385.9 million marks were invested by the federal states for housing, while the central government only invested 69.4 million. In Austria, Vienna city investment was just so much more significant and obvious due to the fact that approximately one third of the population lived in the capital. That this contributed to the lower unemployment figures in Vienna[200] is questionable, as a large portion of Austrian industry and trade was concentrated in the city, naturally lowering its rate of unemployment, compared to the overall rate of the country.

An export support scheme and support for tourism were the only direct state intervention for private enterprises. The export support scheme was mainly for deliveries to the USSR, and in the 30s, directed against the depreciation of Western currencies. Large orders were coming from the Soviet state in the late 20s, especially for expensive modern equipment. However, as this government lacked foreign exchange, payment was very uncertain and business was risky. Western companies were in a difficult situation. On the one hand, payment could not always be expected or ensued reluctantly, but on the other hand, Austrian, as well as German, companies were eager for large and expensive orders from abroad during times of stagnating exports and declining orders. Therefore, the state, and later, on a smaller scale, the city of Vienna and some of the federal states offered a payment guarantee scheme for certain export items, such as electrical engineering goods and other machinery. If there was no payment for deliveries, the Austrian state partially compensated the losses. We will see this in more detail below when discussing company histories.[201] Again, the effect of this was minute, as these costs hardly amounted to 1% of total expenditure.[202]

Another, but more indirect, help of the state for industrial enterprises were tax reductions of various kinds, to make capital formation for investment easier.[203] These laws for tax reduction were already implemented in the early 20s and extended in the second half of the decade. To improve the conditions of capital raising for investment, the state, for example, waived the extremely high taxes on dividend payments and profits. Tax and fee reductions for privately floated industrial loans and bonds were also realised. Needless to say, the impact of this is hardly noticeable, but was certainly not harmful. It did not alleviate the severe structural faults of the domestic capital market and basically left the private firms on their own to raise sufficient capital. To conclude, it can be maintained that the second half of the 20s was a period with the highest state investment rates in Austria.

However, did these public investments really have an effect on growth and was state investment policy unusually restrictive? Certainly the electrical engineering

200 Weber, ibid.

201 See 3.2.7. a.)

202 Fibich, 113 and 114.

203 Bundesministerium für Handel und Wiederaufbau (ed.), *100 Jahre im Dienste der Wirtschaft, Vol. 2. Aus der Tätigkeit des Handelsministeriums in Vergangenheit und Gegenwart*, Vienna 1961, chapter: Die Industriepolitik und Industrieförderung, 56 and 57. See also Wiesbauer, 120–133.

firms benefited from these investments, but, as we shall see below, a big chunk of their orders still came from domestic demand in the form of orders from the hydro-power plants and from demand abroad. It is doubtful if the investments, which affected mainly four or five companies, caused the continuation of economic growth after 1928.[204]

Once again, Austrian public investment behaviour fits into the overall European trend and must be compared with other countries. In fact, Austrian state investment expenditure was not unusually low or restrictive compared to Germany. German state support for the railway was much lower than in Austria. Between the fiscal years 1924/25 and 1928/29, the central government invested only between 300 thousand and 4.4 million marks annually into the railroad, a minute fraction of gross expenditure.[205] In 1929/30, expenditure for the ministry of traffic, the railroad, the expenses for inland waterways, expenses for sea shipping, for roads and for air traffic together, only came to 1.2% of total expenditure.[206] In Austria, the average ratio for the central government amounted to roughly 1.3% in 1930, but that was for the railways only.

To estimate German overall public investment effort and to compare it with Austrian is very difficult, because the expenditure of the German federal states, the municipalities and the Reich central government would have to be included in the calculation. Adding public expenditure for housing, agriculture, industry, trade and traffic for the Reich, the municipalities and the federal states and comparing this figure to NDP, one comes to the result that about 6.6% of net domestic product was invested by the public in the year 1927/1928.[207] This was about 5.6% of GNP at current prices.[208] In fact, the largest invested sum came from the municipalities alone, with nearly 75% of overall public investment. Otherwise, public investment would only have been 1.54% of NDP or 1.4% of GNP at current prices. Comparing Vienna housing investment, state agricultural help and overall investment with Austrian national product one comes to the result that 4% of NDP was invested by the central government and the Viennese city in 1928.[209] That was 3.7% of GNP at

204 Weber: "Es ist nicht von der Hand zu weisen, daß – wie manche Zeitgenossen vermuteten – das Fortdauern der österreichischen Konjunktur über das Jahr 1928 hinaus auf die 'großen Investitionen des Bundes und der Gemeinde Wien' zurückzuführen war." Weber, "Staatliche Wirtschaftspolitik," 544.

205 Statistisches Reichsamt, *Jahrbuch 1930*, vol. 49, 466.

206 Own calculation from Statistisches Reichsamt, *Jahrbuch 1929*, see: expenses for Reichsverkehrsministerium, 418.

207 Own calculation from Statistisches Reichsamt, *Jahrbuch 1930*, 480–484. NDP figure calculated from the average of 1927/28, from Flora, Kraus and Pfenning, *State, Economy, and Society* 2, 337 ff. Adding federal state, municipal and central government investment for "Wohnungswesen" and "Wirtschaft und Verkehr", one comes to the conclusion that 4846.3 million marks were invested in 1927/28. 3633.3 million were only invested by the municipalities!

208 Own calculation from the average GNP figure of 1927 and 1928 (85,645.5 million marks at current prices). See: Albrecht Ritschl and Mark Spoerer, "Das Bruttosozialprodukt in Deutschland nach den amtlichen Volkseinkommens- und Sozialproduktstatistiken 1901–1995," in: *Jahrbuch für Wirtschaftsgeschichte. Volkswirtschaftliche Gesamtrechnungen im internationalen Vergleich*, 2, 1997, 44.

209 Own calculation from Fibich 143, 175 and Weber, "Zum Investitionsverhalten," 539.

current prices.[210] This is lower than in Germany, but this figure excludes investments of all other Austrian municipalities. If Vienna city investment is excluded, then the central government invested 2.3% of NDP or 2.2% of GNP in 1928. That is higher than the German rate of investment for the central government. Thus, Austrian public investment must have been well within the European average, since German public investment policy with its employment of large foreign loans has been considered fairly generous.

In all, Austrian tax burden and public investment behaviour were within the general European trend, which was, in turn, quite restrictive in the late 20s.

3.6. TRADE POLICY AND TRADE, 1925–1930

Another vital aspect of policy-making was trade policy.[211] For all small and advanced industrialised countries, as Austria, foreign trade was very important. The major stimulant of demand were export orders. In these countries, exports had a very high share of national product, while the export rate was declining and much smaller for larger industrialised countries. That did not mean that their economic growth was smaller, though, because a larger proportion of growth was domestically generated by a larger internal market. For example, while in Germany the share of exports of national income was declining from 22.1% in 1913 to 16.3% in 1928,[212] it was slightly rising in the territory of the First Austrian Republic from 22.7% in 1913 to 24.5% in 1928 of GNP at current prices.[213]

	Austria	Belgium	CSR	Denmark
Export Value:	2862	26,697	21,224	1541
Gross National Product:	11,678	48,200 (NDP)	71,400	5268
Export Share of GNP:	24.5%	55.4%	29.7%	29%

	Germany	France	UK	Italy
Export Value:	12,055	51,375	724	14.4
Gross National Product:	88,479	410,000	4899	164.2
Export Share of GNP:	13.6%	12.5%	14.7%	8.7%

Table 3.1.: Relation of exports to gross national product in 1928 (in million national currency at current prices). Source: Data from B.R. Mitchell, *European Historical Statistics 1750–1970*, New York 1978, 295 ff and 407 ff. Data for Austria from Österreichisches Institut für Wirtschaftsforschung, *Monatsberichte* 14, 41, at current prices. Data for Belgium for the year 1927. GNP of the CSR at constant 1929 prices. German GNP at constant 1929 prices.

210 GNP figure from Österreichisches Institut für Wirtschaftsforschung, *Monatsberichte* 14, 39.

211 On trade policy in general and in Germany specifically, see: Matthias Schulz, *Deutschland, der Völkerbund und die Frage der europäischen Wirtschaftsordnung 1925–1933. Beiträge zur deutschen und europäischen Geschichte*, vol. 19, Hamburg 1997.

212 Dietmar Petzina, Werner Abelshauser and Anselm Faust, *Materialien zur Statistik des Deutschen Reiches 1914– 1945. Sozialgeschichtliches Arbeitsbuch*, vol. 3, Munich 1978, 73.

213 Österreichisches Institut für Wirtschaftsforschung, *Monatsberichte* 14, 41.

While the share of exports of national product was much smaller in large countries, it was naturally much greater in smaller nations. This can be seen in table 3.1. The numbers must be viewed with care, because for Belgium net domestic product was taken for lack of data. Thus, its percentage share is too high in comparison with that of the other countries. It is still clear though, that it had one of the highest export rates in Europe. It was followed by the Czechoslovak Republic and Denmark, with nearly a 30% share. Among the small industrialised countries, Austrian exports had the smallest share of national product. Its low export rate could reveal a possible export deficit and a large unexploited export potential, which contributed to its poor performance. It suggests a direct connection between economic growth and export performance in small industrialised countries. While Belgian, Czechoslovak and Danish export rates were high, their economic performance was better than Austrian in the inter-war period. What caused Austrian export performance to be below average? The development of trade structures, direction, tariffs and policy-making is essential to economic performance in small industrialised countries and could possibly provide an answer.

The transformation of trade policy on an international level to intensifying protectionism, after the re-establishment of trade relations among the successor states, which occurred a few years after the end of the war, has been regarded as a major obstacle for economic growth in Austria and Eastern Europe in the late 20s. This seemed to manifest itself in Austria in slow export growth and in a constant trade deficit in the 20s along with an average import surplus of one billion schillings annually. Terms of trade remained passive and export performance improved only slightly, export value increasing about 21%[214] between 1924 and 1928. The following year, the export rate actually declined again. Nevertheless, the Austrian trade structure was better than in most successor states and its per capita export rate was one of the highest among industrialised countries.[215] Furthermore, the trade deficit was largely due to import surpluses in imports of foodstuffs and raw materials, especially coal, while the terms of trade for finished products was highly active.[216] Just as most successor states, apart from Czechoslovakia, Austria suffered from a decline in trade after the war. In Poland and Romania, the levels of trade in 1924 were nearly 50% below their 1913 levels. Hungarian trade per capita level declined 25% below pre-war figures. Bulgaria, Czechoslovakia and Yugoslavia were affected much less or not at all.[217] The Austrian export level never regained pre-war level and was, in

214 Own calculation from Österreichisches Institut für Wirtschaftsforschung, *Monatsberichte* 14, 42.

215 Only Switzerland, Belgium, Great Britain, Sweden and France had higher per capita export rates. Haas, *Außenhandelspolitik*, 4.

216 Karl Bachinger and Hildegard Hemetsberger-Koller, Österreich von 1918 bis zur Gegenwart, in: Wolfram Fischer (ed.), *Handbuch der Europäischen Wirtschafts- und Sozialgeschichte. Band 6. Europäische Wirtschafts- und Sozialgeschichte vom Ersten Weltkrieg bis zur Gegenwart*, Stuttgart 1987, 546. Österreichisches Statistisches Zentralamt, *Der Aussenhandel Österreichs*, 22.

217 Z. Drabek, "Foreign Trade, Performance and Policy," in: M. C. Kaser and E. A. Radice (eds.), *The Economic History of Eastern Europe 1919–1975, Volume 1. Economic Structure and Performance between the TwoWars*, Oxford 1985, 384/385.

1924, nearly 25% below its 1913 level.[218] Thus, on the one hand, Austrian export structure was much more advanced than that of most Eastern European countries, but on the other, growth of outbound trade was limited after the war, as pre-war levels were not reached again. Clearly, there was retarded export potential. While German exports expanded 87%,[219] Austrian grew only 21% between 1924 and 1928.

Examining the increase of protectionism (especially in Eastern Europe) and the relative stagnation of world trade in the inter-war period, and considering the high export dependence of the Austrian economy, there is a large degree of truth to the notion that trade policy harmed economic growth. Nevertheless, protectionism was not so much an intentional aspect of politics, which expressed itself in higher tariffs which retarded growth, but was the expression of a structural problem of the world economy, of overcapacities abroad that caused declining trade and a shift to new, modern production and sales structures. Due to these large scale shifts and distortions of the world industry, vital and influencial national producers in large advanced and in small underdeveloped countries pressed forward economic nationalism and protectionism. This trend was unfavourable for small advanced countries, but essentially trade conditions forced them to turn to protectionist policies as well. Austria was a perfect example of this process, as its policy intentions were the resumption of free trade until the beginning of the depression, but had to adjust its policy as a response to protectionism and structural transformations abroad. Austrian policy only reacted to pressures from the outside. The main effect of the structural changes in the world economy and trade was increased pressure of competition, especially on the older industries and on agriculture. Competitive pressure was particularly great on small countries that suffered from stagnating world-wide market demand, fall of prices and overcapacities in production facilities of many industrial sectors. As a result, domestic pressure from agriculture and from certain sectors of industry forced a policy change in Austria by the mid 20s.

In 1925, the Austrian state introduced new and increased, but still moderate, customs tariffs that were far below the tariffs of the successor states. These tariffs were comparably liberal and were intended as a bargaining tool for future trade negotiations.[220] The goal of Austrian trade policy was still the promotion of international free trade,[221] since the economy was dependent on industrial exports. On this basis, a large number of trade agreements were concluded in 1925 with Germany, France, the Czechoslovak Republic and Yugoslavia. With some of these countries, agreements included unlimited most-favoured nation clauses. It was also possible to attain tariff reductions. In all, new trade contracts did not entail an upswing of Austrian exports to these areas, as the new trade agreements and tariffs were not

218 Own calculation from Österreichisches Institut für Wirtschaftsforschung, *Monatsberichte* 14, 42

219 Own calculation from Statistisches Reichsamt, *Jahrbuch 1930*, 190.

220 The new customs tariffs of 1925 and 1926 were an answer to demands from industry and intented as a bargaining tool against other nations to improve export conditions of Austrian products. The strategy was eventually ineffective, because of Austria's insignificant position as an importer and consumer of foreign goods. See article "Die Zolltarifnovelle," in: *Der Österreichische Volkswirt*, 24.4.1926.

221 Nautz, *Handelspolitik*, 537 ff.

sufficient for the export needs of industry.[222] At the same time, a fall in agricultural prices on the international markets also brought more pressure on policy makers from representatives of Austrian agricultural interests. In 1926 and 1927, Austrian tariffs for agrarian and certain industrial products were raised again, pushing Austrian trade policy increasingly toward protectionism.[223] This development culminated in the customs tariff increases of 1930 and 1931, which marked the country's final move toward protectionism. The new tariffs mostly favoured the interest of agriculture, and many representatives from industries felt disadvantaged. The increasing difficulties for agricultural imports into Austria also caused more difficulties for Austrian industrial products to be exported to the successor states, as these were dependent upon exports in agriculture to maintain the purchasing power to buy industrial products. By and large, Austrian trade policy remained very liberal until the beginning of the depression in 1930.[224] Meanwhile, all of the Central and Eastern European countries isolated their economies more and more, by continuously increasing their import tariff rates.[225]

Despite tariff increases, Austrian rates were still the lowest in all of Europe. In 1927, the average Austrian tariff rate was 18% of value, while it was between 30 and 43% in the successor states.[226] In all of Europe, only in Belgium and in Switzerland were tariff rates lower than in Austria with 11 and 16.8% respectively.[227] In Eastern Europe, protectionism increased substantially in the inter-war period; right after the war under emergency circumstances, and more moderately since the mid 20s until the depression. Only the depression marked the final and radical move to strong protectionism.

At first sight, there seemed to have been two factors that seriously harmed export growth in Austria: Increasing protectionist policies, and the decline and stagnation of Eastern Europe as a market for Austrian finished and semi-finished products. It is true that the countries of the successor states and Eastern Europe remained an important export market for the Austrian economy. But these countries, such as Hungary, Yugoslavia, Poland, Bulgaria and Romania, all had predominantly agricultural economies with the majority of their actively working population employed in this field.[228] Most of their income came from exports of primary agricultural products, while manufacturing had only a small role in their export expansion and as a source of income. Yet, exports in agricultural products were stagnating in the 20s and were depressed in the early 20s and at least until 1926 (balance of trade and prices for agricultural products improved only between 1926 and 1928), mainly contributing

222 Ibid.

223 Kernbauer, *Währungspolitik*, 234 and 235.

224 Österreichisches Statistisches Zentralamt, *Aussenhandel*, 14 and 15.

225 Gross, 107 and 108.

226 See chart "Zollsätze der Nachfolgestaaten 1925 und 1927," in: Fritz Weber, "Die wirtschaftliche Entwicklung," 31.

227 See table 7.63: General tariff levels in Europe 1913–1931, in: Kaser and Radice, *The Economic History of Eastern Europe*, 476.

228 Yugoslavia was with 77% of the working population in agriculture at the high end and Hungary with 54% at the bottom. Drabek, 402.

to the fall of income of these countries and making them less profitable markets for Austrian exports. The world-wide decline in agriculture had caused a fall in prices, a raise of tariff walls for agricultural products, and a fall or at least a stagnation of purchasing power of those countries that heavily depended on exports of primary products. Most affected by these changes were the countries of South America and of Central and Eastern Europe.

Several factors contributed to this process, such as population pressures in these countries which limited productivity and the inability to increase exports in agriculture, instigated by a world-wide agricultural crisis. This was essentially caused by overproduction which was intensified by war and by increasing yields, especially in the US.[229] Moreover, the international market had changed dramatically since the war, as prices constantly dropped and protection was improved in importing industrialised countries that had been able to increase their yields considerably after the war.[230] Another problem was that even the countries with semi-industrial economies, such as Poland and Hungary, were unable to diversify their export structures to counter the dependence on primary products. That would have raised exports which would have contributed to the growth of national income, factors, which in turn, could have made their markets more attractive.[231] Besides the already mentioned decline in agricultural productivity as a result of land reforms after the war, competitiveness of these largely agricultural economies declined more and more. This led to a further decline in income and purchasing power.

This, together with the progressing industrialisation in these countries, made this area a less favourable market for the Austrian export industry than before the war. At the same time, the successor states pursued a policy of industrialisation, which naturally supported the creation of enterprises and plants of the older branches of industry.[232] Due to lack of structures in these countries (apart from the Czechoslovak Republic), such as resources for research, finance and industrial organisation, the production of mostly simple and less modern industries with low technology content grew fairly rapidly in the 20s and 30s. The emphasis was on simple consumer goods industries, such as food processing and textiles industries, on some older capital goods industries, especially iron and steel, and on the extraction of raw materials, like oil in Romania and coal in Poland.[233] This development was especially the case for Poland and Hungary. In these countries, some more advanced producer goods

229 Contemporary economists saw the roots of the agricultural crisis in overproduction, which in turn, was seen as speeded up by the war and essentially caused by intensifying mechanisation of agricultural production in the modern countries. This limited export outlets of the underdeveloped and primarily agricultural exporting countries of Eastern Europe. See: N. Jasny, "Die neuzeitliche Umstellung der überseeischen Getreideproduktion und ihr Einfluß auf den Weltmarkt," in: Deutsches Institut für Konjunkturforschung (ed.), *Vierteljahreshefte zur Konjunkturforschung*, special issue 16, Berlin 1930.

230 Drabek, 406.

231 Ibid, 408.

232 On industrialisation structure and state support in these areas see: Alice Teichova, *Kleinstaaten*, 129 ff.

233 Sidney Pollard, *Peaceful Conquest. The Industrialisation of Europe 1760–1970*, Oxford 1981, 288 ff.

industries also developed, but only with a very low growth rate, such as iron and steel as well as engineering and chemicals.[234] Metallurgy and engineering had quite a substantial share in industrial production in these two countries, with nearly one quarter of overall industrial production. The industrial structure of the even lesser developed countries, as Yugoslavia, Romania and Bulgaria, was largely limited to the extraction and primary processing industries, for example food processing.[235] As a whole, the agricultural sector of the economy continued to play the major role in growth and development in this area.

The consequence for the Austrian economy was that many of its exports companies not only had to deal with lower purchasing power on these markets, but faced severe competition and protective trade barriers in the respective countries. The result was that the older industries in Austria, whose counterparts were supported in the industrialisation process by the governments of Eastern Europe, had declining exports sales or could not export at all any longer to their former essential markets. Not only was there more competition, but the trade tariffs were directed against manufactured products that were now increasingly produced in their own countries. High tariffs (more than 40% of value) were basically directed against the products of the older industries of the already advanced countries, such as textiles, simple engineering and iron and steel products. For example, textile products, which had the largest share of the total value of Austrian exports in the late 20s,[236] had to face a tariff rate[237] of 294.3% of value in Romania, 49.6% in Poland and "only" 30% in Hungary and Yugoslavia.[238] Paper products also suffered from high tariffs, running to 63.1% of value in Poland, 49.6% in Romania and 32.7% in Yugoslavia.[239] For comparison, tariffs ranged between 8.7% in Belgium and 19.4% in the rest of Europe. Thus, the expensively manufactured products of the industrial sectors of the successor states, largely consisting of older industries, were protected by high tariffs. This was part of a vicious circle. The result of the high tariffs was basically an expensive import substitution, which in turn, increased the cost of domestic production and lowered competitiveness in these countries. In connection with missing structures and capital scarcity, the industries of the successor states could never match world-wide productivity and competition and remained dependent on imports of highly advanced and expensive industrial products.

In Eastern Europe, products with a high technological content, such as complex engineering products from the electrical engineering industries and vehicles, enjoyed lower tariffs of only up to 15% of value.[240] Western and Austrian firms of the

234 Alice Teichova, "Chapter 5. Industry," in: Kaser and Radice, *The Economic History of Eastern Europe 1919–1975*, Volume 1, 239–242.

235 Ibid, 242.

236 See calculations below for Austrian exports structure, 2.8.

237 All rates refer to the year 1927.

238 See chart "Zollbelastung in Prozenten des Wertes für Warengruppen," in: The Austrian National Committee, *Zollhöhe und Warenwerte*, 3.

239 Ibid, 15.

240 See chart "Low, medium and high tariff sectors in Romania, Poland, Hungary, Yugoslavia and Bulgaria 1927", in: Drabek, 411.

more modern branches of industry did not face great problems in maintaining their exports to this area, because the tariffs were much lower for their complex products that could not be produced in the lesser developed countries. As stated previously, this is apparent in the tariff structures in Eastern Europe. Metal products faced fairly moderate tariffs of around 30%. In lesser developed Yugoslavia, Poland and Romania, tariffs for engines were only between 11.3% and 23.1% of value.[241] In more developed Hungary and Czechoslovakia, rates were 32 and 33.7% respectively. For agricultural machinery, rates were low (between 14.6 and 19.7%) in Yugoslavia, Poland and Romania. These were naturally much higher in Hungary and Czechoslovakia, where such machines were manufactured. Here, tariffs amounted to 24.9 and 20.2% respectively. In the three lesser developed countries, rates for vehicles were really low, down to 6.3%. Electrical items as consumer goods, such as vacuum cleaners, telephones or boilers suffered from high import duties. Electrical items as investment goods, such as large pieces of machinery (as for example generators) enjoyed moderate rates between 15.1% and 20.5% in the three lesser developed countries. In the countries with electrical engineering industries, Czechoslovakia and Hungary, rates settled around 30%.[242] Expensive consumer goods were probably taxed higher since they were seen as unnecessary and expensive imports, that could put pressure on savings and the balance of payments situation.[243]

However, the importance of the successor states as an export market has been exaggerated and the impact of tariffs must be differentiated. For the majority of the Austrian industrial sectors, trade conditions worsened in the area. For a few advanced sectors, tariffs were of hardly any relevance at all. As Eastern Europe became a less attractive market and the flexibility of the Austrian export industry was low, Austrian exports were only slightly able to re-direct themselves to more advanced markets. Its trade structure remained unbalanced and exports stagnated.

3.7. TRADE STRUCTURES AND DIRECTION

To measure the effects of trade restrictions, high tariffs and progressing overcapacities on export growth in Austria is problematical. Although protectionism in Eastern Europe was rising, the importance of their markets for Austria is questionable. Trade was most intensive with the neighbouring industrialised countries. One of the most important export areas for Austria remained the countries of the successor states and Eastern Europe as a whole, even though their share in Austrian exports declined after 1925.[244] However, besides these, Germany and, to a lesser extent, Italy were also very important trading partners. For analysis, those countries which represented the most important Austrian export markets, should be classified according to their stage

241 The Austrian National Committee, *Zollhöhe und Warenwerte*, 18.

242 Ibid, 19.

243 Drabek states that this kind of protectionism did not enhance industrialisation, since unproductive imports like consumer goods enjoyed substantial annual growth. 413–417.

244 See chart: Import und Export der wichtigsten Länder, in: Nautz, *Handelspolitik*, 550 and 551.

of economic development. Export countries can be separated into three groups: Trade with advanced industrialised, with semi-industrialised, and with underdeveloped countries. Germany, Czechoslovakia and Italy belong to the first group, Hungary and Poland to the second, and Bulgaria, Yugoslavia and Romania to the last group. Another group, belonging to the advanced industrialised countries that imported a large share of Austrian outbound trade were the following countries of Western Europe: Great Britain, France, Switzerland, the Netherlands, Belgium and Denmark. When observing distribution of exports and imports among these groups in table 3.2 and 3.3, the importance of the semi-developed and underdeveloped successor states and of the Eastern European countries for Austrian exports is not as significant. Certainly, the loss of income in these countries due to the fall in agriculture and the progressing simple industrialisation, increasing trade barriers and competition harmed sales, but the importance of these areas for the Austrian economy was declining in the 20s. By and large, over 30% of exports went to the three industrialised, advanced neighbour countries: Germany, Czechoslovakia and Italy. Over 50% of all exports went to the European industrialised countries, the three immediate neighbours and the countries of Western Europe.

Year	Advanced	Semi-industrialised	Underdeveloped	Western Europe	Rest
1924	34.2	18.5	18.2	16.1	13.0
1925	37.6	16.7	16.6	13.2	15.9
1926	34.0	14.3	16.6	15.7	19.4
1927	38.1	15.0	14.9	14.0	18.0
1928	38.8	14.0	14.1	14.4	18.7
1929	38.2	12.3	13.9	16.2	19.4
1930	38.8	10.9	13.4	19.0	17.9

Table 3.2.: Percentage share of groups of countries of the total value of Austrian exports. Source: Calculated from Österreichisches Statistisches Zentralamt, *Aussenhandel*, 31/32. Advanced countries are Germany, Italy, and the CSR. Semi-industrialised countries are Hungary and Poland. Under-developed countries are Bulgaria, Yugoslavia and Romania. The Western European countries are Britain, France, Switzerland, Belgium, Denmark and the Netherlands.

Year	Advanced	Semi-industrialised	Underdeveloped	Western Europe	Rest
1924	44.7	19.2	9.1	12.8	14.2
1925	40.8	19.6	9.4	11.0	19.2
1926	40.4	21.7	10.9	11.5	15.5
1927	39.5	18.3	12.1	12.7	17.4
1928	41.5	17.5	9.4	12.9	18.7
1929	42.7	18.7	8.4	12.2	18.0
1930	42.5	18.4	10.9	11.6	16.6

Table 3.3.: Percentage share of groups of countries of the total value of Austrian imports. Source: Table 3.2

Thus, protectionism in Eastern Europe, where it became especially pronounced, was less significant for Austrian exports. Protectionism, trade barriers, competition and overcapacities among the old branches of industry in the industrialised European countries seemed to be the main factors retarding export potential. Yet, once again, these policies were only a result, only a symptom of changing economic structures in Europe. Since the industrialised countries of Western Europe, Germany and the Czechoslovak Republic were also pursuing protectionist trade policies, their tariffs were more directed against advanced products. Furthermore, the advanced industries in these countries were not only protected against imports, but they were usually more competitive than their Austrian counterparts. For Austrian firms to be able to export to these markets, not only comparable productivity and competitiveness were required, but their products needed to be even more advanced or cheaper than the ones produced in Germany, Czechoslovakia or France, for example, to be able to overcome at first, tariffs and then, domestic competition.

Austrian trade structure changed slightly, to increasing outbound sales of semi-finished and primary products to the Western states and to exports of finished products to the less developed Eastern countries. However, this picture of trade flow is a caricature, to emphasise the change of structures of Austrian exports. By and large, only a minority of overall trade among all countries in Europe and in the world consisted of advanced finished products,[245] but had a greater average portion of trade among the industrialised countries. The change in Austrian trade, though, is expressed in the slow decline of the exports of finished goods during the interwar period. In spite of the low content of advanced finished products, such as electrical goods, motor vehicles or chemicals, in overall European trade, Austria seems to have been in an intermediate position. Primary and semi-finished products, such as magnesite brick and wood, were directed to the West, while advanced machinery and semi-finished products, that were able to surpass Austrian tariffs and could compete on the domestic market, were imported. Only very advanced finished products, such as specialised machinery and automobiles, luxury goods, but also finished textiles, were exported by Austria to the industrialised countries, which also had the purchasing power to afford these items. While Austria imported primary and semi-finished goods from the East, an increasing share of machinery and electrical items were exported to these areas in competition with finished products from the other industrialised countries.

Let us have a detailed look, at first at Austro-German trade flows: For example, the items with the largest share of total imports from Germany were electrical machinery and other machinery (14.6%) in 1928. These items were closely followed by iron and steel products (9.6%) and then by cotton and wool goods (9.2%).[246] Other items were chemicals, paint and fuel. The Austrian tariff and the control of Austrian firms of the domestic market seemed to be able to keep out large numbers of German

245 Nearly 40% of world trade still consisted of exchanges of foodstuffs and raw materials among trading countries. Albert O. Hirschman, "The Commodity Structure of World Trade," in: *The Quarterly Journal of Economics*, Vol. 57, Cambridge, Massachusetts 1943, 574.

246 The following numbers calculated from Österreichisches Statistisches Zentralamt, *Aussenhandel*, chapter: Abschnitt III. Der Aussenhandel nach den wichtigsten Ländern, 71–83.

automobile imports, while domestic firms were unable to counter German imports of machinery. The massive imports of electrical machinery is especially surprising, as Austria had four very large electrical engineering and numerous machine building companies that had a hard time utilising their full capacity.[247] This case shows that superior productivity and competitiveness circumvented tariffs, and that Austrian firms had not raised their productivity to a level comparable to other industrialised countries. In 1928, when the Austrian export level was at its peak, wood was the product with the highest share of total Austrian exports to Germany, with 23.3 %. Then came iron products (5.8%), then (surprisingly), automobiles and engines (5%), and finally cattle (4.7%). Other products exported included fur, skins, woollen yarn, wool wares, leather, metal wares, books and newspapers. Hence, apart from cars, mostly primary and semi-finished products were sold to Germany. Still, the country was one of the largest automobiles markets for Austria.

For imports from Czechoslovakia the case is not quite so clear. Imports consisted mostly of fuels, especially coal, textiles of various sorts, sugar, iron wares and wheat. Here, the source of competition for Austrian textiles firms is obvious, revealing the higher productivity and competitiveness of the Czechoslovak companies. Also, the division of labour between the two nations remained. While a lot of silk goods were imported, Austria exported cocoon to the CSR. In fact, in 1929, it had the largest share of overall Austrian exports to Czechoslovakia, with 11.4%. Other exports items from Austria comprised of silk goods, wood, iron and metal goods, and wool. Only 2.5% of all exports were electrical machinery, 2.47% were other machinery and only 1.8% were chemicals. Trade between Austria and Italy chiefly consisted of various foodstuffs, such as fruit and vegetables from Italy; and wood, wood wares, paper and iron and steel goods from Austria.

Trade with the most important Western European countries, especially with Great Britain, was similar to trade with Germany. The largest portion of imports from Britain were wool and cotton yarn and wares (44% in 1928), and leather, automobiles and engines (5.9%). Austrian exports to Britain were actually quite sophisticated. In 1930, the year with the highest export rate to Britain, nearly 9% of overall exports to that country were silk wares, 13.6% were hats and dresses, 11.6% other textiles, 7.5% leather, 5.5% paper. Even 12.5% consisted of electrical goods, such as light bulbs. Even though Czechoslovakia, Italy and France were fairly advanced countries, trade from and to these countries remained fairly primitive. Imports from France were not very complex and primarily consisted of wool and silk wares and fertiliser. The largest portion of exports to France consisted of wood (40% in 1930), and then paper, magnesite bricks, and few metal and iron wares and even fewer electrical goods. Advanced products were hardly exchanged, suggesting inward oriented growth of electrical engineering, automobiles and machine building industries. A substantial portion of exports consisted of electrical machinery, automobiles and engines only to Germany and Britain.

To the successor states, the structure of trade was a little different. The share of advanced products of total Austrian exports tended to be greater. To semi-industrialised Poland, a great share of exports were machinery and semi-finished goods.

247 See below microeconomic activity of the electrical engineering firms, 3.3.1.

Nearly 15% of Austrian exports to Poland were electrical goods and machinery and other machinery, 16.2% consisted of iron and metal wares, and also nearly 15% were wool products and leather in 1928. Over forty percent of imports from Poland were fuel and 45.8% were foodstuffs. To Hungary, mostly textile wares of various sorts, paper, and iron wares were sold; while imports consisted largely of wheat, cattle, flour, and pigs. In 1929, 15.5% of all exports to Yugoslavia were textiles, 18% were iron and metal wares, and 6.2% were machinery of various sorts. Similar to Hungary, Yugoslavia mainly sold agricultural products like foodstuffs, cattle and fodder to Austria. Trade with Romania was very similar.

Trade flows and export structure were quite complicated. It is hard to see how they were substantially altered by tariff walls. Naturally, countries that were underdeveloped or semi-industrialised raised tariffs for those products that they were producing and exporting themselves, such as semi-finished and primary products. Apart from agricultural products, these were mostly products from the textiles, food processing, paper and iron and steel industries. Tariffs for machinery, electrical engineering machinery and automobiles were lower. In the end, their imports depended on the purchasing power of their markets. The only effect of tariffs was the protection of expensively manufactured products from the old industries. For Austrian companies, there was an indirect impact. Firms of the modern industries naturally suffered less, not only because tariffs designed against their products tended to be lower, but mainly because their products faced less competition in these countries. The situation was reverse for the older industries, mainly because in iron and steel, textiles and paper, large overcapacities existed in all of Europe. Essentially, the advanced industrialised countries were the main trading partners of the Austrian export industry, and were the main cause for the slow growth of exports. These countries not only imposed tariffs, but their industries were much more competitive and productive. They were able to intrude into the protected and poor markets of Eastern Europe and offered serious competition for Austrian export products.

To summarise, it can be maintained that tariffs played a minor and indirect role in changing trade. They only reflected the real economic productivity and development level relations. The higher productivity was, the lower tariffs were, and to a lesser extent were they effective; and same vice versa. The lower economic development and productivity, the greater the necessity for protectionism and the stronger the effects of tariffs were. The main factors were the state of development of the economy of any country setting the rate of competitiveness, productivity of their firms and the purchasing power of their markets. Austria was troubled by two factors. The purchasing power of its former important market stagnated, so trade with other industrialised countries increased compared to the pre-war era. Yet, Austrian productivity and competitiveness had not grown as quickly as in these countries, causing exports to stagnate. Due to its advanced economic structure, Austria could not really raise tariffs high enough to close off its market, but its firms were unable to counter foreign competition effectively enough to dominate their own domestic market. Productivity was generally too low to intrude into foreign markets on a larger scale, that is to countries with greater purchasing power. The structure of its exports contributed to that.

3.8. EXPORT STRUCTURES

Pressure that limited Austrian export growth not only came from outside in the form of increasing competition, overcapacities and tariffs. Another problem for Austrian exports was that it focused on intra-European trade at a time when this was stagnating. Austria entered the stage of the international trade system as an export dependent country at a bad time. Before the war and after the Second World War, international trade grew much faster than in the inter-war period. In fact, during the time between the wars, trade grew much slower than world production.[248] In addition, trade in Europe grew more slowly than world trade. In this situation, Austrian exports were much more focused on trade with European countries than other industrialised European nations. Most advanced countries sold about one-third of their overall exports outside of Europe, [249] while 86.5% of Austrian exports were directed at European trading partners.[250] The stagnation of trade, especially in Europe, also revealed the intensifying inward oriented growth of modern industrial production in Europe during this time, one of the main factors of poor economic performance in small trade dependent countries as Austria. Trade grew especially for advanced finished products and stagnated in the old staple industries of which commodities Austrian exports had a large share.

Hence, the structure of Austrian exports provided a disadvantage for national foreign trade, because is was not as balanced and stratified as that of other advanced industrialised countries and was too reliant on a few commodities of the old and declining industries. Export structure was between that of advanced countries and that of semi-industrialised countries. The share of finished products of total exports was much higher than that of world trade (41% of exports composed of finished goods),[251] almost as high as that of Germany, and within the average of industrialised European countries. The finished product content was slightly declining in the 20s and 30s, but that was not unusual. In France, it was slightly declining as well as in Britain, while in Germany it was increasing at the same time from 71.5% in 1929 to 79.9% in 1937.[252]

However, the biggest problem was that the Austrian export structure was imbalanced. It depended, to a great degree, on a few commodities with high price and demand elasticity, that suffered from world overproduction. Table 3.4 reveals this imbalance of the Austrian export structure compared to the German. In addition, their world market demand and competitiveness had declined. For example, in 1929, nearly one-third (28.3%) of exports consisted of finished and semi-finished tex-

248 Svennilson, 168–202.

249 Calculated from table 49, ibid, 171.

250 For Czechoslovakia the situation was similar with 84%. For the lesser developed countries, trade was basically only intra-European. For example, only 4% of Hungarian exports were sold outside Europe. Ibid.

251 Calculated for 1929 from chart: Der Welthandel (Weltausfuhr) nach Warengruppen, Statistisches Reichsamt, *Jahrbuch 1937*, 145.

252 Berd Höpfer, *Der deutsche Außenhandel 1900–1945. Änderungen in der Waren- und Regionalstruktur*, Frankfurt 1993, 150.

tiles,[253] products which faced high overcapacities and competition on world markets. World export of all textile products only made up 12% of world exports in 1929.[254] Total world production of cotton and rayon textiles increased in the 20s, while total world exports of these products declined slightly, mainly as a result of "Europe's gradual loss of the leading position in the world market"[255] and of increasing capacities outside of Europe, particularly in India, China and Japan. In Belgium, another small industrialised country, exports were more diversified. Overall textile exports only had a share of 15% of all exports.[256]

Austrian Export Commodities	Share of Exports	German Export Commodities	Share of Exports
1. Textiles	28.3%	Advanced Finished Products	17.4%
2. Advanced Finished Products	13.0%	Iron and Metal Goods	15.0%
3. Iron and Metal Goods	12.0%	Textiles	11.8%
4. Wood	11.2%	Coal and Coke	5.5%
5. Paper	6.2%	Paper	2.7%

Table 3.4.: The five most important export items in 1928 and their share of the total value of exports: Data for Austria from Österreichisches Statistisches Zentralamt, *Aussenhandel*. Source: Data for Austrian textiles for 1929. This figure excludes semi-finished textile products. Advanced products include electrical machinery and consumer goods, other machinery, cars and engines, rubber goods and chemicals. Data for Germany from Statistisches Reichsamt, *Jahrbuch 1929*, chart 6 and chart 7, 193–195. All figures for the year 1928. German textiles exclude primary textile products

Almost 12% of Austrian exports were metal and iron goods, and 6.2% were paper and paper products, commodities which also faced considerable structural problems. 11.2% of exports were comprised of unfinished wood, a primary product. A serious credit item for the Austrian economy was the export of advanced finished products, such as electrical machinery, other machinery, cars and engines, rubber wares, and chemicals. Of these, Austria sold a considerably high share of around 13% of overall exports, but was still below world average in trade with advanced finished products of 17.5% . The very high content of sales of automobiles and engines, which made up 2.3% of total outbound trade, is surprising. In Germany, this rate was only 0.38% of all exports. Yet, automobiles and motor bikes combined with all other advanced finished products, amounted to 17.4% of all German exports. Apart from advanced

253 This and the following percentages for Austria calculated from Österreichisches Statistisches Zentralamt, *Aussenhandel*, Abschnitt II. Der österreichische Außenhandel nach den wichtigsten Warengattungen, 36–72. For Germany see: Statistisches Reichsamt, *Jahrbuch 1929*, chart 6. Der auswärtige Handel nach der Gruppeneinteilung des Internationalen Warenverzeichnisses, B. Ausfuhr; and chart 7. Anteil der wichtigsten Waren am auswärtigen Handel, B. Ausfuhr, 193 and 195. All percentages for 1928.

254 Statistisches Reichsamt, *Jahrbuch 1937*, 145.

255 Svennilson, 142.

256 Only the share of metal and metal goods exports was slightly greater. See: Statistisches Reichsamt, *Die Wirtschaft des Auslandes 1900–1927. Einzelschriften zur Statistik des Deutschen Reiches*, No. 5, Berlin 1928, 112.

finished products, where both countries' export rates were quite similar, in Germany, exports were much more diversified and balanced. Thus, the loss or decline of demand of one commodity could be more easily compensated by increasing exports of another. The largest export products after advanced finished manufactures were iron and metal wares, which amounted to only 15% of all German exports. Then came textiles with 9.7%, machinery with 6.8%, chemicals with 6.6%, coal and coke with 5.5%, electrical machinery with 3.6% and then paper with 2.7%.

With the background of declining trade and growth in the old sectors of industry, their structural problems and overcapacities, German export structure was much more favourable and could more easily face the changes. The export group with the highest share of exports were advanced finished products, which enjoyed increasing demand, rising prices on world markets and favourable terms of trade.

In Austria, the export share of all textiles products was, with 28.3%, far too high to be counterbalanced by another export item. Its terms of trade on the world market was declining. World demand for textiles, paper and other smaller manufactured items was contracting, while it was expanding for machinery and transport equipment.[257] This meant that the export structure of European countries had to adjust to the changed structure of commodity demand on world markets. Basically, all semi-finished and finished textiles products, as well as pottery, glass, cutlery, hardware, manufactures of wood and timber, footwear, all leather products and paper and cardboard products counted as those exports items with declining world demand.

In contrast to Austria, most industrialised countries tried to convert their structure of trade away from these commodities with declining demand in the decade after the war. The most successful countries to adapt their trade towards the exports of more machinery and transport equipment were the United States, Sweden and Germany. The United Kingdom, Switzerland, France, Belgium and Luxembourg were also able to decrease the share of textiles and other manufactures with declining demand, but to a much lesser degree. Austria must have been among the countries of the last group which were not as able to adjust as well. The commodities with decreasing world demand, together with all textiles products, roughly made up 43% of Austrian exports in 1928.[258] By the late 30s, the Austrian export structure seemed to have improved, because it became more balanced and stratified.[259] Yet, this was less the result of an adjustment of Austrian trade, than of the general decline of trade and exports in Europe during the 1930s, which will be the topic of the following chapter.

257 Svennilson, 178 and table 53 on 180.

258 Calculated with figures from Österreichisches Statistisches Zentralamt, *Aussenhandel*, Abschnitt II. Export values for wood manufacture for 1929.

259 In 1937 the main export item was still textiles with a 21% share of all exports, then iron and metal wares with 17.6%, then advanced finished products with 11.5%; then wood 10.7%, and then paper with 9.5%. According to Svennilson, the share of the declining commodities was 29%.

4. MICROECONOMIC DEVELOPMENT UNTIL THE BEGINNING OF THE GREAT DEPRESSION, 1925–1930

4.1. FINANCIAL POSITION AND AGGREGATE INVESTMENT BEHAVIOUR OF AUSTRIAN COMPANIES

As especially the Austrian economy was extremely dependent on export trade for demand and employment,[1] the years after stabilisation denoted a brief period of recovery, very moderate expansion and very slow and insufficient adjustment to the new economic circumstances for all industrial sectors. Even though GNP growth rates expanded above the European average between 1924 and 1929 and growth of the industrial sector increased around 40%, Austrian GNP still did not quite reach pre-war production volume and remained below the European average. In 1929, industry was still 2% below 1913 production level, while German production was 24% and world production 76% above pre-war output volume.[2] The overall above average rate of growth of GNP was, to a great degree, due to the fact that the economy began with very low growth levels after the inflation and stabilisation. During the inflation, most firms had lost a substantial part of their pre-war capital assets and financial resources, but had greater production capacity available than before. However, although capacity was greater, plant was often oversized and obsolete. The conditions of production, marketing and sales had changed tremendously due to a number of reasons which lowered profitability and competitiveness for the majority of firms, especially for the ones belonging to the older and traditional sectors of industry. Yet, this was also the only short time span of the inter-war period when investments and depreciation were at least on a level that allowed for a slow growth of production capacity to compensate for ground lost in the war and the inflation. Austrian firms indirectly benefited from the world economic boom of the late 20s, but more moderately than industries in other countries. For Austria, it was not a boom, but only a moderate upswing which gave industrial enterprises still too little time and demand for a serious chance of recovery from war-time and inflationary distortions, with the same symptoms that many other countries experienced. Capacity, production, turnover and sales rose, while earning power and prices declined and unemployment increased, or remained on high levels. The upswing was also, as in many other countries, accompanied by a strong rationalisation, cartelisation and merger movement.

1 Also noted by contemporary economists. See the report on the Austrian economy of the Statistisches Reichsamt, group "Ausländische Wirtschaftsstatistik", *Die Wirtschaft des Auslandes 1900–1927*, 241–258.

2 Rolf Wagenführ, "Die Industriewirtschaft," in: *Vierteljahreshefte zur Konkjunkturforschung*, Berlin 1933, 56.

Year	Austria	Germany
1925	8.1%	6.4%
1926	9.3%	7.0%
1927	8.0%	8.6%
1928	9.7%	8.2%

Table 4.1.: Investment rate in Germany and in Austria (percentage of gross national product at current prices). Source: Data for Germany from Ritschl and Spoerer, "Das Bruttosozialprodukt in Deutschland," and Günther Keiser and Bernhard Benning, "Kapitalbildung und Investitionen in der deutschen Volkswirtschaft 1924 bis 1928," in: Deutsches Institut für Konjunkturforschung, *Vierteljahreshefte zur Konjunkturforschung*, special issue 22, Berlin 1931, 17. Data for Austria from Österreichisches Institut für Wirtschaftsforschung, *Monatsberichte* 14, 41.

Overall the national investment rate reflected the only moderate recovery. It was lower than in 1913 (13%) and lower than in Western European countries, but comparable to that of Germany.

Industrial investment behaviour was far more erratic than total investment pattern during the recovery period. After the highest increases of the value of invested capital among most joint-stock companies with the introduction of reconstructed balances in 1925/26, the average investment rate was with 5% in the second half of the 20s[3] extremely low. It increased from 8% in 1927 to 14% in 1930 to its moderate peak. Highest production and the peak of national income during the inter-war period occurred during the years 1928/29. However, investment was at a low point in those years, and a slow decline in productive capital took place, suggesting that there was no direct correlation between investment rate and industrial growth.[4]

Before 1924/25, the balance sheets were distorted due to inflation. Depreciation and investment had been far too low, which resulted in a deterioration of capital assets and productive capital. Far too low depreciation was a result of the unrealistically low estimated value of productive assets, which in turn, was a sign for much too low depreciation and investment rates during the inflation, which would have inflated their value.[5]

Along with currency reform, in June 1925, the law for the introduction of new balance sheets finally forced joint-stock companies to set their accounting system on realistic values and introduced tax reduction for capital increases of stocks to improve the conditions for the raising of capital.[6] It established a minimum amount of share capital of 100 thousand schillings (minimum par value of 10 schillings) for companies founded before the implimentation of the law, and a minimum of 500

3 Mosser, "Wachstumsstrategie oder Krisenmanagement,“ 106.

4 Ibid, 108.

5 "Die unzureichenden Abschreibungen waren eine Folge der unrealistisch niedrigen Wertansätze der Sachanlagen, die selbst wiederum Zeugnis mangelnder Investitionstätigkeit sind, denn diese hätte dieWertansätze der Sachanlagen inflationiert.“ Mosser, ibid, 111.

6 Kernbauer, *Währungspolitik*, 171 and 172.

thousand schillings (par value of 100 schillings) as minimum share capital for joint-stock companies founded thereafter.[7] With the introduction of the opening balance sheets, based on the new currency, firms were forced to re-value their assets on more realistic bases.

As a consequence, a number of companies which were only benefiting from inflationary conditions had to be dissolved. Moreover, the new gold balance sheet clearly revealed the effects and abuse of inflationary finances, as most joint-stock companies had lost real assets and were financially unsound compared to the pre-war period. According to an analysis of 324 joint-stock companies, conducted by the federal statistical office in 1925, only 36% of total equity capital (capital stock and reserve) consisted of capital reserves, even though the legally prescribed minimum share of reserves was 50%. Of the 144 companies founded in pre-war times, reserves had amounted to 76% of equity capital. The 180 joint-stock enterprises, floated between 1918 and 1925, only had reserves of 24% of equity capital, while the share of liabilities was far greater than for firms established before 1913.[8]

Usually new balance values seemed quite high when looking at the balance sheets of the inflation period and thereafter, but this only appears so because asset values, depreciation and investments were so low before 1924/25. Before stabilisation, only profits and, to a lesser degree, expenses were inflated according to the inflationary process. The value of depreciation was barely inflated. The result was that net profits were artificially high and balance sheet showed a much more positive financial standing. In reality, many firms had lost productive capital. By and large, the new values of the gold balances were quite realistic. With the new currency, managements were interested in realistic values and proper depreciation with rates between 8 and 15% thereafter[9] in order to maintain sufficient productive capital.

Certainly, the large Viennese banks also had to introduce reconstructed balances, but their accounting did not seem to have been as honest. The new balances revealed a substantial loss of their capital basis of about 70% compared to their pre-war value.[10] Since they were interested in attracting foreign, especially Western capital, and in maintaining their large investment engagements in Eastern Europe, the loss of capital presented in the new balance was probably still too moderate, and their actual financial standing was much worse, resulting in the breakdown of the private national banking system in the early 30s.

The new balances allowed an interesting comparison of financial standing of the different sectors of industry of the last pre-war year and the first post-inflation year with reconstructed balances, conducted by contemporary economic journalists.[11] The division of the sectors was fairly rough, but gives an interesting overview. As expected, most joint-stock companies of most industrial sectors had lost a substantial share of their capital stock and reserve and only a few had actually gained. Surpris-

7 Wiesbauer, *Die österreichischen Aktiengesellschaften 1918–1938*, 151.

8 Ibid., 151, 153.

9 Ibid.

10 Kernbauer, *Währungspolitik*, 174.

11 "Die umgestellten Industriebilanzen," in: *Der Österreichische Volkswirt, Die Bilanzen*, 2.4.1927, 302 and 303.

ingly, the firms of the metal mining, general mining and textiles industry had gained in capital reserves and also their net profits had increased. Mining had increased in capital reserves by 42% and textiles by 19%. For the former net profits increased 26% and for the latter 29%. Yet, the debts of these sectors were between 37% and 133% higher than before the war. Regarding mining, this was probably the case, because this branch of industry expanded production due to the scarcity of, and high dependence upon, imports of raw material resources in Austria after the war and the fairly high demand for non-iron metals. Until the mid 20s, textiles sales also did fairly well, but the increase in financial standing seems only so great because 1913 values were quite low as this was a crisis year for textile firms. The paper, electrical engineering and automobile industry experienced only a slight decline in capital stock, but their net profits had decreased by roughly 50%. The machine, iron and steel industries lost up to half of their reserves and only had between 9% and 26% of value of their 1913 net profit income. The construction industry performed the worst in matters of financial standing, largely the result of a fall and stagnation of private investment in housing construction. Contemporaries saw the decline of profitableness as a result of the increased running cost after the war due to higher taxes, social expenditure and first and foremost, the under-utilisation of capacity. The small prospects of a boom and the only very moderate upswing was regarded as a consequence of increased protectionism among the Austrian neighbour countries.

4.2. TRADITIONAL INDUSTRIES

4.2.1. Textile Industry

The textile industry was the most important industry for industrial exports of Austria, providing nearly 30% of all exports in the late 1920s. At the same time, while it remained one of the largest industrial sectors, it was also one of the major contracting industries suffering from international overcapacities and competition. Of the total stock value of more than 1.3 billion schillings of the 739 industrial, trade and financial joint stock companies in late 1926, the textile industry had roughly a share of 8%.[12] More than 7% of the industrial workforce belonged to this branch in the late 20s.[13] It is a perfect example of how much Austrian economic development and performance was dominated by structural faults and changes of the European and world textile industry, and how much it was affected by its dependence on this export commodity. It also shows that international economic policy, i.e. trade protectionism, was a result of the change in world economic structures and that national policy could not have had substantial influence on this development.

a. International Development Despite the financial recovery of the Austrian textile industry by the mid 20s, its production only reached pre-war levels in 1937, with

12 Statistisches Reichsamt, *Die Wirtschaft des Auslandes 1900–1927*, 254.
13 Ibid, 248.

the help of massive protectionism and foreign demand from indirect rearmament. In 1920, it reached only 42.8%, in 1924, 77.6% and in 1929, 89.6% of its 1913 production level, which had been already fairly low.[14] Clearly, this industry belonged to the main stagnating sectors of industrial production in Europe, but remained the dominating industry of a very large share of Austrian exports. Exports of textiles and finished textiles contracted in the late 20s, explaining the stagnation of production. In 1924, textiles goods worth 687 million schillings were exported. By 1929, the value of outbound trade was still only 625.3 million schillings. Of these total exports, finished textile products only constituted a minute fraction.[15]

The contraction phenomenon was the result of a world-wide trend of industrialisation and increase of capacities (explained in chapter 2), from which Europe, as the old core of the industrialised world, suffered most heavily. Among the modern European countries, textile trade of the smallest advanced nations was affected the worst by peripheral industrialisation and competition. Other small countries with a high textiles share of total exports also had declining or stagnating sales. In 1925, the value of outbound Czechoslovak textile products came to 788.6 million German marks. In 1927, it was 855.3 million and in 1929 still only 847.8 million marks. In 1925, Switzerland exported textile commodities worth 639.3 million marks. In 1927, value dropped to 537.7 million and in 1929 to 494 million marks.[16] This development is explicable by an enormous increase of world-wide capacity of production of the older industries, which applied 19th century technology.

The process was similar among all these industries. The textile industry, however, was one of the main representatives which suffered from this transformation. Industrial development and growth stagnated among the matured industries in the old centres of production in Europe, especially in Great Britain, Germany and France, but also in the smaller European states that had been producing textiles manufactures before the war,[17] such as Austria, Switzerland or Belgium. Meanwhile, the periphery, mostly Eastern European and Asian countries, but also the United States, underwent or had undergone industrialisation mainly in these older industries during and after the war. Especially Japan and India had considerably increased their production capacities of textiles.[18]

Contemporary economists divided the industrialising countries of the periphery into three groups:[19] The first group consisted of the countries of the Far East and Africa as part of a colonial empire, mainly South Africa, India, and China. Also New Zealand, Australia and the South American States belonged to this group. The industrialisation effort in this group was confined before the war by the dominance

14 Österreichisches Institut für Wirtschaftsforschung, *Monatsberichte* 14, 12.

15 Österreichisches Statistisches Zentralamt, *Aussenhandel*, 59.

16 Heinz Grünbaum, "Die Welttextilkrise. Zur Umschichtung der internationalen Industriestruktur," in: Institut für Konjunkturforschung (ed.), *Vierteljahreshefte zur Konjunkturforschung*, special issue 24, Berlin 1931, 24.

17 Grünbaum, 10 ff.

18 This was also recognised by contemporaries. See: Ernst Wagemann, *Struktur und Rhythmus der Weltwirtschaft. Grundlagen einer weltwirtschaftlichen Konjunkturlehre*, Berlin 1931.

19 Grünbaum, 11–13.

of European textile products, but set loose during the war by the lack of competition and decline of dependence from Europe during and after World War One. The second group were the countries of Eastern Europe, especially the successor states and Russia, that forced industrialisation mostly due to political reasons, but also because of the decline of markets for primary products in these countries. The last group consisted of Canada, the United States and the European neutrals, countries that were not directly affected by the war, and that took advantage of the sudden cessation of competition from the other European nations involved in the war effort. The last group also had much improved textile industrial plants after the war.

Likewise, the effects of overcapacities were enhanced by increased productivity. World textile raw material production had increased 30% between 1913 and the early 30s, while the production of finished goods increased 40%.[20] The industrialisation trends in the countries of the periphery and higher productivity put tremendous pressure on the older developed Western and Central European textile industry. The outside pressure never allowed full employment in the late 20s and pushed the old European textile industry to the verge of crisis just before the depression set in.[21] As a result, the European countries, as part of the old textiles producers, suffered from stagnating production levels between 1913 and 1926/28. According to Grünbaum, only Austria and Spain slightly overcame pre-war levels, contradicting the numbers from *Volkseinkommen*. However, this was only an artificially high level, since after the loss of textile production capacity to Czechoslovakia, Austrian firms were forced to expand plant capacity insignificantly compared to European capacity. The three largest industrialised countries of Europe, plus the Czechoslovak Republic, Switzerland and Portugal never reached pre-war production levels.

However, the countries of the first group of late industrialisers doubled or nearly tripled their production. The countries of the second group were 30% or 160% above pre-war production levels, and the countries of the last group came between 15% and 81% above pre-war production value.[22] High trade barriers and protectionism, particularly in lesser developed Eastern European countries, were considering the international overproduction that outran demand and resulted in a fierce struggle for markets as well as in a decline of Austria's main export commodity.

Even though Austrian exports heavily depended on textiles, Austrian share of European textile production was small, smaller than the share of the Czechoslovak Republic, Poland, Belgium, Spain and Switzerland. The eight largest producers of textiles (producing 85% of world output) were Great Britain, Germany, France, Italy, Russia, the United States, Japan and India.[23] In 1927 and 1928, gross value of production was highest in the US, with 19,530 million reichsmarks, then Great Britain, with 14,000 million marks, and then Germany, whose production valued between 8000 and 9000 million marks. The value of Czechoslovak production was about 1500, and Polish amounted to between 1000 and 1200 million marks. In comparison, Austrian production value only totalled between 400 and 600 million marks.

20 Grünbaum, 6.
21 Ibid, 11.
22 Ibid, 13
23 Ibid, 8 and 9.

In Hungary, it amounted to 276 million.[24] The industry that produced the main commodity of Austrian exports, therefore, suffered from severe structural problems of the world textile industry and only played a minor role on world markets. Therefore, its international political economic leverage and its influence on prices and markets were insignificant. Since its industry was even smaller than in two of the successor states, Austria had to face severe protectionism in its former markets.

During the first post-war years plenty of orders were available, but Austrian textile firms soon suffered from the immediate effects of disintegration, the loss of former production assets or from the industrialisation of formerly underdeveloped countries. Czechoslovak textiles products formed a major competitor on the Austrian market, while the successor states established and enlarged their own firms and increased trade barriers for Austrian textile products. Before and after the war, most cotton spindles were located in the Czechoslovak Republic, whereas management, trade and a large part of the finishing industry had been situated in Vienna. After the war, the leadership moved to the Czechoslovak Republic, where it set up new production capacities which formed major competition for the Austrian textile industry.[25] Consequently, sales to the areas of the successor states dropped after stabilisation, and Austrian firms increasingly had to turn toward the German market, the industry of which had lost many of its spindles in Alsace Lorraine. This country increasingly imported yarns from Czechoslovakia and Austria. However, more and more spinning factories were founded in Germany and trade barriers for imports increased. Therefore, in general, not only spinning, but also the finishing and other Austrian textile industries began to suffer from the declining export sales in the late 20s.

b. Spitzenindustrie AG The development of the Spitzenindustrie AG,[26] the largest representative of the finished textile producers in Austria, was a perfect reflection of the structural problems of European textile industries as a result of increased capacities and production abroad.

Its workforce had shrunk from 1200 before the war to 400 in 1922. Although its parity was still low, exports declined enormously right after stabilisation of the crown in late 1922. In 1923, sales were between only 30% and 40% of the pre-war level. Virtually every business report thereafter complained about trade policies of the neighbouring countries, which imposed very high import duties that restricted sales. This surely had its justification. The more eastward textiles merchandise was going, the higher import duties. In 1927, in Belgium and Denmark, tariffs were around 14%, in Germany, 24%, in Italy, 18.6% of value, and the general French tariff came to 21.2%. For Austrian products, the French tariff was 70.6%. Apart from the French, average tariffs were far higher in Eastern Europe. In Hungary, Czechoslovakia and in Yugoslavia, it was nearly 30%,[27] in Poland, nearly 50%, and

24 Grünbaum, chart: "Bruttoproduktionswert der Textilindustrie der Welt (ohne China) in den Jahren 1927 oder 1928." 8.

25 *Bilanzen*, 12.3.1927.

26 *Bilanzen*, 10.2.1923, 19.4.1924, 30.5.1925, 9.10.1926, 23.4.1927, 24.11.1928.

27 The company claimed that tariffs in Hungary for its products increased to 300%. Obviously a major exaggeration to support poor performance. *Bilanzen*, 30.5.1925.

in Romania, even 294.3%.[28] Despite these hostile trade conditions, the firm had no choice but to remain heavily dependent upon exports (in 1924, 98% of manufactures were sold abroad), while trade protection of its domestic market was insufficient, as Austria needed to follow the course of free trade. The firm expected positive results from the new Austrian tariffs of 1925, but these turned out to be disappointing to management. For some companies, though, new tariffs seemed to have been helpful. Hutter & Schrantz, mostly an iron and steel processing firm,[29] also owned a weaving mill in Pinkafeld. It was able to increase its number of looms in 1927, due to improving sales and better trade protection. In April, after the conclusion of a trade agreement with the Czechoslovak Republic, higher Austrian tariffs on textile imports were stipulated. In the following trade agreement with Czechoslovakia in August, lower Czechoslovak import tariffs could be enforced.[30] It must also be kept in mind, though, that in 1927 a minor business upswing took place for the international textile industry, lasting until early 1928.

Nevertheless, despite severe trade restrictions, the Spitzenindustrie AG regained its leading position as a finished textiles exporter in Austria and became financially consolidated. Yet, pre-war production was not reached until 1924. Since the successor states' tariffs were much higher, sales were increasingly oriented toward Western Europe and to markets outside of Europe. After stabilisation and the introduction of the reconstructed balance sheets, financial standing deteriorated in 1926. Larger investments had to be carried out. In 1926, 133 thousand schillings were invested for the construction of a new type of weaving mill. Indebtedness increased to 1.61 million schillings, half of which were bank debts. These debts were considerable for a firm with capital stock and reserve of only 2.42 million schillings. Still, compared to pre-war levels, profitability had not declined. In 1927, the Spitzenindustrie experienced strong foreign competition on its domestic market. It was possible to increase turnover and export volume, but profitability declined slightly, due to the fall of prices as a consequence of fierce world-wide competition. In 1928, the very moderate upswing of Austrian production and export of textiles ended, and the following year, the downswing commenced, in accordance with development of other central European textile producers. The German market played a major role for many small European states, and once its demand declined in 1928, textile production dropped.

The case of the textile industry clearly shows the effects of increased industrialisation in countries of the periphery. Austrian exports suffered from overcapacity, protectionism, and fierce competition not only on the international, but also on its own market. Of course, for old stagnating industries of the smaller countries these conditions were more severe, especially since protectionism could not offer help, not even in the short-term. For the industrialising underdeveloped or semi-developed countries of Eastern Europe, protectionism was the only way to support the insufficient and unproductive industries. By and large, these were not as dependent on

28 The Austrian National Committee, *Zollhöhe und Warenwerte*, 3.
29 Mathis, *Big Business*, 375.
30 *Bilanzen*, 16.6.1928.

exports as Austrian firms. In Austria, protectionism was not only harmful because the firms were highly export dependent, but shutting off the domestic market with the help of prohibitive import duties would not even have helped as it did in Eastern Europe or in the three large industrialised countries. It would not have made sense to increase Austrian tariff duties for textile imports since the domestic market was far too small for productive capacity of the textile industry. Export business was the only way out, and tariff raises could have caused serious trade policy retaliation of Austria's most important trade partners. For Germany, Britain and France, tariff raises were advantageous, as their firms were not as reliant on sales abroad and could enjoy the benefits of much larger domestic markets.

4.2.2. Iron and Steel Processing Industry

The iron and steel processing industry also controlled a fairly large section of total exports and belonged to the traditional industries. Structural faults in world and European production did not seem to be as great, since the countries of the periphery could not duplicate production capacity of this industry as quickly and easily as textile production. Nevertheless, also in this case, world-wide overcapacities and overproduction were at the core of structural problems, which resulted in fierce competition for markets and in stagnation in Europe. In the 20s, stagnation and decline in exports of iron wares occurred in Austria. In 1923, export value of iron wares came to 182.9 million schillings, declined in 1924, rose again to its peak in 1925 to 188.9 million, dropped again in 1926 and remained slightly under 170 million schillings in 1928 and 1929. Main customers were Yugoslavia, with a rough share of more than 15% of Austrian iron ware exports, Germany, with slightly less, and Czechoslovakia.[31] Production performance of the iron and steel processing industry was even worse than that of textiles. In 1920, only 24.1% of 1913 production level was achieved, in 1924 only 43.7%. In the period of moderate prosperity, it underwent the greatest production increase to 89.1% of pre-war output level in 1929.[32]

a. Hutter & Schrantz Surprisingly, Hutter & Schrantz,[33] as part of this branch of industry, performed quite well during the 20s, chiefly due to demand for its main products of felt and wire cloth, which supplied the expanding paper producing firms. By 1925, their production and capacity was enlarged in the 20s. At the same time, Hutter & Schrantz' balance sheet value increased by roughly 48% compared to its 1913 value. On the other hand, liabilities had risen above the value of debtors after stabilisation. The increase of debtor value compared to pre-war figures suggests a higher business activity. The profit and loss account also only shows a slightly more negative picture than before the war. In 1925, gross profit was already 82% of the 1913 value. Before the war, 17.7% of gross profit remained net profits. After

31 Österreichisches Statistisches Zentralamt, *Aussenhandel*, 62 and 63.
32 Österreichisches Institut für Wirtschaftsforschung, *Monatsberichte* 14, 12.
33 *Bilanzen*, 10.7.1926, 14.5.1927, 16.6.1928, 4.5.1929, 23.8.1930. See also A.14.

stabilisation, it was 26%. It seems that profitability had increased considerably. Depreciation on plant already amounted to 71% of pre-war value. Until 1929, when gross profit value reached its peak, the development improved moderately, while investment was raised considerably and depreciation on plant rose above pre-war levels. After 1926, interest payment levelled out and remained below investment value. Renumerability also remained fairly high, with 27.6% in 1929.

In 1925, the firm had considerably increased production of its seven plants, and compared to pre-war levels, overall production and turnover had doubled. Production capacity could be utilised fully and turnover increased 10%. Investments were moderate, with 370 thousand schillings, that was 8% of gross profits. Expansion had been possible. In 1925, 3000 workers were employed, compared to 1300 in 1913. In the following year, 1926, investments were on the same level as before. Bank credit was utilised, but was not dangerously high. The firm had 16 million schillings as capital stock and reserve, while bank credit was just 2 million. The following year, capital stock increased to 18.25 million and bank credit could be reduced, while the investment rate had even increased to 16.6% of gross profits and liquidity improved. In 1928, the investment rate stagnated and was at 15.5% of gross profits and the following year, when the depression began, investment was increased again to 21.5%. This shows a considerable self-financing capacity. Investment and depreciation were largely financed by profits, and until 1928, dividend payments could only be moderately increased.

Since production mainly consisted of felt and wire fabric, the firm mostly sold its products to the foreign paper industries. The plants in Czechoslovakia and Hungary largely sold on their own markets, whereas output of the Austrian plants was outbound to other markets. In 1927, foreign sales increasingly went to Soviet Russia and the United States. Hutter & Schrantz was also part of an international cartel of firms in France, Germany and Britain. In the late 20s, highest sales were in the production for paper industries, while the sales of ordinary iron and metal wares stagnated, such as wire and locksmith wares. This clearly fits into the national trend of declining export sales. While investments were at their peak during the inter-war period in 1929, the first signs of the beginning of the depression were noticed in the last month of that year. Domestic consumption of iron and metal wares declined, but was countered by increasing exports in items for the paper industry. Once the international paper industry began to decline during the depression, Hutter & Schrantz was fully hit by the economic downswing.

b. Ditmar-Brünner Another firm of the iron and steel processing industry which enjoyed comparatively high demand was Ditmar-Brünner AG.[34] In contrast to Hutter & Schrantz, balance sheet value of this firm was not even half of its pre-war value. Its financial standing, though, seems to have been quite stable, since debtors permanently remained above creditors value. Moreover, there were no debts when the reconstructed balance sheet was set up. After the reorganisation of its sales organisation, the firm remained, to a great degree, dependent on exports of mass-produced

34 *Bilanzen*, 30.7.1927, 24.8.1929, 7.6.1930. See also A.9.

petroleum lamps and heaters of all sorts. These were mostly sold with success to areas with no, or underdeveloped, electrical supply systems, as in India, China and South American countries. Electrical lamps for industrial buildings and street lighting for orders from the Vienna city municipality were also produced.

After 1925, business did not go quite as well as during inflation times. By 1926, net profit and earning power already began to decline. Export sales were difficult due to strong competition from American, German and Japanese firms. Concentration, rationalisation and modernisation of production became necessary, and an investment programme was started in that year. One plant was shut down and investments were effected for machinery, buildings and an experimental station which measured candle power. In 1926, investments were fairly high, with 474 thousand schillings, i.e. 20.5% of gross profits.

1927 was a crisis year. A strike, initiated by wage demands which occurred exactly during the season of highest sales from the beginning of August until the end of November, caused a major loss of production, sales and income. Only after a 5% wage increase, the strike was terminated, but resulted in a loss of 1.07 million schillings which was covered by taking one million from the capital reserve and from the remainder of the net profit of the previous year. Until the beginning of the depression, the firm was hardly able to recover from the blow caused by the strike. Gross profits remained barely above the value of expenses in 1928 and 1929. In 1930, it was basically balanced. Before the strike, profitability had been 23.7% of gross profit. After the strike, in 1929, it declined to 8%. In spite of this, the proposed investment programme was carried out and finished in 1928. Depreciation was also maintained with the same rate throughout the strike period and thereafter. In the year of the strike, investment was high and came to 640 thousand schillings, that was 38% of gross income. The following year, it still amounted to 35% of gross profit. Production was now concentrated in one plant in Simmering. All bank deposits were used up for investments, and by 1928, a debt of 2.65 million was accumulated. Yet, it was easily covered by capital reserves and stocks of 10.25 million schillings.

During the last year before the depression began, Ditmar-Brünner tried to improve its competitive position on international export markets by changing its production programme increasingly toward technically improved and refined petroleum ovens, cookers and lamps. In 1929, this strategy seemed to work. Export sales increased considerably, and the future outlook was positive. In the late 20s, the company became the leading exporter of petroleum lamps in the world. Main competitors were German and American firms. In the sales of electrical lamps, competition was much greater. About 70% of production was exported, usually to areas outside of Europe, to India, the Eastern Mediterranean, Tunisia, Algeria, Morocco, South America; but also to the Balkan countries, Britain and the Scandinavian countries. Besides trade of its own products, extensive trade was conducted in dishes, glass, porcelain, and iron and metal wares with the help of the firm's export organisation in India and China.

Both firms, Hutter & Schrantz and Ditmar-Brünner, worked under unusual, but favourable conditions. Hutter & Schrantz could rely on fairly steady demand from the international paper industry, whereas Ditmar-Brünner sold simple consumer products with primitive technology to semi-developed or underdeveloped areas. Both companies were also able to maintain investments, even though the former was dealt a heavy blow by a strike, from which it was unable to recover financially. It was necessary to use bank credit for investment, but only to a minor extent. Credit availability did not seem to have limited investment behaviour, which was largely driven by the pressure from international competition to improve productivity. The products of Ditmar-Brünner did not appear to have been able to find demand very easily, since balance sheet, debtors and creditors value was not even one half of pre-war value. In contrast, Hutter & Schrantz found steady and rising sales. Its profitability also improved in the late 20s, but never reached pre-war levels, even though it was able to increase its gross profits value until 1929 to the pre-war value. Earning power of Ditmar-Brünner remained stagnant after stabilisation and never recovered throughout the rest of the inter-war period, whereas its investment rate remained very high.

c. Brevillier This firm[35] was a classical company of the iron and steel processing industry. It produced railway equipment, shaping tools, metal rods as well as bars, screws, malleable iron, hardware and surgical instruments. Compared to the previous two companies, it was much less export oriented, but its profitability was comparable to that of Hutter & Schrantz. Financial standing suffered from stabilisation crisis and high interest rates in 1925 and 1926, but then gross profits almost doubled until 1929. Net profits increased even more dramatically. Between 1925 and 1929, their value rose by 341%. However, it must be kept in mind that the firm started from a very low level in 1925. Gross profit value was just over half the value of 1913 and net profit was barely 15% of the pre-war value. Still, financial standing was quite satisfactory. In 1926, debtors consisted of 10.35 million schillings, while debts just ran to 8.7 million. There was not any short-term bank credit, but instead only a long-term credit in the form of a favourable pound sterling loan. This was reduced to 100 thousand pounds (about 3.4 million schillings) in 1926. The following year, debtors sunk to 6.84 million schillings. In the last two years, it was possible to decrease bank debts, due to an increase in employment. In 1928, overall debts reached about 9 million, which were covered by deposits, securities, debt claims and supplies of 18.5 million schillings. By the next year, the size of the bank loan was insignificant.

Overcapacity remained a big problem after inflation. Between reconstruction and 1929, investment was barely above depreciation value. Thus, the real gain of productive assets in this period was small. A big dilemma was that plants were much too large for the shrunken demand. In 1927, the firm still owned one firm in Poland, one in Hungary and three in Austria, with together about 3000 workers and employees.

In 1926, business activity slightly improved, but utilisation of capacity was only between 25 and 60%. Domestic demand declined. Management saw the main reasons for this development in far too low investment activity of private and public institutions, caused by obstacles of capital formation on the national market.[36] There-

35 *Bilanzen*, 13.8.1927, 25.8.1928, 5.10.1929, 21.6.1930. See also A.6.

36 The decline in domestic demand was justified by the "vollständig mangelnden Investitionstätig-

fore, the firm had to force export sales where prices were depressed. In the next year, turnover increased by one third, of which the Austrian firms had a share of 60%. The Austrian plants exported about 70% of turnover, but prices were so depressed that profits were low. In 1928 and 1929, business improved due to increased domestic demand which was, to some degree, the result of public orders for railway investment in these years. This also caused the share of exports of total sales to decline to 60%. Orders were for various small pieces of railway equipment.[37] In 1928 and 1929, the state invested 88.2 million and 44.3 million schillings for the railway system. Employment rose slightly as Brevillier received orders from a minute fraction of this investment sum.[38] The Austrian plants had a capacity utilisation of 75%. In that year, plants in Poland and Hungary also had more business activity. Turnover of 1929 was between 8 and 10% higher than the year before, even though export share of sales was only between 50 and 60%. Late in the year, a lack of public orders was felt and the firm had to hasten exports sales. During the first half of 1930 business activity was still satisfactory by increasing the rate of exports. Even though public railway investment was at its peak in that year, with 151.8 million schillings, the business report outlook for 1930 specifically stated that a substantial increase in general and in railway investment would improve business. Demand from the public sector declined for Brevillier.

In all, it can be maintained that Brevillier suffered from the structural disproportions of overcapacities in Europe. As production and business activity started from extremely depressed levels right after stabilisation, the rate of growth of production and business remained too low to result in an expansion and improvement of the productive capacity until the beginning of the depression. Essentially, oversized and obsolete capacity were only partially re-employed.

4.2.3. Iron and Steel Producing Industry

As during the inflation, the Austrian iron and steel producing industry, also part of the traditional industries, probably suffered most heavily from international overproduction and overcapacities in the period of moderate prosperity. The structural distortions on the European markets, where production outran consumption, along with comparatively low Austrian productivity, were the main causes for the appalling performance of this sector and not deflationary and restrictive economic policy. Never during the inter-war period was pre-war production level not even nearly reached. In 1920, it was at 20%, in 1924, at 54.4%, and in 1929, at 87.7% of pre-war production level.[39] Export performance was also poor. In 1923, scrap and raw iron worth 15 million schillings were exported. In 1927, it peaked to 25.5 million, and

keit seitens öffentlicher und privater Stellen, hervorgerufen durch die vielfachen Behinderungen jedweder Kapitalsbildung im Inlande.“ *Bilanzen*, 13.8.1927.

37 “Eisenbahnkleinmaterial.“

38 Fibich, 143.

39 Österreichisches Institut für Wirtschaftsforschung, *Monatsberichte* 14, 12.

dropped again to 16.9 million schillings in 1929.[40] The weaknesses of this industry made it much more vulnerable to, and dependent on, international and domestic economic policy. It depended on, and demanded more, from trade and public investment policy, bank credit, and cartelisation, and suffered from these as much as from foreign currency depreciation and high tariffs. Essentially though, these factors, along with deflationary policy, were not the main causes of its stagnation and relative decline, but rather its comparatively low productivity, competitiveness and obsolescence[41] in the face of international overcapacities and distortions.

a. Alpine and International Development Once again, the best example of this branch of industry was the Alpine Montangesellschaft,[42] which had already suffered a hard blow from disintegration, stabilisation and inflation. Production data of this firm are really disillusioning. Due to war and inflation, production of raw ore declined 64% between 1913 and 1924. Coal output dropped 30.5%, raw iron 55%, and rolling mill production 56%. After that, only coal output regained pre-war production levels. The production of raw ore, the main product of the Alpine, only really began to pick up after 1926 and reached its output peak in 1928, with 98% of the pre-war level. In the next year, it declined again and was generally below European levels. In 1928, total production in Austria only reached 63% of the 1913 level. In the same year, in Belgium, for instance, ore production surpassed the 1913 level by 9.2%. Britain attained only 70% of its pre-war level and Germany only 18%, but that was largely due to the loss of mines in Alsace-Lorraine. France surpassed pre-war levels by an incredible 124.4%; but this enormous rise can be ascribed to the annexation of former German territories with rich ore fields. Excluding these, French output was still 30% above 1913.[43]

Alpine raw iron output also reached its production peak in 1928, only attaining 78% of its pre-war level, while world production was 12% above the 1913 level.[44] Alpine rolling mill and coal production reached their output peaks in 1929. Only the latter slightly overcame the 1913 production level, by 1.2%, even though the general trend of the Austrian coal mining industry was better.[45] Yet, coal output only slightly surpassed pre-war production because of Austria's dependence on coal imports.

The financial situation exactly reflected the real economic development of the Alpine. After stabilisation until 1927, gross profits and expenses were nearly equal.

40 Österreichisches Statistisches Zentralamt, *Aussenhandel*, 63.

41 Fiereder, 71.

42 *Bilanzen*, 3.7.1926, 24.7.1926, 31.7.1926, 4.6.1927, 10.9.1927, 3.3.1928, 12.5.1928, 4.5.1929, 31.5.1930. See also A.2 and A.3.

43 Calculated according to numbers from Statistisches Reichsamt, *Jahrbuch* 1933, 50 (international survey).

44 Ibid, 61.

45 Also see production numbers for all of Austria of coal, raw iron and ore output, "Wirtschaftszahlen Österreichs 1923 bis 1938," in: Österreichisches Institut für Wirtschaftsforschung (ed.), *Monatsberichte des Österreichischen Instituts für Wirtschaftsforschung*, issue 10/12, Vienna 1946, 274. For the development of the production of the mining industry see: Österreichisches Institut für Wirtschaftsforschung (ed.), *Monatsberichte des Österreichischen Instituts für Wirtschaftsforschung. Beschäftigung und Produktivität im Österreichischen Bergbau von 1913 bis 1950*, issue 7, Vienna 1950, 7.

Only during the years of highest production and maximum European economic prosperity, 1928 and 1929, very moderate net profits were made, hardly amounting to 12% of the 1913 value. In these years, the best business years after inflation and until the "Anschluss," earning power was very low with 10.5% and 8.9% respectively. At least investment value was above depreciation rate in these years, suggesting that no loss of asset value took place. Indebtedness was far higher than before the war, and the value of debtors was above liabilities only in 1926 and 1927. The biggest German steel concentration, the Vereinigte Stahlwerke, had the majority of Alpine shares (56.66%). It was the successor of the Stinnes combine, the largest coal iron and steel group in Europe and the second largest steel trust in the world.

During the year of the introduction of the reconstructed balance sheets, business activity was low. Only 2 out of 5 blast furnaces and 10 out of 17 open hearth furnaces were active. Between 60 and 70% of output was exported, while prices and demand were declining permanently. Under these catastrophic conditions, management hoped for the improvement of sales conditions with the help of various cartel agreements between Austrian and Czechoslovak iron and steel producers, with the help of the Central European raw steel community and the European rail export cartel.[46] The first cartel, between Austrian and Czechoslovak producers, was based on a bilateral agreement to ensure sales on their respective markets. Alpine controlled the sales of all imported Czechoslovak iron in Austria, whereas it was allowed to sell a certain export quota to Czechoslovakia. Exports to the successor states, as well as to Italy and the Balkans, were also organised. The Czechoslovak companies had a share of 65% of all exports to this area, whereas the Alpine only had a share of 35%. In 1926, Czechoslovak, Austrian and Hungarian iron producing firms formed the Central European cartel, which was enlarged in October to include German, French, Belgian companies and firms from Luxembourg, to form the international raw iron and steel cartel. It functioned until 1931. Its formation was mainly the result of intensified pressure of prices on international markets in the second half of the 20s, which occurred after national groups of producers in Germany had concluded agreements on domestic prices and after French producers had lost their advantage of a forced import quota to Germany in 1925, when the Versailles treaty restrictions on German trade policy autonomy expired.

"The national organisations of steel producers had grown stronger and the German cartel started to apply its dumping policy,"[47] depressing international prices even more. The national group of producers in Europe with the highest productivity, the largest national market and greatest production volume, the German producers, totally dominated this cartel and the European market, because they were able to maintain reasonable earning power and low prices simultaneously. This was not only possible because of greater productivity, but also because the German national cartel, the Stahlwerks-Verband AG, could enforce higher import tariffs against its domestic

46 About this see Bilanzen; and Bachinger and Matis, "Strukturwandel," 120 ff.

47 Svennilson, 128.

processing industry, to support a higher price level on their own market.[48] This way, German exports that were adjusted to very low international prices were subsidised "from the proceeds of sales at high prices in the home market."[49] Such a policy of one group of national producers was only possible in a country with a large market and where only 30% of steel production was exported. Smaller countries, as for example Czechoslovakia, Austria and Belgium, where up to four fifths of production was exported, suffered from this. The international cartel was not really designed to maintain prices to a level acceptable to industries in countries that mainly had to depend on foreign sales. Of course, cartel agreements were not created to cover the much lower productivity and competitiveness of the Alpine. Cartel agreements of this sort were an expression of the economic leverage of national groups of producers on the international market. Companies with high export dependence in small countries were the losers. Furthermore, the European steel cartel only included continental producers and could not limit the development of further capacity in member countries. American and British producers were not part of this cartel. Thus, the actual aim of the cartel, the limitation of output and prices, was not achieved. Prices continued to fall.

In 1925, hopes of Alpine management were also high for the new Austrian tariff rates. The leadership of the firm pushed its lobbyists in political circles in parliament and the government to raise tariffs of iron and ore imports. This led to a conflict with the Austrian iron and steel processing industry. It feared higher raw material prices as a consequence of tariff increases. The following year, the struggle between producers and processors finally culminated in a settlement which stipulated that tariffs were going to be raised moderately, but that the processing firms in Austria were entitled to buy raw iron from the Alpine at world market prices. The tariffs were also compromised by a special bilateral agreement which allowed Czechoslovak firms to export 18% of Austrian iron demand duty free.[50] However, too moderate tariffs and the tight market, shared by numerous cartels, were not the only factors leading to the deterioration of the competitive situation. Until the formation of the international raw iron cartel in 1926, the fall of the French and Belgian franc began to depress world prices for raw iron more, giving the Alpine an even more serious competitive disadvantage.

Until the beginning of the depression, the financial situation did not improve very much. In 1926, debt value was higher than capital stock and reserves. While production in that year was much lower than in 1913, running costs were much higher and prices lower. Investments were too low and obsolete plant capacity could not be fully utilised. Until mid 1926, prices were depressed partially by the falling franc, and once the General Strike in Britain[51] ended, a further decline could be expected. The tariff rate increases of August 1926 on iron and iron wares, even

48 On price development and dumping policy see: Kian Shahidi, *Der Branchen-Lebenszyklus. Eine Untersuchung am Beispiel der deutschen Stahlindustrie*, dissertation, Bern 1997, 244.

49 Svennilson, 127.

50 Bachinger and Matis, "Strukturwandel," 121.

51 Pollard, *Development*, 172 ff.

though they were quite high, running to 30.8% of import value,[52] did not prove to be effective the next year. Mostly, old sales agreements still had to be concluded, including lower prices, making the new tariffs ineffective. Increases of rates were also partially offset by increased freight rates abroad. The only ray of hope was that it was possible to increase the value of investments moderately in the same year, to 8.7 million schillings, and to lower indebtedness by selling coal-pits in Western Czechoslovakia.[53]

Between 1927 and 1929, business improved due to the international upswing of the processing iron and steel industry in Western Europe, which began at the end of 1926.[54] Production could be modernised and extended. Capacity could be utilised to a higher degree, which lowered general running costs. Nevertheless, earning power was still very low, even though the works in Donawitz had an employment capacity of 75%. Running costs were 75% above the pre-war level. Management complained about increased general running costs and particularly about pay rises, although these only made up 2% of general costs. Permanently, management attempted to lower running costs and to increase output and productivity. The Alpine remained dependent on exports during a time when the disintegration of trade progressed and national markets increasingly retrenched. In the first half of 1927, 70% of output had to be exported, but international prices were still too low for the Alpine to make reasonable profits. 72.2% of raw iron output was exported to Germany, Yugoslavia, Italy, Switzerland, and Czechoslovakia. 42% of rolling mill output was outbound, probably because orders from the Austrian railways for rails helped to increase sales on the domestic market. Management counted on the security of several years of railway investment, especially after 1928.

In that year, payment of dividends was resumed, amounting to 2.4 million schillings. That was 11.2% of expenses in 1928. It would probably have been wiser to use this sum for further, highly necessary, investments. The export rate was only 30%, and output and sales nearly reached pre-war levels, but a large portion of domestic sales had to be sold at low world prices, due to agreements with the home processing industry.

During the time of highest sales and output, financial standing was, mildly described, precarious. Debtors equalled the value of liabilities, of which 45% were expensive bank credits. The more bank credits had to be used proportionally to total liabilities, the higher debts service became. With a capital stock of 60 million schillings, the Alpine had bank debts of 10 million, which increased to 16 million in 1929. The dominating bank was the Niederösterreichische Escomptegesellschaft. In the case of the Alpine, the dependence on bank credit was indeed very high. Loans from domestic banks were expensive and not sufficient to finance necessary investments. In 1928 and 1929, these peaked and amounted to 9.4 million and 14

52 The Austrian National Committee, *Zollhöhe und Warenwerte*, 3

53 These were the coal pots and coke works of "Ostrau" in Moravia. Also see: Bachinger and Matis, "Strukturwandel," 124.

54 Iron and steel production was increasing substantially in Germany and Western Europe since November 1926. Statistisches Reichsamt (ed.), *Wirtschaft und Statistik*, vol. 7, no. 1, January 1927, 20.

million respectively, but were still insufficient and too low, considering the amount of running debts.

The sums were used for the enlargement of electricity plants, shaft hauling, a coal dehydration system, the purchase of electrical excavators, mechanical work shops etc. Obviously, productivity of the Alpine was far too low even in the best business years and was not comparable to that of firms in Western Europe.[55] Productivity was not only low because of obsolete equipment, but also because plants were almost always under-utilised. The company was unable to keep up with international market prices. Therefore, in the late 20s, investment was insufficient to raise productivity and was clearly restricted by very heavy indebtedness and difficult credit availability. In addition, the already limited investment was focused on the extension of mining and the production of primary products, instead of on expansion of semi-finished products of rolling mill and steel works production, the sales of which would have been more profitable.

Regarding debt value and form and considering the amount of invested capital, the reason for the lack of investment becomes apparent. Besides running liabilities, and in order to finance investment, but also to re-convert general debts and bank debts, the management had taken up a large bonded debt in the form of a floating loan. It was taken up in 1925, was floated on the American capital market and amounted to 5 million dollars, about 35.5 million schillings at that time. This loan was arranged by the Niederösterreichische Escomptegesellschaft and the New York banking house F. J. Lisman & Co., and was utilised for the extension of the Alpine high grade steel works.[56] By 1927, it roughly amounted to 34.6 million schillings. Its amortisation progressed very slowly, since its value was still 29.4 million in 1936, as it only slighty depreciated due to slow dollar devaluation against the schilling. Considering the value of this debt added to the amount of liabilities, the cost of total debt service each year must have been substantial for the Alpine. During the last three years before the depression, 1927–1929, overall debts were 50.6, 56.2, and 63.2 million schillings respectively, while capital stock and reserve amounted 94.4 million in 1929. This tremendous indebtedness did not allow for investment that would have modernised production assets sufficiently. At the same time, it made the search for investors much more problematical.

In 1929, the last years before the onset of the depression, sales and turnover peaked. By the end of 1928, 13,450 workers were employed. Future prospects were regarded as positive, and a five year investment programme was scheduled for further rationalisation and modernisation. Plans included the construction of a new coal de-hydration plant, new transport equipment and the modernisation of rolling mill production. Steam power was to be fully replaced by electrical energy. Though, not much came of these plans. The first signs of the depression became apparent already by July 1929, when sales of raw iron and ore declined on foreign markets and prices dropped. In autumn, sales on the Austrian market also fell. In 1930, investment had

55 Fiereder, 73.
56 Ibid, 81.

to be cut down and sales fell continuously, even though that year saw the highest public investment for railway construction, with 151.8 million schillings.[57]

To conclude, similar to Brevillier, the development of the Alpine during the moderate upswing of the late 20s, can be regarded as insufficient to be able to adjust to the competitive environment in Europe. The firm was in no way prepared to face international competition on world markets. The main reason for this were overcapacities in all iron and steel processing countries, combined with the lack of comparatively modern equipment of the Alpine. This lack had its roots established already before the war. After war and inflation, this obsolescence in technology could never be made up and subsequent investment was far too low. Heavy indebtedness, apparent after stabilisation, and expensive credit availability from domestic banks did not allow for a higher investment rate. Cartels and tariffs were essentially ineffective in improving the situation, and the firm only indirectly benefited from state investment in railway construction to a minute degree. The problem was clearly a structural one. The Alpine, already in serious financial difficulty after inflation, appeared on the international market when it was shared by more producers with greater productivity and when trade was stagnating. Furthermore, instead of focusing production more on steel production, it increasingly became a supplier of raw iron and ore, making it dependent upon the development of the main European steel producers in Germany.

4.2.4. Steel Producing and Processing Industry

a. Schoeller-Bleckmann and Böhler In 1924, a merger formed the new company Schoeller-Bleckmann Stahlwerke AG,[58] the second largest high grade steel manufacturer in Austria following the Gebrüder Böhler steel works. Their sales performance was much better than that of the Alpine and financial standing was more stable. It is difficult though, to compare the Alpine with advanced steel processing firms. While the Alpine was mostly an iron, ore and coal producer, and to a smaller extent, a manufacturer of steel and finished products, Schoeller-Bleckmann and Böhler, by and large, only produced very high quality, high grade steel finished and semi-finished products with low demand elasticity. As their products were far more advanced and on high demand, these companies suffered much less from international overcapacities.

Unfortunately, detailed information from annual business reports on the development of Böhler[59] in the late 20s is scarce, but its performance seemed to have been similar to that of Schoeller-Bleckmann. Only the development of profitability[60] was contrary. While Böhler still maintained high earning power after stabilisation, with 27% of gross profits in 1926/27, Schoeller-Bleckmann made losses until 1926, or

57 Fibich, 143.
58 *Bilanzen*, 14.11.1925, 7.8.1926, 20.8.1927, 11.8.1928, 22.6.1929, 10.5.1930. See also A.19.
59 *Bilanzen*, 15.12.1928.
60 Turnover profitability calculated from the percentage share of net profits to gross profits.

only came to 18% in 1927. Thereafter, profitability increased to 30% until 1929, while Böhler renumerability dropped to roughly 20%. By and large, the productivity of these companies could compete on international markets, which was revealed by their continuously increasing sales and independence from cartel agreements and high tariffs.

The performance of Schoeller-Bleckmann was also supported by considerable orders from the Austrian railways between 1928 and 1930. The main market, though, was Germany, which underwent economic stagnation in 1925 and 1926 as a result of stabilisation. This was the cause of very low sales and business activity of Schoeller-Bleckmann in these years. In both years, losses of between 9 and 18% of gross profits value were made. Nearly 54% of production was exported in 1925 and 65% the following year. Prices were low and more depressed in 1926 due to the fall of the franc. Constant rationalisation and modernisation was the necessary consequence. Investment costs were substantial between 1925 and 1927, always above gross profits value, making the company one of the most modern equipped, high grade steel producers in Europe. Only by autumn of 1927, did sales on the German market pick up again, allowing for the maintenance of high quantity turnover, but with lower value and another decline in profits.

Finally, in 1927, a small profit of about 18% of gross profits value was possible, but capacity was still only utilised 50%. Sales increased, especially in exports. Only 32% of products were sold on the domestic market. The company also built railway carriages and was able to benefit from orders from the Austrian railways the next year. In fact, orders were large enough to offer employment for the department of railway carriages for the next three years. In 1928, it was possible to pay a dividend of 5%. Employment had improved and turnover increased. The small downswing on the German market, in 1928, was compensated by increased exports to other countries and by increasing the share of sales on the domestic market to 38%. The railway department was well utilised by orders for carriages. Further rationalisation and modernisation was also carried through. The various plants received two open hearth furnaces, three electrical furnaces and one high-frequency furnace, and the steel casting plant was improved. By late 1928, the German market also picked up again, but prices were generally depressed.

In the next year, the financial results and business activity were even better than the year before. Dividend was 6% and earning power had improved to 29.7% of gross profits. Investment was also maintained on a high level. Another modern high frequency furnace was installed. On the domestic market sales picked up, especially because of continuous orders from the railways. The firm was the only steel producer and processor that manufactured wheels for railway carriages in Austria. Most orders for the railways were finished by the end of 1930. In 1929, 62% of turnover value was exported. The manufacture and sales of especially light, high grade steel had become more and more important in the late 20s. Big customers for these products were the large car manufacturers and their ancillary industries. The main market remained the German market.

4.2.5. Mining Industry

a. Veitscher and International Development The Veitscher magnesite works[61] had an overall positive financial development between 1926 and 1929. Financially, it survived war and inflation easily and had a higher capital stock and reserve than before the war, without being diluted from capital increases during the inflation. In 1913, capital stock and reserve was about 14 million schillings. In 1925, it was 18 million, about 87% of balance sheet value. In addition, the firm had a 3 million bank deposit. In 1928, the majority of the joint-stock capital of 10 million schillings was in the hands of the Bodencreditanstalt, which merged with the CA a year later. Another large share of stocks of about one third was in the hands of the French capital group Schneider & Co., Creuzot and the German Danatbank. Yet, these stocks were certainly not a burden when dividend payments in the late 20s were between 10 and 18% and when financial standing was exceptionally stable. Between 1926 and 1929, net profits increased 83%, and profitability, after its peak in 1925 with 48.8%, remained well above 40% until 1930. After the introduction of the reconstructed balance sheet, depreciation on plant was also substantial, never below one million and around one third of gross profits. Debtors remained well above the value of liabilities. The floating of a loan on the British capital market was considered during the stabilisation period 1923/24, when sales were extremely low, but did not become necessary. Investment behaviour was erratic. Usually, the rate was low, apart from peaks in 1926 and 1929. Compared to its finances, real economic development, however, was stagnant.

As the Veitscher share of total Austrian magnesite exports was between 62 and 68%,[62] its export development was exactly commensurate with total Austrian exports in the late 20s. After 1923, they stagnated until 1928 and peaked only in 1929. The high exports sales of 1922/23 were not even nearly reached again for the rest of the inter-war period. After 1922/23, sales, also to the US, never really recovered and remained fairly low. This is even more surprising since profits were higher in the late 20s than before stabilisation. Again, just as before stabilisation, the main customer for Veitscher exports remained the United States, which imported between 31 and 48%[63] of export sales between 1926 and 1929. After the depression, Germany became the main export market.

Whereas financial development was positive and stable, real economic development until 1930 was contracting. The main reason for this was, just as for the iron and steel industries, the existence of overcapacities in magnesite production in the world. This resulted in tariff raises that substantially reduced Veitscher sales to one of its most important markets, the United States. On the European market, competition had also become more fierce, especially when a downswing occurred for the iron and steel industry, as in 1925 and 1926 in Germany, due to currency stabilisation, and in Britain, due to the General Strike. In 1925, turnover and sales were low and a

61 *Bilanzen*, 28.8.1926, 4.6.1927, 5.5.1928, 24.8.1929, 14.6.1930, 4.7.1930. See also A.24.

62 Own calculation from Österreichisches Statistisches Zentralamt, *Aussenhandel*, 49 and Walter, 213.

63 Calculated from Walter, ibid.

further reduction of running costs was not considered possible. American customers had made large orders in December of 1924, but these were cancelled. The same occurred on the European market. Of overall exports, 50% were shipped to the US, 20% to Germany and between 15–18% to France. The rest were sold in Italy, Britain and Belgium. For the European cartel and Veitscher management, the main immediate obstacle were the American tariffs on magnesite imports, which were about 60% of import value. The tariffs on magnesite brick, on the other hand, were quite low almost everywhere in Europe, apart from France.[64]

Management made an effort to get the American iron and steel producers to impel political decision makers to lower import tariffs on European magnesite.[65] Efforts were also made to conclude another delivery agreement with the main American importer, Harbison and General. The conditions of the Americans, including delivery of high quality material only and common delivery with the Austrian-American magnesite corporation in Radentheim, had to be fulfilled. In the next year, an agreement was concluded among Veitscher, Radentheim, and Harbison and General. These three companies also made a common effort to enforce lower US tariffs. The main competitor on the US market and main beneficiary from the high tariffs was the American firm Northwestern Magnesite Co., besides the Canadian exporters of dolomite. The idea was that Harbison and General would buy that part of the Northwestern which produced metallurgic magnesite, so that the firm would concentrate on caustic magnesite production. Since most of the imported material was non-caustic, a reduction of tariffs could be expected after the American iron and steel producers would have lost their main source of domestic metallurgic magnesite supply. In 1926, the American firm Harbison and General bought part of the Northwestern for two million dollars.

The Austrian exporters were supposed to reimburse Harbison and General with lowered prices once US tariffs were reduced. Yet, it never came to that after the US iron and steel producers dropped the question of lowering magnesite tariffs during a hearing in congress in December 1928. The situation worsened for European exporters, when Harbison and General decided to counter Canadian competition with their newly acquired production capacity from Northwestern. Canadian firms had been importing high grade dolomite, a substitute for magnesite which enjoyed much lower import tariffs. In the end, the Austrian exporters concluded a four year agreement with Harbison and General in 1928, stipulating that the Americans would buy an annual minimum quota of 40 thousand tons, of which Veitscher was supposed to have roughly a 50% share. In all, the American market situation for European exporters had deteriorated. The tariff was still high and their main trading partner in the US had its own production capacity. In the second half of the 20s, sales to the US were much lower than before stabilisation. The last agreement came much too late to have any effects, because the depression had already begun.

In 1926, Veitscher production had slightly increased. Still 50% of exports went to the US, where tariffs had dropped to 40% of import value. 30% went to Germany.

64 The Austrian National Committee, *Zollhöhe und Warenwerte*, 15.

65 The following from Walter, 206.

The following year sales were more concentrated on the European market. British firms purchased greater quantities due to the losses from the general coal strike the year before. After stabilisation, sales were the best in 1928 and 1929, just according to the development of world iron and steel production, on which magnesite exports depended. The fierce struggle for market shares and the low utilisation of capacity, which was never more than 40% for Veitscher, was probably not only the result of overcapacities and substitutes for magnesite created during the war.

The overall stagnation of demand for magnesite was also a symptom of the fairly moderate growth of production of the main customer of the magnesite firm, the world iron and steel industry, mostly represented by European and American companies. Between 1927 and 1929, world steel production only increased by 18% and was 51% above the level of 1913 in 1929. Iron production increased in the same period by 13.3% and was only 24% above 1913 levels.[66] The lack of demand due to slow growth of these industries as well as overcapacities were a source for poor economic performance of Veitscher. American tariffs were an expression of this situation and worsened the structural distortion in European magnesite production. Similar to the early 20s, Veitscher was independent of domestic economic development and depended upon the business cycle development of the iron and steel producers of the large industrialised countries. The exact same was the case for the Alpine. Its ore and coal production was largely dependent on the European iron and steel producers.

4.2.6. Paper Industry

a. International Development Besides the wood producing and processing industry, the Austrian paper industry was the only branch of the traditional industries that surpassed pre-war production levels by more than 30% in 1929.[67] Apart from paper and wood, only mining surpassed pre-war levels, but just barely. Until the late 20s, this branch, with about 2% of the total Austrian industrial workforce, was considered one of the most prosperous industries.[68] Still, the international development was also similar here to that of textiles production, where further plant capacities were created and output increased most substantially in countries overseas. The difference in world paper industry development was, though, that the old European producers did not suffer from stagnation symptoms in production as much as the traditional textiles manufacturers. World demand was sufficient to absorb increased production capacities outside of Europe and to make the maintenance of moderate growth in output still possible among the traditional producers in Europe. This was the case at least until the late 1920s. Output still grew most quickly outside of Europe, but the paper industries on the continent were able to enlarge production considerably. Austrian firms clearly benefited from this. This also explains the fairly good performance of

66 Own calculation according to numbers from Statistisches Reichsamt, *Jahrbuch* 1933, 61 (international survey).

67 Österreichisches Institut für Wirtschaftsforschung, *Monatsberichte* 14, 12.

68 Contemporary observers called it one of the "blühendsten Industrien." Statistisches Reichsamt, *Die Wirtschaft des Auslandes 1900–1927*, 249.

Hutter & Schrantz, which delivered felt and wire cloth, mainly for paper producing companies in Austria and abroad.

In Germany, where output was more than 30% above 1913 levels in 1929, the development of paper production was exactly the same as in Austria.[69] In Belgium, production only grew 12%, in Italy 32%, and in the Netherlands, paper and cardboard production grew even up to 83% above pre-war levels. In the Scandinavian countries, growth rates were similar to those in the Netherlands. Between 1913 and 1929, total world production doubled, output grew 80% in the US, grew five times in Canada, and increased seven and a half times in Japan.[70]

In the 1920s, Austrian exports of paper increased continuously, from 61.5 million schillings in 1923 to its peak of 90.4 million in 1929. That was an increase of 47%. Main export countries were Hungary, with a share of 23.3% in 1923 and 18.9% in 1929; Yugoslavia, with a share of around 10%; Britain, around 5%; India, averaged 5.5%; and finally China, with a share of around 6%.[71] Furthermore, Austria exported cellulose, cardboard and various paper goods. Naturally, tariffs were especially high in Poland (63.1%), whose output amounted to around half of overall Austrian production. In Romania and the Czechoslovak Republic, import tariffs were between 30 and 50%. Surprisingly, they were also quite high in Yugoslavia with 32.7%. Hungarian tariffs were relatively moderate among the rates of the successor states, with about a quarter of import value.[72]

b. Leykam-Josefsthaler With more than 3000 workers and employees, Leykam-Josefsthaler AG für Papier- und Druckindustrie[73] was one of the largest paper producing companies in Austria. It benefited from the almost ten year long upswing of paper production in the world until 1930.[74] After the war, the firm sold its plants in Poland and Yugoslavia, which had produced two thirds of overall output. This loss of capacity, though, was already compensated in 1925, by modernisation, plant enlargement and rationalisation at home. Before 1924, Leykam still had one plant in Austria and one in the Czechoslovak Republic. Performance of this firm was contrary to that of Veitscher. While the latter enjoyed great financial standing and good profitability, but stagnating or even declining production, Leykam-Josefsthaler benefited from increasing production, at least until the late 20s, but suffered from low earning power and had an uncertain financial situation. The causes were declining paper and cellulose, increasing wood prices and very high indebtedness.

When scrutinising the profit and loss accounts, the low value of net profits in proportion to gross profits becomes apparent. Only in 1923, 1925 and 1926 were

69 Calculated from production indices in Wagenführ, "Die Industriewirtschaft,“ 56.

70 All numbers calculated from Statistisches Reichsamt, *Jahrbuch* 1933, 76 (international survey).

71 Österreichisches Statistisches Zentralamt, *Aussenhandel*, 52.

72 The Austrian National Committee, *Zollhöhe und Warenwerte*, 3.

73 *Bilanzen*, 16.8.1924, 22.8.1925, 31.7.1926, 23.7.1927, 21.7.1928, 13.7.1929, 2.8.1930. See also A.16.

74 Production numbers of other countries and overall world output verify this development. See Statistisches Reichsamt, *Jahrbuch* 1933, 76

reasonable renumeration rates possible, with 30, 18, and 15%. Before the war, earning power was 23% of gross profits. For all the other years it never surpassed the 7% mark. In 1924, turnover profitability did not even reach one percent. In 1930, clearly the depression hit the company and substantial losses were made. Due to the declining prices and high international competitiveness, constant rationalisation, investment and depreciation was necessary. For example, an investment programme, beginning in 1922, led to the construction of a modern electricity plant that reduced production costs. During the inflation period, high investments were made with the help of several capital increases, allowing for asset value and plant improvement without the necessity of high debts. However, after stabilisation, it was necessary to keep up a high investment rate, leading to high indebtedness. The balance sheet reveals this. After 1925, liabilities were always much higher than debtors. It was not possible to raise sufficient capital on the domestic capital market to finance adequate investment. Thus, the firm had to turn to expensive bank credits, which increased the value of expenses and lowered earning power.[75] Remarkably by 1924, bank credit had increased considerably and first efforts were made to get a long-term foreign loan with lower interests. In the gold balance sheet of 1925, liabilities were only 2.45 million schillings, but the permanent investment, plus the purchase of another plant in 1926, caused debts to increase more than five times. In 1913, liabilities were even higher, but then capital stock and reserve were 30.6 million. In 1925, these were only 12 million.

In 1925, the company received a five year loan worth 150 thousand pounds (about 5.16 million schillings) from a British bank syndicate under the leadership of the Mid-European Corporation. The interest rate was 9.5%. Most of this money was used for investments, but also for the repayment of domestic bank credit. In 1926, another foreign loan was taken up, amounting to 600 thousand dollars (about 4.2 million schillings), increasing overall liabilities to 17.3 million. That was nearly the value of capital stock and reserve. At least almost one third of debts were long-term and no expensive domestic bank loans were utilised. Investment continued to be high until 1929. In 1928 and 1929, debts increased to 19.76 and 22.17 million schillings, of which 11 million schillings consisted of bank credit and the pound sterling loan.

As for most firms, exports progressed very well during inflation times. After reconstruction and policy regime, shift sales abroad became more difficult, but Leykam was soon able to expand export markets, especially outside of Europe. Prices were low, but this was compensated in the short-term by increasing production and reducing costs. The fall of prices for paper products is evident when considering that already by 1923 several plants had reached pre-war output levels, even though gross profit was only 32.8% of pre-war value. In the following two years, output and sales increased again, outrunning pre-war numbers. Capacity was fully utilised. Turnover

75 During the inflation capital was raised with the help of capital increases "und als später die Deroute des inländischen Kapitalsmarktes diesen Weg der Kapitalsbeschaffung verschloß, war die Gesellschaft gezwungen, teures Leihkapital in großem Ausmaß in Anspruch zu nehmen, was die Rentabilität sehr ungünstig beeinflußte." *Bilanzen*, 31.7.1926.

rose 15% annually, while income only increased by 0.5% between 1923 and 1924. This was the result of falling prices. Between the next business years, prices must have stagnated or appreciated because income more than doubled. In these years, 1925 and 1926, expenses did not rise as quickly as gross income.

Most of the time, 60% of sales were exported, chiefly to Great Britain, India, Japan, China, Egypt and to the successor states. Generally, exports did not face any great obstacles, because tariffs must have been low in the Far East and in Britain. Just by the end of 1925, more pressure on prices and increasing competition from Canadian, Scandinavian, and later on, also from Belgian companies was discerned. In the later 20s, another problem for sales was also the beginning political disturbances in the Far East, probably the results of the war between troops of Chiang Kei-Shek and the Warlords in the North of China, between 1926 and 1928, and the communist uprisings after 1927. Even though capacity was fully utilised, a plant had to be shut down because its production costs had become too high. In the late 20s, international competition grew more fierce and prices continued to fall. In 1927 and 1928, low prices caused a decline in gross profits, even though turnover was the same and far higher than before the war. For example, cellulose production in 1928 was 70% above the 1913 level. In the next year, prices for wood kept rising between 15 and 20%, and the upswing of the paper and cellulose industry came to an end.

Thus, even though export sales and turnover were rising until the late 20s, the financial standing of the firm worsened, obvious in increasing indebtedness. In the case of the Leykam- Josefsthaler, the distortions on the Austrian capital market and the high discount rates offered by domestic banks did harm investment growth and performance directly. The main problem was that capital yields for stocks were lower on the stock market, than the yields for bank loans. Thus, companies that were unable to raise sufficient capital themselves from net profits either turned to taking up an expensive bank credit from a domestic bank or attempted to get long-term foreign loans that offered lower interest rates. For Leykam, the main problem must have been the low prices for paper together with a great backlog for modernisation of production. Moreover, Leykam had sold its plant for cellulose production in Yugoslavia during the inflationary period. After 1925, it had to build up new cellulose production plants with expensive credits, because the purchase of this material for the manufacture of paper became too costly. This was also a major factor increasing investment costs and, therefore, overall expenses. Sales and output were rising most of the time, proportionally much higher than gross income. To keep up the spiral of higher production and falling prices, increased productivity and investment was necessary, which caused increasing expenses. At some point in the late 20s, investment costs must have accumulated so much that debt service became a major cost factor of overall expenses. These, in turn, lowered profitability.

c. Neusiedler With between 5000 and 6000 workers and employees, the Neusiedler AG für Papierfabrikation[76] was the largest paper factory in Austria, with large shares

76 *Bilanzen*, 11.11.1922, 13.10.1923, 26.7.1924, 17.10.1925, 12.6.1926, 25.6.1927, 14.7.1928, 7.9.1929, 28.6.1930. See also A.18.

of other plants in the country[77] and in the successor states. In 1924, the branch in Czechoslovakia, the Prager Neusiedler, Vereinigte Papier-, Zellulose- und Holzstoff-fabriken AG, was nationalised, but of its 30,000 shares, the Austrian Neusiedler still kept the controlling majority of 19,153 shares. The Neusiedler also owned a 50% share (72 thousand of a total of 144 thousand) of a paper factory in Romania, the Papierfabrik Petersdorf.[78] So it seems that disintegration only meant a partial loss of productive assets for this firm. Unfortunately, detailed information on profit and loss accounts was not revealed by the management in its annual business reports, and so it is difficult to scrutinise its financial standing and earning power. During the inflation, several capital increases were carried through to pay back bank debts. In 1924, capital stock and reserve made up 53% of balance sheet value. Similar to Leykam, this firm also tried to avoid using domestic credit sources. Three foreign bank loans had been taken up since the publication of the gold balance sheet. These were one Swiss loan of 2 million francs (about 2.7 million schillings) with a discount rate of 8.25% , a 40 thousand pound credit (1.37 million schillings), and a 175 thousand dollar credit (about 1.24 million schillings). Liabilities were still only half of debtors and supplies. By 1926, debts had increased to 19.2 million of which 40% were foreign loans. Since capital stock and reserve were 25 million the next year, the company had considerable debts. Generally, though, its finances were better than those of Leykam.

Although its financial standing was better, production and export performance seemed to have been more moderate than that of Leykam-Josefsthaler. Most of the Neusiedler plants were in Austria and had to import cellulose from factories in the successor states. During the inflation, sales increased and capacity was fully employed, but the imports of cellulose were expensive due to the depreciating Austrian crown. After stabilisation, domestic cellulose production was enlarged and plans were made to build another cellulose plant once capital would be available. In 1924, production was still about one third lower than before the war, but it was possible to increase export sales. Only 40% were sold outside of Austria, and exports were initially not as widely distributed as Leykam's outbound trade. Main sales areas were the successor states (apart from Czechoslovakia and Romania) and the Balkan countries. A small portion of exports also went to Britain and the United States.

However, in the following year, turnover surpassed the pre-war level by 28% , chiefly because of an increase of exports. Suddenly, 75% of production was exported. Output was increased considerably and sold easily, but prices continued to be low. Again, for this firm as well, constant rationalisation and modernisation was necessary to allow for increasing sales with falling prices. Investment was very high in this year only, with a one-time very great peak of 9.33 million schillings. The fall in prices was particularly obvious in 1926, when output rose with capacity utilisation of between 80 and 90%, while gross profits fell 5.8%. In this year, domestic demand was low and an even increased portion of 80% of output was exported. As sales in

77 The company had about one fifth of the shares of the Lenzinger Papierfabrik and shares of the paper factories in Schlöglmühl and of the Theresienthaler. *Bilanzen*, 14.7.1928.

78 In Hungary, the Neusiedler also had shares of the paper factory Goldzieher Géza in Budapest, ibid.

the neighbouring countries became too problematical due to higher tariffs, exports seemed to have been increasingly directed to countries of the Far East. Soon after, exports were sent mainly to China, Japan, India and also to South America. Its plant in the Czechoslovak Republic was largely used for supplying domestic demand and only about one third was exported. The Romanian plant sold all of its production on its home market. Since Neusiedler did not have any plant in Poland, some of its export sales went to this country after 1926.

In 1927 and 1928, once more 80% of output was sold abroad, and the export area was even enlarged to countries like Bulgaria and Italy. These were also the last years when reasonable profits could be made. Plant capacity was utilised up to 80 and 90%, and production facilities of lignin and cellulose were employed to full extent. Similar to Leykam, prices for wood increased while those for paper and cellulose dropped. This considerably reduced the profit margin. In 1927, gross profit only increased by 4.3% and net profit not even by one percent, although production had risen by 11% for paper and 8% for cellulose. While output was raised once again 4% in 1928, gross profits increased only by 1.96% and net profits only 1.4%. The year 1929 meant the end of the moderate boom in paper exports and introduced the beginning of the depression. Prices were depressed and plants had to be shut down.

Essentially, the paper industry also suffered from international overcapacities, just like textiles. The problem was not as acute until the mid 20s, when prices started to fall and competition began to rise. The high pressure to rationalise and to modernise, to maintain productivity on an adequate level to be able to make at least moderate profits, was confined by difficult credit availability. Still, the main problem was not the poor capital market limiting investments, but overcapacities of paper production outside of Europe. These new manufacturers were able to produce cheaper and could keep up with falling prices, although most of them were located outside of Europe and also had to deal with higher transport costs. For Austrian firms to be able to follow the low prices would have meant a major restructuring of production facilities, requiring so much capital that the necessity of investment would have been questionable, even with a well balanced capital market. The distortion of inflation and the capital market only speeded up a process of contraction among the old traditional producers.

4.2.7. Traditional Machine Building Industry

a. Hofherr-Schrantz and Business with Soviet Russia The export performance of the machine building industry was generally positive. Between 1923 and 1929, the value of exports increased 82.3% .[79] Hofherr-Schrantz[80] in Vienna, one of the traditional machine building firms, did not benefit at all from this export upswing. As described in the first chapter, the agricultural machinery producing company suffered heavily from disintegration, inflation and stabilisation. Because of this, productivity

79 Own calculation from Österreichisches Statistisches Zentralamt, *Aussenhandel*, chart: "Ausfuhr von Anderen Maschinen und Apparaten 1923–1937", 68.

80 *Bilanzen*, 18.9.1926, 27.8.1927, 28.7.1928, 1.2.1930, 12.7.1930. See also A.13.

was low, always urging its management to demand higher import tariffs and new trade agreements. These had no results, though, on the company's real economic development.

The financial situation was very unstable and indebtedness was very high. The gold balance account showed a dramatic decline of balance sheet value, debtors and liabilities. The value of capital assets and turnover must have fallen precipitously. Capital stock and reserve amounted to 4.5 million schillings in 1925, of which 3 million were stock capital. In 1913, stock and reserve were about 26 million. In 1925, creditors worth 11.6 million were more than twice as high as debtors, including bank credits running up to 8 million schillings. Thus, bank debts were almost double the amount of available capital stock and reserve. In 1926, bank debt increased, reaching 12 the following and 15 million the next year. That was 69% of all debts, which were by then four times as high as stock and reserve. By 1928 and 1929, debt service payments used up half of gross profits value. The most influential financing banks were the Niederösterreichische Escomptegesellschaft and the Länderbank. In addition to the very high indebtedness, depreciation and investment rates were far too low throughout the 20s, causing a further decline in asset value and productivity. For higher investment rates, bank credit could not be further expanded and capital increases on the stock exchange market were difficult in Austria after 1924 and impossible for a firm with such high debts and meagre sales outlook.

The far too low productivity is obvious when one considers its low profitability. Before stabilisation, the rate was still fairly high with 23%, and then declined to 14% in 1924. In 1925, it was still reasonable with 18.4%, but in the next two years the firm made significant losses. Recovery before 1930 was not possible since the renumeration rate hardly reached 3% until 1929. Therefore, the company ran into the Great Depression with huge debts and low earning power. A breakdown during the depression could be expected.

In 1925, it was still possible to enlarge the export area to Greece, Spain, Italy and South Africa. Yet, this business proved not as profitable as sales at home or to the neighbouring countries, because of expensive freight rates to these areas. Furthermore, widespread sales abroad meant the maintenance of storing larger amounts of stock and the construction of numerous types of machinery, factors which augmented running costs. Of course, the main markets remained in Eastern Europe and Soviet Russia. Since Hofherr's finances, earning power and productivity were so low, business activity and results reacted quickly to any national economic downswings or upswings. This resulted in declining exports, which dropped from 14 to 13.5 million during the next year, as soon as total Austrian exports dropped 11.4% at the same time. Sales especially dropped in Bulgaria (minus 50%), Romania and Poland. Capacity was utilised only to 60%. Management claimed that the 50% tariffs on agricultural machinery particularly harmed exports to Romania. This must have been an exaggeration because customs tariffs on machinery were only 14.6% in this country. Tariffs were only higher in the Czechoslovak Republic and Hungary, where they nearly reached 25% .[81] In Poland, sales dropped because of the regime shift toward drastic stabilisation.

81 The Austrian National Committee, *Zollhöhe und Warenwerte*, 18.

Machinery worth 1.2 million schillings were exported to Soviet Russia, but the terms of payment were very long (up to three years), forcing Hofherr to take up loans. Along with an increase of total Austrian exports of 19.6% in 1927, the company managed to raise its sales abroad. In Poland, the Zloty was stabilised, giving customers in this country greater purchasing power. Business with Soviet Russia doubled and an expansion was deemed possible if the Vienna city municipality would have extended the so-called "Ausfallsgarantie," or deficit guarantee. Since overall exports to Russia had increased (50% in 1925) and Austria had a relatively large share of Russian imports by the late 20s,[82] many firms that had business interests in Russia demanded an export support scheme, or a guarantee for possible losses from foreign business with Russia.

This was deemed necessary as business contracts with communist Russia did not always ensure full or prompt payment for export deliveries, as the country was notorious for its lack of foreign exchange. Most contracts were signed between a Western company and any of the various so-called Russian federal associations of foreign trade, which in turn, were subject to the Russian commissioner of foreign trade. His institution ensured exclusive Soviet government control of all foreign trade.[83] However, even though the federal associations were state controlled, they had private law status, and were, therefore, privately held liable for performing all contract obligations.[84] This way the Soviet government circumvented direct business connections with foreign trade partners and the possibility of state liabilities to foreign Western private enterprises. Thus, although an association could turn out to be unable to pay after large deliveries could have been made by a Western firm, the Soviet government could not be held responsible for pending debts. Thus, many times, the Russian contract partner did not pay for orders that had been made in advance for a few years.

On the other hand, trade with Soviet Russia offered large lucrative export orders during times of high competition on international markets. Furthermore, foreign competition of exports to Soviet Russia, especially from Western Europe and Germany, could afford to grant generous payment conditions to Russia and to the other Eastern European customers, who readily accepted. Austrian firms could not offer such financial favours. Another reason for increasing demand for public export support was that the Austrian banks, among them the national bank, became increasingly

82 Among the small countries trading with Russia, Austria had a high share of total Russian imports in 1929. Austrian share was 2.6%, Belgian 0.5 and Dutch 0.2. The largest importers were Germany (22.1%) and the US (20.1%). See the study of the scientific department of the German nitrogen syndicate (Arbeit der wissenschaftlichen Abteilung des Stickstoff-Syndikates), *UdSSR. Struktur, Industrie, Verkehr, Außenhandel*, Berlin 1939, 62.

83 Foreign trade was controlled by the so-called "Gostorg" (state controlled trade). 90% of imports and 80% of exports were indirectly or directly controlled by the central government. Industrial and agricultural co-operatives and semi-public institutions only conducted foreign trade to a minute degree and were also indirectly controlled by the state. A few private companies and individuals conducted the remainder of foreign trade. Here as well, the state trade office executed some kind of control. See: "Rußland. Section: V. Aussenhandel," in: Statistisches Reichsamt (ed.), *Die Wirtschaft des Auslandes* 1900–1927, 498.

84 Stickstoff-Syndikat, *UdSSR*, 56–57.

reluctant in accepting letters of credit from Russia ("Russenwechsel"), from which payment was uncertain. Therefore, even the national bank began to suggest a public support scheme.[85]

The Austrian central government began to offer an export support scheme after March 1927, with the decision of the national parliament to support Austrian exports to the USSR.[86] The Vienna city municipality followed suit, and in October, concluded to set up a deficit guarantee scheme for exports, but only from Viennese firms to Soviet Russia. The guarantee covered an overall deficit sum of no more than 100 million schillings and only up to 70% of import value. Two federal states followed these examples on a more moderate level. Styria introduced an export support scheme in December 1927 and Lower Austria in March 1928.

In 1927, Hofherr management could reduce losses, and products worth 350 thousand dollars (about 2.5 million schillings) were sold in Russia. In the next year, export, as well as domestic sales picked up, so that the export rate declined to only 50%. Hofherr also began to trade with American tractors, and sales to Russia increased to 500 thousand dollars (about 3.4 million schillings). Aggregate turnover increased nearly 12%, to 16 million schillings. In the last year before the depression set in, turnover increased once more, by 8.75%, or to 17.4 million. Management specifically mentioned that the deficit guarantee of Vienna helped to maintain exports to Russia in this year, although terms of payment were poor. In spite of this moderate upswing in sales, gross and net profit contracted in 1929.

In all, it is clear that economic performance of Hofherr was extremely poor. It did not really follow the upswing of agriculture between 1926 and 1928 in Eastern Europe, when prices for agricultural products were rising for a short time,[87] allowing for higher demand in these areas from increasing purchasing power. In these years, the firm had a large deficit and was still recovering from old debts. Since sales to Russia were only a fraction of total exports, the deficit guarantee was only supportive. The main problems for Hofherr were similar to those of Leykam-Josefsthaler, only much worse. International competition had increased in the 20s, causing prices to fall. Only in France, Czechoslovakia and Hungary were tariffs really a problem. In the other successor states, they were less than 15% and even lower inWestern Europe. The main problem for this firm was its serious lack of productivity and competitiveness. It was not able to make up this backlog because the raising of adequate capital for investment was not possible in the face of substantial debts, amounting to the majority of balance sheet value. It was a classical example of a firm dependent on Austrian bank credit. It probably could not get foreign and cheaper loans because it came out of the inflation with high debts.

b. Engine Factories Probably the firms most directly hit by the changes after the war were the engine factories. Not only were international overcapacities and low

85 Kernbauer, *Währungspolitik*, 239.

86 This was the federal law "über die Förderung der österreichischen Ausfuhr nach der Union der Sozialistischen Sowjet Republiken." Ibid, 241.

87 I.T Berend, "Agriculture," in: Kaser and Radice, *The Economic History of Eastern Europe*, 163 ff.

Austrian productivity a problem, but a shift away from steam powered equipment and machinery to new forms of energy was taking place. After the introduction of the gold balance sheets, the business activity of all locomotives companies was only a fraction of pre-war level. During inflation, it was possible to keep up turnover, but stabilisation clearly revealed overcapacities and obsolescence. Tariff policies were not the problem. Tariffs were fairly moderate in most successor states, with around 25% of value. In Yugoslavia and Germany, they only came to between 8 and 9%.[88]

The main problem was a huge disparity between the production capacities of the locomotive industry and the capacity of absorption of the home market as well as markets abroad. Moreover, Austrian productivity was low. During and after the war, tremendous production overcapacities had been built up in all of Europe and prices for railroad machinery were low. Competition was fierce. The Austrian firms with their backlog in productivity had only a small chance to bid successfully for international invitations of orders from national railways, since firms from abroad could produce and sell under Austrian prime cost prices.[89] Annual production capacity of all four remaining locomotive factories was 400 or more engines, but the federal railways ordered an annual average of only 43 locomotives between 1925 and 1930.[90] As soon as the initial demand of the successor states after war and inflation had been met, sales remained low.

In the period of the moderate boom until 1929, business declined even more, although the manufacturing of new, but fairly simple, machinery had been introduced by some Austrian companies to widen the range of production. Not only was demand of the national federal railway too low, but demand from the successor states remained low as well, apart from a few orders from Russia and the Yugoslavian railway. Austrian exports of all kinds of locomotives, frames and tenders was stagnant and erratic in the late 20s. In 1926, foreign sales peaked, with a value of about 6.6 million schillings, dropped to about 5.3 million in 1927 and fell enormously in 1928 to 1.6 million. The next year it rose back to 5.4 million, but then hit rock bottom during the depression with equipment worth only 5000 schillings sold abroad in 1933.[91] The engine producing industry hardly recovered from that blow.

The AG der Lokomotivfabrik Wiener Neustadt[92] was a good example of this development. Its gross profit value in the business year 1924/25 hardly reached 23% of 1913/14 level. Net profit barely attained 18.5% of pre-war levels. Capital stock and reserve had declined by 40%. Still, bank credit did not exist until 1926/27. In that business year, 40% of liabilities consisted of bank credit, which increased to 85% of all liabilities by 1928. Production costs continuously increased, because of the permanent underemployment of capacity. Depreciation always remained lower than before the war and investment was almost non-existent.

88 The Austrian National Committee, *Zollhöhe und Warenwerte*, 18.

89 Ibid.

90 *Bilanzen*, 6.12.1930.

91 See: Bundesamt für Statistik, *Statistisches Handbuch für die Republik Österreich*, volumes 8–11, Vienna 1927– 1930. And Statistisches *Handbuch für den Bundesstaat Österreich*, volume 15, Vienna 1935. Sections: "Auswärtiger Handel, Ein- und Ausfuhr nach wichtigen Waren."

92 *Bilanzen*, 30.10.1926, 8.1.1927, 21.2.1928, 26.1.1929, 22.3.1930. See also A.17.

After 1925, the company began the manufacturing of boilers, iron and metal casting and parts of simple machinery. A drastic change in the range of production and production plant was avoided, though. Investment was kept to a minimum. Among the Austrian engine factories an arrangement was concluded that allocated a certain quota of federal railway orders to each firm. Still, orders continued to be far too low to offer at least hardly sufficient employment for all companies. Furthermore, Wiener Neustädter was unable to obtain orders from the second most important customer in Austria, the Vienna city municipality, because these were only given to companies within the city limit.

In 1925 and 1926, the railway gave away orders worth 53.6 and 76 million schillings,[93] but still all firms complained of too little employment. In 1926 and 1927, business picked up and turnover nearly tripled from 1.13 to 3.1 million schillings, thanks to increasing orders from the Austrian railway and more exports. Of the orders from the federal railways in 1927 of altogether 40 steam locomotives and the mechanical parts of 10 electrical locomotives, the Wiener Neustädter delivered 21 steam and parts for 10 electrical locomotives. For foreign markets, 25 heavy goods engines and 27 tenders were delivered to the Yugoslavian state railways. In spite of this, its capacity of nearly 100 engines could only be utilised up to 50%. Yet, this year proved to be the best business year after stabilisation. Already in 1927/28, business, profitability and net profit declined slightly. Still the majority of employment came from previous orders and new orders only consisted of 11 locomotives. During the last business year before the depression, 1928/29, no net profit was made. Gross profit had declined 56%, whereas expenses could only be lowered 25%. It was attempted to increase output in the other production branches of machine building, but competition was high and prices too low.

For Wiener Neustädter there was only one reasonable business year after stabilisation, and even then capacity was under-utilised. Its financial standing remained stable, but only because no costly transformation of production was attempted, depreciation was kept far too low and investment rate was almost zero. It pursued a restrictive and conservative policy of retrenchment.

For the larger Wiener Lokomitivfabriks AG,[94] development was very similar, even though it had made greater efforts to widen its production range, which now included steam roadrollers and stationary boiler systems. This locomotive factory was much less export oriented than Wiener Neustädter. The loss of pre-war sales of locomotives could not be compensated. Contrary to many other traditional companies that suffered from war changes, the Wiener was able to maintain the majority of its pre-war capital stock and reserve. In 1913, it amounted to 8.76 million and, in 1925, to 8 million schillings. But this was only possible by strongly raising the value of its productive assets and keeping down depreciation, even though investments during inflation had been moderate. In all, the balance sheet value represented a fairly stable financial status and bank credit did not exist yet. Liabilities increased during the following years, mostly because the federal railways paid for orders in

93 Fibich, 143.

94 *Bilanzen*, 30.10.1926, 17.9.1927, 2.6.1928, 6.12.1930, 24.1.1931, 21.11.1931. See also A.26.

instalments over several years. Thus, the firm had to pre-finance its running production costs on debts. Already by 1926, debts had tripled.

Even though railway orders began to increase slightly in the late 20s, earning power declined constantly. Before the war, profitability was high with 67.4% of gross profit, was at its peak during the inflation in 1923 with 49%, and fell after 1925. In 1926, profitability was only 19.6%, 24% in 1927, and it was down to 14% in 1928. In the next two years, no profits were made, and in 1931, large railway orders increased profitability only slightly to 3.6%. With falling earning power, the financial standing deteriorated as well. By 1930, no more dividend was paid and bank credit had risen to one million. Depreciation was also constantly adjusted downward.

In 1925, turnover fell 33%. Most employment came from repairs, modifications and some export orders from Poland and Bulgaria. Just like for Wiener Neustädter, between the end of 1925 and 1927, business picked up and reached its peak. The Wiener received orders of 55 steam locomotives from the federal railways. Orders for engine frames from Elin, Brown-Boveri, AEG and Siemens, which were manufacturing electrical engines for the federal railways, were also coming in. The department for steam boiler construction delivered high pressure boilers for the Vienna gas works, steam systems for a brewery and for the Lenzinger paper factory. Still, capacity was only utilised between 35 and 40% in 1926. The following year, capacity utilisation was 50%. The hope of the management for increasing orders from more public investment in the national road network, induced it to acquire a patent for the construction of special roadrollers.[95] This hope turned out to be misplaced. In 1928, small export orders came from Soviet Russia, in connection with a deficit guarantee of the city of Vienna. The order included a few heavy locomotives for the construction of the Dnjepr-Stroy hydro-power plant in Russia.

In 1929, profitability was at a low point. Gross profit dropped 23%. After the considerably large orders from the railways in 1926/27, only seven steam and 18 electrical engines were ordered again. The sales of various machinery took over the majority of turnover. Steam boilers, machinery for paper factories and roadrollers were successfully sold. In the last years of the 20s, the Wiener became the leading producer of diesel and steam powered roadrollers in Europe. However, its export orientation was low and it continued to rely too much on a stagnant home market. Only few deliveries were again made to Soviet Russia and Yugoslavia.

The following year, all four Austrian companies of this branch merged into one. The Wiener Lokomotivfabriks AG absorbed the Wiener Neustädter, the Steg and the Krauß Lokomotivfabrik. All useful production facilities were removed from the Steg and the Krauß and installed in the main plant in Floridsdorf. Stock capital was increased from four to 10.66 million schillings and liabilities nearly doubled. Business was at a low point and losses were made. Only two engines for private customers and a mechanical piece for one electric locomotive were produced and delivered. The machinery department produced for the paper industry. Only a few

95 "Sie (Wiener Lokomotiv-Fabriks AG) hat sich aber auch auf den zweitwichtigsten Teil der Investitionspläne des Bundes eingestellt, indem sie das Alleinausführungsrecht der Motorstraßenwalzen nach dem österreichischen Patent Lux erwarb." *Bilanzen*, 2.6.1928.

steam boilers were exported to Yugoslavia. Large state investment for the railways, 151.9 million in 1930, was only noticed by the locomotive industry the next year. Nevertheless, even these substantial sums only allowed for a temporary and moderate rise in business and improvement in financial standing. The depression hit this weak industry heavily, at least by 1932, and it was hardly able to recover.

c. Simmeringer The last firm of the traditional machine building industry which will be discussed is the Maschinen- und Waggonbau-Fabriks AG Simmering.[96] Similar to the engine factories, this company, which mainly produced railway carriages, was naturally also quite dependent on orders from the federal railways. As the previous two firms, Simmeringer also attempted to widen its range of production. Besides carriages, it manufactured steam boilers, coal dust firing systems, steam engines, cable cars, industrial cranes and roadrollers. The management also concluded an agreement with the Foreign Patents Company in London and the Parson & Company in Newcastle for production and sales of patented steam boilers of the Parson system in Austria and Eastern Europe.

Business activity fluctuated violently. After the first large order of 1000 carriages from the railways in 1924, and after deliveries for these orders had been fulfilled by 1925, business declined. The department for the construction of railway carriages was satisfactorily employed until the first half of 1926, but then business activity declined, although the other branches of production received large orders. Yet, the delivery of big steam boilers for the Vienna city gas works, orders for cable cars, cranes and other machinery for industry could not compensate the losses in the railway carriage business. About 90% of total production still came from the manufacture of this product.

The profit and loss accounts clearly revealed the strong dependence of the firm on railway orders. Its financial standing and performance was extremely erratic and in accordance with incoming public orders. After the first large order, gross profit increased dramatically in the business year 1925/26, even though net profit stagnated. Only by late 1927, did railway orders come in, but these were not included in calculations of the financial development of that year. Gross profit declined substantially and were only 55.5% of pre-war value. Only the department of machine building was employed mainly for the delivery of cranes. Half of these were exported to ports in Italy and Greece. Domestic demand came from the Liesinger Brauerei and from a Vienna city power plant for steam boilers.

When in late 1927 and in 1928 orders for 700 passenger, 5450 goods carriages and 200 tramway carriages were accepted, ensuring full employment for three years, turnover and business activity increased. But full capacity utilisation was only possible by late 1928. Income significantly increased over the next two years. Then, gross profit was 63% above 1913 level. In 1928, dividends were raised from 3 to 8%. The machine building department was also well employed. Besides orders for the city of Vienna, 20 cranes were delivered to Argentina and some to Greece. The next year, turnover increased by nearly 27%, four fifths of which were generated by the depart-

96 *Bilanzen*, 29.10.1927, 21.7.1928, 17.8.1929, 12.7.1930, 1.8.1931. See also A.22.

ment of railway carriage production. Even though the depression had affected most companies and was felt by the machine building department, the large public orders from the railways kept the Simmeringer afloat for one more year. The firm was fully employed in 1930, and it was the best business year since the end of the war.

In the long run, though, these public orders were not helpful. At first, financial standing worsened, and then, employment from these orders only lasted for short periods of time. While gross profits sky-rocketed, net gain stagnated. In 1930, net profit was only 97% of pre-war value, even though turnover was much higher. Furthermore, right after 1930, the best business year of the whole inter-war period, the financial standing contracted, resulting in deficits after 1931.

Therefore, to rely on, and to adjust investment primarily to public orders was a great mistake. Even though it had received these large orders, it was not able to sustain itself through the depression without a breakdown. In 1930, as its machine building department conducted sales successfully, it would have been wiser to diversify production, as the Brünn-Königsfelder in Czechoslovakia had done, the largest foreign holding of Simmeringer. Its production capacity was about the size of the Austrian firm, but the department for railway carriages only amounted to 20% of total production capacity. Besides this, the Brünner had departments for machine building, steam boiler construction, and for the manufacturing of equipment for the petroleum industry. It was one of the leading and largest equipper for the oil industry in Europe. While only very small orders came in from the Czechoslovak railways throughout the 20s, Brünner could employ the other departments successfully. It received large orders from the oil refineries in Poland and France (Marseilles). A great disadvantage was that it was hit by the onset of the depression already by 1929, whereas Simmeringer could still sponge off orders from the railways the following year.

4.3. MODERN INDUSTRIES

4.3.1. Electrical Engineering Industry

a. General Development This industrial sector proved to be one of the most stable and crisis resistant industries. For the electrical engineering industry in general, the losses of capital reserves and stocks between the end of the war and stabilisation were quite moderate with a 12% decline. Until the mid 20s, a large proportion of employment from the domestic and foreign markets came from orders of electricity supply companies for the construction of hydro-electrical power plants, from the railways, the Viennese tramways and from the expansion of telephone systems.[97] Since the war, capacities had increased substantially and full employment was not possible and uneven. By the mid 20s, most firms were back to pre-war turnover in value, but not in quantity. This would change in the second half of the 20s, when exports would play an increasing role.

Together with all electricity supply companies, this industrial sector was fairly large with a 12.6% share of overall value of stock of all Austrian joint-stock com-

97 *Bilanzen*, 5.3.1927, "Elektrotechnische Industrie," 254.

panies and a 17.6% share of industrial joint-stock companies in 1926.[98] This share of stock value increased 23% until 1928.[99] Contrary to most traditional industries, the Austrian electrical engineering industry performed extremely well in the second half of the 1920s. Unlike Hofherr, most firms of this branch of industry were able to obtain foreign and cheaper loans for investment when required, because foreign investors showed great interest in this expanding branch.[100] Therefore, availability of capital was fairly easy. This case shows that a lack of investment was not necessarily due to a lack of funds, and that capital could be mobilised by investment opportunities in the large scale application of modern technology, promising future growth and expansion.[101] The emergence and growth of electricity supply companies was a perfect example of this.

b. Electricity Supply Companies The development of electricity generation and supply was at the core of growth of production and increasing demand of electrical engineering products on home markets of advanced countries. Thus, the construction of hydro-electrical power plants was especially important for domestic market demand also in Austria. These construction schemes were basically large long-term public and semi-public investments that offered erratic, but massive employment for the most part of the 1920s. The difficulties of raising capital and of government economic policy, which only half-heartedly supported this development, were not an obstacle. Quite soon after the disintegration of the monarchy, the new Austrian government was interested in enlarging the basis of hydro-electrical power. Two factors favoured this effort: The geography of the country and its dependence on expensive coal imports after 1918. The so-called Wewa,[102] an office of the central government, was established to raise capital for the construction of these plants, organised by several electricity supply companies.[103]

Essentially though, the institution of the central government had difficulty in raising foreign capital, but was able to help with the organisation of the creation of the largest supply companies, the Newag[104] and the Wag.[105] The organisation, partial finance and planning of these and the smaller companies in the other states[106] were taken over by the various Austrian federal states. Thus, all states created their own electricity supply companies, which partially evolved out of the remaining small

98 Statistisches Reichsamt, *Die Wirtschaft des Auslandes 1900–1927*, 254.

99 Own calculation from Bundesamt für Statistik, *Statistisches Handbuch für die Republik Österreich*, volume 11, Vienna 1930, 90/91.

100 Statistisches Reichsamt, *Die Wirtschaft des Auslandes*, 248.

101 Mensch and Schnopp, *Stalemate in Technology*, 61.

102 Wasserkraft- und Elektrizitätswirtschaftsamt (Hydro power and public electrical supply office).

103 See "Elektrizitätslieferungs-Gesellschaften." In: *Bilanzen*, 18.8.1923, 25.8.1923.

104 Niederösterreichische Elektrizitätsgesellschaft (Lower Austrian electrical supply company).

105 Wasserkraftwerke AG (Hydro power works company of Vienna)

106 The companies of the other states were the Oweag in Upper Austria (Oberösterreichische Wasserkraft- & Elektrizitäts AG), the Steweag in Styria (Steirische Wasserkraft- & Elektrizitäts AG), the Salzburger AG für Elektrizitätswirtschaft in Salzburg, the Tiwag in Tyrol (Tiroler Wasserkraft AG) and the Keweag (Kärnter Wasserkraftwerke AG) in Carinthia.

companies founded before or during the war. The states granted these companies generous concessions, such as exclusive control of electricity generation and supply, construction of new plant, easy depreciation of costs via tax reductions and price monopolies. Their system of financing was always the same, either with shares and/or with bonds. Share owners of these companies included the federal states, the large Viennese banks, and large industrial companies which were interested as main consumers of electrical power generation. These institutions were also on the board of directors, usually with the minister presidents of the various federal states as directors. Essentially, these companies were semi-public.

The inflationary process helped significantly in bringing the construction process forward. During the inflation, the investment rate was very high and led to substantial progress in construction. Most of the financing was done on credit. Due to extreme inflation until late 1922, most supply companies were in good standing after stabilisation. High debts, made for construction investment, were essentially depreciated to only a fraction of their pre-inflationary value, while many companies had constructed valuable hydro-power plants. A good example of this development is the Upper Austrian electricity supply company, Oweag. It was founded in 1919, with a share capital of 50 million gold crowns, capital which had not been diluted by inflation yet. The central government participated with ten, the state of Upper Austria with 16, the municipality of the city of Linz with four, and the tramway and electricity supply company of Linz and the Steyr Werke AG,[107] as the main future electricity consumers, with ten million crowns each. Moreover, the Oweag was able to acquire a bond of 600 million and a ten year credit of 100 million paper crowns from Upper Austria and the Bodencreditanstalt. Due to inflation and increasing construction expenses, capital increases and enlargements of the credit and the floating bond had to be carried out in 1921 and 1922.

By the end of the inflation, these sums were extremely inflated, as the company had 22 billion crowns of available capital. Share capital amounted to 4.8 billion crowns, the bond had increased to 7 billion and the rest was credit. Once the inflation was over, these huge sums were enormously depreciated to schillings and only amounted to half a million gold crowns, or 720 thousand schillings. Thus, debts that had helped to increase productive assets substantially were nearly cancelled. And since large productive assets had been accumulated, capital stock could be revalued at a quite high level in the new gold balance sheet of 1925. These companies were clearly winners of the inflationary process. Debts were low, capital assets were enlarged and modernised and further expansion could be expected. Therefore, it was possible to acquire large foreign capital sums already in 1923. Stocks were purchased by a Swiss banking group, under the leadership of the Elektrobank Zurich. This bank group also offered the Oweag a 4.5 million Swiss franc loan. It was also possible to float a two million Swiss franc loan on the domestic capital market. It was bought by two large Viennese banks, an engine factory and AEG Austria. By 1923, the Oweag received income from three finished and running power plants, and was still expanding. The development of the Lower Austrian supply company (Newag) as one

107 In 1919, its name was still Österreichische Waffenfabriks-Gesellschaft Steyr.

of the largest was similar, even though it was officially founded later, in 1922. By 1922/23, it received income and made profits from its nine power plants generating 25 million kilowatts annually.

This development on the regional level resulted in fairly high national growth levels of Austrian electricity supply, offering Austrian electrical engineering companies constant demand. Austrian per capita electricity generation was in the upper European average, behind Belgium and Germany, but higher than in Britain, France, Czechoslovakia or the Netherlands. Nevertheless, compared to other countries with a geographical advantage for hydro-power, as Sweden or Switzerland, Austria was clearly still far behind.[108] There seems to have been a greater Austrian potential of growth for electricity export in the 1920s and for domestic demand of electromechanical machinery.

c. Trade Conditions Until the late 20s, demand from domestic orders for the electrical engineering companies was increasing, but its proportion of total sales declined slightly. The internal shift in economic structure to the application of this new source of energy in small countries did not offer sufficient employment. Domestic demand remained too small for profitable capacity utilisation, in spite of expansion of supply companies' power plants in Austria. And so, all four large Austrian firms had to increase their export sales in order to survive. In the more favourable circumstances after stabilisation, this was possible in the second half of the 20s. The companies could increasingly utilise their capacity of production.

Generally, demand elasticity was low. The change from steam power to the combustion engine and electricity was not only at the core of the above average growth of the electrical engineering industry in industrialised Europe and America, but also central to export growth and demand in the world. Demand for electricity generating equipment, based on hydro-electrical or conventional combustion engine power of all kinds, increased dramatically. Electrical engineering firms, therefore, also the four Austrian firms produced both types. While the exports of steam power generating machines was falling by 36% in the world between 1913 and 1929, it was increasing until 1929 for electrical power machines to a level 47% above pre-war levels. The exports of combustion engines increased even by 81.6% .[109] By far, the largest producers and exporters of electrical power generating machinery were Germany, the United States, Britain and Switzerland. The next largest group of producers were Sweden and France, followed by Italy, the Netherlands and Austria. The latter three had about the same export capacity, varying between a 1.7 and 3.3% share of world trade in electrical goods. Between 1925 and 1929, export growth was the strongest in Germany, with an increase of 43.6%. The American electrical engineering industry was much less oriented to foreign markets and its export sales increased only 15%. Austrian export growth was 30%, well within the European average.[110]

108 See numbers in Statistisches Reichsamt, *Jahrbuch* 1933, 79 and *Jahrbuch* 1936, 89.

109 Wilhelm Heiße, "Die Energiewirtschaft der Welt in Zahlen," in: Deutsches Institut für Konjunkturforschung (ed.), *Vierteljahreshefte zur Konjunkturforschung*, special issue 19, Berlin 1930, 40.

110 Calculated from chart: "Weltausfuhr von Elektrokraftmaschinen nach Ländern," Ibid, 42

Export conditions were favourable, as demand for high-end technology of electromechanical machinery was rising abroad, even though tariffs were moderately high. Surprisingly, import duties on machinery in general were considerable. For example, in Hungary they amounted to 33% of value. Of course, in the Czechoslovak Republic, they were very high, with 46%. In Romania and Yugoslavia, on the other hand, tariffs only came to 23%.[111] Again, those states with the least capabilities to manufacture complex machinery, like Romania or Yugoslavia, imposed relatively low tariffs. Surprisingly, in highly developed countries with advanced and very competitive machine building and electrical engineering industries, import duties were generally also low. These were the industrialised countries in Western Europe, apart from France. In Belgium, they were just 13.2% and in Germany only 10.9%. The only explanation for this must be the relatively small production capacities compared to their large markets and the high competitiveness of their electrical engineering industries. In particular, demand for electromechanical investment goods were high, often times from the supply companies.

For electromechanical goods, tariffs generally varied according to the type of product. Usually, electrical engineering products as capital goods, such as large pieces of machinery for power plant stations, railways and large industrial plant (such as generators and transformers) enjoyed low tariffs in most of the successor states, as well as in Germany and Western Europe. The import duty for generators was 16.8% in Yugoslavia, 20.5% in Poland, and 15.1% in Romania. In Czechoslovakia and Hungary, it was a little higher with 33.2 and 28% respectively. Electromechanical items as consumer goods were taxed heavily, especially telephones, light bulbs and irons. Strangely enough, water boilers enjoyed relatively low import tariffs.[112]

In comparison to other import duties, these tariffs were quite high, especially compared to duties on agricultural machinery. In spite of this, export performance of the Austrian electrical engineering firms was impressive, and there was hardly a need to complain about tariff barriers. While a company such as Hofherr complained about high duties in the neighbouring countries, it actually enjoyed reasonable rates. Whereas the Elin and other firms hardly mentioned foreign import duties, they had to overcome fairly high tariff rates, but still had a successful performance. This situation clearly underlines that protectionist trade policy was of secondary importance for exports of highly complex and advanced industrial goods, and that this was a question of productivity, competitiveness, demand elasticity and market purchasing power.

For the Austrian electrical engineering industry, export value increased from 39.3 million in 1923 to 87.2 million schillings in 1929.[113] That was an increase of nearly 122%, while total Austrian exports only rose 35%.[114] Yet only in 1926, exports of electrical engineering goods stagnated. The major export markets were Germany, the area of the successor states, and the Balkans. Some went to Russia and also to areas outside of Europe. The main competitors on the Austrian market were German

111 The Austrian National Committee, *Zollhöhe und Warenwerte*, 3.

112 Ibid, 19.

113 Österreichisches Statistisches Zentralamt, *Aussenhandel*, 67.

114 Ibid, 12.

firms and on the markets in Eastern Europe, German and American companies, such as General Electric, AEG and Siemens. AEG and Siemens had their largest foreign subsidiary firms in Austria and were, therefore, basically companies generating most of their profits and proceeds for the Austrian economy.

The Österreichische Siemens-Schuckert-Werke and AEG, as the only and largest representatives of their German mother firms, had certain market shares in Eastern Europe delegated by the mother firms. The Siemens plant in Austria was the largest investment of the German Siemens in Central and Eastern Europe.[115] While the Austrian market was much too small for them, these could only export to the areas of South-Central and Eastern Europe. The two subsidiaries of AEG, Telefunken and Osram were also main competitors of the other Austrian firms on the Eastern European market. The former focused on radio production and held a considerable share of the markets in the area between 17 and 74 %. The latter company specialised in bulb manufacture and had plants in Czechoslovakia, Greece and Poland.[116] Siemens had factories in each of the main successor states. Both originally German firms, AEG and Siemens were the main competitors of the only electrical engineering company that was purely Austrian, the "Elin" Aktiengesellschaft für Elektrische Industrie.[117]

d. Elin After substantial expansion of export markets, capacity and foreign holdings during disintegration and inflation times, business activity of Elin was much higher in 1925 than before the war. In 1913, capital stock and reserve amounted to 4.7 and to 6.75 million schillings in 1925. That comprised about 47% of the balance sheet value, which in turn, was about 15% higher than before the war. After the mid 20s, dividends were comparably high, amounting to 10%. Financial standing had been stable before stabilisation and remained in a favourable position thereafter. The balance sheet shows that liabilities nearly reached debtors only by 1927. In all other years, creditors were considerably below the value of financial demands toward others. The profit and loss accounts also revealed a positive and stable development. Most of the time, investments were above depreciation, which also remained fairly stable. In 1929 and 1930, investment rate was considerable, reaching 33% of gross profits value in both years. Earning power performance also remained stable. Before stabilisation, turnover profitableness, the percentage share of net profit to gross profit, was 17.8% in 1923. After currency and balance sheet reconstruction in 1925, it still amounted to 16%. After that, it slightly declined to 14% in 1926 and 13.6% in 1929, while high investments were made. After 1927, balance value rose considerably and was 156.5% above the pre-war level in 1929, suggesting a substantial expansion of business volume and productive capital. Consequently, the firm was

115 Harm Schröter, "Siemens and Central and South-East Europe between the two world wars," in: Alice Teichova and P.L. Cottrell, *International Business and Central Europe, 1918–1939*, New York 1983, 173–191.

116 Ibid, 174.

117 *Bilanzen*, 24.7.1926, 18.6.1927, 9.7.1927, 14.7.1928, 22.6.1929, 13.7.1929, 19.7.1930. See also A.10.

able to encounter the worst depression of all times with a fairly stable financial and business background.

The years 1925 and 1926 were still characterised by stagnation and stabilisation in the Austrian and German economies. Austrian GNP only grew 1.7%. Gross profit of Elin only rose 4.3%, and the main plant was only utilised by 60%. In 1925, only 32% of overall turnover was exported. Business activity and demand was low on the domestic market, which the management blamed on the low investment rate of industry. Orders in Austria came from the large power plant constructions, the railways, postal service and the city municipality of Vienna. The high-frequency department received orders for the electrification of the Arlberg railtrack, for the delivery of several electrical locomotives and their equipment and for various transmission lines. In fact, orders for railway engines were so large that employment for this department was ensured until 1928. From Vienna, Elin received orders for line transformers. The export rate was low, but sales were widely distributed. Due to an arrangement of the Compagnie Hellénique d'Electricité, the power plant in Athens ordered rectifier generators. For the Russian local railway, Baku-Surachani-Sabuntschi, the Elin delivered electrical equipment for 14 motorcoach trains. Its subsidiary sales firms generally performed well. Business was slow in Yugoslavia, but satisfactory in Bulgaria, Greece, Italy and Romania. In Romania, sales were especially good, because of orders from the domestic oil rigging industry. In Poland, sales were favourable during the first half of the year, but then slowed down, because of the sudden depreciation of the Zloty. In Hungary and Belgium, sales declined after import tariffs were raised. Some items were also sold in England.

In the first months of 1927, business activity was still low and capacity was only utilised between 30 and 40%. Yet, after the middle of 1926, sales improved and utilisation was between 70 and 80%. Thus, overall turnover was, in the end, as high as in the year before. The export rate increased. Besides the usual orders on the home market for transformers, generators and transmission lines for power plants, the postal service and the railway, export sales increased in Germany, Britain, Spain and Russia. The Soviet government ordered significant amounts of industrial electrical engines and welding equipment for the state railway system. Business to new export markets in Egypt, Central and South America thrived. Large orders also came from Greek power plants. For the steam turbines of a plant in Philippopel, Elin delivered the electrical equipment as well as built various pieces of equipment for other Greek plants. In combination with the Gefia AG, the Elin received an order worth 250 thousand dollars to begin the construction of a hydro-power plant in Philippopel. The foreign subsidiary firms also competed well. After stabilisation of the Zloty, business in Poland prospered again.

After 1927 until 1929, business in the inter-war period peaked. In 1927, the Elin was able to raise turnover 25%, even though competition grew more fierce. Once more, large orders came from the federal railways and the city of Vienna. Other domestic orders came from power plants of the Steweag, from plants in Innsbruck, Graz, Kitzbühel, from cable car companies and from the Viennese local railways.

New technological development and the beginning of serial production of larger electrical equipment helped to improve sales. The production of the new automatic welding systems and of the new large fibre rectifiers was sold easily. Productivity of Elin must have been very high, since its exports, even to advanced industrialised countries, continued to increase. Sales to Germany, France, Britain, Spain, Russia, Egypt and South America were rising. In the Greek town of Janina, Elin constructed a power plant. In Plovdiv (Bulgaria), a steam generator was installed, and even in Romania, sales remained high, despite the crisis of the oil industry. In Italy, the protectionist policy was successful in preventing large imports of electrical goods. The company had low sales, but was still cabable of receiving large orders for electrical equipment from the tyre producer Michelin.

As business volume, turnover and gross profits (1.1%) rose in 1928, while net profits increased 49.4%, the need for investment capital became acute. Hence, a capital increase was executed, but not for debt coverage. It was employed for anticipatory finance of large projects. A capital increase was very unusual for an Austrian firm in the late 20s, because business activity and interest for new stocks were low on the home stock exchange market. Their profitability and discount rate were at rock bottom. The increase, and therefore, the availability of new investment capital for the management became possible when the Prudential Insurance Company in London bought a very large share of the new active stocks. Finally, the economy slowly began to improve, allowing domestic demand for electrical consumer goods to rise appreciably. Demand from Austrian industrial firms also increased. Not only did power plants and the railways order electrical engines, transformers and accumulator re-chargers, but the Alpine also received two transformers.

The first electrification programme expired in this year. Even though still 44.2 million schillings were invested for overall railway electrification in 1928,[118] the Elin noticed a drop of demand from the federal railways. This deficit in demand, though, was easily offset by increasing export sales. Turnover from foreign sales rose. Sales to Czechoslovakia and Germany increased, especially for welding equipment. Business with Soviet Russia was also rising. Exports experienced a great upswing in the countries of the Far East and South America. The introduction of new patents for the production and manufacture of new items, such as cinematographs and self-cooling oiltransformers, was successful. Many orders for switchboard, power supply systems and for line protection relays came in from Bulgaria and Greece.

In 1929, business was still successful. Gross profit augmented 14.4%. Yet, net profit rose by only 2.4%. This was due mainly to falling business in the later part of the year, and because of massive sums used for investment, which more than tripled to 2.54 million schillings. A new machine building plant was finished in Weiz. The large investments and future investment plans made the utilisation of a bonded debt necessary. It amounted to 220 thousand pounds (about 7.6 million schillings), which were floated on the British capital market with a net interest rate of 8% and a 25 year long running term. The money was also used for further anticipatory credit for large construction schemes, such as power plants. In spite of this loan, indebtedness of

118 It seems that Elin received employment mostly from the first electrification programme which ended in 1928. The second programme was still running until 1930. The investment sum of 44.2 million was mainly for the later programme, Fibich, 146.

Elin was still low. In this year, earning power declined as a result of the depressed business situation in the last quarter, even though considerable orders from public institutions and from domestic firms were still coming in.

Increasingly, the firms in Austria, from the sugar, textile and brewery industries, purchased electrical equipment. Switchboards, transformers, tramway engines, power plant equipment and electrical locomotives were delivered for the Austrian railway and for Vienna. Home demand was falling, though, and was countered by increasing export sales, particularly of special high-end technology equipment. For example, the company was the leading producer of special welding equipment, which enjoyed very low demand elasticity. Therefore, it was still possible to improve overall sales 15%. Exports to Germany, Western European and also to the Scandinavian countries had improved. Sales of wire for generators, rectifiers and light bulbs increased. Transformers and transmission lines were delivered to, and constructed for, Yugoslavia. Several diesel power stations were delivered to Greece. Orders from Russia reached their peak, although the trade concession of the "Russowastorg AG" expired in 1929.

However, business outlook for 1930 was pessimistic. Although, net profit declined 34.5% and gross profit 1.3%, the financial situation still remained acceptable. The invested sum in 1930 of 2.5 million schillings was still very high. A dividend of 8% could still be maintained. A strong deterioration of the financial standing was prevented, because a large backlog of unfulfilled orders remained.

For Elin, trade barriers were of nearly no relevance at all, and even though its profitability was moderate, its future development was considered positive in the 20s. The problems, caused by a small market, high competitive export sales and the finding of new markets, were easily overcome. The difficult availability of capital in Austria also proved to be no problem for Elin, because foreign capital groups were willing to allocate substantial sums for investment, either in the form of purchasing stocks for a capital increase or in the floatation of long-term low interest loans. Why were restrictive trade policies, new and open competitive markets, stagnating home market and capital scarcity less effective than for the Alpine, Hofherr or Brevillier, even though Elin started from a small productive asset basis before the war? The decline of the traditional industrial sectors, to which the former three firms belonged, provides the explanation. The quality of the companies did not decline, but rather, their competitive market environment of their industrial sectors changed substantially due to a structural shift in the world economy.

The next three electrical engineering firms, Siemens, AEG and Brown-Boveri, were much less export oriented than Elin, relied much more on orders from the home market, especially from public and semi-public orders and did not perform quite as well. Still their financial standing was stable.

e. Siemens Post-inflation performance of the largest electrical engineering company in Austria, Siemens-Schuckert,[119] was generally positive. Its earning power was

119 *Bilanzen*, 5.12.1925, 21.8.1926, 2.7.1927, 9.7.1927, 7.7.1928, 6.7.1929, 5.7.1930, 4.7.1931. See also A.21. Siemens Austria had between 6000 and 7000 workers and employees. Elin had between 1500 and 2000.

slightly higher than that of the previous firm. While Elin had higher profitability before stabilisation, Siemens only had 7.9% in 1923. In 1913, it had been 16.7%. Yet, pre-war turnover profitability was quickly recovered. It increased from 9.3% in 1924 to 17.3% in the following year. It peaked in 1930 with 19.4%, which showed that it was hit by the depression a bit later than many firms. The profit and loss accounts revealed a stable development. Between 1925 and 1929, gross profit rose 65% . Investment was erratic, but usually above depreciation. For the balance sheet reconstruction of 1925, large capital reserves were needed. The balance sheet shows a substantial increase of balance sheet value in that year. Value was nearly 60% higher than in 1913, suggesting a massive increase in productive capital. Capital stock and reserves amounted to 50 million schillings, that was about 72% of balance value. Siemens also seems to have used the exceptional circumstances of inflation for investments financed by high credit. Until 1924, liabilities nearly made up balance sheet value, but after the introduction of the reconstructed gold account, debtor value remained above total debts. Investment rate peaked in the last year of the upswing to 24% of gross profits value. Siemens never used a large bank credit, and by the end of 1928 there were no bank debts.

Similar to most Austrian firms, 1925 and 1926 also meant recession business years for Siemens. Even utilisation of capacity was not possible, mainly because of a lack of continuous orders from industry. Orders were mainly from the large power plants in Vienna and Tyrol for large pieces of machinery, from the federal railways for electrical engines and from the federal postal service for transmission lines. Therefore, Siemens increasingly focused production on the manufacturing of special machinery and special designs, such as industrial heating systems or turbo generators. These were not only delivered to power plants in Austria, but also to Czechoslovakia, Poland and to Austrian firms, for example, Alpine and Schoeller-Bleckmann. The majority of sales was still disposed on the domestic market, apart from some orders from power plants in Yugoslavia, Hungary and Romania.

Generally, it can be said that a large portion of employment for Siemens came from semi-public and public orders. Yet, this demand was not sufficient for reasonable and profitable capacity utilisation. This company was much less export oriented than Elin and largely had to rely on increasing industrial investment for electrification in the late 20s. Industrial investment after the recession years of 1925 and 1926 increased and formed a large portion of demand for Siemens. Business activity picked up considerably. Turnover was increased 20% in 1927. General industrial investment experienced an upswing, and large orders came in from domestic companies as well as from firms abroad, besides the usual orders from semi-public power plants, railways, the postal service and the Vienna city. The department for industrial equipment received orders from the textile and sugar industry for all sorts of electrical power systems and from Russia for the complete electrical equipment of the cold storage warehouses in the ports of Odessa and Sevastopol. Other orders were for electrical thermo systems for the heavy industry, special power systems for machine tools and for machinery and engines for the agricultural sector. Deliveries were also made to Bulgaria for large rectifier equipment, to Romania for rail-car equipment, and to Yugoslavia for industrial equipment. Still, exports made up a minor part of overall sales. The moderate upswing in 1927 also allowed for increasing sales of electrical consumer articles. The sales of warm water boilers were especially booming until the beginning of the depression.

In the following two years, business activity reached its inter-war peak, as did most other firms. Besides deliveries for domestic power plants and railways, large orders were coming in as a result of industrial investment. Exports were oriented to the Balkan countries, Hungary, the Czechoslovak Republic and Poland. With the help of the deficit guarantee of the city of Vienna, transformers and machinery were also sold in Russia. However, the majority of turnover increase came from sales in Austria. Only about 20% was exported. In 1929, turnover was increased once more by 10%. A substantial increase in industrial orders was noticed. Deliveries were made to the Plansee Ltd., Alpine and to rubber and paper factories. The Austrian federal railways also made substantial orders for electrification.

Surprisingly, in 1930, the amount of orders from industrial investment increased, constituting a large portion of employment for Siemens, whereas a deficit in orders for railway electrification and power plant construction was felt. This shows that there was no correlation between state railway investment, which was at its peak in 1930 and employment of firms that usually received a large portion of electrification orders.

f. AEG AEG Austria[120] had the poorest performance of all electrical engineering companies. Even contemporary economic journalists were surprised, because the electrical engineering companies generally did quite well after the war. One great disadvantage was that its volume of exports was small compared to total turnover. Moreover, foreign business showed little diversification, similar to Siemens' business. Only between 15 and 25% of production was exported. Management regarded sales on foreign markets as hardly lucrative, because prices were considered too low. Furthermore, it relied to a much greater degree on semi-public and public orders, which offered low market prices. This rigid sales strategy, which was probably due to a large degree to the allocation of sales markets by the German mother firm,[121] resulted in low capacity utilisation and moderate earning power.

Compared to 1913, the production capacity of its plant had been doubled by 1925, but even in the best business years only 50% capacity utilisation was possible. In 1913, profitability had been 36.3% of gross profits value, was still high with 27% in 1923, but declined after 1925 to between 10.2 and 12.3%. It remained on that level until the depression set in. Balance sheet value also dropped dramatically, by 62.5% between 1913 and 1925. In spite of its fairly moderate economic performance, AEG only had to temporarily rely on bank credit. In 1926, it was possible to take up a foreign loan from the CA, the Bodencreditanstalt and from the banking house Blankhart & Co. in Zurich. The loan amounted to seven million Swiss francs (about 9.6 million schillings) with a 25 year long term at 7% interest rate.

120 *Bilanzen*, 24.7.1926, 10.9.1927, 19.5.1928, 25.5.1929, 14.6.1930, 4.7.1931. See also A.1.

121 The German AEG parent firm allocated only a fraction of the Czechoslovak, Yugoslavian, Hungarian, and Polish markets as export areas to the Austrian firm.

During the years of moderate downswing (1925–1926), most of employment came from railway orders and power plant deliveries. Sales for industrial investments were low and a delivery of equipment for electrical harbour cranes to Chile was an exception. Orders of large pieces from electricity supply companies and for the railway resulted in uneven employment of the different departments. Attempts were made to intrude more in foreign markets with the sales of specialised machinery, and deliveries were made to paper, wood, cement and textile firms in the successor states. Similar to the previous two firms, 1927 was also a good business year for AEG. Turnover improved in Austria and in the successor states. Yet again, most of demand was generated at home by the railways and power plants. The department for industrial equipment was under-utilised. Even in the best business years, 1928 and 1929, the most important customers were public institutions.

g. Brown-Boveri The development of the much smaller Brown-Boveri[122] was very similar to AEG, only that its earning power was better. It increased from 11% to 17.6% in 1928. Management was able to avoid heavy bank credit service as well, by converting bank debts into a 1.5 million Swiss francs loan with 7% interest, taken up from its parent company in Switzerland. Once again, the years of 1925 and 1926 meant recession periods, followed by a moderate upswing between 1927 and 1929. Only in these years, was it possible to increase the export rate moderately to 10% of total sales.

In 1928, the Austrian Brown-Boveri, in combination with its Romanian sister company, was able to get an order in the range of 3 or 4 million Swiss francs, to equip a Romanian power plant near Jalomita that supplied Bukarest with electricity. The customer was a recently established electricity supply company, financed by the Escomptegesellschaft, the French bank Banque Coloniale and the Belgian Societé Générale de l'industrie hydraulique. Brown-Boveri also made deliveries of generators, transformers and switchboard systems for Russian gold mines in Siberia, amounting to 90 thousand dollars in these years. Exports to Soviet Russia were strongly enhanced by the deficit guarantee of Vienna. In this case, economic policy had direct effects on sales. Exports also went to most Balkan countries and the Near East. By and large, though, the company relied on home demand. 90% of total turnover was sold in Austria, of which roughly one third came from the railways and the city of Vienna. Business must have gone well at least until the mid 1930s, because management business outlook was surprisingly optimistic until then, expecting future employment from the connection between bank capital and the electrical engineering industry.[123]

Yet, in the business report for 1930, published the next year, the declining activity due to the beginning of the depression was noticed. Turnover shrunk by one quarter, gross profits by nearly 6% and net profits by 16.4%. In this time the low export orientation and high dependence on public orders had negative implications

122 *Bilanzen*, 18.9.1926, 30.4.1927, 30.6.1928, 15.6.1929, 7.6.1930, 1.8.1931. See also A.7.

123 "Man erwartet sich eine günstige Auswirkung von der Zusammenarbeit von Bankverbindung und der Elektrizitätswirtschaft." *Bilanzen*, 7.6.1930.

on financial standing and performance, because the rate of domestic orders declined faster that the rate of export sales.

4.3.2. Motor Industry

a. International Development and Trade Conditions The most significant characteristic of the Austrian automobile industry was its strong export orientation,[124] which was in sharp contrast to the strictly home market and protectionist oriented car manufacture industries of the five large states that dominated world production, the US, Britain, France, Germany and Italy. Ironically, this export concentration, coupled with a lack of comparable international productivity, was essentially one of the main problems of this Austrian industrial sector. It was a perfect example of a modern industrial branch in a small country that did not enjoy the advantages of the equally or more capital and technology intensive mass-producing counterparts in the large industrialised countries. In Europe and the US, car manufacture and sales were strictly tied to the various large domestic markets of the big modern countries, because the sales of these mass-produced durable goods depended upon the limited mass consumption power of the various national economies. In 1938, foreign sales among these five large powers only amounted to 5% of their total exports of motor vehicles, since each group of national producers controlled its own market. Thus, world motor vehicle trade mainly consisted of outbound trade from these large countries to small and/or less developed countries.[125] This tendency was enhanced by protectionist trade policy that supported the interest of national car manufacturers.

The Austrian automobile industry did not fit into this general pattern and directly suffered from the split and controlled structure of foreign markets. Considering the advantageous production and trade conditions of the larger foreign producers, it is surprising that the Austrian manufacturers held their ground as well as they did. There was always a large Austrian export surplus of automobiles. Still, export performance was erratic, revealing its dependence on international business cycles in the countries of its most vital markets, Western Europe and Germany. In 1923 and 1924, export value of all types of vehicles and car engines[126] was at its zenith, with a value of roughly 54 million schillings. This shrunk enormously until the recession year of 1926 to less than half, and rose again until 1928 to 51 million schillings. In 1929, the first recession signs were noticed and export value declined 6%. The change in numbers of automobiles exported was not as extreme and demonstrated the decline of prices by more than half, which forced companies to increase productivity permanently.[127] This decline in prices was enhanced by increasing production of mass-produced smaller and cheaper vehicles. The export sales of the automobile

124 Statistisches Reichsamt, *Die Wirtschaft des Auslandes*, 248.

125 Svennilson, 150–151.

126 This included automobiles, trucks, motorbikes, engines and parts for vehicles of all types.

127 The decline in prices is calculated from the numbers and value of cars exported, according to Österreichisches Statistisches Zentralamt, *Aussenhandel*, 70. The actual export numbers must have been far higher, since Steyr alone produced and exported far more automobiles than the numbers from the Österreichisches Statistisches Zentralamt suggest.

industry was heavily hit by the depression. Until 1933, the number of cars sold abroad shrunk from several thousand to 318.[128] The fact that exported Austrian vehicles were, on average, much more expensive than imported vehicles[129] reveals the lower productivity of Austrian manufacturers.

The main markets, besides the German as the most important, were the Western industrialised countries. Some vehicles were also sold on the markets of the successor states. Trade conditions were generally hostile, as European car manufacturers had been able to exclude their national markets from international competition and imports. The countries with the highest purchasing power, naturally the countries that had automobile industries themselves, imposed the highest import tariffs. In Belgium, tariffs were fairly moderate with 23%, in Britain 33.3%, in Germany and France it was quite high, with around 45% or higher, and tariffs were the highest in Italy with 48%. Austria itself had a considerable import tariff of 40%. Czechoslovakia, with its own developing car manufacturing industry, also offered a high tariff of 45%. Naturally, in the lesser developed successor states, import duties were much lower, apart from Hungarian tariffs. They were between 20% in Yugoslavia and only 5.8% in Romania.[130] Generally, for trucks and motorbikes, duties were slightly lower in all countries.

Year	Germany	GB	France	Italy	Belgium	CSR	Austria	US	World
1926	45.5	198	192	64.8	6	7	5.3	4300.9	5035.2
1927	114.9	211.8	191.3	54.6	6.5	10.2	8.7	3401.3	4159
1928	137.9	211.9	223.6	59.8	8.2	13.2	9.4	4358.7	5203.1
1929	127.9	238.8	245.6	54.1	7	14.7	9.1	5358.4	6277.5

Table 4.2.: Production of automobiles and trucks, 1926–1929 (thousand). Source: Numbers from Statistisches Reichsamt, *Jahrbuch* 1933, 69 (international survey).

Not only the export sales situation was difficult for Austrian vehicle manufacturers. The domestic market was not only far too small for national production facilities, but had a relatively low consumption level. This is evident when comparing number of people per vehicle in different countries in 1929. Among developed countries, Austrian per capita number was by far the highest with 200. In Portugal, it was 224 people per vehicle. Germany was also far below average of industrialised European countries, with 111 people per vehicle. In France, it was only 23, in Britain 35, and in Belgium 66 people per vehicle.[131]

128 All numbers on trade from Österreichisches Statistisches Zentralamt, *Aussenhandel*, 70.

129 Ibid.

130 All tariffs for 1927. The Austrian National Committee, *Zollhöhe und Warenwerte*, 19.

131 Statistisches Reichsamt, *Jahrbuch 1930*, 72 (international survey). For comparison, in the U.S., the number of people per passenger car was only 4.6.

Growth of the Austrian vehicle industry could bear international comparison. The chart below clearly demonstrates to what extent the American industry dominated world vehicle production, with a share of more than 85%. World average production growth rate was roughly 20% between 1926 and 1929, the same as in the US. In Britain, France and Belgium, it was between 17 and 22%. Only in Germany, Belgium, Austria and Italy, production declined as early as 1929. These were also the countries with the highest rates of growth between 1926 and 1928. It was highest in Germany and Austria, with 67 and 44%. Czechoslovakia had the best growth performance of vehicle production, with 52% until 1929. Thus, Austrian growth performance was well above world average, despite difficult trade conditions and a small home market. German growth rates were high, because they started off from a very low level in 1926.

b. Steyr The size of this branch was relatively modest, but not different from other industrialised countries, save the United States. Austrian vehicle producing firms only had a share of 1.8% of overall joint-stock capital or a 2.4% share of industrial joint-stock capital in 1926.[132] This relation did not change in the 1920s.

Financial Standing

With around 6000 workers and employees, the Steyr Werke AG[133] were the dominating automobile producer in Austria. Automobile manufacturing provided at least 70% of total production. The rest consisted of ball bearings, small fire-arms and bicycles. Its unusual balance sheet and profit and loss account development until 1928, suggesting expansionist, risky and aggressive business policy, has already been noted. The development of earning power verifies an increasingly risky and alarming course of business and state of financial standing. Before stabilisation in 1923, the net profit share of gross profit was 27.6%. This ratio declined constantly until 1927, to 16% and finally dropped to less than 6% the next year. The following two years, no balance sheets and profit accounts were published.

Balance sheet value quickly matched pre-war value after it had already reached 81% of the 1913 level in 1925. In 1928, it exceeded this level 42.5%. Its financial standing was quite unstable, as the value of liabilities was far above debtor value and rose just as dramatically as balance sheet value. In the same year, liabilities surpassed pre-war value by 59%. A large portion of this was bank credit. Of the 35.3 million schillings debt burden in 1927, about three quarters consisted of bank debts, which meant that the value of short-term debts was 43% higher than joint-stock capital. In just one year, the debt burden was nearly doubled to almost 58 million, 48 million of which were bank debts. That was more than double the value of capital stock and reserve and 82% of total turnover in 1928. It seems that these huge debts were mainly utilised for permanent and necessary plant enlargement or for improvements

132 Own calculation from chart: "Aktienkapital der Gesellschaften mit Goldbilanzen Ende 1926," in: Statistisches Reichsamt, *Die Wirtschaft des Auslandes*, 254.

133 *Bilanzen*, 10.7.1926, 2.7.1927, 4.8.1928, 27.7.1929, 31.8.1929, 30.11.1929, 11.1.1930, 28.6.1930. See also A.23.

to introduce a new type of car, to adjust to mass production and to attempt to compensate for a backlog in productivity and competitiveness.

Business Activity

Despite the alarming financial development, production, sales and returns were improving annually. The company was extremely export dependent throughout the 20s. After 1925 until the rest of the decade, between 50 and 80% of production was outbound. Even though many industries experienced a moderate downswing in 1926, Steyr plant was utilised to the limit. Output was increasingly adjusted to serial production of mass-produced, cheap cars.[134] Sometimes, up to 30 cars were manufactured daily, about 5000 annually, of which only 1500 were sold on the home market. Turnover increased 25% and production 35%. In 1926, Steyr alone manufactured 94% of the entire Austrian automobile production. The following year, output increased 40%, to 50 cars daily. After 1925/26, domestic consumption began to improve and the company began to use a loan society, Schenker & Co, to improve purchasing conditions for customers and to enhance domestic sales even more. While Steyr would receive full payment from the intermediate financing company, it in turn, received the first instalment of 40% from the customer. So, in the later 20s, an increasing share was sold on the home market. In 1928, for example, the export rate had declined to 50%.

While 1927 was still a good business year (production rose 30%, gross profits 23.6% and net profits 3.3%), the last two years before the onset of the depression revealed its weak and risky financial standing in the face of intensifying international competition and falling prices. At first this development, despite ever increasing sales, turnover, and production, seems strange. By 1928, the heavy burden of servicing huge bank debts was felt. In this year alone, these had increased 60%. Even though turnover and production increased 40%, dividend had to be cut from 10 to 5%. Until then, high dividend was maintained in the hope of increasing the market price of newly issued joint-stock capital. Instead, high dividend distribution only raised debts and interest payments. High rate of production and turnover could only be sustained by offering large price concessions.

In the late 20s, international competition, especially from German, French and American firms, had become extremely fierce. This depressed prices and forced more rationalisation and modernisation. Steyr was simply not able to keep up with the international level of competitiveness and productivity and could hardly follow low international prices. This development revealed the symptoms of the disadvantages of a national producer in a small country. Even though substantial rationalisation had been carried out, Steyr automobiles were too heavy, the frames used up too much material and were too expensive.[135] Often times, cars had to be sold abroad without any profit. The profit and loss account of 1928 reflected this development clearly. Gross profit still rose, by about 17%, while net profit fell 57%. As export sales were

134 This was the Automobiltype XII. Price was about 10 thousand schillings in 1926.

135 During this time the management had great hopes in its new engineer, Ferdinand Porsche, and the new eight cylinder car released in fall 1929.

raised constantly, customs tariffs were not the most important problem at all, as the management stated itself.[136] Still, the company desired higher import tariffs for foreign vehicles. Because outbound vehicles sales for profitable prices became increasingly difficult for Steyr, management attempted to focus more on its subsidiary production of ball bearings and bicycles. The former branch of production had been able to improve its production facilities technically, at least comparable with high international standards and could double output in 1927. Three quarters were sold outside of Austria. Yet, losses in the automobile business could not be recovered.

In 1929, Steyr had to change its business policy completely. A deficit of 24.15 million schillings, that was nearly 30% of balance sheet value, was made. The last type of car, the XX, was an absolute failure. It reached the market far too late and sales stopped altogether in the last three months of 1929. The increasing sales and turnover of ball bearings and bikes could hardly compensate for the losses in the automobile business. Its high debts with the Bodencreditanstalt contributed to the breakdown and merger of this bank with the CA in this year, which in turn, executed the financial reconstruction of the Steyr Werke in the following years.[137] This was mainly done by creating a working pool in combination with the Austro-Daimler-Puch AG, which was also in close financial affiliation to the Creditanstalt. Under the leadership of this bank, the companies merged in 1934. Meanwhile, the large Steyr bank credits were turned into capital stock by the bank. By the end of the depression, the CA held 80% of Steyr stocks.[138]

c. Daimler-Puch The second largest automobile producer in Austria was the Austrian Daimler-Motoren AG.[139] The Puchwerke AG and the Österreichische Flugzeugfabriks AG, a small aircraft company, merged with Daimler in January 1928, forming the Austro-Daimler-Puch AG, which in turn, merged with Steyr in 1934. Financially, Daimler did not perform quite as badly as Steyr. Its development was similar though. Production and sales rose, while the company suffered from high indebtedness and insufficient productivity.

After its crisis year of 1924, when the company made a deficit, it was not able to recover financially. Earning power remained very low, between 2 and 5%, until the merger. The balance sheet showed highly increased liabilities compared to pre-war values. After 1925, the greater part of balance sheet value consisted of liabilities. For example, in this year the balance value was 17.7 million. Of this sum, only 1.8 million were capital stock and reserve and more than 14 million were debts of various kinds. Productive assets only had a value of 4.3 million. The heavy burden of indebtedness is obvious in the great share of interest payments of gross profits. In 1924, almost 75% of gross profits were spent on interest payments. Until the merger, it was almost always more than half. Financial standing was very weak and investment for substantial modernisation remained too low.

136 "Die Ausfuhr nach Deutschland ist günstig, trotz eines Wertzolles in Deutschland von 25% ." *Bilanzen*, 4.8.1928.

137 Mathis, *Big Business*, 297.

138 Ibid.

139 *Bilanzen*, 2.10.1926, 28.5.1927, 23.6.1928, 31.8.1929. See also A.8.

Contrary to Steyr, Daimler export and overall sales performance was weak, mainly because it produced large luxury automobiles. In Austria, the market for such products was far too small and foreign import tariffs seemed to have been quite high. The management complained about high foreign tariffs and insufficient protection of the home market. According to the management's business report, exports to Germany and Britain were nearly impossible in 1925. Sales to Poland were also stagnant because of the falling Zloty. 1926 was also a difficult year and earning power was very low. The decline of the French franc and the lira might have supported stagnant business activity.

After more rationalisation and disposing of various shares and holdings in 1927, production and sales picked up. Capacity was utilised up to 75%. 40% of output was exported under difficult conditions. In the following year of the merger, it was possible to reduce bank debts from 18 to 10 million. The merger with the Puchwerke AG[140] brought a reduction of expenses for sales organisation and general administration. In addition, the new subsidiary branches of production from Puchwerke, motorbikes and bicycles, resulted in a better distribution of risk and a higher export rate of up to 60% for automobiles and 30% for motorbikes. In this time, the Austro-Daimler Puchwerke produced one fifth of Austrian car and 95% of Austrian motorbike output. Financially, the merger was also positive, raising profitability from 2.4 to 17% in 1928. Debts were still quite high, though. Of the 19.5 million liabilities, 14.5 million were still bank debts, while capital stock and reserve only amounted to 5.71 million.

1929 was a critical year. Business stagnated and financial standing worsened. Sales and turnover were a bit higher than the year before, but profit declined. Output of cars stagnated, while motorbike production increased 30%. Prices were much lower than the previous year, and many car dealers in Germany, Czechoslovakia and Poland collapsed. Liabilities increased substantially, to nearly 33 million, 18 million of which consisted of bank debts. When the pooling agreement with Steyr was concluded in 1930 and the depression was dawning, the main Austrian car and motorbike manufacturers were in serious financial difficulties, closely boundup with large, influential, but financially ill, Austrian banks that held large shares of capital stocks of these firms in the hope of an economic upswing.

Lack of competitiveness and productivity seemed to have been the main problems that Steyr and Daimler-Puch suffered from in the 20s. While their turnover, sales and production increased and capacity was fully utilised, income declined and indebtedness and debt service costs reached unbearable heights. The question is if this had mainly to do with a serious lack of capital after inflation, if available funds would have enabled these two companies to follow the international market situation, with falling prices, and why it was not possible to turn expensive bank credit into long-term foreign loans. As we have seen above, this is what many other firms had done. It seems that capital was essentially not the only main problem. The European market situation gave these firms from a small country a natural disadvantage. As the main car producers were situated in large countries with large well-funded and

140 *Bilanzen*, 27.8.1927, 23.6.1928, 10.3.1928, 31.8.1929, 26.7.1930.

protected markets, it was much easier for them to increase productivity and to keep up with falling prices on international markets. Low export or even dumping prices could be compensated by higher sales at home with higher prices. Steyr and Daimler-Puch did not have this option of countering unprofitable export sales with increasing domestic sales. Their dependence on unfavourable exports, combined with a small and weak home market, seemed to have been the greatest problem. Essentially, under these unfavourable sales conditions, it was much more difficult to find investors at home or abroad. The best solution would have been to focus on the production of specialised products that had low demand elasticity on international markets.

d. Austro-Fiat The much smaller, mainly utility vehicle producing, companies, Austro- Fiat and Gräf & Stift, were less prone to crisis and financial breakdown simply because the production and sales of these vehicles were much less risky as already noted in the first chapter. Besides, the domestic market was large enough for their relatively small production capacities. These firms could rely on steady and slowly rising domestic demand in the period of the relative upswing in Austria and Europe in the late 1920s. Rationalisation and modernisation pressure was also not as great as that for car manufacturing. Export played a minor role until 1926/27. After 1927, though, export increased and until 1930 general business activity expanded considerably. Mainly trucks and buses were sold on the home market, and some abroad, to the successor states or Russia. In accordance with positive real economic development, financial standing was stable.

For example, profitability rate of Austro-Fiat[141] always remained surprisingly high, thanks to the lack of high pressure to increase productivity permanently, only slowly falling home market prices and fairly steady demand. The firm possessed neither bank debts nor high interest payments. It financed investment and anticipatory credit and advance deliveries, which were offered to customers, with several capital increases carried through in the late 20s. Earning power increased from 18.5% in 1923 to 38% in 1929. Even in 1931, it was still at 26%. Between 1926 and 1930, gross profits increased 55 % and net profits 46%. Financial standing was also stable after 1923. Liabilities usually remained well below debtors' value. Moreover, dividends with 15%, were pretty high. They were reduced in 1930 to only 12%.

Austro-Fiat almost exclusively concentrated on supplying its home market until 1927. Thereafter, business expanded quickly and export sales rose. In many years, a large portion of home market demand came from public institutions, the postal service, the army and the Vienna city municipality. In 1926, business activity grew only slowly and turnover increased 10%. Some trucks were sold to the markets of the successor states. The following year, 60% of production consisted of a three-quarter ton truck and the rest was a three ton truck mainly for orders from the postal service. In 1928, about one tenth of output was for public orders. Because of high import tariffs in Czechoslovakia and Hungary, the management granted construction licenses, to the I. Walter & Co AG in Prague and to the Hungarian Maschinen- und Waggonfabriks-AG in Raab. While sales and turnover increased in the late 20s,

141 *Bilanzen*, 14.5.1927, 12.5.1928, 21.9.1929, 29.3.1930, 3.5.1930. See also A.5.

prices began to fall rapidly. In 1928, turnover was raised 30%, and prices fell 10%. It was still easily possible to raise productivity in order to to keep up with market price development.

One quarter of output was sold abroad, to the successor states and even to Russia. 1929 and 1930, when Steyr, Daimler and Puch began to feel the beginning of the depression and the first signs of their weak financial standing, these years were still a time when business was improving for Austro-Fiat. The recession began to hit the more market and consumer sensitive automobile industry first. To keep up with enlarged business in 1929, a capital increase was carried out. Production increased 20% to 1000 vehicles. The only way the recession tendencies of late 1929 and 1930 were felt was in the form of slightly falling prices and a stop of cash payment. Almost all sales had to be done on credit. Usually customers were granted monthly instalments of up to 18 months. In 1930, terms of payment had to be extended to even two years.

e. Gräft & Stift This enterprise[142] was not quite as successful as Austro-Fiat, but enjoyed a fairly stable development. Its financial standing was satisfactory, but not secure. Profitability remained low after stabilisation. Before the war, its rate was about 34%, was around 10 or 12% until 1926, and remained between 8 and 10% until 1929. Had the management already accumulated large liabilities before the war, after introduction of the gold balance sheet, liabilities increased to alarming heights. After 1926, their share of balance value was always more than half. In 1929, it was 60%. Yet, not even half of total liabilities (6.5 million) consisted of bank debts (2.7 million). The main investor was the Creditanstalt, which only held a minority of shares. Contrary to Steyr, the controlling majority of Gräf & Stift shares remained in the hands of the proprietors Karl, Franz and Heinrich Gräf, who were also president, directors and members of the board of directors.[143]

Until 1928, only about 10% of output was exported and up to 20% was sold to public institutions. This changed completely when large orders came from Soviet Russia, amounting to 45% of turnover. Deliveries were supported by the public deficit guarantee, because full payment was not certain and could take between two and four years. Capacity was fully employed and overall turnover rose 40%. In 1930, the onset of the economic downswing was noticed. This could have been postponed by accepting further orders from Russia, but the termination of deficit guarantees by the city of Vienna and the central government made this impossible. Moreover, public orders for utility vehicles stopped altogether in this year. These losses in domestic and export sales could hardly be counteracted by the small amount of export sales to other countries, such as Switzerland and Turkey. The company also had great difficulty to face competition on foreign markets, because it could not offer extended terms of payments. Italian firms were able to offer up to four year long payment schemes and German producers made large price concessions.

142 *Bilanzen*, 15.9.1928, 1.11.1930, 17.10.1931. See also A.11.

143 Mathis, *Big Business*, 127.

Thus, Gräf & Stift was able to benefit from state and municipal support. Of course, both utility vehicle manufacturers also benefited from public orders to some degree. Though, this was not the primary cause of their relative stability. Public orders, at utmost, only came to 20% of demand and exports to Russia were only effective for two years. Development of utility vehicle producers was fairly stable, because they did not have to encounter the productivity and competitiveness pressures that Steyr was exposed to. Prices of utility vehicles were also falling, but not as dramatically as for automobiles, and the rate of productivity increase did not have to be so rapid. Moderate investment and funding sufficed. Furthermore, the export rate and price pressure on the home market were lower than that for car production.

4.3.3. Rubber industry

a. International Development The last branch of the modern industry to be discussed is the rubber industry, as the largest sector within the Austrian chemical industry. Similar to all producers in small countries, it was certainly highly dependent on foreign trade, but only played a minute role on international markets, which was dominated by the huge chemical trusts in the US, Germany and Britain. After the chemical industry in Europe and the US had experienced enormous expansion during the war, in the inter-war period it underwent a large scale process of concentration and rationalisation as well as structural distortions of some of its production branches. The outcome was the formation of such massive industrial combines as the German IG-Farben, the British Imperial Chemical Industries Ltd. and the American Du Pont. This process was mainly the result of its increasing high capital intensity, its emphasis on research and development and massive application of complex technology. Not only was there a trend toward large scale industrial groups, "but also the location of production in countries with a large domestic market. In this respect, the large industrial countries enjoy[ed] a great advantage, since they can continue to sell on a large scale even after the special benefits accruing from an early start have been exhausted and exports tend to decline, for the reason that they can fall back on a protected home market."[144]

Although it was a modern industry and in spite of the advantages of large home markets, many production branches of the international chemical industry suffered from tremendous structural imbalances. Before the war, the German chemical industry was the largest and most advanced in the world. Yet, under the auspices of a policy of self-sufficiency, the other large industrialised countries attempted to recover lost ground for the backlog of certain, allegedly nationally vital, chemical production capacities during the war and in the 20s. Thus, production of synthetic dyestuffs, fibres and of fertilizer and explosives (through nitrogen synthesis) enormously expanded in Europe and the US in the 20s, creating large international overcapacities. As a consequence, these various massive national production capacities were only sustainable in the framework of protectionist trade policies.[145]

144 Svennilson, 162.

145 Gottfried Plumpe, "Unternehmen und Industriesektoren in der Weltwirtschaftskrise im interna-

Retrenchment, extreme protectionism and international cartels followed in the late 20s and thereafter.

At first sight, it is surprising that the chemical industry of a small country was not severely affected by this development and still performed extraordinarily well. However, in contrast to the world chemical industry in general, the Austrian rubber industry, the largest sector within the national chemical industry, was clearly able to benefit from two special conditions. Since it principally produced rubber goods, it did not suffer significantly from international overcapacities, because the rubber production branch remained dependent on imports of natural caoutchouc. The creation of national synthetic rubber production, again as part of the policy of self-sufficiency, only became relevant in the late 30s and during the Second World War. Another special feature of the Austrian rubber industry was the fact that its plants were located in several small countries, enabling this sector to dominate markets in Eastern Europe.

However, the domination of the markets of the successor states was not their only advantage. This industry was still able to keep up with international competitiveness and falling prices, because its export performance can be considered positive, despite fluctuations. At first sight, its export performance seemed to have been stagnant. The peak of export volume was already reached in 1923. Excluding 1923, clearly an exceptional year dominated by low inflationary crown parity, it rose 5% until 1929. The maximum of export value was reached in 1929, with 41 million schillings. Between 1923 and 1929, the value of exported rubber goods increased 19.5% or only 5.8% between 1924 and 1929.[146] Therefore, the export performance of the Austrian rubber industry can still be considered positive, because performance in 1923 distorted the picture of the general development of the 20s.

The fact that an export growth of barely 6% was possible until the depression, showed that this industrial sector was still able to hold its ground on international markets, despite its weak position as a comparably small national producer. That this was possible in the 20s, is chiefly explained by the fact that demand of its main product, automobile tyres, benefited from the spread of passenger cars and trucks and the general upswing of the motor industry during this time. In fact, the economic situation of the rubber industry was closely interconnected with the upswings and downswings of the motor industry.[147] Since general large scale application and production of vehicles in Europe took place in the 20s, even rubber goods producers in small countries underwent a moderate upswing. In the 30s, when the boom of the motor industry was restricted to some industrialised authoritarian states and world tyre production suffered from temporary overcapacities, conditions for the Austrian rubber industry deteriorated. It stagnated and had great difficulty to hold its own when prices dropped.

tionalen Vergleich. Das Beispiel der chemischen Industrie," in: Otto Büsch and Peter-Christian Witt, *Internationale Zusammenhänge der Weltwirtschaftskrise. Präsentation aus Anlaß einer Fachkonferenz*, Berlin 1994, 182–183.

146 Own calculation from Österreichisches Statistisches Zentralamt, *Aussenhandel*, 71.

147 Svennilson, 148.

In the 20s, however, trade conditions were acceptable. Prices declined only slowly and European tariff structures for rubber goods seemed to have been similar to those of electrical goods. Rubber products as simple consumer goods, such as toys or clothes, generally suffered from higher tariffs, while more complex goods such as tyres, as a rubber good for pneumatic equipment, benefited from the rising demand of automobiles and enjoyed more favourable import duties.[148] Generally, tariffs were high in France, the successor states, and low in the rest of Western Europe and Germany. By and large, exports of pneumatic equipment, such as tyres as the main product, must not have encountered great trade obstacles anywhere, neither in the area of the successor states nor in Western Europe or in Germany. Rates were between 10 and 24.9%.

b. Semperit This company, with a workforce of between 7500 and 8000 the largest industrial combine manufacturing rubber products in Eastern Europe,[149] was nearly the only representative of this industry. The rubber processing industry in Austria had stock capital of 23.2 million schillings in 1928,[150] that was roughly 2% of the value of all industrial joint-stock companies. As early as 1925, stock capital of Semperit alone amounted to 16 million. By and large, its financial standing and economic performance can be described as very positive, in spite of the moderate growth of national export value and volume.

The substantially increased balance sheet value, revealed in the reconstructed balance sheet account of 1925, reflects large expansion of Semperit during and after the war. Financial standing was slightly more negative than before 1913, with liabilities exceeding debtors approximately 11%. The value of liabilities and debtors had increased considerably compared to the last pre-war year, suggesting higher business activity and active turnover. The following year, 1926, value of creditors and debtors was balanced again, and thereafter accounts due would remain far below debtor value, a sign for fairly stable financial standing. The only weakness of the balance sheet was the high proportion of bank debts of total liabilities. They came to more than 16 million in 1925. This was about the sum of stock capital. Yet, the management was able to dispose of bank credit, as many of the electrical engineering firms, by taking up a long-term foreign loan. Two years later, a 1.4 million dollar loan (about 10 million schillings) was taken up, arranged by theWiener Bankverein and the Niederösterreichische Escomptegesellschaft. The issue contributed 8.8 million schillings, enabling Semperit to repay a large portion of bank debts. All balance sheet values increased until 1929, showing that Semperit business activity was growing in the late 20s. The growth of business activity also meant increased expenses, especially for the enlargement of the sales organisation and subsidiary firms abroad. Thus, by 1929, liabilities had climbed to more than 17 million, 40% of which consisted of bank debts. Rising competition and turnover, and falling prices

148 See chart in The Austrian National Committee, *Zollhöhe und Warenwerte*, 13.

149 This includes the workforce of factories outside of Austria. *Bilanzen*, 6.8.1927, 7.4.1928, 28.7.1928, 2.11.1929, 13.9.1930, 14.11.1931. See also A.20.

150 Bundesamt für Statistik, *Statistisches Handbuch für die Republik Österreich*, volume 11, 1930, 90/91.

required increasing investment, especially after 1927. The peak occurred in 1929, when more than 1.5 million were invested for new equipment and machinery for pneumatic products.

Profit and loss accounts reflected the 1920s business cycle. Gross profit stagnated until 1927. Then it shows fairly even growth of gross profit and expenses until 1929. Net profits grew much more moderately, but profitableness was high and very stable. It was usually well above 20% until 1929. This was not even harmed by the development of raw material prices, which reduced overall income growth. Large quantities of unvulcanised rubber, the main raw material product necessary for production, had been acquired for a high price, while prices fell after 1926. The price also fell in 1927 and remained low the following year.[151] That meant that finished rubber products, manufactured with expensive raw materials had to be sold for a lower price, causing a loss in income. Many rubber companies were affected by this and some had substantial losses.

In the late 20s, the export rate fluctuated, but always composed of more than half of total sales. In 1926, about 60% of output was exported. Export areas consisted of all the successor states, the rest of the Balkan countries, Western Europe, Germany and overseas countries. After 1925, turnover, sales and export increased continuously, while foreign competition grew more fierce, especially from the US. The American rubber industry, besides the automobile industry, had the highest growth levels among all American industrial sectors and was able to increase its export volume considerably. Between 1924 and 1927, the export volume of tyre covers, for instance, was raised 52.5% .[152] Naturally, a large portion of this export was directed to Europe and put pressure on European rubber processors. Semperit also suffered from this. Because American firms had the advantage of a large and strong home market, they were able to put more pressure on the price level of international markets. At the same time, US tariffs for rubber goods imports were augmented.[153]

1927 was a weak finanical year. Turnover had increased 20%, but cotton prices rose 50%, cutting profits. Still, constant rationalisation made a reduction of product prices possible. Thus, in spite of increasing international competition, 1928/1929 were good business years, supported by a strong winter that enhanced sales of rubber clothes and boots. In 1928, volume of sales increased 25% and value 10%. Nearly 70% of output was exported. In the following year, value of turnover reached its all-time peak of 86 million. At the same time, management complained about increasing protectionism and insufficient Austrian import tariffs.

1930 marked the onset of the depression, although the volume of turnover was even higher than in 1929. The main symptoms of the recession were rapidly falling raw material prices of unvulcanised rubber (down to 14% of pre-war price) and

151 Statistisches Reichsamt (ed.), *Wirtschaft und Statistik*, volume 9, numer 22, Berlin, November 1929, 911.

152 Calculated from Statistisches Reichsamt, *Die Wirtschaft des Auslandes*, 552.

153 "Amerikanische Fabriken, die sich früher vom europäischen Markt ferngehalten haben, liefern nun zu weit niedrigeren Preisen, als sie in Amerika selbst verlangt werden, dagegen sperren die Vereinigten Staaten sich immer stärker ab. So wurde der amerikanische Wertzoll auf Bälle, in denen die Semperit einen Weltruf genießt, von 30 auf 70% erhöht." *Bilanzen*, 6.8.1927.

cotton, which slightly eroded financial standing. Not only the value of raw material stocks, but also product prices dropped dramatically between 30 and 50%. That was partially below primary cost prices. Export rate was at 67% of overall sales. In spite of this alarming development, no deficit was made. Profitability was still 12.5%, dividend 6% and investment was still considerable, with nearly one million schillings for technical improvement and rationalisation.

4.4. CONCLUSION

Thus, did restrictive currency policy, resulting from the effort to re-establish or maintain the gold standard parities, bank policy and heavy capital inflow, low public investment, and international protectionist trade policy limit economic growth and performance? Was the upswing in Austria in the late 20s an artificial boom induced by monetary injection? Was there a causal connection between these policies and low investment rate?

In general, these economic policies on a national level always barely had any direct influence on the problems that the Austrian industrial sectors were suffering from. There is no doubt that industrial investment rates were low in this period and seriously contributed to low economic performance. But investment rates were only a symptom of a stagnating economy. The question is if the availability of capital, to some extent influenced by economic policy, determined this low investment and performance. Generally, it can be stated that this depended on individual cases and that there were clear, distinctively different courses of growth and development between companies belonging to traditional and modern industries, supporting the theory of interconnection between economic stagnation and lack of innovation or a lack of their large scale application. If an enterprise was among the modern industries, it was usually export oriented, had comparably high productivity levels and enjoyed low demand elasticity. For these firms the negative impact of restrictive policies was very limited. For almost all companies of the traditional sector the opposite was true. This phenomenon was not a result of economic policy, but rather a consequence of large scale structural distortions.

Considering the varying performances of companies influenced by many other factors than capital availability, currency parities, state investment or trade tariffs, a reasonable assumption seems to be that national structural transformations in the developed countries and international structural transformations were the dominating factors determining growth and development. Companies seemed to have been influenced to a greater degree by comparable productivity, international overproduction, overcapacities, demand elasticity and the application of new technologies. Still, policy goals, with results such as an unstable fixed exchange rates system, strong distortion on capital markets and no compensating state investment, had considerable impact. For the limited data scrutinised here, it is reasonable to state that this impact seems to have been largely in the form of supporting or enhancing the dominating structural distortions.

Usually, the main problems for Austrian industrial joint-stock companies were based on the two structural distortions described above. The greater the impact of either of these distortions and transformations, the more any company was subjected to the negative sides of economic policy of the 1920s. Moreover, Austrian firms had the great disadvantage of being part of a small, limited and relatively poor domestic market. Therefore, their political economic leverage against other national groups of producers was low on an international level. For example, Alpine was directly affected by overproduction and overcapacities of the iron and steel producing industries in Europe and the US due to war, inflation and technological improvement. In addition, the largest Austrian firm had been heavily hit by the effects of disintegration, war and inflation. Therefore, it was introduced to a fierce international market when its productivity was low. Unlike the most influential German national producers of iron and steel, it had no large domestic market ensuring that employment would rise to a level that would have allowed for at least reasonable utilisation of capacity and to enable it to follow falling international prices. Because of these unfavourable circumstances, discrimination of its products in the form of high import duties abroad was severe; it was even affected by dumping prices from the fall of the franc and could not take advantage from international cartel agreements. Quite the opposite, it suffered from these. Naturally, business outlook was meagre, and therefore, it was very difficult to receive substantial amount of reasonable credit. This was a vicious circle. While dependence on export sales was great, at the same time productivity, sales and capacity utilisation were low, while debts were already quite high after stabilisation. Reasonable profits, depreciation and investment could only be made when capacity was fully utilised. As expectations were meagre and demand low, no investor was seriously interested in granting sufficient capital to a company that already suffered from high debts and whose sales prospects were grim. To reiterate, a lack of investment capital was not the primary problem, but instead the lack of profitable investment opportunities. Alpine certainly did not offer these.

For Leykam-Josefsthaler the problem was very similar. Huge sums would have been necessary to make up for the backlog in productivity. Yet again, the company mainly came into this situation because of greatly increased production outside and inside of Europe. It was still possible to raise production, but that was absolutely necessary in order to maintain profits when prices were constantly declining. Hofherr had a very similar financial problem. For the Veitscher magnesite works, the essential problems were again international overcapacities and overproduction, especially in the US. Besides this, it was directly hit by the slow growth of the international iron and steel industries. Increasing tariffs in the US were only a political reaction of American magnesite producers to these tendencies. Since it was easier to reduce the costs for mining magnesite when demand was falling, finances could be kept quite stable.

The traditional machine building industry stagnated also because of large international production overcapacities. Protectionism and disintegration of the former market of the Empire only speeded up this process. Furthermore, the decline of the capacity of absorption of markets in the East coupled with higher competition from Western European producers were the main factors contributing to the contraction. Another factor was the application of new technology for machine building. Demand for systems which depended upon steam power was stagnating. For this lack of orders, the admittedly very limited and too low demand from the state railways could not compensate. For Simmeringer, it was a mistake to rely on and to hope for orders from the federal railways.

Similar to the period of disintegration and inflation, the only firms of the traditional industries which performed surprisingly well were Hutter & Schrantz and Ditmar-Brünner. This was largely due to their successful export orientation and manufacturing of fairly simple products. Again the former benefited from the upswing in the production of the paper industry, while the latter sold simple mass-produced consumer products all over the world. Böhler and Schoeller-Bleckmann also performed well, largely because both companies manufactured high grade steel and steel products with low demand elasticity. Their technological specialisation in this field enabled them to sell their products even on the markets of the advanced industrialised countries. Again, these enterprises were not strongly affected by protectionism, credit scarcity, or by a lack of more state investment. They had been able to adjust to long-term structural shifts.

For the modern industries, economic policies were much less effective. Management was not compelled to cry for political support in the form of import tariff increases. And expensive short-term bank credit could be avoided. This was especially the case for the electrical engineering and the rubber industry, but to a lesser degree for the vehicle manufacturing industry. The first definitely benefited from public investment for railway electrification, but this was not the main factor contributing to stable development. Demand from semi-public investment for the construction of power plants from supply companies in Austria and abroad probably constituted a greater part of overall employment. In the later 20s, increasing exports and demand from rising industrial investment also formed a considerable part of employment. In spite of substantial import tariffs directed against electromechanical goods, export sales were not limited by these. Capital availability was also fairly easy, because this industry offered promising investment opportunities in the form of an even greater scale of future application of electromechanical technology. Bank credit was converted into long-term foreign loans or capital increases could be carried out with the help of domestic or foreign banks.

The Austrian automobile industry enjoyed high growth rates of production and sales, until the bubble burst in 1928. The main problem stemmed from the national structural shifts taking place in industrialised countries. In Austria, this change was incomplete and retarded because it lacked a large and capital rich consumer market. In a way, Steyr suffered from similar problems as the Alpine, while its production performance was far better. The disproportion between production capabilities and its home market, forced this enterprise to focus on export sales at a time when European trade of automobiles was almost completely limited to sales on the various national markets of the large advanced countries. The little outside trade that took place was pressured by falling prices, enhanced by large national producers of the US, Britain, France, and to a lesser degree, of Germany. For these, in turn, it was much easier to increase production and competitiveness. Unless Steyr would have changed its policy, i.e. by reducing the size of production facilities, changing or specialising production, it was only a matter of time before it would not have been able to keep up with fierce international competition. Regarding these circumstances, it is surprising that Steyr was able to adjust and increase production, especially after war and inflation.

To conclude, it is clear that the role of national and international economic policy in affecting performance and development has been exaggerated. Its impact has only enhanced the results of long-term structural shifts that were the main causes for stagnation and contraction of some sectors of industry in the 1920s. The policy goals of returning to the gold standard and dramatic regime shift for stabilisation only seemed to have had direct results on microeconomic development in 1925 and 1926, when most companies were struck by the sudden change and experienced a moderate recession. Unbalanced currency parities in the late 20s only had a minor impact. Only when the franc fell dramatically in 1926, was the competitive situation of some enterprises, usually from the traditional industries, harmed. The inability to adopt to long-term structural changes, enhanced by conservative policies, can be seen as one of the primary causes of poor performance in Europe and in Austria.

PART III

5. THE GREAT DEPRESSION, 1929–1938. NATIONAL ECONOMIC POLICIES, PERFORMANCE AND STRUCTURAL CHANGES

5.1. POLICY AND DETERMINANTS OF MACROECONOMIC DEVELOPMENT

The course, intensity, length and impact of the Great Depression were impressive. For the industrialised world, its impact lasted from the late 20s until the beginning of the Second World War. Even though most countries reached their peak of national product in 1929, the first signs of a recession were already noticeable by 1928. The summer of 1932 proved to be the definite nadir for most economies.[1] Until then, the loss of world production, declining 31.4% between 1929 and 1932 and not recovering pre-crisis level until late 1935,[2] was more than twice as great as during the shorter depression in 1920/21.[3] Some national economies still grew until 1930 and even until 1931, and then declined until 1935. At first, a reduction in industrial production took place in Central Europe, Germany, Poland, Austria, Belgium, Hungary and the Czechoslovak Republic. Outside of Europe, in the US, Canada and South America, the industrial crisis was noticed by the turn of 1929/30. In France, Sweden and in countries that were just beginning to industrialise, the recession was not felt until 1931, with the onset of the crisis of the international capital and currency system. Nearly all industrialised countries were unable to attain pre-crisis production levels until 1937/38.

As the crisis primarily hit the industrial sector, after an enormous drop of agricultural prices, the severity of the depression on the national income of a national economy was chiefly determined by its state of development and rate of interconnection into the world economy and trade. Therefore, the greater the share of the industrial sector of total national product, the greater the impact of the depression on economic growth. This is obvious when looking at total European performance. The total European level of GNP declined only 4.5% between 1929 and 1932. Yet, excluding the USSR (a country with a planned and still developing economy exempted from world-wide economic trends), European GNP decline was 9.5%. The fall of GNP was even greater for industrialised Europe. It was 14.5%, and excluding Great Britain, 18.2%. Since the American economy was highly industrialised, with a

1 For a description of the course of the depression until 1933 see: League of Nations, Economic Intelligence Service (ed.), *World Economic Survey 1932–1933*, Geneva 1933, 11–17. And: League of Nations (ed.), *World Production and Prices 1925–1933*, Geneva 1934, 5–7.

2 Own calculation from Deutsches Institut für Konjunkturforschung (ed.), *Wochenbericht des Instituts für Konjunkturforschung*, vol. 6, no. 7, Berlin, May 1933, 30 and *Wochenbericht*, vol. 10, no. 2, Berlin, January 1937, 10.

3 Deutsches Institut für Konjunkturforschung (ed.), *Wochenbericht des Instituts für Konjunkturforschung*, vol. 5, no 41, Berlin, January 1933, 167–168.

decline of national product of 31% between 1929 and 1933, the fall was even more dramatic than in Europe.[4]

However, because another determinant of performance in the 30s was the rate and level of growth of industrial production before 1929, some advanced countries were not as heavily struck as others. Those countries with fairly rapid growth, starting from high or low levels in the early 20s, and with a relatively large industrial sector, were afflicted the worst. Therefore, according to rate and level of growth and development, roughly four groups of countries with specific performances can be distinguished. The first consists of those countries where the severity of the crisis was particularly harsh, because growth rates and level of development were comparably high. Another factor influencing the performance of two of these countries was the rapid and unstable nature of their upswing in the late 20s, due to the long-term effects of war and inflation. These countries were Germany, Austria and the United States. Between 1929–1932, American industrial production dropped 45%, Austrian 39.6%[5] and German 39%.[6] Until 1933, German GNP declined 19.5% and Austrian 22.5%.[7]

The second group includes those countries whose economies were advanced, but experienced a moderate or belated and prolonged recession. These are Britain, France and Italy. Britain's industrial decline was only 17%, mainly because of its poor rate of growth in the 1920s. Therefore, the fall of national product amounted to a moderate 2.3% until 1933.[8] GNP of France fell 12.5% until 1933, greater than in Britain, but more moderately than in Germany, the US or Austria. Its fairly high level of growth until 1929 combined with its comparably small industrial sector, whose production declined 31%, were probably the main reasons for this moderate decline. Moreover, the French economy was much less export market oriented than, for example, Germany, and therefore much less affected by the precipitous decline of trade until 1932. Yet, it suffered much longer from the depression than most other industrialised countries except for Austria. Remarkably, France reached its nadir of national product in 1936, by which time it had fallen more than 18% since 1929.[9] Italy seemed to have been affected by the crisis in a similar fashion, but recovered sooner than France. Italian industrial production fell 23.6% until 1932,[10] but GNP had reached its low already in 1931, with a fall of only 8.8%.

The third group incorporates the smaller countries. Unlike Austria, the decline of national product was not so great for most smaller advanced countries. However,

4 Paul Bairoch, "Europe's Gross National Product: 1800–1975."

5 According to calculation from table: "Die Zahlen der Woche. Die industrielleWeltproduktion", in: Deutsches Institut für Konjunkturforschung, *Wochenbericht 1937*, 143.

6 Figures for industrial production calculated from chart: "Die industrielle Weltproduktion nach Ländern", in: Deutsches Institut für Konjunkturforschung, *Wochenbericht*, vol. 6, no 7, May 1933, 30.

7 Percentages for GNP calculated from Mitchell, 407 ff. And Österreichisches Institut für Wirtschaftsforschung, *Monatsberichte* 14, 42.

8 GNP value for the United Kingdom. From table 10: "Volume of total national Product at Market Prices", in: Bairoch, "Europe's Gross National Product."

9 Mitchell, 411.

10 Own calculation from Deutsches Institut für Konjunkturforschung, *Wochenbericht* August 1933.

many of these countries also did not attain pre-crisis levels of national product until the late 30s. Belgium experienced a fall of national product of about 11%, while industrial output declined 37%. Denmark reached its GNP low in 1934 with a fall of 10.5%. Swedish national product fell 8.8% and Swiss by 4.8% until 1932. Denmark declined 5% until 1933. Only the Scandinavian countries experienced a reasonable recovery. Since the economies of most countries in Eastern Europe were underdeveloped, the sharp falls of industrial production (Poland -46%, Hungary -38.4%) affected their national product only moderately. It dropped between about 3% and 10%.[11]

The countries of the periphery, Russia, Japan, India, Canada and to some degree South American states, represent the last group. As these countries still had comparatively small industrial sectors that enjoyed rapid expansion, based on the international structural transition of increasing peripheral industrialisation of traditional industries, their national product and manufacturing output were only negligibly, or not at all, struck by the depression. They recovered much faster and had much higher growth rates. Moreover, the process of industrialisation that had progressed rapidly during the war and in the 20s, offering greater competition for the traditional European industries, carried on nearly unrestrained during the depression. In the years of the worst industrial decline, Japan and India, for example, augmented their share of world industrial capacity 10% and 25% respectively. Soviet Russia was probably able to double its capacities. In India, this extension of production capacity was still, to a great degree, based on the enlargement of fairly simple consumer goods industries, mostly textile manufacturing. In Russia, as well as Japan, though, it was possible to improve and enlarge capital investment industries, while the rest of the world suffered from crisis. Whereas for many European countries production had fallen to only half of pre-war levels or barely reached pre-1913 output in 1932, the new industrialisers in the periphery reached levels far above those of 1913. While production in Chile was only 3% above 1913 levels, Canadian industrial output was nearly 30% higher. India almost doubled, while Japan and Russia more than tripled their industrial output until 1932.[12]

The figures 5.1 and 5.2 roughly reveal the interconnection between the state of development of various economies and the severity of the depression in several countries for industrial production.

Thus, structural pre-conditions predetermined, to a great degree, how a national economy was afflicted by the depression. However, these were not the only factors, as to varying degrees long-range political and monetary processes since the First World War also influenced performance in the depression, at least until 1933. In some cases, structural factors played a greater role in inducing performance than political and monetary factors. In other cases, long-term political and monetary mechanisms were also of great relevance, especially for the former Central Powers. It was certainly not a mere coincidence that those major countries that had lost the

11 Bairoch, ibid.

12 See charts in League of Nations, *Industrialization and Foreign Trade*. And chart "Die industrielle Produktion in wichtigen Ländern," in: Deutsches Institut für Konjunkturforschung, *1. Beilage zum Wochenbericht*, vol. 10, no 2, Berlin January 1937.

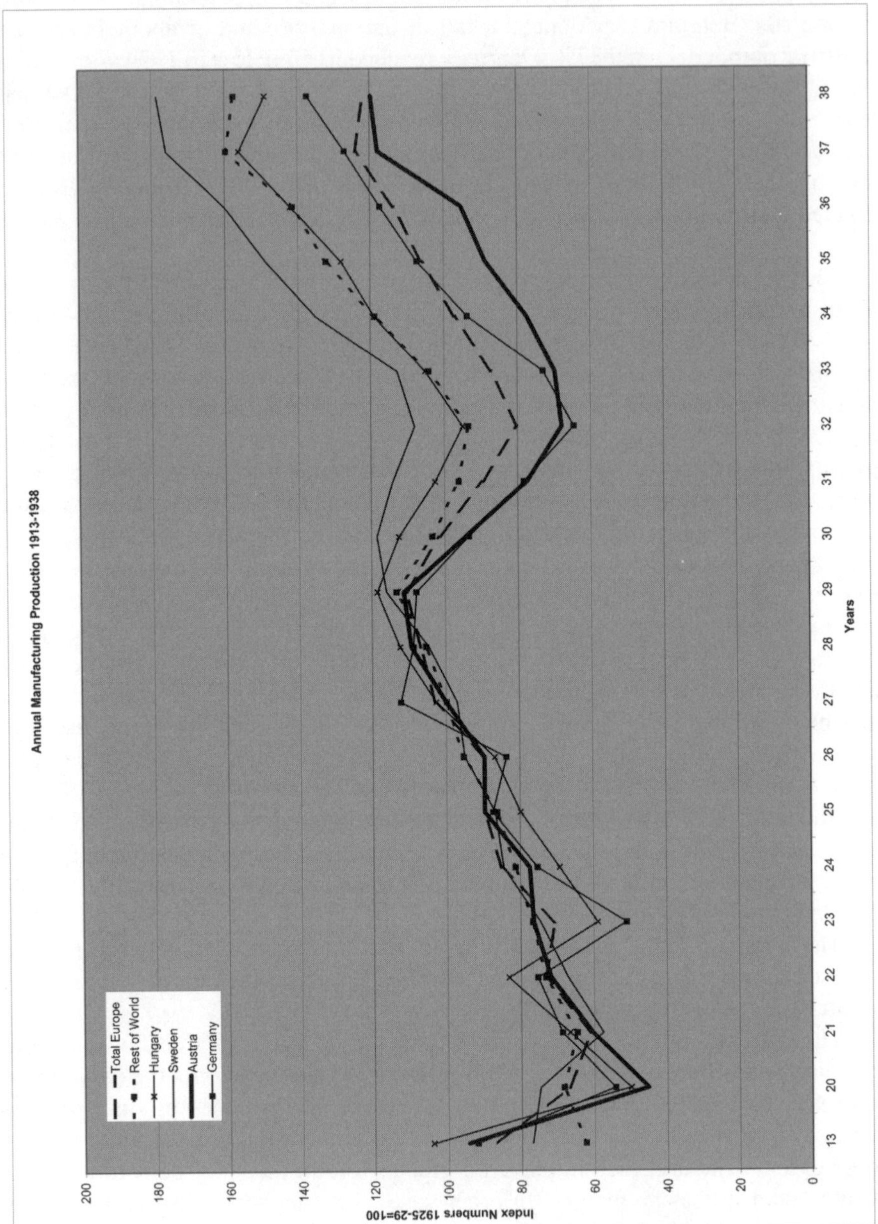

Figure 5.1.: Annual Manufacturing Production 1913–1938, 1925–1929=100. Source: Svennilson, 304– 305. And League of Nations, *Industrialization and Foreign Trade*, 140–143.

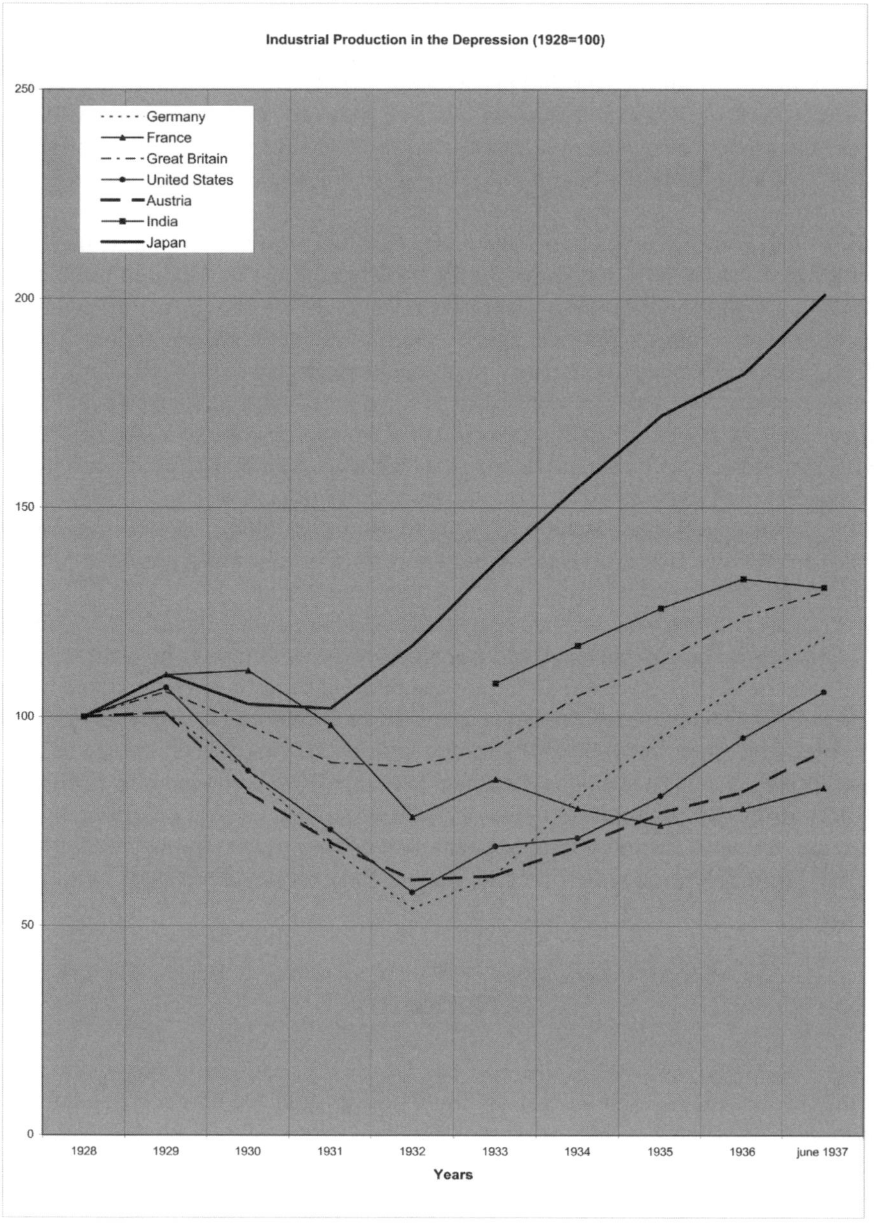

Figure 5.2.: Industrial Production during the Depression (1928=100) Source: „Die Zahlen der Woche. Die industrielle Weltproduktion," in: Deutsches Institut für Konjunkturforschung, *Wochenbericht*, vol. 10, no.26, 1937.

war, suffered from inflation, capital scarcity and large scale foreign capital inflow, experienced the severity of the depression most intensely.

Nevertheless, political and monetary factors of a long-term nature only worsened the economic downturn, especially for Germany and Austria, but were not the main causes of the severity of the recession in these countries. Policies during the depression were similar everywhere and also supported the decline. In all countries, the nature of economic policy was ad hoc, arbitrary and based on the search for short-term solutions. Policies were the political expression and reaction of the interests of various national producers that were under extreme market pressure as the consequence of distorted long-term structural transformations. Even though these efforts which employed the tools of protectionism (of trade limitation and monetary and currency manipulations) only enhanced the structural deficiencies, national producers regarded economic nationalism and retrenchment as the best solutions. The result was a recovery after 1933 purely based on domestically oriented growth and was in many cases merely based on compensating for a backlog in the industrial revolution of the 20s and on uneconomical rearmament demand. National economies that could not generate this type of growth by the advancing process of creative destruction, suffered from stagnation. After 1933, only extreme economic policy measures of fascist and communist states had positive short-term results on the growth of national product, but this expansion was short-lived and deformed.

Policies of the other countries remained orthodox and hardly affected economic development, whereas performance remained to be determined by structural preconditions. Overall, structural distortions, supported by policies, helped to create an economic environment, in which, for large national sectors in various countries an efficient, economically viable, functioning and market oriented economic development, progress and growth was no longer possible. Retrenchment and nationalism had destroyed efficient international division of labour, created overpriced, inefficient national markets and a collapsed, barely recovering international market which suffered from overproduction in some sectors and excessively low prices.

5.2. STANDARD THEORIES OF THE CAUSES OF THE GREAT DEPRESSION

Many contemporary economists[13] in the US saw the initial cause of the Great Depression as the stock market crash and believed that the severity and length of prolonged recession was due to currency and banking troubles in Europe. Yet, today, it seems clear that the Great Crash only inaugurated the crisis by reducing primary wealth, enhancing business pessimism and intensifying structural weaknesses.[14] It was not the main cause of the onset, nor of the length and severity of the depression. The increasing policy reaction to the implications of the war and the negative results

13 Sumner H. Slichter, "The Period 1919–1936 in the United States: Its Significance for Business Cycle Theory," in: *The Review of Economics and Statistics*, Vol. 19, No. 1, Part 1, February 1937, 1–19.

14 John Kenneth Galbraith, *The Great Crash 1929*, London 1980 (first edition 1954), 168–194.

of political intervention were also recognised by contemporaries. The disturbances of the First World War and all subsequent state interventions and policies, for example the return to the gold standard, were seen as the major causes of an extreme disturbance of economic equilibrium leading to the greatest depression of all times.[15]

With the luxury of hindsight, many historians and economists have attributed the main causes for, and the severity and length of, the depression to false economic policy as well, and often resorted to theories of economic disequilibrium, which were regarded as being caused by the breakdown of the financial system, either emphasising overproduction, underconsumption or profits squeeze theories.[16] A great number of theories concerning the depression exist, but roughly three standard theoretical approaches can be distinguished, all roughly in agreement that the crisis originated in the United States and that it was mainly due to economic policy errors.[17] Basically, none of these theories ignore the factors and arguments of the other, just the emphasis on certain aspects are accentuated and the theoretical pre-conceptions differ considerably. Somehow or other, it is an exercise of deduction.

The first theory is the monetarist approach mainly represented by Milton Friedman and Anna Schwartz.[18] Monetarists, as well as most representatives of the demand hypothesis, believe that the depression was primarily of domestic origin in the US and that the distortions and weaknesses of the international monetary and trade system were only secondary factors. Essentially driven by deflationary Federal Reserve currency policy and banking crisis, the stagnation of the money supply in the US between 1926 and 1929, its contraction by 2.6% in the autumn of 1930 and by 33% in the spring of 1933, are considered by the monetarists as the primary

15 "Es ist mithin eine richtige Erkenntnis von hohem und praktischem Wert, daß beinahe die gesamteWirtschafts- und Finanzgeschichte der letzten fünfzehn Jahre aus Interventionen bestand, deren üble Folgen nachher nicht ausgeblieben sind. Aber diese Interventionen waren nicht die Ursache der Krise. Richtig ist nur, daß diese zum Teil völlig falsch und kurzsichtig durchgeführten Interventionen die Lösung der Krise weit hinausgeschoben haben. Diese Hinausschiebung war jedoch keineswegs sinnlos: Die Urintervention war der Weltkrieg selbst gewesen. Alle Interventionen der Nachkriegszeit waren zum Teil nur kostspielige und opferreiche Mittel, die letalen Folgen dieser brutalsten aller Gleichgewichtsstörungen von der Gesellschaft abzuwehren. Zum anderen Teil freilich haben sie überflüssigerweise neue Störungen bewirkt, die die Folgen der Urintervention noch verschärften." Only by 1933 there was an awareness of the impossibility of return to pre-war conditions. The same author wrote: "Die Rückkehr zur Goldparität in England ist das eigentliche Symbol dafür, mit welcher Ahnungslosigkeit vor kaum zehn Jahren darangegangen wurde, nach den Vorkriegsplänen an einer Weltwirtschaft weiterbauen zu wollen, deren Fundamente in den Tiefen durch die Kriegsjahre ausgehöhlt worden waren." Karl Polanyi, "Der Mechanismus der Weltwirtschaftskrise," in: *Sonderbeilage des Österreichischen Volkswirt anlässlich der Vollendung seines 25. Jahrganges*, Vienna 1933, 4 and 5.

16 Heinrich Knoche, *Die Wirtschafts- und Sozialpolitik der Regierungen Brüning, Papen, Schleicher und Hitler in den Jahren der Weltwirtschaftskrise von 1938/30–1934*, dissertation, Marburg 1989, 24–32.

17 Volker Hentschel gives an excellent summary of these theories in his article: "Große Depression undWirtschaftspolitik. Sachzwänge und Handlungsspielräume," in: Wolfram Fischer (ed.), *Sachzwänge und Handlungsspielräume in der Wirtschafts- und Sozialpolitik der Zwischenkriegszeit*, St. Katharinen 1985, 13 ff.

18 Milton Friedman and Anna J. Schwartz, *A Monetary History of the United States 1867–1960*, Princeton 1963.

causes of the depression. This contraction is said to have brought a major decline of economic growth by the reduction of investment and demand.

The second thesis, the demand hypothesis, enjoyed great popularity, especially since Keynes laid the foundation with his attempt to prove his theory on the causes and course of the depression. It emphasises the aspect of underconsumption, and regards an autonomous decline in demand for consumption and investment goods, which unleashed an increasing deflationary process, as the main cause for the depression.[19] It is in strict contradiction to the monetarists' explanation. While they see the decline in the money supply in the US as the major cause for the dramatic drop in aggregate demand and income, the representatives of the Keynesian approach see the fall in income and demand as the basis for the contraction of money supply. The demand hypothesis has several versions of explanations for the cause of the fall in aggregate demand. Demand dropped because of one, or a combination, of the following factors: A decline in capital investment, a decline in demand of consumer durable goods, a fall of activity in private housing, or because of a drop of exports.

An interesting Marxist version of the demand theory, which does not emphasise national economic policy, is the hypothesis of Baran and Sweezy.[20] Employing a more structural approach, these authors see a direct connection between the rise of large oligopolistic corporations, the decline of small economic units and the "inherent tendency of the American economy towards depression and stagnation."[21] Simply explained, the theory implies that the continuously expanding American corporations were able to receive an increasing share of corporate income in the late 19th and early 20th centuries. Corporate income and profits rose disproportionally higher than workers income, causing a distortion in the distribution of income which created an "increasing imbalance between investment expenditures and consumption expenditures."[22] Simultaneously, prices were "sticky" (artificially maintained on high levels) due to the monopolistic nature of large corporations and cartels. These factors, in turn, entailed a profit incentive to increase capital investment which enlarged capital stock. Therefore, the production of consumption goods increased faster than aggregate demand, because wage increases were not so high as the growth of profits. This lag of aggregate demand was seen as the primary cause of stagnation and depression. Baran and Sweezy argue that the Great Depression did not begin until the early 30s, because "the tendency towards insufficient demand in this period was offset by epoch-making innovations and World War I."[23] Large scale investment in the railroad and government investment in the war were able to offset deficient consumer demand for durable goods until the late 1920s. Keller partially verifies the thesis of declining labour and increasing capital income. Between 1923 and

19 Hentschel, 15–16. One of the main representatives is W. W. Rostow, *The World Economy. History & Prospect*, Austin 1978.

20 Paul Baran and Paul Sweezy, *Monopoly Capital: An Essay on the American Economic and Social Order*, New York, 1966.

21 Robert R. Keller, "Monopoly Capital and the Great Depression: Testing Baran and Sweezy's Hypothesis," in: *Review of Radical Political Economy*, 7 (4), 1975, 65.

22 Ibid.

23 Ibid.

1929 corporate share of national income rose from 19.6% to 25.5%, while workers' share dropped from 77.9% to 72.9%.[24] At its root, Baran and Sweezy's hypothesis is essentially a theory of long-term structural economic transformations, to which we will refer later.

Another underconsumption theory places emphasis on the contraction of demand for durable goods, which was much more dependent on income elasticity than on demand of traditional 19th century consumer goods. Again, this explanation implies a strong structural approach. The durable consumer goods industries (cars, electrical appliances and products from the chemical industries) had become new leading growth sectors of the US economy. Once more, the emphasis is placed on the insufficient growth of labour income, whereas corporate income was rising disproportionally high. Consequently, the US experienced a profit inflation which was not compatible with inadequate durable goods demand. Profits and investment for capital goods were high, until the availability of investment opportunities shrank. Increasingly profits were utilised for speculation on the stock market, while consumption power of the masses did not keep up with increasing production. Sooner or later, this development led to a severe crisis.[25] Another author[26] has placed emphasis on the unusual build-up of household liabilities before 1929 and claimed that the severity of the depression was strongly enhanced by the deterioration in household balance sheets. Once the stock market crashed, the value of household financial and asset holdings declined dramatically, whereas private debt service rose. This, in turn, would have explained the dramatic drop in aggregate demand between 1929 and 1930 in the US, when consumer durable expenditure fell by more than 20% and residential housing expenditure by 40%.

The third major theory, in some respects compatible with previous theories and mainly represented by Charles Kindleberger,[27] finds the deficiencies of the weak international economic and currency system as the primary causes of the depression. The malfunction of the gold standard mechanism and the shifting role of Britain and the US after the war are considered as the essential components of this weakness. As the new leading economic and financial power, expected to act as a lender of last resort to countries in financial crisis, the US did not take up this position properly. The international financial and economic system broke down in the face of an economic crisis in the US and could not keep world markets from protectionism and competitive devaluation. The crisis was disseminated to the rest of the world, because the international finance system was incapable of maintaining international long-term credit flows, as the Bank of England had done before 1914. Hence, the depression continued to spread, especially to those countries that had depended on these credit flows in the 1920s, in particular Germany, Austria, Eastern Europe, and many other countries in the periphery.

24 Ibid, 66.

25 Underconsumption theories are discussed by Hentschel, 33.

26 Frederic S. Mishkin, "The Household Balance Sheet and the Great Depression," in: *The Journal of Economic History*, Vol. 38, No 4, 1978, 918–927.

27 Charles Kindleberger, *Die Weltwirtschaftskrise 1929–1939*, Munich 1973.

It was also not possible to help countries, such as Germany, Austria, Great Britain and many primary producing countries, which suffered from severe currency crisis in 1931. The American monetary policy and capital market made a major contribution to the destruction of the deformed, unstable and precarious European financial system, by reversing the credit flow of the 20s. For example, the United States reduced international dollar liquidity between 1929 and 1932 from 7.4 to 2.4 billion dollars. Between 1930 and 1933, America withdrew 2.7 billion dollars from abroad in the form of short-term credits, severely increasing the deflationary pressure on other economies.[28] This, in turn, contributed to the severity and length of the crisis all over the world, especially in Germany and Austria. For Britain and France, the decline of export demand is regarded by many historians as a main cause for the spread of the depression in these countries.[29] In regard to the spread of the depression, the monetarists would emphasise the reduction or stagnation of the money supply in European economies, which were initiated by US credit withdrawals, whereas the supporters of the demand hypothesis would consider the spread of the crisis from the US as caused by a decline of export demand. This reduction in real economic demand is seen as a cause for the fall in the money supply in Europe. Thus, overall, the third major theory, placing importance on international interconnections, just like the monetarists, also finds the primary cause and severity in wrong policy measures, which in turn, caused the severe economic downturn.

Most other "historical" theories also regard deflationary economic and monetary policy as the primary reason of the onset and severity of the economic breakdown.[30] Peter Temin[31], for example, largely regards parallel deflationary policy by governments and central banks, with the goal to reconstruct and maintain the gold standard system, as the main factor producing the depression.[32] In this view, the deflationary policy measures in Germany and the US are specifically considered as major factors contributing to the causes of the crisis. Reichsbank credit restrictions, attempting to limit foreign lending in 1928, are said to have initiated the decline in industrial activity in Germany that year. In the US, Federal Reserve credit restriction in 1929, against increasing speculation, is said to have caused a decline in activity. Moreover, the ideology of contemporary economic thought, believing that the remedies for the recession were deflationary measures, is seen as the primary cause of the severity of the depression. Just as the depression was brought about by deflationary policy, the causes of the recovery are mainly seen in a regime shift in economic policy in late 1932 and 1933 in the US and Germany.

28 Hentschel, 35.

29 Ibid, 36.

30 For example, Maddison, "Economic Policy and Performance," 457–466.

31 Peter Temin, *Lessons from the Great Depression. The Lionel Robbins Lectures for 1989*, Cambridge, Massachusetts 1990. Gottfried Haberler can also be considered as one of the main proponents of this view. See: Haberler, "The World Economy, Money, and the Great Depression 1919–1939," in: *Selected Essays of Gottfried Haberler*, London 1985, 363–403.

32 Eichengreen also sees the breakdown of the gold standard as one of the main factor causing the depression. *Golden Fetters*.

The new expansionist policies, which encouraged consumption and investment in these countries, are said to have turned those economies around and was supposed to have been "powerful enough to arrest world-wide decline."[33] France, on the other hand, did not recover in the 1930s, because it adhered to the gold standard and consequently, to deflationary policies. The franc was, therefore, overvalued, especially after 1933 and restricted French exports. Britain's recovery is to a large degree explained by its abandonment of the gold standard and the subsequent devaluation of the pound in September 1931. Eichengreen and Sachs claim that there was a direct connection between competitive devaluation, adherence to the gold bloc in the 30s and economic performance and recovery from the depression.[34] Individual currency devaluation has been considered as helpful to growth, while the adherence to gold, as France had done until 1936, or insufficient devaluation, like Austria in 1931, limited recovery. This paper conjectures that these policies were certainly helpful in bringing about only very moderate and incomplete recovery and poor performance, but were not the main reasons. All of these arguments either look upon the phenomenon of crisis as a stable economic system being struck by a major shock of deflationary policy, or as an unstable system being affected by a minor weak shock.

5.3. STRUCTURAL APPROACH: THEORETICAL CONCEPTS APPLIED

This section does certainly not attempt to explain the cause of the Great Depression; rather, it only suggests that structural shifts in the economy constituted a weak system that was shaken by policy measures, and that performance during the crisis and the rate of recovery, to a large degree, depended on structural pre-conditions. Performance was only supported by policy. The empirical base for an analysis of the causes is too small, as the crisis began and spread in the largest economy of the world, the US, and as Austria was merely an importer of the depression. Notwithstanding that, suggestions for explaining the causes of the severity, length of economic stagnation and incomplete recovery in the 1930s can be made. This section also attempts to analyse and compare the impact and role of policy on economic development.

The problem of intentionalist explanations lies in their almost complete lack of consideration for shifts in economic structures, constraints and circumstances. The decision-making of economic subjects is seen as a static, repetitive process regardless of structural changes, influenced by expectation changes due to policy regime shifts, interest rates, devaluation and credit availability. Yet, the stimuli, incentives and pressures imposed on them by structural circumstances are often neglected. The depression and the recovery were very unusual phenomena that demand more causal factors than deflationary monetary policy, the breakdown of the gold standard, lack of international economic co-operation and protectionism. In many ways, these were symptoms of, and policy reactions to, the deterioration of real economic conditions and long-term structural shifts.

33 Temin, 105.

34 Barry Eichengreen and Jeffrey Sachs, "Exchange Rates and Economic Recovery in the 1930s," in: *Journal of Economic History*, 45, 1985, 925–946.

Other major, but more unconventional theories,[35] are those that could be classified as structural theories. Some contemporary economists already looked at long-term structural causes of the depression, and nurtured a theory that combined a type of neo-classical equilibrium hypothesis with long-term structural transformations. In this view an unstable economic equilibrium had been created by combining modern industrialisation under conditions of a free market economy with increasing monopolisation and planless state interventionism. This unstable system is said to have become more vulnerable to financial and political crisis and to business cycle downswings.[36]

Baran and Sweezy's, some other demand theories, and Mensch' hypothesis of "technological stalemate"[37] are modern theories that come very close to the structural approach, since they include structural economic shifts, such as the development and impact of corporate structures, investment from new innovations or the stagnation of old and the rise of new industries. Again, these ideas go back to Schumpeter's theories of long cycles. *In this view, the depression was mainly caused by endogenous, repetitive disruptions of the capitalist process, which vary in intensity and length. These disturbances are caused by reorientation and shifts for industrial re-adjustments with the introduction of new technologies, production processes and services in economic structures. Recessions are regarded as the primary symptoms of these disturbances.* In the case of the Great Depression, a recession of a long-term Kondratieff cycle (enduring between 48 and 60 years) coincided with that of a mid-term Juglar (lasting seven to twelve years) and a short-term Kitchin cycle (with a duration of about three to five years).[38]

As Schumpeter stated himself, these patterns of cycles with periods and dates are not to be taken seriously and primarily had the purpose of illustration.[39] *The*

35 Another theory places emphasis on the declining rate of population growth in the 1920s and the stagnation of growth of the labour force. I find it difficult to accept that this is supposed to have induced a reduction in investment great enough to have caused a major depression. See for example: Clarence L. Barber, "On the Origins of the Great Depression," in: *Southern Economy Journal*, 44 (3), 1978, 432–456.

36 See lecture of Professor Colm in Dresden 1932, "Deutschland und die Weltkrise," in: Franz Boese (ed.), *Schriften des Vereins für Sozialpolitik*, vol. 187, Munich 1932, 36–51.

37 Gerhard Mensch, *Das technologische Patt. Innovationen überwinden die Depression*, Frankfurt a. M. 1975.

38 Joseph A. Schumpeter, *Konjunkturzyklen II*, chapter XV. Until the Second World War, three Kondratieff cycles have been discerned. The last to be observed lasted from 1897 and ended in a downswing until 1939. Between 1787 and 1932, economists have counted 11 Juglar cycles. See: Walter Assenmacher, *Konjunkturtheorie*, 8th edition, Munich 1998, 17–18. The pattern of a fourth Kondratieff cycle after World War Two has not been proven. Therefore, the long-term cycle theory is rejected by many economists today. The distinction between Juglar and Kitchin cycles is also disputed nowadays. Jürgen Heubes, "Juglar-, Kondratieff- und Kitchin-Zyklen," in: *Wirtschaftswissenschaftliches Studium*, vol. 9, 1980, 383–385.

39 "*Dieses* Schema hat lediglich illustrative Bedeutung, und die Daten haben nichts zu besagen." Schumpeter, *Konjunkturzyklen II*, 936. This statement did not mean, however, that Schumpeter himself did not take his own theory seriously as Haberler stated. Haberler, *The World Economy*, 388. In contrast, Aldcroft seems to trust in the "traditional periodicity of cyclical activity". See: *The European Economy*, 3rd edition, 65–66.

central theme of this theory is the constant repetition of a revolution within industrial structures at the core of the evolutionary process of capitalism, largely unrestrained by political or intentional events. The long-term Kondratieff cycle was merely the expression of this long-term shift of industrial structures. Schumpeter clearly saw monetary and policy effects as secondary in this process, and only as accentuating or limiting crisis symptoms.[40] *This section will again attempt to employ these ideas of changing economic structures, to combine them with the accumulating effects of policy results and structural distortions occurring in the 1930s, as the main factors driving the economic process forward, and determining performance in the 20s as well as the severity of the depression and the course of recovery in the 30s in Austria and various other countries. Contrary to Schumpeter, though, this paper does not suggest that the problem was the end of a long cycle coinciding with short-term business cycles, but the disturbance of the "second industrial revolution" which was partially due to war and inflation, obvious in distortions of economic structures in many countries.*

This approach is similar to a structural theory which attempts to explain poor recovery during the 30s in the US. The process of industrial revolution to new production methods, products and consumption, is called secular transition. The author[41] regards a disturbance in this industrial secular transition of the American economy, to be observed since the financial collapse starting in 1929, as the main cause of "a decade of poor macro-economic performance"[42] in the US. The main features of secular transition are changes in consumption, investment and employment trends towards mass consumer durable goods markets and increasing growth and investment of certain industries. Within this structural explanation of American economic stagnation, the insufficient growth of the "dynamic sectors"[43] is also recognised, causing a "structural employment problem"[44] and insufficient demand.

This phenomenon of disturbed or distorted changing structural shifts, or secular transition, partially due to war, inflation and further supported by economic policy

40 "Der Kapitalismus ist also von Natur aus eine Form oder Methode der ökonomischen Veränderung und ist nicht nur nie stationär, sondern kann es auch nie sein. Dieser evolutionäre Charakter des kapitalistischen Prozesses ist nicht einfach der Tatsache zuzuschreiben, daß das Wirtschaftsleben in einem gesellschaftlichen und natürlichen Milieu vor sich geht, das sich verändert und durch seine Veränderung die Daten der wirtschaftlichen Tätigkeit ändert; diese Tatsache ist zwar wichtig und diese Veränderungen (Kriege, Revolutionen usw.) bedingen oft auch eine Veränderung der Industrie, sie sind aber nicht ihre primäre Triebkraft. Auch ist dieser evolutionäre Charakter nicht einer quasiautomatischen Bevölkerungs- und Kapitalzunahme oder den Launen des Geldsystems zuzuschreiben, von denen genau das gleiche gilt. Der fundamentale Antrieb, der die kapitalistische Maschine in Bewegung setzt und hält, kommt von den neuen Konsumgütern, den neuen Produktions- und Transportmethoden, den neuen Märkten, den neuen Formen der industriellen Organisation, welche die kapitalistische Unternehmung schafft." Cited in Mensch, *Das technologische Patt*, 18; from Schumpeter, *Kapitalismus, Sozialismus und Demokratie*, 4th edition, Munich 1950, 136–137.

41 Michael A. Bernstein, *The Great Depression. Delayed recovery and economic change in America, 1929–1939*, Cambridge, Massachusetts 1987.

42 Ibid., 20 and 30.

43 Which are called "modern industries" in this study.

44 Bernstein, 31.

during the depression, is at the core of the argument here, even though it is very difficult to quantify as it is problematical to delineate structural changes with available statistics.

Considering the structural faults on national and international levels in the late 20s, it seems more likely that an already very unstable economic system, suffering from distortions in shifting structures, was affected by strong monetary and deflationary policy shocks. This impact on an already weak system, combined with an extreme turn to economic nationalism, caused the length and severity of the Great Depression. This extreme move toward economic nationalism did not allow for a restoration of a functioning international economic system. The problem of previous arguments was that the main pre-occupation was on an intentional level, largely concerning policy-making and monetary mechanisms. Long-term structural changes in economic systems are seen as a permanent process in economic development. Constantly weak sectors of the economy are taken over by new technologies and services and goods, consumption habits, etc. Thus, economists regard this permanent process as irrelevant when attempting to explain and analyse growth and stagnation. This constant structural shift has been neglected in attempts to understand the depression.

The change in structure was enhanced and distorted by inflation and war in Europe and the world. In addition, the shift in advanced, industrialised economies suffered from an inherent, endogenous weakness before the depression, in the form of increasing dependence on consumer purchasing power, unprecedented in history, which was not fully established and lacked proper security of a more ideal distribution of income.[45] In combination with these structural distortions and weaknesses, deflationary economic policies had catastrophic effects. The desire and policies to return to the gold standard were actually the right measures in the years after the war. To establish a system of fixed exchange rates would enhance trade, growth and international division of labour.

Right after the negative currency experiences of the 30s, Nurkse[46] concluded that uncontrolled floating exchange rates systems are not desirable. Today, this view is largely shared. It is doubtful that policy measures designed to maintain the gold standard, harmed growth in the 1920s to such an extent, that it would have formed the main foundations of the Great Depression. Overvalued pound and undervalued franc were not vital reasons for the depression. The main problem was that it was impossible to combine national social and economic policy interests with international policy goals to uphold currency parities. In the 1920s, the choice was made to favour the interest of influential financial institutions, because the balance of political power favoured banks and producers instead of labour. After the Second World War, it was possible to return to a system of pegged exchange rates with the Bretton Woods system. The implementation of these systems was mainly possible because of two reasons: First, there was a willingness in various national economies to increase

45 This point is emphasised in: Walt Whitman Rostow, *The World Economy. History & Prospect*, Austin 1978, Part Three. Trend Periods, 15. 1920–1936, 203–229.

46 Ragnar Nurkse, *International Currency Experience*, Geneva 1944.

state involvement and spending to such a degree, that it allowed for the simultaneous pursuit of the policy goal of pegged currencies and the goal of meeting the needs and demands of national social and economic policies; and secondly, economic growth and development progressed rapidly and smoothly enough to provide for the basis of such a double edged policy. In the 1920s, this was not the case.

5.3.1. Structural Transformation during and after the Depression and the Spread of Economic Nationalism

Contemporaries were aware of structural changes, but did not see their exact quality, long-term developments, results and implications. The process of creative destruction, as described by Schumpeter as a constant process of industrial change, suffered from accelerating distortion and was slowed down during war and inflation. In spite of this general deceleration and deformation, the structural transformations on national and international levels carried on rapidly in the 20s. As we have seen in chapter 2, the shift towards increasing industrialisation outside of Europe put pressure on traditional industries in Europe. At the same time, the national structural transformation of advanced economies to new industries was insufficient, evident in the inability of the modern industrial sectors to absorb the declining rate of growth of the old industries. These grew only very moderately or suffered from stagnation and overcapacities, while their share of national product was still considerable. This phenomenon is especially obvious in the case of Britain. This process enhanced moderate protectionism, but did not grow on such a scale that it would have been harmful to international trade, division of labour and specialisation. Hence, in the 20s, policy was still mainly a reaction to real economic developments.

During the depression, however, the pressure from new industrialising countries grew, and much more importantly, the structural distortions in the advanced national economies increased and eventually became uncontrollable. In most European countries, the increasing endogenous structural weaknesses of the economy combined with a major international monetary and financial breakdown led to an exogenous, severe shock resulting in a long and deep depression. After 1931, the crisis was primarily supported by a combination of further structural distortions enhanced by recession pressure and economic policy measures. Now, all sectors underwent severe production decline. In particular, the modern, durable goods industries were hit hard. After the nadir, and until the war, the structural distortions were not adjusted. On the contrary, they were further supported by protectionist national policies in almost all countries. This was one of the main reasons for insufficient recovery in the decade before the Second World War. During the depression and in the 30s, therefore, policy became more and more not only a reactionary force to economic distortions, but increasingly contributed to false and stagnating development and structural disequilibria.

5.3.2. Contraction of Trade, Industrialisation in the Periphery and Concentration on National Economies

The dramatic contraction, following stagnation of world trade in 1930s, and the eventual breakdown of the system of multilateral trade,[47] was another reason for the severity of the depression. Value of world trade contracted even more than industrial output, and volume of trade almost as dramatically as world industrial production. Value shrunk by more than 50%, volume by almost 30%, whereas world export declined about 60% between 1928 and 1932.[48] Trade in value and volume never recovered from this blow until after the war. After 1933, world production increased again due to an upswing of industrial domestic markets, but world trade never came close to the growth rate of industrial production.[49] The decline of trade was not the primary cause of the depression,[50] but its decline and further protectionism which perpetuated trade stagnation was a major factor for its length and severity.

Naturally, countries whose economic well-being depended on foreign trade were heavily hit by this process. Therefore, as strict deflationary policy certainly supported stagnation, the main reason for inadequate Austrian recovery and performance in the 30s was the contraction of international trade, as growth of the Austrian national product was highly dependent on exports and, therefore, on international trade. Figure 5.3 shows the interconnection between declining world and European trade and Austrian foreign trade.

After the introduction of further extremely restrictive trade restrictions, devaluation and direct state support of certain sectors before 1933, a return to open economies and a resumption of world trade on a pre-crisis scale was no longer possible. Industrial and agricultural interests in the large countries that had been supported by state protection and intervention during the 20s and the depression, were now very well sheltered within national borders and did not want to abandon their artificial advantages.[51] *This development resulted in increasing distorted growth of national industries in the 30s, aided by government investment and, later on, by large scale rearmament.*

Thus, there were three vital features of the 30s that were, at first, a reaction to, and then a major supporter of, these structural deformation: 1.) a dramatic contraction

47 W.S.Woytinsky and E.S.Woytinsky, *World Commerce and Governments. Trends and Outlook*, New York 1955, 87.

48 Deutsches Institut für Konjunkturforschung, *Wochenbericht*, vol. 6, no. 32, 1933, 138. Also see "Die Lage des Welthandels", in: *Wochenbericht*, vol. 10, no. 26, 1937, 143–144.

49 "Weltproduktion und Welthandel," in: *Wochenbericht*, no. 43, October 1937, 249 ff.

50 Carl-Ludwig Holtfrerich, "Weltwirtschaftskrise und Aussenhandel. Forschungsstand und Forschungsaufgaben," in: Otto Büsch and Peter-Christian Witt (ed.), *Internationale Zusammenhänge in der Weltwirtschaftskrise. Präsentationen aus Anlaß einer Fachkonferenz*, Berlin 1994, 53–69.

51 This is also partially maintained by a League of Nations study. "When the impact of capital withdrawals had exhausted itself and the financial panic subsided, vested interests had been created on the basis of the new orientation of production and trade, anxious to consolidate the situation created by recent government protection measures." League of Nations, Economic Intelligence Service (ed.), *Europe's Trade. A Study of the Trade of European Countries with Each other and with the Rest of the World*, Geneva 1941, 79.

and stagnation of trade and increase of protectionism; 2.) a shift away from international division of labour, production, exchanges of goods and services to nationalistic economies and inward, domestic oriented growth, especially in Europe. This was closely interconnected with the shift and concentration of growth away from some modern sectors back to more traditional sectors of industry in the old industrialised countries supported by government intervention. 3.) Another change and important development continuing from the 1920s was the increasing development, growth and competition of and from industries in underdeveloped and semi-developed countries in the periphery, whereas growth in the old industrialised countries in Europe and the US was stagnating. How much was performance of the advanced countries affected by this process, and did it contribute to the stagnation of trade?

The drastic contraction and stagnation of trade during and after the depression, as well as the move toward nationalistic and protectionist economies and the increasing growth of, and competition from, new industrialising countries was clearly noticed by contemporaries. One economist called this process "[eine] eindeutige Ausrichtung aller wirtschaftlichen Vorgänge und Formen, kurz des gesamten Wirtschaftssystems auf den Primat und die Lebensnotwendigkeit der Nation [...]."[52]

Lucien Brocard noticed increasing international economic interlocking and concentration in 1933; but at the same time he also discerned a greater tendency of increasing economic nationalism,[53] harming Europe and resulting from intensifying industrialisation in the US, India, Japan, Australia and Eastern Europe. The process would lead to a decline in international division of labour and specialisation and to a rise of self-contained national economies. This tendency would limit international solidarity, co-operation and economic interconnection, which would aggravate economic and political contradictions. This prediction would prove to be quite precise.

For some contemporaries, increasing protectionism was, to a large degree, the result of peripheral industrialisation. This holds only partially true for the 1930s. Increasingly competitive industrialisation in the periphery only revealed the move to national economies and protectionism in the advanced core of the world economy.

Before and after the First World War, trade in manufactured articles had increased commensurately with the increase in output of manufactures in the world. This trend was broken by the depression. In the 1930s, "there was a large difference between the world movements of manufacturing and trade in manufactured goods over the period (1926/29–1936/38): the former increased by 33% and the latter fell by 12%."[54] Generally, the growth of world trade remained far behind the growth of industrial production in the world throughout the 1930s. World industrial production

52 Hans Kretschmar, "Ökonomische Theorie, Nationalwirtschaft und 'Interventionismus'," in: *Weltwirtschaftliches Archiv. Zeitschrift des Instituts für Weltwirtschaft und Seeverkehr an der Universität Kiel*, vol. 38, 1933, 334–355.

53 Lucien Brocard, "Die Tendenz zur Nationalwirtschaft und die internationalen Beziehungen," in: *Weltwirtschaftliches Archiv*, vol. 38, 1933, 317–333.

54 League of Nations, *Industrialization and Foreign Trade*, 94.

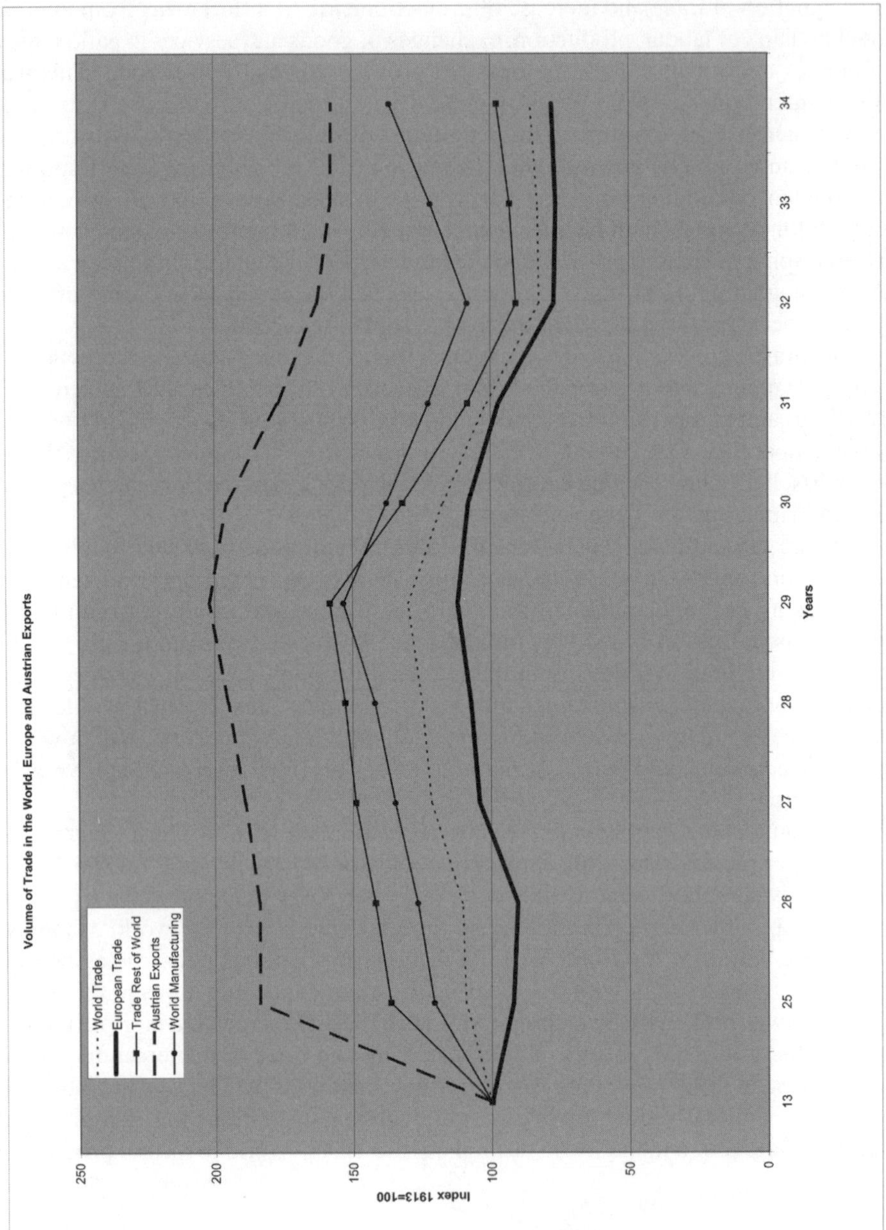

Figure 5.3.: Volume of Trade in the World, in Europe and of Austrian Exports. Source: Ernst Hickmann and Karlheinrich Rieker, *Statistisches Handbuch des Deutschen und internationalen Aussenhandels 1936*, Berlin 1936, 6. And Österreichisches Institut für Wirtschaftsforschung, *Monatsberichte* 14, 43. And League of Nations, *Industrialisation and Foreign Trade*, 134.

was nearly 20% above the 1929 level in late 1936, but volume of trade was still 10% and value of trade still about 30% below its pre-crisis level.[55]

This process was primarily the result of the concentration of industrialised countries on national economies, supported by the attempt of national economic policies to focus on the "restoration of employment and business activity"[56] at home. Since governments could only apply their policies on a national level to alleviate the effects of economic crisis at home, these measures were only able to restore "new national equilibria"[57] to a limited degree, and enhanced the disintegration of international economic relationships. Moreover, trade among the industrialised countries contracted, while trade between the core and periphery had increased in the period starting from the beginning of recovery until 1938. The underdeveloped periphery countries had increased their production and export of primary products as well as of traditional finished products to the industrialised countries, while the mutual trade of industrialised countries stagnated.[58] Thus, whereas nations in the periphery increased their share of trade and production in the world, the industrialised countries in Europe and the US increasingly shut off their production and trade among each other and focused on their home markets. At the same time, the competition for exports of finished products of the industrialised countries increased, since the primary goods producing countries had been able to augment their share of world exports of finished products by about 32% between 1913 and 1937.[59] In particular, Japan and Canada were able to increase their share of world exports of finished goods.

Hence, to some contemporaries it appeared that advancing industrialisation outside of the old industrialised countries increased competition in the exports and sale on domestic markets of finished products and contributed to stagnation in the highly developed countries. It seemed as if their trade balance, as well as their economic growth, was harmed, as advanced countries with limited natural resources, i.e. most industrialised countries in Europe, relied on a balance of exports of manufactured articles, as well as on a balance of imports of primary products in order to maintain continuous economic growth. Hence, since advanced countries had more difficulty selling their finished products in a hostile international trade environment, they turned to economic warfare and reduced their capital export. In order to ensure and finance continuous imports of necessary primary products and to sustain debt service payments, they limited imports of products not vital to development and promoted exports of manufactures.[60] Other methods included increased import substitution.

However, progressing industrialisation abroad only seemed to be the problem on a superficial level. Before the war, economic growth was not limited at all by

55 See diagramme "Welthandel und Weltindustrieproduktion", in: Deutsches Institut für Konjunkturforschung, *Wochenbericht*, 1937, 144.

56 Cited and paraphrased from League of Nations, *Europe's Trade*, chapter: Summary of Tendencies During the Thirties, 79 ff.

57 Ibid, 96.

58 Richard Seiler, "Strukturwandlungen des Welthandels. Ein Beitrag zur Frage: Industrialisierung und Außenhandel," in: *Schriften des Instituts für Konjunkturforschung, Vierteljahreshefte zur Wirtschaftsforschung*, vol. 13, no. 2, Hamburg 1938/39, 155–171.

59 Ibid, 164.

60 League of Nations, *Industrialization and Foreign Trade*, 97.

industrialisation abroad,[61] even though this process was taking place at the same rate before 1914. Furthermore, the increase of the share of world exports in finished products of industrialising countries from 11.2% in 1913 to 16.3% in 1937[62] does not seem to be large enough to be considered a major factor in harming world trade on this scale, and to induce old industrialised Europe and the US to focus exclusively on their own respective national economies and domestic growth. A study from the League of Nations showed that under normal conditions, imports of manufactures from old industrial countries to the periphery were not likely to decline because of industrialisation abroad. Only the structure of these imports tended to change, because demand in the newly industrialising countries diversified. Since this industrialisation process progressed slowly, the advanced countries usually had no difficulty in adopting their production and exports according to changing demand.[63] In other words, their process of changing economic structures easily kept up with, or was ahead of, changes abroad. In the inter-war period, though, competition from industrialisation abroad clearly became a problem for many traditional sectors of industry in Europe.

Competition from periphery countries was not in itself the problem for trade and development for most industrial sectors in Europe. However, the inability of the advanced countries to adjust trade to changing demand was a symptom of their disturbed development. Essentially, trade deteriorated in the 30s not only because of "disturbances in international economic relationships,"[64] but because the acute economic crisis in the early 30s had caused a severe policy shock and had further increased the structural distortions that limited economic development, the capitalist process of creative destruction and growth since the war. This process must have progressed too slowly, insufficiently and was distorted in Europe and the US. Naturally, the adoption of new types of innovations, products, production processes, goods and services in the old industrialised countries did not work as smoothly as before 1913. New industries were not adopted on a wide enough scale and were incapable of compensating the decline of the old industries, partially due to the adoption of these old production processes and products in the industrialisation effort of the periphery countries. Thus, the development of industrialisation outside of Europe and the US only became a problem after the process of creative destruction was malfunctioning in the old industrialised, advanced countries after the war.

61 Ibid, 106.
62 Seiler, 164.
63 League of Nations, *Industrialization and Foreign Trade*, 117.
64 As claimed by the League of Nations' study in 1945. Ibid, 106.

5.4. DEFLATIONARY POLICY REACTION TO MONETARY CRISES: THE BEGINNING OF THE RETREAT TO ECONOMIC NATIONALISM

It is very problematical to discuss the breakdown of the world financial system in the early 30s and to combine it with a structural theory of economic growth and development. The financial breakdown was a short-term process, whereas structural theories can only be verified by observing and interpreting long-term economic phenomena. Nevertheless, to understand the spread of nationalistic economies, further structural distortion, slow recovery in the 30s and performance of various European countries after the catastrophic events of 1931, it is necessary to comprehend the breakdown of the international currency system and the spread and causes of deflationary economic policy until 1931. Portions of policy measures will be discussed to show their actual short-term and long-term effects and their weaknesses. Then, we shall turn to alternative, real economical, structural explanations of policy and performance in various European countries after 1933.

There is no doubt that a major crisis in the international financial system, which began in 1928 and reached its peak with the breakdown of the gold standard system in late 1931, contributed, to a great degree, to the causes and severity of the depression. The collapse of this credit system was also one of the main initiating forces spreading the crisis.[65] However, it cannot explain the severity, nor the length of, economic stagnation in the 30s. The monetary crisis initiated a tremendous deflationary process, which introduced the dramatic, maximum withdrawal of economic activity to the pure national sphere. This withdrawal process existed only subliminally in the 20s, but fully implemented itself after 1930. *After the peak of financial crisis in mid-1931, the most catastrophic financial year,[66] large obsolete and traditional sectors of national economies, with the help of national policies, first, began to adjust to this process of deflation, and secondly, abused policy measures in order to maximise the retreat to economic nationalism. Once this process was finished, it was difficult to turn back to a liberal, international economic system, since the structurally distorted industrial sectors had accommodated themselves with retrenchment and protectionism, and were unable or unwilling to accept the burden of painful adjustment to an international competitive environment.*

The restrictive US Federal Reserve monetary policy, which began to cut US foreign lending from the summer of 1928 onward, had major international repercussions.[67] Central banks in the world, especially in the regions that had enjoyed large US capital imports,[68] which included the debtor nations in South America and Eu-

65 "Die geographische Verschiebung und dadurch zeitliche Hinausschiebung der Krise geschah mit Hilfe eines in der Nachkriegszeit zur Entfaltung gelangten Kreditmechanismus von einzigartiger Kapazität und Spannkraft." Polanyi, 1933, 5.

66 A Harvard economist called this crisis "the profound financial disturbance which has been the oustanding characteristic of the year 1931." J. B. Hubbard, "European Economic Conditions in the Year 1931," in: *The Review of Economic Statistics*, Vol. 14, No.1, 1932, 24.

67 The following brief review on monetary crisis is based on Eichengreen's excellent monography, *Golden Fetters*, chapters 6–9. And Aldcroft, *The European Economy*, 3rd edition, 65–77.

68 For an account and brief analysis of the extent and quality of US investment abroad in the 20s and

rope, in particular Germany, Austria, Hungary and other Eastern European nations, were forced to follow this restrictive policy, because capital inflow from the US declined at a time when many South American, German, Austrian and other Eastern European national and private banks heavily relied on foreign lending. This had a huge, world-wide, destabilising and deflationary impact, especially as demand from the industrialised countries declined and primary commodity prices fell dramatically in 1929. The commodity exporting countries that suffered from great indebtedness and debt service payments, were hit hard by the fall in demand of primary products and subsequent decline of foreign exchange income from export sales. They had to turn to deflationary policy measures as well, in order to defend their gold parity and balance of payments equilibrium.

Falling commodity prices were not the only factor that accelerated the spread and intensity of deflationary policy. In Central Europe, the main problem seemed to have been restricted capital availability after the breakdown of massive American lending. Since lending from the US diminished and Austrian, German and Eastern European banks continued to service their debts to maintain the facade of credibility, their gold and foreign exchange reserves fell. Therefore, popular fears that national banks would have to go off gold increased. With vivid memories of the recent catastrophic inflation in mind, capital flight to allegedly saver currencies, such as the franc or the dollar, began to endanger gold parities in Germany, Austria, Hungary and Britain. The main problem, according to Eichengreen, was that central banks could not act as domestic lender of last resort. As soon as central bank officials would induce liquidity to the large banks in danger, "they signalled that they attached higher priority to the stability of the banking system than the defence of the gold standard. Depositors rushed to get their money out of the country in advance of devaluation. Any liquidity injected into the banking system just leaked back out as the inevitable balance-of-payments crisis loomed."[69] The only way out would have been international co-operation in the form of an internationally concerted co-ordinated credit operation to support any national bank by granting it greater liquidity, so that it could help its endangered national banking system without running out of reserves.

Since the BIS (Bank for International Settlements), founded in 1930, did not enjoy Federal Reserve participation and was simultaneously responsible for German reparations transfers and central bank co-operation, the credits that it had been granted, and the credits that it could offer, were too small and essentially ineffective. According to Eichengreen, large scale international lending to Europe and its breakdown, and the dramatic decline in prices and the lending problem for the primary commodity producing countries essentially caused, at first, severe deflationary policies and eventually, the breakdown of the gold standard system in these areas. Finally, the central banks under pressure had "to choose between stability of the domestic banking system and maintenance of the gold standard."[70] Banking crises

the spread of deflationary policy during the depression see: W.S. Woytinsky and E.S. Woytinsky, *World Commerce*, 201–211.

69 Eichengreen, *Golden Fetters*, 259.

70 Ibid, 285.

in Germany and Austria and liquidity problems in other debtor countries in Central Europe had major repercussions on the financial situation of Britain. As the Bank of England had given large credit to these areas, it was heavily hit by the cessation of debt service in these countries and could only maintain sterling gold parity with the help of US credits. This did not halt the fall of its gold reserves, and Britain went off the gold standard in September 1931.

Policy options and reactions to this international monetary crisis were similar[71] and always resulted in a withdrawal to economic nationalism. Between 1929 and 1931, most countries reacted with a passive classical liberal and observant policy. As the domestic financial and economic recession carried on, it was still regarded as a normal crisis. The central banks reacted with credit restrictions. In order to defend the gold parity, most governments reacted with increasing taxes and cutting of spending to follow the doctrine of balanced budgets, fiscal order and currency stability. The primary commodity exporting countries could attempt to raise exports and restrict imports, although this action enhanced a further fall of commodity prices. Trade policy became only slightly more protectionist during this initial phase of the depression. Once these policies were ineffective in 1929 and 1930, many countries stopped their debt service payments altogether in order to save valuable foreign exchange. In early 1931, a slow upswing was expected. When the recession turned into a major depression during the spring and summer of 1931, policy became more extreme. The last measure after 1931 was devaluation and the suspension of the gold standard for a national currency. With drastic exchange and trade control, this was often done only de facto, in order to keep up the facade of gold parity, as was the case in Austria and Germany. Hand in hand with currency measures, trade protection was dramatically accelerated on a world-wide scale.

After the nadir was reached by mid-1932, not only debtor nations, but most governments in Europe along with the US, had reduced their policies to nationalist and protectionist measures. With the attempt to exclude their market as much as possible from international trade, the countries' austerity policy of fiscal retrenchment and protectionist trade policies had turned their economies into besieged economies. Throughout the 1930s, these policy restrictions prevailed. Compared to the period 1925–1930, it is clear that economic policies in the 30s had far greater direct impact on economic development and growth. While the breakdown of the international financial system and deflationary policy reactions were the initial cause for the spread and severity of the depression and economic nationalism, only extreme policy decisions and measures in the authoritarian states after 1931/32 would determine the rate of recovery and performance in the 30s.[72]

71 Eichengreen summarised three policy options. Ibid, 230–232. For another comparison and summary of debtor countries' policy reaction see: Herbert Matis and Dieter Stiefel, *Die Weltwirtschaft. Struktur und Entwicklung im 20. Jahrhundert*, Vienna 1991.

72 This view is contrary to Eichengreen's conclusion: "Nineteen thirty-two was the year of transition. Countries that had not yet abandoned the gold standard had to decide whether to do so. Countries that had already suspended gold convertibility had to decide whether to adopt expansionary initiatives or maintain their passive policy stance. Such critical policy decisions would condition the course of economic recovery from the Great Depression." Eichengreen, *Golden Fetters*, 287.

5.4.1. Capital Flight and Currency Crisis until 1931

Now we will turn to a comparison of national economic policies during the initial phases of the crisis to reveal the international trend of turning toward economic nationalism and the similarity of these policies despite different performances. Traditionally, descriptions of economic policy have been used to show their implications on economic performance, to point out the direct interconnection between policy and performance. Here, it is attempted to present policy measures in the 30s as a reaction to economic crisis, which only aggravated the situation by contributing to the disintegration of international economic co-operation and enhancing structural distortions.

Policy reaction to the fall of prices and breakdown of trade as well as foreign lending in Austria took the classical course of development, as described above, for most debtor countries with pending collapse of the gold standard. Breakdown of lending led first to a major bank crisis, then to capital flight and finally to a currency crisis. Once the balance of payments situation dramatically deteriorated and debt service payments to foreign countries increased without a compensating inflow of capital from abroad the main Austrian banks came under tremendous liquidity pressure. In May 1931, this development culminated in a major financial crisis for the largest Austrian bank, the Creditanstalt.[73] In other countries, similar bank panics and breakdowns occurred, as in Hungary for example. Yet, the crisis of the Creditanstalt meant the collapse of one of the largest deposit and investment banks in Central Europe. In the light of Austrian universal banking policy, which had attempted to maintain its financial influence over the territories of the former empire, this bank maintained substantial financial interests and shares in eleven banks and about 40 industrial enterprises in Eastern Europe, plus shares of many domestic companies. 40% of its loans and advances were invested outside of Austria. Since it had already absorbed large Viennese banks on the verge of collapse, e.g. the Bodencreditanstalt in 1929, the CA was the largest and one of the last banks pursuing this risky and expansionist pre-war policy on feet of clay. With insufficient funds, short-term borrowing in the West and long-term lending for industrial ventures in the East and at home, CA business strategy had to break down once international lending contracted with the onset of depression.[74] Many of its foreign and domestic short-term loans and deposits were withdrawn, entailing the bank's illiquidity.

Despite its strict orthodox approach to economic policy-making, the Austrian state decided to conduct a large scale interventionist financial policy. Since it was believed that up to three quarters of Austrian industry depended on the CA,[75] and

73 This paragraph is partially based on: Dieter Stiefel, "The Reconstruction of the Credit-Anstalt," in: Alice Teichova and Philip L. Cottrell (eds.), *International Business and Central Europe 1918–1939*, 415–430. And Stiefel, *Finanzdiplomatie und Weltwirtschaftskrise. Die Krise der Credit-Anstalt für Handel und Gewerbe 1931*, Frankfurt 1989.

74 Other reasons for its breakdown were the losses it made due to the merger with the collapsed Bodencreditanstalt and the losses of falling stocks of many of its industrial shares. Creditanstalt-Bankverein (ed.), *Ein Jahrhundert Creditanstalt-Bankverein*, Vienna 1957, 208.

75 Haas, Außenhandelspolitik, 8.

since this breakdown initiated a currency crisis, the government readily agreed to intervene in order to reconstruct the bank financially. In reality, 68.75% of Austrian industry had financial connections to the CA, but only 13.75% were actually so far in debt to the bank that they would have collapsed with it.[76] The losses of 140 million schillings, declared on May 8, proved to be far too low, and essentially the state had to take over the CA debts to the national bank of 571 million and debts to foreign creditors of 210 million. Moreover, the capital share had to be reduced to a minute fraction of its original value, and the state signed new shares of 71 million. The state, therefore, virtually became the owner of the bank.[77]

Before cancellation of shares, a very large portion of the bank shares and the majority of credit had been owned and granted by foreigners, mainly from the US, Britain, France and the European neutrals. Therefore, the reconstruction operation was not a mere national problem, but meant a strong involvement of influential Western capital groups. Now, the financial, economic, domestic and international political situation became extremely mixed up and complex. Since the Austrian government was keen on stopping further capital outflow and re-establishing credibility in the hope of future active financial support,[78] foreign capital share holders of cancelled shares enjoyed favourable treatment. While the state bore the greatest losses, foreign shares were devalued only 25%. Meanwhile, foreign creditors had formed the "Austrian Credit-Anstalt International Committee," with the goal to repatriate their CA investments as soon and painlessly as possible. Since the CA financed withdrawals by discounting drafts from the national bank, the government also became the principal creditor of the CA. In the end, this turned out to be what the socialists called, "privatisation of profits and socialisation of losses."[79] After it had proclaimed a guarantee of 1.2 billion schillings on all deposits and foreign liabilities of the CA in June, under very heavy financial losses, the government hoped that capital would remain in, or return to, Austria and that the country would regain international financial credibility.[80] With its massive financial intervention, the state still expected a return to normalcy, even though this capital flight and banking crisis, interconnected with orthodox policy reaction in all countries, meant the first step toward protectionism, economic nationalism and retrenchment.

In Germany, the path to economic nationalism was introduced almost the exact same way, only that it came much sooner. Exactly as in Austria and many Eastern European countries, foreign capital inflow, borrowing on a short-term and lending on a long-term basis, played an important role for capital accumulation and investment for banks and enterprises in Germany. Once international lending contracted after 1928 and collapsed around the turn of 1930/31, a national banking crash introduced a currency crisis. Also, in this case, the government, expecting a return to normalcy, pursued an orthodox economic policy which entailed an enormous financial intervention as an attempt to maintain gold standard parity. The banking crisis occurred

76 Stiefel, "Reconstruction," 418.
77 Weber, "Staatliche Wirtschaftspolitik," 546.
78 Stiefel, "Reconstruction," 420.
79 Ibid, 418.
80 Ibid, 423. Kernbauer, *Währungspolitik*, 300.

in July, when one of the largest German banks, the Darmstädter und Nationalbank, declared insolvency after the CA had crashed in May.[81] Credibility in the parity of the reichsmark declined and massive capital flight took place, endangering exchange and gold reserves of the Reichsbank.

With the emergency decree of July 13, 1931, the state declared a deficit guarantee in order to fulfil the bank's foreign obligations and liabilities. In contrast to the Austrian course of events, though, Germany was not as co-operative to its foreign creditors. A moratorium, lasting until September, was declared, and exchange control was introduced immediately. In the following year, the state reconstructed the national banking system. Capital stock was cancelled, new stocks issued, purchased by the government, and several large banks were merged. Now, a large portion of the national banking system was in public hands and control. For example, the state had a 95.4% share of the largest German bank, the Dresdner Bank.[82] Again, the consequences of this policy were a deterioration of credibility in the national financial system and the introduction of economic nationalism.

In Britain, the crisis of the financial system was not quite as extreme. It also led to retrenchment and protectionism, but to a much more moderate degree. The already unstable and difficult return of the pound to its pre-war gold parity, combined with the stabilisation of the undervalued franc, low exports after 1926, the investment boom in the US stock market which drew funds away from London, and continuous stagnation before the depression, resulted in exchange rate difficulties and crises in Britain even before the depression set in.[83] Between 1925 and 1929 the discount rate had to be set relatively high (up to 6%) by the Bank of England, in order to attract capital to maintain an at least moderate amount of liquid reserves. Another problem, making the maintenance of the gold parity more difficult, was the more than tenfold increase of the national debt since 1914. Annual state debt service payments amounted to about 7% of national income.[84] This burden lowered confidence in a balanced budget, lowered credibility to sustain gold parity, and strained funds. Essentially, British financial resources were too small to resist larger capital outflow, while international co-operation and support was not forthcoming. On the one hand, funds were drawn away from London, especially to the American stock market after 1928, and on the other, capital repatriation from Europe to the US induced increasing British lending to Germany and Central Europe, further pressuring British funds.

In addition, the concentrated effect of declining US lending to Europe and the fall of prices for primary producing countries resulted in falling debt service payments from debtor countries inside and outside of Europe to Britain. Liquidity crises in debtor countries also "caused governments to liquidate sterling balances traditionally maintained in London, thereby aggravating the drain of gold and foreign

81 Gustav Stolper (continued by Karl Häuser and Knut Borchardt), *Deutsche Wirtschaft seit 1870*, Tübingen 1964, 131–137. Fischer, *Deutsche Wirtschaftspolitik 1918–1945*, 42. Hallgarten and Radkau, 192. Petzina, *Zwischenkriegszeit*, 98 ff. Knoche, 118 ff.

82 Knoche, 122.

83 Alec Cairncross and Barry Eichengreen, *Sterling in Decline. The Devaluations of 1931, 1949 and 1967*, Oxford 1983, 44–82.

84 Pollard, *Development*, 126.

exchange [...]".[85] Therefore, sterling gold standard parity stood on feet of clay. After the collapse of the American stock market boom, the currency situation in Britain was only temporarily relieved. Hoping for a resurgence of international capital flows as capital returned to London after October 1929, bank interest rate was lowered to 3% until May 1930.[86] Yet, this was only a temporary phenomenon, and eventually, sterling had to go off gold. Although the money supply still rose slightly in 1930, monetary policy could not be relaxed as much as desired, because of restrictions imposed on it by the attempt to sustain the gold standard system, when, at the same time, the foreign exchange situation of sterling continued to be precarious.

The British Treasury, as well as the Bank of England, regarded the resurgence of capital flow from the US as a chance to relax monetary policy. Meanwhile, Chancellor of the Exchequer, Philip Snowden, tried to balance the budget by all means, even though the depression had already caused a decline of revenue and an increase of unemployment relief expenditure.[87] Until the financial crisis of 1931, the labour government, under Ramsay McDonald, focused on international financial problems and the contraction of trade, instead of on domestic economic policy measures. It was still believed that adherence to orthodoxy would maintain the gold standard system, which in turn, would allow for an international economic revival and a return to normalcy. The consequence, so it was thought, would be recovery of international trade and British exports. Therefore, fiscal orthodoxy was deemed necessary, whereas devaluation was still out of the question. Even as late as March and July 1931, Keynes and the Macmillan Committee urged the government to balance the budget in order to sustain credibility and confidence in the pound gold parity and dissuaded from devaluation.[88]

5.4.2. Restrictive Economic Policy in Austria and Germany, 1931–1933

Neo-liberal policy reaction to the collapse of the international economy, which had changed already to restricted trade, moderate protectionism, collective bargaining, more sensitive markets and mass consumption, almost automatically entailed massive retreat of national economies to domestic activity. In some countries retrenchment was supported by conservative, later authoritarian governments, and by agricultural and certain industrial interest groups within these states. Due to short-term economic advantages, these interests groups inadvertently advocated deformed growth until the mid 30s, as they had suffered most from the social concessions made after the war and in the 20s and from the effects of the depression. In Germany and in Austria, as well as in some Eastern European countries, this process was particularly pronounced, since the crisis favoured the creation of fascist and proto-fascist

85 Cairncross and Eichengreen, 48.

86 Susan Howson, *Domestic Monetary Management in Britain 1919–1938*, Cambridge 1975, 66–74.

87 Ibid.

88 Peden, 90. Cairncross and Eichengreen, 60–61.

regimes. In contrast, in France, the depression caused serious political uprisings, but no regime shift.

As further capital flight, depletion of foreign exchange reserves of the Austrian national bank and the intensification of the currency crisis continued, state efforts to support the national banking system were in vain. The more faith and credibility in the national and public financial systems deteriorated, the more acute the currency crisis became. Since capital outflow persisted between the spring and autumn of 1931, gold reserves of the Austrian national bank shrank, and the gold standard parity of the schilling was endangered. The national currency was only covered by short-term loans from the BIS and the Bank of England. After foreign creditors had their way and the guarantee was declared, the government was forced to resign after strong oppositional political pressure mounted.

In order to maintain or recover credibility, to keep gold standard parity and to be in accordance with the rules of classical economic theory, it was believed that only three policy options remained, apart from a moratorium. They entailed severe political and economic consequences and initiated an extreme economic withdrawal process. The first of the measures deemed necessary was the enforcement of a balanced budget with the support of tax raises and expenditure cuts. The second policy measure was the procurement of foreign capital funds to allow for continuing finance of capital flight and debt servicing. The implementation of strict exchange control as a makeshift solution was considered the final option.

The first two measures went hand in hand. Both policy actions were supported by the government and strongly demanded by the League of Nations' principal powers. Without a balanced budget, the League would not have permitted the floatation of another international loan. The enforcement of both measures not only entailed strong domestic political opposition, but introduced the end of parliamentary democracy in Austria. However, the government could count on strong political support for orthodox policy, even after an authoritarian regime was established, from the main representatives of Austrian employers.[89] Big business interest was in favour of tax cuts and reduction of social expenditure, because it was believed that this would introduce lower and more flexible labour costs and provide a better basis for keeping up with international competitiveness. Exactly as politicians and economists, employers could not ascertain a connection between interventionist or anti-cyclical policy and increase of aggregate demand and economic recovery.

Not only were the government, economists and Austrian entrepreneurs in favour of orthodox policy, but generally, the social democratic opposition agreed to these restrictive principles, at least until late 1932. Political opposition occurred as soon as restrictive policy harmed the interests of a certain socio-economic group. Thus, when employment relief was to be cut, the socialist opposition demanded concessions and exemptions. When expenditure for farming support was to be cut, agricultural

89 See: Gerald Sturmayr, "Industrielle Interessenverbände: Ringen um Einheit," in: Emmerich Talos (ed.), *Handbuch des politischen Systems Österreichs. Erste Republik 1918–1933*, Vienna 1995, 339–352. And: Karl Haas, "Industrielle Interessenpolitik in Österreich zur Zeit der Weltwirtschaftskrise," in: Österreichische Gesellschaft für Zeitgeschichte (ed.), *Jahrbuch für Zeitgeschichte*, Vienna 1978, 97–126.

interests opposed aspects of economic policy. Despite these problems, in 1932, Austria was able to cut state investment altogether and restricted total state expenditure 19%.[90] It was, therefore, one of the few countries in Europe that balanced its budget during that crucial year. Eventually, the state established new sources of revenue income that were not in accordance with socio-economic principles, but instead, augmented taxes where the weakest political opposition could be expected and where crisis symptoms were aggravated. Whereas employers were favoured, demand was curtailed by cuts of social relief and increases of excise duties.

Generally, enforcement of this restrictive policy was executed under strong international political pressures and constraints, despite its socio-economic implications and political opposition at home. International political pressure, from the League of Nations and the guaranteeing states, helped the Austrian government to enforce strict fiscal policies. The principal Austrian creditor nations, represented by the League, not only protected their financial interest, but also supported these orthodox policy measures, because they were employed in their countries as well and were seen as a co-ordinated effort to re-establish the pre-crisis economic system. A prospective loan was only reluctantly granted, and only as long as Austria continued to pursue an orthodox economic policy.

For the Austrian government and those interest groups benefiting from its conception of crisis management, this course of economic policy seemingly had some advantages. However, there were also great disadvantages. On the one hand, strict currency policy seemed to help Austrian debtors. As long as the schilling was stable and was possibly overvalued, debt servicing could be easier. On the other hand, internal political pressure mounted, against balancing the budget, orthodox economic policy and the handing over of national autonomy in matters of economic policy-making to League of Nations officials.

As the Austrian government had great difficulty in attaining a balanced budget and was strained by extreme financial pressure, it took until the summer of 1932 until the guaranteeing states of the League were able and willing to sign an agreement which permitted a future floatation of another international loan. Until then, international political differences further complicated the situation. France was only willing to grant credit after Austria renounced the Austro-German customs union project of March 1931.[91] Moreover, other states were only inclinable to grant credit after the Austrian state had declared an unlimited guarantee for foreign Creditanstalt deposits. Again, the Financial Committee of the League put together a reconstruction plan

90 The following paragraph about the struggle between the enforcement of a balanced budget and the sociopolitical opposition is based on Dieter Stiefel, *Die große Krise in einem kleinem Land. Österreichische Finanzund Wirtschaftspolitik 1929–1938*, Vienna 1988. Percentage value, see 33 ff. Austria was not the only country that was able to balance its budget. Britain had a budget surplus and Germany did not have a significant deficit.

91 Representatives of Austrian industry were also against the customs project since they feared a loss of international financial credibility and support. The automobile and metal producing and processing industries also feared increasing German competition. Frank Wittendorfer, *Industrie, Banken, Politiker und Verbände in Österreich im Widerstand gegen die Wirtschaftspolitik des Jahres 1931. Dargestellt am Beispiel des deutsch-österreichischen Zollunionsprojektes*, dissertation, Innsbruck 1986.

demanding a balanced budget, the termination of state investment, and increased taxes. On September 21, 1931, chancellor Karl Buresch accepted the demands from the League. The conservative Christian democrats even suggested the enforcement of restrictive economic policy by emergency degree and the exclusion of parliament. The League's committee supported this suggestion.[92] Still, the emergence was not enacted yet, as parliament reluctantly ratified the highly restrictive budget reconstruction law on October 3.

1932 proved to be a difficult year. Tax receipts were much lower than expected, and expenditure cuts, especially the reduction of social spending, were more oppressive than anticipated. After further short-term stop gap loans had been granted by France and Britain, the Protocols of Lausanne were finally concluded in July, allowing Austria to float another League loan in the next year. The stipulations of the Geneva Protocols were repeated, and Austria once more lost its economic and financial autonomy. Had it already been problematic to receive sufficient support from parliament to ratify the Protocols of Lausanne, with the continuous severity of the depression and its social costs, the economic policy of the Dollfuß government and the League was increasingly pressured by heavy socio-political criticism in late 1932. The Dollfuß administration, as well as the Financial Committee, began to regard political opposition to their policy as an obstacle to successful reconstruction of public finances and restoration of financial credibility, which was seen as a prerequisite of recovery.

The impossibility of receiving sufficient political support for an economic policy that in actuality accentuated the crisis, pushed the legitimacy of a new state that had become increasingly involved in social welfare and the economy to its limits.[93] The commitment of the state for social relief, the interconnection of the state and the national economy, and the sensivity of tax receipts to economic fluctuations, had considerably increased since pre-war times. Therefore, fiscal retrenchment and economic orthodoxy in times of severe economic crisis were only possible when political opposition was at first threatened and then eliminated. In the beginning, the government received hesitant support from parliament, but as the crisis continued, opposition continued to mount. Then, the government threatened to demand dictatorial powers from the president in order to enforce its economic policy. All the same, parliament still went along in 1932 and agreed to further restrictive measures to avoid dissolution.

This extorted co-operation deteriorated in late 1932 and early 1933 when the economic and political crisis and the restrictive policy reaction did not find an end. The political confrontation over distribution of the contracting national product reached its peak. Finally, the government was able to implement an authoritarian regime in March 1933, after a weak parliament with a disillusioned social democratic party dissolved itself. The government could do this with the assistance of those interests groups and parties in favour of further restriction and harsh currency

92 Extensively on the politics of the second League of Nations' loan: Grete Klingenstein, *Die Anleihe von Lausanne. Ein Beitrag zur Geschichte der Ersten Republik in den Jahren 1931–1934*, Graz 1965, 50 ff.

93 See for the following: Stiefel, *Die große Krise*, 96 ff.

policy: Big business, banks, foreign creditors and the League of Nations' financial committee. Utilising an enabling act from the war economy of World War One, further deflationary orthodox policy was enforced after 1933.

Historians have seen a direct connection between the first orthodox measures to counter the crisis, the budget reconstruction law of 1931, the Protocols of Lausanne of 1932, the dissolution of parliament and the authoritarian enforcement of economic policy in early 1933.[94] The economic importance of the balanced budget and the foreign loan was actually minute. The Lausanne loan, finally floated in 1933, only amounted to 300 million schillings, 64% of which were used only for financial purposes. 200 million alone were for the repayment of state debt to the national bank. Only 36% were utilised for small investments and ineffective work creation programmes.[95] Its only importance lay in the enforcement of extremely orthodox policy and consequential economic nationalism by the government and various interest groups with the support of the power of the League and the guaranteeing states.

Once this process was finished in the first half of 1933, the final measures to turn to complete protectionism had been concluded. Basically, the enforcement of classical non-interventionist policy in the face of a severe economic crisis not only aided the emergence of a fascist regime, but the implementation of restrictive economic nationalism in a small and trade dependent country.

In Germany, the enforcement of a balanced budget and fiscal retrenchment, under the governments of Heinrich Brüning, Franz von Papen and Kurt von Schleicher, also resulted in retreat of economic activity to the national economy and the rise of a fascist regime. At the bottom, economic policy was the expression of the attempt to create the pre-conditions of an upswing, according to neo-liberal principles, although there was no inherent mechanism of self-regulation in the economic system[96] which had rapidly transformed since pre-war times. Furthermore, in order to suggest a direct connection between problematical reparations payments and weak German economic performance to the Entente powers, economic policy was partially subordinated to revisionist reparations policy. Here as well, policy was strongly supported by agricultural and certain industrial interests groups against mounting oppositional political pressure. These main interest groups also expected a partial reversal of the "revolution of 1918," i.e. reduction of wages, taxes and social expenses, and did not shrink back from the dissolution of parliamentary democracy to enforce restrictive neo-classical economic policy, again viewed as the tool to create the basic conditions for an economic revival.[97] Interestingly enough, the representatives of traditional industries, such as iron, steel and coal, were more inclined to restrictive, authoritarian and repressive enforcement of policy. The modern and expansive industries, for instance electrical engineering and machinery, tended more toward a moderate,

94 Ibid, 118–119.

95 199–200.

96 Petzina, *Zwischenkriegszeit*, 102.

97 Bernd Weisbrod, *Schwerindustrie in der Weimarer Republik. Interessenpolitik zwischen Stabilisierung und Krise*, Wuppertal 1978, chapter: Ausblick: Die Schwerindustrie in der Weltwirtschaftskrise, 479–501.

co-operative, expansionist, and labour friendly approach of socio-economic policy-making.[98]

Orthodox policy in Germany did not require the support of the League of Nations. Instead of using outside pressure from the League to compel parliament to accept restrictive fiscal measures, the Brüning administration enjoyed plenty of support from the two strong economic interest groups so that it could utilise emergency decrees, authorised by article 48 of theWeimar constitution in order to enforce drastic cuts of state expenditure, increased mass consumption taxes and strict deflationary currency policy. Yet, even in this case, economic policy was not quite free from foreign pressures and demands as Germany still depended on credit from abroad, especially from France. To get loans and credit extensions, for example, Germany was also forced to renounce its intentions of an Austro-German customs union. In order to receive foreign loans from influential American financial circles for the desolate German railways, the German government was forced to increase employee contribution payments for unemployment relief and to reduce central government redistribution of tax to the Länder.[99]

Further measures of orthodox policy were the reduction of prices, interest rates and wages by state decree in late 1931.[100] With the same motives as in Austria, to regain credibility in the financial system, everything was done to balance the budget. New taxes were introduced and expenditure was vigorously cut. Despite these harsh measures, it was not quite possible to balance the budgets of 1931 and 1932, because the financial gains from the new and increased taxes were more than offset by higher expenditure for unemployment relief. Compared to 1929, budget deficits were reduced, but still amounted to 670 and 170 million reichsmarks in these two years.[101] Not all measures were restrictive. Before the beginning of the crisis, the state had already subsidised large corporations in financial need. In this time, state transfer subsidy payments, not only for banks, but also for the iron and steel industry, as well as to large country estates in Eastern Germany, rose dramatically.

In May 1932, the new government, under Papen, came to power. It became increasingly authoritarian and restrictive, in favour of employers and to the disadvantage of labour. In June, another emergency decree enforced a 23% reduction of unemployment relief and a 15% cut of welfare support. More taxes were introduced for lower income groups. In September, the system of collective bargaining was dissolved. At the same time, employers enjoyed tax reduction in the form of the so-called tax vouchers, which could be used as waivers for future taxes.[102] The new government under Schleicher, since December 1932, was not quite as restrictive. Similar ideas of corporate state as later implemented in Austria, with stronger political integration of trade unions, were developed. Creation of currency and the introduction of a few, but ineffective, work creation programmes were the first signs

98 Knoche, 172 and 173
99 Ibid, 77.
100 Ibid.
101 Ibid, 62 ff.
102 Ibid, 144–152

of a slow move to more expansionist policies.[103] However, the actual policy regime shift came with the accession of power of the Nazis in 1933.

5.4.3. Economic Policy in Britain and France, 1931–1933

In France and Britain, policy reaction also remained strictly orthodox, but its political consequences were milder. Both countries attempted to balance their budgets, cut expenditure and raised taxes. As French domestic prices were above world prices, especially after pound devaluation, France adhered to strict deflationary policy.[104] Until 1933, budget deficits were minute and only rose substantially thereafter.[105]

Even though the pound was devalued in September 1931, Great Britain also adhered to orthodox economic policy during the depression. The Treasury view was strictly orthodox and against ideas of counter-cyclical economic policy. The budget of 1931 included heavy increases of direct and indirect taxation, while expenditure cuts were made in unemployment benefits and payments to civil servants. Public work programmes were sporadic, ineffective and often abruptly stopped. From 1932 onward, public policy became a bit less restrictive, possibly because of going off gold, higher tariff incomes and the conversion of the War Loan, which lowered state debt service payments. However, only in 1931 did the budget turn into a deficit. Until 1938, Britain had a substantial budget surplus of up to 45 million pounds. British recovery in the 1930s, therefore, cannot to be attributed to deficit spending and expansionist economic policy.[106]

5.4.4. Conclusion

All major European countries reacted to the depression in a very similar fashion until 1933. Policy reaction was orthodox and extremely restrictive in nearly all spheres of economic policymaking. Under the principles of neo-classical theory and policy only a very few options were available. In Germany, Austria and Central Europe these were either a moratorium, enforcement of a balanced budget with expenditure cuts and tax raises and eventually, complete national retrenchment, incorporating exchange control. As the depression hit these countries severely and the financial crisis was the worst in these areas, these measures tended to entail the breakdown of parliamentary democracy. This was the result of the struggle of socio-economic interest groups over enormously shrinking national incomes. In France and Britain, the depression was not as severe. Therefore, to find a socio-political compromise, while still following classical policy options, proved much easier. These kinds of policies, in the face of severe international economic crisis, and the breakdown of the international financial system, ensued a policy of economic nationalism after

103 Ibid, 159–169.

104 Caron, 262. Kemp, 58. Fohlen, 113.

105 Statistisches Reichsamt, *Jahrbuch* 1938, 261 (international survey).

106 Pollard, *Development*, 133–134.

1931, and even more extremely after 1933. This policy is visible in extreme trade restrictions, and after 1933, in national economic growth directly supported by government intervention. The depression initiated a withdrawal of economic activity to the national economies. These policies strongly supported this process, and after 1933, made a return to normal international economic relations impossible.

5.5. THE TOOLS OF ECONOMIC NATIONALISM AND RETRENCHMENT: TRADE RESTRICTIONS, DEVALUATION, EXCHANGE CONTROL AND CLEARING SYSTEMS

5.5.1. Conditions of Protectionism

As a consequence of the economic and financial crisis, and the increase of further structural distortions in national economies, the persistent rise of economic nationalism and trade protection of the 1920s was sustained in an extreme manner during the depression and until the war.[107] These policies, in turn, further hastened structural disequilibria and economic nationalism. As in the 20s, the main motive for trade restriction was the protection of agriculture and of many national, and usually traditional, sectors of industry from outside competition by equalising lower "productivity of labour, land, and capital of a national economy with the superior productivity of other countries [...]".[108] The dramatic fall of world prices, more extreme for primary products than for manufactures, led to even greater competitive pressure from outside. This was especially the case for many traditional industries that had suffered from overcapacities and insufficient adjustment before 1930.

Interconnected with this process, countries needed to limit imports to maintain their balance of payments. Yet, the desire for the rate of protectionism and trade restriction depended on the relative export dependence, the relative size and state of traditional sectors and agriculture and, therefore, on the relative competitiveness of a national economy on world markets. The lower total productivity, the greater the tendency for, and political pressure to favour, an increase of protectionism. This, in turn, was determined to a great degree by the rate of permanent economic adjustment and change, i.e. on the rate of progress of the "process of creative destruction" that had taken place since the war in any national economy. Therefore, tariffs and trade

107 For a good contemporary description of trade restriction and protectionism in the early 1930s see: Henry Chalmers, "The Depression and Foreign Trade Barriers," in: *The Annals of the American Academy of Political and Social Science. The World Trend Toward Nationalism*, Volume 174, Philadelphia, July 1934, 88–106.

108 Heinrich Liepmann, *Tariff Levels and the Economic Unity of Europe. An Examination of Tariff Policy, Export Movements and the Economic Integration of Europe, 1913–1931*, reprinted in Philadelphia 1980 (1st edition: London 1938), 360. Instead of structural, competitive and productive differences among various economies, many historians have traditionally regarded international political insecurity, the trade cycle and the breakdown of the gold standard system as the main causes of the rise of trade barriers. See for example: H. W. Arndt, *The Economic Lessons of the Nineteen-Thirties*, London 1972 (1st edition 1944), 274.

restrictions were essentially "a weapon against technical progress,"[109] *or against the industrial revolution of the inter-war period. They were also a reflection of the level and rate of technical progress and development.*

In underdeveloped industrialising countries, still dependent on agriculture and with highly uncompetitive industries, the desire for a high rate of trade restriction was naturally great. In large advanced countries that had undergone a relatively poor or insufficient adjustment process in the 20s and still had a comparably large agricultural sector, like France, Italy, to some degree, Germany, and certainly all Eastern and South-Eastern European countries, the pressure to implement a fairly high degree of restriction was high. For the US and Britain, pressure for protectionism was great, but relatively smaller compared to the other two groups. Even though it was against their export interests, small countries which also had undergone only very limited economic adjustment and with high dependence on exports, as Austria, had no choice but to follow the general protectionist trend hesitantly, in order to avoid an overflow of cheaper imported foreign goods on their home markets.

Thus, the level of trade restriction depended on the relative rate of competitiveness, which, in turn, was determined by the level of economic development and progress of structural adjustment to changing economic conditions. Whether this trade restriction was supported by devaluation of currency or by direct commercial restrictions did not really matter for performance and recovery. After the depression and in the 30s, protectionist policy was not only a reactionary policy and did not only depend on the level of development of an economy. Some authoritarian states utilised protectionism as an active and vital part of the policy of economic nationalism and preparation for war.

To find a direct correlation between trade restrictions and economic performance is complicated, for the structure and effects of tariffs, devaluation, exchange controls and clearing systems are highly complex. Even more intricate is the attempt to find an interrelation between these policies and structural changes, because the short-term nature of policies is difficult to link to long-term structural developments and shifts. However, the more dependent on trade an economy was, the greater the effects of protectionism on a country.

5.5.2. Tariffs, Quotas and other Import Restrictions

At first, the traditional weapon of national trade protectionism was applied: Import tariff increases. As the depression became more severe, prices fell more and more and pressure on agriculture and industry mounted. Import duties were augmented everywhere, until their level was far higher in 1931 than in the late 1920s. Soon aggressive tariff policy proved to be insufficient. After 1931 most states, especially those whose need for protection was greatest, completely turned away from multilateral trade and the most-favoured nation principle. Once the full severity of the crisis was felt, old trade agreements were circumvented with bilateral regional and

109 Ibid.

preferential agreements. Quotas, direct import restrictions and barter trade became the principles of commercial policy after 1931 and for the rest of the decade, limiting international trade.

As the first signs of a downswing were obvious in the form of quickly falling agricultural prices, those countries whose economies still had a considerably large share of agricultural production were the first to react with higher tariffs for agricultural products. Already by 1929, tariffs were raised in Germany, France, Italy, as well as in some Eastern European and Scandinavian countries.[110] Since the US was one of the largest importers in the world, its tariff raises of the following year had much greater implications for many other countries, perhaps not necessarily economically, but more in the form of policy retaliation. The Hawley-Smoot Tariff, introduced in 1930, considerably raised import duties for agricultural products and manufactures. It might have given some short-term advantages to some American industries, but it was essentially ineffective. The fall of international prices continued and most countries reacted with retaliatory protectionist measures.[111] Still, compared to tariffs and trade restrictions in Europe, rates in the US were moderate.

a. Eastern Europe Tariff increases in Eastern Europe were the highest. The rest of Europe had followed the principle of most-favoured nation treatment and contractually bound customs tariffs in the 20s, under the leadership of the Franco-German trade agreement of 1927, whereas there had already been an implementation of an autonomous and highly protectionist trade system in the late 20s in Eastern Europe. During the depression, a new and more radical kind of protectionism was introduced in this area.[112] As these countries had comparably unproductive industrial and agricultural production and suffered heavily from credit contraction after 1929, they strongly resorted to tariff protection. Tariff wars took place between Germany and Poland, and Czechoslovakia and Hungary. From 1927 to 1931, the already high industrial tariffs were raised between 13 and 37% .[113] As agricultural prices had dropped the most and a large share of these countries' national product depended on the agricultural sector, Austrian exports were particularly hard hit by these tariffs. Tariff increases were most extreme for foodstuffs. Between 1927 and 1931, duties rose 59.5% in Poland, 106% in Hungary, 137% in Yugoslavia, 152% in Romania and exceptionally, 438% in Bulgaria.[114]

b. Austria Austria moved only reluctantly to the policy of extreme protectionism. Its policy was mainly a reaction to tariff increases and import restrictions of its most important commercial partners and to pressures from its home industries that suffered from declining prices and cheap imports. As a small export oriented country with a small home market, Austria was primarily interested in lowering international

110 League of Nations, *Commercial Policy*, 52.

111 Woytinsky, 260.

112 Gross, 108.

113 In Bulgaria, the Czechoslovak Republic, Hungary, Romania, and Yugoslavia. Poland actually decreased duties for manufactured goods. Kaser and Radice, 460.

114 Numbers calculated from Liepmann, 413.

trade restrictions and boosting its exports. Since, in the face of depression, an opposite trend in international commercial policy took place, the country was forced to retaliate in order to protect its small domestic market, thereby sacrificing the main policy target: advancing of exports.[115] As in many countries, no well planned effort of protectionism existed. Initially, trade policy consisted only of short-term, ad hoc, measures whose intention was the limitation of imports and the pressing forward of a boost of exports as much as possible. In regard to agriculture, this policy did in fact have some success, as domestic prices were artificially pegged to high levels. Naturally, the first tariff policy reaction to the crisis concerned agricultural duties, since world prices in this sector fell most precipitously. With the fourth customs tariffs increase, which came in effect July 27, 1930, a compromise between industry and agriculture was attempted. For agriculture, price guarantee duties were enforced against imports, and for industry further protective duties were implemented.[116]

Since import duties of many articles were still tied to various trade agreements under the auspices of the most-favoured nation principle, these tariff increases did not have any great implications. With the fifth customs tariff increase, enforced shortly after the preceding raises, however, agricultural as well as industrial tariffs were augmented substantially by circumventing the most-favoured nation treatment principle. This was done with the help of regional, preferential agreements. Many agricultural duties were doubled and sometimes even more than doubled. Customs tariffs for cereals, for example, rose from 3.7% in 1927 to 96% of value of import prices in 1931. Other foodstuffs duties more than tripled. Generally, duties for semi-manufactured articles doubled. For finished products the average increase was around 10%.[117] Aggregate tariff burden on imports rose 51% between 1929 and 1932.[118] Now, a proper, highly protectionist customs system was in force, contributing, to a great degree, to relatively higher price levels in Austria, compared to world market price levels.[119] Moreover, particularly agricultural interest had been catered, in favour of the interests of the Austrian export industry. While world prices and trade further declined, in the course of 1931, increased tariffs no longer offered sufficient protectionism. Similar to other nations, Austria turned to bilateral preferential agreements, import quotas and direct restrictions. In several trade agreements, import quotas were fixed with or without preferential tariffs.[120]

c. Germany The political compromise over lower tariffs between the German export industry and agriculture, finally concluded in 1928, broke down during the depression. Trade and tariff policy was no longer liberal and export oriented. To increase economic nationalism and protectionism, policy became a mixture of uncoordinated and short-sighted measures without any substantial long-term positive effects.[121]

115 Haas, Außenhandelspolitik, 38
116 Ibid, 31 ff.
117 Liepmann, 391.
118 Own calculation from Haas, Außenhandelspolitik, 39.
119 Österreichisches Statistisches Zentralamt, *Aussenhandel*, 17–18.
120 Ibid.
121 Wilfried Feldenkirchen, "Deutsche Zoll- und Handelspolitik 1914–1933," in: Hans Pohl (ed.),

Those industrial, and in particular, agricultural sectors that suffered most from falling world prices and were the least competitive intensified their political pressure to bring about a stronger effort of economic nationalism and protectionism. Eventually, policy was in no way co-ordinated or subjected to a long-term plan. As in Austria, the move toward protectionism progressed quickly during the depression, with the help of many ad hoc policies. Whereas tariffs for industrial products had been raised substantially until 1927, they remained stable until 1931. Since many industrial branches became increasingly dependent on exports, tariff raises for industrial products remained moderate between 1927 and 1931, and even during the depression. For example, duties for textiles only rose from 25.5% in 1927 to 35.4% in 1931. Duties for vehicles declined. Import duties on agricultural products, however, were augmented notably after 1929,[122] and especially in 1930. For instance, duties on cereals rose from 26.3% to 149%.[123]

Nevertheless, the following year an enabling act permitted the government to raise even higher import duties for semi-finished as well as finished products. This measure deviated from existing trade agreements and entailed also an increase for most tariffs imposed on manufactures. In 1932, the so-called maximum tariff was introduced. It was imposed on goods from states which raised higher tariffs against imports from Germany than from third countries. After the devaluation of the pound and various other currencies, pegged to sterling, Germany also raised higher compensation import duties, this time against goods from states with devaluated currencies. The final and official move away from any contractually bound tariff policy and toward an arbitrary and autonomous policy came with the tariff act of 5 July 1934.[124]

d. Britain Similar to the rest of Europe, Britain also had partially moved away from a free trade policy already before the depression. The McKenna duties, introduced during the war, and the Dyestuffs Importation Act of 1921 were the first trade policy moves toward increasing protectionism,[125] mostly as a consequence of structural industrial distortions due to the war. These were the first British duties on imported manufactured goods. Other tariffs that came into effect in the 20s were clearly designed to protect Britain's traditional industries and reflected its structural weaknesses.[126]

Protectionism in Britain was seriously introduced after the pound was devalued in 1931. Higher import duties were imposed in November 1931 with the Abnormal Importations Act and, in early 1932, with the Import Duties Act. The first act gave the

Vierteljahrschrift für Sozial- und Wirtschaftsgeschichte, Beiheft No. 80, Die Auswirkungen von Zöllen und anderen Handelshemmnissen auf Wirtschaft und Gesellschaft vom Mittelalter bis zur Gegenwart, Stuttgart 1987, 346–356.

122 Liepmann, 113–120.

123 For tariffs percentages see ibid, 401.

124 Guido Radio von Radiis, *Die deutsche Außenhandelspolitik unter dem Einfluß der Devisenbewirtschaftung von 1931 bis 1938*, Vienna 1939, 48–50.

125 Cairncross and Eichengreen, *Sterling in Decline*, 17–18.

126 Liepmann, 131–133.

Board of Trade the power to impose tariffs of 100% on products that were imported in "abnormal quantities." Apart from other general tariffs,[127] with the new Ottawa Agreements Act of 1932 and Imperial Preference, Britain focused its foreign trade more within its Empire, while discriminating increasingly against trade with other regions.[128] In order to maintain high agricultural prices, further prohibitive import duties came into effect in 1932. As tariffs did not suffice for protectionism, a complex system of import controls was introduced in the 30s.

e. France As the French economy was hit by the depression slowly and belatedly, France began to introduce a highly protectionist policy in progressing stages, but also without any coherent concept.[129] Trade policy was quite passive in the beginning, reacting to increasing restrictions and falling prices abroad. It was solely led by the motives of high protectionism in order to limit the inflow of imports as much as possible, even when legal and international contractual stipulations and provisions were violated. Again, these were ad hoc measures, as an immediate reaction to the pressures of national industries and agriculture from the unexpected severity of the depression. By authorities, the policy was considered only as a temporary emergency action, since its goal was not self-sufficiency.

Although France was hit by the crisis quite late, the first signs of the depression already had an effect on agriculture by the summer of 1929.[130] This sector, already protected by tariffs, showed crisis symptoms throughout the 20s. This chiefly had to do with weaknesses within the farming sector. Production was inefficient and too expensive. Price levels were too high. When agricultural world prices dropped sharply in 1929 and coincided with domestic overproduction of wheat and wine, higher tariffs were introduced. Between early 1931 and the summer 1932, the whole agricultural sector was intensely affected by depression. Industry proved to be much more resistant.[131] In 1930, mild recession tendencies were noticed, due to a reduction of exports and an increasing inflow of goods on the French market from countries already suffering from recession. As the economic situation deteriorated outside of France, the price difference between domestic and foreign prices rose. This was also enhanced by the support of agricultural prices with tariffs. Therefore, with the 28% decline of the volume in French exports of finished goods, and the simultaneous 28.6% rise of the volume of imports, between 1929 and 1931, the potential of industry to sell excess products abroad dropped.[132] Production and employment fell, and supported by financial crisis in the summer, the industrial sector was severely hit by the depression from mid 1931 onwards. The situation deteriorated further until early 1932.

127 See Deutsches Institut für Konjunkturforschung, *Wochenbericht*, no. 28, 1932, 115.

128 Cairncross and Eichengreen, 19–20. And Peden, 100–102. Pollard, *Development*, 119–124.

129 Achim Tobler, *Die französische Handelspolitik in der Weltwirtschaftskrise (Herbst 1929 bis Frühjahr 1936),* dissertation, Heidelberg 1938, 164 ff.

130 Ibid, 5–9.

131 Ibid, 10–13.

132 Own calculation from Tobler, chart on page 12.

Despite the economic decline and deterioration of trade conditions, tariff policy was not facilitated to a great extent in order to keep out imports. Between 1927 and 1931, tariffs were only moderately raised. The main reason for relatively low duties was a complex multilateral system of commercial treaties, to which about 70% of all tariff rates were still tied. This system was established by the Franco-German trade treaty of 1927, which term was running until 1935.[133] Because France did not have an autonomous, but a contractually bound tariff system, a greater tariff raise would have entailed a restructuring of the whole set of French multilateral international trade agreements and contracts.[134] Instead of utilising tariffs, French protectionist policy increasingly relied on quotas and direct import volume restrictions. Besides higher tariffs, in the spring and summer of 1932, import restrictions and compulsory import licenses for many agricultural products were implemented. Import quotas became one of the most important protectionist measures in France and were enforced for a large range of semi-finished and finished products. Moreover, laws enforcing the utilisation of a certain quota of domestic wheat, for wheat processing, came into effect at the same time.[135] Another form of protectionism was direct state export support in the form of export deficit guarantees or export bounties,[136] and the adoption of an exchange compensation tax after the devaluation of sterling in September 1931.[137]

Along with this, the destruction of French involvement in multilateral trade progressed without any coherent planning. Again, measures were ad hoc and short-term. Between the beginning of 1931 and March 1932, most existing trade agreements had been undermined or became irrelevant, because of national restrictions and preferential commercial crisis contracts with Eastern and South-Eastern European countries. After extreme protectionism, the international conflicts from reciprocal trade limitations and the breakdown of the old trade agreements, new commercial treaties were concluded from the beginning of 1934 onward, with the USSR, Spain, Britain, Portugal, Switzerland, Germany, Austria and various other countries. These new agreements were so-called "crisis contracts," which left much greater independence to national governments to prescribe tariffs independently, ignoring the principles of most-favoured nation treatment. These contracts permitted the imposition of quotas, import restrictions, as well as the introduction of autonomous customs policies, unbound by any multilateral international trade agreements with far higher tariff levels than before 1931.[138] Between 1927 and 1931, tariffs for foodstuffs nearly tripled, and average duties for manufactured goods rose more than 14%.[139]

133 Liepmann, 124 and 125.

134 Tobler, 44.

135 Deutsches Institut für Konjunkturforschung, *Wochenbericht*, vol. 5, no 28, October 1932, 112–114.

136 Tobler, 123.

137 Julian Jackson, *The Politics of Depression in France, 1932–1936*, Cambridge 1985, 31.

138 Tobler, 124–149.

139 Liepmann, 385.

5.5.3. Exchange Control and Clearing Systems

As part of economic policy and protectionism, exchange control was not a novelty. During the war, extensive controls had been erected in many belligerent countries. After the war, exchange control was reintroduced in Austria in July 1922,[140] after the drastic inflationary process was stopped and was cancelled after currency reform. Due to the war economy and currency depreciation, strict exchange control in various forms was in effect in Germany between 1917 and 1924. Only a government decree of February 1927 finally lifted all limitations on dealings with foreign exchange. During and after the depression, only in Germany and Eastern Europe were extremely strict exchange control systems introduced that seriously harmed trade.

Closely interconnected with exchange control were clearing systems and clearing agreements among countries with controlled currencies. This was another measure which certainly must have harmed trade to a greater degree and made a return to international free trade much more difficult. After 1931, an increasing share of foreign trade in Germany, Austria and central Europe was conducted through clearing agreements.

In two countries that participated in a clearing agreement, importers paid the equivalent value of their imports to their national bank. Exporters would receive the value of their exports from their own national bank in their national currency. The two national banks would then enumerate mutual obligations and debts. Under normal circumstances a credit margin would be included in the system. In the 1930s, however, when countries suffered from a lack of foreign exchange, authorities tried to keep deliveries and deliveries in return on par, to avoid any clearing assets or debts. Advances were usually not granted. Basically, it was attempted to avoid the exchange and transfer of only those foreign currencies whose parity was artificially maintained. Therefore, countries that kept parity with the help of exchange control, Eastern Europe, Austria and Germany, or had an artificially high currency parity, as France, had to use clearing systems for trade among themselves. Hence, trade among some of these countries nearly turned into barter trade. In order to avoid the involvement of currency exchange for the conduct of the exchange of goods, trade was drastically distorted and limited. Though, commerce with these countries and countries with floating exchange rates, like the US or Britain, was conducted without controls.

a. Austria In Austria, it became necessary to introduce exchange control once again, after measures already taken following the bank crashes in 1931 did not suffice to stop capital flight and the depletion of national bank reserves. Between April 30 and October 7, the bank lost foreign exchange worth 847.9 million schillings.[141] To maintain gold parity and to stop the outflow of capital, it became necessary to implement exchange control. Quite late, in October 1931, after the bank had already

140 See "439. Verordnung: Beschränkung des Handels und Verkehres mit ausländischen Zahlungsmitteln," in: *Bundesgesetzblatt für die Republik Österreich*, no. 91, Vienna 1922, 879.

141 Kernbauer, *Währungspolitik*, 323.

lost a substantial amount of its reserves, it was decided to enforce centralised foreign exchange control in order to stabilise the schilling. On the 9th, the decree for trade and commerce with foreign exchange and capital transfers with foreign countries was enacted.[142] From now on, only certain authorised banks were allowed to buy and sell foreign exchange. The Austrian national bank controlled this system and determined the schilling value of any foreign currency. Receipt and ownership of foreign exchange had to be notified to the bank and had to be sold to it. Moreover, the national bank had to be notified of any export sales, and the exporter was obliged to sell foreign exchange from the proceeds of foreign sales to the bank. Nobody was permitted to grant credit to foreigners, neither in foreign nor in domestic currency. The purpose of these restrictions was to control reserves, maximise the inflow and minimise the outflow of foreign exchange, which was necessary to finance imports and to keep or replenish central bank reserves for the artificial maintenance of the schilling gold parity.[143] In the long run, it could not be maintained, and in July 1933, the schilling was fixed at 79% of its former gold parity.[144]

However, the limitations of these measures on trade should not be overestimated. Eventually, Austrian exchange control proved to be effective only to a very limited degree[145] and seemed to harm trade to a small extent. The public, many politicians and of course the export industry were against this system and regarded it as superfluous. Eventually, it was never possible for authorities to control capital transfer over the borders completely, as the system had too many loop-holes. Export proceeds of foreign exchange only amounted to 10 or 20% of the actual value of overall exports. This was due to several reasons. First of all, the so-called "certificate system" allowed about 1700 firms to use their export proceeds for the purchase of raw materials and other goods from abroad. This way, central bank control was circumvented. Secondly, after September 1931, many export deals abroad were concluded in the real international, much lower, market value of the schilling. That meant that the artificially overvalued parity did not have a significant effect on the Austrian position of export competitiveness.

Besides introducing exchange control, Austria concluded numerous clearing agreements. In December 1931, and January 1932, agreements were signed with Switzerland, Hungary,[146] Italy and Yugoslavia. In the following years, further agreements were signed with France (1933), Germany (1934), Romania (1935) and Poland (1936). Agreements that did not entail a full clearing system, i.e. agreements that controlled capital transfers in connection with compensation and quota systems, were concluded with Bulgaria, Greece and Turkey.[147] Until 1937, half of the value of

142 "306. Verordnung: Devisenbewirtschaftung," in: *Bundesgesetzblatt für die Republik Österreich*, no. 80, Vienna 1931, 1681 ff.

143 For a good explanation of the exchange control mechanism see: "Devisenzwangswirtschaft," in: *Der Österreichische Volkswirt*, 17.10.1931, 61–62.

144 Österreichisches Statistisches Zentralamt, *Aussenhandel*, 16.

145 The following account on the ineffectiveness of the exchange rate system is partially based on: Kernbauer, *Währungspolitik*, 325–327.

146 For detailed information see Dr. Hellmann, "Clearingverträge mit der Schweiz und Ungarn," in: *Bilanzen*, 26.12.1931, 135–137.

147 Haas, Außenhandelspolitik, 16–17.

total foreign trade was conducted through clearing systems.[148] However, since there were various methods to circumvent the policy measures, the main contribution to the fall of exports after 1931 and its slow recovery must be ascribed to the collapse of foreign trade and the focus of most industrialised countries on national economies in the 30s. The artificial schilling parity, which overvalued the currency, and direct exchange control only had minor implications on trade. Clearing agreements certainly limited trade among the countries forced to resort to this measure.

b. Eastern Europe The depression and the following deflationary contraction had the strongest real economic implications in Eastern Europe. It resulted in extremely protectionist and nationalistic economic policy in this area. All Eastern European countries, including the successor states of the Austro-Hungarian Empire, had imported a substantial amount of foreign credit between 1924 and 1928, mainly from the US, Britain, France, Sweden, Switzerland and various other Western European countries.[149] Nearly 50% of all debts were made in the post-war era. Apart from Czechoslovakia, all debtor countries utilised half of this capital to finance their import surplus; 40% to finance debt service of previous debts and 10% to buy gold.[150] In Yugoslavia and Bulgaria, capital imports were almost exclusively used for debt services. As capital imports contracted and then nearly terminated, debt service payments became higher than the inflow of new foreign loans. This was especially difficult when agricultural prices and exports also began to contract until 1932. For the Czechoslovak Republic, Hungary and Yugoslavia, volume of exports declined between 10 and nearly 50% between 1928 and 1932.[151]

The deflationary effect of this process on underdeveloped countries with large and insufficient agricultural sectors, as well as the comparatively low productivity and competitiveness of their industrial sectors, caused the whole region to turn to extreme prohibitive protectionism and economic nationalism, supported by large sectors of society.[152] It entailed complete retrenchment of domestic markets and internally oriented growth. Customs tariffs no longer sufficed to detain industrial imports, and the few agrarian preferential duties and quotas granted by Germany and other Western European states, after an international conference in 1930, turned out to be far too limited to be effective.[153] Hence, all Eastern European countries applied quotas, licensing systems, direct import restrictions, exchange control and clearing systems in an extreme way. For example, in May and July of 1932, Romania introduced exchange control and barter trade for payments to Czechoslovakia. The

148 Kernbauer, *Währungspolitik*, 408.

149 "Das Donauproblem III," in: Deutsches Institut für Konjunkturforschung, *Wochenbericht*, vol. 5, no. 8, Berlin, 1932, 30.

150 The following on capital inflow to Eastern Europe from: Rudolf Nötel, "International Capital Movements and Finance in Eastern Europe 1919–1949," in: *Vierteljahrschrift für Sozial- und Wirtschaftsgeschichte*, vol. 61, 1974, 79 ff.

151 Ibid, 86.

152 Jan Kofman, "Economic Nationalism in East-Central Europe in the Interwar Period," in: Henryk Szlajfer (ed.), *Economic Nationalism in East-Central Europe and South America 1918–1939*, Geneva 1990, 200.

153 Ibid, 110. Liepmann, 350.

latter limited exchange allocation for imports from Austria, Yugoslavia, Greece, Hungary and Bulgaria, and in general for certain import products.[154] Poland, Romania, and Bulgaria imposed import quotas and licensing systems in 1932 and 1933. In Yugoslavia, Bulgaria and Hungary, 70% of trade was conducted through clearing systems. By 1937, it was up to 80% for Romania. Only the Czechoslovak Republic and Poland used clearing arrangements only to a small degree.[155]

The result was a complete breakdown of international free trade in this area: "With exchange controls the multilateral system of payments collapsed and was to a large extent replaced by bilateralism."[156] A system of preferential trade arose among certain regions, dominating volume and direction of trade according to "creditor or debtor position of countries."[157] Tendencies of economic nationalism turning toward self-sufficiency and declining international specialisation intensified. To circumvent the complex system of exchange controls, clearing agreements between countries regulated bilateral trade. With its extensive and effective exchange control and clearing systems, reminiscent of a planned economy, Germany became the primary trading partner of most Eastern European countries in the 30s. Its tools were an overvalued currency and an artificially high price level. For agricultural products from Eastern Europe, Germany offered favourable prices above world market levels, at least until the beginning of increasing trade with this area. In return, German machinery and other capital goods were traded for foodstuffs and primary products.[158]

c. Germany Exchange control was most extreme in Germany. It was also the first industrialised country to introduce this measure in the war. As in Austria and in the Eastern European countries, it was, at first, only a reaction to the catastrophic effects of the depression. In the beginning, just a mild version of exchange control was introduced, and only after 1933 did it become a central and indispensable element of foreign trade policy.

Contemporaries distinguished among four levels of exchange control.[159] The first and mildest level lasted from the summer of 1931 until July 1933. Its primary objective was only the surveillance of capital flow and the termination of capital flight. To re-establish German credibility and to maintain artificial gold parity, the government introduced mild exchange control, and the central bank increased the discount rate from 7 to 10% on July 15, 1931.[160] On August 8, credit was even more restricted by raising the discount rate to 15%. The import and outflow of foreign exchange was centralised by the German national bank and controlled by a few banks

154 Deutsches Institut für Konjunkturforschung, *Wochenbericht*, vol. 5, no. 28, October 1932, 112–114.
155 Kaser and Radice, 450–452.
156 Ibid, 435.
157 Ibid.
158 Gross, 112–113. Kaser and Radice, 444 ff.
159 Harald Lossos, "Bilanz der deutschen Devisenbewirtschaftung," in: *Münchener Volkswirtschaftliche Studien*, vol. 29, Jena 1940.
160 Hardach, *Weltmarktorientierung*, 139. Kernbauer, *Währungspolitik*, 321–322. "Notverordnung über den Verkehr mit ausländischen Zahlungsmitteln vom 15. Juli 1931."

specified by the Reichsbank. Trade with foreign exchange was only permitted on the official Reichsbank mark parity.[161] Moreover, offices for exchange control were set up within the revenue offices of the Länder in August 1931. Germans and foreigners could only dispose of their exchange, reichsmark and obligations after official permission had been granted. This was only done for the payment of vital imports (i.e. essential raw materials), for the payment of imports from agreements and treaties concluded before the implementation of exchange control, and for debt amortisation and service. Every exporter had to report all exchange dealings to the Reichsbank monthly. Over time the system of control became more and more strict. Permission to utilise foreign exchange was also limited to debt service. The definition of vital imports was more closely defined. After February 1932, foreign exchange was only granted to 50% the of essential import level of the year 1930/31. Only as part of Nazi economic planning were the last three far more restrictive levels of exchange control introduced.

d. France France did not have to turn to exchange control, since large scale capital outflow did not take place and the central bank held ample reserves of gold and foreign exchange. Notwithstanding that, a clearing system was established. With the increasing application of exchange control in other countries in 1931 and the consequential problematic transfer of exchange from these countries to French exporters, the imports from these countries to France were limited to import concessions. As a reaction, in early 1932, France introduced a clearing system for foreign exchange based around and controlled by the Parisian Chamber of Commerce. Similar to other countries, this system implied complicated procedures for the settling of accounts, control of the actual business transactions and of import and exports. Clearing transactions were conducted with Germany, Austria, Italy, Turkey, Greece, Hungary, Bulgaria, the Baltic countries and various South American countries. The application of the clearing system resulted in a reduction of debts of foreign trading partners in the French balance of payments, but naturally, this system entailed great friction for trade transactions and limited foreign trade even more.[162]

5.5.4. British Devaluation

Instead of strict exchange control, some Western countries turned to devaluation in order to support their trade balance. Initially, devaluation was a reaction to international financial crises in 1931. After these events, competitive devaluation became another form of protectionism and import restrictions as a classical component of the beggar-thy-neighbour policy. The intention was to boost exports and to limit imports by inflating the external value of the currency at the expense of other nations and hence, to improve and relieve the competitive position of the national export industry and the national balance of payments position. This process resulted in the break-

161 See on exchange control in Germany: Radio von Radiis, 11 ff.
162 Tobler, 150–161.

down of the system of fixed exchange rate parities, the gold standard. Currencies were now freely floated and maintained artificially low for national advantage.

In the case of Britain, both motives were relevant. The Central European banking crisis of the summer of 1931 entailed a loss of confidence in sterling and led to a major withdrawal of exchange reserves and gold from London from mid July onwards. Sterling parity could be sustained until September by using credits from France and the US in August and by raising the discount rate.[163] Yet, speculation and the run on pound continued as the new budget proposals did not settle confidence. Reserves were running out, and the only options left were either devaluation, drastic import restrictions or further credits from abroad to continue the financing of capital outflow. On September 21, Britain decided to suspend the gold standard and devaluated the pound 25% to the dollar.[164] Most other countries whose currencies were pegged to gold followed. Immediately succeeding this move, the Bank of England and the Treasury used the suspension of the gold standard rules and restriction on policy to conduct a policy of cheap money. As it was not any longer necessary to attract foreign funds, the bank rate was reduced to 2% by June 1932, and the Treasury established the Exchange Equalisation Account (EEA).[165] It was an account with Treasury funds managed by the central bank to even out strong exchange rate fluctuations of the freely floating pound. The goal was a cheap money policy to support British export industries by keeping the exchange rate artificially low![166] The old parity had been $ 4.86, but after 1931 the bank attempted to maintain the dollar parity at 3.40, even though speculation was moving against this trend already in early 1932, when it was back to 3.70.

The pound devaluation of 1931 and cheap money policy have been considered as one of the main factors contributing to economic growth and above average economic recovery in Britain after the depression. In fact, British domestic price levels did decline, as compared to international prices, but only offered a very brief competitive advantage. The actual advantage of a favourable exchange rate was only short-lived, as many other countries, among them Britain's most important trading partners, also turned to devaluation. The export advantage was quickly lost and lasted only for a few months. In September 1932, value of exports of finished products was actually 14% lower than the year before. Imports were not limited at all and actually increased in late 1931.[167] The British trade position was not at all supported by sterling devaluation. The slow increase of exports in 1932 and 1933 could be mainly attributed to the general world-wide recovery of trade in these months.[168]

163 Peden, 90 ff

164 Cairncross and Eichengreen, 66–72, 85. Peden, 90–92. Howson, 75–78.

165 Howson, 86–89. Cairngross and Eichengreen, 80 ff.

166 Peden, 97–98.

167 See "England und Japan. Probleme der Währungsentwertung," in: Deutsches Institut für Konjunkturforschung, *Wochenbericht*, vol. 5, no. 31, Berlin 1932, 123–125.

168 For a very detailed contemporary analysis see: Hanns von Mühlenhoff, "Die englische Währungsabwertung und die wirtschaftlichen Wechsellagen. Untersuchung des gegenwärtigen Aufschwungs der englischen Wirtschaft," in: Arthur Spiethoff (ed.), *Beiträge zur Erforschung der wirtschaftlichen Wechsellagen Aufschwung, Krise, Stockung*, issue 18, Jena 1939, 50–57.

Following sterling devaluation and British attempts to maintain a low parity, world-wide competitive devaluation ensued in the following years.[169] More than twenty countries depreciated their currencies with sterling. All countries within the Empire, Scandinavian as well as Eastern European countries depreciated.[170] Since sterling depreciation gave Indian and British textile products in South East Asia a price advantage of between 20 and 30% , Japan devaluated the yen on December 13, 1931. Its value declined more than 50% until October 1932.[171] Without any apparent pressure, the US went off gold and depreciated the dollar 47% in March and April 1933. Already by late 1931, the 25% depreciation of sterling to the dollar had declined to 13%. In 1932, the pound appreciated even against countries still on gold.[172] After the depreciation of the dollar in 1933, the pound rate to the dollar was even higher than after 1925, as it appreciated to around $ 5 for the rest of the decade. In effect, the mark and the franc were also devalued to the pound.[173]

5.5.5. Conclusion

Indeed, extremely restrictive policy measures negatively affected international trade and certainly supported the decline of foreign trade. In countries where the necessity for protection was the greatest, foreign trade suffered the most. This was mainly the case in Eastern Europe. As Austria remained interested in expanding its exports, exchange control remained fairly mild and ineffective. The same can be said for this policy in Germany until 1933. Thereafter, though, it became a central aspect of focusing recovery on the national economy and became increasingly harmful to trade. British and French protection was also more effective in consolidating reduced international trade relations after 1933. For the large national economies, it was much easier to resist the slow recovery of international trade. Therefore, these retaliatory policies could be counterbalanced by national recovery policies and domestic oriented growth after 1933.

5.6. ECONOMIC POLICY, PERFORMANCE AND STRUCTURAL DISTORTIONS AFTER 1933

To tell and interpret the story of economic policy and performance in the 1930s proves a difficult task. To find a direct correlation between a certain type of policy and performance is complicated inasmuch as performance was determined by many

169 See list "Einfuhrhemmungen im Ausland," in: Deutsches Institut für Konjunkturforschung, *Wochenbericht*, 1932, 111–112.

170 Cairncross and Eichengreen, 85.

171 *Wochenbericht*, 1932, 125.

172 Cairncross and Eichengreen, 85–86.

173 I. Drummond, "Britain and theWorld Economy 1900–1945," in: Roderick Floud and Donald McCloskey (eds.), *The Economic History of Britain since 1700. Volume 2: 1860 to the 1970s*, Cambridge 1981, 301.

factors. Yet, it is certain that the implications of economic policy on economic development and growth were much greater in the decade after the depression than in the 20s.

After policy reactions to the implications of the depression were formed, contemporaries divided the main countries into groups of currency systems, in which they were operating by 1933, and which resembled their analogue policy reaction to the crisis. It was distinguished among four groups.[174] The first group are the so-called gold bloc countries, including France, Belgium, Italy, the Netherlands, Switzerland and Luxembourg. The countries that maintained their gold parity artificially (de jure), with strict exchange controls and clearing systems, Germany, Austria, many underdeveloped Eastern European countries and Italy after 1934, formed the second group. Some European countries such as Greece and Czechoslovakia depreciated their currencies and introduced exchange controls. These constituted the third group. The fourth group of countries devalued their currencies and had free exchanges. These were the countries that were able to maintain liberal economic systems; most prominent among them the US, Great Britain, the British Dominions, Sweden and Norway. Within these systems, trade was intensified. Britain and France increased imperial trade, while Germany focused on Central and Eastern Europe. "Gold bloc" countries also enlarged their mutual trade.[175]

It has been claimed that recovery "was in general not shared by the members of the 'gold bloc' in which the painful process of deflation was pursued right up to 1936."[176] The decision of which of these options was chosen depended on numerous factors, and a certain option did not necessarily entail a greater tendency toward stagnation or growth. In some cases these policies were chosen with the aim of achieving short-term national advantages, but were chiefly determined by the economic position and leverage of large socio-economic interest groups, such as agriculture and various industrial sectors. For the first group of countries, the decision to maintain gold parity was probably supported by a fear of the consequences of another inflation, as in France and Belgium. Countries that had experienced strong inflations and were in a weak financial position during the 20s, like Germany and Austria, were even more reluctant to devalue. Circumstances were opposite in the US and Britain. Both devalued in the early 30s.

A few years later, 1938/39, in the light of another, but minor recession, contemporaries did not necessarily divide the most important industrialised countries into groups of currency systems, but spoke of a division of the world economy into authoritarian states and the area of the liberal economies.[177] It was noticed that the countries of the second group, Germany, Italy, Japan and also Poland, enjoyed higher growth rates and greater economic expansion in spite of contracting foreign trade,

174 According to League of Nations, *Commercial Policy*, 69.

175 Ibid, 70 and 71.

176 Ibid, 68.

177 "Die Wirtschaftslage der Welt (Dezember 1938)," in: Deutsches Institut für Konjunkturforschung (ed.), *Schriften des Instituts für Konjunkturforschung. Vierteljahreshefte zur Wirtschaftsforschung*, vol. 13, Hamburg, 1938/39, 281–304.

while countries of the last group, mainly the United States and the "liberal European industrial states" like Britain, France, Sweden, and the Netherlands, partially suffered from economic stagnation. Economists noticed that a coherent world-wide economic development did not seem to exist any longer. Instead, they found that regional "national business cycles,"[178] increasingly dependent on state influence, determined general world economic growth. Authoritarian states were hardly touched by the recession of 1937/38, while in the US, Canada and Belgium, production shrank between 18 and 23%. In Britain, it dropped about 10%.[179] The strong inclination toward economic nationalism, its harmful effects and internally oriented domestic growth were also apparent to some contemporaries.

This division of authoritarian states and states with liberal economies came closer to a reasonable allocation of a certain trend of policy to economic performance. Generally, three types of policies correlating with similar performances can be distinguished among the modern advanced countries: The semi-planned economies of fascist states, first and foremost among them Nazi Germany; the half hearted Keynesian approach to, and still orthodox, policy of the liberal states, especially the United States, Sweden, and Britain; the third type were the strictly deflationary and orthodox economic policies of the gold bloc countries, primarily France, but also of semi-fascist Austria. Essentially, the economies of all these groups suffered from structural long-term distortions, enhanced by economic nationalism. Yet, some policies tended to support this process much more than others. This process was independent of the mere quantitative growth of national income.

5.6.1. Policy and Performance in Authoritarian States: Germany, Italy and Japan

The authoritarian states were the most prominent practitioners of a policy of economic nationalism which resulted in a mixture of planned economic systems and liberal markets. Economic nationalism of authoritarian states, especially in the case of Germany and Japan, had its origins in the desire to achieve a self-sufficient military or defence economy (Wehrwirtschaft) in order to prepare for war and military expansion. However, it did not have the characteristics of a full war economy. Theoretically, it had its origins in a typical economic doctrine of the 1930s which was a reaction to the depression and the apparent failure of liberal economics and free trade.[180] The consequences of this extreme policy were a strong subjugation of

178 "[...] nationale Konjunkturen, die ihrerseits wieder in wachsendem Maß von den wirtschaftspolitischen Entscheidungen des Staates abhängen." Ibid, 285–286. Austria was not included in this study as it had been incorporated into Germany by the time of publication of this article.

179 Ibid, 282.

180 Dieter Petzina, "Autarkiepolitik im Dritten Reich. Der nationalsozialistische Vierjahresplan," in: Hans Rothfels and Theodor Eschenburg (eds.), *Schriftenreihe der Vierteljahreshefte für Zeitgeschichte*, no. 16, Stutgart 1968, 197. Petzina called this mixed policy "staatliche Kommandowirtschaft," ibid. On the anti-liberal economic doctrine see for example: Felice Guarneri (president of the Bank of Rome), "Autarkie und Außenhandel," in: Andreas Predöhl (ed.), *Kieler Vorträge gehalten im Institut für Weltwirtschaft an der Universität Kiel*, vol. 65, Jena 1941.

the economies of fascist countries to structural distortions and an almost complete exclusion from world trade, compared to their previous rate of interconnection in the world economy and the position of the states with free market economies. Authoritarian states only benefited from this policy in the short-term and until the war, and only in the manner that expansion of the economy took place on a more superficial level and in quantitative terms. These countries enjoyed fairly high levels of domestic growth and rapidly falling unemployment. In the long run, though, this policy was not sustainable socio-economically. It was bound to lead to aggressive expansion and war.

a. Germany The main and most important proponent of this extremely radical trend of economic nationalism and unbalanced distorted growth was, of course, Nazi Germany. While countries such as Britain and the US enjoyed moderate expansion, steadily rising productivity and competitiveness supported by the natural capitalist process, above average German economic growth after 1933 can be to a large extent directly attributed to expansionist government policy. Besides the effects of the ordinary upswing after the summer of 1932, as part of a natural upswing of the business cycle movement, the rapid German economic expansion and enormous rise in employment, between 1933 and 1936, was mainly caused by public investment-led growth, state expenditure and fiscal concessions to raise domestic demand and investment.[181] Work creation programmes did not have any long-term growth effects, but helped to cut the initial high unemployment. The main generators of fast recovery, until 1936, were massive, government financed, construction and road building programmes and government supported motorisation, combined with the multiplication and accelerator effects which the expansion of these sectors had on other industrial branches.[182]

Rearmament became a major motor of economic growth only after 1935/36, with the introduction of the Second Four Year Plan under Göring. Between 1932 and 1935, total government expenditure rose from 7.3 billion to 28.2 billion reichsmarks. In 1935, public expenditure amounted to about 34% of GNP.[183] Had rearmament expenditure only made up an insignificant portion of national product and up to about one quarter of total expenditure until 1935, thereafter, it was more than tripled. By 1939, it accounted for 23% of GNP.[184] In macroeconomic terms, the results were impressive: between 1933 and 1938 German GDP grew nearly 56%. In Britain, a country with a favourable performance in the 30s, it was only 21%, and in the US 33%.[185] French GDP only grew 3.24%.

181 According to Richard J. Overy, *The Nazi Economic Recovery 1932–1938*, London 1982, 65.

182 On motorisation in the Third Reich see: Richard J. Overy, *War and Economy in the Third Reich*, Oxford 1994, 68–89. See also Richard Overy, „Cars, Roads, and Economic Recovery in Germany, 1932–8," in: *The Economic History Review*, Vol. XXVIII, No. 3, 1975.

183 Réne Erbe, *Die nationalsozialistische Wirtschaftspolitik 1933–1939 im Lichte der modernen Theorie*, Zurich 1958, 34 and Overy, *Recovery*, 42.

184 Overy, *War and Economy*, 202.

185 Own calculation from Angus Maddison, "Measuring Long Term Growth and Productivity

At first glance, German performance seemed to have been extraordinary. However, while growth in the free Western economies was still chiefly generated by increasing and new domestic consumer demand through a rise of real incomes or by regenerating export sales, in Germany, consumer demand and exports were indirectly sharply curtailed by state policies. Even though some of the modern industries expanded rapidly, in Germany, growth was only to a minor degree brought about by "the normal development of technical and organisational change,"[186] i.e. a steady shift in industrial structures to modern and more productive modes of production. The structural industrial transition turned out to be not as forceful and profound as before 1929 and after 1945.[187] The primary cause for this phenomenon lay not necessarily in state investment itself, but in the type and nature of state investment and in the government controls necessary to maintain these types of investments, direct and indirect rearmament. Public investment-led growth entailed intensifying strict state control of the economy and could only be achieved by growing structural economic distortions. To understand the causes for increasing imbalances in economic structure, it is necessary to look at the motives and functions of control and planning.

Economic Control

The main problems of the indefinable economic organisation of Nazi Germany were inherent in its nature to turn away from a free market economy, toward a semi-planned economy system, in which large portions of supply and demand were state controlled. The government did not simply incite economic revival through spending and public investment and let recovery take its course naturally. It directly controlled recovery, initially by increasing consumption and lowering unemployment with plain, work intensive, employment creation programmes. Once recovery was underway after 1935/36, its course was directed toward establishing a war economy and self-sufficiency. This could only be attained by indirectly diverting financial, material and productive resources away from private domestic consumption, and by redirecting resources from foreign trade and consumer industries to capital investment industries vital for direct and indirect rearmament.

The majority of government investment and expenditure was financed by deficit spending and public debt. The latter was maintained by inconsiderate utilisation of credit from the domestic capital market, as foreign funds were not available. The former was financed by issuing short-term government bills[188] to be repaid in five years with the anticipated increase of revenue, after recovery would have been underway.[189] Directing private activity to certain sectors of production, extremely lowering private consumption and exports at the same time and financing this system

Change on a Macroeconomic Level," in: Rainer Fremdling and Patrick K. O'Brien (eds.), *Productivity in the Economies of Europe*, Stuttgart 1983, 107–123.

186 Overy, *Recovery*, 54. The following also from Overy's excellent introduction and collection of articles in: *War and Economy*.

187 Overy, *Recovery*, 54.

188 These were the famous Mefo bills, Overy, *Recovery*, 45. Petzina, *Wirtschaftspolitik*, 68–71.

189 Overy, *Recovery*, 45.

without igniting an inflationary process, made the implementation of a system of close state controls of prices, wages and foreign trade necessary.

By the mid 30s, an intensification of state control and planning was required, because of two reasons. First of all, slowly, the profit and long-term economic interests of vital conservative industrial circles, especially of heavy industry, began to contradict and disagree with the state's reckless policy of limited foreign trade, channelled private production and consumption, and rapid rearmament output at all costs. Influential industrial circles were interested in returning to a more free market economy and a revival of German involvement in international trade, and did not place long-term confidence in the rearmament boom.[190] Secondly, the policy of recovery, via rapid rearmament, threatened to endanger the raw material basis and capital funds of the economy. Government reaction was even more direct involvement and control in the economy after 1936. Control manifested itself in two ways which complemented each other: Increasing control of domestic production and consumption, as the main tool to achieve the goals of rearmament and autarky. The second, complementary type of control was total supervision of all foreign trade, to receive material and capital from abroad.

Excluding the German economy from world trade and competition was a major aspect of economic policy that slowed down and distorted the structural shift in the 30s. Since recovery was achieved solely through domestic oriented growth, the economy was no longer exposed to world-wide competition and pressure to modernise. Many industries were now sheltered behind extremely protective trade barriers and control and could rely on state demand. In the long run, this was one factor that lowered productivity. The modern and highly competitive export industries only contributed to growth after 1933 by focusing on the home market, whereas it would have been more profitable and productive in the long run to participate in world trade. On the one hand, this certainly had to do with the slow recovery of world trade in the 30s. But on the other, this process was intensified by German trade and recovery, deformed by government investment. It diverted economic activity and resources away from exports sales to domestic consumption.[191]

In Germany, the system of exchange and trade control became much more rigid, strict and effective during the 30s than anywhere else. Exchange control became a vital aspect of economic policy-making, of the effort to focus on growth of the national economy. It became an essential part of Nazi economic planning and preparation for a limited war economy.[192] It already showed its implication on trade as soon as world economic recovery set in. By 1933, German exports had already stagnated and import demand risen, whereas trade of other industrial countries had begun to expand again. Following the 64% decline in the value of German exports between 1929 and 1933, the low export rate not even barely recovered its pre-crisis level.

190 Overy discusses the struggle between large private enterprises and government policy and state control in *War and Economy*, chapter 3–, 93–118.

191 Ibid, 88.

192 On German trade policy and war preparation see: Eckart Teichert, *Autarkie und Großraumwirtschaft in Deutschland 1930–1939. Außenwirtschaftspolitische Konzeptionen zwischen Wirtschaftskrise und Zweitem Weltkrieg*, Munich 1984, 48 ff.

The actual nadir of the value of overall exports was reached in 1934. Export rates of vital industries had declined between 1932 and 1934, even though international trade began to recover again. For example, for car manufacturing, the export rate had fallen from 21 to 8%, from 29 to 18% for the iron industry, and from 49 to 16% for the machinery industry.[193] Until 1938, the value of German exports only increased 26%.[194] Already by 1934, the German trade balance was passive.

At this time, foreign exchange to purchase vital raw materials became very tight, while exports, whose sales would have raised income of foreign funds, could not be allowed to regenerate freely on a normal scale. This was not possible, because production was largely for domestic purposes, i.e. indirect and direct rearmament. The only options were to allow free foreign trade or to turn to complete trade control. Since the former would have strongly compromised rearmament programmes, the latter policy option was chosen. Still, the growth of rearmament had to be limited, as the lack of raw materials and foreign exchange became alarming with increasing recovery. At some point, trade policy actually attempted to boost export sales, especially of expensive military equipment and aircraft, in order to allow for sufficient accumulation of foreign exchange to be able to buy vital imports.[195] Therefore, after 1934, the last three levels of exchange control were introduced.[196] These became more extensive, attempting to affect and control every aspect of German-international economic relations. Their main goals were the total interruption of capital flow, limitation of trade flow and total control of all foreign trade.

Trade was even more restricted after the mid 30s, at a time when it once again became increasingly profitable for many industrial sectors, including heavy industry, to turn back to higher exports. Yet, from then on the German export rate was artificially low, primarily because production items were designated for domestic use. Concentrating production on domestic purposes, though, required strict import and export controls. To achieve complete control of external trade, allocation of imports and restriction of exports, policy measures already in effect were simply utilised and extended. Restrictive tariff policy, import restrictions, exchange control and clearing systems that were implemented initially as a reaction to the financial and commercial breakdown in the depression, became central and permanent tools of trade policy after 1933.

Between 1933 and 1935, several new decrees and laws concerning trade and exchange control were introduced. In addition, a centralised government exchange control office was established. By the late 30s, very complex, rigorous systems of exchange controls, quotas and import limitations were in effect. Exactly as in

193 "Der Anteil der Ausfuhr an der deutschen Industrieproduktion," in: Deutsches Institut für Konjunkturforschung, *Wochenbericht*, vol. 8, no. 15, 1935, 50.

194 Own calculation from Hans-Erich Volkmann, "Außenhandel und Aufrüstung in Deutschland 1933 bis 1939," in: Friedrich Forstmeier und Volkmann (eds.), *Wirtschaft und Rüstung am Vorabend des Zweiten Weltkrieges*, Düsseldorf 1975, chart on 85.

195 The basic simple principle was depicted by Schacht as follows: "Nicht mehr kaufen als bezahlt werden kann und in erster Linie das kaufen, was notwendig gebraucht wird." Cited in: Volkmann, 89.

196 See Lossos.

Austria, foreign trade, free of monetary exchange, had to be introduced in the form of bilateral clearing systems or barter trade. By late 1937, Germany had concluded clearing agreements of various kinds with 34 countries. That meant that about 80% of German foreign trade was conducted within its international clearing system.[197] The implications of this radical policy were a greater decline of the German export rate than for other countries. Though the export share of national product had still been around 16% until 1931, it dropped quickly thereafter to between roughly 5.3 and 7% of national product in the late 1930s.[198] In 1937, value of exports was only at 6.7% of GNP.[199] In contrast, the decline of the export rate in other large and small countries was milder. Between 1929 and 1937, Austrian export rate declined from 23 to 17.6%.[200] The British rate dropped only from 11.5 to 9.5%.[201]

The main form of control was, of course, direct or indirect government control of domestic production and consumption for rearmament. Indirect control simply manifested itself in large scale state investment and orders. The implementation of the Second Four Year Plan was a form of direct state control and ownership. With the foundation of the Reichswerke, the Four Year Plan began to control more than half of all industrial investment after 1936. This was a holding company of various large and small enterprises of the iron and steel industry in and outside of Germany that had been brought into state ownership, partially by coercion. The main companies were the AG für Erzbergbau und Eisengesellschaften, and after the take-over of Austria, the Alpine Montangesellschaft. It incorporated many enterprises of the heavy industry that were located in the newly occupied territories of Germany, such as the Skoda Werke in occupied Czechoslovakia. Moreover, it also incorporated a number of firms for synthetic fuel and rubber production which were slowly expanded after the mid 30s.[202] The main goal of the Reichswerke was the improvement of the level of self-sufficiency through diminishing German import dependence of ore supplies and other raw materials.

Industrial Structural Distortions

The overall consequence of intensifying state control and planning was the suffering of industry and agriculture from the problems and inefficiencies of a nearly planned, isolated economy. The results were further structural economic distortions and a slowing down of the natural process of progressing to modern modes of production, services and consumption. In the long run, the gap of productivity and competitiveness between Germany and other advanced industrialised countries widened.

How did this distortion manifest itself? Part of it became apparent, for an advanced country, in an outstanding, disproportionate shift of demand away from con-

197 Radio von Radiis, chapter 5 and page 77.

198 See Teichert, table in footnote 53, chapter 2, 279. My own calculation of export rate is slightly higher. See below subtitle: 4.7.2.

199 Own calculation from data at current value, from Ritschl and Spoerer, 44 and Volkmann, 85.

200 Current value, Österreichisches Institut für Wirtschaftsforschung, *Monatsberichte* 14, 41.

201 Current value, from: Mitchell, *European Historical Statistics*, 307 and 416.

202 Wolfgang Birkenfeld, *Der synthetische Treibstoff 1933–1945. Ein Beitrag zur nationalsozialistischen Wirtschafts- und Rüstungspolitik*, Göttingen 1964.

sumer goods to capital goods and industrial raw materials. This resulted in a higher and disproportionate growth of production of capital goods and an expansion of investment industries.[203] The long-term consequences were large overcapacities and low productivity. There certainly was a strong structural shift to modern industrial sectors, such as car, aircraft and chemicals production, without which such dramatic recovery would not have been possible. Nevertheless, this process only played a secondary, basic role, did not progress under normal economic conditions and was greatly slowed down, exaggerated or distorted in most sectors. In the case of the motor industry, it simply compensated for a backlog that had its roots in slow development before the depression. In the case of the aircraft industry, huge overcapacities only for rearmament were created, without any future economic considerations. In addition, the transition to modern industries only took place in sectors that were in alignment with general rearmament programmes. For instance, the German electrical engineering industry, in other countries a sector that was rapidly expanding, actually suffered from stagnating, and in the later 30s only slightly rising, sales, even though its workforce was slowly expanding. In 1937, the value of total sales was still 22% below the 1929 level.[204]

Productivity did not only decline because the economy was almost cut off from the world market. As demand shifted away from consumer goods and was, to a great degree, state generated, in general, the short-term necessity of companies for growth of productivity and competitiveness declined. As Overy stated, productivity declined "[b]ecause the state assumed increasing responsibility for the economy, and for large areas of investment in particular, the normal market pressures for improving efficiency and for innovating were often lacking."[205] In many sectors, expansion of production was only reached by utilising the equipment that had been invested in the late 20s and had formed huge overcapacities during the depression.

The decline of productivity and competitiveness can be observed by the relative fall of investments. Considering the rate of recovery, the level of private industrial investment was low, revealing insufficient investment in modern production equipment. Even though German GDP of 1928 was 13% and industrial production was 8% below 1936 levels, aggregate investment rate, i. e. the share of all investments of national income, had been much higher in the 20s.[206] Moreover, not only had the investment rate declined, but the structure of aggregate investment was changed and distorted. The share of overall investment of capital goods industries rose from 65% in 1928/29 to 80% in the years 1936–1939, whereas the share of consumer goods industries' investment declined commensurately. Between 1928 and 1939, volume of industrial investments of capital goods industries rose 156%. Volume of investment

203 According to Overy the heavy industrial sector increased 200% between 1932 and 1938, while consumer industries only expanded 38%. *Recovery*, 31 and 54.

204 "Der Auslandsabsatz der elektrotechnischen Industrie," in: Deutsches Institut für Konjunkturforschung, *Wochenbericht*, vol. 9, no. 20, 1936, 77–78. And: Länderrat des Amerikanischen Besatzungsgebiets (ed.), *Statistisches Handbuch von Deutschland 1928–1944*, Munich 1949, 302–303.

205 Overy, *Recovery*, 56.

206 According to the Statistisches Reichsamt, aggregate investment was even 22% higher in 1928 than in 1936. Calculated from *Jahrbuch* 1938, 566.

of consumer industries hardly increased 20% .[207] The result was a disproportionate expansion of capital goods industries and a structural imbalance of investments.

This phenomenon reveals the incompleteness, inefficiency, and distortion of the structural transformation of the productive sector in the 30s. By and large, only the productivity of the German heavy industry was slightly higher than in Britain. It was considerably lower than in the US. The heavy industrial sector improved and expanded, even though world-wide overcapacities had existed even during the boom period of the late 20s. However, generally the rise in productivity of modern industrial sectors was slow. It suffered from inefficient use of capital, labour and technology, since the type of demand did not generate a great incentive to modernise and rationalise. Moreover, many firms were subsidised by the state. German per capita production in most consumer industries, also of advanced industries, like radio or car manufacturing, was lower than British, and far lower than US, productivity. For example, American productivity of car production was more than four times greater than German. British productivity in the 30s also increased faster than in Germany.[208]

An interesting example of the distorted process of modern industrial development was German car manufacturing. Great importance for recovery has been attributed to the considerable increase of the German motor industry after 1933. Thanks to the rapid general upswing, a backlog of motorisation and government support, this industry recovered quickly from the depression. Already by 1935, car output was 36% above the peak of production level in the 20s.[209] It was one of the most important modern sectors that led the slow structural shift, as its production expanded by more than 230% between 1933 and 1938.[210]

However, the relevance of this expansion should not be overestimated since this increase mainly made up for lost ground of the 20s. In that decade, France was, without doubt, Europe's largest car producer, closely followed by Britain. In 1928, German car manufacturing reached its production peak in the 20s, with only 108,100 units, this reflected just about 65% of British and 48% of French output level. During the depression, German output shrunk dramatically, whereas British production maintained a fairly high level, and French production only fell moderately. In the 30s, Britain clearly had the leading automobile industry in Europe,[211] followed by France and leaving Germany still far behind.[212] Hence, in the early 30s, German production started from fairly low levels and capacity lay idle. Therefore, a quick expansion of car manufacturing could be achieved without having to undergo a considerable shift in industrial structure, i.e. a massive expansion of the car industry itself. The Ger-

207 Petzina, *Autarkiepolitik*, 184–185.

208 See L. Rostas, "Industrial Production, Productivity and Distribution in Britain, Germany and the United States," in: *The Economic Journal*, Vol. 53, 1943, 46 and 49.

209 "Die Kraftfahrzeugkonjunktur im vierten Aufschwungsjahr," in: Institut für Konjunkturforschung, *Wochenbericht*, special issue, vol. 9, no. 19, 1936, 2.

210 Own calculation from Overy, *Recovery*, 55.

211 Jonathan Wood, *Wheels of Misfortune. The Rise and Fall of the British Motor Industry*, London 1988, 56.

212 Also see chart of vehicle output under 5.3.2. of this study.

man automobile industry expanded quickly and car output rose to significant levels only by the second half of the decade. Nonetheless, it still did not reach British, and only slightly overtook French, output levels. In 1936, it was at nearly 68% of British production and about 13% above French production.[213] Even though Germany had the largest population, in 1938, German total stock of vehicles only amounted to 80% of French and 75% of British numbers of registered vehicles.[214]

The aircraft industry, which was probably the leading industry of the modern sectors, is another good example of rapid, but inefficient expansion. The expansion of its productive sector and production was truly remarkable after 1933. Its workforce expanded from about 5000 in 1933 to more than 110,000 by mid 1936, when it became larger than car manufacturing.[215] Whereas the motor industry employed more than 140,000 workers in 1938,[216] the workforce of the aircraft industry had expanded to about 204,000.[217] From the very beginning, the rapid build-up of this industry was geared toward war preparation. This entailed an excessive expansion of production, without consideration of market viability. Intentionally, under the auspices of the new military doctrine of maintaining a "constant airforce," the creation of large plant overcapacities was planned without any long-term economic considerations. This doctrine abandoned the idea of stockpiling large stores of military aircraft far before the event of mobilisation, but meant a constant readiness of the industry to be able to follow the still fairly low demand of civilian aircraft production, as well as maintaining the capability to fulfil military orders for the latest modern combat aircraft with the potential onset of war.

Since this policy could only be fulfilled as long as large overcapacities existed, these rearmament plans had to be performed against the principles of general market mechanisms and economic rationalism. This massive capacity extension could not be financed by aircraft enterprises under market conditions.[218] Many firms that worked for airforce rearmament contracts recognised that these large overcapacities and long-term underutilisation were dangerous for operating efficiency. Siemens, for example, only reluctantly followed the demands of the airforce ministry to invest in expansion of its aircraft engine plants. In the long run, management considered engine production economically unreasonable.[219] To be able to keep up the pace of rearmament, though, further state involvement in aircraft production and investment for plant expansion was inevitable, especially after 1935. Again, the overall result, were only small progress in production techniques, low productivity and low capac-

213 Percentages calculated from international surveys in Statistisches Reichsamt, *Jahrbuch 1933*, 69 and *Jahrbuch 1937*, 81.

214 Own calculation from table 39, Svennilson, 147.

215 Lutz Budraß, *Flugzeugindustrie und Luftrüstung in Deutschland 1918–1945*, Düsseldorf 1998, 377 ff. Overy cites different employment numbers, *War and Economy*, 61.

216 Ibid, 88.

217 Williamson Murray, *The Luftwaffe 1933–45. Strategy for Defeat*, Washington 1996, chapter: Origins and Preparation.

218 Budraß, 338.

219 "Dem Flugmotorenbau fehle auf Dauer jedwede wirtschaftliche Grundlage." Ibid, 384.

ity utilisation in the 30s.[220] German productivity was as low as the notoriously inefficient aircraft industry of Soviet Russia. It produced the largest number of aircraft (8000) in 1937, followed by Germany (5800). In both countries the relation of one manufactured aircraft to the workforce was about 1:20. In most Western countries, where output was much lower, productivity was higher. In Britain, it was 1:17.8. In Italy and the US, the relations were 17.6 and 11 respectively. Only in France, productivity was comparable to that of Germany or Russia.[221]

State control and rearmament forced a disproportional expansion of this industry, whose capacity could only be utilised for war production. Rapid growth certainly supported the progress of one of the most dynamic, modern and advanced growth sectors of the German economy. It also supported the growth of the electrical engineering, chemical, light metal and machine building industries. Yet, this process did not take place along economically viable and efficient lines. These industries would not have been prepared to stand on their own in world markets against the far more competitive American aircraft and British motor industries. In some cases, production capacities were not only far too large for the market, but production itself was much too expensive. Essentially, the final products of the most modern and largest German industries were not designed for productive use, i.e. products which would have directly helped the progress of future consumption or new transport. In the case of the aircraft industry this process was especially pronounced. This type of production was only profitable in the short run, but only because demand of this expansive equipment was government financed. In the long run, it was a process of investing and wasting material, capital and labour to manufacture expensive and unproductive weapons systems only to be wasted in warfare. Over a longer period, this development was not only harmful to a few enterprises, but to the whole aircraft industry itself.

The same can be said for other large and traditional industrial sectors, especially heavy industry. The expansion of the iron and steel industry was purely domestically oriented and depended, almost exclusively, on rearmament orders. Employment of the Krupp enterprise alone expanded from a workforce of about 43,000 in 1933/34 to 101,113 in 1938/39. The result was a huge build-up of production facilities, whose capacity was utilised predominantly for military output. Krupp military output more than tripled between 1933/34 and 1938/39. At the same time exports of the German coal, iron and steel industry declined about 80%, and profits fell rapidly after 1938. Krupp net profits dropped 46% until 1939/40.[222] To industrial leaders, it was clear that growth, purely based on rearmament, did not have any long-term future prospects. However, the state had increasingly taken direct control of large sections of heavy industry. Rearmament production of Krupp, for example, was directly controlled by the Wehrmacht bureaucracy.[223]

220 "Während die Leistungen der nach 1932 konstruierten Flugzeuge sprunghaft anstiegen, waren die Fortschritte in der Produktionstechnik wenig spektakulär." Ibid, 405.

221 Own calculation from Budraß, table 18, 376.

222 Numbers and percentages calculated from Overy, *War and Economy*, table 3.3, 117 and table 4.3, 138.

223 Overy, *War and Economy*, 137.

Summarising, it can be said that Germany is one of the very few examples where performance can be directly attributed to a certain type of policy. It should be noted however, that only an extreme policy, severely distorting the economic structure of an advanced industrialised country, could have had such great implications. Again, only extreme policies in the inter-war period entailed results on real economic development.

b. Italy and Japan These two countries will only be discussed briefly, but are included here to show that similar processes of extreme policy and economic distortions took place elsewhere, especially when massive rearmament took place. Soviet Russian development was probably very similar. Its case it not included here, though, since that would have entailed a discussion of communist economic planning, for which the framework of this study is too limited.

A very similar process of extreme nationalist economic policy, supporting growth in the short run, but distorting economic development in the long run, took place in Japan and Italy. For the latter, though, this process was quite mild and hardly visible, due to various factors. One of such was the weakness of control of the regime over influential socio-economic interests groups. Another factor was the relatively low level of Italian industrialisation. The agrarian sector was still quite large, many industrial sectors were obsolete, and Italy was highly dependent on imports, including semi-finished imports. Like so many other states, the country tried to shelter its weak industries and moved to harsh protectionism as a reaction to the depression. Even manufactured goods were exposed to high tariffs.[224] After the proclamation of Western sanctions, as a reaction to the Abyssinian war, these measures were further extended in the framework of a more radical policy of self-sufficiency.[225]

All the same, state control and rearmament did not go nearly as far as in Germany, and the policy of autarky remained the main feature of economic policy-making in Italy. Direct state investment remained on low levels. In the 30s, overall state expenditure remained stagnant and only increased 3.3% between 1932/33 and 1937/38. In the same time span, military expenditure only rose 3.7%.[226] All out efforts for rearmament only came after 1938, entailing that Mussolini found his country unprepared for his schemes of military expansion during the war. Until then, investment for industrial development took priority before rearmament. By and large, economic policy seemed to have had small implications for Italian performance, whose growth remained relatively low. Between 1933 and 1938, GNP only grew 16.5%.[227]

In Japan, however, the situation was wholly different. Here, policy makers regarded Nazi German economic planning and war preparation as a model. Also Japan, truly executed economic nationalism as a major component of aggressive military and economic expansion. This country enjoyed the highest growth of industrial production

224 Liepmann, 386.

225 On policy in Italy see: Angela Raspin, "Wirtschaftliche und politische Aspekte der italienischen Aufrüstung Anfang der dreißiger Jahre bis 1940," in: Forstmeier and Volkmann, *Wirtschaft und Rüstung*, 203–221.

226 Own calculation from Statistisches Reichsamt, *Jahrbuch 1937*, 261 (international survey).

227 Own calculation from Bairoch, "Europe's Gross National Product," table 18.

in the world in the 30s. Between 1929 and 1936, it increased more than 65%.[228] Certainly, though, this impressive growth can only be attributed to economic policy to a minor degree. This country was still in the process of industrialising and started from a low level of industrial development. Like most industrialising periphery countries, Japanese growth still depended on the development of the older traditional industries such as some heavy industry, but mainly on textiles. The economic structure was still marked by strong imbalances. Agriculture, employing always more than 40% of the labour force, remained, by far, the largest sector. Distribution of income was extremely uneven as industry and trade contained oliogopolistic features, dominated by a few influential family clans, the Zaibatsu. At the same time, neither a domestic consumer market,[229] nor a substantial middle class existed.

Japan became one of the main competitors against the advanced Western countries on the world textile market. Until 1936, growth was based on cheap exports, primarily again textiles, and cheap and simple consumer goods. These products were sold at dumping prices in Asia, the US, the British colonies, and Africa. About 11% went to Europe.[230] To some degree, the boost of exports was supported by taking the yen off gold in 1931. The already low-priced Japanese products became even cheaper, especially in the US. Textile prices fell by half.[231] Yet, textile manufacturing did not necessarily make exports cheap, but instead, low labour costs.

From 1936 onward, rearmament and a policy of self-sufficiency began to really affect economic development directly. There was a movement away from export-led growth to domestic growth focused on the expansion of military output. Between 1931/32 and 1936/37, the share of military spending of overall state expenditure had already risen from 31 to 47%.[232] After the war had expanded to China in 1937, the Japanese economy was extremely strained, because rearmament production was expanded at a time when production capacity had already been fully utilised.[233] The result was a further disproportionate expansion of production capacity in favour of heavy capital goods industries. Growth was also focused on Japan's primary sphere of economic interest, the yen bloc area of Manchuko, Korea, Formosa and, after 1937, part of China. Shortly before the war against the US, this was to become Japan's so-called Co-Prosperity Sphere.

Until then, heavy industry, the small motor and aircraft industry, machine building and shipbuilding expanded production due to large-scale rearmament orders. Aircraft companies and car manufacturing enterprises, such as Nissan, expanded with the help of direct government intervention and partial state ownership. Cartelisation

228 "Industrielle Weltproduktion," in: Deutsches Institut für Konjunkturforschung, *Wochenbericht*, vol. 10, no. 2, 1937, 12.

229 On industrial structures, ownership and policy see: Bernd Martin, "Aggressionspolitik als Mobilisierungsfaktor. Der militärische und wirtschaftliche Imperialismus Japans 1931 bis 1941," in: Forstmeier and Volkmann, *Wirtschaft und Rüstung*, 222–245.

230 "Japans Vormarsch auf dem Weltmarkt," in: *Wochenbericht*, vol. 9, no. 5, 1936, 19 ff.

231 Bernd Martin, "Wirtschaftliche Konzentration und soziale Konflikte in Japan," in: Dietmar Rothermund (ed.), *Die Peripherie in der Weltwirtschaftskrise: Afrika, Asien und Lateinamerika 1929–1939*, Paderborn 1982, 215.

232 G. C. Allen, *A Short Economic History of Modern Japan*, New York 1981, 141.

233 "Totale Kriegswirtschaft in Japan," in: *Wochenbericht*, vol. 12, no. 26, 1939, 155–157.

and industrial concentration of vital sectors was an essential aspect of this process. Exactly as in Germany, all vital industrial, material, financial and labour resources were directed by the state to concentrate on preparation for war, resulting in what has been called "state monopoly capitalism."[234] Therefore, extensive controls of the capital market, production, consumption and foreign trade were implemented. The system of rearmament finance was similar to Schacht's reflationary capital generation with the help of government bonds. Simultaneously, investments of light and consumer industries, not directly necessary for this effort, were curtailed by excluding them from the capital market.[235] This type of internal expansion, only possible by diverting production away from exports to domestic purposes, was very problematic for a country that highly depended on imports and foreign trade.

In Japan, the process of state and military influence over the economic structures seemed to have been even greater than in Germany. Consumption was also restricted to a far greater degree, while extreme military spending, beginning in the mid 30s, led to intensifying inflation. A shift also took place in Japan, entailing a disproportional expansion of capital investment industries at the expense of consumer industries. In the early 40s, the Japanese economy was already suffering heavily from structural distortion. By that time, a return to peace production and consumption, without help from the outside, would have been no longer possible.[236]

5.6.2. Policy and Performance in the Liberal States: Britain and France

Policy and performance in countries with liberal economies were completely different from development in authoritarian states. Unlike Germany, economic policy here only had mild implications on the secular long-term trend of economic transition and development. There also was no apparent connection between a certain policy option and the level and rate of recovery. Half-hearted Keynesian measures were only implemented in the US and Sweden, where growth rates were relatively high, but fluctuating. However, fairly rapid recovery could take place without mediocre interventionist policies. In Britain, a country where orthodox economic policy prevailed, rapid growth took place in the 30s. In France, on the other hand, where fiscal orthodoxy was also practised until 1936, performance was poor. Generally, it is problematical to ascribe similar policies to both countries, because there were substantial differences in monetary policy. However, even though Britain devaluated its currency much sooner and more effectively than France, devaluation had mild results in both cases. Monetary policy played only a minor role in changing economic performance, and in the long run structural transformations were the main factors determining recovery.

a. Britain In contrast to the 1920s, British economic performance after 1932 was exceptional, as not only its rate, but also the level of recovery was remarkable. Al-

234 Martin, "Konzentration," 219.
235 Martin, "Aggressionspolitik," 234.
236 Ibid, 240.

though there was a slump in 1937/38, between 1932 and 1938, industrial production increased 42%.[237] Until 1937, before the downswing, industrial production rose 64%.[238] In Sweden, for example, it grew 69%, but it started off from a level 14% below British industrial production in 1932.[239] British GNP rose 24%, that was 3.4% annually. In the 20s, annual growth had only been 1.3% .[240] This performance, even though not as dramatic as in Germany or Japan, was remarkable when one considers that the economy took off from fairly high levels of growth and development in the early 30s as the depression had much milder effects in Britain than in many other countries. This outstanding performance among the liberal states was basically achieved without government intervention and despite continuous orthodox and restrictive economic policy. Britain was one of the few countries that resorted to economic nationalism, protectionism and state investment only in a very mild way. There was no deficit spending, and compared to all other European countries, tariffs were relatively low. Nor did any large scale government spending take place[241] until rearmament in the late 30s. Some have even regarded fiscal policy as slightly deflationary, because there was almost a constant budget surplus.[242]

The goal of government policy remained the maintenance of a balanced budget. Not only was traditional orthodoxy the cause for this, but pure financial necessity. Unlike the US, with its ample gold reserves and balance of payments surplus, Britain could simply not afford huge government expenditure without the maintenance of an economic system of direct, extensive controls at the same time. A very large increase in spending would have entailed far greater imports and possibly capital flight. The country would have run into great balance of payments difficulties and perhaps currency problems. Therefore, large-scale deficit spending, an effective Keynesian expansionist policy, to relieve the unemployment problem and to raise national income, would only have been possible when Britain would have closed off its economy with the help of vigorous control measures, as Germany had done in the 30s.[243]

Between 1931/32 and 1932/33, total state expenditure was curtailed by about 4%. Thereafter, expenditure only increased 7.8% until 1937/38. Spending for economy and infrastructure was slightly raised after 1933, but was cut again after 1936/37.[244] A number of policy measures, such as sterling devaluation, cheap money policy, tariffs after 1932, and direct help to some of the old staples industries, have been regarded as one of the main stimulants for growth.[245] However, government

237 Own calculation from A. E. Musson, *The Growth of British Industry*, Norfolk 1978, 277.

238 Peden, 107.

239 Own calculation from Mitchell, 181.

240 Own calculation from Mitchell (constant 1938 prices), 416.

241 H.W. Richardson, "The Economic Significance of the Depression in Britain," in: *The Journal of Contemporary History*, vol. 4, no. 4, 1969, 13.

242 Peden, 92–100.

243 T. Thomas, "Aggregate demand in the United Kingdom 1918–45," in: Floud and McCloskey, *The Economic History of Britain since 1700*, Cambridge 1981, 338.

244 Statistisches Reichsamt, *Jahrbuch 1937*, 261 (international survey).

245 Lomax, 17.

financial help for reconstruction, reorganisation and scrapping of some of the old staples, as shipbuilding and coal mining, was sporadic and too small to have had substantial influence.[246] Neither can exports be considered as a main factor for growth, since its share of national product slightly declined.[247] As mentioned above, currency devaluation in 1931 had only short-term effects and enhanced the competitiveness of British exports, but just until many other countries depreciated until 1933. The only real long-term advantage was that future policy of monetary authorities was freed from the constraints imposed by the adherence to gold standard rules under unfavourable conditions, which had resulted in restrictive currency policy between 1925 and 1931.[248] A policy of cheap money could be pursued thereafter, with lower exchange rates, lower discount rates of around 2%, between 1932 and 1937, and easy credit availability. To strengthen business confidence at the same time, the budget remained balanced.

Structural Transformation and Performance

The economic boom until 1937 was primarily a domestic private investment boom,[250] driven by an intensifying structural shift. As mentioned above, in the 20s, this transformation to modern expanding sectors and the change of the productive capacity of the traditional industries to more modern modes of production was slow and insufficient. It seems that the British economy made up the lag of structural transition in the 30s, surprisingly almost without any government interference. Certainly, cheap money policy supported this process.[251] However, this transformation mainly took place in the framework of a post-depression business cycle upswing, without such extreme structural distortions as in Germany and was driven by compensating for a backlog in industrial modernisation. Demand came from private investment, consumption and a steadily rising, but low export rate.

This development was a stratified and complex process, about which only a superficial discussion can be conducted here. The industrial shift must have been most pronounced in Britain, since this process has not been as clearly recognised in other countries. The shift from old to new, or from declining to expanding industries, is a standard, but not uncontested view developed already right after the Second World War and in the 60s by a number of British historians.[252] Generally, this process was also recognised and interpreted by contemporaries in the 30s. It has also been well documented and described. Surprisingly, in Germany, Austria and France, this view

246 Musson, 288–289.

247 Pollard, *Development*, 56.

248 Cairncross and Eichengreen, 102.

249 Mühlendorf, 131.

250 Peden, 108.

251 "Although cheap money is in itself incapable of inducing recovery, it proved a highly important contributory influence in England [...]," A.E. Kahn, *Great Britain in the World Economy*, New York 1946, 263.

252 See literature in Pollard, *Development*, 53 and 54. See also: Richardson, 8–12. One of the earliest proponents of this view was probably Kahn. One of the contestors of the traditional recovery school is B. W. E. Alford, "New industries for old? British industry between the wars," in: Floud and McCloskey, *The Economic History of Britain since 1700*, 308–331.

of structural shift and distinction of performance among industrial sectors was hardly made by contemporaries and historians. Here, the process was not as pronounced, as it was either slowed down, distorted in certain periods or overshadowed by crises and extreme policy regime shifts.

Clearly, the expanding industries, such as the motor, electricity, electrical engineering, rayon, rubber and other chemicals industries, were again the leading modern growth sectors. Yet, as these provided only 19% of output in 1935 and only amounted to an equal share of industrial employment in 1938,[253] the explanation of rapid recovery must go beyond a simple shift from old traditional industries to modern expanding industries. The application of new technologies took place not only among the new sectors, but also stimulated, to varying degrees, the traditional industries, such as coal, iron and steel, textiles and shipbuilding, as well as house building and construction.

Musson has described this "second industrial revolution" by looking at the change of production and investment patterns before and after the First World War.[254] At first, British pre-war trends of high growth were reversed during the twenties by the market forces and war distortions which formed the pressure that led to a change of industrial structures and technology. Breaking the general trend was not only possible because of wartime disturbances, but also because investment before the war was concentrated on quantitative, but not on qualitative labour and capital input in the traditional sectors. Pre-war expansion and investment was still concentrated on, and over-committed to, enlarging the application of old technology and production processes already in use. Productivity gains were small. After the war this investment trend was reversed, but did not lead to continuously high levels of growth. As the industrial concentration on the old sectors had been high and their level of productivity and modernisation was low, the structural transformation was difficult after the war and resulted in stagnation. Pre-war retardation of the most important industries turned into stagnation and decline among traditional sectors. Their capacities were too large and obsolete. Plants had to be downsized before production could be modernised. At the same time, labour and capital was invested to enlarge and improve production of the modern sectors, whose expansion could not yet counterbalance the decline of contracting industries. This partially explains the high levels of unemployment and low rate of growth in the 20s.

In the 1930s, however, the "second industrial revolution" showed positive results, and growth recovered to pre-war levels. The older sectors of industry had completed the scrapping and reduction of obsolete production plant and increasingly applied, inspired and pressured by the expanding sectors, modern modes of production, based on chemicals, electricity and the internal combustion engine. The new sectors simply carried on the process of investment and production expansion of the 20s. Overall, the recovery process and structural changes were obvious in a clear shift of investment from old to new industries and to new forms of production

253 Musson, 277–278.

254 Musson, 270–271. Of course he was not the first one to suggest this explanation. See also: Kahn, especially Part Two.

among the old sectors. Increasing structural changes and improvement also became obvious in higher productivity. In the 30s, productivity growth of British manufacturing industry experienced a breakthrough, and was higher than in Germany and the US.[255]

The most important growth industries were the electrical engineering, electricity supply and the motor industry. In the 20s, electricity consumption per head was behind other advanced countries, but in the late 30s it was nearly equal.[256] By 1938, electrification had progressed so far that about 65% of British households were wired.[257] As in all advanced countries, general electrification offered a whole range of sources for demand. Factory plant, street lighting and the railways started to apply electricity and electrical engineering products. Production increased 71% between 1932 and 1938. Until 1937, the electrical engineering industry employed about 367,000 workers,[258] even slightly larger than its German equivalent, whose workforce roughly numbered 359,000.[259] In the 1930s, it partially made up its backlog of modernisation in technology and organisation that had existed before the war and in the 20s. Large companies, like the British Thompson-Houston Ltd, lost part of their dependence on American innovation and technology. Following closely behind the American and German industries, the British electrical engineering industry became the third largest producer of electrical goods in the world.[260]

The motor industry had also greatly expanded, producing by far the greatest number of vehicles in Europe in the late 30s. Its production rose 111% after the depression. In 1937, it still outstripped German production by over 180,000 units.[261] British car and truck manufactures dominated the home market and were profitable at the same time, although still far from American productivity levels.[262] The number of people whose employment was directly and indirectly connected with the motor industry in the late 30s has been estimated 1.3 million.[263]

Growth of industries that could not directly be attributed to modern technologies and whose production had been based on the first industrial revolution, finally began to pick up in the 30s and some outstripped pre-war output levels by 1938. Three old staples industries, textiles, shipbuilding and coal, did not recover after the crisis. Textiles, the largest industrial employer in the 30s besides building and contracting, suffered heavily from the breakdown of world trade and did not reach 1913 production levels. Also, shipbuilding suffered from the precipitous fall of trade and declined

255 Pollard, *Development*, 53. Rostas, table VII, 49.

256 Pollard, *Development*, 59.

257 Musson, 356.

258 Pollard, *Development*, 60.

259 Länderrat des Amerikanischen Besatzungsgebietes (ed.), *Statistisches Handbuch von Deutschland 1928–1944*, Munich 1949, 302.

260 Arno Mietschke, "Technisches Humankapital in der britischen Elektroindustrie der Zwischenkriegszeit: Die British Thompson-Houston Co. in vergleichender Perpektive," in: *Zeitschrift für Unternehmensgeschichte*, vol. 40, Stuttgart 1995, 115–118.

261 Own calculation from Statistisches Reichsamt, *Jahrbuch 1938*, 83 (international survey).

262 Wayne Lewchuk, "The Motor Vehicle Industry," in: Bernhard Elbaum and William Lazonick (eds.), *The Decline of the British Economy*, Oxford 1986, 142–149.

263 Kahn, 110.

after the depression. Coal mining was seriously challenged by electricity and oil, and stagnated as well.[264] Production in the 30s never reached pre-crisis levels.

Building, contracting and construction materials, though, already enjoyed considerable growth in the 20s, when output more than doubled. By 1937, production was 21% above 1929 level.[265] Iron and steel recovered pre-crisis output in 1934,[266] and outstripped pre-war production levels by 12% in 1938. The steel industry, which had suffered from substantial overcapacities and underutilisation until the depression, benefited from the general upswing of the largest traditional markets after 1932, shipbuilding and heavy steel, but also from the building, construction and canning industries. Demand from the modern sectors, however, automobiles and aircraft still only constituted a small portion of overall demand for steel products.[267] The upswing of the steel industry in the 30s was substantial. Dropping export sales of the inter-war period were "more than counterbalanced by expansion of the home market."[268] Whereas output hardly increased until 1929, steel production had risen from 7.6 million in 1913 to 13 million tons until 1939.[269] This shows how a large market could offset declining international trade.

Rearmament, basically concentrated on the building-up of the navy and air force, only began to affect the economy in the late 30s. The moderate boom of iron and steel after 1935, can be, to some degree, attributed to rearmament orders.[270] In that year, rearmament expenditure began to pick up slowly, but was minute compared to German efforts. Between 1933 and 1938, the government was determined to finance the majority of rearmament costs with tax income and to keep disturbances of the rearmament effort on the normal economic process to a minimum.[271] Even though military expenditure increased from almost 114 million to 253 million pounds between 1934/35 and 1938/39,[272] its share of net national product in 1938 and 1939 was only 7 and 15% respectively.[273]

The greatest initial implication of military expenditure was probably on the aircraft industry, which enjoyed rapid expansion after 1935. Until then this industry, with its many small firms, had to rely on small orders from the RAF and support from the air ministry. However, unlike the distorted and disproportional growth in Germany, the British aircraft industry grew according to normal demand conditions

264 Musson, 298–299.

265 Musson, 277.

266 Pollard, *Development*, 70.

267 Steven Tolliday, "Steel and Rationalisation Policies, 1918–1950," in: Bernard Elbaum and William Lazonick, *The Decline of the British Economy*, Oxford 1986, 83.

268 Musson, 302.

269 Musson, 303.

270 Pollard, *Development*, 70. Mühlendorf saw great implications of British rearmament on industry already from 1934 onward, "Währungsabwertung," 102.

271 Norman H. Gibbs, "Das britische Aufrüstungsprogramm 1933 bis 1939 und das Ausmaß seiner Abhängigkeit von der Entwicklung in Deutschland," in: Volkmann and Forstmeier, *Wirtschaft und Rüstung*, 251.

272 Statistisches Reichsamt, *Jahrbuch 1937*, 261 and *Jahrbuch 1938*, 275 (international survey).

273 Pollard, *Development*, 214. Peden, 131.

until rearmament orders set in in the late 30s. It remained a minor industry until the mid 30s with about between 30,000 to 35,000 employees.[274]

In conclusion, it is clear that British economic growth and development was largely unaided by government intervention. The only positive aspect of economic policy after 1931 was cheap money policy, which did not initiate the recovery process, but supported it. Another important feature of British recovery was that it was mainly driven by a long-term secular trend of economic modernisation, concentrated on domestically oriented growth and not distorted by state investment for military expansion.

b. French Devaluation and Performance While most countries went off gold in 1931 after Britain had suspended its gold parity, France pursued a policy of deflation, refrained from devaluation, and remained on the gold standard for various reasons. The problematical development of government finances, the difficulty of accepting and distributing the burden of the war costs, the dramatic course of inflation and stabilisation until 1926, fear of another inflation and social disorder in a paralysed French bourgeois society, were probably the main reasons for inflexible and rigid policy-making. All sections of the middle class, the Bank of France and even many exporters were against any currency experiments. With the help of orthodox economic policy, the government attempted to do anything in order to maintain trust and confidence in the national currency and public finance.[275]

World prices were already far lower than French wholesale prices before 1931, but after the devaluation of sterling and the fall of the dollar in 1933, the disparity between French home and world prices grew, increasing the competitive disadvantage for French export industries and the pressure to change currency policy. While the depression continued, taxes were raised, state expenditure was cut to balance the budget and the reliance on central bank advances increased, especially from 1935 onwards.[276] For the rest of the 30s, the various governments attempted to find a balance between growing social and armament expenditure, the stipulations of orthodox finance and the maintenance of the franc gold parity.[277] Still, the resulting overvaluation of the franc certainly helped to prolong the depression in France, but was not the main cause of the length of the depression in this country, since devaluation only offered temporary relief.

After the administration of Albert Sarraut had resigned in November 1933, the deflationary policy of the following years, most vigorously enforced by the administrations under Pierre Étienne Flandin and Pierre Laval, was terminated with the election of the Popular Front government in May 1936, under the leadership of Léon Blum.[278] A lack of internal aggregate demand, seemingly due to a reduction of purchasing power, was seen as the origin of the crisis by the new government. An economic programme was drawn up, using the American New Deal as a model. The

274 Pollard, *Development*, 61. Musson, 350. Kahn, Table 7, 107.
275 Kemp, 102 ff.
276 Eichengreen, *Golden Fetters*, 372.
277 See Jackson.
278 Kemp, 115 ff.

following social reforms of June and August gave concessions to labour by enforcing the 40 hour week, higher wages, paid holiday and more workers' rights. Besides encouraging domestic demand, the implementation of a cheap money policy by the national bank was also considered as a major stimulus for economic revival.

Eventually, though, the advantages of increasing demand and a lower discount rate were more than offset by an increase of production costs and rising prices. There still remained reluctance to lower the exchange rate, but as wage and production costs increased, as a consequence of the social reforms, French price levels rose again. The credibility in the increasing deficit of government finance and in the stability of the currency was again questioned as capital and gold left the country. Finally, France turned to devaluation on September 26, 1936.[279] To ensure that no retaliatory dollar and sterling devaluation would take place, the franc was devalued only 25%. As part of the Tripartite Agreement with Britain and the US of the same year, this measure was presented as an alignment of the franc to the dollar and pound,[280] which it was essentially.

Contemporary economists noticed only a slight improvement of France's economic condition, following depreciation. For Switzerland and the Netherlands, countries that devalued their currencies at the same time, the same was observed. However, the slight upswing was due to increasing sales, as a reaction of the population to pending price increases after devaluation. An improvement of the competitive position in foreign trade was noticed only temporarily for all countries that abandoned the gold bloc.[281]

The positive effects of devaluation did not last very long. Even though French price level was 8%, the Dutch 2% and the Swiss 9% below the British domestic price level right after depreciation, this advantage was soon lost by December 1936. This was mainly due to rising price levels in all three former gold bloc countries, as costs of imports, wages and production rose. In France, the rise of domestic prices was most pronounced, and soon the competitive advantage of devaluation was lost altogether.

In the long run, devaluation did not really bring any improvement in performance. Production performance remained erratic and no recovery occurred. Between 1935 and 1936, manufacturing production increased 6.2%, without a currency advantage. The following year, it increased another 6% and dropped 7.4% in 1938,[282] partially as a consequence of another milder world-wide depression in 1937/38. Eichengreen has attributed the failure of French devaluation to "rising real costs of production and falling profitability. With higher wages putting upward pressure on costs, there was little incentive to expand production. With higher costs putting upward pressure on prices, there was little improvement in the terms of trade. Hence

279 "Das Ende des 'Goldblocks'," in: Deutsches Institut für Konjunkturforschung, *Wochenbericht*, vol. 9, no. 39, Berlin, October 1936, 153–154. Eichengreen, *Golden Fetters*, 377.

280 Ibid, 380. Kemp 122–124.

281 "Die Wirtschaftsentwicklung in Frankreich, den Niederlanden und der Schweiz seit der Abwertung," in: *Wochenbericht*, vol. 10, no. 6, Berlin, February 1937, 29.

282 Own calculation from League of Nations, *Industrialization and Foreign Trade*, 140.

little increase in exports occurred."[283] Not only "years of deflation" were responsible for the ineffectiveness of economic policy, in an environment in which France was surrounded by retrenched national economies. The fact that devaluation and the Blum experiment of 1936 did not show serious positive implications indicates that the problems of the economy were rooted much deeper and suggests that the real cause for economic stagnation lay in structural deficiencies.

Structural Deficiencies

There were three main reasons for French resistance to the depression and persistent stagnation after 1931. First, as industrial production was mostly affected by the crisis, the existence of a still fairly large and backward agricultural sector that was not highly dependent on exports, helped to limit the fall of GNP. The agricultural sector always had a higher share of national product than industry. In 1927, it was 19%, declined in the depression to 12.8% and rose again in 1933. Industry's share was 13.9% in 1927, and dropped to 8.8% of national product in 1933.[284] It was a small wonder that a sharp industrial recession did not affect French performance as severely as it did more advanced countries, as Germany, the US or Austria. After the industrial sector had retrenched and adjusted to the moderate demand of the domestic market, its competitive position had deteriorated until 1936 and could hardly contribute to a rise in aggregate demand, investment and recovery thereafter.

Secondly, the peculiar structure of industry, on the one hand, had the effect that the country was hit by depression quite late, and on the other, that recovery was not forthcoming. It had undergone a rapid transformation in the 20s, with modernisation and concentration, but French industry still consisted of only a fairly small number of large industrial combines that had undergone the industrial revolution to mass production, high capital intensity, specialisation and had a productivity comparable to that of Germany or Britain. This is apparent in the low value of French per capita manufacturing, not comparable to other large advanced countries. Gross value of French per capita manufacturing was the lowest among the large industrialised countries, not even half of that of the US and comparable to that of Sweden, the Netherlands or Denmark.[285]

Moreover, the boom period in the 20s seemed not to have been long enough for a sufficient transformation of the industrial structure that could have affected productivity of larger sectors of industry. In spite of the existence of large car manufacturers and steel producers, the industrial sector was dominated by small artisan firms that were able to resist recessions easier than big capital and investment intensive companies. These smaller firms focused on their home market. It was easier for them to reduce running costs and investment during the depression. While the obsolete sectors could deal with recession, the collapse of exports and general stagnation over several years resulted in a decline of competitiveness of the larger and

283 Eichengreen, *Golden Fetters*, 385.

284 Tobler, calculated from chart: development of French national income, 192.

285 See table 11: Manufacturing Production and Trade in Manufactured Articles per head of Population in 1926– 1929, in: League of Nations, *Industrialization and Foreign Trade*, 84.

modern industries[286] that were more dependent on international trade. That was the main reason for continuing industrial stagnation, despite a short upswing in 1933 and devaluation in 1936.

Third, as French national income was not so dependent on income from export sales as other industrialised countries, at least as long as industry and agriculture could turn to an active home market, it was affected by depression only by 1931. This is obvious when considering that national product grew despite the fact that export sales dropped. Even though the value of export declined nearly 16% between 1926 and 1929, GNP increased 11.5% in the same period.[287] Between 1929 and 1935, value of French exports declined almost 70%. Meanwhile, GNP at constant prices only fell 17.2% and industrial production 32.7%. In 1929, exports still had a share of 11% of national product, and fell to about 4% in 1935. The importance of foreign trade clearly fell dramatically. Many industries were now sheltered behind trade restrictions in their home market, whereas the export industry did not have the same weight as in other national economies. Those economic interests groups that represented the majority of industry and agriculture, peasants, artisans and smaller industrial units, applied political pressure to limit foreign competition with duties, quotas and other restrictions. Some well organised producers limited output while raising prices. The results were high domestic price levels and a small and uncompetitive export industry.

Primarily, the unusual structure of the French economy combined with the implications of non-interventionist and deflationary policy seemed to have been the main determinants of the late beginning of the depression and slow recovery. That France had not fully developed into a highly industrialised country, with overall comparative productivity and competitiveness is not only obvious in the large agricultural sector, but also in the modest, compared to Germany and Britain, low unemployment figures in the 30s.[288] The connection of the workforce to agriculture must have been still fairly close, as the overall number of the workforce was decreasing. Industry and agriculture clearly retrenched to their home market and France increasingly became a sheltered and retrenched national economy.

One of the main problems was that the economy was not advanced enough to sustain internal growth, because no major structural adjustment took place in the 30s. Another obstacle to growth was that, contrary to the new authoritarian states, France did not turn to extensive government spending and investment to compensate its structural deficiencies. In addition, economic policy strongly enhanced and supported the tendency of retrenchment of agriculture and industry toward a protected, nationalist and inward oriented economy, in which the process of structural adjustment was distorted and stagnated.

286 Kemp, 101–102.

287 Own calculation from Mitchell, 304 and 411. Admittedly the decline in export is in current prices. In volume the drop was more moderate. Also see numbers from Hickmann and Rieker, *Statistisches Handbuch*, 261–263.

288 Kemp, 109.

5.7. POLICY AND PERFORMANCE IN AUSTRIA

By the late 1920s, Austrian economic policy had become a bit more progressive. State investment for infrastructure and social relief increased. During the crisis and thereafter, however, this was reversed and policy strictly adhered to orthodox financial principles, extremely limiting active state intervention. Austria truly remained one of the most conservative countries in matters of economic policy.

After the dissolution of parliament in March 1933, the neo-liberal principles of a balanced budget, stable currency and prices, with the objective to maintain or regain international financial credibility, dominated economic policy-making in Austria until early 1938. With similar motives as the French government, fear of inflation and loss of credibility, Austria decided to remain on the gold standard, at least de jure. De facto it could not afford to maintain gold convertibility and was one of the countries that only artificially sustained gold parity with the help of exchange controls and clearing systems. Hence, its currency policy was somewhat of a mixture between French deflationary policy and German currency control. The approach to economic policy-making was similar as in 1922. The government legitimised its policy by calling the League of Nations for help.

In the 30s, Austrian deflationary economic policy, under the conduct of the proto-fascist "Ständestaat" (corporate state), has not only been harshly criticised by German contemporaries,[289] but also by many modern scholars. It is certainly true that it was strictly neo-liberal, reactionary and saw its main goals in a balanced budget and currency stability. In the decade of the depression, the interests of foreign creditors and employers were supported by government policy, while income of labour and domestic consumption stagnated.[290] Economic policy basically refrained from any kind of counter-cyclical interventionist policy. The small work creation programmes largely had only propaganda purpose, were essentially ineffective, and the investment loans floated by the government were too small to have an impact. They were predominantly utilised for deflationary debt servicing. This course of policy, in contrast to the more counter-cyclical measures increasingly applied elsewhere, has been regarded as one of the main causes for poor recovery in the 30s. Furthermore, in historiography, a direct connection has been drawn between this policy, economic misery in the 30s and the apparent ease of the take-over of Austria by National Socialist Germany in March 1938.[291]

289 For example: Deutsches Institut für Konjunkturforschung, "Österreichs Wirtschaftsnot und Wirtschaftspolitik vor der Eingliederung in das Reich," in: *Schriften des Instituts für Konjunkturforschung. Vierteljahreshefte zur Wirtschaftsforschung*, vol. 12, no. 4, 1937/1938, 387–398.

290 See for example: Siegfried Mattl, "Die Finanzdiktatur. Wirtschaftspolitik in Österreich 1933–1938," in: Emmerich Talos and W. Neugebauer (eds.), *„Austrofaschismus". Beiträge über Politik, Ökonomie und Kultur 1934– 1938*, Vienna 1984, 133–155.

291 "Die langandauernde Depression, die Massenarbeitslosigkeit und der Rückgang des allgemeinen Lebensniveaus wurden von großen Teilen der österreichischen Bevölkerung mit Erbitterung regristriert, zumal sich im benachbarten Deutschland schon seit der Mitte der dreißiger Jahre eine deutliche wirtschaftliche Wende anzubahnen schien. All dies trug nicht wenig zu der erwartungsvollen Stimmung bei, mit der der Einmarsch der deutschen Truppen im März 1938 in Österreich aufgenommen wurde." Weber claimed that the Austrian 'Ständestaat' strove for "das

An explanation such as this is near at hand when regarding the appalling Austrian economic performance. Austrian growth and performance were very poor during and after the depression. Besides the US and Germany, it experienced the harshest downswing in 1932. Industrial production dropped as enormously as in Germany and the US, and value of exports declined 45.5% between 1929 and 1933, when it finally reached its absolute low point of the inter-war period.[292] In 1937, it still had only reached 76% of pre-crisis export value and only 86.5% of GNP level. Therefore, in view of the apparent direct interdependence between the decline of national income and falling exports, it is surprising that so much of this economic decline has been attributed to orthodox Austrian economic policy during and after the depression, and that so little attention has been paid to comparable international development.

As there certainly was a strong connection between Austrian economic stagnation, the rise of an authoritarian government and the "Anschluss," it is an overstatement to claim that economic policy was directly responsible for poor performance, and in turn, directly for Nazi success. *Again, while it is certainly true that deflationary policy harmed recovery, it is suggested here that its role has been overestimated. First of all, policy and its results were not a whole lot different from economic policy in most other, economically more successful, industrialised countries, save the countries with authoritarian fascist regimes.[293] Therefore, there must be another explanation for poor recovery. Moreover, an expansionist policy was hardly possible, because economic policy-making was restricted by financial and social constraints. Secondly, since policy could only function in the small framework of the Austrian national economy, its potential impact in the case of more expansionist measures would have been small. In other words, effective counter-cyclical policy was not possible in a small and export dependent country surrounded by high tariff walls and other trade restrictions. The scale of fiscal expansion and spending necessary to counteract the deficit of foreign demand would have been far too large to be realised. Thirdly, it is argued that poor performance can be mainly attributed to structural shifts and distortions described above. They manifested themselves in the formation of economic nationalism outside of Austria, resulting in a major contraction and then stagnation of trade, Austrian exports, and of capital supply. This in turn resulted in a stagnation of progress of the Austrian export structure, composition and direction, not providing an incentive to industrial development. Unlike the larger industrialised countries, Austrian industry did not have the option to turn to domestically stimulated growth and development. A stimulus for structural*

Gegenteil der keynesianischen Krisenlösung des Nationalsozialismus." Weber, Wirtschaftspolitik, 550 and 548.

292 Calculated from Österreichisches Institut für Wirtschaftsforschung, *Monatsberichte* 14, 42

293 Stiefel claims that international economic theory and policy had changed radically in the 30s, but that Austria had not adjusted to this at all: "Die Weltwirtschaftskrise wurde allgemein als Wendepunkt in Wirtschaftstheorie und Wirtschaftsauffassung betrachtet. Zwischen 1930 und 1935 liegen in der Wirtschaftspolitik Welten. Nicht aber so in Österreich. Die österreichische Wirtschaftspolitik hatte aus der Weltwirtschaftskrise keine Schlüsse gezogen." Stiefel, *Konjunkturelle Entwicklung*, 80. Fritz Weber claims that basically only Austria clung to a policy of balanced budget and stable currency. "Investitionsverhalten," 547.

transformation and growth could only come from outside, i. e. increasing demand from its most important trading partners. This does not mean, however, that a more expansionist policy would not have been possible at all, or would not have alleviated the situation. Spending, especially for social welfare, the unemployed or for investments for industrial modernisation, would have been possible, but would not have greatly improved Austrian recovery.

5.7.1. Austrian and European Policy in Comparison

To compare government spending policies of countries in which economic structures and financial circumstances were completely different is quite difficult. Generally, though, the principles of a balanced budget, currency and price stability, which have been regarded as a particularly Austrian feature,[294] were also upheld in almost all free market economies in Europe, at least until large scale rearmament began after 1936. Of course, Austrian policy was extremely orthodox compared to the spending policy of the rearming authoritarian states, Russia and the US. Certainly, Austrian policy was highly restrictive, but not much more so than in Great Britain, France and all other gold bloc countries.[295] As we have seen above, France tried its utmost to keep its deficit to a minimum and followed a deflationary policy until 1936. Britain was able to maintain a considerable budget surplus during most of the 30s. As in Austria, in both countries government investment and work creation programmes were small and ineffective.

It is very complicated to compare government spending in the 30s. According to contemporary figures from the German statistical office, Austrian spending seems to have been within a group of countries with average increases in spending. Only American, German and Russian spending behaviour was truly expansionist. In Austria, spending policy was as restrictive as British, Italian, and Czechoslovak policies. Between 1932 and 1936, Austrian spending for economy and infrastructure increased 13.5%. Meanwhile, it rose 20.8% in Britain, 8.6% in Italy and only 6.1% in Czechoslovakia. Until 1937, Austrian public spending behaviour was even more generous than in the Czechoslovak Republic, Italy and Britain, where expenditure even slightly dropped. At the same time, Belgium tripled and France more than doubled its spending for economy and infrastructure. Until 1937, total government spending among this group of countries with generally low government expenditure increased the most in Belgium (17.5%) and France (17%), followed by Britain (9%). Austrian and Italian total public expenditure rose 4.3 and 3.3% respectively. In contrast, total public spending in the US increased 38%, 124% in Germany and even 216% in Soviet Russia.[296]

294 Mattl, 142.

295 Butschek does not regard Austrian economic policy as particularly restrictive and accentuates employment creation programmes of the 30s that resulted in deficits amounting to between 1.7% and 2.7% of GNP. *Die österreichische Wirtschaft im 20. Jahrhundert*, Vienna 1985, 56.

296 All percentages calculated from Statistisches Reichsamt, *Jahrbuch 1937*, 260–265 (international survey). Figure for Germany calculated from Overy, *Recovery*, 42.

Credit availability in different European countries was much more similar in the 30s than in 20s, as international capital markets lay idle. Generally, interest rates were very low everywhere. In this atmosphere, Austrian currency policy also does not appear to have been unusually deflationary or restrictive. Germany had a discount rate of 4%. Belgium and Britain had the most favourable rates of between 2 and 3%. Austrian central bank interest rate was only a bit higher than the French, which was between 3.5% and 5%.[297] The Austrian national bank dropped its discount rate to 4% in early 1935, the lowest level since its foundation.[298]

According to Kernbauer, there was also no restrictive effect from the Austrian central bank money supply. In the 30s, the index of the volume of central bank money was always higher than GNP index.[299] Between 1932 and 1937, volume of central bank money increased 20.6%, while GNP grew 7.8%.[300] The stock of money had already been increased substantially in the 20s and until the depression, when it remained on a stable level. Between 1933 and 1937, it was expanded considerably once again by 11%.[301] This was an expansion according to economic growth. GNP grew 11.6% in the same time span.[302]

The reluctant currency devaluation after 1931 has often been regarded as deflationary. Currency stability has been made directly responsible for declining and stagnating Austrian exports.[303] Between 1931 and 1933, the devaluation of the schilling was milder than in most countries that artificially adhered to the gold parity. Austria also did not participate in the general movement of currency devaluation in 1935 and 1936 of almost all gold bloc countries. Until September 1936, these countries had depreciated between 13.5 and 32.5%.[304]

However, the schilling seemed to have been overvalued only after 1936, when the economy actually began to thrive again. Moreover, as we have seen, devaluation in France only had a temporary positive effect on the competitive position. Until then, the artificial overvaluation of the schilling was less harmful than often believed. Eventually, the privately conducted foreign exchange business after 1932, allowed between importers and exporters, already devalued the schilling 25%.[305] During the depression and until 1935/36, the schilling parity, compared to Austria's most important trading partners, remained stable and favourable. The schilling par-

297 Statistisches Reichsamt, *Jahrbuch 1938*, 256–257 (international survey). Butschek also regards Austrian interest rate as moderately low. *Die österreichische Wirtschaft im 20. Jahrhundert*, 57.

298 *Bilanzen*, 23.3.1935, 189.

299 Kernbauer, *Währungspolitik*, 402.

300 Ibid. Own calculation from Österreichisches Institut für Wirtschaftsforschung, *Monatsberichte* 14, 42.

301 Butschek, *Die österreichische Wirtschaft im 20. Jahrhundert*, 57.

302 Own calculation from Österreichisches Institut für Wirtschaftsforschung, *Monatsberichte* 14, 42.

303 Kernbauer, "Österreichische Währungs-, Bank- und Budgetpolitik in der Zwischenkriegszeit," 564 and 568.

304 Kernbauer, *Währungspolitik*, 402–403.

305 Reprint of a series of articles in the *Manchester Guardian Commercial* between July 1936 and January 1937, "The Economics of Isolation," in: *The Annals of the American Academy of Political and Social Science. The United States and World War*, Vol. 193, Philadelphia 1937, 172.

ity against the French and Belgian franc almost remained stable until 1935, when the French franc actually appreciated against the schilling. The exchange rate with one of Austria's most important trading partners, Germany, was favourable. The reichsmark actually appreciated considerably after 1934, by roughly 30%, as a result of strict German exchange control. The same can be said for the Swiss franc, which appreciated against the Austrian currency after 1934. The Italian lira fluctuated in the 30s, but had, on average, a higher parity than in the 20s. The Zloty fluctuated and the Lei, Lew and Dinar slightly depreciated against the schilling. Only the dollar (–41% between 1932 and 1935) and the pound (roughly –25% between 1931 and 1935) seriously depreciated against the schilling, but only a fraction of Austrian exports was sold in these countries.[306] For example, only between 1.5 and 2.5% of Austrian exports went to the US in the 30s.[307] Apart from its parity to the reichsmark, the schilling was only seriously overvalued after 1936, so that most European currencies had devalued against the schilling.

Compared to 1930, depreciation in 1936 ranged from only 5% for the Lei to 32% for the lira.[308] In all, it is hard to believe that these currency fluctuations were the primary reason for stagnant Austrian exports and growth after the depression, especially since devaluation only seriously disfavoured Austrian exporters after 1936, when parts of Austrian industrial sectors had recovered their 1929 level of production. In fact, despite apparent overvaluation, exports rose 28% in 1937. Furthermore, the stable Austrian schilling made foreign debt servicing much easier and improved the balance of payments position as imports had become cheaper or remained stable.

Even if the Austrian government had been willing to pursue an expansionist policy, it was limited by practical constraints.[309] Its small gold and foreign exchange reserve and substantial and permanent balance of payments deficit would not have permitted the state to raise enough capital funds to conduct an at least half-way effective counter-cyclical policy without triggering an inflation. This was especially the case as credibility was low after the major financial crisis of 1931. Even with conservative fiscal policy, about half of all foreign exchange liabilities were withdrawn from Austria between 1932 and 1937.[310] Besides capital scarcity, the country had sustained a large trade deficit in the 20s, which could only be lowered substantially until 1937. Even Great Britain, a much larger country with much greater capital funds, could not pursue an expansionist policy, due to similar, but less severe financial limitations. The only option available to the Austrian government would have been reckless reflationary credit expansion for state investment, similar to that in Nazi Germany. However, in the light of bank crashes, credibility crisis and fear of inflation an expansionist monetary policy was out of the question.[311]

306 Schneider, Schwarzer and Denzel, *Währungen der Welt II*, 280–317.

307 Österreichisches Statistisches Zentralamt, *Aussenhandel*, 80.

308 Kernbauer, *Währungspolitik*, 405.

309 See also Borchardt's arguments of policy constraints in Germany in 1930/31, chapter 2. Butschek discusses this argument, *Die österreichische Wirtschaft im 20. Jahrhundert*, 55.

310 Dieter Stiefel, "Utopie und Realität. Die Wirtschaftspolitik des Ständestaates," in: *Tirol und der Anschluß. Vorraussetzungen, Entwicklungen, Rahmenbedingungen 1918–1938*, Innsbruck 1988, 413.

311 Contrary to this argument, März and Szecsi (page 330) believe that it would have been possible

Not only was capital scarcity a constraint to policy-making, but also the large deficit of the balance of payments combined with the collapse of the financial system, international lending and trade, strongly reduced the room for manoeuvre of recovery policies. In the 1920s, Austria had an average annual import surplus of approximately up to half a billion schillings, which was, besides invisible exports and the sale of foreign assets, largely financed by the inflow of long-term and short-term foreign capital. From 1924 until 1929, annual trade deficits had amounted to between 6 and 12% of national product.[312] Between 1924 and 1930, the country received long-term foreign credits running to 1116.6 million schillings. By the end of 1930, short-term foreign credits amounted to 1750 million schillings.[313] In April 1931, shortly before the onset of the international financial crisis, the Austrian banks held short-term credits worth 822 million schillings.[314] Naturally, the contraction of international lending beginning in 1928 and the complete breakdown of international lending after mid-1931, coinciding with a collapse of international trade and exports, hit Austria severely and had a massive deflationary impact. The result was a serious constraint on policy-making after 1933.

5.7.2. Trade Dependence and Performance in Austria and Europe

Even if an expansionist policy would not have been constrained by financial problems, it would not have been possible to counteract the massive deficit of demand from foreign trade. Whereas Germany or the United States could utilise deficit spending to spark off domestic demand, in Austria, this option was not available. Advanced small countries partially experienced the secular shift, but usually did not enjoy higher demand and growth, firstly, because other nations practised economic nationalism and shut off their markets, and secondly, because small countries were unable to compensate the deficit of demand from trade. To understand this process, it is necessary to look at the development of Austrian and European export rates and national growth after 1932. The first distinctive change is certainly the decline of the share of exports of national income in all countries. For a comparison, we will use 1936, a year when considerable recovery from the depression had taken place (see table 5.1.)

Between 1928 and 1936, average export rates of the smaller countries declined faster than those of the larger industrialised countries. That advanced small countries

to utilise state credit for large work creation programmes after 1933/34. Many authors also resent that a large portion of the international loan of 175 million schillings floated by the state in 1933 (Trefferanleihe) was used for debt service. These sums, however, even if they had been completely employed to direct investment and work creation, were far too small to have had any impact on recovery. Weber, "Staatliche Wirtschaftspolitik," 547. Butschek agrees with my view. *Die österreichische Wirtschaft im 20. Jahrhundert*, 57.

312 Österreichisches Institut für Wirtschaftsforschung, *Monatsberichte* 14, 25. This study referrred to "verfügbares Güter- und Leistungsvolumen," which was roughly equal to GNP.

313 Kernbauer, *Währungspolitik*, 245.

314 "Das Donauproblem II," in: Deutsches Institut für Konjunkturforschung, *Wochenbericht*, vol. 5, no. 6, Berlin 1932, 24.

relied heavily on foreign trade for economic growth can be seen in the lower growth rates of these countries, at a time when foreign trade was stagnating. Although the average export rate (20%) was substantially higher, the average growth rate of Austria, Belgium, Czechoslovakia and Denmark was just 10.3%. It is also interesting to note that the most industrialised successor states of the Austro-Hungarian Empire had a much lower export rate than advanced small countries in Western Europe. This reveals their still lower level of integration into the modern international economic system of trade, and provides yet another reason for their poor performance.

	Austria	Belgium	Czechoslovakia	Denmark
Export Value	1379	19,745	8036	1327
Gross National Product	9319	59,800	64,900	6543
GDP Growth Rate 1932–1937	7.8%	9.7%	9.7%	14%
Export Share of GNP	14.8%	33%	12.4%	20%

	Germany	France	UK	Italy
Export Value	6550	15,492	441	5.5
Gross National Product	79,171	371,000	5100	126.6
GDP Growth Rate 1932–1937	50.4%	7.8%	23%	16.4%
Export Share of GNP	8.3%	4.2%	8.6%	4.4%

Table 5.1.: Relation of exports to national product and growth in 1936 (in million national currency at current prices). Source: Data from Mitchell, *European Historical Statistics*, 295 ff and 407 ff. Data for Austria from Österreichisches Institut für Wirtschaftsforschung, *Monatsberichte* 14, 41, at current prices. Data for Belgium for the year 1927. GNP of Czechoslovakia at constant 1929 prices. GDP growth rates 1932–1937 calculated according to data from Maddison, "Measuring Long Term Growth," 114–115. GDP growth rate of Czechoslovakia calculated from Mitchell, 410. GNP of Germany according to figures from Ritschl and Spoerer, "Das Bruttosozialprodukt," 44

The large countries, Germany, France, the United Kingdom and Italy enjoyed an average rate of growth of 24.4%, even though their average value of exports was only 6.4% of national income. In the 20s, their average export rate had been twice as high. Their growth rate was higher, because most of these countries were able to focus economic expansion on the resources and demand of their large domestic markets. Trade was of only secondary importance to them. It was far easier to incite sufficient domestic demand for higher growth and structural change, than in national economies where production facilities were essentially not only designed to supply the domestic market, but also to generate income from exports to foreign markets. Moreover, a reduction of trade also hit a small country more severely, because export industries everywhere suffered much more from contracting trade than industries producing for home markets.[315] As Austria had a relatively large export industry, the country's vulnerability to the decline of international trade in manufactured and semi-finished articles was far greater than in almost all other industrialised coun-

315 League of Nations, *World Production and Prices 1925–1933*, 6.

tries. Small countries simply could not turn to the option of concentrating growth on their national economies with the help of policy, since the home market was far too small for domestic production capacities. This phenomenon is one major alternative explanation for poor Austrian performance.

The processes of contracting world trade, domestically oriented growth, retrenched, protectionist, nationalist economies and trade restriction among the large industrialised countries in the 30s, combined with the naturally high export rate of small advanced countries, were the main factors contributing to Austria's economic decline and inability to recover.

For the Austrian government, therefore, it was impossible to compensate a loss of foreign trade demand that amounted to around 20% of national income, which was the average annual value of exports in the 20s, or about half of Austrian industrial production, the usual portion of industrial output sold abroad.[316] As export demand dropped dramatically already in 1930 and hardly recovered after 1933, Austria was heavily hit by the massive decline of world trade. Recovery was barely possible when volume of world trade only slowly recovered. In 1936, it only reached 86% of the value of world trade and only 59% of its 1929 level.[317] Value of Austrian exports in 1936 only reached 60.4% of its pre-depression level, but was still higher than the value of exports of most European industrialised countries, which on average, only reached about 46.5% of their 1929 export value level.[318] The vital difference, though, is that many of these countries were not as dependent on foreign trade. When Austrian export figures increased considerably in 1937, it was mainly due to higher foreign demand from greater armament expenditure in neighbouring countries, especially Italy and Germany.

Therefore, the major source of income and most important generator of a multiplication and accelerator effect for growth and structural change, export sales, was harshly curtailed by the precipitous reduction of imports of its most important trading partners. The consequence was a fatal loss of export demand that could not be compensated. In the period of most dramatic export contraction, between 1929 and 1933, the average annual deficit of export demand, compared to its 1929 level, amounted to more than 707 million schillings. That was about 6% of 1929 GNP. In the worst year, 1933, the export demand deficit amounted to 1037 million schillings. Between 1934 and 1937, the average annual export deficit compared to 1929 level was even 850.5 million. It would have been impossible for national economic policy to even attempt to substitute this loss, neither before nor after 1933. For the Austrian government that would have entailed the compensation of a loss of aggregate demand of more than 6.2 billion schillings between 1930 and 1937![319] Only the annexation of Austria, the ensuing incorporation into the German economy and aggressive economic policy

316 Kernbauer, *Währungspolitik*, 289.

317 Deutsches Institut für Konjunkturforschung, *Wochenbericht*, no. 26, 1937, 146.

318 Own calculation from Österreichisches Institut für Wirtschaftsforschung, *Monatsberichte* 14, 42, and *Wochenbericht*, no. 26, 1937, 146. This is the average taken from 11 industrialised European countries as calculated by the German business cycle research institute.

319 All values in 1937 schillings. Numbers calculated from Österreichisches Institut für Wirtschaftsforschung, *Monatsberichte* 14, 42.

brought a compensation for the massive deficit of demand. In 1937, the theoretical deficit of demand amounted to 549 schillings compared to the 1929 export level.[320] The following year, after the Nazi take-over, the Austrian economy benefited from 750 million schillings worth of German state orders and investments, or nearly 8% of 1937 GNP.[321] In 1939, unemployment in Austria was virtually wiped out.

5.7.3. Export Structure and Direction

Austrian recovery and progress of industrial modernisation was not only slowed down by decline and stagnation of exports, but also by a stagnation of the structure of trade demand and trade direction. This was a direct result of structural distortions and concentration of growth and development in domestic markets of Austria's most important trading partners. This expressed itself in the highly protectionist trade policy described earlier. As we have observed in chapter 2, in the 20s these processes, which began to harm Austrian exports, mainly occurred in the under-developed and semi-developed successor states and other Eastern European countries. The hastened transformation toward increasing industrialisation, harsh protectionism and consequential overproduction were the main causes. Since these countries did not absorb the majority of Austrian foreign trade and most other areas in Europe formed moderately free trade areas, generally foreign demand was still the main source of progressing growth and industrial development in Austria until 1930.

After 1933, though, these processes of distorted structural shifts occurred, to varying degrees, in almost all countries and were accompanied everywhere by trade restrictions. Moreover, as noted above, Austria's immediate neighbours and most vital trading partners, Italy and Germany, were the main representatives of these changes. The overall consequence for Austria was not only a decline, but a further distortion and dislocation of its main source of demand. This, in turn, directly affected the domestic process of secular structural change. The main point is that, unlike the larger advanced European countries, the Austrian economic structure was directly affected by changes among its neighbouring countries. When these experienced distorted structural shifts, Austria also underwent a similar process. However, in the 30s, this shift could result in higher demand and growth in the large countries, because the transformation was, as already noted, domestically generated and concentrated. Not so in Austria, because the stimulation from stagnating and static foreign demand was far too low for higher rates of growth, as well as for progress in industrial change.

When examining the export structure of the 30s, this development is evident. Taking the year 1936 to scrutinise the export structure, the first distinctive characteristic is the static, unchanging, or slightly deteriorating, composition and direction of foreign trade (see table 5.2). Basically, the unbalanced structure of exports remained unchanged. There was no substantial demand for new types of products and ser-

320 Calculated from ibid, 42.

321 Butschek, *Die österreichische Wirtschaft im 20. Jahrhundert*, 60. Felix Butschek, *Die österreichische Wirtschaft 1938 bis 1945*, Vienna 1978, 57.

vices that would have forced large sectors of the economy to adopt new production methods, new technology and to increase productivity. Once foreign demand finally increased in 1936 and 1937, it was mainly demand for products used for rearmament, which certainly did not help improving and advancing industrial structures in Austria. This type of demand increased in the mid 30s, simply because the rearming states were fully utilising their industrial capacity by this time.

	Export Commodity	Share of Total Exports
1.	Textiles	26.8%
2.	Iron and Metal Goods	15.3%
3.	Advanced Finished Products	12.3%
4.	Wood	8.8%
5.	Paper	7.9%

Table 5.2.: The five most important export items in 1936 and their share of the value of overall exports. Source: Own calculation from Österreichisches Statistisches Zentralamt, *Aussenhandel,* 36–72. Percentage share of textiles excludes semi-finished textile products. Advanced finished products includes electrical machinery and consumer goods, other machinery, cars and engines, rubber goods and chemicals. Data for paper for 1937.

For some sectors of the Austrian industry, this development meant that demand increased for exports of raw materials (e.g. wood, magnesite and iron ore) or for semi-manufactured products (e.g. raw iron and steel). Therefore, there was hardly a need to adopt new production methods, and usually only the older, more traditional branches of industry benefited. Furthermore, demand was still so low that the industrial sectors benefiting from new demand, could simply re-employ idle capacity. No necessity for an improvement of productivity and competitiveness existed. When analysing company development below, this process is obvious. As in the 20s, textile products were still the dominant export item. Unlike 1928, though, iron and metal goods became the second most important products sold abroad. The share of advanced finished products had slightly declined.

The direction of Austrian trade also remained static (see tables 5.3 and 5.4). The only marked difference was a greater importance for outbound trade of Western European industrialised countries and a declining reliance on imports from Germany and Italy.

Year	Advanced: G/It/CSR	Semi-industrialised: H/P	Under-developed: B/Y/R	Western Europe:	Rest:
1928	38.8	14.0	14.1	14.4	18.7
1936	36.8	14.1	13.1	17.9	18.1

Table 5.3.: Percentage share of groups of countries of the total value of Austrian exports in 1928 and 1936. Source: calculation from Österreichisches Statistisches Zentralamt, *Aussenhandel*, 34. Advanced countries are Germany, Italy and the CSR. Hungary and Poland are regarded as semi-industrialised countries. Under-developed countries are Bulgaria, Yugoslavia and Romania. The Western European countries trading with Austria are Britain, France, Switzerland, Belgium, Denmark and the Netherlands.

Year	Advanced: G/It/CSR	Semi-industrialised: H/P	Under-developed: B/Y/R	Western Europe:	Rest:
1928	41.5	17.5	9.4	12.9	18.7
1936	33.0	15.2	14.7	14.3	22.8

Table 5.4.: Percentage share of groups of countries of the total value of Austrian imports in 1928 and 1936. Source: see Table 5.3. [279]

Year	textiles	iron and metal goods	advanced products	rest	exports
32	204.7	94.9	101.1	363.7	764.4
33		100.1	101.3	341.5	772.6
34		121.0	110.1	396.3	857.0
35		126.2	111.2	428.0	895.0
36		133.7	112.6	475.0	951.0
37	254.7	213.8	135.9	612.5	1216.9

Table 5.5.: Exports of textiles, iron and metal goods and of advanced finished products in million schillings, 1932–1937. Source: All values calculated from Österreichisches Statistisches Zentralamt, *Aussenhandel*, 36–72. Value of exports only include merchandise traffic and excludes services (blind exports). For textiles, data is only available for two years. Advanced finished products are electrical machinery, other machinery, cars and engines, rubber and chemicals. Due to lack of data, for chemicals the average export values of 1932 and 1937 have been taken for each year.

Thus, not only was there a substantial retardation of growth from the fall of overall exports, but there was also no incentive for larger changes in industrial structures, from a possible variation and improvement of the composition and direction of trade, i.e. a shift to an increasing share of advanced products or more highly developed markets. Such a change and improvement of trade demand could usually be expected within ten years, or during an upswing. Moreover, the development of export demand in the 30s only offered a moderate incentive of growth and change for traditional industries, and only a very small incentive to growth for modern industries. This process is revealed in table 5.5.

Whereas advanced products' volume of exports only rose moderately and had a declining share of exports, goods from traditional industries, raw materials and semi-manufactured goods either maintained a high portion of overall exports or doubled and tripled their export volume. One of the most important export items, textiles, expanded more than 24%. Exports of iron and metal goods increased 125%. The goods from traditional industries and raw materials and semi-manufactured goods (under the heading "Rest" in the table above) also made up an increasing portion of overall exports. Their volume rose nearly 70% and their overall share rose from 47.6% to more than 50% between 1932 and 1937. The main items were wood, wood products and paper (274 million schillings in 1937), whose share of overall exports remained around 20%. Other vital exports items were magnesite, magnesite brick and raw iron (68 million schillings in 1937). Sales of magnesite and magnesite brick were doubled and more than tripled. The overall export share of iron and metal goods increased from 12.4 to 17.7%, between 1932 and 1937. At the same time, even though their volume expanded 34.4%, advanced finished products' growth started from very low levels, and their share of total exports declined from 13 to 11%.

5.7.4. Conclusion

In conclusion, it is clear that the main causes for Austrian economic stagnation cannot be found in economic policy deficiencies. First of all, there were strong policy constraints to expansionist measures. Secondly, Austrian economic policy was within the average trend of policy-making of other, economically more successful, European countries. Thirdly, there were no possibilities to alleviate the massive main problems of recovery, as these mostly lay outside of the sphere of action of Austrian policy makers. The main reasons for poor performance was mainly the high vulnerability of small countries to declining and stagnating international trade, which caused a massive underutilisation of industrial production capacity. That Austria was affected by these problems more than most other small advanced countries was not surprising, considering that its level of productivity and competitiveness was already low in the late 20s. The decline and the shift of foreign demand to more basic goods and products of the traditional industries accentuated the deceleration of the secular transition of industrial structures or the "process of creative destruction." There were only a few incentives to invest in new technology and innovation, as the motivation and pressure from demand to improve productivity and competitiveness and to change production methods were low. In the fifth and last chapter, we will observe this process of stagnating shift of industrial structures when analysing company history in the 30s.

6. ECONOMIC RECOVERY, STRUCTURAL DISTORTIONS AND MICROECONOMIC DEVELOPMENT IN AUSTRIA DURING THE DEPRESSION UNTIL 1938

6.1. GENERAL DEVELOPMENT AND INVESTMENT BEHAVIOUR

In this chapter, we want to analyse how and if budget, currency and trade policy in Austria and abroad harmed microeconomic development during depression and recovery. It is also interesting to understand how enterprises dealt with severe crisis shocks.

As in nearly all countries, in Austria, the depression and incomplete recovery in the 30s proved a serious catastrophe for all industrial sectors. Not only did they undergo an unprecedented slump, but almost all enterprises were unable to recover from this blow before 1938. Pre-depression investment, demand and production levels were never reached again. Production capacity remained under-employed and unchanged. It is safe to say that the process of secular transformation of increasing growth of new industries and application of new technologies drastically slowed down, if not stopped altogether in the 1930s. The retreat of Austria's most important trading partners to economic nationalism and domestic growth and the protectionist economic policies that went along with this process, directly harmed Austria's export oriented enterprises. Furthermore, the export demand structure reflected the effort of rearmament of its immediate neighbours and distorted economic development as it tended to favour growth of traditional heavy industries. Surprisingly though, most enterprises survived the depression and were able to cope and adjust to stagnating growth and development in the 30s.

Performance of different industrial sectors was quite different. By and large, the traditional consumer industries tended to stagnate, while basic industries and capital goods industries enjoyed higher rates of growth. Between 1933 and 1937, growth rates of most industrial sectors were considerable. However, this only appears so, because production of nearly all branches had fallen so low until 1933. Starting off from incredibly low production levels after precipitous decline, vehicles production, for example, expanded nearly five times. Iron production increased 166%, iron and steel processing 98%, output of the paper industry rose 22% and textiles and leather output rose 49%.

However, when comparing production levels of 1929 and 1937, the picture is wholly different. Almost all industrial sectors had still not recovered pre-depression production levels by 1937. The iron and steel processing industry, the wood industry, the chemical industry and the vehicle manufacturing industry were still all roughly around 30% below 1929 production levels. Only mining, oil, magnesite and the iron producing industry nearly recovered pre-crisis output levels. Among other traditional industries only paper (7.8%) and textiles (17%) surpassed pre-depression levels. Of the modern industries only electricity supply expanded output (17.6%).[1]

Since capacity was under-utilised and business activity low, the incentive for investment and depreciation was also low. Between 1933 and 1937, aggregate investment rose from 473 million to 721 million, but only reached 57% of the already low 1929 investment level. Annual investment rate was merely between 5.1 and 7.4%, whereas it had been 9.9% in 1929.[2] Whereas productive capital asset had been moderately increased in the later 20s with investment rates of between 5 and 10%, there was an actual reduction of capital asset during the depression. Thereafter, low profit prospects induced companies to lower depreciation and investment. Its rate was below 5%, which resulted in general stagnation and deterioration of productive assets.[3]

6.2. TRADITIONAL INDUSTRIES

6.2.1. Iron and Steel Producing Industry

The effects of policy and long-term structural distortion were once again most noticeable among the traditional industries, especially the iron and steel producing industry. Because this industry benefited from policies of rearmament, it underwent a process of distortion due to disproportionate expansion in the late 30s. Its production capacities remained under-employed until the mid 30s and enjoyed a sudden and enormous spurt of demand after 1936. This recovery, based on a rearmament boom, was short, uncertain and stood on feet of clay. Furthermore, it was not predicated on viable economic considerations.

Even though the iron and steel producing sector did not quite reach pre-depression levels, it had, besides vehicle manufacturing, the highest production growth rate between 1933 and 1937. In 1937, the production level of iron ore in Austria, which just about reached the 1929 level, was actually well above the European average. Most states began to rearm quite late and output levels were high only in the authoritarian states. In France, output performance was even lower than in Austria. Production was about a quarter below pre-crisis level. Czechoslovak output was nearly 38% below the 1929 level. Of the large liberal advanced countries, only Britain barely surpassed 1929 output, with only 7.5% above pre-crisis level. Contrary to that, Germany, undergoing its substantial rearmament-led recovery, was able to recover its iron ore production level already by 1936 and surpassed the 1929 output level by more than half in the following year.[4]

1 Own calculation from Österreichisches Institut für Wirtschaftsforschung, *Monatsberichte* 14, 12; and Statistisches Reichsamt, *Jahrbuch 1938*, 83 and 85 (international survey).

2 Österreichisches Institut für Wirtschaftsforschung, *Monatsberichte* 14, 18–19.

3 Mosser, "Wachstumsstrategie," 106–112.

4 For Austria, see *Monatsberichte des Österreichischen Instituts für Wirtschaftsforschung*, issue 10/12, Vienna 1946, 107. For data for the rest of Europe see Statistisches Reichsamt, *Jahrbuch 1938*, 64 (international survey). Especially for Germany see: "Die Eisenindustrie im Jahre 1936," in: Statistisches Reichsamt (ed.), *Wirtschaft und Statistik*, vol. 17, no. 22, 1937, 882–883.

In Austria, raw iron output was 16% below and raw steel production 3% above pre-depression levels in 1937. Production substantially surpassed 1929 output levels only after it was integrated into the German war economy in 1938.[5] Nevertheless, this performance was still far better than output performance of most European countries. In Belgium, raw steel production in 1937 was just 94% of 1929 output. Raw iron production was still 5% lower than in 1929. In France, raw steel output was 81.5% and raw iron 76% of the 1929 production. Italy only barely recovered pre-crisis raw steel production. Even US output remained far below 1929 levels. Only German (+21%) and British (+34.5%) raw steel production recovered considerably. German raw iron production was 20.5% and British 12% higher than in 1929.[6]

It seemed that the world iron and steel producing industries were only barely able to recover. By and large, most iron and steel producers experienced an unprecedented decline of production until 1932 and a fast and drastic upswing between 1932 and 1937, but were unable to match late 1920s production. Generally, substantial excess capacities persisted and only those industries in countries enjoying a massive upswing and rearmament demand experienced high growth.[7] In general, for European production, export played a decreasing role, as national producers focused on home markets. The Austrian industry, however, continued to depend upon, and benefited from, foreign demand.

International trade in, and prices of, raw iron and steel were organised by the international raw steel export community, a successor organisation of the international raw steel community of the 20s. It was founded in 1933 and enlarged in 1935 (also including the British and Polish national producers), by which time it controlled nearly all European iron exporters and between 80 and 85% of world iron exports.[8] The largest Austrian producer, Alpine, concluded agreements with this organisation.[9] However, Austrian export performance was low and erratic overall. Export volume recovered and surpassed pre-crisis level only by 1937 (+49%), the year when rearmament demand really began to pick up. Until 1935, export of raw iron remained stagnant and only a fraction of the volume and value of the 20s.[10]

a. Alpine The Alpine Montangesellschaft,[11] producing the majority of Austrian raw iron and ore, remained one of the most dominating enterprises in the Austrian

5 "Wirtschaftsprobleme undWirtschaftserfolge in der Ostmark," in: Deutsches Institut für Konjunkturforschung, *Wochenbericht*, vol. 12, no. 21, Berlin 1939, 137.

6 Statistisches Reichsamt, *Jahrbuch 1938*, 75 (international survey). For Austria see: *Monatsberichte*, issue 10/12, Vienna 1946, 107. For Germany also see: *Statistisches Handbuch von Deutschland*, 188, and Overy, *War and Economy*, 117.

7 See the report on the international iron producing industry: "Die Eisen schaffende Industrie des In- und Auslandes im Juni/Juli und im Halbjahr 1937," in: Statistisches Reichsamt (ed.), *Wirtschaft und Statistik*, vol. 17, no. 15, 1937, 621–622.

8 "Zur Neuordnung der internationalen Eisenverträge," in: Deutsches Institut für Konjunkturforschung, *Wochenbericht*, vol. 8, no. 39, Berlin 1935, 153.

9 Bachinger and Matis, "Strukturwandel," 136.

10 Österreichisches Statistisches Zentralamt, *Aussenhandel*, 63.

11 *Bilanzen*, 1.8.1931, 4.6.1932, 24.6.1933, 16.6.1934, 30.6.1934, 1.12.1934, 28.9.1935, 11.4.1936,

economy, with about 5% of total industrial capital stock, or 21% of capital stock of all iron and metal producing joint stock companies in 1932.[12] The shock of the depression on output and performance was indeed tremendous. It was a sad story of simultaneous decline, basically among all branches of production. All future plans of investment, rationalisation and modernisation had to be discarded. Especially the programme of electrification could not be carried out.

Financial Standing

Throughout the recovery period of 1925–1929, it had not been possible to raise productivity and competitiveness to international standards, and profits remained low. The company hardly consolidated by the late 20s and still had low profit margins. The depression shattered even these small improvements. Had it already been difficult to make an at least small profit in the late 20s, in 1931, it was barely possible to balance losses and income. As business declined between mid 1929 until late 1933, it was possible to reduce expenses commensurately to falling gross profits only until 1931. Thereafter, expenses could not be further reduced, entailing massive annual deficits of between 6.7 and 7.5 million schillings. These were covered by capital reserves. It took until 1936 to make a very small profit. Before the crisis, profitability had been slightly less than 10%. Thereafter, it did not recover until 1936, when it reached only 2.6% of gross profits.

Even these poor financial results could only be maintained by drastically cutting all expenses, especially labour costs and investments. The workforce was reduced from 13,400 to 4000 until June 1932. Investments were cut 91% between 1929 and 1931. In 1936, when production had recovered, investments were still only 21% of their 1929 level. The already low average annual investment had been nearly 9 million in the 20s. In the depression decade, it was not even a third of this sum. As a result of sudden massive Italian and German rearmament demand, investments only recovered in 1937 to 20 million schillings. Certainly depreciation was also reduced, but after 1931 its rate was maintained on a higher level than before 1929.

Even though the Alpine already had financial difficulties in the period of relative prosperity, surprisingly its financial standing did not seriously worsen immediately during the depression. In the first catastrophic year, 1931, it was possible to reduce bank debts by half. Total debts were still easily covered by outstanding debts and stocks. Bank debts and bonded debt were only about half of capital resources. However, liabilities remained well above debtors value until 1936. Although business declined, creditors value remained high. The financial standing deteriorated once the company had to sustain three years of consecutive massive losses and altogether five years of no profit. In 1933, finances seriously worsened. Excluding foreign loans, overall debts increased to 28.5 million, 13.3 of which were bank debts. Thus, total

27.6.1936, 1.8.1936, 5.9.1936, 2.1.1937, 20.3.1937, 17.4.1937, 12.6.1937, 3.7.1937, 7.8.1937, 25.9.1937, 25.12.1937. See also A.2 and A.3.

12 Own calculation based on Alpine stock capital (60 million schillings) share of overall joint stock capital as listed in: Bundesamt für Statistik, *Statistisches Handbuch für den Bundesstaat Österreich*, vol. 15, 1935, 112.

debts amounted to half of capital stock (60 million) and to nearly a third of capital resources. Not even the dollar devaluation in 1933 resulted in a reduction of the five million dollar loan that had been floated in the mid 20s, since this bond was signed on gold dollars.[13] Therefore, parity remained 7.1 schillings to one dollar, even though market parity was 4.9 to one or even lower thereafter.[14] Bond value remained 35 million schillings.

Until 1935, financial standing did not improve. Bank debts, for example, still amounted to 12 million schillings. To cover losses, capital reserves had dropped from about 34 to 20 million. The only positive aspect was the fact that debt service expenses had declined by about a third, due to reduction of the discount rate. Due to slowly recovering business activity, financial standing began to improve only by 1936. Rising income and the first profit in six years enabled management to quickly lower bank credit to 1.7 million schillings. To further reduce debt service payments, a portion of the shares of the dollar bond was purchased. Overall debts had declined to about half of their very high 1929 level. In the last two years before annexation, the profit and loss account and the balance sheet were nearly consolidated.

Business activity

In 1931, the decline of the domestic and international markets and the reduction of public and industrial investment had direct implications on Alpine business activity. Sales dropped precipitously. Sales of finished iron and steel products declined between 30 and 35%, and sales of raw iron by half. Export of iron ore came to a standstill. Sales of coal could only be kept up by reducing prices. Net turnover of exports fell from 100.9 to 70.7 million schillings. The volume of unfilled orders shrunk by one fifth. Capacity utilisation of raw steel output dropped from 65 to 43%. Electricity consumption dropped 23%. By far, the worst year was 1932, when public and private investments were the lowest. In May, the Alpine had to blow out the only blast furnace still in operation in all of Austria. The value of total turnover was only one third of its highest post-war level and only a fraction of capacity was employed. Productivity continuously dropped. Meanwhile, management practised a harmful price policy when it attempted to cushion the drop of profits by maintaining relatively high price levels. Prices were not reduced commensurately with declining sales. The result was that its exports nearly stopped altogether, whereas imports of raw iron actually increased, in spite of protective tariffs and declining domestic sales.[15] Thus, the share of Alpine sales of domestic sales decreased, while that of foreign producers, who offered far lower prices, was rising.

In 1933, business activity of the Alpine still did not consolidate itself even though the European iron and steel industry had surpassed its trough and experienced symptoms of a slight upswing. The decline of raw ore production was the most precipitous. Until 1933, it dropped 86%. Raw iron output declined about 81%. Rolling

13 In the US, the Alpine unsuccessfully instituted proceedings against bond holders.

14 Schneider, Schwarzer and Denzel, 315.

15 Between 1931 and 1932, volume of import of raw iron increased from 31,500 to 44,900 tons, while value of imports declined 47%. Österreichisches Statistisches Zentralamt, *Aussenhandel*, 62.

mill production reached its nadir in 1932, after having declined 75%. Coal output was only slightly touched by the depression and recovered already after 1931. Apart from coal, all branches of production did not even nearly recover by 1936. Such declines were not unusual in the depression. Iron output declined in the US and Germany more than 80%, in France, Italy and Britain by around 50%, and in Belgium by about a third. Raw iron and steel output experienced similar declines.

However, although production declined just as fast in other industrialised countries, large advanced countries enjoyed an upswing a year sooner than in Austria. Raw iron, steel and ore production increased substantially already between 1932 and 1933 in Germany, Britain and France. Only the production of small advanced countries was not within this trend. In Belgium and Austria, for instance, output continued to decline. As always, for Austria the decline was stronger. Alpine raw ore and steel production, which constituted 80% of Austrian output, dropped 13 and 6.4% respectively. Only steel output rose by about 10%, far lower than in the larger countries. Alpine turnover was still 3% below 1932 value and 64.4% below the value of turnover of 1929.

Poor performance, in spite of European wide recovery, was mainly the result of the natural disadvantage of producers with large capacities in small countries that could not expand their export business. While large producers in Germany and Britain could rely on an expanding and protected home market, the Alpine was unable to increase sales, because it was not possible to raise exports correspondingly. The decline of Alpine exports, in turn, was the main cause of the decline of sales and employment. In 1932 and 1933, only between 11 and 13% of turnover consisted of export sales. Since 1929, volume of raw iron export sales had dropped from 43 million to 4.2 million tons! Volume of semi-finished iron and steel exports decreased more than half. Moreover, Alpine did not only have the disadvantage of a small market and collapsing exports, but its low productivity, combined with little financial reserves to sustain substantial income deficits, resulted in a continuously reckless price policy that cut foreign and domestic sales even more. Whereas world prices collapsed between 1929 and 1933, Alpine management maintained constant raw iron prices and even increased price level of bar iron. Basically, the company augmented the natural disadvantages of its market position. The consequence was that all blast furnaces and ore mining lay idle between December 1932 and May 1933.

The year 1934 finally meant a feeble but steady rise of production and sales for the Alpine, even though a deficit could still not be avoided. Yet, the slow rise of state investments hardly contributed to the slight improvement of business. How little public investments for the railway infrastructure were effective in the 30s can be seen when considering the relation of public orders to production capabilities. The state almost doubled overall investments from 44.6 to 96.7 million, of which 28.7 million schillings were designated for railway construction.[16] However, this sum only generated an order of 19,000 tons of railway track material, while Alpine rail production capacity was about 500,000 tons annually!

16 Fibich, 143.

In 1935, production increased slowly and prices fell. Export sales increased 79% in the framework of bilateral barter trade agreements with Czechoslovakia and Hungary. Ore was exported in return for coke from Czechoslovakia and flour from Hungary. Exports to Italy also increased, partially as a result of the Protocols of Rome concluded in March 1934. An essential component of these agreements, as part of the attempt of the proto-fascist Austrian government to obtain foreign political support against domestic and German National Socialist, as well as domestic social democrat political pressure,[17] was the conclusion of several preferential trade concessions between Italy, Austria and Hungary. These countries granted one another preferential tariffs and freight rates in the framework of further bilateral barter trade agreements.[18] Other factors that helped to increase exports were the upswing of the Italian and German iron and steel processing industries as a result of state investment-led recovery and slowly increasing rearmament in these countries.

In 1936 and 1937, the Alpine seriously benefited from recovery and rising rearmament in Germany and Italy, whose involvement in the Abyssinian war increased its imports of semi-finished goods and raw materials. Production and sales increased considerably and substantial profits were made. The majority of exports was conducted in the framework of further barter transactions. With the largest German steel works cartel and holder of the majority of Alpine stocks, the Vereinigte Stahlwerke, an agreement was concluded in 1936 for the delivery of high grade steel worth 600 thousand reichsmarks (1.3 million schillings), as well as 83,500 tons of ore, 7500 tons of raw iron and 15,000 of dross (Martinschlacke) in return for 80,000 tons of coke. Altogether, German orders in this year amounted to 10 million schillings. The barter agreement, running for five years, enabled employment of two blast furnaces. Moreover, 66,200 tons of ore were delivered to Hungary in return for imports of flour, pork and pigs. 15,000 tons of raw iron and 10,000 tons of semi-finished material were exported to Italy. Substantial amounts of ore were also exported to the booming rearmament industry in Czechoslovakia. Alpine management also hoped for increasing demand of iron ore from Britain and Germany, as a consequence of a shortage of supplies of Spanish ore after the escalation of the civil war. However, these countries were able to meet their demand elsewhere, in particular, from Sweden.

In the last year before the "Anschluss," Alpine exports for rearmament production in Europe boosted. Austrian exports of raw iron expanded 76%. Austrian ore production increased 84%, raw iron and steel output rose by more than half. Finally, in the spring of 1937, the Alpine steel works could almost fully employ their capacity. Twelve out of 14 open-hearth furnaces were employed. Iron ore production was also fully utilised. By December, the workforce had expanded to 16,000. In the first five months of the business year, Alpine ore output was 37% higher than in 1936. Production of raw iron, steel and semi-finished material was 50% higher and prices improved. In July 1937, the volume of unfilled orders ensured full employment for at

17 Adam Wandruszka, "Zwischen den Weltkriegen," in: Silvio Furlani and Adam Wandruszka, *Österreich und Italien. Ein bilaterales Geschichtsbuch*, Vienna 1973, 249–250.

18 Österreichisches Statistisches Zentralamt, *Aussenhandel*, 79.

least six months. Foreign demand skyrocketed and management could choose among the most favourable foreign orders. Until this year, the Alpine had been more than happy to fulfil any foreign order, but with dramatically increasing foreign demand for armament in 1937, unprofitable orders could be turned down.[19] For instance, the Alpine declined an order from Yugoslavia for the delivery of railway tracks, since it would have entailed the granting of a seven year term credit. An order from Britain was refused, because profit margins would have been small due to high delivery costs. Meanwhile, new barter transactions were concluded with the German Stahlwerke, including the annual delivery of one million tons of iron ore. By now, Germany was the second biggest export market of the Alpine, with a share of 16%. Sales to Italy also increased. Journalists and businessmen praised the boom and acclaimed the participation of Alpine production in the world-wide upswing.[20]

However, the upswing and Alpine recovery in 1937 stood on feet of clay! The sudden and massive demand of basic iron, steel products and ore was almost exclusively due to the inability of German and Italian, and to some degree, Hungarian and Czechoslovak, iron and steel producers to keep up with the massive increase of demand for rearmament production in these countries. This was especially obvious in Germany, where terms of deliveries had to be extended to 12 or even 16 months between 1933 and 1939.[21] Yet, as contemporaries knew, rearmament production could not go on indefinitely and this upswing would have been only sustainable in the event of war. The massive rise of demand could be followed by a sudden depression. Consequently, businessmen did not trust the boom and, just as many representatives of heavy industry in Germany in 1937, feared over-expansion, overcapacities and misinvestment in the case of an abrupt end of the boom once rearmament demand would decline. Even though employment of three blast furnaces was ensured for the first quarter of 1938, already in September 1937, a slight mitigation of the upswing was noticed, partially because of political instability in Europe. Though, it was mainly a result of a lack of foreign exchange in the authoritarian states that were focusing production and consumption on domestic growth and increasingly lagged income from export sales to finance their expensive imports.[22] Italy and Germany contemplated a reduction of demand. Italy, for instance, attempted to obtain an increasing portion of its supply from the Czechoslovak Republic, because the parity

19 "Während früher ein erbitterter Kampf um den Absatz jeder einzelnen Tonne Eisen geführt werden mußte, in welchen die Alpine ohne den direkten und den indirekten – im Weg des Stahlverein wirksamen – Schutz der internationalen Abmachungen aufs schwerste benachteiligt gewesen wäre, ist nunmehr die Nachfrage so lebhaft, daß die Werke mit den Lieferungen nicht nachkommen können." See: "Alpine undWeltkonjunktur," in: *Der Österreichische Volkswirt*, 17.4.1937.

20 "Von der Alpine Montan kann man sagen, daß ihr der vielberufene Anschluß an die Weltkonjunktur gelungen ist." Ibid.

21 Kian Shahidi, *Der Branchen-Lebenszyklus*, 199.

22 In contrast, contemporary journalists regarded political unrest in Europe, the war in China and difficulties within clearing systems as the main causes: "[...] die kriegerischen Ereignisse im Fernen Osten, die politische Unruhe in Europa und die Clearingschwierigkeiten sind auf den Geschäftsgang der Alpine Montan nicht ohne Einfluß geblieben." See: "Notizen: Alpine Montan an der Jahreswende," in: *Der Österreichische Volkswirt*, 25.12.1937.

of lira and Czechoslovak crowns was more favourable. In all, future prospects of raw iron sales were uncertain and sales of iron and ore to more distant markets in Europe would not have been possible due to high freight costs.

Generally, the downfall and slow recovery of the Alpine during and after the depression were not unusual in Europe. Only large advanced countries were able to incite large domestic demand that entailed an expansion of iron and steel production massive enough to enlarge and modernise capacities. As a consequence, the Alpine, like producers in other small countries, could only start to recover when demand outran production capabilities in Germany and Italy. Until then, its already low productivity declined even further and productive assets stagnated. The first barter trade agreements, as symptoms of rearmament demand from countries with controlled economies, brought a slight upswing, but capacity was still under-utilised. Meanwhile, state investments and currency instabilities had little direct effect on business. Full employment of the old and idle production capacity was only possible in 1937. By this time, production and employment levels of 1929 were attained once again. The 1930s remained a time of stagnation and decline without great structural changes in the Austrian iron and steel producing industry. Only shortly before the "Anschluss," the first signs of an uncertain upswing, structural transformation to modernisation and over-expansion based on rearmament were visible.

6.2.2. Steel Producing and Processing Industry

a. Schoeller-Bleckmann

Financial Standing

More than a year later than the Alpine, the largest high grade steel producers in Austria felt the impact of the depression in late 1930. Since its earning power, productivity and finances had been relatively stable in the late 20s, Schoeller-Bleckmann[23] went through the depression fairly unscathed. It did not suffer financial and economic difficulties of the magnitude of the Alpine. Earning power had been nearly 30% in 1929, and declined to 12.7% in 1930. Gross profits decreased by almost half and net profits were not even one forth of their 1929 value. However, although business activity was declining, very large investments were effected. Even though the company had large losses in 1931 and 1932, a slight profit was already made in 1933. The deficit in 1931 of 2.9 million was covered with capital stock and reserves of 13.7 million schillings. The following year the financial situation became precarious as the capital reserve shrunk to 6.8 million schillings. It would have been very difficult to sustain another year of massive losses. That would have entailed the raising of further loans.

Two thirds of joint stock capital was in the hands of the banking house Schoeller and the Creditanstalt, which was also the principle creditor of Schoeller-Bleckmann.

23 *Bilanzen*, 22.8.1931, 20.8.1932, 9.12.1933, 14.7.1934, 9.7.1935, 5.12.1936, 27.11.1937. See also A.19.

The breakdown of the bank did not seem to have had any immediate effects on business, nor did it lead to a remission of debts, which in fact, increased 18.6% between 1930 and 1932. For the rest of the 30s, the level of debts and bank credit only slowly lowered. In spite of these financial difficulties, profitability increased after 1933. In 1934 and 1935, net profit made up 18% of gross profits. In 1936, the company was almost back to pre-crisis profitability levels and surpassed 1929 gross profits value by 39%. The highest net profit of the inter-war period was reached.

Business Activity
The depression made itself felt at first at home, since the first great deficits of demand came from the domestic market while the share of exports of total turnover increased from 62 to 68%. The business report pointed out two reasons for slackening home demand. For one thing, employment from large orders for railway carriages placed in 1928 was exhausted. Secondly, by 1930, the boom of car manufacturing that had been stimulating substantial demand for finished steel products came to an end, as this branch also began to be affected by the depression. And so, capacity utilisation declined to 40%. In 1931 exports, the great majority of which went to Germany, slumped. Turnover share of exports was still 66%. The total volume of turnover declined 23%.

1932 was the worst business year. Average capacity utilisation was only 22% and volume of turnover declined another 34%. Since Schoeller-Bleckmann was highly dependent on export sales, the decline of foreign currency contributed to declining income. Demand from the Austrian home market deteriorated much more than export business. Due to the stop of all public investments, the firm did not receive any orders from the Austrian railways. A reaction to this was an even stronger emphasis on its export business and on the sales of highly advanced products with low demand elasticity. Foreign business share of total turnover increased from 66 to 71%. This policy was successful and resulted in the maintenance of the value of total turnover in spite of declining prices.

The following year, the company fortunately enjoyed moderate recovery based largely upon export sales alone. The domestic market did not offer any incentives for recovery, as there was no change in low and stagnating demand. Based on intensive export business of high quality advanced finished products, turnover increased monthly. Total volume of turnover increased 25%, of which between 70 and 80% was sold abroad. However, the fall of the pound and dollar parity had the disadvantage that prices did not rise proportionately to the volume of sales. Exports to Japan and Russia slowed down, whereas sales to South America, the British colonies and Spain were stimulated. Sales to Germany had to be conducted within the framework of the Austro-German clearing system, i. e. sales of high quality steel in Germany were corresponding to the value of raw material imports from that country. Utilisation of productive capacity increased from 22 to 45%.

In the next years until 1938, the company enjoyed considerable recovery through rearmament driven exports sales, even though currency fluctuations and exchange control caused some problems to international trade. Schoeller-Bleckmann fully participated in the world-wide upswing, especially of heavy industry, because of its expansive and forceful export business of high quality products with low demand elasticity.

The year 1934 brought a remarkable increase of turnover and profit (+66%). This year, not only exports increased (+25%), but also domestic market sales rose considerably (+40%). Orders from the railways and private industry came in. Even though lower dollar and pound parities depressed prices, between 70 and 80% of turnover was exported once again, mainly to Europe, but also to India, the Far East and South America. The decline of the Czechoslovak crown did not increase competition, nor did it lower demand from that country. A major stimulant of demand from abroad was increasing international rearmament.[24] Capacity utilisation was still quite low, between 50 and 55%. Even though full capacity could not be used, the year 1935 was considered a good business year. Volume of export turnover continued to increase, but export proceeds remained low because of currency devaluation. In spite of exports to Germany within the scope of barter agreements, exchange control and clearing systems and currency fluctuations with trade to countries with liberal economies, volume of exports still increased. Sales to Italy were especially favourable. As a whole, 80% of turnover was sold abroad. The only great disadvantage of clearing arrangements was delayed payment of outstanding foreign debts. Payments from Hungary and Italy took up to between nine and five months.

The last business report before the annexation of Austria was once again quite positive. In 1936, an increase of turnover of 15% was possible. The development of exports was very positive as well, in spite of the massive and widespread devaluation of the gold bloc countries in autumn of 1936. Income losses resulting from falling currencies were minute, as most of foreign business was conducted in schilling or pound. Right after the wave of devaluation, management was more afraid of decreasing competitiveness, than of falling prices, since foreign competitors usually had to compensate parity differences with price increases. The wave of depreciation in 1936 only offered short-term advantages of competitiveness to foreign companies.[25] After a few months either Schoeller-Bleckmann had been able to lower costs and prices, or foreign counterparts were forced to raise their prices as imports and labour became more cost intensive in their countries. Business development in 1937 was similar to that of the Alpine. In the first half of 1937, sales continued to increase, but stagnated thereafter, because of clearing difficulties and lack of foreign exchange in the authoritarian states. The war in China also harmed exports. Sales stagnated on world markets, probably because of the general minor recession of 1937/1938 in the US and Britain.

To summarise, it can be stated that Schoeller-Bleckmann saw through the depression quite well and enjoyed considerable and better recovery than the Alpine.

24 "Die internationale Rüstungskonjunktur dürfte auf den Halbfabrikantenbedarf mit von Einfluß gewesen sein." *Bilanzen*, 6.7.1935.

25 "Durch die Abwertung vom Herbst des Berichtjahres war der ausländische Wettbewerb zwar nur vorübergehend begünstigt, immerhin dauerte es einige Monate, bevor dessen Vorsprung eingeholt wurde, was teils durch Herabsetzung der eigenen, teils durch Steigerung der fremden Selbstkosten, teils durch Zurücktreten gewisser im Inland besser beschäftigten Lieferstaaten vom Weltmarkt geschah." *Bilanzen*, 27.11.1937.

The main reasons for this were its already high profitability and competitiveness in the 20s, the quality and continuously high demand of its products and its intensive policy of export expansion and progressing adoption of new technology. Export orientation was particularly the right choice when considering that domestic market demand was stagnating in the 30s. These conditions increased the company's resistance to structural deficiencies and obstacles that were a result of nationalist policies, such as currency fluctuations and trade restrictions at home and abroad.

6.2.3. Iron and Steel Processing Industry

Unlike Schoeller-Bleckmann, the following three companies of the iron and steel processing industry belonged to the traditional producers of this sector. Demand of their products was not nearly as high as for high grade steel products. They also highly depended upon export sales and were heavily hit by the decline of international trade during the depression. Export peak had already been reached in 1927. Between 1929 and 1932, value and volume of exports of iron goods declined 65%.[26] Some of these companies were affected by this slump more than others. Once again, this depended on productivity, competitiveness, demand elasticity and relating to this, export policy.

a. Hutter & Schrantz

Financial Standing

In spite of depression, it was possible for Hutter & Schrantz[27] to improve its financial situation in the 30s. Had the value of liabilities always been higher than the value of debtors in the 20s, this relation could be reversed after 1930. In 1930, value of debts and debtors was balanced and debt servicing declined. In 1932, the value of interest payments declined 54%, and bank credit was eliminated. Between 1929 and 1933, value of liabilities could be substantially reduced (-86%). The only restriction of the depression on finances was the end of an increase of dividend payments, which had been 10% in 1929. However, in 1931, it still amounted to 8%. At the same time, the level of depreciation could be maintained on a high level. Yet, investment rate declined. In the 20s, annual average investment had been more than 670 thousand schillings; in the 30s, it was only 159 thousand. In spite of falling gross profits, capital stock and reserve only slightly declined from 18.65 million in 1930 to 15.54 million schillings in 1935.

In the worst years, 1929 to 1933, value of gross profits only dropped 40%. This enabled management to lower expenses nearly as fast (-35%) while maintaining profitability on considerably high levels. It dropped from 27.6% of gross profits to 17% in 1932. It recovered thereafter to around 25% in 1934 and 1935.

26 Österreichisches Statistisches Zentralamt, *Aussenhandel*, 62.

27 *Bilanzen*, 23.8.1930, 6.6.1931, 14.5.1932, 7.10.1931, 14.4.1934, 23.11.1935, 4.1.1936, 18.7.1936. See also A.14.

Business Activity
First signs of economic decline were noticed in late 1929. Just like Schoeller-Bleckmann, management immediately focused on concentrating sales on export markets. Again, the worst decline in sales was on the Austrian home market. The following year, the level of sales could be maintained by further concentrating on exports and lowering prices. Now the massive investments of 1929 to increase productivity paid off, since price declines only mildly affected earning power. Gross profits only fell 2%. In the next two years, sales fell simultaneously on domestic and export markets. In 1931 turnover declined 12% and even more in 1932. However, currency depreciation only had minute effects on income. In 1933, when turnover fell only 3%, more than 40% of production was exported, mainly to the successor states, Germany, Finland and Sweden. Overseas markets were North and South American countries.

Already in the first two months of 1934, the company enjoyed a turnover increase of 24%. The main stimulant was the international paper industry. Capacity utilisation was very high with 80%. Export rate was 40%, even though trade restrictions, especially of metal cloth to the US, lowered sales. This was compensated by increasing sales to South American markets. Competition did not harm sales, as its export items were of high quality and well established on international markets. By the mid 30s, the company was able to increase the volume of sales, while prices were declining. Thus, gross profits remained stagnant, whereas volume of turnover increased.

The major advantages of this firm were its international export orientation and its stratified production. Metal and wire cloth were sold to the large or expanding paper and textiles industries; various types of simple iron and steel goods were produced and cotton goods were sold for private and increasing public consumption at home. Another advantage was its high investment rate and consequential modernisation in the 20s, giving it sufficient productivity to keep up with falling prices in the 30s. Furthermore, it was easier to circumvent freight difficulties and trade restrictions, because it owned production facilities in Austria, the Czechoslovak Republic and Hungary.

b. Ditmar-Brünner

Financial Standing
Financially, Ditmar-Brünner,[28] one of the largest exporters of petroleum lamps in the world, was hit by the depression much harder than the previous company. Still, its financial standing was not alarming. The main reason for financial decline seemed to have been its already low profitability after the strike in 1927 and low investments in the 20s. Yet, the debt situation remained stable and liquidity was satisfactory. Gross profits declined quickly in the depression as a result of falling sales. Between 1929 and 1932, profit value dropped 45% and recovered thereafter only slowly. Gross profits value of 1927 was only surpassed in 1935. Profitability, already only 8% in 1929, never recovered from the deficits in 1931 and 1932. In spite of these difficul-

28 *Bilanzen*, 10.10.1931, 21.5.1932, 19.8.1933, 7.7.1934, 13.7.1935, 29.2.1936, 10.10.1936, 15.1.1938. See also A.9.

ties, bank debts remained low and the balance sheet and profit and loss account were stable. By 1936, bank credits were cleared off.

Business Activity

The positive business outlook of 1929 was soon disillusioned. In 1930, various factors besides the general effects of the crisis, disturbed exports (70% of total sales), such as political unrest in India and currency problems in the Far East. These losses were compensated by an increase of sales of petroleum ovens, for which new sales markets could be found, especially in France and its colonies. The management attempted to cushion the continuous decline of sales by incorporating new export items in its production process, such as torch light batteries and other types of electric lighting. Due to falling demand and dropping prices, Ditmar-Brünner further concentrated on exports of cheap mass consumption products. By 1933, when the decline of export sales came to a halt in autumn, between 70 and 80% were exported. Again the main force of recovery did not come from the home market, and capacity was still only utilised 50%. A large portion of export increase came from rising sales of simple petroleum heaters and cookers, especially in Italy, Spain, Portugal and France. The Russian export market had been lost, as the Russian industry was now capable of manufacturing these items itself. Other main export markets were South America and Central and Eastern Asia, where increasing Japanese competition was noticed.

In the mid thirties, the company was affected by the consequences of the depreciation of dollar and pound. While an increasing share of turnover was conducted abroad (up to 80%), volume of turnover and capacity utilisation rose, but the value of turnover and profits continued to stagnate. To compensate the losses of sales in heaters and cookers, and also to react to rising rearmament demand, production became more diversified and modern, to include such items as metal components for gas-masks, home cinematographs and electrolytic capacitors for radio sets. In 1935, the company bought a German-owned plant for gas defence equipment situated in Austria,[29] in order to be able to manufacture complete sets of gas-masks from 1937 onwards. With this shift in production, management successfully reacted to changing demand, away from simple consumer goods of petroleum lighting and heaters, and could maintain and increase its volume of export sales. Whereas export of its old traditional goods to India, Burma and Ceylon decreased because of Japanese competition and peripheral industrialisation, Ditmar-Brünner was able to increase sales of more complex goods to more advanced markets, as home cinematographs, and radio set and gas-mask components found increasing demand in Europe. Sales to Italy also rose, because of increasing armament orders.

Since France had become an important export market and because the franc devaluation was expected before September 1936, the company had taken preventive monetary measures well in advance. Months before the actual devaluation, it had been possible to change French business transactions from franc to dollar or pound. However, the international movement of currency depreciation in the gold

29 This was the so-called "Oesterreichische Gasschutz GesmbH."

bloc countries seriously diminished profits in 1936 and 1937, while turnover and production had increased. The currency declines were so harmful, because the price declines abroad affected exports at the time of highest sales. Furthermore, a very large portion of its exports went to gold bloc countries.

Overall, it can be stated that Ditmar-Brünner performed well in the thirties, as a result of its successful export and business policy which adjusted to shifting demand. The firm did not earn great profits, but was, at least, able to maintain liquidity and kept debts at an acceptable minimum.

c. Brevillier

Financial Standing

The profit and loss accounts of this traditional producer of iron and metal goods clearly revealed the impact of the depression. Already in late 1929, Brevillier[30] was struck by the depression. The level of profitability declined precipitously, from around 30% in the late 20s to 7.5% in 1930. Between 1931 and 1933, the company suffered substantial losses which were covered by declining reserves. Between 1929 and 1932, gross profits fell 70% and did not surpass 1927 value until the last year of the period of investigation. In the mid 30s, earnings capacity could not be recovered and remained between 8 and 16%. The financial standing, though, could still be called stable. In spite of losses, liabilities remained below debtor value. Even though bank debts increased from one million schillings in 1930 to two million in 1931 and 2.57 million in 1933, a slow process of liquidation of indebtedness took place thereafter. Bank credit was reduced from 2.63 million in 1934 to 1.59 million the following year and to 777 thousand in 1936. The consequences, however, were a low investment rate, slightly declining debts and a stable rate of depreciation. While financial markets were stable in the 30s and the discount rate low, Brevillier conducted a conservative financial policy to reduce debts. Investments were so low that there was hardly a modernisation of plant. Capital assets stagnated, as well as volume of business. Indirectly, this is revealed in declining balance sheet value.

Business Activity

As mentioned in chapter 4, the company's export orientation was comparably low and declined further in the 30s. Therefore, it was hit by a declining domestic market much more than Hutter & Schrantz and Ditmar-Brünner. By late 1929, turnover value shrunk between 25 and 30%. Until May 1930, business moderately revived, followed by a sudden drop of orders. The termination of railway orders was especially noticed. Domestic market demand contracted the most, while exports (still 50–60% of total turnover) still offered substantial employment, even though demand for screw steel and iron and steel goods, its main products, declined. Capacity utilisation of the various plants in Austria, Hungary, and Poland fell below 50% and never really recovered. Compared to 1929, total turnover in 1930 had dropped nearly 30%. In 1931, turnover declined another 18% and in 1932, even 32%. Some plants had to be

30 *Bilanzen*, 21.6.1930, 17.1.1931, 5.9.1931, 17.1.1931, 4.4.1931, 10.9.1932, 30.9.1933, 18.8.1934, 22.6.1935, 3.10.1936, 13.11.1937. See also A.6.

shut down, and short-time work was introduced. Mainly because of low productivity, exports (which mostly went to Europe but also South America, India and Australia) were harmed by import restrictions, exchange control, and allegedly, by increasing competition from abroad due to currency depreciation. Yet, main competitors were Swedish and Belgian firms, which actually did not have a currency advantage at this time. In 1932, sales on foreign markets declined more (-38%) than in the various home markets (-30). Contrary to the previous two companies, Brevillier did not force exports, but, in the face of increasing foreign competition on international markets, attempted to concentrate on the domestic market. Nearly 70% of total turnover was sold in the home markets of its production facilities.

The dollar depreciation in 1933 did not have any immediate effects on its business. In this year, it was possible to halt the decline of turnover, which remained on appallingly low levels, entailing low employment. Recovery began quite late, in the first half of 1934, when turnover rose 20%. The main drive of recovery came from home markets, while it was very difficult to maintain the level of export sales against foreign firms situated in countries with devaluated currencies. Thus, the export share of turnover dropped again to 31%. By the mid thirties Brevillier was still far from recovery as capacity in all three countries was only utilised around 50%. In 1935, total turnover only increased 10%, while export share declined again (-25%). Whereas other firms moved away from the home market, Brevillier management continued to complain about harsh foreign competition and trade restrictions. The small increase in business activity was purely based on the very moderate expansion of the Austrian market. In 1936, management worried much about devaluation in gold bloc countries and feared more losses of export sales. Once again, turnover only increased 7%, and in 1937, only 12%, while export share of turnover dropped to 20%. Trade restrictions and currency fluctuation were blamed for poor performance.[31] Instead of focusing on increasing productivity and competitiveness to participate in the upswing of the international markets, management pursued a conservative and careful policy of retrenchment to its stagnant home market, hoping for pending revival of railway and private demand for traditional products of high demand elasticity.

6.2.4. Mining

Veitscher

The world economic depression had catastrophic effects on production and sales performance of the highly export dependent Austrian magnesite industry, as its main customer, the world iron and steel producing industry, went through a dramatic decline in the early 1930s.[32] Total Austrian magnesite exports declined from almost

31 "Das Auslandsgeschäft war nach wie vor beeinträchtigt durch die zahlreichen den freien Waren- und Geldverkehr hemmenden Beschränkungen, die zum Teil sogar zugenommen haben. Die internationale Wettbewerbslage der Gesellschaft war zeitweise auch durch die Währungsabwertungen von Konkurrenzländern ungünstig beeinflußt." *Bilanzen*, 13.11.1937.

32 Hermann, 77.

120,000 to 33,000 tons in 1932. The largest customer of the Veitscher[33] magnesite works, the American iron and steel industry, reduced its demand 94% between 1929 and 1932.[34] The dissatisfying import agreements of 1929 with Harbison and General had to be discarded in the face of crisis.[35] In this period, Veitscher production shrunk 79%, total Austrian production 68%,[36] whereas world magnesite output only dropped 38%.[37] After 1931, Austria was overtaken by Soviet Russia as the largest producer of magnesite in the world.

Financial Standing

Financially, the blow was, by far, not as heavy. The financial standing of Veitscher remained excellent and could easily resist crisis shocks, even of this magnitude, although gross profits declined from almost 4.2 million to one million schillings between 1929 and 1932. The firm was unable to lower expenses accordingly, the result being a minor deficit of 40 thousand schillings in 1932. Management was also forced to lower the dividend from 18 to 6% in 1931. The entailing increase of creditor value was easily covered by substantial financial reserves. Already by 1933, a profit of 613 thousand schillings was made and in 1936 pre-crisis remunerativeness level was reached again. After 1932, gross and net profits recovered steadily, surpassing 1928 levels in 1936. Furthermore, the company had large bank deposits and value of liabilities remained well below debtor value. Management could also afford to pay very high rates of dividends. Whereas only 110 of the 297 large Austrian enterprises (with a capital stock of one million or more) could pay a dividend at all, and the majority of which only disbursed between 3 and 8%,[38] Veitscher was able to grant an impressive 20% dividend in 1937.[39] With this financial background it was easily possible to maintain depreciation and investments on sufficiently high levels, enabling management to modernise and increase the value of capital assets, even though capacity was under-utilised most of the time. Value of productive capital increased from 13.5 million to 17.5 million between 1924 and 1937, including total depreciation of 12.5 million schillings.[40]

Business Activity

By mid 1930, a deterioration of demand was noticed as a result of declining iron and steel production abroad. Yet, this was still a minor blow compared to the following two years, when capacity utilisation of the world iron and steel industry declined to 25%. In 1931, Veitscher magnesite production was only a third of its 1929 volume.

33 *Bilanzen*, 14.6.1930, 4.7.1931, 28.5.1932, 15.7.1933, 19.5.1934, 16.2.1935, 13.5.1935, 4.4.1936, 30.1.1937, 15.5.1937. See also A.24.

34 Österreichisches Statistisches Zentralamt, *Aussenhandel*, 49.

35 Walter, 208.

36 Own calculation from Statistisches Reichsamt, *Jahrbuch 1938*, 72 (international survey).

37 Own calculation from Hermann, 31.

38 Data for 1935. Bundesamt für Statistik, *Statistisches Handbuch für den Bundesstaat Österreich*, vol. 17, Vienna 1937, 85.

39 Walter, 217.

40 Ibid, 218.

Three of the four plants had to be shut down. Export sales to the US dropped 70% and to all other markets 45%. In 1932, export sales, declining another 46%, reached rock-bottom.

The company experienced an upswing in 1933. Austrian exports nearly doubled and the American iron and steel works were again the main customers. Also, British iron and steel producers substantially increased demand. However, the rise of profits was not proportionate to the increase of production and sales, mainly because of falling prices. These were, to some degree, the result of the dollar depreciation. Although production and sales were rising and financial development was positive, recovery was progressing very slowly. Still, in the next year, only 26% of capacity was utilised. This slow upswing was commensurate to the slow recovery of the world iron and steel industry.

Similar to the development of the Alpine, Veitscher production naturally benefited also from the rearmament boom starting in the mid thirties. From 1935 onwards, production and export sales finally started to pick up, and markets began to change, reflecting the shift of demand and structural distortion in Europe. Whereas American demand stagnated after 1933, demand from iron and steel producers in the authoritarian states, enjoying large scale public investment from military orders, boosted. Between 1933 and 1937, German producers bought between 31 and 44% of Austrian magnesite exports.[41] Total exports more than doubled. In the same time span, Austrian magnesite production increased more than 60%, reaching nearly 400 thousand tons in 1937, about 91% of 1929 output.[42] Only Soviet Russian production was higher. The majority of total Austrian exports went to the rearming states in Europe. Veitscher exports increased 74% between 1933 and 1937, surpassing 1928 volume.[43] Furthermore, magnesite brick, about a third of total value of sales, were delivered to Germany, France, Britain, the Scandinavian countries, India and South Africa. Total Austrian brick export doubled after 1933.[44] Although capacity utilisation was still only 40%, in 1935 and 1936 Veitscher production and export sales experienced a massive expansion. The importance of the American market for Austrian magnesite producers declined, as only a fraction of sales went to the US market. It was well protected by tariffs and was now completely in the hands of the Northwestern and Canadian importers.

Thus, similar to the iron and steel producing and processing industry, the performance of the Austrian magnesite industry was largely determined by the development of its foreign markets.

41 Österreichisches Statistisches Zentralamt, *Aussenhandel*, 49.
42 Statistisches Reichsamt, *Jahrbuch 1938*, 72 (international survey).
43 Walter, 213.
44 Österreichisches Statistisches Zentralamt, *Aussenhandel*, 50.

Year	Austria	Belgium	Poland	Germany	Britain	France	Japan
1932	85.7	67.0	57.5	79.2	90.2	60.6	108.2
1933	88.4	63.6	60.0	90.7	97.6	74.5	127.3
1934	110.1	52.7	67.4	98.7	100.3	63.7	141.6
1935	127.2	67.5	71.1	91.0	106.8	65.7	147.2
1936	143.9	77.5	73.0	98.0	114.3	67.2	143.1

Table 6.1.: Production index of textile industries in various countries (1928=100). Source: "Die Lage der Textilindustrie im Ausland," in: *Wochenbericht*, no. 12/13, 1937, 72.

6.2.5. Textile industry

a. General Development Unfortunately, microeconomic data for the textile industry in the 30s are not available, but general statements about this important branch can be made. Excluding clothing manufacture, the textile industry had a share of total industrial capital stock which hardly declined, from 9 to 8.8% between 1932 and 1935.[45] Hence, it remained one of the most important industrial sectors in the 30s. Of more than 6200 Austrian enterprises, still 671 were textile manufacturers of various types.[46]

As shown in table 6.1, production performance of the Austrian textile industry in the 1930s was well above world average. The main reasons for this were a change in the speed, volume and range of the two world-wide structural shifts taking place in the inter-war period and probably the extremely low utilisation of Austrian production capacities in the late 20s. First of all, increasing industrialisation of textile manufacturing in the periphery slowed down in the mid thirties, disburdening international textile markets of competitive pressures. In addition, the shift to modern modes of production within national textiles industries, which was part of the second major transformation, was too small to affect textile production as a whole. Apart from a slow process of technical and organisational improvement of the traditional textile industry, new products and methods were only applied reluctantly and on a small scale.

Production of the world textile industry only slowly moved away from using cotton to the application of rayon and mixed fabrics as raw materials. Before the First World War rayon was hardly used for textile production "and even at the end of the twenties it represented only a fraction of the consumption of cotton. It was not until the thirties that the consumption of rayon took on large proportions."[47] This application was most pronounced in large advanced countries, with the markets and capital to support such adjustments, and in some peripheral, late industrialising countries. A massive increase of rayon production took place in Japan, which became

45 Own calculation from: Bundesamt für Statistik, *Statistisches Handbuch für den Bundesstaat Östereich 1935*, 112, and 1937, 83.

46 *Handbuch 1937*, 66.

47 Svennilson, 141.

the largest producer in the world in 1936. Output not only expanded in Canada, the US, Germany, Britain, France and Italy, but also in smaller countries, such as Czechoslovakia, Poland and Switzerland.[48]

However, the application of modern production modes in the textiles industry was a slow process and the expansion of rayon output began to slow down in the 30s.[49] After 1933, the cotton textile industry, basically representing the traditional sector, still provided the majority of world textile production and exports. Between 1936 and 1938, total textile production amounted to 40,800 million square yards, of which rayon and mixed fabrics only constituted 5300 million. Of total world exports of textile, rayon and mixed fabrics production only had a share of 9.5%.[50] Therefore, world-wide productivity increases and expansion of production was not as great as in other industries, leaving more room for the recovery of traditional producers in the 30s that had been strongly underemployed in the late 20s, such as the Austrian textile industry.

At the same time, the international structural change, the pressure from rising production of late industrialising countries on international markets, started to slow down by the mid 30s. Increase of output and production capacities in countries that had massively expanded, such as Japan, India, and Canada were reaching their peaks. Meanwhile, general recovery after 1933 in the old industrialised countries, in particular in Germany, Britain and also in the US, took place. In these countries, consumption and demand for textile products increased, allowing for a moderate expansion in output of traditional producers in Europe.[51] Pressure for protectionism of national producers in Europe must have abated, even though the share of exports of total world production declined from 27% in the late 20s to 18% in the late 30%.[52]

In the 1930s, the comparably small Austrian textile industry experienced a moderate upswing. It benefited from these processes of slow application of modern modes of production and intensifying stagnation of production expansion in the periphery, as the speed of world production and capacity enlargement slowed down. However, although it was still one of the most important Austrian industrial sectors, with an export share of nearly 27% in 1936, its production and export expansion was far too moderate to support a better national economic performance.

The main reason for this phenomena was not the rate, but the volume and level of the upswing in the 30s. Like many other sectors, it started from the very low levels

48 Statistisches Reichsamt, *Jahrbuch 1937*, 85 and *Jahrbuch 1938*, 92 (international survey). See also: Deutsches Institut für Konjunkturforschung , "Textilwirtschaft," in: *Vierteljahreshefte zur Wirtschaftsforschung*, vol. 12, no. 2, 1937, 210. On the development of the international rayon industry after World War One see: Eva Flügge, "Kunstseidenindustrie. Der internationale Aufbau der Kunstseidenindustrie und seine Folgen," in: Hermann Schumacher (ed.), *Wandlungen in der Weltwirtschaft*, no. 3, Leipzig 1936. See also: Fritz Grotius, *Die deutsche Kunstseidenindustrie, ihre Produktionsbedingungen, ihre Entwicklung und Marktstellung*, dissertation, Emsdetten 1938.

49 Flügge, 111.

50 Own calculation from Svennilson, 142.

51 Deutsches Institut für Konjunkturforschung, "Die Lage der Textilindustrie im Ausland," 70–72.

52 Svennilson, 142.

of the depression and only barely surpassed 1913 production levels in the late 30s. Although output of its most important product, cotton yarn, considerably surpassed the 1929 level already in 1935,[53] capacity was still under-utilised. The main reason for this was the extremely low level of production even in the late 20s. Therefore, the seemingly considerable expansion after 1932, was based on very low starting levels. Thus, in order to be able to incite an expansion and modernisation process, and to act as a major stimulant for the Austrian economy in the 30s, the textile industry would have required far higher demand than existed in the moderate boom period in the late 20s or in the pre-war period. The result was that a large scale structural change of the textile industry, i.e. expansion and modernisation of production facilities, was hardly necessary. Under-utilised capacity just had to be re-employed.

Moreover, textile exports not only stagnated in the 20s, but, in spite of recovery in the 30s, never again reached already low pre-crisis levels. While volume of Austrian exports rose to a minute degree, value declined 9% between 1924 and 1929. In the 30s, the fall of prices was even more pronounced. Between 1932 and 1937, volume of textile exports increased 47%, whereas value only rose 25%. In addition, volume and value of exports in 1937 were still far below 1929 levels.[54] Volume increased to more than 38,000 tons, but was still 16.4% below the 1929 level. Only the rate, but not the volume, of Austrian expansion of textile production was well above world-wide average.

6.2.6. Paper Industry

a. International Development This sector, incorporating 344 enterprises with a 6,5% share of total industrial capital stock,[55] was much smaller than the textile industry. Its foreign trade and production performance was far less successful. Total value and volume of exports and production declined until 1936, and only moderately recovered in the last year before the „Anschluss." Its main products were paper, cardboard, lignin and cellulose. Production growth of the former two items was below the world and European averages. Until 1936, it was still one fifth below, and in 1937, it was only 4% above pre-depression levels. In Norway, the Netherlands, and Czechoslovakia, production performance was comparably poor. At the same time, German (+20%), Belgian (+24), or Italian (+49) output levels were much higher. Austrian output of lignin and cellulose, though, was well within world average. Between 1929 and 1937 it expanded 26%. In Germany, the US and Japan, production growth ranged from 19.7 to 31.6%.[56]

While relative production volume was probably greater, generally the relative rate of production growth in the paper industry was far lower than that of textiles, because it basically stagnated until 1936. Whereas, in the 30s, textile production

53 In 1935, output was 13.5 % above 1929 level. Own calculation from: Bundesamt für Statistik, *Statistisches Handbuch für den Bundesstaat Österreich 1937*, 68 and 79.

54 Österreichisches Statistisches Zentralamt, *Aussenhandel*, 59.

55 Data for 1935. *Handbuch*, 1935, 66 and 83.

56 All values calculated from Statistisches Reichsamt, *Jahrbuch 1938*, 92.

expansion hardly started from low 1929 levels and barely surpassed 1913 production for the first time in 1937, output of the paper sector had already reached a high level before the crisis, far above 1913 production volume. It had experienced an upswing of foreign sales and production lasting nearly 10 years, which came to an abrupt halt in 1929.[57] Production of paper and cardboard expanded 18.3% in the second half of the 20s[58]; by this time the industry had already undergone substantial expansion. In 1930, though, moderate growth changed to stagnation, and then turned into crisis. And just as in many other industries, output declined in the depression and did not recover after 1933. From this year until 1936, production virtually stagnated, with a growth rate of 0.4%.[59] Only in the very last year of Austrian independence did total production slowly increase, to 44.3% above pre-war, or only 7.8% above pre-depression levels,[60] partially as a result of demand outrunning production capacities in countries with intensifying rearmament.[61]

It is interesting to note that the pattern of inter-war production performance of moderate growth rates in the 20s and stagnation in the 30s was not in accordance with performance of the world paper industry. While Austrian production expanded less than 20%, world production increased 40% between 1925 and 1929. When Austrian production stagnated, world output augmented 30% between 1933 and 1937.[62] Again, this phenomena can be explained by increasing production capacities in the periphery countries and in large advanced countries. The former benefited from their own protected markets and from high competitiveness on world markets, while national producers in the old industrialised countries took advantage of their large, protected domestic markets with high purchasing power. Once again, national producers with large capacities in small advanced countries suffered from this process, as international market pressures increased and producers were unable to evade to home markets to find sufficient demand and acceptable prices. By and large, this explains the poor export, and therefore also, poor production performance of the Austrian paper industry.

Similar to all other industrial branches, this sector was highly dependent on foreign trade. In 1936, for example, 60% of output were exported.[63] The development of production clearly reflected the extremely poor export performance and the precipitously falling prices in the 30s. Export volume dropped drastically and increased only slightly. Therefore, the main reason for the sad decline of the paper industry must be primarily sought in declining foreign trade, resulting from exogenous structural transitions.

57 *Bilanzen*, 20.6.1931.

58 This covers the period 1925–1929. Calculated from Statistisches Reichsamt, *Jahrbuch 1931*, 42.

59 Own calculation from *Jahrbuch 1938*, 92.

60 Österreichisches Institut für Wirtschaftsforschung, *Monatsberichte* 14, 1913. According to figures from *Jahrbuch 1938*, Austrian paper and cardboard output surpassed pre-crisis level only 3.8% in 1937.

61 "Konjunktur der Papierindustrie," in: *Bilanzen*, 20.1.1937 and 5.6.1937.

62 Own calculation from *Jahrbuch 1931*, 42; and *Jahrbuch 1938*, 92.

63 "Nöte der Papierindustrie," in: *Bilanzen*, 4.7.1936.

Year	Paper Production	Paper Export Volume	Paper Export Value	Lignin and Cellulose Production	Lignin and Cellulose Export Volume	Lignin and Cellulose Export Value
1929	230	111	90	328	113	46
1932	201	95	51	283	102	24
1933	201	96	47	310	120	26
1934	199	96	47	319	132	31
1935	197	89	40	335	155	34
1936	179	82	37	336	168	41
1937	232	117	58	414	186	59

Table 6.2.: Production and export value and volume of paper, lignin and cellulose in Austria, 1929–1937 (in thousand tons and million schillings). Source: *Jahrbuch 1938*, 92. *Aussenhandel*, 51–52.

Lignin and cellulose export volume and value only barely recovered volume and value of the late 1920s, and surpassed these considerably only by 1937, when its trade volume became larger than that of paper. Until 1936, however, value of exports remained well below pre-crisis level. The development of paper exports was alarming. It continued to decline until 1936, when it reached its absolute low point in the inter-war period, and it surpassed the volume of the 1929 level only slightly in 1937. The only positive aspect of foreign trade was that exports of both production branches was affected by the depression rather late. Whereas trade values declined after 1929, volume still expanded until 1931.

b. Leykam-Josefsthaler

Financial Standing

Having sustained great market pressure, very high debts and declining earning power in the late 20s, poor income from foreign trade in paper products during the depression and thereafter, struck Leykam-Josefsthaler[64] heavily. Already in the late 20s, profitability did not surpass 7% and dividends could not be disbursed. Due to large investments, already by 1929 debts had amounted to more than 22 million schillings, including bank credits of 13 million. High debts and debt servicing made it very difficult for management to lower expenses, as income declined precipitously due to the depression. Thus, between 1930 and 1934, the company suffered substantial deficits of altogether more than 15 million. In 1931 alone, the loss amounted to 7.8 million schillings, that was almost half of capital stock and reserve, which had already shrunk due to deficits in 1930. As a consequence, basically the capital stock and reserve of nearly 18 million schillings was completely consumed by the mid 30s, although sterling depreciation had led to a decrease of bonded debt.

In 1933, the principal shareholders, the CA, the Böhmische Union Bank and the Hartmann group, demanded financial reconstruction, but were divided over who was to carry the burden. Hartmann wanted the banks to grant remission of debts, whereas the banks demanded a depreciation of stock capital. Finally, in 1934, the

64 *Bilanzen*, 2.8.1930, 19.1.1932, 13.1.1934, 24.7.1937. See also A.16.

balance sheet was reconstructed. Stock capital was devalued by 4 million schillings for debt amortisation, and revaluated to its original amount. The new stocks were purchased by the main shareholding banks. Only after 1935 was the profit and loss account barely balanced, with negligible net profits thereafter. In 1936, debts still came to more than 13 million schillings, far above debtor value. At least it had been possible to lower long-term bank credits, whose terms ran until 1949, to less than 9 million and short-term credits to 1.26 million. Basically, the highly indebted company was barely able to survive the depression financially. In the late 30s, all financial reserves had been used up and, needless to say, depreciation and investments had been far too low.

Business Activity
After 1930, Leykam-Josefsthaler suffered from the crisis of international markets. Demand and prices declined dramatically. While production was still expanded in 1931, prices for paper dropped 10% and for cellulose between 12 and 15%. Home market and export demand fell simultaneously. Leykam export was particularly hard hit by the losses of sales in China and India. The following year, competition also grew more fierce, as a result of sterling devaluation. Exchange control systems in Austria and Hungary began to disturb trade, as it became increasingly problematic to receive debt claims and to make deliveries. For the first time production was restricted and only one plant worked full-time. In 1933, business improved slightly, while prices still declined. Trade agreements with Italy and Hungary made exports to these markets easier.

By the mid 30s, export share of turnover had only barely declined, even though prices were low. Still, nearly half of paper and three quarters of cellulose output were outbound. A large portion of foreign trade was now conducted through clearing agreements. As for many Austrian industries, the year 1937 brought a sudden considerable improvement of demand and prices. Again, this can be, to a great extent, attributed to the armament boom of the late 30s. Prices stabilised and cellulose production was completely disposed of, and orders for 1938 were already available. All factories were fully employed, and plans were made to modernise the main factory.

c. Neusiedler
Financial Standing
Even though it had substantial debts in the late 20s, this company[65] probably was one of the most financially consolidated firms in this industrial branch. Between 1926 and 1930, capital stock and reserves amounted to 25 million schillings. Shortly before the depression, it had not carried out any large scale investments and enjoyed high liquidity since debtor value was about 10% above creditor value. Therefore, annual income deficits in the 30s were far lower than for Leykam, ranging between 200 and 320 thousand schillings. 1932 and 1934 were peak years when annual losses

65 *Bilanzen*, 28.6.1930, 20.6.1931, 17.9.1932, 12.8.1933, 24.11.1934, 19.10.1935, 2.11.1935, 17.10.1936, 13.3.1937, 13.7.1937. See also A.18.

amounted to 590 and 910 thousand respectively. Even though Leykam was a far smaller firm, its overall deficits totalled more than 15 million, while total losses of Neusiedler only came to 2.2 million, at least until 1935. On the other hand, deficits were more persistent, because losses were still made until that year. The business report for 1936 is unclear regarding the financial situation, but it appears that again, another loss was made. Soon after 1930, hidden reserves were fully consumed and management had no choice but to use capital stock and reserve to cover annual losses. The result of persistent deficits was that depreciation and investments could not be made between 1931 and 1936.

Business Activity

Already in 1929, Neusiedler experienced declining business. Production had to be reduced and gross profits declined 15% and net profits 25.7%. This was mainly due to falling export demand, which was especially harsh, because up to 80% of output were sold abroad. In contrast, the Prager Neusiedler, its largest foreign holding, was initially only mildly hit by the depression, as it was not affected by the deterioration of foreign markets to such a great extent. It still sold 80% of its products on the Czechoslovak market. For Neusiedler, domestic sales also began to stagnate in 1930, and export sales continued to decline, while prices dropped between 20 and 30%. Total turnover fell one quarter. Production was curtailed and the export rate was down to 50%. In 1931, business worsened. Prices declined another 30%. From then on, only 40% of output or less was exported. Export direction of paper shifted away from the markets nearby, the successor states and the Balkans, to markets overseas, such as South America, South Africa, China and Australia. Sales of cardboard increasingly went to Egypt and India instead of Britain, whose industry had expanded its cardboard production capacity.

The next two years marked the low point of the depression for Neusiedler. Value of turnover, falling 20% in 1932 and another 17% in 1933, reached less than half of the 1928 level. Since that year, market prices had fallen more than 50%. The downfall had greater implications on paper and lignin, than on cellulose production. Between 1929 and 1933, paper output declined 34%, and until 1932, lignin production dropped 32%. Cellulose output fell only 20% until 1932. In the Austrian plants, seven out of fourteen paper machines lay idle.

After these catastrophic years, recovery was long in coming. In 1934, total value of turnover dropped again, from 20 to 18.5 million and one third of capacity lay completely idle. The rest was utilised up to 80%. International market prices were remarkably low and export business remained a losing business, although currency devaluation did not have harmful implications, as most of foreign trade was transacted in schillings. Nevertheless, many other Austrian paper producers had to terminate foreign trade altogether. Not only continuously falling prices, but also trade restrictions and national policies of self-sufficiency limited foreign trade income opportunities and profitability. As for Leykam, export business became more costly as deliveries to Hungary and Italy, with which Austria had signed preferential trade agreements in 1934, were problematic. The main problem was low international demand, but exchange control and clearing systems only worsened the situation.

Although customers in these countries promptly fulfilled payments, clearing banks took weeks and months for remittance. Problems with exports to these countries mounted in the next years. While deliveries were still made, Austrian enterprises would not receive payments for months, because outstanding debts of clearing transactions rose due to transfer difficulties. For instance, Hungarian clearing debts increased from 7.5 million in November 1935 to 13.5 million in 1936. Rising sales to Italy during the period of sanctions on Italian trade, imposed by the League of Nations,[66] also did not pay off. Italian clearing debts to Neusiedler alone mounted to 9 million schillings in 1935 and reached 12 million in 1936.

Furthermore, the importance of the Hungarian and Italian markets declined, as both countries made strong efforts to increase production capacity of their respective paper industries. The Hungarian paper industry doubled its capacities, and Italy, reacting to the sanctions, intensified its policy of self-sufficiency, in order to become independent of cellulose imports. In 1935, foreign trade did not improve at all. Sales of cardboard, for example, lost some old export areas altogether. Exports to Egypt came to an end, because of fierce German competition, and sales to Turkey stopped, as this country also established its own paper industry.

Due to these massive difficulties of foreign trade, Neusiedler, as so many other national producers in other countries, focused its attention on the stagnating home market, increasing domestic sales to more than 65% of output. A central part of this policy was the participation in an international paper cartel in 1935, the contract terms of which were running until 1940. Even though the share of total sales allocated by the cartel only offered employment for one third of production capacity, it ensured at least slightly rising or stable prices. However, in the long run, these efforts only helped to prevent rising deficits, but could not improve the course of business. Paper production still decreased another 5% in 1936. Value of turnover dropped 17%.

d. Summary Clearly, business activity of the paper producers reflected the international market development. Prices and demand declined until the mid 30s, and recovery only began to take place by 1937. Basically, the Austrian paper industry was not only a victim of the depression, but of large scale and rapid international structural changes in the 30s. In the 20s, it could still increase productivity and competitiveness to keep up with fierce international market pressure due to massive expansion of the international paper production capacities. This was a process of national producers in former import countries quickly expanding their production capabilities. Unlike a similar process taking place in the textile industry, this development in the paper industry speeded up in the 1930s and exposed firms, especially in small export dependent countries, to massive market pressure during the period of the greatest depression. Therefore, recovery was not forthcoming, in spite of sufficient financial reserves and investments before 1929. It was impossible to maintain, not to speak of extending, exports. Therefore, investments and depreciation were low. The structure of the productive assets of this industry hardly changed, as

66 This was a reaction of the Western powers to the Italian attack on Abyssinia in October 1935.

it remained permanently underemployed. Again, currency devaluation, exchange control and other policy devices were a minor issue for economic performance, but only aggravated the situation.

6.2.7. Traditional Machine Building Industry

Economic performance of this industrial sector was appalling. It was heavily hit by the decline of foreign trade and never recovered. In the depression, level of employment dropped from 42 to 22% and only rose to 32% in 1935. Estimated total output of this sector declined to less than half by 1932.[67] Value and volume of export dropped 75% until 1932, increased only 35% until 1935 and dropped again 21% in 1936. In the next year, volume was barely back to one third and value to about 38% of 1929 export levels.[68]

a. Hofherr-Schrantz

Financial Standing

For the period after 1930, only limited information on Hofherr-Schrantz is available.[69] The already low earning power, deficits in the late 20s, minute profits in 1928 and 1929, and very high debts, led to a complete financial breakdown of this firm during the depression. Already in 1930, gross profit shrank one third and the company made substantial losses of nearly 1.2 million schillings. Between 1931 and 1933, total losses amounted to 12.2 million schillings. With small capital stock and reserve of only 4.3 million (including 3 million joint-stock capital) and debts amounting to 20.7 million (of which 14 million were bank credits), Hofherr was unable to sustain such losses. The firm was at the mercy of its financing banks. Until 1935, tenacious negotiations for financial reconstruction took place with the main creditor banks, which also held the majority of stock capital. Two of these banks, the Länderbank and the Industriekredit AG,[70] were willing to remit debts, whereas foreign banks, the Bulgarian-Italian bank and the Banque Franco Belge, only reluctantly released Hofherr liabilities. This behaviour was understandable when eventually, total debts of 17 million had to be remitted. Share capital was reduced from 3 million to only 75 thousand schillings and was revaluated to its original value thereafter. The new shares were taken up by the creditor banks.[71]

Business Activity

The international decline of agriculture certainly was the main factor affecting Hofherr export sales in the depression. In 1930, export business to Russia had to

67 Bundesamt für Statistik, *Statistisches Handbuch für den Bundesstaat Österreich 1937*, 75.

68 Own calculation from Österreichisches Statistisches Zentralamt, *Aussenhandel*, 68.

69 *Bilanzen* 12.7.1930, 19.12.1931, 14.1.1933, 27.7.1935. See also A.13.

70 This was the reconstructed successor bank of the Niederösterreichische Escomptegesellschaft. Besides foreign shares, it also had shares of Hofherr, Alpine, Simmeringer, Bleiberger Bergwerk, Semperit, Schwechater, Ditmar-Brünner and Union Baugesellschaft. *Bilanzen*, 11.5.1935.

71 Mathis, *Big Business*, 153.

be restricted, although this country expanded its imports of agricultural machinery and equipment from 61 million to 83 million reichsmarks in 1930.[72] Hofherr simply could not continue deliveries to this market, as terms of payment were long and risks were too high. At the same time, the deficit guarantee of Vienna was running out and the state deficit guarantee scheme did not provide an adequate substitute. Thus, only products worth 150 thousand dollars (about 1.1 million schillings) were sold in Soviet Russia. In all other export areas, such as Czechoslovakia, Poland, Italy, Spain, Romania and Bulgaria, the fall of agricultural prices everywhere harmed sales directly. Total value of turnover dropped one quarter.

The year 1931 was, of course, even worse. Management made desperate attempts to cushion the effects of economic decline by intensifying rationalisation and trying to diversify its production. In the late 20s, some new and more simple production branches had been introduced, such as the production of home cooking ovens, water pipes, simple household appliances, cigarette machines, and brake pads for tramways. But these items only amounted to one fifth of sales. Now, during the depression, the manufacturing of combine harvesters began, of which only four were delivered to Argentina. Markets were closed for such expensive products, especially as they had to compete against cheaper American products. Of course, these efforts came too late as purchasing power of all markets continued to drop. Emergency decrees that helped to extend or lower debt payments in many agricultural countries contributed to deficits. In Bulgaria, for example, emergency laws permitted a reduction of annual repayment of outstanding foreign debts to 10% of value.

Eventually, as its main Eastern European markets continued to suffer from the depression, Hofherr-Schrantz barely recovered until 1937 and was bought up by the largest German producer of agricultural machinery in 1938.[73]

b. Engine Factories

Business Activity and Financial Standing

The engine factories that had merged into the Wiener Lokomotivfabriks AG[74] in 1930 were probably the only machine building sector whose downfall in the depression was postponed because of public railway investment. Since the relatively large railway orders until 1927, business had been declining in the late 20s. Falling sales combined with the merger in 1930 resulted in the first minor deficit. However, the government railway investment of 151.8 million schillings in 1930, the largest publicly invested sum in the First Republic,[75] showed its mild, but indeed helpful, implications on business activity in 1931 and enabled the Wiener to balance its profit and loss account for one more year. While all other production branches, machine and steam boiler building, steam roller manufacture and the iron foundry, had only very little employment, value of turnover of engine production doubled. The Austrian railway ordered 35 steam engines, ten tenders and part of the mechani-

72 "Das Rußlandgeschäft in der Weltwirtschaftskrisis," in: Deutsches Institut für Wirtschaftsforschung, *Wochenbericht*, vol. 5, no. 12, 1932, 54.

73 Mathis, *Big Business*, 153.

74 *Bilanzen*, 24.9.1932, 18.11.1933, 21.8.1937. See also A.26.

75 Fibich, 143.

cal equipment of 18 electrical engines. This demand, though, only enabled partial capacity utilisation for a short period of time.

Already by the following year, employment from these orders ran out. Only the delivery of mechanical equipment continued until 1932. State investment and export sales reached rock-bottom, and turnover value dropped to one third of its 1931 level. As business remained depressed until 1937, it was impossible to lower expenses. From this time on, losses occurred at least until 1936, amounting to roughly 2.8 million schillings. Until 1937, hopes for rising employment from new state railway investments were shattered. However, in spite of this, the financial standing of this company was stable. Losses were covered by capital reserves of 3.25 million, which declined to 680 thousand. The balance sheet still revealed high liquidity as creditor and debtor values were balanced.

Finally, business began to thrive suddenly in 1937, after the first railway orders in nearly five years had come in the year before.[76] The Wiener had employment from orders for 26 electrical engines and 20 steam coaches. Other branches of production enjoyed slow and moderate recovery as well once the domestic market demand from moderate private investment began to pick up in this year. Steam boiler manufacturing and machine building for the paper and sugar industries especially benefited from this.

c. Simmeringer

Business Activity and Financial Standing

Similar to the engine factories, the Simmeringer,[77] whose manufacturing emphasis was on carriage production, was highly dependent upon public railway orders. Therefore, as large orders came in, 1930 was the best business year of the inter-war period. As soon as public investment declined and railway orders terminated in 1931, business and finances declined rapidly. The deficit of public orders could not be counterpoised by the machine building department, and so total turnover dropped from 32 million to 17 million. Whereas gross profits nearly declined more than 60% and net profits nearly 80%, it was just about possible to balance the income account. In 1932, the department of carriage production lay almost idle, and even though the department of machine building delivered a high pressure boiler plant, a steam turbine and cranes, a deficit of 240 thousand still could not be avoided. Turnover declined to 7 million schillings.

In the following years, no proper business report was published. Although a financial reconstruction was carried through in 1933, the company kept having losses. In 1936, the annual deficit amounted to half a million. Planned exports to Bulgaria were a failure, because of fierce international competition and price struggles. Export prices were below prime cost prices. Since the mid 30s, the machine building section was satisfactorily employed, but the main branch of production was continuously under-utilised. The concentration of Austrian carriage production with the take-over of

76 "1936 brachte der AG endlich die ersehnten Bestellungen auf Dampfloks, 'worauf sie ein halbes Jahrzehnt vergebens gewartet hatte, [...]'". *Bilanzen*, 21.8.1937.

77 *Bilanzen*, 1.8.1931, 9.7.1932, 2.12.1933, 30.6.1934, 19.11.1934, 21.11.1936, 8.5.1937, 16.10.1937. See also A.22.

the majority of the Grazer Waggon- und Maschinenfabriks AG shares in 1934,[78] did not improve the business situation. The main problem remained the lack of railway orders. A moderate improvement of business only came with an order of 378 cargo carriages and six diesel motorcoaches in 1937. However, these orders still remained far too small to bring a substantial rectification of the financial situation.

d. Summary The companies of the traditional machine building sector suffered most from the depression. As their production processes and products were obsolete already in the 20s, they were unable to sustain sufficient domestic and foreign sales in the depression. The only moderate recovery of the late 20s hardly gave them a chance to improve and adjust their production to international standards. In addition, to rely heavily on public railway orders was clearly a mistake. Even the relatively large state investments of the year 1930 only offered short-term employment. In all, it can be stated that these firms hardly participated in the industrialisation process of the 20s and 30s. As new and modern products substituted the products of these firms and as the purchasing power of the traditional markets of these firms deteriorated, capacity of the engine factories, of Hofherr and of Simmeringer remained utterly underemployed and unchanged.

6.3. MODERN INDUSTRIES

6.3.1. Electrical Engineering Industry

a. International Development In the 1930s, there was a considerable expansion of electricity supply in all advanced and developing countries. The rate of expansion varied, according to the volume and rate of expansion and development before 1929. In Austria, however, the rate of expansion of electricity supply between 1929 and 1937 seemed to have been one of the lowest. While in the Netherlands, Switzerland and Belgium growth rates were 30% and above, in Austria there was only an expansion of barely 18%. In Britain and Germany rate of expansion was between 60 and more than 100%.[79]

The increase of production of electrical machinery and goods in the 30s must have been primarily based on domestic growth and demand, while the importance of foreign trade for national producers world-wide declined. During the depression and thereafter, world trade in electrical goods of all sorts suffered heavily from the decline and slow recovery of world trade and the fall of prices (see table 6.3). Of course, this fact was particularly hard for the export dependent Austrian electrical engineering industry, which was more intensely affected than electrical engineering elsewhere. While the Austrian value of exports of this industrial sector expanded 122% in the 20s, it continuously dropped until 1933 and hardly recovered thereafter. Value of exports declined more than 56% between 1929 and 1937. Volume of

78 Mathis, *Big Business*, 285.
79 Own calculation from Statistisches Reichsamt, *Jahrbuch 1938*, 85.

Year	Value of Austrian Exports	Value of German Exports	Value of World Exports	Index of Value of Austrian Exports	Index of Volume of Austrian Exports	Index of Value of German Exports	Index of Value of World Exports	Index of Volume of World Exports
1929	51.5	639	2294.8	100	100	100	100	100
1930	50.7		2181.4	98.5	107.5		95.1	96.9
1931	39.4		1648.7	76.5	69.4		71.8	78.6
1932	21.2	354	1012.2	41.2	38.9	55.4	44.1	53.0
1933	18.9	249	834.9	36.7	35.5	39.0	34.6	52.6
1934	19.9	226	866.3	38.6	42.5	35.4	37.8	62.8
1935	15.9	233	904.0	30.9	36.6	36.5	39.4	70.0
1936	17.3	266	1000.8	33.6	45.3	41.6	43.6	80.8
1937	22.4	328	1236.0	43.5	84.0	51.3	53.9	95.8

Table 6.3.: Exports of electrical products of Austria, Germany and of the world in million reichsmarks, and indices of value and volume of exports (1929=100). Source: Data for Austria calculated from: Österreichisches Statistisches Zentralamt, *Aussenhandel*, 67. Austrian export value in schillings converted into reichsmarks at current exchange rates according to Schneider, Schwarzer and Denzel, 286. The decline of the value of Austrian exports in 1935 and 1936 was in reality not as pronounced as indicated here, because the mark appreciated against the schilling in these years. Data for Germany from *Statistisches Handbuch von Deutschland*, 302. Data for world development from: "DerWelthandel in elektrotechnischen Erzeugnissen," in: Deutsches Institut für Wirtschaftsforschung, *Wochenbericht*, vol. 12, no. 20, Berlin 1939, 126.

exports only declined 16%, not quite reaching 1928 level. Volume of world exports of electrical products, though, nearly recovered until 1937.

Trade conditions were almost equally poor for other countries, but again national producers in large countries were able to take advantage of their home markets. This was especially the case for Germany, where rearmament supported this process. German export value, for example, also dropped nearly by half, a bit stronger than value of world exports. Meanwhile, value of German production only shrank 22% until 1937 and its workforce slightly expanded.[80] Compared to 1928, total sales had increased 19% until January 1938. Domestic sales of German electrical engineering companies increased 36.8%, whereas export sales dropped more than 40%. This indicates that it was possible for the German electrical engineering industry to evade declining foreign trade and divert sales to the domestic market. Furthermore, also this industrial branch benefited from massive rearmament demand. In the late 30s, between 50 and 80% of employment of some companies was generated by rearmament orders.[81] However, just like the representatives of the German heavy industry, Siemens, for example, did not trust the state investment-led boom and feared over-expansion.[82]

Even though it was an important industry with a 7.6% share of capital of all Austrian industrial joint-stock companies in 1935,[83] the Austrian electrical engineering export industry played a minor role in world markets and faced fierce competition. The German industry still remained the most important exporter of electrical products, with a more than 26% share of world exports. It was followed by the US (25.5%), Britain (19.5%), and the Netherlands (8%). The Austrian export industry ranked number ten in the world with only a 1.9% share of world exports in 1937. Thus, it was still behind the industries of Japan, Sweden, Belgium and Luxembourg, Switzerland and France.[84] Therefore, not only did this industrial sector suffer from slow expansion of electricity supply at home, but it was also strongly affected by the decline of trade, whereas its economic leverage on world markets was negligible.

However, in the 30s, it proved to be most worthwhile for Austrian companies, when business policy was strongly trade oriented. Certainly this industry[85] was severely hit by the termination of public orders from Vienna, the federal states and the railway in 1930 and 1931. During the depression, domestic sales declined much more rapidly than export sales, which remained largely unaffected by exchange control systems and other trade restrictions, at least in the early 30s. Hence, the most trade oriented of the four major Austrian companies also enjoyed the most favourable economic performance. While public investments for electrification came to a com-

80 Länderrat des Amerikanischen Besatzungsgebietes, *Statistisches Handbuch von Deutschland*, 302.

81 Wilfried Feldenkirchen, *Siemens, 1918–1945*, Munich 1995, 134, 137–138.

82 Ibid., 328.

83 Bundesamt für Statistik, *Statistisches Handbuch für den Bundesstaat Österreich 1937*, 83. Including electrical supply companies, the share was 26%.

84 Institut für Wirtschaftsforschung, *Wochenbericht*, vol.12, no.20, 1939, 127.

85 The following information on the electrical engineering industry is from general reports in *Bilanzen*: 16.7.1932, 26.8.1933, 25.8.1934, 27.4.1935, 24.5.1935, 22.8.1936, 2.10.1937.

plete halt in 1932, and the domestic private industry almost stopped all investments, some of the electrical engineering companies, among them first and foremost Elin, were able to focus their business on export sales in order to limit the effects of the depression. Until 1934, AEG, Siemens and Brown-Boveri made deficits, while the independent Elin, pressing its foreign business forward, made small profits.

Generally, for all companies, the 1930s were difficult years. Since the home market remained stagnant, the companies had to increase their export rate, even though foreign trade was not nearly as buoyant and smooth as in the late 20s. Moreover, currency fluctuation and competition from counterparts in the large countries constituted huge problems. International markets had contracted, national markets were much more in the grip of national producers and protectionist policies, and foreign trade competition was fiercer than ever, explaining the contradiction of development between volume and value of exports. Thus, this situation for relatively large companies with a small market was a dilemma. The only options remained to wait for reviving public and private investment, or to press relatively unprofitable export trade forward, which remained one of the most vital pillars of business that kept this industry going in difficult times. In order to withstand unfavourable trade conditions, increasing specialisation of export items with low demand elasticity was necessary. By and large this industry was damaged by the decline of trade, national retrenchment and structural distortions, but the nature of its advanced products and its export orientation allowed it to stay afloat relatively well. Very moderate recovery only came in the late 30s, with slow increases in public and semi-public investment and participation in the international rearmament boom. It should be noted, though, that also the large German electrical engineering companies, benefiting from the four year plan, were only able to recover volume of production after the mid 30s and value of turnover in the last few years of the decade.[86] The German AEG, for instance, only surpassed 1928 value of turnover in 1939.[87]

b. Elin

Financial Standing

The Elin,[88] the second largest electrical engineering company during the late 20s,[89] tumbled into the depression with stable finances and consolidated export business. Debts and bank credit were small, especially because a sterling loan was used. The balance sheet revealed the abrupt halt of rapid expansion of business in 1929 and 1930. Balance sheet value declined 26% until 1934. Its financial standing, however, remained very stable. Value of liabilities was always well below debtor value. The balance also shows the capital gain from the depreciation of the bonded sterling debt in 1931. It fell 2.36 million schillings. Unlike almost all other Austrian companies of the traditional and modern industries, Elin was able to balance its profit and loss

86 Feldenkirchen, *Siemens*, 327–328.

87 Gert Hautsch, *Der Elektrokonzern AEG-Telefunken. Untersuchungen zum Verhältnis von Wirtschaft und Politik am Beispiel eines westdeutschen Großunternehmens*, Bremen 1982, 41.

88 *Bilanzen*, 29.8.1931, 30.7.1932, 26.8.1933, 25.8.1934, 31.8.1935, 16.11.1935, 19.9.1936, 16.10.1937. See also A.10.

89 Mathis, *Big Business*, 92.

accounts and made minor profits in the depression and throughout the 30s without having to undergo a profound financial reconstruction. In 1930, gross profits only declined 1.4% and net profits only 26%. After 1931, minute net profits and small investments were made. It was possible to avoid deficits not only because of excellent financial standing and stable business in 1929, but also because it was possible to cut expenses drastically: 9% in 1931 and even 20% in 1932. Furthermore, after 1933, the company still benefited from a reduction of debt service, because of sterling depreciation. It also took advantage of profits from depreciation of the sterling bond. In spite of increasing turnover after 1933, it was not possible to make higher net profits as prices continued to be depressed.

Business Activity

Notwithstanding business decline on the Austrian market already in late 1929, management was still able to increase turnover, by forcing an increase of export sales, especially of highly developed finished products. As the recession worsened in 1930, and demand from private and public domestic orders weakened, in particular from the construction of hydro-power plants, it became expedient to press export business forward even more. Permanent search for employment on foreign markets had highest priority. In 1930, 60% of turnover was sold abroad. Transmission lines and a power plant, including a transformer station, were built in Poland. A transformer was delivered to Bulgaria, and a diesel power plant was set up in Greece. In 1931, when business continued to worsen, Elin management continued to make the right policy choice, and remained focused on foreign markets, whereas the other electrical engineering firms were contractually bound by their parent companies to limit diffusion of their exports. For Elin, orders from Yugoslavia, Egypt, and South Africa increased. Soviet Russia, augmenting its total value of imports of electrical machinery and other electrical engineering products to 116 million reichsmarks in 1931, still remained an especially important customer.[90]

1932 and 1933 were the most difficult years. Again, domestic demand declined much more than foreign demand. Particularly, foreign demand of special and highly developed products, such as specific welding equipment and various types of rectifiers, were able to stand their ground on international markets. Manufacture of such products and also of incandescent lamps remained stable. With expansive and aggressive export business, it was possible to limit the drop of total value of turnover (-35%) only to the year 1932. Very new types of welding sets, allowing the construction of large sized steel supporters, were sold in the Netherlands. A large diesel power plant was delivered to the Assuan dam. The city power system of Guirga, Egypt, was extended. From Bulgaria, the Elin accepted orders for a 20 kilometre transmission line and a transformer station. In Poland and Yugoslavia, rectifier plants and high voltage rectifiers were constructed.

The low mark of domestic sales in 1933 was well compensated by reviving exports in the second half of the year. Once again, most successful were the sales of highly developed special products of electrical engineering, such as welding equip-

90 Deutsches Institut für Konjunkturforschung, "Das Rußlandgeschäft," 1932, 54. In fact, in 1931, the value of total Russian imports reached their peak. See: Stickstoff-Sydikat, *UdSSR*, 62.

ment. To be able to maintain and increase export business and competitiveness after 1933, the company enlarged its range of production of other highly developed electrical items. Research and development of high quality technology was advanced. The machinery department developed more than one hundred new products, among them new types of electrolytic rectifiers, stage-selector switch controls, protective switches for electric motors, special oil drilling engines, high powered squirrel-cage motors, direct-current machinery and new electric stoves. Management remarked that currency and trade restrictions were less harmful to business than the year before, even though the dollar was devalued.[91] Foreign sales became more and more far reaching until 1938, as exports went to 54 different countries. Within 80% of these, business improved. Between 65 and 80% of total value of turnover was exported. While sales to Russia declined after 1932, deliveries and construction to the Near and Far East, South America and South Africa could be extended. For instance, high voltage rectifiers were set up in Cracow, and some were constructed for radio stations and for the state owned telephone company in Warsaw.

In 1934, still no substantial profit was made, even though capacity was utilised between 65 and 70% and export business was expanding. Continuously falling prices remained the main problem on international markets. Between 1934 and 1935, average prices of electrical machinery dropped around 16% and those of other electrical products 10%. Even the huge German electrical engineering industry required supreme effort to keep up the profitableness of foreign trade.[92] Yet, Elin could expand foreign trade, and export business was successful. The main markets remained the industrialised Western European countries, the Near East, the Balkans, Italy, South Africa and other areas overseas. According to management, export sales only declined in areas where either political unrest (as in Spain) or extreme currency devaluation coincided with harsh intensification of trade restrictions (as in Denmark and Czechoslovakia). Also, by the mid 30s, orders from public investment slowly began to increase again. Elin did switchgear installations for the railway plant in Mallnitz and made a few deliveries to Viennese power plants.

While there was hardly any stimulation from the Austrian home market, in 1935 and 1936 foreign sales continuously rose, so that the rectifier and neon light factories had to be enlarged. In both years turnover increased 15%. The export rate was augmented to 80% of turnover. However, competition on world markets had become more fierce with currency depreciation of the gold bloc countries and government export bounties directly supporting foreign competitors. Profit margins could not be raised. Research and development was enforced, while management continued to expand foreign trade to new overseas markets. In 1936, the extension of export business stopped. The export rate went slightly below 80%. In the following year, public investment finally offered increasing employment, but business remained focused on markets abroad until the war.

91 "Das ist eine für das Jahr der Dollarabwertung bemerkenswerte feststellung." *Bilanzen*, 25.8.1934.

92 "Der Auslandsabsatz der elektrotechnischen Industrie," in: Deutsches Institut für Konjunkturforschung, *Wochenbericht*, vol. 9, no. 20, Berlin 1936, 77–78.

c. Siemens

Financial Standing

Even though economic performance of this firm[93] was not as positive, its financial situation remained excellent throughout the 30s. Since it had been the main supplier of the Austrian home market in the 20s, export sales only played a minor role. They only came to 20% of turnover value in 1929. Under pressure, the export rate was reluctantly raised in the 30s, but by and large, sales abroad remained of secondary importance. Since home market demand declined much more than foreign demand in the depression, Siemens' petty foreign trade orientation is the main explanation for the continuous and extreme under-utilisation of plant capacity, and therefore, the primary cause of deficits in the 30s.

In 1929, earning power had still been 19%. In 1931, it was still possible to balance the profit and loss account. Between 1932 and 1936, however, total annual losses amounted to 6.2 million schillings. The profit and loss report of 1936 is deceiving, because the balance was reconstructed. In fact, in 1936, a deficit of 380 thousand schillings was made. Yet, the company could rely on ample financial resources of 51.2 million of capital stock and reserve, accumulated in the 20s. Furthermore, large bank deposits existed, while debtor value was always well above value of liabilities. Liabilities and balance sheet value declined incessantly between 1928 and 1936 as a result of the decrease of business volume. In 1932, expenses were especially oppressive since large indemnity payments of 1.75 million had to be made for laid-off workers and employees. But financial standing could be considered save, as capital stock and reserves still made up more than 48 million, while debts amounted to 8.06 million only.[94] Although turnover began to increase once again in 1934, value of gross profits only recovered in 1935. By that year, losses were not covered by capital reserves any more, but with capital accumulation from price gains of their own stocks (1.64 million) and from gains in currency speculation. Generally, the financial situation remained very stable. Depreciation was declining, but investments seemed to have been higher than those of other electrical engineering companies.

Business Activity

Due to the fact that Siemens mainly relied on domestic private and public investment from power plant construction and railway electrification, its business was exceptionally weakened by the lack of public expenditure. By way of contrast, the Hungarian Siemens, one of its subsidiary firms, could only maintain satisfactory business levels due to state investment for the electrification of the railway track between Budapest and Hegyeshalom. Although the Austrian government also went ahead with large railway investments in 1930, Siemens' department for the manufacture of railway equipment lacked orders in that year. Only the cable and metal producing plants were fully employed. The majority of demand came from the various power plants in the federal states and Vienna, the postal service and the partial

93 *Bilanzen*, 4.7.1931, 16.7.1932, 26.8.1933, 1.9.1934, 24.8.1935, 22.8.1936, 2.10.1937. See also A.21.

94 "Die Gesellschaft kann also noch manchen Stoß leicht aushalten." *Bilanzen*, 26.8.1933.

electrification of production of a few private enterprises. In addition, the company installed the lighting system of the Austrian parliament. In 1930, turnover value still dropped only 15%.

In subsequent years, the decline of public investment really made itself felt. In 1931 Siemens ran out of employment from previous orders, and total turnover fell another 30%. Capacity utilisation was only 40%. Turnover kept declining the next two years. In 1932, employment of plant capacity dropped to 30% and reached an all time low of 25% in 1933. The worst contraction was noticed by the department for industrial electrification. Foreign trade was advanced and exports amounted to about half of total turnover, which in turn, dropped again 30% in 1933. Semi-public supply companies hardly invested at all this year, but export business picked up a little with the sale of special equipment.

Once employment opportunities from the railways and electricity supply companies slowly extended, moderate recovery in the mid 30s progressed painfully sluggishly. Management quickly concentrated sales on its home market after a short upsurge of foreign sales in 1934. An improvement of business was experienced when Siemens finally benefited from a modest upswing of its home market and continued to maintain export rates on the unusually high level of more than half of its turnover. However, sales only increased 10% and capacity utilisation just rose 5%. Export business remained difficult as prices progressively declined, especially in countries that devalued their currencies. Outlet areas abroad were the allocated markets of the successor states and the Balkan countries, but also Palestine. Some special constructions were even sold in Germany. As in 1935 and 1936, the majority of turnover was again generated at home, its value only increased 17 and 12%. Employment of plant capacity was still at the order of 40 and 50%. Contracts and orders came from Viennese and federal supply companies for extension and modernisation of plant and from the railways for electrical railcars and engines. Deliveries of electrical heating systems, machinery and turbines were also made to private industrial sectors, such as the textile, mining, iron and steel and paper industries. As a result of a limited stimulation in house-building in Vienna and in some of the provincial cities, demand for electrical household appliances, such as hot water boilers and electrical stoves and ovens, intensified as well. For most industries, 1937 finally saw a serious step towards substantial recovery. Already in the first eight months, turnover increased 40%, excluding deliveries to the railways.

d. AEG

Financial Standing

Due to large excess capacities, very limited export business and small financial reserves, the AEG was struck the hardest by the depression.[95] With total net annual losses of more than about 12.7 million schillings between 1931 and 1936, financial development in the 30s can truly be called catastrophic. This not only suggests poor and insufficient accounting, and inadequate gold balance sheet preparation in 1925,

95 *Bilanzen*, 14.6.1930, 4.7.1931, 23.7.1932, 16.9.1933, 18.4.1936, 5.9.1936, 9.10.1937. See also A.1.

but also that financial reconstruction would have been necessary well before the economic downswing. Liabilities climbed more than 40% until 1934, and surpassed debtor value 85%. Since 1929, gross profits had declined 78%. In the worst year, 1932, expenses amounted to more than twice as much as gross profits. A major factor that contributed to its weak financial standing and downfall in the depression was the fact that the majority of stock and reserve capital came from the Swiss franc loan taken up in 1926. In 1931, capital stock and reserves amounted to 10.76 million schillings, 8.87 of which consisted of the Swiss franc loan. Moreover, annual deficits could only be covered by these reserves. Thus, basically massive losses were covered by large long-term debts. Hence, already by the next year, reserves dwindled to 7.92 million schillings.

After another two years of deficits, the balance had to be reconstructed in 1935. Until then, total gross deficit was about 18.7 million schillings. Primarily they consisted of all annual losses until then (11.7 million), and of other losses from special depreciation on capital assets, losses from foreign currency depreciation, write-offs of debt claims, and losses from the appreciation of the Swiss bond against the schilling. Massive deficits and reconstruction were financed by a large reduction of share-capital, the giving away of left over reserves, the waiving of all debt claims by AEG Berlin and by the sale of foreign holdings. Finally, the value of depreciation was raised to adequate levels and a proper reserve could be built up, which provided the money to cover that year's loss of almost 700 thousand schillings. The 1936 balance sheet and profit and loss account were deliberately non-transparent, because management attempted to depict the depreciation of the Swiss franc loan, amounting to almost 950 thousand, as a profit. Thus, reported gross profits of 2.4 million, actually only came to 1.45 million. This way, it was possible to represent a loss of only four thousand schillings, although the actual loss was far higher than in 1935, running to 953 thousand schillings. Therefore, financial standing did not recover at all, despite large scale reconstruction.

Reconstruction of the German parent company was carried out in similar fashion. In 1936, value of capital stock was reduced one third and revaluated to 120 million reichsmarks.[96] It had also suffered from equally poor accounting and bad financial policy towards its associated companies in the 20s, resulting in massive losses during the depression. Even though its business decline was similar to that of Siemens, total losses of the German AEG were far higher, amounting to 120 million reichsmarks, of which only 60.6 million were due to normal reduction of business in the crisis.[97]

Business Activity

Economic performance was equally poor. The main reason was that AEG plunged into the depression at a time when its business and financial standing were already low. Like Siemens, sales policy was rigid, mostly focusing on moderate demand of the home market in the late 20s. Dependence on public orders was high, profitability

96 Hautsch, 41.

97 Feldenkirchen, *Siemens*, 127 and 128.

and export rate (15–25%) were low, whereas capacity employment had already been only 50% in the period of moderate prosperity. A large portion of employment in 1930 came from large government railway investments. Two freight engines were delivered, eleven engines were still being built and other electrical railway equipment was ordered. Orders from supply companies and private enterprises also came in. Three transformers, 19 crane sets and equipment of 13 special cranes were sold in Russia.

However, to maintain business volume and to prevent financial deterioration, this employment was too small. Total turnover dropped already 10% and capacity utilisation was less than half. As the volume of domestic public orders shrank, and export sales almost completely terminated, employment of capital assets and turnover continued to decline in the following years. In 1931 and 1932, utilisation was down to 20–30%. In 1932, turnover dropped 40%. Subsidiary firms in Czechoslovakia and Hungary also made massive losses.

Even after 1935, business activity had not even nearly approached pre-crisis levels. Similar to Siemens, nearly all of the very modest home demand came from public orders and some from private industrial investment. For example, one mine engine was delivered to the Graz-Köflacher, one to the Alpine and one to a tobacco factory. Few deliveries were also made to the chemical, steel, sugar and paper industries. As the railways and various supply companies finally increased their investments, domestic sales began to pick up in the following two years. Coal dust firing systems, high frequency furnaces and rectifiers met with approval on the market. Yet, it was impossible to employ capacity to an adequate degree, since management only relied on stagnating home demand and did not make any efforts to advance foreign trade. There was no financial and general recovery until 1937.

e. Brown-Boveri

Financial Standing

The financial situation and business activity of this firm,[98] the smallest electrical engineering joint-stock company, developed somewhat contrary to Siemens. Siemens suffered from low plant employment and could not really revive business, but enjoyed stable financial standing. Brown-Boveri, on the other hand, was at least able to recover capacity utilisation by expanding foreign sales, but could not maintain stable finances and required reconstruction. As business reports, and profit and loss accounts appeared unusually positive in the depression and thereafter, they seemed to have been palliated by management. Although the balance sheet revealed drastic contraction of business volume between 1929 and 1931, losses were prevented. In spite of a 63.6% decline of gross profits from peak to trough, only very moderate annual losses were made between 1932 and 1934, running to 1.2 million schillings. These were seemingly well covered by capital stock and reserve, which still had amounted to 6.95 million in 1931. No short-term bank credits had been taken up until then, and only the Swiss bonded debt and other foreign liabilities appreciated.

98 *Bilanzen*, 1.8.1931, 23.7.1932, 4.11.1933, 8.9.1934, 21.9.1935, 14.11.1936, 21.11.1936, 9.1.1937, 23.10.1937. See also A.7.

It seems that shareholder interests favoured deference of a necessary and speedy financial reconstruction. Moreover, management attempted to prevent higher losses by fraudulently altering the balances and keeping expenses below absolute minimum, i. e. avoiding sufficient depreciation of plant and investments. Apart from unclear possible financial advantages for shareholders and management, the main motives of deference of the balance reorganisation were apparently uncertain future economic prospects as a result of political instability in Germany and Austria.[99] The 1935 balance finally had to be reconstructed. According to the business report issued in 1937, deficits of the Austrian Brown-Boveri only came to 290 thousand schillings. Yet, actual losses ran to 6.5 million, because they included a massive backlog of depreciation (6.4 million). This huge loss was covered by capital reserves, remission of debts (2.25 million) by the Swiss parent company and the Industriekredit AG, and reduction of shareholder capital (2.8 million). Because of the disintegration of the gold bloc, the burden of the Swiss franc loan also eased, more than 600 thousand schillings. At the end of this process, all liabilities were barely covered by the remainder of capital stock and reserve, and losses of 1.45 million were still outstanding. Overall, the financial situation in the 30s can be called precarious.

Business Activity
The comparatively high level of capacity utilisation and turnover can be attributed to a very flexible sales policy. In the late 20s, Brown-Boveri heavily relied on ordinary public orders, and its export rate was only between 15 and 25% of turnover value. When turnover dropped precipitously in the depression (25% in 1930, 50% in 1931, and another 48% in 1932), management augmented its export rate quickly, up to 60% after 1932. In 1933, the decline of turnover could finally be cushioned. Essentially, this had been possible due to a moderate increase of foreign trade, mainly to Russia, and to Eastern and Western Europe. Since Russian terms of payment could be up to 21 months, export expansion would not have been possible without support of the state export guarantee. Already in 1930, most of foreign sales went to Soviet Russia. During the depression, it intensified, reaching its peak in 1932 when the equipment for two tube rolling mills in Nikopol was ordered and equipment and machinery were delivered to a power and a transformer station in Bulgaria. Exports to Western countries, especially of control systems, also increased again in 1933. In this year, the oil producing industry in Romania was also an important customer, ordering electric motors, switchgear systems and installation material for refineries.

Although only a fraction of the workforce was employed in 1934, turnover rose 20% and capacity utilisation was back to 60%. Total income was not even half of the 1929 value, because of losses caused by deficits of the Romanian subsidiary com-

99 "Der Vorsitzende der Generalversammlung äußerte sich in sehr pessimistischem Sinn über die allgemeine Geschäftslage. Durch die Ereignisse in Deutschland und Österreich habe sich die politische Unsicherheit wesentlich verschärft. [...] Eine Wendung zum Besseren sei erst von einer Klärung der politischen Lage zu erwarten. [...] Angesichts der absoluten Gefahr, Maßnahmen zu treffen, die sich in Zukunft als ganz verfehlt erweisen können, habe die Verwaltung davon abgesehen, eine Sanierung der Bilanz vorzuschlagen, bleibe dagegen andauernd beschäftigt, durch geeignete Mittel ein weiteres Anwachsen der Verluste hintanzuhalten." *Bilanzen*, 8.9.1934.

pany. In addition, income from deals with Russian traders, conducted in US dollars, lost value in 1933, as the dollar depreciated after March 1933. Like Siemens and AEG, Brown-Boveri also mainly relied on the home market since the mid 30s, and only enjoyed very limited recovery. Value of turnover remained unsatisfactory, as 60% of business was again concentrated on moderate private, semi-public and public investment of the home market.[100] Even in 1936, turnover increased only 20%, even though 70% of capacity was employed. The main reasons for this poor financial result were the incredible fall of international and home market prices, supported by the wave of currency depreciation of the gold bloc countries.

6.3.2. Motor Industry

a. International Development

Although in all countries average growth rates of vehicle production were higher than total industrial production,[101] the world vehicle industry, which tripled its output after the depression, did not recover pre-crisis levels until 1937 (see table 6.4). Production performance of national producers in authoritarian states was, by far, the best, partially because their production and consumption started from comparably low levels, and partially because public policy supported these increases. Between 1932 and 1937, Germany increased output more than six times, Italy two and a half times, and Russia even more than eight and a half times. Compared to 1929, Germany augmented its output 155%, Italy 39% and Russia about 129 times! As the only country with a liberal economic system, British performance (+113%) was truly remarkable. Most other European producers, and not even the United States, did not recover 1929 output levels. Until 1937, French output was still only 16% and American just a little more than 10% below pre-crisis levels. As expected, the producers in small advanced countries tended to experience the worst declines of output. In 1937, Czechoslovak production was nearly 5%, Austrian 33%, and Belgian production even 79% (in 1936) below 1929 level.

As in the 1920s, most of production growth was based on national demand, while foreign trade stagnated. Vehicle manufacturers in large countries retrenched to their domestic markets and were protected by high import duties. For example, of its vehicle production of more than 240,000 in 1935, Germany only exported around 23,500 automobiles and trucks, not even 9.5% of total output.[102] By far, the most trade oriented manufacturers of the larger countries were British producers, export-

100 "Als gut kann aber der Geschäftsgang mangels zureichender Aufträge der öffentlichen Körperschaften immer noch nicht bezeichnet werden [...]. Die Zukunftsaussichten der Österr. Brown-Boveri hängen wie die Aussichten der gesamtem heimischen Elektroindustrie von der privaten und öffentlichen Investitionstätigkeit ab. Die große Hoffnung bleibt die Elektrifizierung der Bundesbahnen." *Bilanzen*, 9.1.1937.

101 "Die Kraftfahrzeugsaison 1936," in: Deutsches Institut für Konjunkturforschung, *Wochenbericht*, special issue, vol. 9, no. 34, Berlin 1936, 3.

102 Own calculation from: "Die Kraftfahrzeugkonjunktur im vierten Aufschwungsjahr," in: Deutsches Institut für Konjunkturforschung, *Wochenbericht*, special issue, vol. 9, no. 19, Berlin 1936, 2.

Years	Germany	GB	France	Italy	Soviet Russia	Belgium	CSR	Austria	US	World
1929	127.9	238.8	245.6	54.1	1.7	7.0	14.7	9.1	5358.4	6277.5
1930	96.0	236.6	230.7	42.7	8.5	4.7	16.8	3.2	3355.9	4126.5
1931	77.6	226.3	209.2	29.3	20.6	3.2	17.0	4.4	2389.7	3048.6
1932	51.6	232.7	180.7	29.1	25.4	2.2	13.6	2.4	1370.7	1977.0
1933	105.5	286.3	198.2	42.0	49.7	1.4	10.0	1.2	1920.0	2675.7
1934	174.7	342.5	198.2	44.8	72.5	0.7	9.9	2.1	2753.1	3735.8
1935	247.1	403.7	178.6	49.2	97.1	0.8	10.0	3.1	3946.9	5126.7
1936	301.9	461.4	209.3	51.1	137.0	1.5	12.0	6.4	4454.1	5815.8
1937	326.5	507.7	206.7	75.1	220.0	–	14.0	6.1	4809.0	6350.3

Table 6.4.: Production of automobiles and trucks, 1929–1937 (thousand). Source: Figures from Statistisches Reichsamt, *Jahrbuch* 1937, 81 and 1938, 83 (international survey). Numbers from Mitchell, *European Historical Statistics*, slightly differ; 278–280.

ing about 98,500 vehicles, or 19.4% of output amounting to 14% of the value of the world market.[103] However, the majority of this export went to the Empire countries, where it benefited from preferential tariffs. Furthermore, the British market was highly protected by the McKenna duties, imposing a tariff of 33.3% on imported cars,[104] hardly giving a chance to small national producers with lower productivity. Export rate of the French car industry was probably around 10% in 1936.[105]

Of course, for big national producers in large modern countries, declining foreign trade was, by far, not as harmful as it was to export dependent producers in small advanced countries. In large countries that underwent an economic boom and where the number of persons per car was still high, producers still enjoyed unsatisfied private and public demand in their home markets. This was the case for Germany, Italy and Russia. In large countries in which economies underwent stagnation or moderate recovery and where the number of people per car was very low, producers naturally faced low demand, saturated markets and a slow increase of output. This especially occurred in the US,[106] but also in France. Britain clearly experienced an exceptional boom in the 30s, and producers benefited from higher demand than in the late 20s. Between 1926 and 1929, production rose 20%, while between 1934 and 1937, it still increased more than 48%.

Very large national producers in the authoritarian states and Britain not only benefited from large markets, but also enjoyed the combined advantage of massively reduced unit prices and a reduction in the cost of car ownership. In the US market, this process had been fully exploited already in the 20s. In the case of a general upswing, these price reductions entailed a sudden spurt in demand. While number of units produced after 1933 increased in nearly all countries, the perfection and spread of mass production resulted in continuously declining prices. In Germany, for example, average car prices in 1935 were 25% below 1929 prices.[107] In 1937, they were 56% below pre-war prices.[108] The British industry was able to reduce car prices even more. In 1935, motor vehicles were about one third cheaper than in 1929.[109] Whereas volume of 1929 production was surpassed quite early in some countries, value of production never recovered in the 30s or was only slightly surpassed. Even in Germany, the large advanced country with the highest growth rate, output value of 1928 was only barely surpassed (+10.2%) in 1936.[110]

103 Musson, 346.

104 Musson, ibid.

105 According to sources from Heidrun Edelmann, *Vom Luxusgut zum Gebrauchsgegenstand. Die Geschichte der Verbreitung von Personenkraftwagen in Deutschland*, Frankfurt a. M. 1989, chapter 5, footnote 113. Edelmann estimated the German export rate to have ranged between 6.7 and 7.5% in 1935 and 1936, and the British 17%.

106 A study from the German business cycles research institute also pointed this out: Deutsches Institut für Wirtschaftsforschung, *Untersuchungen zur Kraftverkehrsplanung im europäischen Großwirtschaftsraum. I. Die Ausrüstung des europäischen Großwirtschaftsraums mit Kraftfahrzeugen und die Triebkräfte der europäischen Kraftverkehrsentwicklung*, unpublished manuscript, Berlin 1941, 112.

107 Deutsches Institut für Konjunkturforschung, "Die Kraftfahrzeugsaison," 4.

108 Edelmann, 165.

109 "Die Kraftfahrzeugsaison," 4.

110 Own calculation from: Deutsches Institut für Konjunkturforschung, "Die 'jungen' Industriezweige," in: *Wochenbericht*, vol. 10, no. 7, Berlin 1937, 33.

Consequently, foreign sales of the Austrian motor industry were heavily hit by the combined effect of declining prices, because of ever increasing international productivity, and collapsing and stagnating trade, resulting from national retrenchment of producers in large advanced countries. One of the main problems was that small national producers with small home markets were unable to lower prices as much as large national producers in Germany or Britain, not to speak of manufacturers in the US. Moreover, there was a huge disparity between home and export market prices, so that, for most producers, prices at home were far more profitable. For instance, for most German companies, export sales actually resulted in deficits, which could only be compensated by increased and higher priced domestic sales. Therefore, in order to have any capability to export, the home market of any national producer had to be large enough to expand the volume of domestic sales to an extent that allowed a dramatic reduction of production costs through rigorous extension of mass production, rationalisation and modernisation. Thus home market sales were bearing the unit costs for losses or low income of export sales.[111] As it was very difficult even for the German vehicle manufacturing industry to benefit from this process,[112] it proved to be impossible for the Austrian industry to raise competitiveness of production capacities to international standards. In 1937, the average price of one exported Austrian car was still 39% higher than that of an average imported foreign vehicle.[113] This way, Austrian firms were unable to make profits from foreign trade, and had no choice but to retrench to their home market as well.

Thus, export of Austrian vehicles and engines underwent a major crisis in the 30s. Between 1928 and 1932, value of exports dropped from 51 to 6.5 million schillings. Volume declined nearly as extremely. Thereupon, there was no recovery at all. In 1937, value of exports was still more than 72% and volume 60% below 1928 levels.[114] Therefore, the only option for Austrian producers remained to attempt to regain control over and retrench to the domestic market, and to hope for reviving international trade. Yet, the Austrian domestic market did not offer an adequate compensation, because poor home market demand had declined in the depression and only slowly recovered again until 1937. The number of licensed new vehicles per annum were only back to 4700 and 5700 vehicles by 1936 and 1937. In contrast, most smaller countries had higher annual demand. For instance, in Norway and Switzerland it was between 6000 and 12,000. Even in underdeveloped Portugal, the number for annually licensed cars and trucks was between 4000 and 5000. In the large developed countries figures ranged between 160,000 to more than 400,000 annually.[115] In Austria, therefore, as in all other small advanced countries, production levels of the late 30s were far below pre-crisis output levels. This process is reflected in the development of automobile companies.

111 Home market sales as "Kostenträgerin für die Exportverluste." Cited in Edelmann, 195.

112 Edelmann, 170 and 194. Only Opel, as part of the foreign holding of General Motors, was able to profit from export sales.

113 An average Austrian car came to 4976 schillings, whereas an imported vehicle amounted to 3558 schillings. Own calculation according to figures from Österreichisches Statistisches Zentralamt, *Aussenhandel*, 70.

114 Calculated from ibid, 70.

115 See Statistisches Reichsamt, *Jahrbuch 1937*, 106 and *Jahrbuch 1938*, 114.

b. Steyr-Daimler-Puch AG

Financial Standing

As the highly indebted Steyr[116] had conducted a risky business policy in the late 20s, it underwent a massive financial breakdown already in 1929, entailing a deficit of more than 24 million schillings. Only after slow state reconstruction enabled the Creditanstalt to stabilise Austria's largest automobile producer financially, it was possible to balance the profit and loss account in 1932 and thereafter. Massive remittance of debts, capital stock reduction and revaluation had been necessary. The balance sheet reveals a 31% reduction of liabilities, the majority of which included bank credit. Until 1933, it was almost possible to balance the value of creditors and debtors.

Also, the Austro-Daimler-Puchwerke,[117] which merged with Steyr in 1934, had been running massive debts which had to be lowered by debt remittance of the Creditanstalt, capital stock reduction and subsequent revaluation. After the merger, capital stock was raised to 13.2 million schillings, and the reduced debts of Daimler-Puch, still running to 13 million in 1933, had to be assumed. However, thanks to improving business after 1935, it was possible to reduce bank debts considerably. In spite of financial breakdown in the depression and difficult trade conditions, the renamed Steyr-Daimler-Puch made surprisingly high profits in 1935 and 1936. Profitability was with 12 and 20% well above the level of the late 20s.

Business Activity

Unfortunately, Steyr did not publish detailed business reports between 1929 and 1931. In the late 20s, the company must have produced well above 6000 automobiles, of which a fluctuating share of roughly 50 or 80% was exported. Until 1932, conditions had rapidly changed. The workforce had been reduced from 6200 to less than 1500. Although the company continued to provide nearly all of Austrian car output, its home market share declined and remained on low levels. Moreover, its export rate had dropped to 50% or less. In this year, Steyr sold 1800 cars (some of which had been on stock),[118] of which only far less than 500 were outbound sales.[119] The main export areas remained Germany, Hungary, Poland and Switzerland. Promising orders from Brazil and Portugal had been lost. Total domestic sales amounted to 2268 cars, of which Steyr had sold only 1368. Thus, its home market share was slightly more than 60%.

In 1933, turnover value increased 20%, but net profits and total exports still declined. The export rate of car sales increased to 50%. Two thirds of ball bearing sales were exported. The home market share continued to decline, while the propor-

116 *Bilanzen*, 5.3.1932, 3.12.1932, 17.12.1932, 7.1.1933, 25.2.1933, 17.6.1933, 23.9.1933, 20.10.1934, 20.1.1935, 20.7.1935, 8.8.1936, 24.10.1936, 26.6.1937. See also A.23.

117 *Bilanzen*, 26.7.1930, 25.11.1933, 19.5.1934, 22.9.1934. See also A.8.

118 Total car output was 1725. Bundesamt für Statistik, *Statistisches Handbuch für den Bundesstaat Österreich 1937*, 75.

119 Total number of exported Austrian cars was 432. Steyr must have sold the majority. Österreichisches Statistisches Zentralamt, *Aussenhandel*, 70.

tion of imported products increased. Of the 1433 brand-new automobiles licensed in Austria,[120] Steyr only had a share of 45%.

After the merger in 1934, Steyr-Daimler-Puch basically constituted the only automobile as well as the only motorcycle producer in Austria. It was the largest company, besides the Alpine and Semperit. It took over the manufacture of the large, more luxurious Daimler cars, the output of which had amounted to 800 units in 1929, and of Puch motorcycles, the production of which had run to 7000. The Daimler factory in Wiener Neustadt was closed and in September all production capacities were concentrated in Steyr. In spite of this concentration, competitiveness did not improve and business only slowly began to pick up. Foreign trade stagnated and did not surpass its 1931 level until 1937. In 1934, total sales only increased 20%, of which half was generated by car manufacture, 30% by bicycle and motorbike output and the rest by ball bearing and car battery production. Steyr's domestic market share slightly augmented. Nevertheless, of the more than 1700 licensed new automobiles, its share was still just 54%.

In the next two years, production could be raised more than 150%, finally allowing for higher capacity employment and acceptable profitability. The majority of this still slow upswing was based on rising demand of the home market, due to moderate general recovery, a reduction of car running costs, and a massive decrease of Austrian automobile prices. While it introduced the low cost, mass-produced compact car,[121] Steyr gained an increasing share of home market sales, rising approximately from 59% in 1935 to 82% in 1936. At the same time export volume stagnated until 1936. Export rate was only around 10%. In 1935, total turnover value increased 30% and capacity was utilised 75%. The following year, employment of car manufacture was up to 70% and up to 100% for motorcycle production. Total turnover increased 43%.

Thus, only after the mid 30s was the volume of home demand large enough to introduce profitable mass production of cheap cars. This process, in turn, enabled Steyr to regain control of its home market, which had been flooded by cheaper imported cars well into 1935. Moreover, home sales of mass-produced compact cars proved to be far more profitable than export sales of larger obsolete cars in the late 20s. Earning power had considerably improved, and in 1936 net profit was 24% above its highest pre-crisis value in 1927. However, Austrian car manufacturing was still far from full capacity utilisation as volume of output was still 40% below 1929 level. Furthermore, because of its disadvantages as a national producer with a small domestic market, Steyr was unable to compete on international markets and could not revive its once lively, but unprofitable export business. Therefore, even though Steyr must have considerably modernised and improved its production facilities in the 30s, there was still a great potential for expansion and productivity increase.

120 Bundesamt für Statistik, *Statistisches Handbuch für den Bundesstaat Österreich 1937*, 123.
121 This was the Steyr 50.

c. Austro-Fiat

Financial Standing

Financial standing of this company,[122] the largest utility vehicle manufacturer in Austria, was exceptionally stable before and after the depression. It was probably more consolidated than Elin or Veitscher. Even though, in real economic terms, it was heavily hit by the depression (massive reduction of output, sales and income), it never ran a deficit, could fully reinvest all depreciation and always had a bank deposit that was higher than its liabilities. However, turnover profitability shrunk from around 30% in the late 20s to around 5% until 1934 and 10% after the mid 30s.

Compared to the balance sheets, profit and loss accounts much more clearly revealed the drastic reduction of business activity. Only the decline of liabilities indirectly showed shrinking production and sales. Income, though, fell precipitously and did not recover. Until 1934, gross profits decreased 70% and net profits 96%, as expenses could only be reduced commensurately with falling income until 1931. In spite of the fact that until 1936 income had still not recovered at all, it was possible to pay dividends of 12 and 8% in 1930 and 1931, and to resume dividend payment of 5% in 1936. Furthermore, total debts never amounted to more than 11% of capital stock and reserve, whereas bank deposit only declined from 840 thousand in 1932 to 440 thousand schillings in 1936. Even contemporary journalists were amazed at the permanently stable financial situation, in spite of low sales and capacity employment.[123]

Business Activity

How was this possible? The main reasons for this seemingly contrary development were the complete retrenchment to the domestic market and the different nature of utility vehicle production. As already noted in chapter four, in contrast to motorcar manufacturing, utility vehicle production was far less risky and capital intensive. Even though prices of these products were also falling, home and international market pressure was far lower. The necessity to massively invest and to press export sales forward was not so great as for Steyr. Therefore, it was possible to pursue a safe business policy in the late 20s, that enabled management to avoid debts, accumulate capital and run into the recession with stable finances. The relation of the capacity of Austrian production and the market was also more favourable. In contrast to Steyr in the 20s, it was not necessary to resort to foreign sales in order to utilise capacity adequately, and so retrenchment to the apparently safe home market provided plenty of income, at least for a certain time span. Had the home market depression lasted longer, this business policy would have been questionable.

Although Austro-Fiat was able to maintain a home market share of between 30 and 44% in the 30s, and this policy of retrenchment and safety resulted in stable finances, it contributed, to a large degree, to catastrophic production and sales performance by augmenting the effect of stagnating home market demand. Since there

122 *Bilanzen*, 9.5.1931, 16.4.1932, 14.10.1933, 16.12.1933, 26.5.1934, 1.6.1935, 4.1.1936, 25.4.1936, 6.6.1936, 26.6.1937, 8.1.1938. See also A.5.

123 Own bank deposits were hardly touched, "[...] eine für ein Unternehmen der Automobilindustrie bemerkenswerte Unabhängigkeit vom Bankkapital." *Bilanzen*, 26.6.1937.

had been no massive effort of modernisation and rationalisation in the 20s, no heavy investment and debts had been necessary.[124] On the other hand, this also had the effect that it was impossible after the depression to rise up to international levels of competitiveness. Thus, the incredibly low and stagnating home demand for trucks in the 30s could not be compensated at all by increasing export sales. In the late 20s, at utmost, only 25% of turnover was exported. In the 30s, there were basically no export sales at all. The overall result was that production, sales and income of this company hardly recovered at all until 1936.

The car industry started to be affected by the depression in 1929, but Austro-Fiat only started to notice a 15% reduction of turnover in 1930. Prices and terms of payment, in some cases extending to longer than two years, began to worsen. During the first three quarters of 1931 sales were satisfactory, but declined rapidly thereafter. Volume of turnover slightly increased, whereas value declined. The real crisis came in 1932, when turnover value shrunk 50%. The majority of this decline could be attributed to falling sales of commercial vehicles. Production and sales of engines, fire engines, and gear-wheels as well as of the Viennese subsidiary carbody construction company Weiser & Co., held their ground much better. Only the fire-fighting and utility vehicle equipment producing firm, Wilhelm Knaust & Co. für Feuerlöschgeräte und Spezialaufbauten für Nutzfahrzeuge GesmbH, made a small deficit.

Primarily because of the stagnant home economy, Austro Fiat suffered in the following years from the low replacement rate of commercial vehicles on the market. Noticing the lower number of people per vehicle and higher sales in other European countries, management never was tired of blaming car and fuel taxes, and other legal regulations for poor Austrian demand.[125] In 1933, the relation of newly sold trucks and buses to total national stock was only 3%, which was equivalent to a vehicle life-span of 33 years. Under normal conditions, though, average lifespan was eight years, and in other countries, replacement rate was between 10 and 15%. In the late 20s, the company had roughly produced 1000 vehicles annually. In this year, total Austrian sales of commercial vehicles dropped 36%, and Austro-Fiat could only sell 236 trucks and buses. Value of total turnover did not shrink more than 20%, but only because the other branches of production offered some kind of compensation. Hope for higher sales in autumn 1934 were shattered. The general decline did not stop. Total Austrian sales and production reached an all time low, dropping another 12%. Austro-Fiat only sold 211 vehicles. Capacity employment was 25%.

Although manufacture of different and more modern types of trucks and buses was extended, even in 1935 and 1936 business remained appallingly depressed. Growth that took place remained so low that capacity was still far from full employment. In these years value of turnover increased 25% and 18%, but still only 285 and 275 vehicles were sold. Sales were still more than 50% below their already

124 Journalists of the *Der Österreichische Volkswirt* regarded its conservative policy as positive, since finances remained excellent even in 1932: "In ihrer finanziellen Verfassung bietet sie jedoch ein Beispiel dafür, daß die Krise selbst ein von der Verschlechterung der Wirtschaftslage stark getroffenes Unternehmen nicht erschüttern mußte, wenn es sich von gesunder Expansion und unwirtschaftlichen Schulden freigehalten hat." *Bilanzen*, 14.10.1933.

125 "Automobilfeindliche Gesetzeslage."

crisis-ridden level of 1931. Due to low international market prices, Austro-Fiat continued to refrain from export sales altogether. Business of the subsidiary firms was more favourable, but as they only generated 30% of total turnover, they could not compensate for stagnating utility vehicles sales.

d. Gräft & Stift

Financial Standing

Contrary to the previous company, Gräf & Stift[126] did not experience such a steep decline of production and sales. However, unlike Austro-Fiat, its finances were precarious, led to deficits and required balance sheet reorganisation in 1934. Already in the late 20s, financial standing was unsafe, as its earning power was low and liabilities were relatively high. Although management forced amortisation of debts after 1930, bank debts still amounted to 2.5 million schillings in 1933 and 2.78 million in 1935. In 1931, it was still possible to balance profits and losses, but in the following two years, deficits were made, running to 465 thousand schillings. The balance sheet was adjusted in 1934. Debtor value and stocks were depreciated, and losses were covered. The Creditanstalt lowered the interest rate of its outstanding debts to 4%.

Business Activity

Since exports to Soviet Russia and public orders stopped altogether, turnover began to decline in 1930. Due to a more flexible business policy, the deterioration of the domestic market could be compensated in the first phase of the depression. In 1931, total exports still came to 35% of sales and business with Russia (25% of total sales) could be revived thanks to a renewal of the state export guarantee. Therefore the decrease of turnover (-10%) was relatively mild. As for most other companies, 1932 was the worst year. As the export rate dropped to between 10 and 15%, low home market sales could not be countered. Total turnover decreased 40%. But management still hoped for reviving business and efforts of rationalisation were maintained. Production was concentrated, plants had to be shut down, but were prepared for full re-employment, and some products were re-introduced, such as large passenger cars. In spite of these endeavours and increasing deliveries of spare parts to Russia, turnover declined another 14% in 1933.

Economic development in the following years is unclear. Recovery seems to have been poor, but a little better than for Austro-Fiat. To move away from depressed utility vehicle business, the company continued to diversify its production range in the mid 30s. A licence contract was concluded with the Ford Motor Co. in Cologne. At this time, initial products, like pig-iron casting, body sheet, electrical equipment and carburettors were also manufactured and delivered to Ford in Germany.

126 *Bilanzen*, 17.19.1931, 12.11.1932, 23.9.1933, 15.9.1934, 29.8.1936. See also A.11.

6.3.3. Rubber Industry

a. International Development

The international rubber industry, as part of the chemical industry, was, by far, the most competitive, productive and capital intensive industrial sector in the inter-war period. As it highly depended upon the growth of the motor industry, the massive application of automobiles in the 20s supported the dramatic expansion of the rubber industry only until 1929. Since the Americans dominated world car production, increased car output and had the largest market with the lowest number of people per car, the US rubber industry was undoubtedly the greatest producer in the world. Its practical production capacity expanded from 45.6 thousand in 1921 to 91.6 thousand tyres per annum in 1929.[127] Even though it still chiefly supplied its large domestic market, it had the greatest share of world trade. In the 20s, large and highly productive plant capacities amounted in the US, and in the modern industrialised European countries, prices rose until 1926, and the quantity and quality of tyres continuously improved.

Conditions completely changed after the depression. Corresponding to declining production and sales of automobiles due to the depression and partial saturation of markets in nearly all advanced countries, apart from the authoritarian states and Britain, output of the rubber industry moderately declined until 1932 and stagnated in the 30s. In addition, as all advanced countries had been able to built up their own chemical industry, overcapacities amounted and international market pressure intensified. Despite dropping international market prices, the industrialised fascist countries only aggravated the situation by increasing the expansion of their rubber industries in the late 30s, also with the creation of synthetic rubber plants.[128] Once again, this economic policy effort was not compliant with rational economic considerations, but was strongly influenced by the policy of self-sufficiency and rearmament. In relation to this policy, the backlog boom in automobile output in Germany only had secondary importance.

The combined effect of depression, disproportional expansion and temporary overcapacities entailed an immense deterioration of international market conditions, resulting in a precipitous decline of prices of rubber goods. In the US, for example,

127 John Dean Gaffey, "The Productivity of Labour in the Rubber Tire Manufacturing Industry", in: Faculty of Political Science of Columbia University (ed.), *Studies in History, Economic and Public Law*, No. 472, New York 1968 (first published in 1940), 60.

128 IG-Farben only began limited production of buna (sythetic rubber) in 1935. Wille A. Boelcke, *Die deutsche Wirtschaft 1930–1945. Interna des Reichswirtschaftsministeriums*, Düsseldorf 1983, 166. During the war, 97% of German tyre output was based on the use of buna as a basic material for production. Peter Schäfer, *Wettbewerb und technischer Fortschritt in der deutschen Reifenindustrie*, dissertation, Aachen 1968, 131.

129 Calculated from Gaffey, 54 and 50.

130 Micheal J. French, *The U.S. Tire Industry. A History*, Boston 1991, 61.

131 "Zur Lage am Kautschukmarkt," in: Deutsches Institut für Konjunkturforschung, *Wochenbericht*, vol. 9, no. 18, Berlin 1936, 69.

value of output dropped from 900 million in 1926 to 406 million dollars in 1936, although the amount of renewal sales only dropped 20% in this period.[129] Rubber prices of the American market, the largest and most influential in the world, dropped from 20.6 cents per pound in 1929 to 3.5 cents in 1932, i. e. minus 83%.[130] On the London exchange, the market prices declined 72%.[131] The Austrian export dependent rubber industry, mainly represented by Semperit, directly suffered from this deterioration of international market conditions. That it still performed comparably well in spite of its weak position as a producer of several small countries is surprising. This phenomenon can be mainly attributed to the mild decline in the depression and moderate recovery of production volume of the world rubber industry until the mid 30s. Rubber demand only dropped 15% until 1931, and already by 1935, the world rubber processing industry consumed 20% more raw rubber than in 1929, and prices slowly recovered. Until May 1936, they were back to between 71 and 77% of their 1929 level.[132]

b. Semperit

Financial Standing

Compared to the motor industry, Semperit[133] performed relatively well during and after the depression. Since the decline of production and turnover was only mild, the stable, but not excellent, financial situation did not deteriorate. In spite of massive bank debts of 30 million schillings (capital stock and reserve amounted to about 24.5 million), mostly from the subsidiary companies, no deficits were made nor was balance sheet reconstruction necessary. In 1932, these debts had been reduced to 25 million and to 9 million in 1937. Other liabilities, proved in the balance sheets, could be reduced by one third until 1936. Whereas it was actually possible to improve the balance sheets, the profit and loss accounts deteriorated. By permanently reducing running costs, it was only barely possible to make minor profits. Though turnover profitability had been up to 26% in the late 20s, it declined to around 2.5% in the 30s. Reflecting the real economic development, the worst financial year was 1932, when earnings capacity of turnover was merely 0.7%. In 1936, it was only back to 4%. However, accounting was honest, and fairly high rates of investment and depreciation were maintained.

Business Activity

The main cause for declining income was continuously falling prices. At the same time Semperit only experienced a mild drop and then recovery of the volume of turnover and production. When regarding national foreign trade of rubber goods, this positive performance seems odd. While volume of exports of Austrian rubber goods declined 42% until 1932 and hardly recovered at all, value dropped more than 60%, and fell even more until 1937.[134] One reason for the surprisingly positive development of Semperit and its prevention of losses, was a permanent effort of modernisa-

132 Ibid.

133 *Bilanzen*, 14.11.1931, 8.10.1932, 21.10.1933, 27.10.1934, 25.1.1936, 26.9.1936, 6.11.1937. See also A.20.

134 Own calculation from Österreichisches Statistisches Zentralamt, *Aussenhandel*, 71.

tion and rationalisation, reducing unit costs to declining prices. Furthermore, flexible business policy, thanks to the distribution of several large subsidiary companies in various successor states, favourable sales conditions and relatively stable demand also contributed to steady development in the 30s. This was partially supported by the recovery of the European motor industry after 1933. Another advantage was its ability to manufacture and export a wide range of products at low costs.

The subsidiary companies in Czechoslovakia and Hungary, almost enjoying the status of monopoly firms,[135] and the ones in Poland and Yugoslavia, could mainly rely on supplying their domestic markets, whereas the Austrian production facilities were not only focused on their home market, but also on export business. Emphasis of production and sales orientation was altered according to demand.

By 1930, the drop of prices became apparent, as volume of turnover still increased while value dropped 10%. In the following two years, value of production and turnover continued to decline. Gross profits dropped 19% until 1932. Nevertheless, the fall was not dramatic, and by concentrating production, expenses could be kept below income, although volume of production and turnover remained constant. In 1931, only sales of the Austrian factories dropped, because these mainly supplied foreign markets. Foreign sales not only became more problematic due to import restrictions, but also because of expanding production facilities in countries that represented important export areas. Besides Germany and Switzerland, these consisted of the Netherlands, Spain, Egypt and Turkey. Thus, the export rate declined from 67 to 40%, and the share of total turnover, generated by Austrian plants, dropped from 72% in 1929 to less than 50%. Polish, Czechoslovak and Yugoslavian firms, now providing the majority of turnover, were still able to expand sales.

As exchange control systems, tariffs and import licence procedures became more extensive in 1932, and market pressures with increasing competition from Japanese and Polish producers mounted, prices kept falling and export sales worsened. Sales to the US, for instance, resulted in losses. Moreover, because Semperit conducted most of its export business in foreign currency, it had to sustain income losses from currency depreciation in late 1932. Essentially, though, profits dropped because prices kept declining. The export rate was still only 40%. Volume of turnover was sustained, meanwhile, value dropped another 15%. However, profits and losses were balanced, all of the firms in the successor states made it through the worst year without losses and substantial investment and depreciation were effected.

Since the fall in the depression was moderate, recovery was mild and slow. Although the total workforce had been reduced to 5000, it was already back to between 7500 and 8000 in the following year. Even though the Austrian home market showed no signs of recovery, there was a considerable recovery of business during the second half of 1933, because of reviving foreign sales. Volume of turnover was the highest up to date. Mostly the Austrian factories benefited from this as their capacity employment increased to 70%. They provided 55% of turnover, whereas the Czechoslovak firm, the Matador Gummiwerke AG, had a 33% share. However, market pressures continued to increase, because of rising production and exports from other countries, especially Germany and Japan. Also tariffs and currency fluctuations

135 Mathis, *Big Business*, 271.

worsened market conditions. Value of turnover still dropped 11.3%. That gross profit was nearly back to its 1931 level can only be ascribed to drastic rationalisation and modernisation entailing a substantial increase of productivity. This enabled Semperit to avoid losses, although international prices kept falling.

Even though 1934 did not bring full recovery and prices remained depressed, capacity employment was still 70%, as output remained relatively high. Export business continued to expand and the Austrian plants experienced a production rise of 10%. Their share of turnover rose to 60%. Value of foreign sales of rubber tyres nearly doubled, from 570 thousand schillings to 1.07 million schillings. Germany, importing tyres worth 520 thousand, was the main customer. It was an advantage that the Semperit export structure was very diversified. Losses in the sales of one product could be compensated by augmenting exports of other items. Other important export items were rubber footgear, nearly worth 3 million schillings, sealing material (2.6 million), bathing-caps (690 thousand), soft rubber goods (3.1 million) and ebonite goods (2.7 million).

Despite its ability to keep up a high level of capacity employment, 1935 was still a year of stagnation. Total value of turnover only increased 1%. International competition became more fierce, especially because national producers in Germany and Japan could sell at dumping prices, benefiting from public export bounties to increase the national stock of foreign exchange. Export rate was only 30%. Gross profit dropped 5.6%. Moderate recovery only came in the last two years of Austrian independence. In 1936, gross profit rose 12.6%. The Austrian plants increased foreign sales and the export rate of the whole industrial combine was back to 50%. The Yugoslavian and Czechoslovak firms also enjoyed a positive course of business. Until November, turnover of 1937 finally made substantial advances and grew 18%. Management contemplated to take up distribution of dividend once again.

6.4. CONCLUSION

6.4.1. Determinants of Performance of Modern and Traditional Industries

The analysis shows that numerous factors influenced financial and real economic performance. Generally though, companies belonging to the modern sectors, or companies with a strong commitment to foreign trade, tended to perform better than those that retrenched to the stagnant home market or only produced traditional goods. Modern companies that did not attempt to force foreign trade also performed poorly. Usually, traditional firms had to be export oriented to have a chance of survival. Retrenchment was always the wrong choice. Generally though, in the 1930s, there was no chance for anyone to expand and make larger profits.

The broad financial development seems to verify the hypothesis that modern sectors tended to weather the depression better than others. Of the nearly 20 companies[136] analysed here, only four did not make any deficits at all. Three of those belonged to the modern industrial sectors. These were Elin, Semperit and Austro-

136 Including textile firms, which certainly ran into deficits in the 30s.

Fiat. The only traditional firm without losses was Hutter & Schrantz. The two paper producers, all three traditional machine manufacturers, and Siemens and AEG ran deficits at least until 1936. Thus, the paper and traditional machine building industries financially experienced the worst performances. As its production level was appallingly low, also in real economic terms the traditional machine building sector endured the worst performance, primarily because it suffered from low productivity, manufactured traditional products, and retrenched to its home market.

To come to a conclusion about real economic development, i.e. production performance, the expansion of productive assets or the introduction of new products, is more difficult. Yet once again, those firms with the most flexible and export oriented business policy tended to do well. These did not necessarily have to be enterprises belonging to the modern sectors. Schoeller-Bleckmann, Hutter & Schrantz, Ditmar Brünner, Elin and, to some degree, Brown-Boveri and Gräf & Stift chiefly based their slow and partial recovery on outbound trade. Companies that retrenched to the domestic market, such as Brevillier, the engine producers, Simmeringer, Siemens, AEG, and Austro-Fiat always experienced low capacity utilisation, low turnover, low production, but not necessarily massive deficits. Enterprises that had enjoyed very stable finances in the 20s and pursued a policy of retrenchment, made it through the depression quite well financially. Brevillier and Austro-Fiat are good examples of this case.

Some companies in industrial sectors that suffered from particularly harsh structural distortions, underwent crisis periods. This was the case even though some of those were well within the average European production performance, tended to be trade oriented and attempted to increase productivity. The best examples of this case are the firms of the paper sector. Both companies, Leykam-Josefthaler and Neusiedler, sold the majority of their turnover abroad, but still made major deficits throughout the decade. The main reason was the steep drop of prices due to expanding production capacities of the paper industry in the periphery and in some large advanced countries. The Alpine was in a similar position. It only began to recover pre-crisis levels of production, turnover and investment after capacities of the neighbour states were fully employed. The textile industry also suffered from increasing production abroad. Although its export rate and production growth after 1932 was quite high and the expansion of capacities in the periphery slowed down, it hardly reached pre-war output levels in the late 30s.

6.4.2. International Competitiveness and Retrenchment

Nearly all industrial sectors suffered from a disadvantage of competitiveness on international markets. This was mainly due to stagnant foreign trade and a disproportion between relatively large production capacities and a small domestic market. As already mentioned, this phenomenon was especially pronounced and harmful because of a process of retrenchment and structural distortion in the large advanced countries and the successor states. Since restrictive trade policies were a political expression of this process, they consequently did have in many cases harmful results on export sales of Austrian companies.

In contrast, the deflationary shock of the financial breakdown of 1931 and currency devaluation only had minor direct long-term effects. Depending on the sizes of loans and the currency in which foreign loans were floated, and on the distribution of a company's outbound trade, depreciation could be harmful or positive to various degrees. In many cases appreciation and depreciation of foreign liabilities tended to cancel each other out. Export competitiveness was only affected negatively in very rare cases, and usually when real economic productivity was comparably low anyway. The collapse of the CA also did not seem to have had any long-term negative direct consequences. State intervention, leading to the reconstruction and concentration of the Austrian banking system, was beneficial and helped to financially reorganise and reconstruct the balances of those enterprises that were unable to sustain deficits.

Whereas monetary crises had minor implications, national retrenchment of Austria's most important trading partners was harmful to export performance. Moreover, this was intensified by the fact that national producers of large advanced countries were able to outperform most Austrian firms on international markets, since their domestic markets allowed a compensation of often unprofitable export sales. The availability of large protected markets with greater purchasing power also facilitated the introduction of mass production and increasing competitiveness.

Even the modern Austrian industrial sectors suffered from this phenomenon, as only the most competitive and advanced companies were able to expand export business by supreme effort. This was only possible for Semperit and Elin, whose business policy was excellent. Flexible and forced exports of advanced high-quality products, introduction of new and better products with the help of R & D, the introduction of a diversified production range, and a constant effort to increase productivity and competitiveness were the secrets to moderate business performance in the 30s. For the classical heavy industrial sector, iron and steel producing, the disadvantages of a small home market were soon apparent in the 20s, since already then the Alpine was hardly able to follow low international market prices and just made minor profits. Only with massive foreign military demand in the second half of the 30s were minor profits possible. A similar phenomenon was noticeable for car manufacturing. Steyr-Daimler-Puch attempted to keep up with unprofitable export trade in the 20s, and nearly had to completely terminate outbound sales in the 30s. Luckily it was able to control its home market after it had introduced cheaper mass-produced cars in the mid 30s.

Overall, it can be asserted that performance of all Austrian industrial sectors was determined by their international position as minor national producers with a small and impotent home market, compared to their foreign counterparts. This naturally entailed a serious disadvantage of competitiveness, especially in a hostile environment which tended to confine trade. Only a few companies were able to break out of this position of constraint. In all, it seems that the constant revolution of industrial structures, the process of transformation and reorientation to new types of production, production methods and consumption, was enormously restrained in the 30s by distortion of structural transformations, the establishment of economic retrenchment and economic nationalism. Production and business of nearly all enterprises stagnated until the mid 30s. They only *began* to recover in 1936/37!

7. CONCLUSION

To come to reasonable conclusions and to find basic determinants of, and the interrelation between, European economic development and policy of such a stratified and turbulent time as the inter-war period, that included inflation, harsh policy regime shifts and the Great Depression, is truly a challenge, and perhaps, presumptuous. Nevertheless, the following pages represent the attempt to sum up the main conclusions of this study.

7.1. LONG-TERM TRANSFORMATIONS

As this work employs a structural theoretical approach based on Schumpeter's endogenous growth theory, two main structural transformations can be discerned that determined economic development in Europe and Austria specifically.

I. National shifts: The main determinant of economic growth and development was a long-term secular, industrial structural transformation within the modern and advanced European economies and the US. This long-term shift from old and traditional 19th century to new and modern 20th century production and consumption processes occurred at different rates in various advanced countries. It was determined by the application of new technology of traditional industries (such as iron and steel, coal, textiles, paper and traditional machine building) and by the large scale application of innovations of the late 19th century (chemicals, electricity and the combustion engine) that formed the basis for the emergence of modern industrial sectors (such as the motor, electrical engineering and chemical industries). In addition, this transformation was also determined by the emergence and dissemination of mass consumption markets with high purchasing power and favourable distribution of wealth. This was the "second industrial revolution" of the 20s and 30s.

1. This permanent shift was disturbed and distorted in Europe. This distortion was partially intensified by war and inflation. Moreover, the process of development toward the classical 20th century economy entailed the concentration of economic growth and development on advanced large national economies, i.e. inward oriented growth and development. The lower the rate and level of economic growth, the greater the tendency to turn to economic nationalism and retrenchment, especially in the 30s. As a whole, these processes led to low growth rates and investment, slow development and expansion of the productive sector, and massive overcapacities and underemployment among the traditional industrial branches in Europe. In contrast, growth rates, employment, and development and expansion of the productive capacity of the modern sectors tended to be higher. Yet, they could not compensate for lower growth and development of the older sectors, which partially contributed to lower growth of the national income.

II. International shifts: The second long-term structural transformation was intensifying expansion of industrialisation in the world economic periphery and the advanced countries outside of Europe, such as the US and Canada. The most prominent areas of intensifying industrialisation in the periphery were in particular the British colonies, especially India, then China, Japan, Russia, some South American and also Eastern European countries. This process of peripheral industrialisation was supported by the war, as the traditional European domination of markets was temporarily chequered. Peripheral industrialisation was primarily based on the emergence, growth and development of the classical traditional industries of the 19th century. Thus, those industrial sectors that stagnated in Europe, began to expand rapidly in the periphery in the 20s and 30s. Besides the still relatively small size of their industrial sectors, rapid industrialisation of traditional industries was the second most important reason why countries in these areas were only slightly afflicted by the Great Depression.

1. As the "process of creative destruction," i.e. the second industrial revolution, was disturbed and distorted in Europe, peripheral industrial production became a major competitor of the stagnant European traditional industries in world markets. The effects of overcapacities of European traditional industries were intensified by market pressure from industries in the periphery.

III. Overall repercussions: The result of increasing global industrialisation and distorted changes within the advanced countries in and outside of Europe was the decline of Europe's economic strength and weight in the world. This went along with contraction, stagnation and a lower growth rate of international trade. As development of advanced economies became more inward oriented, international trade grew slower than industrial production. This process was detrimental to economic growth and development in small export oriented countries. Thus, the Austrian economy was not only strongly affected by war and inflation, but was mainly negatively influenced by long-term and world-wide structural shifts

7.2. A STRUCTURAL APPROACH TO POLICY AND PERFORMANCE IN EUROPE AND AUSTRIA

With these theoretical concepts and overall changes in mind, we will now attempt to define the determinants of economic policy and performance in the inter-war period.

I. Economic performance: Performance was determined by a variety of factors, of which the most prominent was the impact of the two structural transformations on the various national economies. This impact, in turn, depended on the state of development of a national economy, its size, its competitiveness and productivity, as well as the severity of the effects of war and inflation.

1. As growth and development were more inward oriented and trade contracted, generally, large advanced countries tended to undergo the transformations easier than small advanced countries. As Austria was a small advanced export dependent country with a small domestic market and relatively large national producers with

little economic leverage on international markets, it was extremely difficult to face the structural transformations. The country suffered intensely from their negative impacts, such as overcapacities and mounting market pressure. In addition, while it was only possible for a few Austrian companies to keep up with international competitiveness and productivity, international demand hardly offered a stimulus to economic growth and development in small countries. The Austrian export structure remained unchanged and imbalanced, more productive foreign national producers continued to dominate markets of large advanced countries and the quality of Eastern European markets deteriorated. Simultaneously, the small Austrian home market could not compensate for the deficiencies of international demand. The overall result was stagnant economic growth.

2. Large countries, such as Germany, France and Great Britain, were partially able to counterbalance the deterioration of international market demand and generated domestic economic growth. Their performance was determined by the rate of the industrial revolutions in their economies. France enjoyed rapid but insufficient industrial transformation in the 20s. Due to its still relatively low level of development in comparison with other large modern economies, it was belatedly hit by the depression and was unable to generate substantial recovery in the 30s. Britain, on the other hand, suffered from stagnation in the 20s, since it inherited disproportionally large and obsolete traditional industrial sectors. As its rate of growth was low, it was only mildly affected by the depression. In the 30s, the British industries made up the backlog of development and generated rapid growth based on the second industrial revolution on their home market.

3. Germany and Austria experienced similar development, which was particularly different from development in the other advanced countries. Similar, but more extreme as in France, in Germany it was not possible to find a socio-economic consensus for stabilisation right after the war. Therefore, this country not only underwent inflation, but experienced hyperinflation. After a national and international stabilisation consensus was established, the economy continued to suffer from the after-effects of distortions from inflation and stabilisation. The process was similar in Austria. Austrian and German erratic economic growth and development were disturbed until the onset of the Great Depression by the inability to find a socio-economic stabilisation consensus soon enough to prevent inflationary distortions, i.e. oversized and obsolete traditional sectors, slow expansion of modern industries and comparatively low general competitiveness and productivity. Finally, after inflations had caused havoc among these countries' economic structures, stabilisation consensus was reached, but could only be enforced with the help of highly restrictive, deflationary and essentially harmful economic policy. Eventually, Germany and Austria only slowly reintegrated into the world economic system and only attained insufficient adjustment to the new conditions. The industrial revolutions in these countries hardly began to flourish. The low level, but high rate of growth in the late 20s entailed only an overall slow rise of the national income. Thus, the political struggles of the distribution of national income in Germany and Austria became extreme between 1929 and 1933 and led to the breakdown of parliamentary democracy in both countries.

Since Germany enjoyed the benefits of a large national economy, National Socialist economic policy could turn to reckless anti-cyclical and expansive economic policy. The general upswing of the world economy, massive state investments and the recovery of lost ground in the 20s initiated rapid, and later distorted, economic recovery. In Austria, the proto-fascist regime was unable to turn to such policy measures, because of the impossibility of a small country to compensate for the massive annual deficits of foreign demand in the 30s. Unlike the larger advanced nations, the Austrian economy was unable to move to complete retrenchment and inward growth. Since world, and especially European, trade only slowly expanded and the large advanced countries turned to extreme economic retrenchment, international market demand only slowly recovered. Thus, growth of the Austrian economy remained extremely depressive and only began to expand after some industrial sectors benefited from large scale rearmament demand from its neighbouring countries after the mid 30s.

II. Economic policy: European and Austrian economic policy remained orthodox and neo-liberal throughout the inter-war period. In the 30s, European economic policy only slightly changed among the liberal states and only became half-heartedly interventionist. Only policy in the authoritarian states massively intervened in their economies. However, by and large, economic policy rarely directly influenced performance and was generally a reaction to the large scale structural shifts. Policy was an expression of the competitive position of a national economy. It tended to support and intensify structural shifts. Only very extreme policies that intervened on a massive scale and were supported by national, and in some cases international, socio-economic consensus tended to have a great direct impact on economic performance.

1. The disintegration of the Austro-Hungarian Empire only had minute long-term effects on trade patterns, on the influence of Austrian companies in the area, and on the organisation and ownership conditions of Austrian assets in Eastern Europe. Only a few Austrian companies lost capital and productive assets and some enterprises even increased their economic power. War, disintegration and inflation only intensified the process of industrialisation and market deterioration in the area of the successor states.

2. The inflationary policy measures in Austria and other European states had indeed a tremendous and ambivalent impact on economic development and growth. Inflations were harmful as only the most successful industrial sectors could benefit from them. Generally, in the long run, it led to structural distortions whose repercussions continued to dominate and depress ensuing growth and development. Yet, inflationary policies were not intentional. Governments whose economies and societies were extremely negatively affected by the war, were constrained in their policy-making by enormous socio-economic pressure of inflation consensus.

3. Stabilisation, the attempt to re-establish the gold standard and restrictive neo-liberal economic and monetary policies until the depression can be summarised as the essential components of an enormous European-wide reactionary movement of influential socio-economic groups against the left political and economic revolutions that had occurred after the war and during the inflation. After 1924/25, rightist

governments were back in power, whose policies were heavily supported by big national producers in the advanced countries. These were the representatives of big business, influential financial circles and agriculture. The conservative governments, backed up by big business, banks and agriculture, pursued the attempt to restore the favourable status quo of the pre-war era by attempting to employ the same traditional tools of economic and currency policy. These, in turn, were constrained by the impossibility to compromise the rules of the gold standard, imposed on currency policy, with the obligations of national social and economic policies, while many countries suffered from insufficient or stagnant growth of national income. Essentially, policies were ineffective and only intensified the social and economic problems that their countries suffered.

4. The general trend of trade policy toward protectionism was a direct reaction to the results of the two long-term structural transformations. Since they caused massive overcapacities among many traditional sectors (in particular iron and steel and textiles) and inward oriented growth of modern industries which required large markets with high purchasing power (in particular the motor industry), competitive pressures increased in the inter-war period. Naturally, countries whose economies just began to industrialise and countries whose economies incorporated large obsolete traditional industrial sectors specifically suffered from this pressure. Therefore, the most influential national producers in these countries urged their governments to augment tariff protection for their industries. The lower the relative competitiveness and productivity of the industrial sectors and agriculture of any country, the greater the tendency to intensify protectionism. Since the structural distortions increased during the depression, the problems of overcapacities and competitive pressures intensified. The main reaction was that governments, even in small and export dependent countries, were forced to introduce extreme protectionism, which included higher tariffs, import quotas, exchange control, clearing systems or currency devaluations. In the long run, this development resulted in the maintenance of many unproductive European industrial sectors.

Generally, protectionism incorporated a system of import controls that discriminated only against products of certain industrial sectors. Countries in the periphery that were industrialising naturally discriminated against products that their own industries fabricated and hauled. Therefore, export business of advanced countries that were able to adjust to changing international market conditions most successfully, i.e. countries whose modern sectors were comparatively large and whose traditional industries were relatively productive, was afflicted the least by increasing protectionism. The development of foreign trade of Austrian companies clearly reflected this mechanism. As their products were in high demand on foreign, and in particular underdeveloped, markets, modern and advanced Austrian enterprises were hardly touched by mounting protectionism, while companies of the traditional sectors clearly suffered from rising tariffs.

4. During the Great Depression, the structural distortions, i.e. the slow shift to modern production methods in addition to massive obstinate overcapacities among the traditional sectors, intensified. The initial policy reaction of all governments was similar. Until the summer of 1931, it remained passive because policy makers and

national producers still believed in a return to normalcy. After the international financial crisis and further economic downswing, orthodox policy reactions introduced the turn to extreme retrenchment and protectionism. Without experience, theoretical concepts and with the hope of an automatic economic recovery, governments, with the support of the most influential financial, producer and agricultural interest groups, enforced restrictive neo-liberal economic policy. This was executed against mounting left political opposition. Instead of introducing exchange control, Britain, and later France, turned to devaluation because of a loss of confidence in their fiscal policies and national currencies. Yet, currency depreciation only provided short-term relief, because the competitive position of their industries and price levels were determined by their level of productivity, which in turn, was conditioned by the ability of their industries to adjust to the "process of creative destruction." Only after the depression came to an end and slow recovery set in, few governments introduced anti-cyclical policies.

5. After the depression, only extreme economic policy of Nazi Germany was effective in generating rapid economic growth. Until the mid 30s, it was in accord with traditional financial and industrial interests. However, once policy turned to strict monetary control, trade control, direct government intervention in production and rapid disproportionate rearmament, economic growth and development became extremely distorted. In the long run, this led to a decline of productivity, competitiveness, underdevelopment of consumer industries and overexpansion of capital investment industries.

7.3. ECONOMIC POLICIES AND MICROECONOMIC DEVELOPMENT IN AUSTRIA

I. Growth and development of Austrian companies reflected the two structural long-term transformations and were largely determined by these. Naturally, exactly as for whole national economies, main determinants of growth and development were comparable productivity, international competitiveness, demand elasticity and the level and rate of the successful application of new technology. Most economic policy measures were of secondary importance to performance.

1. The companies of the traditional sectors tended to experience the negative implications of the structural changes much stronger. Most of these were directly affected by competition of modern sectors, peripheral industrialisation, overcapacities in Europe and the deterioration of their formerly vital markets. Therefore, these firms were not only severely hit by the depression, but were also much more affected by economic policy measures, such as stabilisation policies, protectionism, currency devaluation, tight money policies and restrictive public investment. Especially the Alpine, Veitscher, the engine factories, Simmeringer, Hofherr, Enzesfelder and Brevillier were heavily hit by the negative effects of structural shifts. While these enterprises were large national producers in Austria, their economic leverage on international markets was small. The only exception constitutes Veitscher.

Generally, business policy of the traditional companies that suffered from structural changes was static, and some adhered to retrenchment. Some companies were even directly affected by certain economic policy measures, such as trade agreements, tariffs or public investment behaviour. In addition, as their future business prospects were often poor, capital availability was extremely restricted in many cases. Bank dependence remained high. Nearly all of these firms suffered from overcapacities, low productivity and competitiveness. Yet, while their productive capacity hardly improved and did not expand, their financial standing did not necessarily have to be poor.

2. The companies belonging to the modern sectors tended to face the massive structural changes and crises much better than traditional industries. Generally, economic policy was of secondary importance to performance of these Austrian companies. In spite of crises and poor trading conditions, most of these firms were able to expand and modernise their output, productive capacity and export volume slowly, based on the massive application of new technology. The companies of the electrical engineering industry and the rubber industry fared the best. Due to the nature of the world motor industry, dominated by large producers in large advanced countries with great market advantages, the financial standing of the small Austrian motor industry was poor. In addition, its production was erratic. However, it weathered changes and crises surprisingly well. Despite massive market pressures, Steyr was able to expand its production and foreign sales in the 20s. After the depression, it was able to reconquer its domestic market.

Modern Austrian companies that pursued a flexible and extremely export oriented business policy generally enjoyed favourable performance. The most prominent and successful companies were Elin and Semperit. Not only did their financial standing improve and their production increase, but they were also able to expand and modernise their productive sector. AEG, Siemens and the utility vehicle producers were modern enterprises that stuck to a policy of retrenchment. Generally, unlike most traditional companies, at least a few of the modern firms were able to keep up with international productivity and competitiveness.

3. Not only modern companies performed well. The few enterprises of the traditional sectors that followed a highly flexible and foreign trade oriented business policy tended to experience relatively favourable development. Usually companies that had been export oriented before the First World War, possessed foreign holdings and enjoyed low demand elasticity belonged to this group of firms. Hutter & Schrantz, Ditmar-Brünner, and to a lesser degree, Schoeller- Bleckmann and Gebrüder Böhler can be counted to this group of companies. These four performed extremely well on international markets and expanded their productive assets.

APPENDIX

TIME SERIES DIAGRAMS OF PROFIT AND LOSS ACCOUNTS AND BALANCE SHEETS

LIST OF FIGURES

AEG Union Elektrizitäts-Gesellschaft

Profit and Loss Account (in thousand schillings)

Years	13	23	24	25	26	27	28	29	30	31	32	33	34	35	36
Gross Profits	5622	2957	3490	4183	3636	4264	4318	4492	3972	2552	2299	983	974	1437	2400
Expenses	3581	2146	2635	3570	3265	3815	3786	3958	3604	3847	5257	4793	4005	2135	2404
Exchange depreciation															949
Investment				520	350	130	303	360							
Net Profits	2040	811	855	613	371	449	532	534	369	-1245	-2948	-3810	-3032	-698	-4

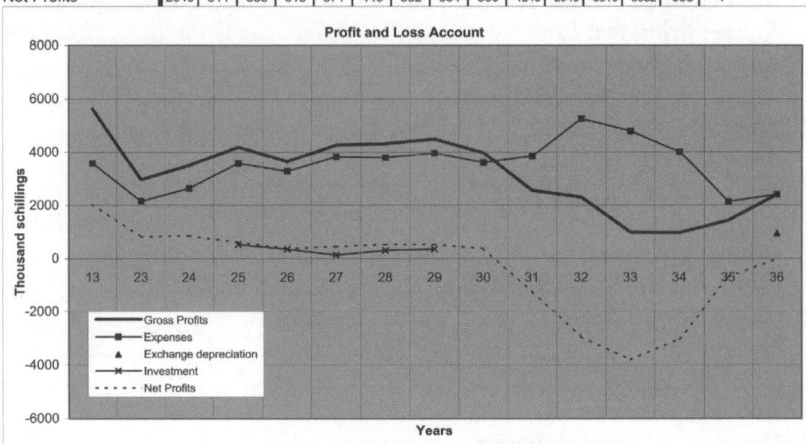

Balance sheet

Years	13	23	24	GB	25	26	27	28	29	30	31	32	33	34	RB	35	36
Balance sheet value	59249	10243	13834	22222	27370	26982	28611	30223	31551	28848	24632	20854	22171	26104	15049	12691	12227
Capital stock and reserve	25920	3600		12000	12000	12000	12000				10760	7920					
Extraordinary losses															13960		
Debtors	26215	8195	10055	7497	5602		9313	11056	11047	10347	8014	5267	3715	5250	4922	2738	2943
Liabilities (creditors)	29604	5760	8913	9070	13945	4351	5854	7295	9170	6854	4332	3979	5432	9694	5451	2938	3555
Bonded debt (Swiss franc loan)						9598	9598	9437	9262	9077	8875	8661	8432	8188	5496	5495	4547

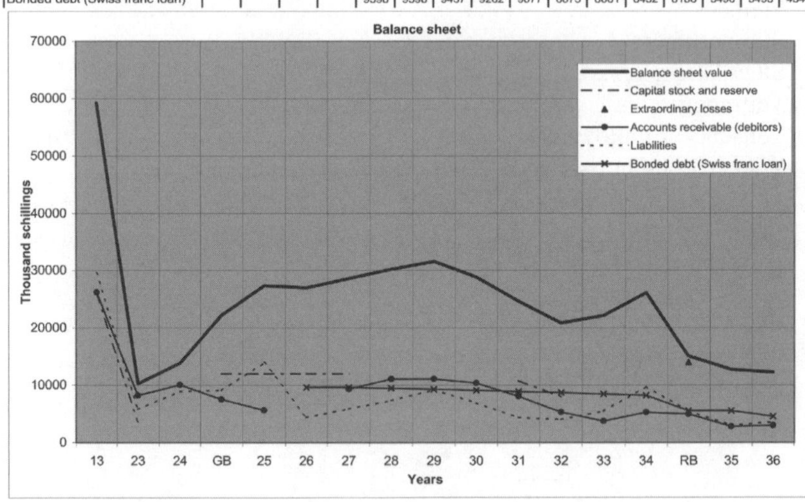

Figure A.1.: AEG Union

The Österreichische-Alpine Montangesellschaft

Profit and Loss Account (in thousand schillings)

Years	13	23	24	25	26	27	28	29	30	31	32	33	34	35	36
Gross Profits	40915	10627	11483	13242	14003	16068	23988	28901	23086	16558	9493	8537	14867	16794	23164
Expenses	19289	7822	11269	13136	13999	16006	21478	26337	23085	16558	16240	16088	17038	16794	22616
Depreciation	5201	506	1615	2380	3124	5287	8128	10128	7442	4455	4881	5123	5858	6123	12170
Investment		5400		8700	5800	7700	9400	14000	11060	1220	2110	5920		1430	2880
Net Profits	21626	2806	213	106	4	80	2510	2564	1	0	-6748	-7551	-2171	0	594

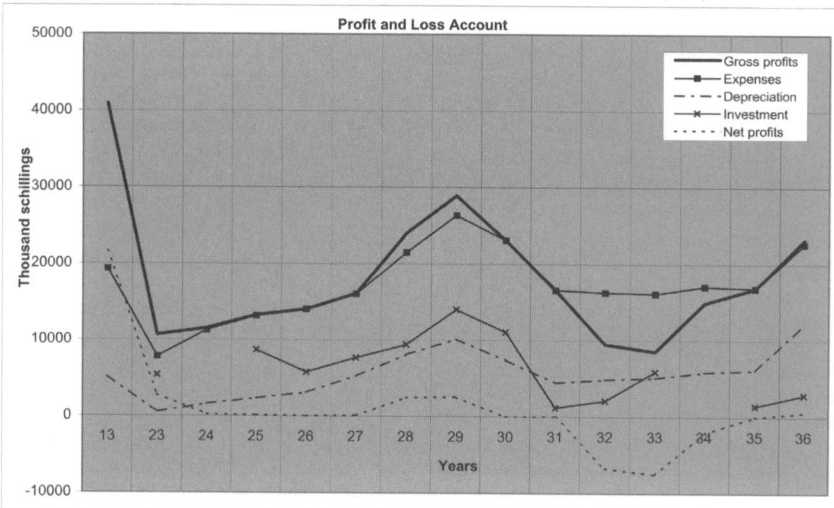

Profit and Loss Account

Years	18	19	20	21	22
Gross Profits	4,057	3,77	12,6	54,1	36,76
Expenses	3,26	2,7	9,71	48,05	31,3
Depreciation	0,54	0,6	0,77	1,31	6,7
Investment					13,54
Net Profits	0,79	1,07	2,85	6,05	0,48

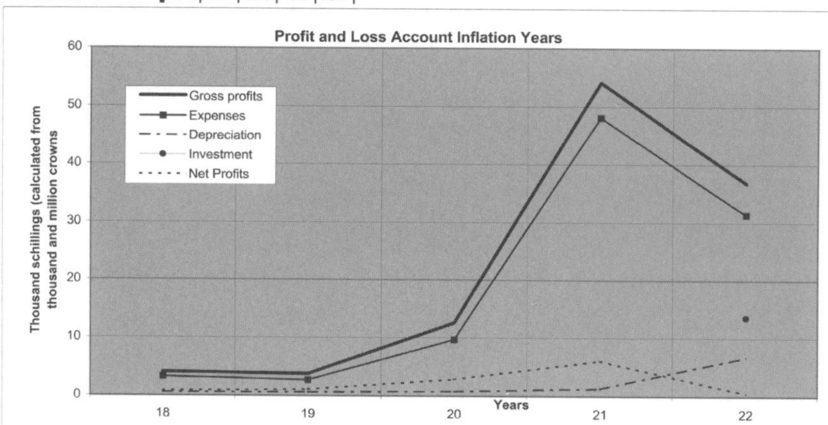

Figure A.2.: Alpine: Profit and Loss Account

The Österreichische-Alpine Montangesellschaft

Balance sheet (in thousand schillings)

Years	13	22	23	24	GB	25	26	27	28	29	30	31	32	33	34	35	36
Balance sheet value		28287	65694	79894	138063	160594	148271	154039	153172	160706	158260	146596	138216	141087	132557	132373	122896
Debtors	7924	18497	29050	22560	13212	17592	13212	20743	21949	19606	15607	12879	9872	11754	11288	14409	13497
Liabilities (creditors)	5325	16717	17712	33722	35884	22875	10833	16087	22112	29575	30392	19287	18112	28546	22185	24040	14767
Bonded debt	546							34579	34152	33694	33204	32671	32202	32202	32202	30154	29401

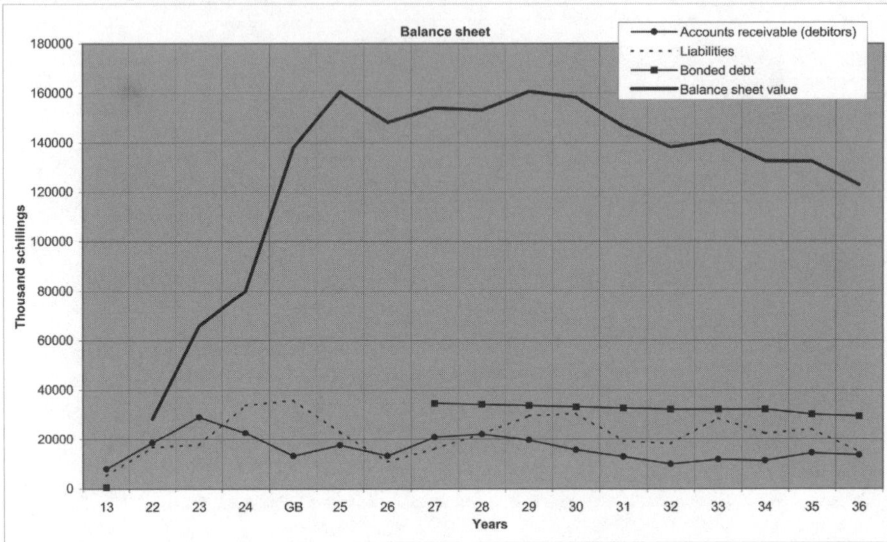

Balance sheet

Years	18	19	20	21
Balance sheet val	17,6	24,9	58,26	417,9
Debtors	2,35	8,1	29,65	368,5
Liabilities	6,6	4	34	397,8

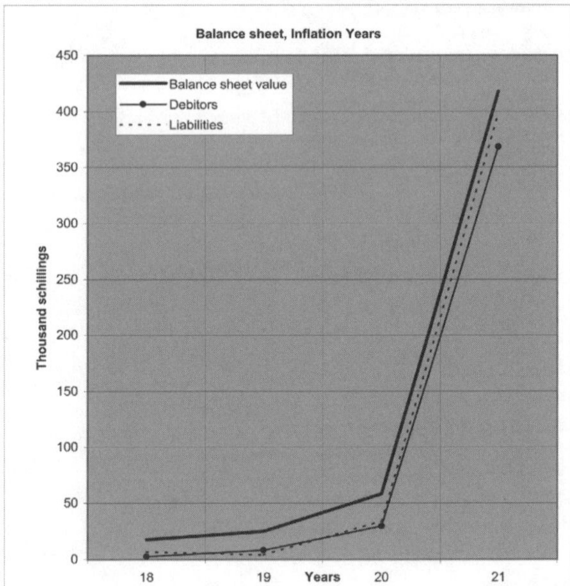

Figure A.3.: Alpine: Balance sheet

Österreichische-Alpine Montangesellschaft Production Data

Years	12	13	19	20	21	22	23	24	25	26	27	28	29	30	31	32	33	34	35	36
Coal	12068	11352	6407	7176	6823	8899	8493	8386	10032	9819	9419	10722	11459	9197	8851	10160	10455	10516	10783	10901
Raw ore	18744	19534	2443	4285	6795	10840	12045	7066	10250	10871	15847	19131	18666	11734	5111	3068	2660	4640	7726	10201
Raw iron	5835	5866	594	980	2143	3142	3398	2649	3799	3303	4303	4583	4575	2846	1447	955	879	1309	1932	2479
Rolling mill production	3312	2455	706	847	1326	2001	1983	1462	1947	1958	2203	2796	2887	2178	1314	719	781	1212	1343	1482

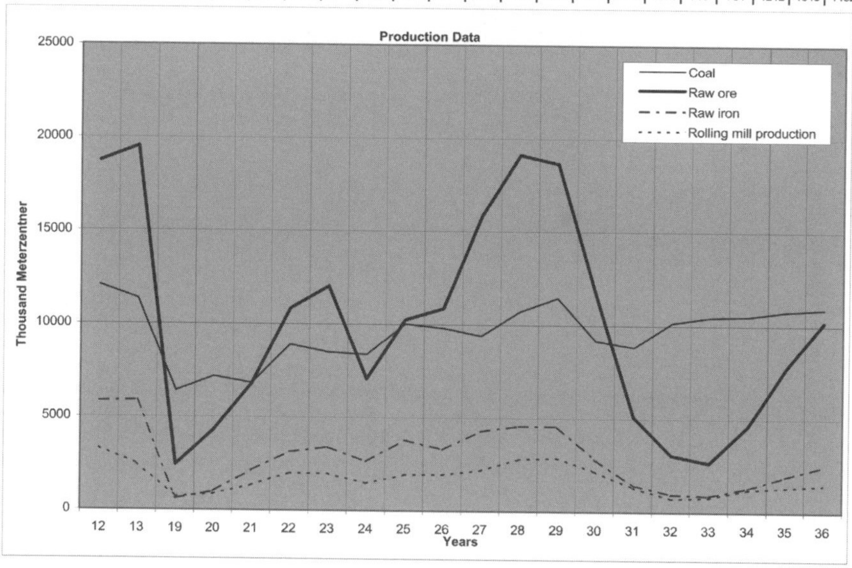

Employment Alpine Montangesellschaft

Years	13	22	27	28	29	30	31	32	33	34	35	36	37
Workforce	14681	17700	12033	13450	13400	11600	7600	6818	6954	6269	6792	9387	16000

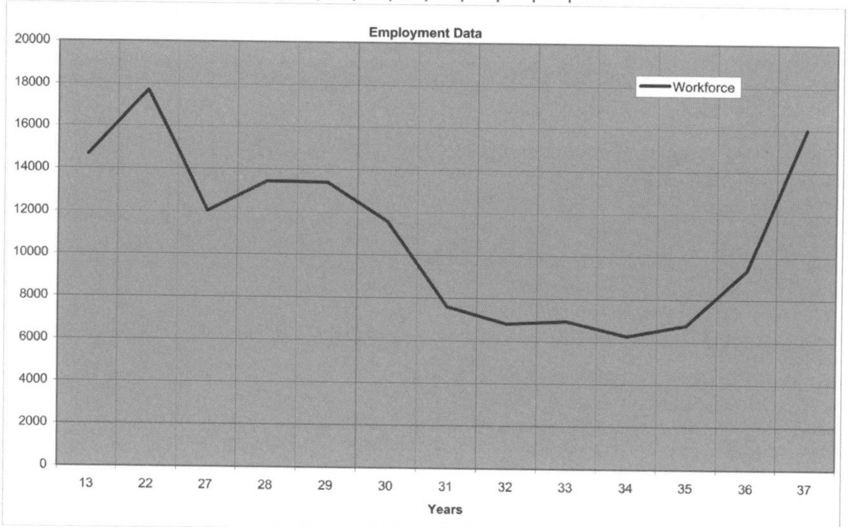

Figure A.4.: Alpine: Production Data

Österreichische Automobil-Fabriks-AG, vormals "Austro-Fiat"

Profit and Loss Account (in thousand schillings)

Years	13	22	23	24	25	26	27	28	29	30	31	32	33	34	35	36
Gross Profits	1886	1126	1393	919	1168	1175	1405	1953	2364	2633	1790	1317	753	748	794	933
Expenses	1426	995	1138	667	758	694	887	1123	1480	1736	1315	1246	708	715	714	837
Investments						100	67	318	560		210	91	89	100		
Net Profits	461	131	255	252	410	481	518	830	913	898	475	71	45	33	80	95

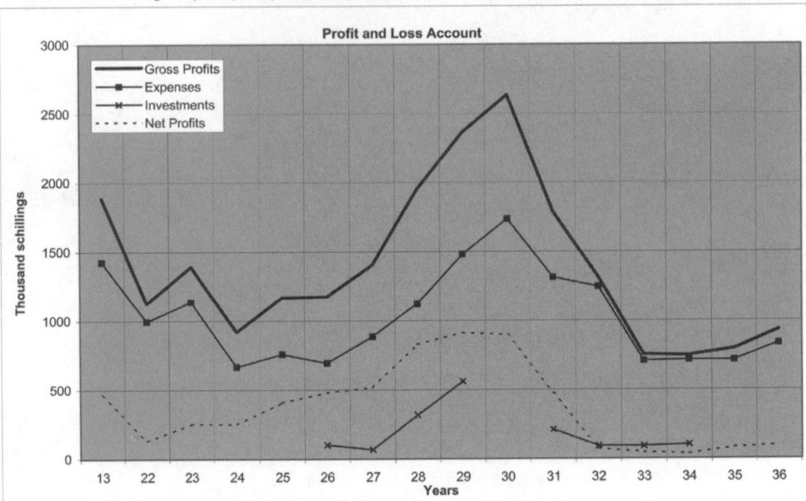

Balance sheet

Years	13	22	23	24	GB	25	26	27	28	29	30	31	32	33	34	35	36
Balance sheet value	7796	2142	3168	4255	6246	6494	7102	5998	7936	9665	10085	9953	9167	8802	8833	9366	9889
Debtors	2619	4,5	1204	2357	2435	3214	3720	2452	3402	3774	4449	4382	3754	3869	3786	3972	4265
Liabilities (creditors)	3966	967	1013	316	836	987	1985	2217	2168	3378	1330	1473	848	236	244	556	984

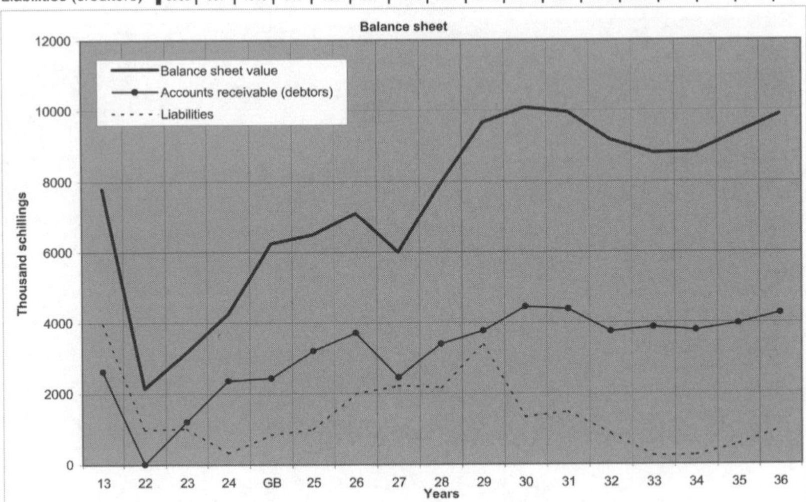

Figure A.5.: Austro-Fiat

Schrauben- und Schmiedewaren AG Brevillier & Co. Und A. Urban und Söhne

Profit and Loss Account (in thousand schillings)

Years	13	22*	23	24	25	26	27	28	29	30	31	32	33	34	35	36
Gross Profits	6002	507	1551	2252	3226	3127	3613	4674	6165	3870	2428	1860	2012	3069	3227	3694
Expenses	2579	338	1198	1908	2718	2374	2660	3204	4413	3579	3266	3538	2620	2833	2785	3101
Exchange losses															124	266
Depreciation on plant		29,4	30	61	625	351	592	679	698	733	647	1289	751	724	556	593
Investment					800		550	800	740	600	77			220	380	500
Net Profits	3424	170	353	344	508	752	954	1470	1732	290	-839	-1678	-608	237	442	592

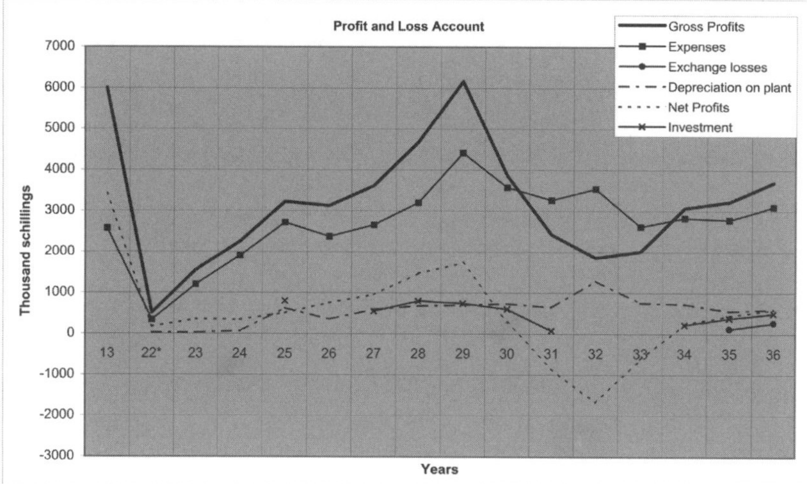

Balance sheet

Years	13	22*	23	24	GB	25	26	27	28	29	30	31	32	33	34	35	36
Balance sheet value	36115	3151	4083	7244	25983	28231	28252	27090	29785	28771	27338	24215	24135	22352	21614	21580	21648
Debtors	8003	1293	2182	5072	7531	10047	10350	8680	11206	9874	9181	6571	6650	6499	6905	6316	5701
Liabilities (creditors)	2519	2904	3607	6676	6460	8519	8212	6843	9013	7502	7252	4826	5340	5235	4869	4393	4156

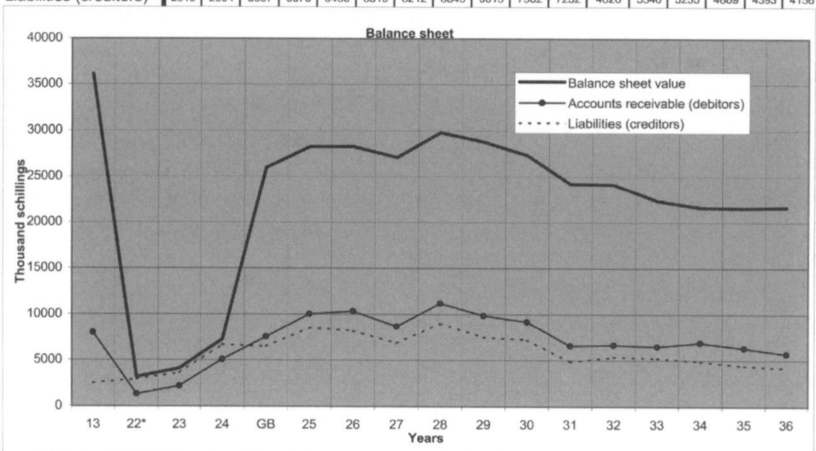

*The year 1922 includes only 10 months

Figure A.6.: Brevillier

Österreichische Brown-Boveri Werke AG

Profit and Loss Account (in thousand schillings)

Years	13/14	22/23*	24	25	26	27	28	29	30	31	32	33	34	35***	35**	36
Gross Profits	925	3535	3730	4307	4127	4319	5441	6212	5851	4274	2262	2497	2825	2475	2475	2636
Expenses	1686	3051	3190	3838	3576	3568	4484	5251	5048	4016	3092	2816	2880	8969	8969	2634
Depreciation on plant						195	249	276	267	219	193	188	189	6356	147	60
Investments						157	230	360	70	0	47	42				
Net Profits	-762	483,6	545	469	550	751	958	961	803	257	-830	-318	-56	-290	-1445	2

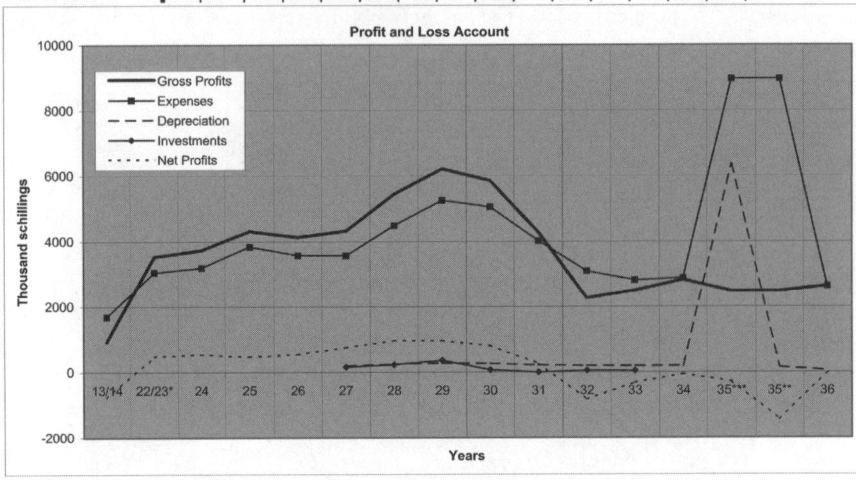

Balance sheet

Years	13/14	22/23*	24	GB	25	26	27	28	29	30	31	32	33	34	35	36
Balance sheet value	11929	6485	5613	11657	14613	15621	17660	18193	18374	15889	11708	11233	11650	11923	9943	9684
Debtors	5662	4539	3860	3658	5907	6897	7788	9826	9779	7932	5137	5992	6307	7241	4344	4401
Liabilities (creditors)	4883	3566	2194	2717	2563	5546	5717	7115	7732	5180	1880	2390	2236	2576	3482	3313
Bonded debt							2055	2055	2055	2055	2055	2507	2522	2537	1875	1863

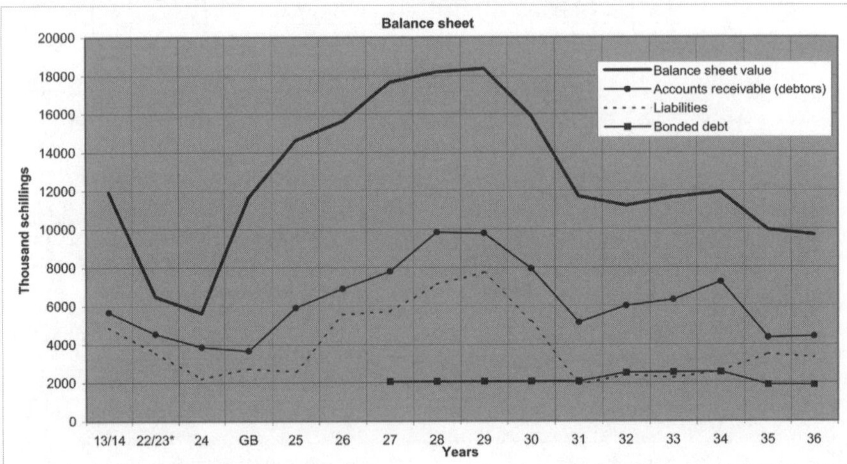

*1922/23 includes 18 months. **Reconstructed account of 1935. ***Total Losses, including depreciation backlog, amounted to 6,494 million schillings

Figure A.7.: Brown-Boveri

Österreichische Daimler Motoren AG und Puchwerke AG

Profit and Loss Account (in thousand schillings)

Years	13	22	23	24	25	26	27	27*	28	29
Gross Profits	1103	517	1628	1351	1492	1575	1486	2067	3474	3720
Expenses	683	323	1218	1444	1434	1544	1449	1949	2882	3297
Interests	269	273		1005	798	231	884	1077	1173	1791
Investments									630	1000
Net Profits	421	194	410	-935	58	30	36	232	592	423

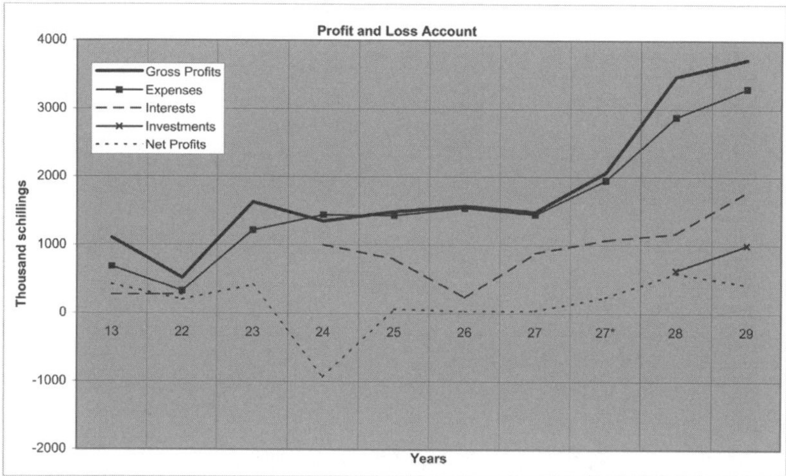

Balance sheet

Years	13	22	23	24	25	GB 26	26	27	27*	28	29
Balance sheet value	14095	6243	14493	18160	17789	20193	21628	16364	22904	26301	31047
Debtors				8777	7385	8534	10053	4784	5257	5105	8444
Liabilities (creditors)	6474	5415	9457	13458	14149	16506	17940	12640	16374	19870	24638

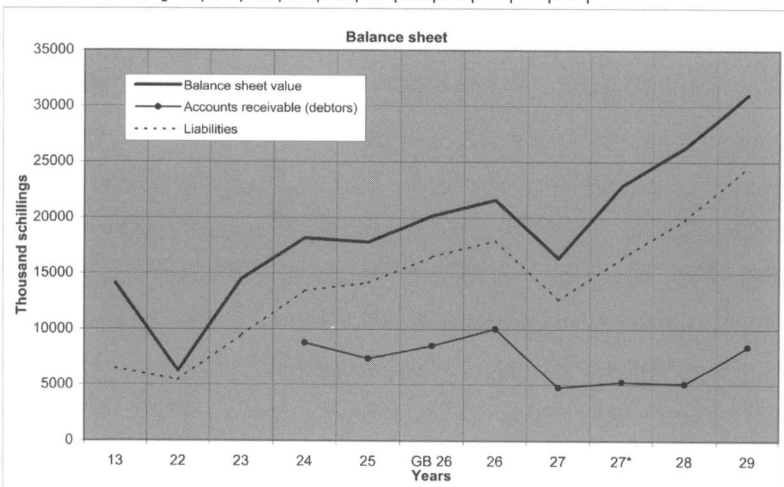

*Merger of Daimler and Puch in 1927

Figure A.8.: Daimler-Puch

Lampen- und Metalwarenfabriken R. Ditmar, Gebr. Brünner AG

Profit and Loss Account (in thousand schillings)

Years	13	22/23	23/24	24	25	26	27	28	29	30	31	32	33	34	35	36
Gross Profits	3748	883	2052	2246	2212	2307	1674	1907	2087	1987	1442	1152	1643	1605	1712	1643
Expenses	2405	558	1464	1618	1575	1760	1744	1840	1919	1975	1823	2952	1628	1590	1692	1620
Depreciation on plant		38	40	194	194	370	410	437	427	402	381	1813	316	228	365	293
Net Profits	1344	325	588	629	637	547	-70	67	169	12	-381	-1800	15	16	20	23

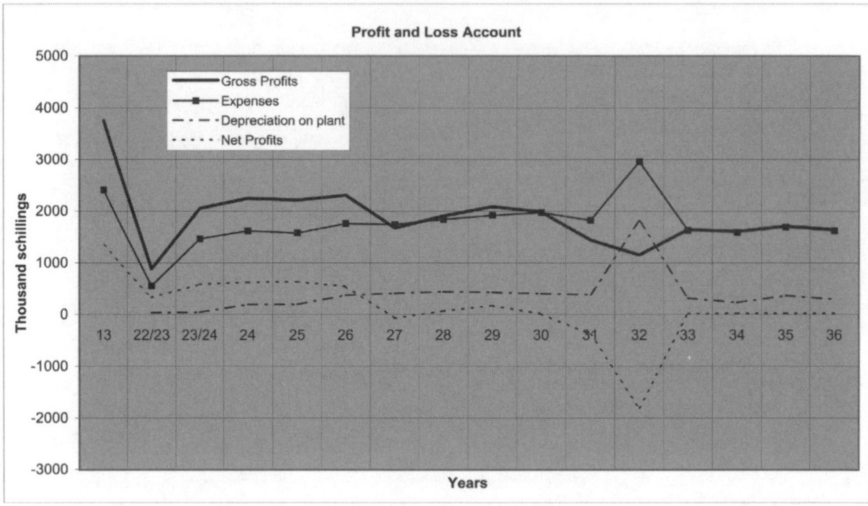

Balance sheet (in thousand Schillings)

Years	13	23/24	24	GB	25	26	27	28	29	30	31	32	33	34	35	36
Balance sheet value	26323	1699	2172	12857	13447	13592	12526	12913	12811	12745	12311	10363	10552	10179	9619	9361
Debtors	12247	962	1400	3685	3141	3307	3082	3609	3514	3344	3076	3019	3266	3292	3074	3173
Liabilities (creditors)	11069	923	1199	1604	1553	1773	2276	2650	2380	2302	2060	2101	2276	1887	1207	1026

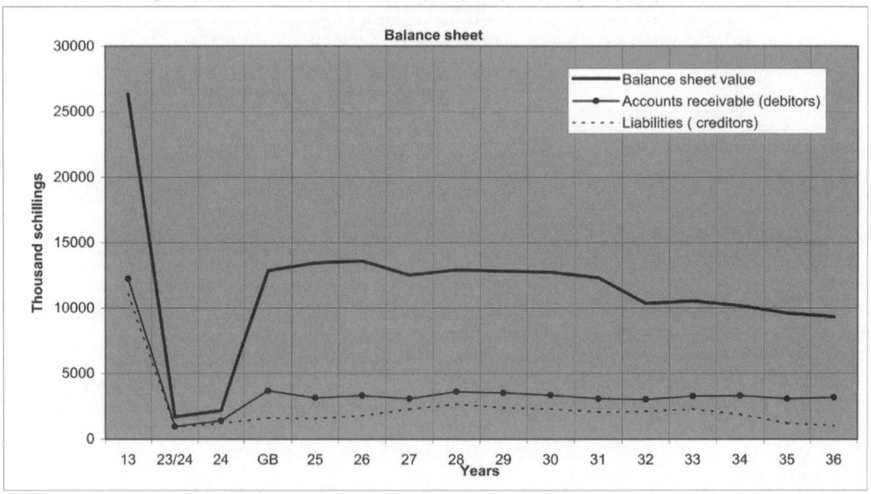

Figure A.9.: Ditmar-Brünner

"Elin" Aktiengesellschaft für Elektrische Industrie

Profit and Loss Account (in thousand schillings)

Years	13	23	24	25	26	27	28	29	30	31	32	33	34	35	36
Gross Profits	3125	2491	3515	4004	4486	6598	6669	7627	7525	6277	4749	4236	4196	4361	4457
Expenses	2932	2048	2960	3370	3853	5623	5655	6589	6754	6162	4713	4196	4154	4321	4344
Depreciation	413	157	179	222	328	428	477	598	708	560	318	332	399	442	540
Interest	268	74	257	232	184	196	54	194	458	598	542	579	495	412	422
Investment				300	240	700	730	2540	2500	390	0		120	180	300
Net Profits	192	443	555	635	633	678	1013	1037	771	115	36	40	41	40	113

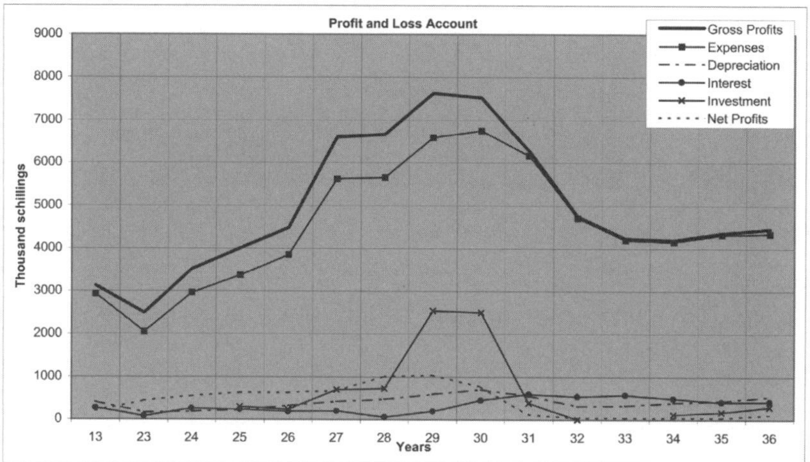

Balance sheet

Years	13	23	24	GB	25	26	27	28	29	30	31	32	33	34	35	36
Balance sheet value	11359	8421	9950	13047	12460	14527	17066	21135	29135	28583	26135	24007	21891	21535	22755	23335
Debtors	3936	3666	5263	4737	5054	4637	5514	7049	10816	10732	10023	8967	7615	7113	7751	7428
Plant under construction		1427	1452	1452	574	900	1571	1330	1989	766	399	42	83	344	386	308
Liabilities (creditors)	6090	1272	2519	3413	1960	1749	5215	4799	6051	6565	5922	4310	3637	3273	4715	4926
Bonded debt (Sterling loan)									7625	7589	5224	5027	5560	4862	4756	4620
Bond depreciation									379		348	333	318	303	288	273

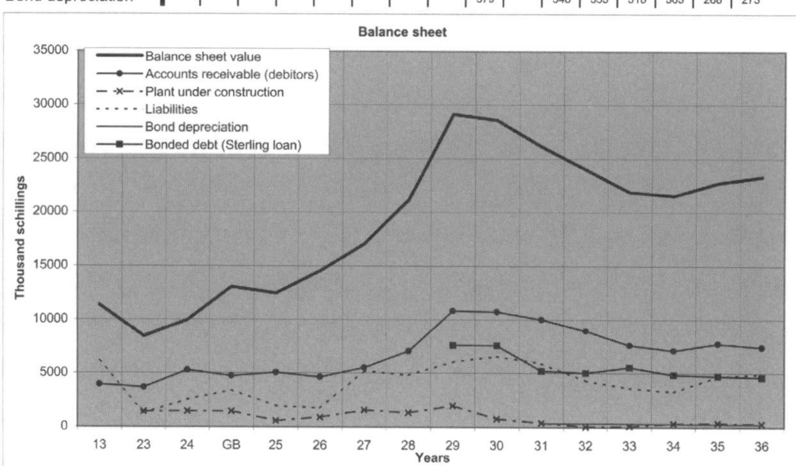

Figure A.10.: Elin

Wiener Automobilfabrik AG vorm. Gräf & Stift

Profit and Loss Account (in thousand schillings)

Years	13	24	25	26	27	28	29	30	31	32	33	34	35
Gross Profits	1094	1582	1401	1523	1803	1910	1880	1729	1502	1054		310	630
Expenses	724	1420	1230	1368	1645	1759	1702	1628	1489	1379			
Net Profits	370	162	171	155	158	150	177	101	12	-325	-140		

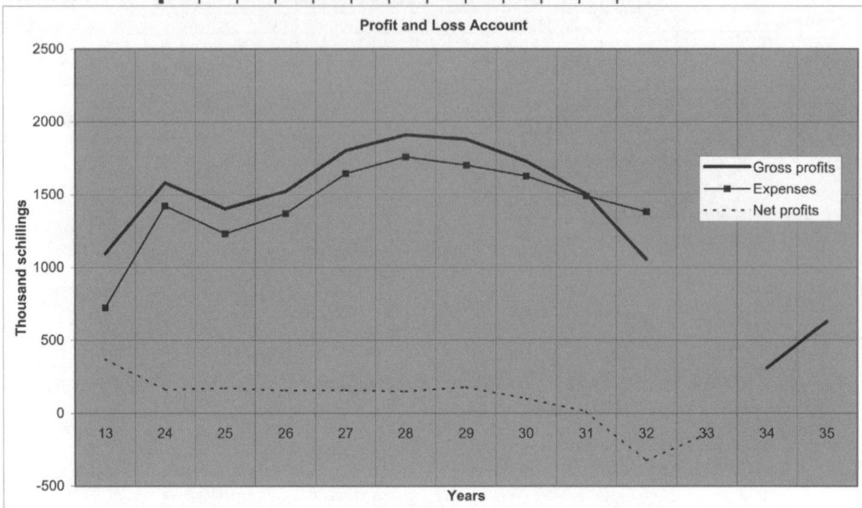

Balance sheet

Years	13	GB	25	26	27	28	29	30	31	32	33	34	35
Balance sheet value	5233	4705	4773	6332	8308	10495	10695	11058	9518	7570			
Debtors	733	1368	1073	1537	2119	1509	3574	2607	2510	831	1070	1100	1150
Liabilities (creditors)	2421	1455	1253	2662	4531	6531	6490	6740	5109	4260	4090	4420	3620

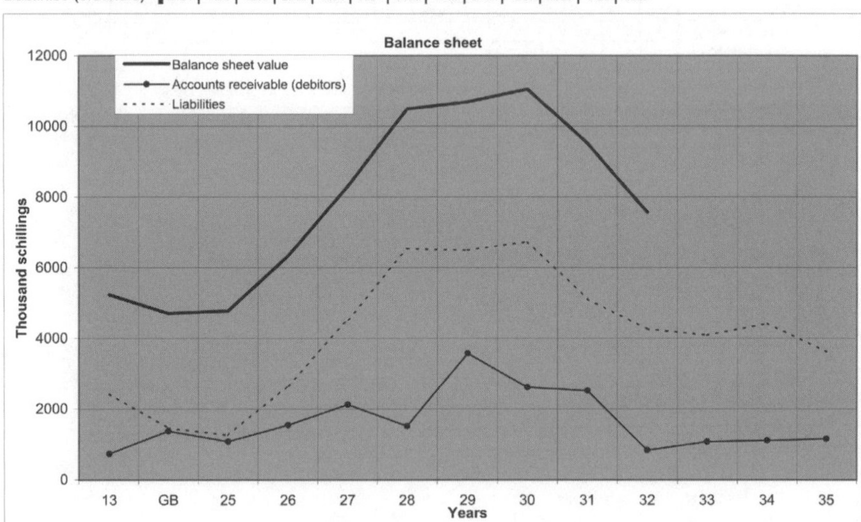

Figure A.11.: Gräf & Stift

Felten und Guileaume, Fabrik elektrischer Kabel, Stahl- und Kupferwerke

Profit and Loss Account (in thousand schillings)

Years	13	22	23	24	25	26	27	28	29	30	31	32	33	34	35
Gross Profits	4998	1157	1835	2204	2576	3574	4775	4889	5210	4921	3835	2182	1645	2021	2613
Expenses	2360	818	1036	1328	1683	2216	3056	3007	3234	3160	2718	2090	1784	1570	1930
Depreciation	585	0,9	0	0	244	360	867	541	694	921	929	821	719	666	759
Investment					320	530	710	610	1010	1760	210		320	170	250
Net Profits	2632	340	800	876	892	1357	1718	1882	1977	1771	1117	92	-139	450	680

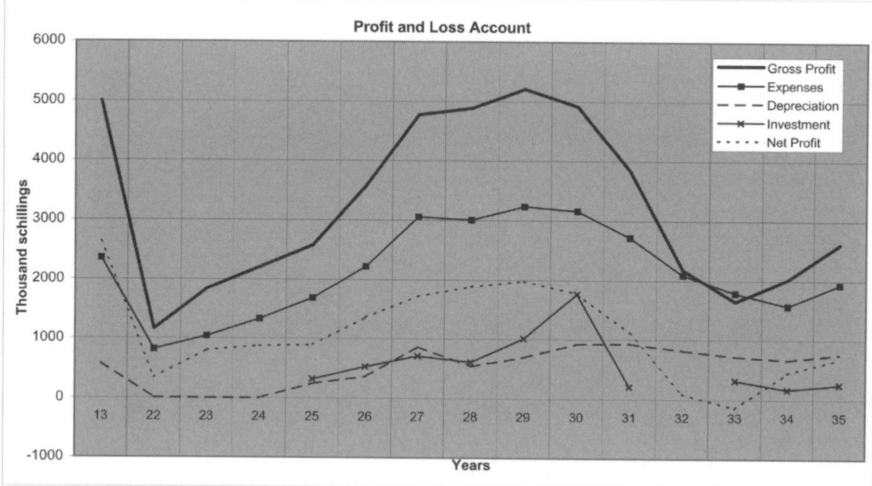

Balance sheet

Years	13	22	23	24	GB	25	26	27	28	29	30	31	32	33	34	35
Balance sheet value	25281	3567	5470	6254	19350	20790	21949	25315	27421	28499	26119	26341	23997	19984	20514	20477
Debtors	4458	1940	2550	3041	3041	3271	6182	9036	10720	11471	9004	9713	8347	4533	4618	4346
Liabilities (creditors)	4537	2376	3500	4090	4286	5496	4476	6651	8762	8033	5347	4736	3867	3269	2869	2315

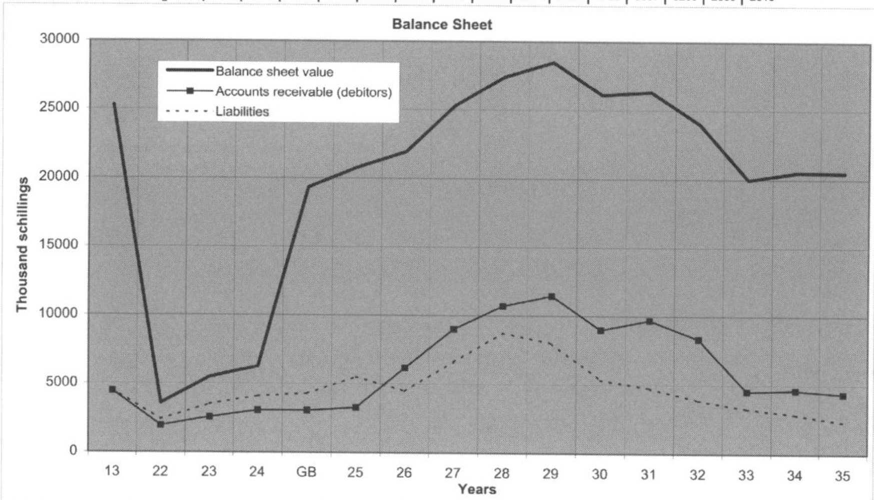

Figure A.12.: Guilleaume

Hofherr-Schrantz-Clayton-Schuttleworth, landwirtschaftliche Maschinenfabrik AG in Wien

Profit and Loss Account (in thousand schillings)

Years	13	21	22	23	24	25	26	27	28	29	30
Gross Profits	4775	17	380	977	1589	2143	1886	2019	1969	1962	670
Expenses	3031	13,3	250	751	1368	1747	2105	2039	1902	1903	1864
Interests							1287	1144	1042	950	847
Investment							528	350		200	
Net Profits	1744	3,76	129	225	221	395	-218	-20	56	59	-1193

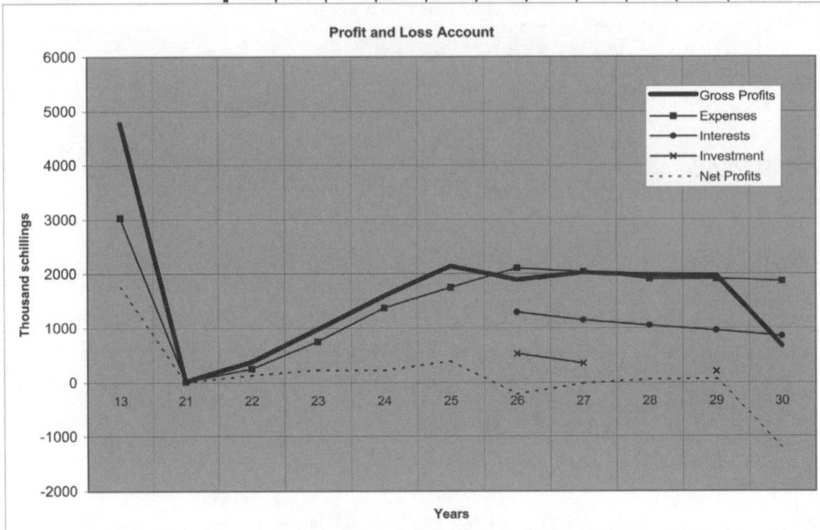

Balance sheet

Years	13	21	22	23	24	GB 25	25	26	27	28	29	30
Balance sheet value	68466	166,6	3655	6843	9860	12251	16600	20158	22046	26612	25945	26514
Accounts receivable (debtors)	23583	52,2	951	1262	2441	3221	4168	5853	6923	10435	8004	9690
Liabilities (creditors)	40355	108	3405	4821	7746	7592	11693	15632	17545	20772	20047	20731

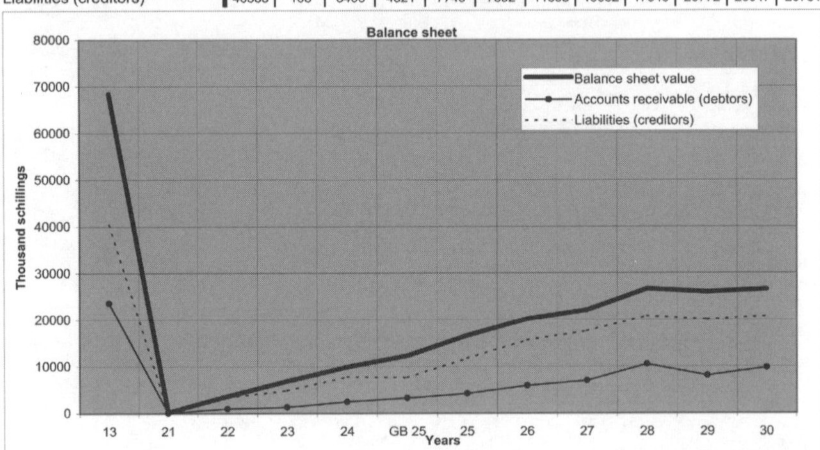

Figure A.13.: Hofherr

Hutter & Schrantz AG Siebwaren und Filztuchfabriken

Profit and Loss Account (in thousand schillings)

Years	13	22	23	24	25	26	27	28	29	30	31	32	33	34	35
Gross Profits	5599	822	2498	3540	4609	4677	4988	5364	5914	5804	5122	3938	3606	3178	3274
Expenses	4604	515	1497	2511	3406	3391	3560	3739	4282	4444	3889	3269	2798	2362	2454
Interests	134	44	177	544	744	561	472	454	592	471	354	162			
Depreciation on plant	746	21	53	109	531	650	884	931	999	916	919	853	749	502	439
Investment					370	370	830	832	1270	350	190		330	230	46
Net Profits	995	307	1000	1030	1202	1285	1428	1625	1632	1360	1233	669	808	816	820

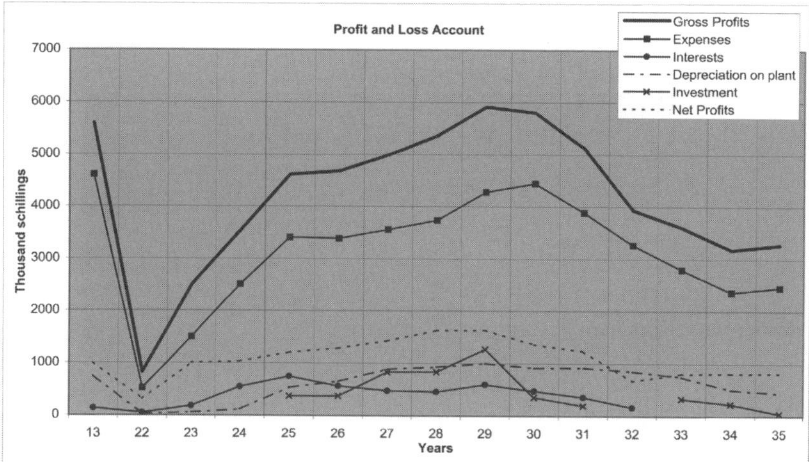

Balance sheet

Years	13	23	24	GB	25	26	27	28	29	30	31	32	33	34	35
Balance sheet value	17775	4755	8082	26264	26770	26056	26812	28936	28926	26013	24344	21896	17985	18211	19089
Debtors	5790	2368	5427	8479	8681	5564	4741	6241	6616	5498	5149	3540	3857	5041	5269
Liabilities (creditors)	4308		3410	9706	9091	8486	6739	8546	8312	5447	3903	1892	1128	1241	1432

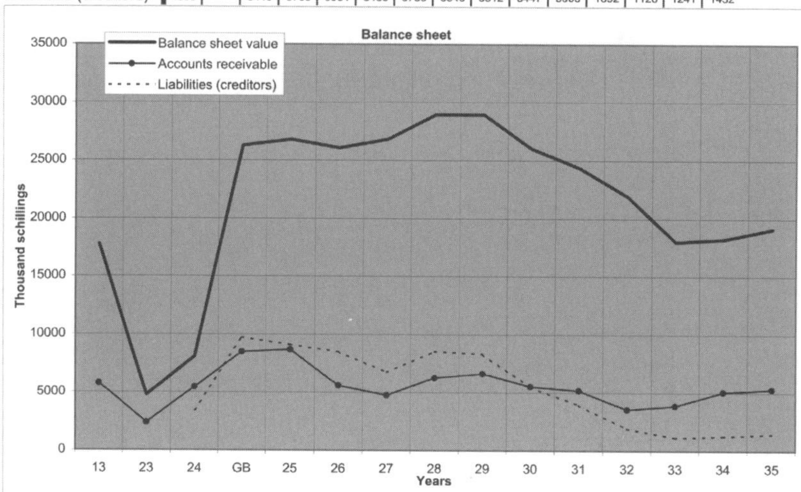

Figure A.14.: Hutter & Schrantz

Hutter & Schrantz AG Siebwaren und Filztuchfabriken

Profit and Loss Account, Inflation Years (in thousand schillings)

Years	18	19	20	21
Gross Profits	1,24	2,3	9,3	45,2
Expenses	1,1	2,02	7,9	40,3
Interests			0,23	1,8
Depreciation on plant	0,084	0,085	0,29	0,62
Net Profits	0,173	0,29	1,33	4,9

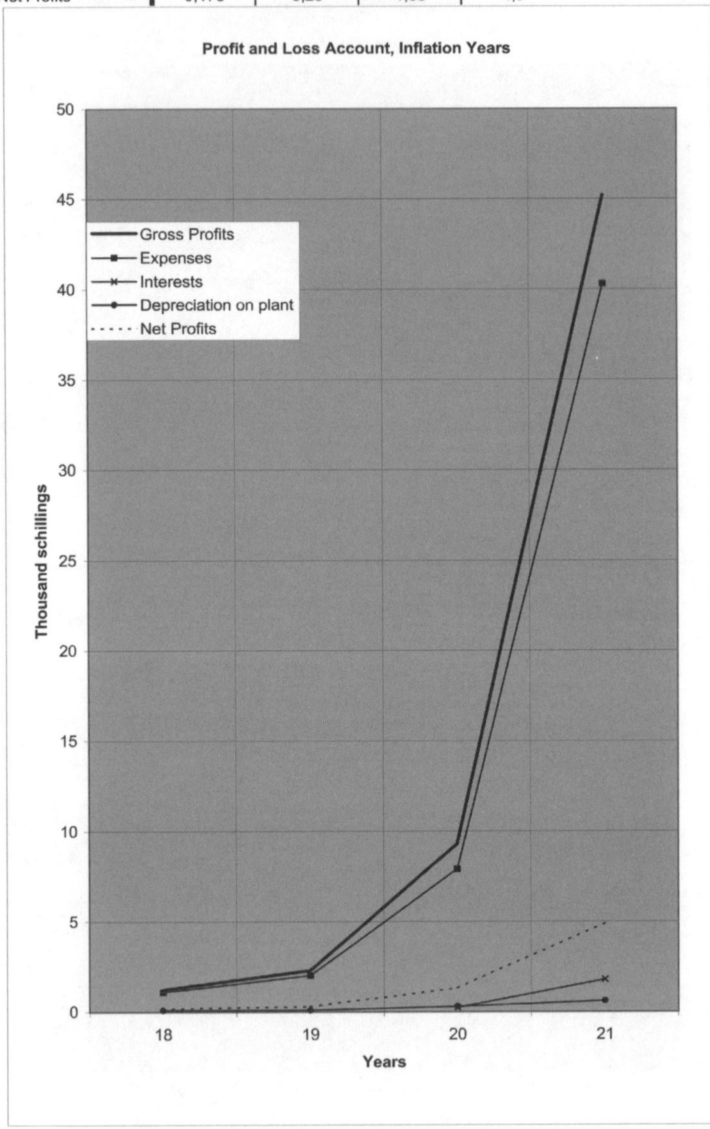

Figure A.15.: Hutter & Schrantz: Inflation

Leykam-Josefsthaler AG für Papier- und Druckindustrie

Profit and Loss Account (in thousand schillings)

Years	13	22	23	24	25	26	27	28	29	30	31	32	33	34	35	36
Gross Profits	3450	384	1134	1140	2930	4389	3866	4015	4465	3094	1707	2259	2363	2700	3465	3699
Expenses	2608	307	799	1129	2400	3753	3591	3737	4393	5130	9583	3568	4682	4575	3442	3668
Depreciation on plant		32,7	58	152	352	863	821	871	1019	546	1207		1869	1722	1123	1409
Investment					5500	1230	1130	3450	1560						120	420
Net Profits	801	48	335	10	531	636	275	278	72	-2046	-7831	-1248	-2319	-1875	23	31

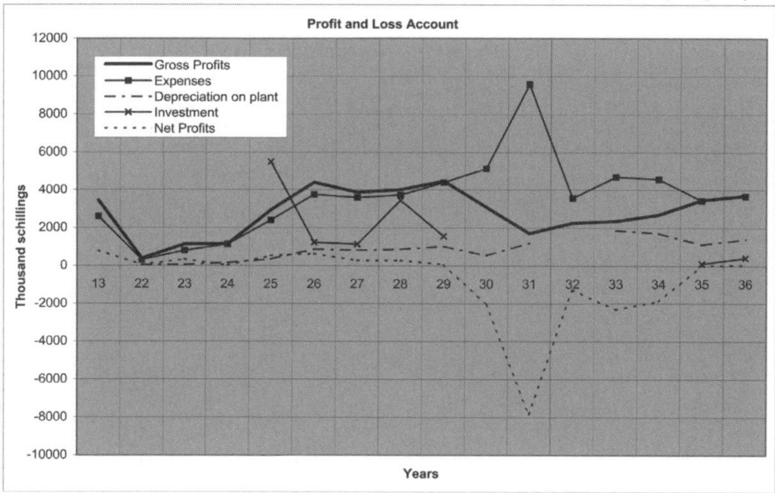

Balance sheet

Years	13	23	24	GB	25	MB*	26	27	28	29	30	31	32	33	34	35	36
Balance sheet value	47792	5461	14127	20160	30104	36693	36709	38132	41632	45032	41811	43553	40279	40454	36068	37639	37628
Debtors	7973	1680	2644	2704	5666	8672	6293	6911	6536	7509	5043	3623	4043	3845	4530	5977	5628
Liabilities (creditors)**	16060	1814	2368	2449	6166	12710	11200	12122	14583	17000	13549	18450	18695	20453	14665	15090	13639
Bonded debt***					5174	5174	5174	5174	5174	5174	5174						

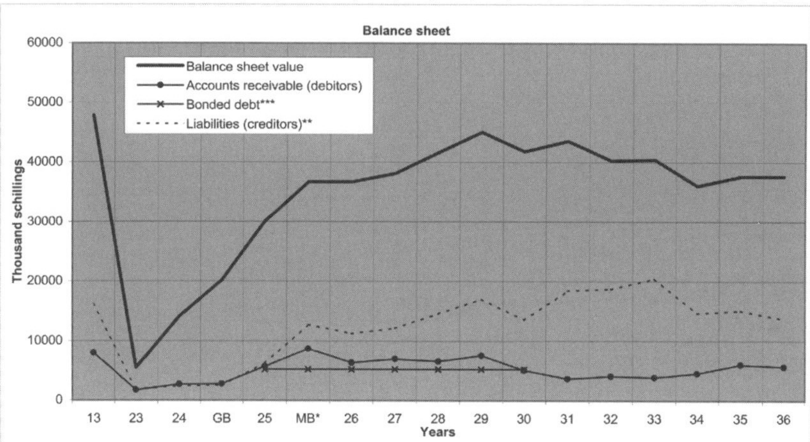

*Merger Balance **Including bonded debt value from 1931 onwards ***Sterling credit

Figure A.16.: Leykam-Josefsthaler

AG der Lokomotivfabrik, vormals S. Sigl, Wiener Neustadt

Profit and Loss Account (in thousand schillings)

Years	13/14	18/19	19/20	20/21	21/22	22/23	23/24	24/25	25/26	26/27	27/28	28/29
Gross Profits	1436	-11,4	68	362	457,6	839		329	354	533	564	250
Expenses	827	21,5	15,6	115,6	273,7	245		216	198	291	327	244
Net Profits	611	-22,6	52	246,6	184	594		113	156	242	237	6

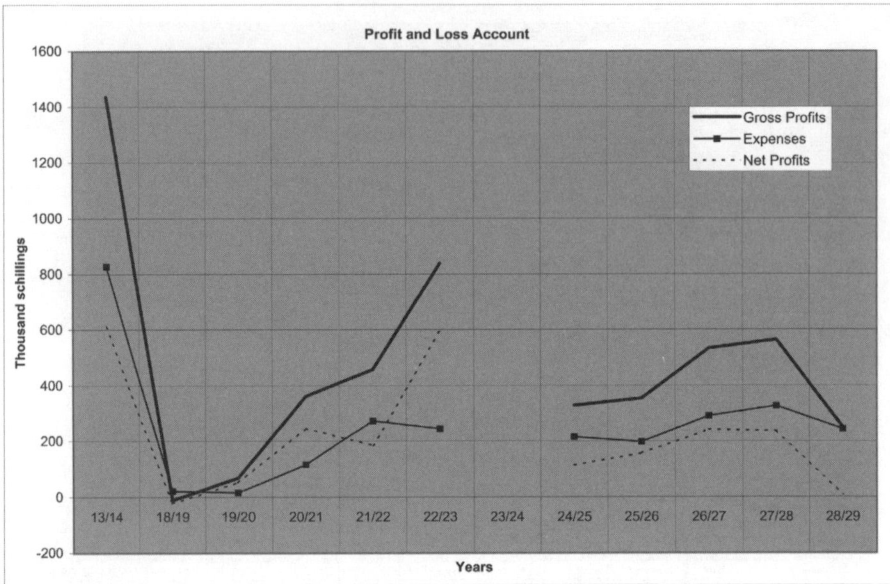

Figure A.17.: Lokomotivfabrik Wiener Neustädter

Neusiedler AG für Papierfabrikation

Profit and Loss Account (in thousand schillings)

Years	24	25	26	27	28	29	30	31	32	33	34	35	36
Gross Profits		2079	1965	2054	2095	1782	1401					200	460
Net Profits	4417	1539	1413	1427	1448	1076	527			-200	-910	-200	

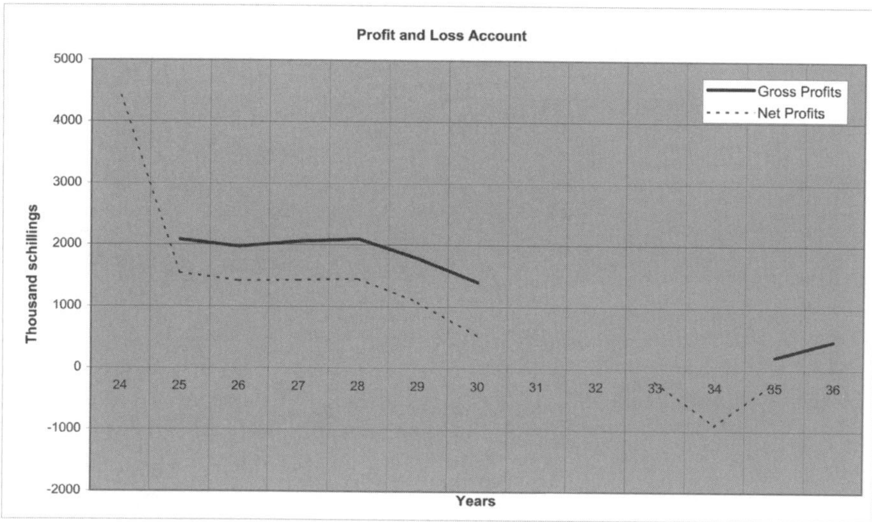

Balance sheet

Years	13	GB	25	26	27	28	29	30	31	32	33	34	35	36
Balance sheet value	36167	33599	37035	42140	45602	48855	47952	44204	42456	40869	40006	40093	38961	37348
Debtors	9017	13525	16017	19167	19715	21390	18019	15364	15215	14346	13311	12892	12184	11644
Liabilities (creditors)	12057	8241	9327	13902	16874	19356	17845	13782	12184	10904	10630	11094	10873	9001

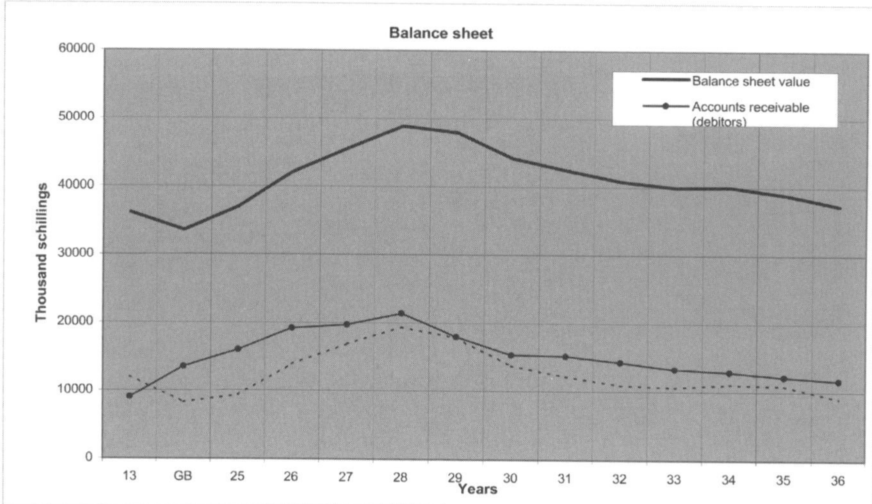

Figure A.18.: Neusiedler

Schoeller-Bleckmann Stahlwerke AG

Profit and Loss Account (in thousand schillings)

Years	22	23	24	25	26	27	28	29	30	31	32	33	34	35	36
Gross Profits	884	325	473	270	285	547	1345	1467	796	-2397	-4069	797	1321	1671	2036
Expenses	243	153	158	294	338	448	971	1031	694	2912	4089	735	1075	1367	1477
Depreciation	58	105	132	243	285	320	694	727	384	472		715	985	1247	1267
Investment				1210	990	682	779	890	1990				590	390	950
Net Profits	641	172	314	-25	-52	98	374	436	101	-2912	-4070	34	246	304	559

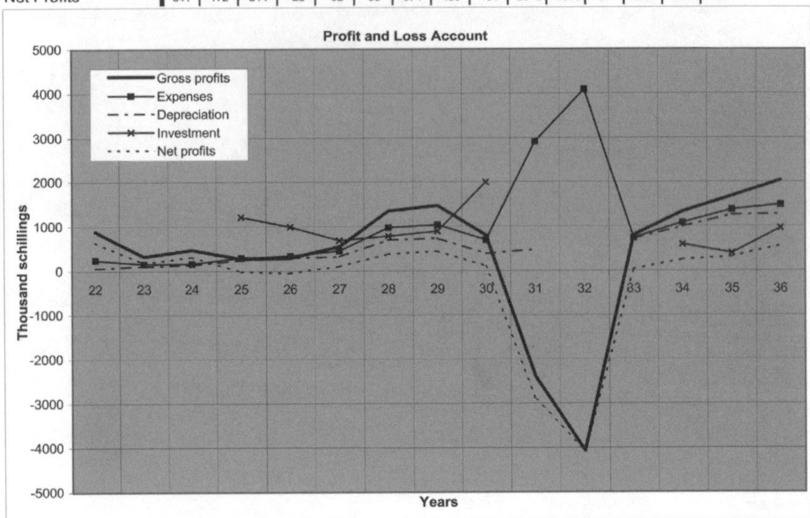

Balance sheet

Years	22	23	24	GB	25	26	27	28	29	30	31	32	33	34	35	36
Balance sheet value	10516	15647	20988	28258	33717	34594	39438	39447	41092	37959	38399	32706	32072	34724	38365	38484
Debtors	1908	8755	11720	11225	12792											
Bank credit	6864	8179	13549	14588	19753	20292	19766	19146	19957	16867	18154	20011	19394	21133	22986	21079

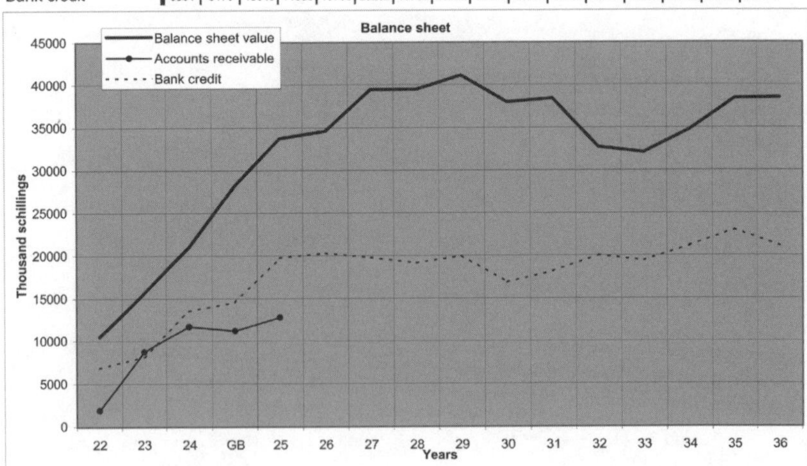

Figure A.19.: Schoeller-Bleckmann

"Semperit", Österreichische-amerikanische Gummiwerke AG

Profit and Loss Account (in thousand schillings)

Years	13	23	24	25	26	27	28	29	30	31	32	33	34	35	36
Gross Profits	6653	4430	7048	7112	6576	6036	7202	8346	7183	7207	6763	7246	7431	7016	7899
Expenses	5443	3406	5157	5318	6591	4501	5138	6144	6101	7028	6432	7071	7269	6842	7583
Investment				153		80	630	1570	900	720	1210			300	590
Net Profits	1210	1025	1890	1794	1341	1535	2020	2141	1083	179	49	175	162	175	316

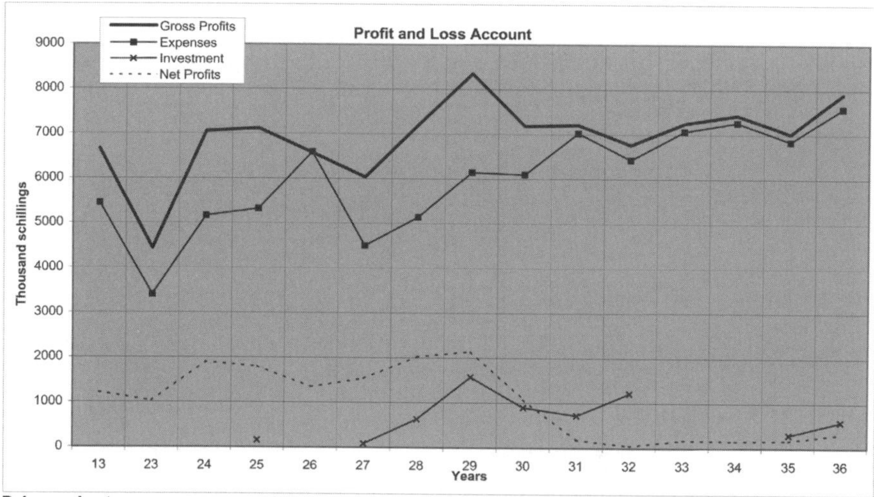

Balance sheet

Years	13	23	24	GB	25	26	27	28	29	30	31	32	33	34	35	36
Balance sheet value	29514	9917	24620	38854	42011	40855	41426	44287	46221	43952	43952	41352	41044	41088	40992	39760
Debtors	7212	6595	18477	13074	14722	15276	16514	19145	20912	20217	20810	18336	20290	16440	17013	16425
Liabilities (creditors)	6025	4334	10788	14709	16179	15499	12915	15290	17193	15653	16543	13904	12918	13351	13080	11530
Bonded debt	1320						2955	2904	2597	2597	2597	2597	3116	3076	3076	3076

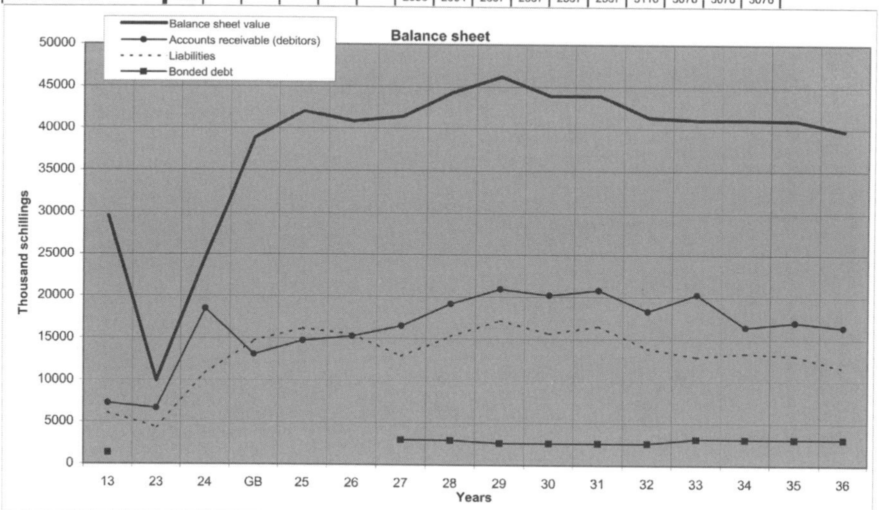

Figure A.20.: Semperit

Österreichische Siemens-Schuckert Werke

Profit and Loss Account (in thousand schillings)

Years	13	22	23	24	25	26	27	28	29	30	31	32	33	34	35	36
Gross Profits	23603	2367	5713	8390	10576	10816	11661	14151	17432	16052	11375	6337	4481	4405	4717	6565
Required capital reserves					21125							3124	2876	1886		
Expenses	19655	2160	5264	7609	8747	8973	9752	11641	14142	12935	11318	9682	7357	6292	5571	5712
Depreciation		93	228	729	1044	1279	1383	1949	3316	2199	1912	1752	1689	1265	660	510
Investment					2500	2370	460	1487	4200	1620	530	0	160	320	330	920
Net Profits	3948	207	449	781	1829	1843	1909	2510	3289	3118	56	-221	-2876	-1886	-854	854

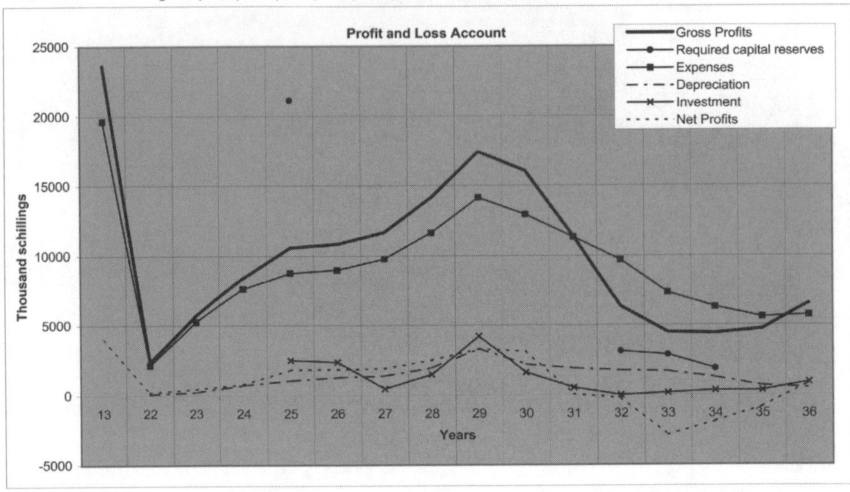

Balance sheet

Years	13	22	23	24	GB	25	26	27	28	29	30	31	32	33	34	35	36
Balance sheet value	28848	10629	22433	25375	72088	69264	72541	75016	81108	73619	70207	63091	56175	53888	47083	46538	44206
Debtors	54300	6674	10508	12530	25366	25838	25421	36049	38472	29165	30072	27863	28890	31952	26626	23317	22571
Liabilities (creditors)	57144	9486	21150	23670	22088	17435	20522	22709	27343	18813	15369	11328	8062	8674	3739	3195	3862

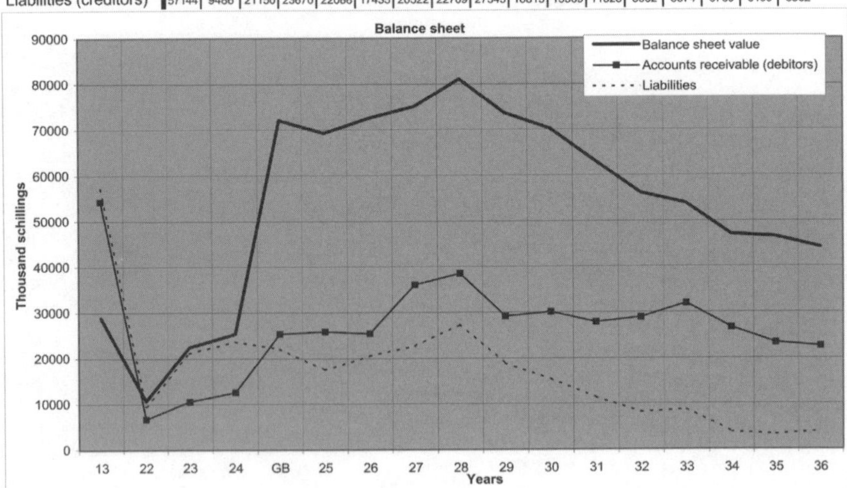

Figure A.21.: Siemens

Machinen- und Waggon- Fabrik AG Simmering

Profit and Loss Account (in thousand schillings)

Years	13	20/21	21/22	22/23	23/24	24/25	25/26	27	28	29	30	31	32
Gross Profits	2226	6,55	60,5	627	1619	1853	2542	1237	1817	2218	3635	1323	710
Expenses	1565	2,5	20,6	222	788	963	1671	901	1270	1636	2985	1190	960
Depreciation on plant		0,7	2,2	33	130	106		167	327	529	1810	538	530
Investment							520	210	230	750	1600	220	156
Net Profits	667	3,94	39	405	831	890	871	336	547	582	649	133	-240

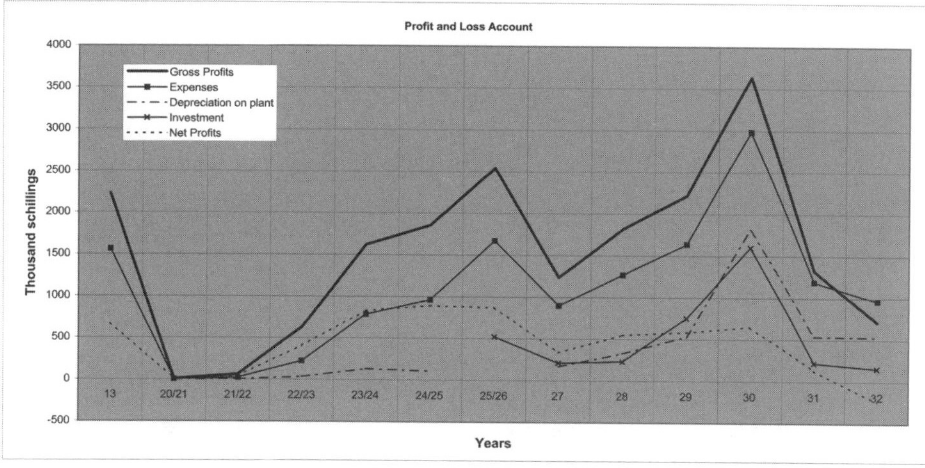

Figure A.22.: Simmeringer

Steyr Werke AG and Daimler Puch

Profit and Loss Account (in thousand schillings)

Years	13/14	21	22	23	24	25	26	27	28	29	30	31	32	33	MB34*	35	36
Gross Profits	8400	60	1577	3496	5353	7169	9099	11911	14395			3299	6126	4598	7355	9256	11708
Expenses	4380	42	1137	2531	4136	5484	7248	9997	13571			5635	6073	4568	7037	8125	9330
Depreciation on plant						1191								672	872	1333	1280
Investment						1870	1210								290	810	250
Net Profits	4019	19	440	965	1217	1685	1850	1914	824			-2354	52	31	318	1131	2377

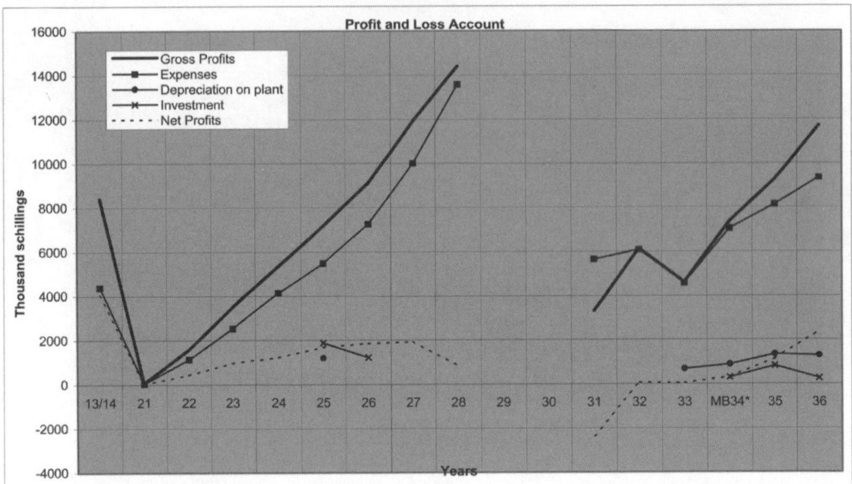

Balance sheet (in thousand Schillings)

Years	13/14	21	22	23	24	25	26	27	28	29	30	31	32	33	MB34*	34	35	36
Balance sheet value	48450	65,4	7541	10996	15253	43656	56483	62561	84187			44958	35870	31652	39361	39010	40303	45704
Debtors	12722	23,5	2596	4890	4864	8511	8598	12082	18725			6545	7129	10687	11745	9364	11821	13168

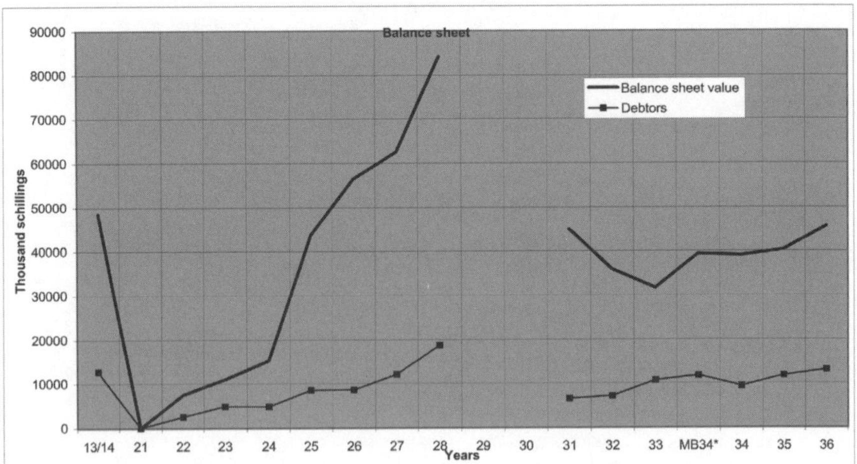

*Merger Balance

Figure A.23.: Steyr Werke

Veitscher Magnesitwerke AG

Profit and Loss Account (in thousand schillings)

Years	20/21	21/22	22/23	23/24	25	26	27	28	29	30	31	32	33	34	35	36
Gross Profits	9,92	193,8	1864	1946	3612	2683	3073	3319	4174	4070	2279	1093	2241	2791	3206	3412
Expenses	5,54	116	1189	1415	1849	1548	1625	1691	2094	2125	1818	1133	1628	1835	1890	1718
Depreciation on plant	0,11	0,11	0,1	0,1	1071	1011	1047	1042	1269	1379	1391	1023	1395	1456	1142	664
Investment				222	200	820	77	110	1640		140				60	150
Net Profits	4,43	77,77	675,1	531,2	1763	1136	1448	1628	2080	1945	461	-40	613	956	1316	1694

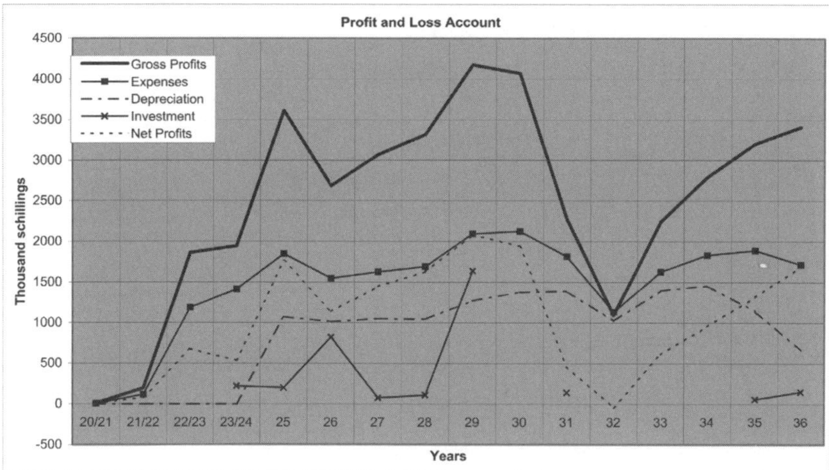

Balance sheet

Years	20/21	21/22	22/23	23/24	25	26	27	28	29	30	31	32	33	34	35	36
Balance sheet value	19,54	210,3	2555,4	1458	20576	23364	22371	23778	26887	25157	21919	21349	22531	24119	22803	24330
Debtors	8,75	103,9	1742,3	756,3	4601		8824	10988	14470	13145	10001	10412	14131	17287	15854	18340
Liabilities (creditors)	7,13	38,3	866,6	798,9	2573	1810	2340	2131	5065	4803	3156	3194	3887	5113	4834	5899

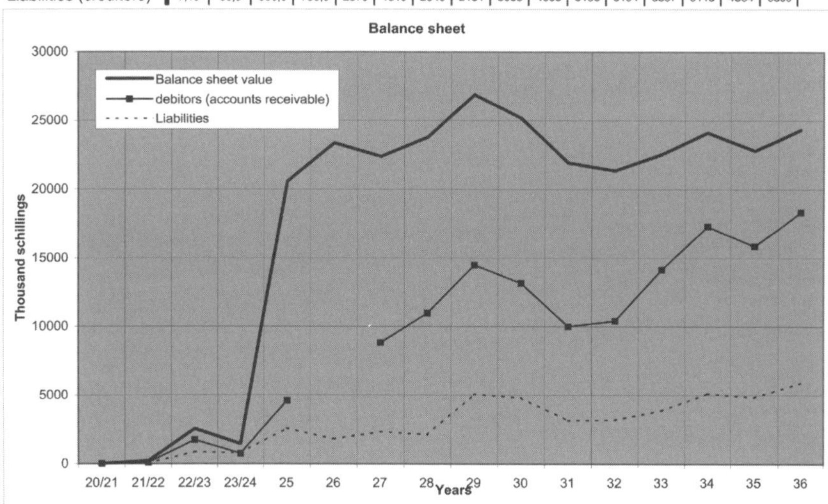

Figure A.24.: Veitscher

Veitscher Magnesitwerke AG

Employment

Years	22	25	26	27	28	29	30	31	32	33	34	35	36	37
Workforce*	2300	1300	1250	1450	1450	1690	1450	476	292	670	812	987	1000	1150

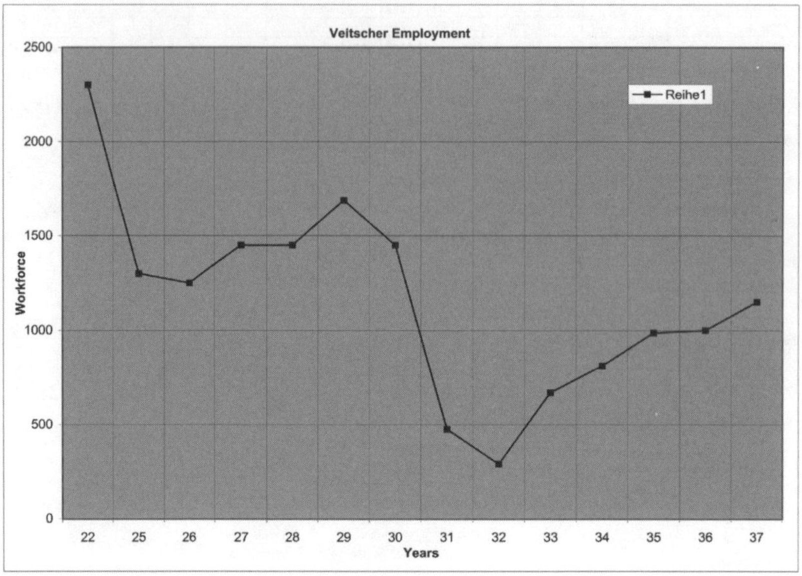

*Approximate figures

Figure A.25.: Veitscher: Employment

Wiener Lokomotiv-Fabriks AG

Profit and Loss Account (in thousand schillings)

Years	13	22	23	24	25	26	27	28	29	30	31	32	33	34	35	36
Gross Profits	3432	686	2134	1590	887	1160	1459	1240	959	621	1537	366	125	165	445	738
Expenses	1119	401	1089	979	546	932	1113	1065	954	636	1481	924	1157	1006	921	908
Depreciation		50	63	50		349	459	347	313		695		398	374	326	290
Net Profits	2313	285	1045	611	341	228	347	175	5	-15	56	-393	-912	-840	-476	-170

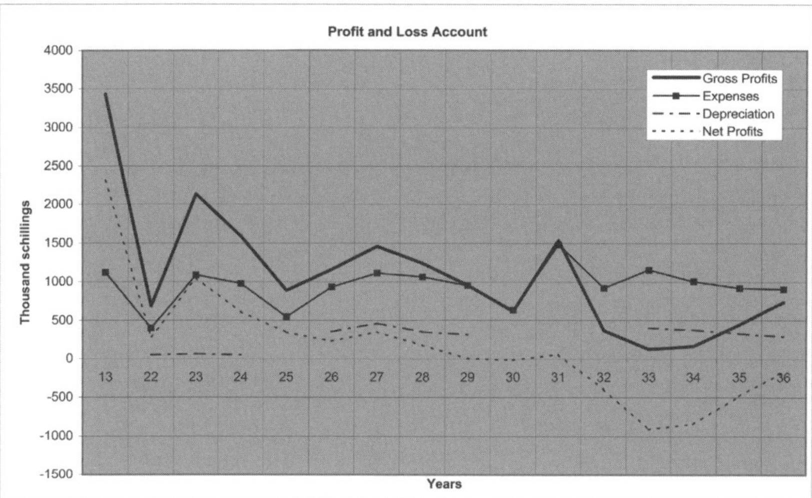

Balance sheet

Years	13	22	23	24	GB	25	26	27	28	29	30*	31	32	33	34	35	36
Balance sheet value	14273	2009	3556	3250	9769	9420	11435	11939	12704	10387	18379	17982	12997	11802	11501	10583	10110
Debtors	4206	702	1847	1698	2224	2609	1901	3756	4211	2510	3878	6057	3188	1351	1656	1876	3084
Liabilities (creditors)	2079	878	1501	1485	1605	1013	3139	3499	4432	2277	4375	3922	2149	953	1901	1823	1826

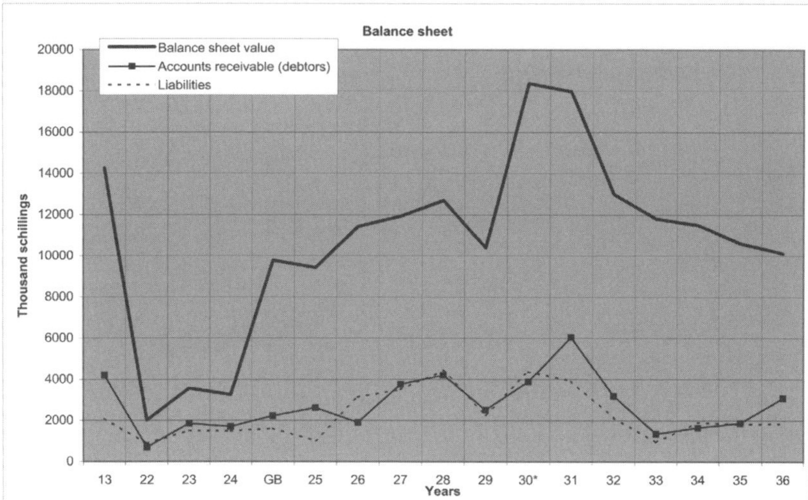

Figure A.26.: Wiener Lokomotiv-Fabrik

BIBLIOGRAPHY

Abelshauser, Werner, and Dietmar Petzina, "Zum Problem der relativen Stagnation der deutschen-Wirtschaft in den zwanziger Jahren," in: Hans Mommsen, Dietmar Petzina and Bernd Weisbrod (eds.), *Industrielles System und politische Entwicklung in der Weimarer Republik*, vol. 1, Düsseldorf 1974.

Abelshauser, Werner, and Dietmar Petzina, "Krise und Rekonstruktion. Zur Interpretation der gesamtwirtschaftlichen Entwicklung Deutschlands im 20. Jahrhundert," in: Wilhelm Heinz Schröder and Reinhard Spree (eds.), *Historische Konjunkturforschung. Historisch-Sozialwissenschaftliche Forschungen. Quantitative sozialwissenschaftliche Analysen von historischen und prozeß-produzierten Daten*, vol. 11, Stuttgart 1981.

Abelshauser, Werner (ed.), *Die Weimarer Republik als Wohlfahrtsstaat. Zum Verhältnis von Wirtschafts- und Sozialpolitik in der Industriegesellschaft*, Stuttgart 1987.

Aghion, Philippe, and Peter Howitt, *Endogenous Growth Theory*, Cambridge, Massachusetts 1998.

Aldcroft, Derek H., and Peter Fearon (eds.), *Economic Growth in Twentieth-Century Britain*, Suffolk 1969 (first published in 1964).

Aldcroft, Derek H., *Die zwanziger Jahre. Von Versailles zur Wall Street, 1919–1929*, Munich 1978.

Aldcroft, Derek H., *The British Economy between the Wars*, Oxford 1983.

Aldcroft, Derek H., *The European Economy 1914–1990*, 3rd edition, London 1995.

Alford, B.W.E., "New industries for old? British industry between the wars," in: Roderick Floud and Donald McCloskey (eds.), *The Economic History of Britain since 1700. Volume 2: 1860 to the 1970s*, Cambridge 1981.

Allen, D.C., *A Short Economic History of Modern Japan*, New York 1981.

Ardt, Sven (ed.), *The Political Economy of Austria*, Washington, D.C., 1982.

Armengaud, André, Sidney Pollard and Guido L. de Brabanter, "DieWirtschaft: Großbritannien, Irland, Frankreich, Belgien, die Niederlande, Luxemburg, 1914–1980/83," in: Wolfram Fischer (ed.), *Handbuch der Europäischen Wirtschafts- und Sozialgeschichte. Band 6. Europäische Wirtschafts- und Sozialgeschichte vom Ersten Weltkrieg bis zur Gegenwart*, Stuttgart 1987.

Arndt, H.W., *The Economic Lessons of the Nineteen-Thirties*, London 1972 (1st edition 1944).

Assenmacher, Walter, *Konjunkturtheorie*, 8th edition, Munich 1998.

Ausch, Karl, *Als die Banken fielen. Zur Soziologie der politischen Korruption*, Wien 1968.

Bachinger, Karl, and Herbert Matis, "Strukturwandel und Entwicklungstendenzen der Montanwirtschaft 1918–1938", in: Michael Mitterauer (ed.), *Österreichisches Montanwesen. Produktion, Verteilung, Sozialreformen (Sozial- und Wirtschaftshistorische Studien)*, Vienna 1974.

Bachinger, Karl and Herbert Mathis, "Die österreichische Nachkriegsinflation 1918–1922," in: *Beiträge zur Historischen Sozialkunde*, No. 3, 1986.

Bachinger, Karl, and Hildegard Hemetsberger-Koller, "Österreich von 1918 bis zur Gegenwart," in: Wolfram Fischer (ed.), *Handbuch der Europäischen Wirtschafts- und Sozialgeschichte. Band 6. Europäische Wirtschafts- und Sozialgeschichte vom Ersten Weltkrieg bis zur Gegenwart*, Stuttgart 1987.

Bachinger, Karl, "Teil II: Österreich 1918–1945. 4. Der Staat und die Wirtschaft," in: Karl Bachinger, Hildegard Hemetsberger-Koller and Herbert Matis (eds.), *Grundriss der österreichischen Sozial- und Wirtschaftsgeschichte von 1848 bis zur Gegenwart*, Vienna 1987.

Bachinger, Karl, and Vlastislav Lacina, "Wirtschaftliche Ausgangsbedingungen", in: Alice Teichova and Herbert Matis (eds.), *Österreich und die Tschechoslovakei 1918–1938. Die wirtschaftliche Neuordnung in Zentraleuropa in der Zwischenkriegszeit*, Vienna 1996.

Bairoch, Paul, "Europe's Gross National Product: 1800–1975," in: *The Journal of European Economic History*, 2, Vol. 5, 1976.

Balderston, Theodor, "The Origins of Economic Instability in Germany 1924–1930. Market Forces Versus Economic Policy," in: *Vierteljahrschrift für Sozial- und Wirtschaftsgeschichte*, Volume 69, 1982.

Balderston, Theodor, *The Origins and Course of the German Economic Crisis. November 1923 to May 1932*, Berlin 1993.

Baran, Paul, and Paul Sweezy, *Monopoly Capital: An Essay on the American Economic and Social Order*, New York 1966.

Barber, Clarence L., "On the Origins of the Great Depression," in: *Southern Economy Journal*, 44 (3), 1978.

Benedikt, Heinrich (ed.), *Geschichte der Republik Österreich*, Vienna 1977.

Berend, I.T., "Agriculture," in: M. C. Kaser and E. A. Radice (eds.), *The Economic History of Eastern Europe 1919–1975, Volume I. Economic Structure and Performance between the Two Wars*, Oxford 1985.

Berger, Peter-Robert, *Der Donauraum im wirtschaftlichen Umbruch nach dem Ersten Weltkrieg. Währung und Finanzen in den Nachfolgestaaten Österreich, Ungarn und Tschechoslovakei 1918–1929*, dissertation, Vienna 1982.

Berger, Peter, "The Austrian Economy, 1918–1938," in: John Komlos (ed.), *Economic Development in the Habsburg Monarchy and in the Successor States (East European Monographs*, No. 280), New York 1990.

Bernstein, Michael A., *The Great Depression. Delayed recovery and economic change in America, 1929–1939*, Cambridge, Massachusetts 1987.

Birkenfeld, Wolfgang, *Der synthetische Treibstoff 1933–1945. Ein Beitrag zur nationalsozialistischen Wirtschafts- und Rüstungspolitik*, Göttingen 1964.

Bloomfield, Jonathan, "Surviving in a Harsh World: Trade and Inflation in the Czechoslovak and Austrian Republics 1918–1926," in: Gerald D. Feldman, Carl-Ludwig Holtfrerich, Gerhard A. Ritter and Peter-Christian Witt (eds.), *Die Erfahrungen der Inflation im Internationalen Zusammenhang und Vergleich (The Experience of Inflation. International and Comparative Studies)*, New York 1984.

Boelcke, Wille A., *Die deutsche Wirtschaft 1930–1945. Interna des Reichswirtschaftsministeriums*, Düsseldorf 1983.

Bombach, G., H.J. Ramser, M. Timmermann and W. Wittmann (eds.), *Der Keynesianismus I. Theorie und Praxis keynesianischerWirtschaftspolitik. Entwicklung und Stand der Diskussion*, New York 1976.

Borchardt, Knut, "Zwangslagen und Handlungsspielräume in der großen Weltwirtschaftskrise der frühen dreißiger Jahre," and "Wirtschaftliche Ursachen des Scheiterns der Weimarer Republik," in: Knut Borchardt (ed.), *Wachstum, Krisen und Handlungsspielräume der Wirtschaftspolitik (Studien zur Wirtschaftsgeschichte des 19. und 20. Jahrhunderts)*, Göttingen 1982.

Bordes, Walré de, *The Austrian Crown. Its Depreciation and Stabilisation*, London 1924.

Brocard, Lucien, "Die Tendenz zur Nationalwirtschaft und die internationalen Beziehungen," in: Andreas Predöhl (ed.), *Weltwirtschaftliches Archiv. Zeitschrift des Instituts für Weltwirtschaft an der Universität Kiel*, vol. 38, 1933.

Brusatti, Alois, *Österreichische Wirtschaftspolitik vom Josephinismus zum Ständestaat*, Vienna 1965.

Budraß, Lutz, *Flugzeugindustrie und Luftrüstung in Deutschland 1918–1945*, Düsseldorf 1998.

Bundesamt für Statistik (ed.), *Statistisches Handbuch für die Republik Österreich*, Vienna 1927–1932.

Bundesamt für Statistik (ed.), *Statistisches Handbuch für den Bundesstaat Österreich*, Vienna 1935–1937.

Bundesgesetzblatt für die Republik Österreich, "439. Verordnung: Beschränkung des Handels und Verkehres mit ausländischen Zahlungsmitteln," no. 91, Vienna 1922.

Bundesgesetzblatt für die Republik Österreich, "306. Verordnung: Devisenbewirtschaftung," no. 80, Vienna 1931.

Bundesministerium für Handel und Wiederaufbau, *100 Jahre im Dienste der Wirtschaft. Vol. 2. Aus der Tätigkeit des Handelsministeriums in Vergangenheit und Gegenwart*, Vienna 1961.

Büsch, Otto, and Peter-Christian Witt (eds.), *Internationale Zusammenhänge in der Weltwirtschaftskrise. Präsentationen aus Anlaß einer Fachkonferenz*, Berlin 1994.

Bussière, Eric, "The Evolution of Structures in the Iron and Steel Industry in France, Belgium, and Luxemburg: National and International Aspects, 1900–1939," in: Francois Crouzet (ed.), *The Economic Development of France since 1870*, Vol. 2, Aldershot 1993.

Butschek, Felix, *Die österreichische Wirtschaft 1938 bis 1945*, Vienna 1978.

Butschek, Felix, *Die österreichische Wirtschaft im 20. Jahrhundert*, Vienna 1985.

Butschek, Felix, "Präkeynesianismus in Österreich," in: *Wirtschaft und Gesellschaft*, 19, 1993.

Butschek, Felix, "External Shocks and Long-Term Patterns of economic growth in Central and Eastern Europe", in: David F. Good (ed.), *Economic Transformations in East and Central Europe. Legacies from the Past and Policies for the Future*, New York 1994.

Cairncross, Alec, and Barry Eichengreen, *Sterling in Decline. The Devaluations of 1931, 1949 and 1967*, Oxford 1983.

Caron, Francois (Translated from the French by Barbara Bray), *An Economic History of Modern France*, London 1979.

Chalmers, Henry, "The Depression and Foreign Trade Barriers," in: *The Annals of the American Academy of Political and Social Science. The World Trend Toward Nationalism*, Volume 174, Philadelphia, July 1934.

Cipolla, Carlo M. (ed.), *The Fontana Economic History of Europe. Volume 5. The Twentieth Century*, Sussex 1977.

Cipolla, Carlo M. (ed.), *Europäische Wirtschaftsgeschichte. The Fontana Economic History of Europe in 5 Bänden, Deutsche Ausgabe herausgegeben von Knut Borchardt, Die europäischen Volkswirtschaften im zwanzigsten Jahrhundert*, Stuttgart 1980.

Colm (no first name stated), "Deutschland und die Weltkrise," Lecture printed in: Franz Boese (ed.), *Schriften des Vereins für Sozialpolitik*, vol. 187, Munich 1932.

Creditanstalt-Bankverein (ed.), *Ein Jahrhundert Creditanstalt-Bankverein*, Vienna 1957.

Crouzet, Francois (ed.), *The Economic Development of France since 1870*, Volume 2, Aldershot 1993.

Davis, Joseph S., "Economic and Financial Progress in Europe, 1924–25," in: *The Review of Economic Statistics and Supplements*, Vol. 7, Cambridge, Massachusetts 1925.

Dellin, L.A.D., *Bulgaria*, New York 1957.

Der Österreichische Volkswirt, 1918–1938.

Der Österreichische Volkswirt, "Zur Wirtschaftslage," 17.4.1926.

Der Österreichische Volkswirt, "Die Zolltarifnovelle," 24.4.1926.

Der Österreichische Volkswirt, "Die neuen Zollsätze," 1.5.1926.

Der Österreichische Volkswirt; "Die umgestellten Industriebilanzen," 2.4.1927.

Der Österreichische Volkswirt, "Die österreichische Industrie im Jahre 1929," 21.12.1929.

Der Österreichische Volkswirt, "Devisenzwangswirtschaft," 17.10.1931.

Der Österreichische Volkswirt, "Der Mechanismus der Weltwirtschaftskrise," *Sonderbeilage des Österreichischen Volkswirt anlässlich der Vollendung seines 25. Jahrganges*, Vienna 1933.

Der Österreichische Volkswirt, "Alpine und Weltkonjunktur," 17.4.1937.

Der Österreichische Volkswirt, "Notizen: Alpine Montan an der Jahreswende," 25.12.1937.

Deutsch, Otto, and Alexander Vértes, *Aufbau nicht Abbau*, Vienna 1932.

Deutsches Institut für Konjunkturforschung, "Das Donauproblem", in: *Wochenbericht des Instituts für Konjunkturforschung*, vol. 5, no. 4, 1932.

Deutsches Institut für Konjunkturforschung, "Das Donauproblem II", in: *Wochenbericht*, vol. 5, no. 6, 1932.

Deutsches Institut für Konjunkturforschung, "Das Donauproblem III", in: *Wochenbericht*, vol. 5, no. 8, 1932.

Deutsches Institut für Konjunkturforschung, "Das Rußlandgeschäft in der Weltwirtschaftskrisis," in: *Wochenbericht*, vol. 5, no. 13, 1932.

Deutsches Institut für Konjunkturforschung, "Einfuhrhemmungen im Ausland", in: *Wochenbericht*, vol. 5, no. 28, 1932.

Deutsches Institut für Konjunkturforschung, "England und Japan. Probleme der Währungsentwertung", in: *Wochenbericht*, vol. 5, no. 31, 1932.

Deutsches Institut für Konjunkturforschung, "Die industrielle Weltproduktion", in: *Wochenbericht*, vol. 5, no. 35, 1932.

Deutsches Institut für Konjunkturforschung, "Die Weltwirtschaft Ende 1932", in: *Wochenbericht*, vol. 5, no. 38/39, 1932.

Deutsches Institut für Konjunkturforschung, "Die Industrieproduktion in der Welt", in: *Wochenbericht*, vol. 6, no. 7, 1933.

Deutsches Institut für Konjunkturforschung, "Die Industrieproduktion der Welt", in: *Wochenbericht*, vol. 6, no. 19, 1933.

Deutsches Institut für Konjunkturforschung, "Krisenbilanz der Weltproduktion", in: *Wochenbericht*, vol. 6, no. 41, 1933.

Deutsches Institut für Konjunkturforschung, "Die Kraftverkehrswirtschaft", in: *Wochenbericht*, special issue, vol. 6, no. 45, 1933.

Deutsches Institut für Konjunkturforschung, "Der Anteil der Ausfuhr an der deutschen Industrieproduktion," in: *Wochenbericht*, vol. 8, no. 15, 1935.

Deutsches Institut für Konjunkturforschung, "Zur Neuordnung der internationalen Eisenverträge," in: *Wochenbericht*, vol. 8, no. 39, 1935.

Deutsches Institut für Konjunkturforschung, "Der Welthandel," in: *Wochenbericht*, vol. 8, no. 48, 1935.

Deutsches Institut für Konjunkturforschung, "Die Industriekonjunktur im Jahr 1935," in: *Wochenbericht*, vol. 8, no. 51/52, 1935.

Deutsches Institut für Konjunkturforschung, "Japans Vormarsch auf dem Weltmarkt," in: *Wochenbericht*, vol. 9, no. 5, 1936.

Deutsches Institut für Konjunkturforschung, "Zur Lage am Kautschukmarkt," in: *Wochenbericht*, vol. 9, no. 18, 1936.

Deutsches Institut für Konjunkturforschung, "Die Kraftfahrzeugkonjunktur im vierten Aufschwungsjahr," in: *Wochenbericht*, special issue, vol. 9, no. 19, 1936.

Deutsches Institut für Konjunkturforschung, "Der Auslandsabsatz der elektrotechnischen Industrie," in: *Wochenbericht*, vol. 9, no. 20, 1936.

Deutsches Institut für Konjunkturforschung, "Die Kraftfahrzeugsaison 1936," in: *Wochenbericht*, special issue, vol. 9, no. 34, 1936.

Deutsches Institut für Konjunkturforschung, "Das Ende des 'Goldblocks'," in: *Wochenbericht*, vol. 9, no. 39, 1936.

Deutsches Institut für Konjunkturforschung, "Textilwirtschaft," in: *Schriften des Instituts für Konjunkturforschung. Vierteljahreshefte zur Wirtschaftsforschung*, vol. 10, no. 2, 1937.

Deutsches Institut für Konjunkturforschung, "Die industrielle Produktion in wichtigen Ländern," in: *Wochenbericht*, first special issue, vol. 10, no. 2, 1937.

Deutsches Institut für Konjunkturforschung, "Die industrielle Weltproduktion," in: *Wochenbericht*, first special issue, vol. 10, no. 2, 1937.

Deutsches Institut für Konjunkturforschung, "Die Wirtschaftsentwicklung in Frankreich, den Niederlanden und der Schweiz seit der Abwertung," in: *Wochenbericht*, vol. 10, no. 6, 1937.

Deutsches Institut für Konjunkturforschung, "Die 'jungen' Industriezweige," in: *Wochenbericht*, vol. 10, no. 7, Berlin 1937.

Deutsches Institut für Konjunkturforschung, "Die Lage der Textilindustrie im Ausland," in: *Wochenbericht*, vol. 10, no. 12/13, 1937.

Deutsches Institut für Konjunkturforschung, "Die Zahlen der Woche. Die industrielle Weltproduktion" and "Die Lage des Welthandels," *Wochenbericht*, vol. 10, no. 26, 1937.

Deutsches Institut für Konjunkturforschung, "Welthandel und Weltindustrieproduktion", in: *Wochenbericht*, vol. 10, no. 26, 1937.

Deutsches Institut für Konjunkturforschung, "Die Lage des Welthandels", in: *Wochenbericht*, vol. 10, no. 26, 1937.

Deutsches Institut für Konjunkturforschung, "Weltproduktion und Welthandel", in: *Wochenbericht*, vol. 10, no. 43, 1937.

Deutsches Institut für Konjunkturforschung, "Die industrielle Weltproduktion in den letzten Monaten", in: *Wochenbericht*, vol. 10, no. 43, 1937.

Deutsches Institut für Konjunkturforschung, "Österreichs Wirtschaftsnot und Wirtschaftspolitik vor der Eingliederung in das Reich," in: *Schriften des Instituts für Konjunkturforschung. Vierteljahreshefte zur Wirtschaftsforschung*, vol. 12, no. 4, 1937/1938.

Deutsches Institut für Konjunkturforschung, "Die Wirtschaftslage der Welt (Dezember 1938)," in: *Schriften des Instituts für Konjunkturforschung. Vierteljahreshefte zur Wirtschaftsforschung*, vol. 13, 1938/39.

Deutsches Institut für Konjunkturforschung, "Die deutsche elektrotechnische Industrie," in: *Wochenbericht*, vol. 12, no. 4, 1939.

Deutsches Institut für Konjunkturforschung, "Der Welthandel in elektrotechnischen Erzeugnissen," in: *Wochenbericht*, vol. 12, no. 20, 1939.

Deutsches Institut für Konjunkturforschung, "Wirtschaftsprobleme und Wirtschaftserfolge in der Ostmark," in: *Wochenbericht*, vol. 12, no. 21, 1939.

Deutsches Institut für Konjunkturforschung, "Totale Kriegswirtschaft in Japan," in: *Wochenbericht*, vol. 12, no. 26, 1939.

Deutsches Institut für Wirtschaftsforschung, *Untersuchungen zur Kraftverkehrsplanung im europäischen Großwirtschaftsraum. I. Die Ausrüstung des europäischen Großwirtschaftsraums mit Kraftfahrzeugen und die Triebkräfte der europäischen Kraftverkehrsentwicklung*, unpublished manuscript, Berlin 1941.

Die Bilanzen, 1920–1938.

Die Bilanzen, "Elektrifizierungs-Gesellschaften," 18.8.1923 and 25.8.1923.

Die Bilanzen, "Elektrotechnische Industrie," 5.3.1927.

Die Bilanzen, "Die Goldbilanzen der Industriegesellschaften," 30.4.1927.

Die Bilanzen, "Nöte der Papierindustrie," 4.7.1936.

Die Bilanzen, "Konjunktur der Papierindustrie," 20.1.1937 and 5.6.1937.

Dimsdale, N.H., "British Monetary Policy and the Exchange Rate 1920–1938," in: W. A. Eltis and P. J. N. Sinclair (eds.), *The Money Supply and the Exchange Rate*, Oxford 1981.

Drabek, Z., "Foreign Trade Performance and Policy," in: M. C. Kaser and E. A. Radice (eds.), *The Economic History of Eastern Europe 1919–1975, Volume I. Economic Structure and Performance between the Two Wars*, Oxford 1985.

Drummond, I., "Britain and the World Economy 1900–1945," in: Roderick Floud and Donald McCloskey (eds.), *The Economic History of Britain since 1700. Volume 2: 1860 to the 1970s*, Cambridge 1981.

Edelmann, Heidrun, *Vom Luxusgut zum Gebrauchsgegenstand. Die Geschichte der Verbreitung von Personenkraftwagen in Deutschland*, Frankfurt a. M. 1989.

Eichengreen, Barry, "Did Speculation Destabilize the French Franc in the 1920's?' In: Francois Crouzet (ed.), *The Economic Development of France since 1870*, Volume 1, Aldershot 1993, (first published in 1982).

Eichengreen, Barry (ed.), *The Gold Standard in Theory and History*, New York 1985.

Eichengreen, Barry, and Jeffrey Sachs, "Exchange Rates and Economic Recovery in the 1930s," in: *Journal of Economic History*, 45, 1985.

Eichengreen, Barry, "The Bank of France and the Sterilisation of Gold, 1926–1932," in: Francois

Crouzet (ed.), *The Economic Development of France since 1870*, Volume 1, Aldershot 1993 (first published in 1986).

Eichengreen, Barry, *Golden Fetters. The Gold Standard and the Great Depression, 1919–1939*, Oxford 1995.

Eichengreen, Barry, *Vom Goldstandard zum Euro. Die Geschichte des internationalen Währungssystems*, Berlin 1997.

Eigner, Peter, "Die Verflechtung zwischen den Wiener Großbanken und der Industrie 1855 bis 1938," in: Herbert Matis (ed.), *Historische Betriebsanalyse und Unternehmen. Festschrift für Alois Mosser*, Vienna 1997.

Ekel, Robert B., and Robert F. Hébert, *A History of Economic Theory and Method*, 2nd edition, New York 1975.

Elbaum, Bernhard, and William Lazonick (eds.), *The Decline of the British Economy*, Oxford 1986.

Eltis,W.A., and P. J. N. Sinclair (eds.), *The Money Supply and the Exchange Rate*, Oxford 1981.

Enderle-Burcel, Gertrude, and Eduard Kubu, "Die österreichisch-tschechoslowakischen Handelsbeziehungen in der unmittelbaren Nachkriegszeit," in: Alice Teichova and Herbert Matis (eds.), *Österreich und die Tschechoslovakei 1918–1938. Die wirtschaftliche Neuordnung in Zentraleuropa in der Zwischenkriegszeit*, Vienna 1996.

Erbe, Réne, *Die nationalsozialistische Wirtschaftspolitik 1933–1939 im Lichte der modernen Theorie*, Zurich 1958.

Faltus, Josef, and Alice Teichova, "Die Nachkriegsinflation. Ein Vergleich," in: Alice Teichova and Herbert Matis (eds.), *Österreich und die Tschechoslovakei 1918–1938. Die wirtschaftliche Neuordnung in Zentraleuropa in der Zwischenkriegszeit*, Vienna 1996.

Federn, Walter, "Zwanzig Jahre 'Österreichischer Volkswirt'," in: *Der Österreichische Volkswirt*, 29.9.1928.

Feldenkirchen, Wilfried, "Deutsche Zoll- und Handelspolitik 1914–1933," in: Hans Pohl (ed.), *Vierteljahrschrift für Sozial- und Wirtschaftsgeschichte, Beiheft Nr. 80, Die Auswirkungen von Zöllen und anderen Handelshemmnissen auf Wirtschaft und Gesellschaft vom Mittelalter bis zur Gegenwart*, Stuttgart 1987.

Feldenkirchen, Wilfried, *Siemens, 1918–1945*, Munich 1995.

Feldman, Gerald D., and Heidrun Homburg, *Industrie und Inflation*, Hamburg 1977.

Feldman, Gerald D., *Iron and Steel in the German Inflation 1916–1923*, New Jersey 1977.

Feldman, Gerald D., Carl-Ludwig Holtfrerich, Gerhard A. Ritter and Peter-Christian Witt, "Einführung. Inflation und Wiederaufbau in Deutschland und Europa 1914 bis 1924. Ein Forschungsprojekt," in: Gerald D. Feldman, Carl-Ludwig Holtfrerich, Gerhard A. Ritter and Peter-Christian Witt (eds.), *The German Inflation Reconsidered. A Preliminary Balance*, New York 1982.

Feldman, Gerald D., Carl-Ludwig Holtfrerich, Gerhard A. Ritter and Peter-Christian Witt (eds.), *The German Inflation Reconsidered. A Preliminary Balance*, New York 1982.

Feldman, Gerald D., Carl-Ludwig Holtfrerich, Gerhard A. Ritter and Peter-Christian Witt (eds.), *Die Erfahrungen der Inflation im Internationalen Zusammenhang und Vergleich (The Experience of Inflation. International and Comparative Studies)*, Berlin 1984.

Feldman, Gerald D., "Der Historiker und die deutsche Inflation," in: *Beiträge zur Historischen Sozialkunde*, No. 3, 1986.

Feldman, Gerald D., "Politik, Banken und der Goldstandard in der Zwischenkriegszeit," in: Manfred Pohl (ed.), *Vom Goldstandard zum Multireservewährungsstandard. Neuntes Nationales Symposium zur Bankengeschichte am 18.10.1985, im Hause der Deutschen Bank A.G.*, Frankfurt am Main 1987.

Fibich, Alexander, *Die Entwicklung der österreichischen Bundesausgaben in der Ersten Republik (1918–1938)*, dissertation, Vienna 1977.

Fiereder, Helmut, "Die Österreichisch-Alpine Montangesellschaft (OeMAG) von 1881 bis 1938. Technologie, Konzernierung und besitzrechtliche Verhältnisse im alpenländischen Hüttenwesen," in: *Scripta Mercuaturae*, vol. 15, no. 1, 1981.

Fischer, Wolfram, *Deutsche Wirtschaftspolitik 1918–1945*, 3rd edition, Opladen 1968.

Fischer, Wolfram, "Die Weimarer Republik unter den weltwirtschaftlichen Bedingungen der Zwischenkriegszeit," in: Hans Mommsen, Dietmar Petzina and Bernd Weisbrod (eds.), *Industrielles System und politische Entwicklung in der Weimarer Republik*, vol. 1, Düsseldorf 1974.

Fischer, Wolfram, *Weltwirtschaftliche Rahmenbedingungen für die ökonomische und politische Entwicklung Europas 1919–1939*, Wiesbaden 1980.

Fischer, Wolfram, (ed.), *Sachzwänge und Handlungsspielräume in der Wirtschafts- und Sozialpolitik der Zwischenkriegszeit*, St. Katharinen 1985.

Fischer, Wolfram, (ed.), *Handbuch der Europäischen Wirtschafts- und Sozialgeschichte. Band 6. Europäische Wirtschafts- und Sozialgeschichte vom Ersten Weltkrieg bis zur Gegenwart*, Stuttgart 1987.

Flora, Peter, Jens Alber, Richard Eichenberg, Jürgen Kohl, Franz Kraus, Winfried Pfenning and Kurt Seebohm, *State, Economy, and Society in Western Europe 1815–1975. A Data Handbook in two Volumes. Volume 1. The Growth of Mass Democracies and Welfare States*, Frankfurt 1983.

Flora, Peter, Franz Kraus and Winfried Pfenning, *State, Economy, and Society in Western Europe 1815–1975. A Data Handbook in two Volumes. Volume 2. The Growth of Industrial Societies and Capitalist Economies*, Frankfurt 1987.

Floud, Roderick, and Donald McCloskey (eds.), *The Economic History of Britain since 1700. Volume 2: 1860 to the 1970s*, Cambridge 1981.

Flügge, Eva, "Kunstseidenindustrie. Der internationale Aufbau der Kunstseidenindustrie und seine Folgen," in: Hermann Schumacher (ed.), *Wandlungen in der Weltwirtschaft*, no. 3, Leipzig 1936.

Fohlen, Claude, "Die Entwicklung Frankreichs," in: Carlo M. Cipolla, *Europäische Wirtschaftsgeschichte. The Fontana Economic History of Europe in 5 Bänden, Deutsche Ausgabe herausgegeben von Knut Borchardt, Die europäischen Volkswirtschaften im zwanzigsten Jahrhundert*, Stuttgart 1980.

Forstmeier, Friedrich, and Hans-Erich Volkmann (eds.), *Wirtschaft und Rüstung am Vorabend des Zweiten Weltkrieges*, Düsseldorf 1975.

Freihsl, Hans, *Bahn ohne Hoffnung. Die österreichischen Eisenbahnen von 1918 bis 1938. Versuch einer historischen Analyse*, Vienna 1971.

Fremdling, Rainer, and Patrick K. O'Brien (eds.), *Productivity in the Economies of Europe*, Stuttgart 1983.

French, Micheal J., *The U.S. Tire Industry. A History*, Boston 1991.

Fridenson, Partick, "French Automobile Marketing 1890–1979," in: Francois Crouzet (ed.), *The Economic Development of France since 1870*, Volume 2, Aldershot 1993 (first published in 1981).

Friedman, Milton, and Anna J. Schwartz, *A Monetary History of the United States 1867–1960*, Princeton 1963.

Furlani, Silvio, and Adam Wandruszka, *Österreich und Italien. Ein bilaterales Geschichtsbuch*, Vienna 1973.

Gaffey, John Dean, "The Productivity of Labour in the Rubber Tire Manufacturing Industry," in: Faculty of Political Science of Columbia University (ed.), *Studies in History, Economic and Public Law*, No. 472, New York 1968 (original publication in 1940).

Galbraith, John Kenneth, *The Great Crash 1929*, London 1980 (1st edition 1954).

Gibbs, Norman H., "Das britische Aufrüstungsprogramm 1933 bis 1939 und das Ausmaß seiner Abhängigkeit von der Entwicklung in Deutschland," in: Friedrich Forstmeier and Hans-Erich Volkmann (eds.), *Wirtschaft und Rüstung am Vorabend des Zweiten Weltkrieges*, Düsseldorf 1975.

Good, David F. (ed.), *Economic Transformations in East and Central Europe. Legacies from the Past and Policies for the Future*, New York 1994.

Gross, Hermann, "Mitteleuropäische Handelspolitik 1890–1938 und der Donauraum.", in: *Der Donauraum. Zeitschrift des Forschungsinstitutes für den Donauraum*, vol. 7, 1962.

Grotius, Fritz, *Die deutsche Kunstseidenindustrie, ihre Produktionsbedingungen, ihre Entwicklung und Marktstellung*, dissertation, Emsdetten 1938.

Grünbaum, Heinz, "Die Welttextilkrise. Zur Umschichtung der internationalen Industriestruktur," in: Deutsches Institut für Konjunkturforschung (ed.), *Vierteljahreshefte zur Konjunkturforschung*, special issue 24, Berlin 1931.

Guarneri, Felice, "Autarkie und Außenhandel," in: Andreas Predöhl (ed.), *Kieler Vorträge gehalten im Institut für Weltwirtschaft an der Universität Kiel*, vol. 65, Jena 1941.

Haas, Ernst, *Die Außenhandelspolitik der ehemaligen Republik Österreich während der Weltwirtschaftskrise bis zum Anschluß unter besonderer Berücksichtigung der Handelsvertragspolitik*, dissertation, Hochschule für Wirtschafts- und Sozialwissenschaften, Nürnberg, Würzburg, 1939.

Haas, Karl, "Industrielle Interessenpolitik in Österreich zur Zeit der Weltwirtschaftskrise," in: Österreichische Gesellschaft für Zeitgeschichte (ed.), *Jahrbuch für Zeitgeschichte*, Vienna 1978.

Haberler, Gottfried, "The World Economy, Money, and the Great Depression 1919–1939," in: *Selected Essays of Gottfried Haberler*, London 1985.

Hallgarten, W.F., and Joachim Radkau, *Die Deutsche Industrie und Politik von Bismark bis in die Gegenwart*, Frankfurt a.M., 1974.

Hardach, Gerd, *Weltmarktorientierung und relative Stagnation. Währungspolitik in Deutschland 1924–1931*, Berlin 1976.

Hardach, Gerd, and Sandra Hartig, "Der Goldstandard als Argument in der internationalen Währungsdiskussion," in: *Jahrbuch für Wirtschaftsgeschichte. Währungs- und Finanzgeschichte*, 1, 1998.

Hautsch, Gert, *Der Elektrokonzern AEG-Telefunken. Untersuchungen zum Verhältnis von Wirtschaft und Politik am Beispiel eines westdeutschen Großunternehmens*, Bremen 1982.

Heiße, Wilhelm, "Die Energiewirtschaft der Welt in Zahlen," in: Deutsches Institut für Konjunkturforschung (ed.), *Vierteljahreshefte zur Konjunkturforschung*, special issue 19, Berlin 1930.

Hellmann (no first name stated), "Clearingverträge mit der Schweiz und Ungarn," in: *Bilanzen*, 26.12.1931.

Henning, Friedrich-Wilhelm, *Das industrialisierte Deutschland 1914–1992. 8. Auflage*, Munich 1993.

Hentschel, Volker, "Große Depression undWirtschaftspolitik. Sachzwänge und Handlungsspielräume," in: Wolfram Fischer (ed.), *Sachzwänge und Handlungsspielräume in der Wirtschafts- und Sozialpolitik der Zwischenkriegszeit*, St. Katharinen 1985.

Hermann,Walter, *Der Magnesit in der Weltwirtschaft unter besonderer Berücksichtigung Österreichs. Eine wirtschaftsgeographische Untersuchung*, Vienna 1937.

Hertz, Friedrich, *Ist Österreich lebensfähig?* Vienna 1921.

Hertz, Friedrich, "Zahlungsbilanz und Lebensfähigkeit Österreichs," in: *Schriften des Vereins für Sozialpolitik*, vol. 167, M.J. Bonn (ed.), *Probleme der deutschen Zahlungsbilanz*, Munich and Leipzig 1925.

Hertz, Friedrich, *The Economic Problem of the Danubian States. A Study in Economic Nationalism*, London 1947.

Heubes, Jürgen, "Juglar-, Kondratieff- und Kitchin-Zyklen," in: *Wirtschaftswissenschaftliches Studium*, vol. 9, 1980.

Hickmann, Ernst, and Karlheinrich Rieker, *Statistisches Handbuch des Deutschen und internationalen Aussenhandels 1936*, Berlin 1936.

Hirschman, Albert O., "The Commodity Structure of World Trade," in: *The Quarterly Journal of Economics*, Vol. 57, Cambridge, Massachusetts 1943.

Hoffman, Robert, "Die wirtschaftlichen Grundlagen der britischen Österreichpolitik 1919," in: *Mitteilungen des Österreichischen Staatsarchivs*, 30, 1977.

Holtfrerich, Carl-Ludwig, "Die deutsche Inflation 1914–1923 und ihre Verteilungswirkungen," in: *Beiträge zur Historischen Sozialkunde*, No. 3, 1986.

Holtfrerich, Carl-Ludwig, "Weltwirtschaftskrise und Aussenhandel. Forschungsstand und Forschungsaufgaben," in: Otto Büsch and Peter-Christian Witt (eds.), *Internationale Zusammenhänge in der Weltwirtschaftskrise. Präsentationen aus Anlaß einer Fachkonferenz*, Berlin 1994.

Höpfer, Berd, *Der deutsche Außenhandel 1900–1945. Änderungen in der Waren und Regionalstruktur*, Frankfurt 1993.

Horn, Norbert, and Jürgen Kocka (eds.), *Recht und Entwicklung der Großunternehmen im 19. und frühen 20. Jahrhundert*, Göttingen 1979.

Howson, Susan, *Domestic Monetary Management in Britain 1919–1938*, Cambridge 1975.

Hubbard, J.B., "European Economic Conditions in the Year 1931," in: *The Review of Economic Statistics*, Vol. XIV, No.1, 1932.

Jackson, Julian, *The Politics of Depression in France, 1932–1936*, Cambridge 1985.

James, Harold, "Die Währungsstabilisierung 1923/24 in internationaler Perspektive," in: Werner Abelshauser (ed.), *Die Weimarer Republik als Wohlfahrtsstaat. Zum Verhältnis von Wirtschafts- und Sozialpolitik in der Industriegesellschaft*, Stuttgart 1987.

James, Harold (ed.), *The role of banks in the inter-war economy*, Cambridge 1991.

Jasny, N., "Die neuzeitliche Umstellung der überseeischen Getreideproduktion und ihr Einfluß auf den Weltmarkt," in: Deutsches Institut für Konjunkturforschung (ed.), *Vierteljahreshefte zur Konjunkturforschung*, special issue 16, Berlin 1930.

Kahn, A.E., *Great Britain in the World Economy*, New York 1946.

Karner, Stefan, Ingris Kubin and Micheal Steiner, "Wie real war 'Mitteleuropa?' Zur wirtschaftlichen Verflochtenheit des Donauraumes nach dem Ersten Weltkrieg," in: *Vierteljahrschrift für Sozial- und Wirtschaftsgeschichte*, vol. 74, no. 2, 1987.

Kaser, M.C., and E. A. Radice (eds.), *The Economic History of Eastern Europe 1919–1975, Volume 1. Economic Structure and Performance between the Two Wars*, Oxford 1985.

Keiser, Günther, and Bernhard Benning, "Kapitalbildung und Investitionen in der deutschen Volkswirtschaft 1924 bis 1928," in: Deutsches Institut für Konjunkturforschung (ed.), *Vierteljahreshefte zur Konjunkturforschung*, special issue 22, Berlin 1931.

Keller, Robert R., "Monopoly Capital and the Great Depression: Testing Baran and Sweezy's Hypothesis," in: *Review of Radical Political Economy*, 7 (4), 1975.

Kemp, Tom, *The French Economy 1913–1939. The history of a decline*, London 1972.

Kerekes, Lajos, *Von St. Germain bis Genf. Österreich und seine Nachbarn 1918–1922*, Budapest 1979.

Kernbauer, Hans, and Fritz Weber, "Die Wiener Großbanken in der Zeit der Kriegs- und Nachkriegsinflation (1914–1922)," in: Gerald D. Feldman, Carl-Ludwig Holtfrerich, Gerhard A. Ritter and Peter-Christian Witt (eds.), *Die Erfahrungen der Inflation im Internationalen Zusammenhang und Vergleich*, Berlin 1984.

Kernbauer, Hans, and Fritz Weber, "Von der Inflation zur Depression. Österreichs Wirtschaft 1918–1934," in: Emmerich Tálos and W. Neugebauer (eds.), *"Austrofaschismus". Beiträge über Politik, Ökonomie und Kultur 1934–1938*, Vienna 1984.

Kernbauer, Hans, and Fritz Weber, "Multinational banking in the Danube basin: the business strategy of the Viennese banks after the collapse of the Habsburg monarchy," in: Alice Teichova, Maurice Lévy-Leboyer and Helga Nussbaum (eds.), *Multinational enterprise in historical perpective*, Cambridge 1986.

Kernbauer, Hans, *Währungspolitik in der Zwischenkriegszeit. Geschichte der Oesterreichischen Nationalbank von 1923–1938*, Vienna 1991.

Kernbauer, Hans, "Österreichische Währungs-, Bank- und Budgetpolitik in der Zwischenkriegszeit," in: Emmerich Tálos, Herbert Dachs, Ernst Hanisch and Anton Staudinger (eds.), *Handbuch des politischen Systems Österreichs. Erste Republik 1918–1933*, Vienna 1995.

Kernbauer, Hans, "Zur österreichischen Wirtschaftspolitik in der Ersten Republik: Ein Überblick," in: Alice Teichova (ed.), *Banken, Währungen und Politik in Mitteleuropa zwischen den Weltkriegen*, Vienna 1997.

Keynes, John Maynard, "Essays in Persuasion, 1931. The Economic Consequences of Mr. Churchill, (written right after the return to gold in 1925)," in: Sidney Pollard (ed.), *The Gold Standard and Employment Policies between the wars*, London 1970.

Kienböck, Viktor, *Das österreichische Sanierungswerk*, Vienna 1925.

Kindleberger, Charles, *Die Weltwirtschaftskrise 1929–1939*, Munich 1973.

Kindleberger, Charles P., "A Structural View of the German Inflation," in: Feldman, Gerald D., Carl-Ludwig Holtfrerich, Gerhard A. Ritter and Peter-Christian Witt (eds.), *Die Erfahrungen der Inflation im Internationalen Zusammenhang und Vergleich (The Experience of Inflation. International and Comparative Studies)*, Berlin 1984.

Kindleberger, Charles P., "Banking and Industry between the Two Wars: An International Comparison," in: *The Journal of European Economic History*, Vol. 13, No. 2, special issue, 1984.

Klemperer, Klemens von, *Ignaz Seipel. Christian Statesman in a Time of Crisis*, Princeton 1972.

Klingenstein, Grete, *Die Anleihe von Lausanne. Ein Beitrag zur Geschichte der Ersten Republik in den Jahren 1931–1934*, Graz 1965.

Knoche, Heinrich, *Die Wirtschafts- und Sozialpolitik der Regierungen Brüning, Papen, Schleicher und Hitler in den Jahren der Weltwirtschaftskrise von 1928/30–1934*, dissertation, Marburg 1989.

Kofman, Jan, "Economic Nationalism in East-Central Europe in the Interwar Period," in: Henryk Szlajfer (ed.), *Economic Nationalism in East-Central Europe and South America 1918–1939*, Geneva 1990.

Komlos, John (ed.), *Economic Development in the Habsburg Monarchy and in the Successor States (East European Monographs*, No. 280), New York 1990.

Korsch, Andreas, "Der Stand der beschäftigungspolitischen Diskussion zur Zeit der Weltwirtschaftskrise in Deutschland. II. Die Ausereinandersetzung mit der zeitgenössischen Wirtschaftslehre," in: G. Bombach, H.J. Ramser, M. Timmermann and W. Wittmann (eds.), *Der Keynesianismus I. Theorie und Praxis keynesianischer Wirtschaftspolitik. Entwicklung und Stand der Diskussion*, New York 1976.

Krengel, Rolf, *Das Deutsche Institut fürWirtschaftsforschung (Institut für Konjunkturforschung) 1925–1979*, Berlin 1986.

Kretschmar, Hans, "Ökonomische Theorie, Nationalwirtschaft und 'Interventionismus'," in: Andreas Predöhl (ed.), *Weltwirtschaftliches Archiv. Zeitschrift des Instituts für Weltwirtschaft und Seeverkehr an der Universität Kiel*, vol. 38, 1933.

Kroll, Gerhard, *Von der Weltwirtschaftskrise zur Staatskonjunktur*, Berlin 1958.

Kusternig, Andreas, (ed.), *Beiträge über die Krise der Industrie Niederösterreichs zwischen den beiden Weltkriegen (Studien und Forschungen aus dem Niederösterreichischen Institut für Landeskunde*, vol. 7), Vienna 1985.

Ladner, Gottlieb, *Seipel als Überwinder der Staatskrise vom Sommer 1922. Zur Geschichte der Entstehung der Genfer Protokolle vom 4. Oktober 1922*, Vienna 1964.

Länderrat des Amerikanischen Besatzungsgebiets (ed.), *Statistisches Handbuch von Deutschland 1928–1944*, Munich 1949.

Landes, David S., *The Unbound Prometheus*, Cambridge 1969.

Layton, Walter T., and Charles Rist, *Die Wirtschaftslage Österreichs*, Vienna 1925.

League of Nations, Economic Intelligence Service (ed.), *World Economic Survey 1932–1933*, Geneva 1933.

League of Nations (ed.), *World Production and Prices 1925–1933*, Geneva 1934.

League of Nations, Economic Intelligence Service (ed.), *Europe's Trade. A Study of the Trade of European Countries with Each other and with the Rest of the World*, Geneva 1941.

League of Nations, Economic, Financial and Transit Department (ed.), *Commercial Policy in the Interwar Period: International Proposals and National Policies*, Geneva 1942.

League of Nations, Economic, Financial and Transit Department (ed.), *Industrialization and Foreign Trade*, reprinted by the United Nations, New York 1948 (originally published in 1945).

League of Nations, Economic, Financial and Transit Department (ed.), *The Course and Control of*

Inflation. A Review of Monetary Experience in Europe after World War I, reprinted edition, New York 1978 (original publication: 1946).

Lewchuk, Wayne, "The Motor Vehicle Industry," in: Bernhard Elbaum and William Lazonick (eds.), *The Decline of the British Economy*, Oxford 1986.

Liepmann, Heinrich, *Tariff Levels and the Economic Unity of Europe. An Examination of Tariff Policy, Export Movements and the Economic Integration of Europe, 1913–1931*, reprinted in Philadelphia 1980 (1st edition: London 1938).

Lindenlaub, Dieter, "Maschinenbauunternehmen in der Inflation 1919 bis 1923. Unternehmenshistorische Überlegungen zu einigen Inflationstheorien." in: Feldman, Gerald D., Carl Ludwig Holtfrerich, Gerhard A. Ritter and Peter-Christian Witt (eds.), *The German Inflation Reconsidered. A Preliminary Balance*, New York 1982.

Lomax, K. S., "Growth and Productivity in the United Kingdom," in: Derek H. Aldcroft and Peter Fearon (eds.), *Economic Growth in Twentieth-Century Britain*, Suffolk 1969 (first published in 1964).

Lossos, Harald, "Bilanz der deutschen Devisenbewirtschaftung," in: *Münchener Volkswirtschaftliche Studien*, vol. 29, Jena 1940.

Maddison, Angus, "Economic Policy and Performance in Europe 1913–1970," in: Carol M. Cipolla (ed.), *The Fontana Economic History of Europe, Volume 5, The Twentieth Century*, Sussex 1977.

Maddison, Angus, "Measuring Long Term Growth and Productivity Change on a Macroeconomic Level," in: Rainer Fremdling and Patrick K. O'Brien (eds.), *Productivity in the Economies of Europe*, Stuttgart 1983.

Maier, Charles S., *Recasting Bourgeois Europe. Stabilisation in France, Germany, and Italy in the Decade after World War I*, New Jersey 1975.

Manchester Guardian Commercial, reprint of a series of articles between July 1936 and January 1937, "The Economics of Isolation," in: *The Annals of the American Academy of Political and Social Science. The United States and World War*, Vol. 193, Philadelphia 1937.

Martin, Bernd, "Aggressionspolitik als Mobilisierungsfaktor. Der militärische und wirtschaftliche Imperialismus Japans 1931 bis 1941," in: Friedrich Forstmeier and Hans-Erich Volkmann (eds.), *Wirtschaft und Rüstung am Vorabend des Zweiten Weltkrieges*, Düsseldorf 1975.

Martin, Bernd, "Wirtschaftliche Konzentration und soziale Konflikte in Japan," in: Dietmar Rothermund (ed.), *Die Peripherie in der Weltwirtschaftskrise: Afrika, Asien und Lateinamerika 1929–1939*, Paderborn 1982.

März, Eduard, *Österreichische Bankpolitik in der Zeit der großen Wende 1913–1923. Am Beispiel der Creditanstalt für Handel und Gewerbe*, Vienna 1981.

März, Eduard, and Maria Szecsi, "Stagnation und Expansion. Eine vergleichende Analyse der wirtschaftlichen Entwicklung in der Ersten und Zweiten Republik," in: *Wirtschaft und Gesellschaft*, 2, 1982.

Mathis, Franz, *Big Business in Österreich. Österreichische Großunternehmen in Kurzdarstellungen*, Vienna 1987.

Mathis, Franz, "Das Jahr 1918 und die österreichischen Großunternehmen. Neubeginn oder Kontinuität?' in: O. Pickl and R. Metlar (eds.), *Zerfall und Integration*, Vienna 1995.

Matis, Herbert, "Disintegration and multi-national enterprises in Central Europe during the post-war years (1918–23)", in: Alice Teichova and P.L. Cottrell (eds.), *International Business and Central Europe 1918–1939*, New York 1983.

Matis, Herbert, and Dieter Stiefel, *Die Weltwirtschaft. Struktur und Entwicklung im 20. Jahrhundert*, Vienna 1991.

Matis, Herbert, (ed.), *The Economic Development of Austria since 1870*, Aldershot 1994.

Matis, Herbert (ed.), *Historische Betriebsanalyse und Unternehmen. Festschrift für Alois Mosser*, Vienna 1997.

Mattl, Siegfried, "Die Finanzdiktatur. Wirtschaftspolitik in Österreich 1933–1938," in: Emmerich

Tálos and W. Neugebauer (eds.), *"Austrofaschismus." Beiträge über Politik, Ökonomie und Kultur 1934–1938*, Vienna 1984.

McClokey, Donald N., and J. Richard Zecher, "How the gold standard worked, 1880–1913," in: Barry Eichengreen (ed.), *The Gold Standard in Theory and History*, New York 1985.

Meister, Rainer, *Die große Depression. Zwangslagen und Handlungsspielräume der Wirschafts- und Finanzpolitik in Deutschland 1929–1932*, Stuttgart 1991.

Mensch, Gerhard, *Das technologische Patt. Innovationen überwinden die Depression*, Frankfurt a. M. 1975.

Mensch, Gerhard, and Reinhard Schnopp, "Stalemate in Technology, 1925–1935: The Interplay of Stagnation and Innovation," in: Wilhelm Heinz Schröder and Reinhard Spree (eds.), *Historische Konjunkturforschung. Historisch-Sozialwissenschaftliche Forschungen. Quantitative sozialwissenschaftliche Analysen von historischen und prozeß-produzierten Daten*, volume 11, Stuttgart 1981.

Mietschke, Arno, "Technisches Humankapital in der britischen Elektroindustrie der Zwischenkriegszeit: Die British Thompson-Houston Co. in vergleichender Perpektive," in: *Zeitschrift für Unternehmensgeschichte*, vol. 40, Stuttgart 1995.

Mises, Ludwig, *Die Ursachen der Wirtschaftskrise*, Vienna 1931.

Mishkin, Frederic S., "The Household Balance Sheet and the Great Depression," in: *The Journal of Economic History*, Vol. 38, No 4, 1978.

Mitchell, B.R., *European Historical Statistics 1750–1970*, New York 1978.

Mitterauer, Michael (ed.), *Österreichisches Montanwesen. Produktion, Verteilung, Sozialreformen* (*Sozial und Wirtschaftshistorische Studien*), Vienna 1974.

Moggridge, D. E., *British Monetary Policy, 1924–1931: The Norman Conquest of $ 4.86*, Cambridge 1972.

Mommsen, Hans, Dietmar Petzina and Bernd Weisbrod (eds.), *Industrielles System und politische Entwicklung in der Weimarer Republik*, vol. 1 and 2, Düsseldorf 1974.

Mosser, Alois, *Die Industrieaktiengesellschaft in Österreich 1880–1913. Versuch einer historischen Bilanz- und Betriebsanalyse*, Vienna 1980.

Mosser, Alois, "Wachtumsstrategie oder Krisenmanagement? Vom Investitionsverhalten der österreichischen Industrie in der Ersten Republik," in: Andreas Kusternig (ed.), *Beiträge über die Krise der Industrie Niederösterreichs zwischen den beiden Weltkriegen (Studien und Forschungen aus dem Niederösterreichischen Institut für Landeskunde*, vol. 7), Vienna 1985.

Mosser, Alois, and Alice Teichova, "Investment behaviour of industrial joint stock companies and industrial shareholding by the Österreichische Credit-Anstalt: inducement or obstacle to renewal and change in industry in inter-war Austria," in: Harold James (ed.), *The role of banks in the interwar economy*, Cambridge 1991.

Mühlenhoff, Hanns von, "Die englische Währungsabwertung und die wirtschaftlichenWechsellagen. Untersuchung des gegenwärtigen Aufschwungs der englischen Wirtschaft," in: Arthur Spiethoff (ed.), *Beiträge zur Erforschung der wirtschaftlichen Wechsellagen Aufschwung, Krise, Stockung*, issue 18, Jena 1939.

Murray, Williamson, *The Luftwaffe 1933–45. Strategy for Defeat*, Washington 1996.

Musson, A.E., *The Growth of British Industry*, Norfolk 1978.

Natmeßig, Charlotte, *Britische Finanzinteressen in Österreich: Die Anglo-Österreichische Bank*, Vienna 1998.

Nautz, Jürgen, *Die österreichische Handelspolitik der Nachkriegszeit 1918–1923. Die Handelsvertragsbeziehungen zu den Nachfolgestaaten*, Wien 1994.

Nautz, Jürgen, "Between Political Disintegration and Economic Reintegration. Austrian Trade relations with the successor states after World War I", in: David F. Good (ed.), *Economic Transformations in East and Central Europe. Legacies from the Past and Policies for the Future*, New York 1994.

Nötel, Rudolf, "International Capital Movements and Finance in Eastern Europe 1919–1949," in: *Vierteljahrschrift für Sozial- und Wirtschaftsgeschichte*, vol. 61, 1974.

Nötel, Rudolf, "Money, Banking and Industry in Interwar Austria and Hungary," in: *Banks and Industry in the Interwar Period. The Journal of European Economic History*, vol. 13, number 2, special issue, Fall 1984.

Nurkse, Ragnar, *International Currency Experience*, Geneva 1944.

Österreichisches Institut für Konjunkturforschung, *Monatsberichte des Österreichischen Institutes für Konjunkturforschung*, 1st volume, Vienna 1927.

Österreichisches Institut für Wirtschaftsforschung, "Wirtschaftszahlen Österreichs 1923 bis 1938," in: *Monatsberichte des Österreichischen Instituts für Wirtschaftsforschung*, issue 10/12, Vienna 1946.

Österreichisches Institut für Wirtschaftsforschung, *Monatsberichte des Österreichischen Instituts für Wirtschaftsforschung. Beschäftigung und Produktivität im Österreichischen Bergbau von 1913 bis 1950*, issue 7, Vienna 1950.

Österreichisches Institut für Wirtschaftsforschung, *Monatsberichte des Österreichischen Instituts für Wirtschaftsforschung, special issue 14, Österreichs Volkseinkommen 1913 bis 1963*, Vienna 1965, 5.

Österreichisches Statistisches Zentralamt, *Der Aussenhandel Österreichs in der Zeit zwischen den beiden Weltkriegen. Beiträge zur österreichischen Statistik*, issue 1, Vienna 1946.

Otruba, Gustav, *Österreichs Wirtschaft im 20. Jahrhundert*, Munich 1968.

Otruba, Gustav, "Die Entwicklung des Böhler Konzerns vom Ersten Weltkrieg bis zur Gegenwart," in: *100 Jahre Böhler Edelstahl, 1870–1970*, Vienna 1971.

Overy, Richard J., "Cars, Roads, and Economic Recovery in Germany, 1932–8," in: *The Economic History Review*, Vol. 28, No. 3, 1975.

Overy, Richard J., *The Nazi Economic Recovery 1932–1938*, London 1982.

Overy, Richard J., *War and Economy in the Third Reich*, Oxford 1994.

Peden, G. C., *British Economic and Social Policy. Lloyd George to Margaret Thatcher*, Oxford 1985.

Petzina, Ditmar, "Autarkiepolitik im Dritten Reich. Der nationalsozialistische Vierjahresplan," in: Hans Rothfels and Theodor Eschenburg (eds.), *Schriftenreihe der Vierteljahreshefte für Zeitgeschichte*, no. 16, Stutgart 1968.

Petzina, Ditmar, *Die deutsche Wirtschaft in der Zwischenkriegszeit*, Wiesbaden 1977.

Petzina, Ditmar, Werner Abelshauser and Anselm Faust, *Materialien zur Statistik des Deutschen Reiches 1914–1945. Sozialgeschichtliches Arbeitsbuch*, vol. 3, Munich 1978.

Plumpe, Gottfried, "Unternehmen und Industriesektoren in der Weltwirtschaftskrise im internationalen Vergleich. Das Beispiel der chemischen Industrie," in: Otto Büsch and Peter Christian Witt, *Internationale Zusammenhänge der Weltwirtschaftskrise. Präsentation aus Anlaß einer Fachkonferenz*, Berlin 1994.

Pohl, Manfred (ed.), *Vom Goldstandard zum Multireservewährungsstandard. Neuntes Nationales Symposium zur Bankengeschichte am 18.10.1985, im Hause der Deutschen Bank A.G.*, Frankfurt am Main 1987.

Polanyi, Karl, "Der Mechanismus der Weltwirtschaftskrise," in: *Sonderbeilage des Österreichischen Volkswirt anlässlich der Vollendung seines 25. Jahrganges*, Vienna 1933.

Pollard, Sidney, *The Development of the British Economy, 1914–1980*, 3rd edition London 1962.

Pollard, Sidney, (ed.), *The Gold Standard and Employment Policies between the wars*, London 1970 (first published in 1957).

Pollard, Sidney, *Peaceful Conquest. The Industrialisation of Europe 1760–1970*, Oxford 1981.

Radiis, Guido Radio von, *Die deutsche Außenhandelspolitik unter dem Einfluß der Devisenbewirtschaftung von 1931 bis 1938*, Vienna 1939.

Raspin, Angela, "Wirtschaftliche und politische Aspekte der italienischen Aufrüstung Anfang der dreißiger Jahre bis 1940," in: Forstmeier, Friedrich, and Hans-Erich Volkmann (eds.), *Wirtschaft und Rüstung am Vorabend des Zweiten Weltkrieges*, Düsseldorf 1975.

Redmond, J., "The sterling overvaluation in 1925: a mulitlateral approach," in: *Economic History Review*, 2nd series, volume 37, 1984.

Renndorfer, Friedrich, *Ignaz Seipel. Mensch und Staatsmann. Eine biographische Dokumentation*, Vienna 1978.

Resch, Andreas, and Zdenek Sládek, "Integrations- und Desintegrationstendenzen. Die Handelsbeziehungen 1921–1937," in: Alice Teichova and Herbert Matis (eds.), *Österreich und die Tschechoslowakei 1918–1938. Die wirtschaftliche Neuordnung in Zentraleuropa in der Zwischenkriegszeit*, Wien 1996.

Richardson, H.W., "The Economic Significance of the Depression in Britain," in: *The Journal of Contemporary History*, vol. 4, no. 4, 1969.

Ritschl, Albrecht, and Mark Spoerer, "Das Bruttosozialprodukt in Deutschland nach den amtlichen Volkseinkommens- und Sozialproduktstatistiken 1901–1995," in: *Jahrbuch für Wirtschaftsgeschichte. Volkswirtschaftliche Gesamtrechnungen im internationalen Vergleich*, 2, 1997.

Rostas, L., "Industrial Production, Productivity and Distribution in Britain, Germany and the United States," in: *The Economic Journal*, Vol. 53, 1943.

Rothermund, Dietmar (ed.), *Die Peripherie in der Weltwirtschaftskrise: Afrika, Asien und Lateinamerika 1929–1939*, Paderborn 1982.

Rothschild, K.W., *Austria's Economic Development between the Two Wars*, London 1947.

Rostow, Walt Whitman, *The World Economy. History & Prospect*, Austin 1978.

Sandgruber, Roman, *Ökonomie und Politik. Österreichische Wirtschaftsgeschichte vom Mittelalter bis zur Gegenwart*, Vienna 1995.

Sargent, Thomas J., "Die Beendigung vier großer Inflationen", in: Feldman, Gerald D., Carl-Ludwig Holtfrerich, Gerhard A. Ritter and Peter-Christian Witt (eds.), *Die Erfahrungen der Inflation im Internationalen Zusammenhang und Vergleich (The Experience of Inflation. International and Comparative Studies)*, Berlin 1984.

Sattler, Barbara, *„Der Deutsche Volkswirt" 1926–1933*, dissertation, Kiel 1982.

Sauvy, Alfred, *Histoire Économique da la France entre les deux guerres. De l'armistice a la dévaluation de la Livre (1918–1931)*, Fayard 1963.

Sayers, R.S., "The Return to Gold 1925," in: Sidney Pollard (ed.), *The Gold Standard and Employment Policies between the Wars*, London 1970 (first published in 1957).

Schäfer, Peter, *Wettbewerb und technischer Fortschritt in der deutschen Reifenindustrie*, dissertation, Aachen 1968.

Schausberger, Norbert, *Der Griff nach Österreich*, Vienna 1978.

Schmidt, C.T., *German Business Cycles, 1924–1933*, New York 1934.

Schmukler, Nathan, and Edward Marcus (eds.), *Inflation through the Ages: Economic, Social, Psychological and Historical Aspects*, New York 1983.

Schneider, Jürgen, Oskar Schwarzer and Markus A. Denzel (eds.), *Währungen der Welt II. Europäische und nordamerikanische Devisenkurse (1914–1951)*, Stuttgart 1997.

Schöpfer, Gerald, "Möglichkeiten einer aktiven Konjunkturpolitik im Österreich der zwanziger Jahre," in: *Geschichte und Gegenwart*, 2, 1983.

Schröder, Wilhelm Heinz, and Reinhard Spree (eds.), *Historische Konjunkturforschung. Historisch-Sozialwissenschaftliche Forschungen. Quantitative sozialwissenschaftliche Analysen von historischen und prozeß-produzierten Daten*, volume 11, Stuttgart 1981.

Schröter, Harm, "Siemens and Central and South-East Europe between the two world wars," in: Alice Teichova and P.L. Cottrell, *International Business and Central Europe, 1918–1939*, New York 1983.

Schuker, Stephen A., *The End of French Predominance in Europe. The Financial Crisis of 1924 and the Adoption of the Dawes Plan*, North Carolina 1976.

Schulz, Matthias, *Deutschland, der Völkerbund und die Frage der europäischen Wirtschaftsordnung 1925–1933. Beiträge zur deutschen und europäischen Geschichte*, vol. 19, Hamburg 1997.

Schumpeter, Joseph A., *Kapitalismus, Sozialismus und Demokratie*, 4th edition, Munich 1950.

Schumpeter, Joseph A., *Konjunkturzyklen. Eine theoretische, historische und statistische Analyse des kapitalistischen Prozesses*, 2nd volume, Göttingen 1961.

Seidel, Hans, "The Austrian Economy: An Overview," in: Sven Ardt (ed.), *The Political Economy of Austria*, Washington, D.C., 1982.

Seiler, Richard, "Strukturwandlungen des Welthandels. Ein Beitrag zur Frage: Industrialisierung und Außenhandel," in: *Schriften des Instituts für Konjunkturforschung, Vierteljahreshefte zur Wirtschaftsforschung*, vol. 13, no. 2, Hamburg 1938/39.

Shahidi, Kian, *Der Branchen-Lebenszyklus. Eine Untersuchung am Beispiel der deutschen Stahlindustrie*, dissertation, Bern 1997.

Slichter, Sumner H., "The Period 1919–1936 in the United States: Its Significance for Business Cycle Theory," in: *The Review of Economics and Statistics*, Vol. 19, No. 1, Part 1, February 1937.

Spitzmüller, Alexander, ...*und hat auch Ursach es zu lieben*, Vienna 1955.

Stankovsky, Jan, "Foreign trade in Austria and East-Central Europe. Retrospective and perspective", in: David F. Good (ed.), *Economic Transformations in East and Central Europe. Legacies from the Past and Policies for the Future*, New York 1994.

Statistische Reichsamt (ed.), *Statistisches Jahrbuch für das Deutsche Reich*, 1924–1938.

Statistisches Reichsamt (ed.), *Wirtschaft und Statistik*, vol. 7, no. 1, January 1927, 20.

Statistisches Reichsamt (ed.), *Die Wirtschaft des Auslandes 1900–1927. Einzelschriften zur Statistik des Deutschen Reiches*, no. 5, Berlin 1928.

Statistisches Reichsamt (ed.), *Wirtschaft und Statistik*, volume 9, no. 22, Berlin, November 1929.

Statistisches Reichsamt (ed.), *Internationaler Steuerbelastungsvergleich. Die Steuer- und Soziallasten der gewerblichen und kaufmännischen Betriebe in Deutschland, Frankreich, Großbritannien, Italien, Österreich und den Vereinigten Staaten von Amerika. Einzelschriften zur Statistik des Deutschen Reichs*, Berlin 1933.

Statistisches Reichsamt, "Die Eisen schaffende Industrie des In- und Auslandes im Juni/Juli und im Halbjahr 1937," in: *Wirtschaft und Statistik*, vol. 17, no. 15, 1937.

Statistisches Reichsamt, "Die Eisenindustrie im Jahre 1936," in: *Wirtschaft und Statistik*, vol. 17, no. 22, 1937.

Steiner, Friedrich, "Erster Teil. Notenbankpolitik und staatliche Anleihepolitik in den österreichisch-ungarischen Nachfolgestaaten," in: *Schriften des Vereins für Sozialpolitik*, vol. 166, Munich and Leipzig 1924.

Stickstoff-Syndikat (ed.), *UdSSR. Struktur, Industrie, Verkehr, Außenhandel*, Berlin 1939.

Stiefel, Dieter, *Konjunkturelle Entwicklung und struktureller Wandel der österreichischen Wirtschaft in der Zwischenkriegszeit, Forschungsbericht Nr. 135*, Vienna 1978.

Stiefel, Dieter, "The reconstruction of the Credit-Anstalt," in: Alice Teichova and Philip L. Cottrell (eds.), *International Business and Central Europe 1918–1939*, New York 1983.

Stiefel, Dieter, "The Great Depression in a Small Country. Austria, the World Economic Crisis of the 1930's and its Significance for the Present Day," in: Herbert Matis (ed.), *The Economic Development of Austria since 1870*, Aldershot 1994 (first publication: Budapest 1986).

Stiefel, Dieter, "Utopie und Realität. DieWirtschaftspolitik des Ständestaates," in: *Tirol und der Anschluß. Vorraussetzungen, Entwicklungen, Rahmenbedingungen 1918–1938*, Innsbruck 1988.

Stiefel, Dieter, *Die große Krise in einem kleinem Land. Österreichische Finanz- und Wirtschaftspolitik 1929–1938*, Vienna 1988.

Stiefel, Dieter, *Finanzdiplomatie und Weltwirtschaftskrise. Die Krise der Credit-Anstalt für Handel und Gewerbe 1931*, Frankfurt 1989.

Stolper, Gustav, *Deutschösterreich als Sozial- und Wirtschaftsproblem*, Vienna 1921.

Stolper, Gustav, "Der Friedensvertrag von St. Germain in seinen wirtschaftlichen Wirkungen," in: *Schriften des Vereins für Sozialpolitik*, Vol. 162, Gustav Stolper (ed.) *Deutsch-Österreich. Neue Beiträge über seine wirtschaftlichen Verhältnisse*, Munich and Leipzig 1921.

Stolper, Gustav, (continued by Karl Häuser and Knut Borchardt), *Deutsche Wirtschaft seit 1870*, Tübingen 1964.

Sturmayr, Gerald, "Industrielle Interessenverbände: Ringen um Einheit," in: Tálos, Emmerich (ed.), *Handbuch des politischen Systems. Erste Republik 1918–1933*, Vienna 1995.

Svennilson, Ingvar, *Stagnation and Growth in the European Economy*, United Nations, Economic Commission for Europe, Geneva 1954.

Szlajfer, Henryk, (ed.), *Economic Nationalism in East-Central Europe and South America 1918–1939*, Geneva 1990.

Tálos, Emmerich, and W. Neugebauer (eds.), *"Austrofaschismus." Beiträge über Politik, Ökonomie und Kultur 1934–1938*, Vienna 1984.

Tálos, Emmerich, Herbert Dachs, Ernst Hanisch and Anton Staudinger (eds.), *Handbuch des politischen Systems. Erste Republik 1918–1933*, Vienna 1995.

Teichert, Eckart, *Autarkie und Großraumwirtschaft in Deutschland 1930–1939. Außenwirtschaftspolitische Konzeptionen zwischen Wirtschaftskrise und Zweitem Weltkrieg*, Munich 1984.

Teichova, Alice, "Versailles and the Expansion of the Bank of England into Central Europe," in: Norbert Horn and Jürgen Kocka (eds.), *Recht und Entwicklung der Großunternehmen im 19. und frühen 20. Jahrhundert*, Göttingen 1979.

Teichova, Alice, and P.L. Cottrell, *International Business and Central Europe 1918–1939*, New York 1983.

Teichova, Alice, "A Comparative View of the Inflation of the 1920s in Austria and Czechoslovakia", in: Nathan Schmukler and Edward Marcus (eds.), *Inflation through the Ages: Economic, Social, Psychological and Historical Aspects*, New York 1983.

Teichova, Alice, "Die Wirtschaftspolitik der kleinen Nationen in Mittel- und Osteuropa. Sachzwänge und Handlungsspielräume in der Zwischenkriegszeit", in: Wolfram Fischer (ed.), *Sachzwänge und Handlungsspielräume in der Wirtschafts- und Sozialpolitik der Zwischenkriegszeit*, St. Katharinen 1985.

Teichova, Alice, "Chapter 5. Industry," in: M. C. Kaser and E. A. Radice (eds.), *The Economic History of Eastern Europe 1919–1975, Volume 1. Economic Structure and Performance between the Two Wars*, Oxford 1985.

Alice Teichova, Maurice Lévy-Leboyer and Helga Nussbaum (eds.), *Multinational enterprise in historical perpective*, Cambridge 1986.

Teichova, Alice, "Die Inflation der 1920er Jahre in Mitteleuropa im Vergleich," in: *Beiträge zur Historischen Sozialkunde*, No. 3, 1986.

Teichova, Alice, *Kleinstaaten im Spannungsfeld der Großmächte. Wirtschaft und Politik in Mittel- und Südosteuropa in der Zwischenkriegszeit*, Vienna 1988.

Teichova, Alice, "Rivals and Partners: reflections on banking and industry in Europe, 1880– 1938," in: *European Industry and Banking Between the Wars. A Review of Bank-Industry Relations*, Leicester 1992.

Teichova, Alice, "Kontinuität und Diskontinuität: Banken und Industrie in Mitteleuropa im 20. Jahrhundert," in: *Österreichische Zeitschrift für Geschichtswissenschaften*, vol. 4, no. 4, 1993. Also in: David F. Good (ed.), *Economic Transformations in East and Central Europe. Legacies from the Past and Policies for the Future*, New York 1994.

Teichova, Alice, and Herbert Matis (eds.), *Österreich und die Tschechoslovakei 1918–1938. Die wirtschaftliche Neuordnung in Zentraleuropa in der Zwischenkriegszeit*, Vienna 1996.

Teichova, Alice (ed.), *Banken, Währungen und Politik in Mitteleuropa zwischen den Weltkriegen*, Vienna 1997.

Temin, Peter, *Lessons from the Great Depression. The Lionel Robbins Lectures for 1989*, Cambridge, Massachusetts 1990.

Thalmann, Friedrich, "Teil III. Die Wirtschaft in Österreich," in: Heinrich Benedikt (ed.), *Geschichte der Republik Österreich*, Vienna 1977.

The Austrian National Committee of the International Chamber of Commerce (Österreichisches Nationalkomitee der Internationalen Handelskammer) (ed.), *Zollhöhe und Warenwerte. Eine vergleichende Studie über die Höhe der Zollbelastung für 402 Waren in 14 europäischen Staaten*, Vienna 1927.

The Economist, January 12, 1935.

Thomas, T., "Aggregate demand in the United Kingdom 1918–45," in: Roderick Floud and Donald McCloskey (eds.), *The Economic History of Britain since 1700*, Cambridge 1981.

Tobler, Achim, *Die französische Handelspolitik in der Weltwirtschaftskrise (Herbst 1929 bis Frühjahr 1936),* dissertation, Heidelberg 1938.

Tolliday, Steven, "Steel and Rationalisation Policies, 1918–1950," in: Bernard Elbaum and William Lazonick, *The Decline of the British Economy*, Oxford 1986.

Volkmann, Hans Erich, "Außenhandel und Aufrüstung in Deutschland 1933 bis 1939," in: Friedrich Forstmeier and Hans Erich Volkmann (eds.), *Wirtschaft und Rüstung am Vorabend des Zweiten Weltkrieges*, Düsseldorf 1975.

Wagemann, Ernst, *Struktur und Rhythmus der Weltwirtschaft. Grundlagen einer weltwirtschaftlichen Konjunkturlehre*, Berlin 1931.

Wagenführ, Rolf, "Die Industriewirtschaft. Entwicklungstendenzen der deutschen und internationalen Industrieproduktion 1860 bis 1932," in: Deutsches Institut für Konjunkturforschung (ed.), *Vierteljahreshefte zur Konkjunkturforschung*, special issue 31, Berlin 1933.

Walter, Friedrich, *Veitscher Magnesitwerke Actien-Gesellschaft 1881–1951*, without data on location and year.

Wandruszka, Adam, "Zwischen den Weltkriegen," in: Silvio Furlani and Adam Wandruszka, *Österreich und Italien. Ein bilaterales Geschichtsbuch*, Vienna 1973.

Ward, Benjamin, "National Economic Planning and Policies in Twentieth Century Europe 1920–1970," in: Carlo M. Cipolla (ed.), *The Fontana Economic History of Europe. Volume 5. The Twentieth Century*, Sussex 1977.

Weber, Fritz, "Die österreichische Bankenkrise und ihre Auswirkungen auf die niederösterreichische Industrie," in: Andreas Kusternig (ed.), *Beiträge über die Krise der Industrie Niederösterreichs zwischen den beiden Weltkriegen* (*Studien und Forschungen aus dem Niederösterreichischen Institut für Landeskunde*, vol. 7), Vienna 1985.

Weber, Fritz, "Universal banking in inter-war Central Europe," in: Harold James (ed.), *The role of banks in the inter-war economy*, Cambridge 1991.

Weber, Fritz, "I. 2. Die wirtschaftliche Entwicklung" in: Emmerich Tálos (ed.), *Handbuch des politischen Systems Österreichs. Erste Republik 1918–1933*, Vienna 1995.

Weber, Fritz, "Staatliche Wirtschaftspolitik in der Zwischenkriegszeit. Zum Investitionsverhalten der öffentlichen Hand 1918–1938," in: Emmerich Tálos (ed.), *Handbuch des politischen Systems Österreichs. Erste Republik 1918–1933*, Vienna 1995.

Weisbrod, Bernd, *Schwerindustrie in der Weimarer Republik. Interessenpolitik zwischen Stabilisierung und Krise*, Wuppertal 1978.

Wiesbauer, Helmut, *Die österreichischen Aktiengesellschaften 1918–1938, unter Berücksichtigung betriebswirtschaftlicher und rechtlicher Aspekte*, dissertation, Linz 1977.

Wittendorfer, Frank, *Industrie, Banken, Politiker und Verbände in Österreich im Widerstand gegen die Wirtschaftspolitik des Jahres 1931. Dargestellt am Beispiel des deutschösterreichischen Zollunionsprojektes*, dissertation, Innsbruck 1986.

Wood, Jonathan, *Wheels of Misfortune. The Rise and Fall of the British Motor Industry*, London 1988.

Woytinsky,W.S., and E.S.Woytinsky, *World Commerce and Governments. Trends and Outlook*, New York 1955.

Wright, J. F., "Britain's Inter-War Experience," in: W.A. Eltis and P. J. N. Sinclair (eds.), *The Money Supply and the Exchange Rate*, Oxford 1981.

Zacchia, Carlo, "International Trade and Capital Movements 1920–1970," in: Carlo M. Cipolla (ed.), *The Fontana Economic History of Europe. Volume 5. The Twentieth Century*, Sussex 1977.